The Ministers Manual

SEVENTY-THIRD ANNUAL ISSUE

THE MINISTERS MANUAL

1998 EDITION

Edited by

JAMES W. COX

Jossey-Bass Publishers • San Francisco

Editors of THE MINISTERS MANUAL

G. B. F. Hallock, D.D., 1926–1958
M. K. W. Heicher, Ph.D., 1943–1968
Charles L. Wallis, M.A., M.Div., 1969–1983
James W. Cox, M.Div., Ph.D.

Translations of the Bible referred to and quoted from in this book may be indicated by their standard abbreviations, such as NRSV (New Revised Standard Version) and NIV (New International Version). In addition, some contributors have made their own translations and others have used a mixed text.

Other acknowledgments begin on page 337.

Substantial discounts on bulk quantities of Jossey-Bass books are available to corporations, professional associations, and other organizations. For details and discount information, contact the special sales department at Jossey-Bass Inc., Publishers (415) 433–1740; Fax (800) 605–2665.

For sales outside the United States, please contact your local Simon & Schuster International Office.

Jossey-Bass Web address: http://www.josseybass.com

 Manufactured in the United States of America on Lyons Falls Turin Book. This paper is acid-free and 100 percent totally chlorine-free.

Library of Congress Cataloging Card Number
25-21658
ISSN 0738-5323
ISBN 0-7879-0882-7

FIRST EDITION
HB Printing   10 9 8 7 6 5 4 3 2 1

CONTENTS

PREFACE

This seventy-third annual issue of *The Ministers Manual* is the first for Jossey-Bass Inc., Publishers. It is clear to me that this publisher is committed to maintaining the quality and usefulness of the *Manual* that have characterized its record across the years. In addition, Jossey-Bass proposes to make this annual volume, if possible, even better. The publisher's scrupulous attention to the many details of my task as editor has made this task in some respects more difficult but more promising.

A productive conference with my new editor in San Francisco last year led to some changes that should make *The Ministers Manual* more useful. Section II reflects the most significant changes. The Lectionary Message for each Sunday is first rather than last, and, while it focuses on one biblical text, it cites the other readings for the day. Also, two illustrations follow each lectionary message. These illustrations are in lieu of a formerly separate section.

A new feature in Section II is Hymn Suggestions. In it, both classical and contemporary hymns appropriate to the season and often highlighting the Scripture lessons for the day are listed and annotated.

I wish to thank the many persons who make this book possible. Without their contributions, such a volume would hardly be possible. The Southern Baptist Theological Seminary, where I have taught since 1959, has provided valuable secretarial assistance in producing the manuscript. The present volume was word-processed by Beth Beauchamp, with the assistance of Ja-Rhonda Staples and Linda Durkin. To all of these people and the authors and publishers whose works I have quoted and highlighted, I am deeply grateful.

James W. Cox
The Southern Baptist Theological Seminary
2825 Lexington Road
Louisville, Kentucky 40280

SECTION I.
General Aids and Resources
Civil Year Calendars for 1998 and 1999

1998

JANUARY
S M T W T F S
1 2 3
4 5 6 7 8 9 10
11 12 13 14 15 16 17
18 19 20 21 22 23 24
25 26 27 28 29 30 31

FEBRUARY
S M T W T F S
1 2 3 4 5 6 7
8 9 10 11 12 13 14
15 16 17 18 19 20 21
22 23 24 25 26 27 28

MARCH
S M T W T F S
1 2 3 4 5 6 7
8 9 10 11 12 13 14
15 16 17 18 19 20 21
22 23 24 25 26 27 28
29 30 31

APRIL
S M T W T F S
1 2 3 4
5 6 7 8 9 10 11
12 13 14 15 16 17 18
19 20 21 22 23 24 25
26 27 28 29 30

MAY
S M T W T F S
1 2
3 4 5 6 7 8 9
10 11 12 13 14 15 16
17 18 19 20 21 22 23
24 25 26 27 28 29 30
31

JUNE
S M T W T F S
1 2 3 4 5 6
7 8 9 10 11 12 13
14 15 16 17 18 19 20
21 22 23 24 25 26 27
28 29 30

JULY
S M T W T F S
1 2 3 4
5 6 7 8 9 10 11
12 13 14 15 16 17 18
19 20 21 22 23 24 25
26 27 28 29 30 31

AUGUST
S M T W T F S
1
2 3 4 5 6 7 8
9 10 11 12 13 14 15
16 17 18 19 20 21 22
23 24 25 26 27 28 29
30 31

SEPTEMBER
S M T W T F S
1 2 3 4 5
6 7 8 9 10 11 12
13 14 15 16 17 18 19
20 21 22 23 24 25 26
27 28 29 30

OCTOBER
S M T W T F S
1 2 3
4 5 6 7 8 9 10
11 12 13 14 15 16 17
18 19 20 21 22 23 24
25 26 27 28 29 30 31

NOVEMBER
S M T W T F S
1 2 3 4 5 6 7
8 9 10 11 12 13 14
15 16 17 18 19 20 21
22 23 24 25 26 27 28
29 30

DECEMBER
S M T W T F S
1 2 3 4 5
6 7 8 9 10 11 12
13 14 15 16 17 18 19
20 21 22 23 24 25 26
27 28 29 30 31

1999

JANUARY
S M T W T F S
1 2
3 4 5 6 7 8 9
10 11 12 13 14 15 16
17 18 19 20 21 22 23
24 25 26 27 28 29 30
31

FEBRUARY
S M T W T F S
1 2 3 4 5 6
7 8 9 10 11 12 13
14 15 16 17 18 19 20
21 22 23 24 25 26 27
28

MARCH
S M T W T F S
1 2 3 4 5 6
7 8 9 10 11 12 13
14 15 16 17 18 19 20
21 22 23 24 25 26 27
28 29 30 31

APRIL
S M T W T F S
1 2 3
4 5 6 7 8 9 10
11 12 13 14 15 16 17
18 19 20 21 22 23 24
25 26 27 28 29 30

MAY
S M T W T F S
1
2 3 4 5 6 7 8
9 10 11 12 13 14 15
16 17 18 19 20 21 22
23 24 25 26 27 28 29
30 31

JUNE
S M T W T F S
1 2 3 4 5
6 7 8 9 10 11 12
13 14 15 16 17 18 19
20 21 22 23 24 25 26
27 28 29 30

JULY
S M T W T F S
1 2 3
4 5 6 7 8 9 10
11 12 13 14 15 16 17
18 19 20 21 22 23 24
25 26 27 28 29 30 31

AUGUST
S M T W T F S
1 2 3 4 5 6
8 9 10 11 12 13
14 15 16 17 18 19 20
21 22 23 24 25 26 27
28 29 30

SEPTEMBER
S M T W T F S
1 2 3 4
5 6 7 8 9 10 11
12 13 14 15 16 17 18
19 20 21 22 23 24 25
26 27 28 29 30

OCTOBER
S M T W T F S
1 2
3 4 5 6 7 8 9
10 11 12 13 14 15 16
17 18 19 20 21 22 23
24 25 26 27 28 29 30
31

NOVEMBER
S M T W T F S
1 2 3 4 5 6
7 8 9 10 11 12 13
14 15 16 17 18 19 20
21 22 23 24 25 26 27
28 29 30

DECEMBER
S M T W T F S
1 2 3 4
5 6 7 8 9 10 11
12 13 14 15 16 17 18
19 20 21 22 23 24 25
26 27 28 29 30 31

Church and Civic Calendar for 1998

JANUARY

1 New Year's Day
  The Name of Jesus
5 Twelfth Night
6 Epiphany
18 Confession of St. Peter
19 Martin Luther King Jr. Day
25 Conversion of St. Paul

FEBRUARY

1 National Freedom Day
2 Presentation of Jesus in the
  Temple
  Groundhog Day
3 Four Chaplains Memorial Day
12 Lincoln's Birthday
14 St. Valentine's Day
16 Presidents' Day
22 Washington's Birthday
24 St. Matthias, Apostle
25 Ash Wednesday

MARCH

1 First Sunday in Lent
8 Second Sunday in Lent
15 Third Sunday in Lent
17 St. Patrick's Day
19 Joseph, Husband of Mary
22 Fourth Sunday in Lent
25 The Annunciation
29 Fifth Sunday in Lent

APRIL

5 Palm/Passion Sunday
  Daylight saving time begins
5–11 Holy Week
9 Maundy Thursday
10 Good Friday
11 Passover
12 Easter
14 Pan-American Day
17 St. Patrick's Day
19 Orthodox Easter
25 St. Mark, Evangelist

MAY

1 Law Day
  Loyalty Day

  May Day
  St. Philip and St. James, Apostles
1–5 Cinco de Mayo Celebration
10 Mother's Day
12 Purim
25 Memorial Day
31 The Visitation of Mary
  First Day of Shavuot

JUNE

11 St. Barnabas, Apostle
14 Children's Sunday
21 Father's Day
24 The Nativity of St. John the
  Baptist
29 St. Peter and St. Paul, Apostles

JULY

1 Canada Day
4 Independence Day
22 St. Mary Magdalene
25 St. James, Apostle

AUGUST

3 Civic Holiday (Canada)
6 The Transfiguration
14 Atlantic Charter Day
15 Mary, Mother of Jesus
24 St. Bartholomew, Apostle
26 Women's Equality Day

SEPTEMBER

6 Labor Sunday
7 Labor Day
13 National Grandparents' Day
  Rally Day
14 Holy Cross Day
17 Citizenship Day
21 First Day of Rosh Hashanah
  St. Matthew, Apostle and
  Evangelist
29 St. Michael and All Angels

OCTOBER

4 World Communion Sunday
5 Sukkoth
11 Laity Sunday

12 Columbus Day (observed)
    Thanksgiving Day (Canada)
16 World Food Day
18 St. Luke, Evangelist
23 St. James, Brother of Jesus
24 United Nations Day
25 Daylight saving time ends
31 National UNICEF Day
    Reformation Day
    Halloween

NOVEMBER

1   All Saints' Day
2   All Souls' Day
8   Stewardship Sunday
11 Armistice Day
    Veterans Day
    Remembrance Day (Canada)
22 Bible Sunday

26 Thanksgiving Day
29 First Sunday of Advent
30 St. Andrew, Apostle

DECEMBER

6   Second Sunday of Advent
13 Third Sunday of Advent
14 Hanukkah
29 Fourth Sunday of Advent
21 Forefathers' Day
    St. Thomas, Apostle
24 Christmas Eve
25 Christmas
26 Boxing Day (Canada)
    St. Stephen, Deacon
27 St. John, Apostle and Evangelist
28 The Holy Innocents
31 New Year's Eve
    Watch Night

The Revised Common Lectionary for 1998

The following Scripture lessons are commended for use in public worship by various Protestant churches and the Roman Catholic Church and include first, second, and Gospel readings, and Psalms, according to Cycle C from January 4 to November 22 and according to Cycle A from November 29 to December 27. (Copyright 1992 Consultation on Common Texts.)

Jan. 4: Jer. 31:7–14; Ps. 147:12–20; Eph. 1:3–14; John 1:(1–9) 10–18.

EPIPHANY SEASON

Jan. 11 (Epiphany Sunday): Isa. 60:1–6; Ps. 72:1–7, 10–14; Eph. 3:1–12; Matt. 2:1–12.
Jan. 18: Isa. 62:1–5; Ps. 36:5–10; 1 Cor. 12:1–11; John 2:1–11.
Jan. 25: Neh. 8:1–3, 5–6, 8–10; Ps. 19; 1 Cor. 12:12–31a; Luke 4:14–21.
Feb. 1: Jer. 1:4–10; Ps. 71:1–6; 1 Cor. 13:1–13; Luke 4:21–30.
Feb. 8: Isa. 6:1–8 (9–13); Ps. 138; 1 Cor. 15:1–11; Luke 5:1–11.
Feb. 15: Jer. 17:5–10; Ps. 1; 1 Cor. 15:12–20; Luke 6:17–26.
Feb. 22: Gen. 45:3–11, 15; Ps. 37:1–11, 39–40; 1 Cor. 15:35–38, 42–50; Luke 6:27–38.
Feb. 25 (Ash Wednesday): Joel 2:1–2, 12–17;

Ps. 51:1–17; 2 Cor. 5:20b–6:10; Matt. 6:1–6, 16–21.
Mar. 1 (Lent): Deut. 26:1–11; Ps. 91:1–2, 9–16; Rom. 10:8b–13; Luke 4:1–13.
Mar. 8: Gen. 15:1–12, 17–18; Ps. 27; Phil. 3:17–4:1; Luke 13:31–35.
Mar. 15: Isa. 55:1–9; Ps. 63:1–8; 1 Cor. 10:1–13; Luke 13:1–9.
Mar. 22: Josh. 5:9–12; Ps. 32; 2 Cor. 5:16–21; Luke 15:1–3, 11b–32.
Mar. 29: Isa. 43:16–21; Ps. 126; Phil. 3:4b–14; John 12:1–8.

HOLY WEEK

Apr. 5 (Palm/Passion Sunday): Mark 11:1–11; Ps. 118:1–2, 19–29; (Passion) Isa. 50:4–9a; Ps. 31:9–16; Phil. 2:5–11; Luke 22:14–23:56.
Apr. 6 (Monday): Isa. 42:1–9; Ps. 36:5–11; Heb. 9:11–15; John 12:1–11.
Apr. 7 (Tuesday): Isa. 49:1–7; Ps. 71:1–14; 1 Cor. 1:18–31; John 12:20–36.
Apr. 8 (Wednesday): Isa. 50:4–9a; Ps. 70; Heb. 12:1–3; John 13:21–32.
Apr. 9 (Thursday): Exod. 12:1–4 (5–10), 11–14; Ps. 116:1–2, 12–19; 1 Cor. 11:23–26; John 13:1–17, 31b–35.
Apr. 10 (Good Friday): Isa. 52:13–53:12; Ps. 22; Heb. 10:16–25 (alt.); Heb. 14–16; 5:7–9 (alt.); John 18:1–19:42.

Apr. 11 (Holy Saturday): Job 14:1–14 (alt.); Lam. 3:1–9, 19–24; Ps. 31:1–4, 15–16; 1 Peter 4:1–8; Matt. 27:57–66 (alt.); John 19:38–42 (alt.).

SEASON OF EASTER

Apr. 11–12 (Easter Vigil): Gen. 1:1–2, 4a; Ps. 136:1–9, 23–26; Gen. 7:1–5, 11–18; 8:6–18, 9:8–13; Ps. 46; Gen. 22:1–18; Ps. 16; Exod. 14:10–31; 15:20–21; Exod. 15:1b–13, 17–18 (resp.); Isa. 55:1–11; Isa. 12:2–6 (resp.); Bar. 3:9–15, 32–4:4 (alt.); Prov. 8:1–8, 19–21; 9:4–6 (alt.); Ps. 19; Ezek. 36:24–28; Pss. 42–43; Ezek. 37:1–14; Ps. 143; Zeph. 3:14–20; Ps. 98; Rom. 6:3–11; Ps. 114; Luke 24:1–12.

Apr. 12 (Easter): Isa. 65:17–25; Ps. 118:1–2, 14–24; Acts 10:34–43 or 1 Cor. 15:19–26; John 20:1–18.

Apr. 19: Acts 5:27–32; Ps. 118:14–29; Rev. 1:4–8; John 20:19–31.

Apr. 26: Acts 9:1–6 (7–20); Ps. 30; Rev. 5:11–14; John 21:1–19.

May 3: Acts 9:36–43; Ps. 23; Rev. 7:9–17; John 10:22–30.

May 10: Acts 11:1–18; Ps. 148; Rev. 21:1–6; John 13:31–35.

May 17: Acts 16:9–15; Ps. 67; Rev. 21:10, 22–22:5; John 14:23–29.

May 24: Acts 16:16–34; Ps. 97; Rev. 22:12–14, 16–17, 20–21; John 17:20–26.

SEASON OF PENTECOST

May 31 (Pentecost): Acts 2:1–21 or Gen. 11:1–9; Ps. 104:24–34, 35b; Rom. 8:14–17; John 14:8–17 (25–27).

June 7 (Trinity): Prov. 8:1–4, 22–31; Ps. 8; Rom. 5:1–5; John 16:12–15.

June 14: 1 Kings 21:1–10 (11–14), 15–21a; Ps. 5:1–8; Gal. 2:15–21; Luke 7:36–8:3.

June 21: 1 Kings 19:1–4 (5–7), 8:15a; Ps. 42; Gal. 3:23–29; Luke 8:26–39.

June 28: 2 Kings 2:1–2, 6–14; Ps. 77:1–2, 11–20; Gal. 5:1, 13–25; Luke 9:51–62.

July 5: 2 Kings 5:1–14; Ps. 30; Gal. 6:(1–6) 7–16; Luke 10:1–11, 16–20.

July 12: Amos 7:7–17; Ps. 82; Col. 1:1–14; Luke 10:25–37.

July 19: Amos 8:1–12; Ps. 52; Gal. 1:15–28; Luke 10:38–42.

July 26: Hos. 1:2–10; Ps. 85; Col. 2:6–15 (16–19); Luke 11:1–13.

Aug. 2: Hos. 11:1–11; Ps. 107:1–9, 43; Col. 3:1–11; Luke 12:13–21.

Aug. 9: Isa. 1:1, 10–20; Ps. 50:1–8, 22–23; Heb. 11:1–3, 8–16; Luke 12:32–40.

Aug. 16: Isa. 5:1–7; Ps. 80:1–3, 8–19; Heb. 11:29–12:2; Luke 12:49–56.

Aug. 23: Jer. 1:4–10; Ps. 71:1–6; Heb. 12:18–29; Luke 13:10–17.

Aug. 30: Jer. 2: 4–13; Ps. 81:1, 10–16; Heb. 13:1–8, 15–16; Luke 14:1, 7–14.

Sept. 6: Jer. 18:1–11; Ps. 139:1–6, 13–18; Philem. 1–21; Luke 14:25–33.

Sept. 13: Jer. 4:11–12, 22–28; Ps. 14; 1 Tim. 1:12–17; Luke 15:1–10.

Sept. 20: Jer. 8:18–91; Ps. 79:1–9; 1 Tim. 2:1–7; Luke 16:1–13.

Sept. 27: Jer. 32:1–3a, 6–15; Ps. 91:1–6, 14–16; 1 Tim. 6:6–19; Luke 16:19–31.

Oct. 4: Lam. 1:1–6; Ps. 137; 2 Tim. 1:1–14; Luke 17:5–10.

Oct. 11: Jer. 29:1, 4–7; Ps. 66:1–12; 2 Tim. 2:8–15; Luke 17:11–19.

Oct. 18: Jer. 31:27–34; Ps. 119:97–104; 2 Tim. 3:14–4:5; Luke 18:1–8.

Oct. 25: Joel 2:23–32; Ps. 65; 2 Tim. 4:6–8, 16–18; Luke 18:9–14.

Nov. 1: Hab. 1:1–4; 2:1–4; Ps. 119:137–144; 2 Thess. 1:1–4, 11–12; Luke 19:1–10.

Nov. 8: Hag. 2:1–9; Ps. 145:1–5, 17–21; 2 Thess. 2:1–5, 13–17; Luke 20:27–38.

Nov. 15: Isa. 65:17–25; Isa. 12; 2 Thess. 3:6–13; Luke 21:5–19.

Nov. 22 (Christ the King): Jer. 23: 1–6; Luke 1:68–79; Col. 1:11–20; Luke 23:33–43.

ADVENT AND CHRISTMAS SEASON

Nov. 29 (Advent): Isa. 2:1–5; Ps. 122; Rom. 13:11–14; Matt. 24:36–44.

Dec. 6: Isa. 11:1–10; Ps. 72:1–7, 18–19; Rom. 15:4–13; Matt. 3:1–12.

Dec. 13: Isa. 35:1–10; Luke 1:47–55; James 5:7–10; Matt. 11:2–11.

Dec. 20: Isa. 7:10–16; Ps. 80:1–7, 17–19; Rom. 1:1–7; Matt. 1:18–25.

Dec. 25 (Christmas Day): Isa. 9:2–7; Ps. 96; Titus 2:11–14; Luke 2:1–14 (15–20) or Isa. 62:6–12; Ps. 97; Titus 3:4–7; Luke 3:(1–7), 8–20 or Isa. 52:7–10; Ps. 98; Heb. 1:1–4 (5–12); John 1:1–14.

Dec. 27: Isa. 63:7–9; Ps. 148; Heb. 2:10–18; Matt. 2:13–23.

Four-Year Church Calendar

	1998	1999	2000	2001
Ash Wednesday	February 25	February 17	March 8	February 28
Palm Sunday	April 5	March 28	April 16	April 8
Good Friday	April 10	April 2	April 21	April 13
Easter	April 12	April 4	April 23	April 15
Ascension Day	May 21	May 13	June 1	May 24
Pentecost	May 31	May 23	June 11	June 3
Trinity Sunday	June 7	May 30	June 18	June 10
Thanksgiving	November 26	November 25	November 23	November 22
Advent Sunday	November 29	November 28	December 3	December 2

Forty-Year Easter Calendar

1998 April 12	2008 March 23	2018 April 1	2028 April 16
1999 April 4	2009 April 12	2019 April 21	2029 April 1
2000 April 23	2010 April 4	2020 April 12	2030 April 21
2001 April 18	2011 April 24	2021 April 4	2031 April 13
2002 March 31	2012 April 8	2022 April 17	2032 March 28
2003 April 20	2013 March 31	2023 April 9	2033 April 17
2004 April 11	2014 April 20	2024 March 31	2034 April 9
2005 March 27	2015 April 5	2025 April 20	2035 March 25
2006 April 16	2016 March 27	2026 April 5	2036 April 13
2007 April 8	2017 April 16	2027 March 28	2037 April 5

Traditional Wedding Anniversary Identifications

1 Paper	7 Wool	13 Lace	35 Coral
2 Cotton	8 Bronze	14 Ivory	40 Ruby
3 Leather	9 Pottery	15 Crystal	45 Sapphire
4 Linen	10 Tin	20 China	50 Gold
5 Wood	11 Steel	25 Silver	55 Emerald
6 Iron	12 Silk	30 Pearl	60 Diamond

Colors Appropriate for Days and Seasons

White. Symbolizes purity, perfection, and joy, and identifies festivals marking events in the life of Jesus, except Good Friday: Christmas, Epiphany, Easter, Eastertide, Ascension Day; also Trinity Sunday, All Saints' Day, weddings, funerals. Gold also may be used.

Red. Symbolizes the Holy Spirit, martyrdom, and the love of God: Good Friday, Pentecost, and Sundays following.

Violet. Symbolizes penitence: Advent, Lent.

Green. Symbolizes mission to the world, hope, regeneration, nurturance, and growth: Epiphany season, Kingdomtide, Rural Life Sunday, Labor Sunday, Thanksgiving Sunday.

Blue. Advent, in some churches.

Flowers in Season Appropriate for Church Use

January. Carnation or snowdrop.
February. Violet or primrose.
March. Jonquil or daffodil.
April. Lily, sweet pea, or daisy.
May. Lily of the valley or hawthorn.
June. Rose or honeysuckle.

July. Larkspur or water lily.
August. Gladiolus poppy.
September. Aster or morning star.
October. Calendula or cosmos.
November. Chrysanthemum.
December. Narcissus, holly, or poinsettia.

Historical, Cultural, and Religious Anniversaries in 1998

Compiled by Kenneth M. Cox

10 years (1988). *February 24:* U.S. Supreme Court overturns a lower court award to Rev. Jerry Falwell against Larry Flynt's *Hustler* magazine, finding free speech protections for parodies and satire involving public figures. *April 25:* Israeli court sentences retired U.S. autoworker John Demjanjuk to death for Nazi death camp war crimes. *July 3:* U.S. Navy shoots down Iranian passenger jet, killing 290. *October 1*: Mikhail Gorbachev consolidates power by assuming the Soviet presidency.

25 years (1973). *January 22:* U.S. Supreme Court decides in *Roe* v. *Wade* that states may not prevent abortions during the first six months of pregnancy. *January 28:* Cease-fire signed in Paris ends direct involvement of U.S. troops in Vietnam. *May 8:* Siege at Wounded Knee, South Dakota, ends as occupying Indians surrender under terms of cease-fire. *June 9:* Secretariat wins the Belmont Stakes by thirty-one lengths to become thoroughbred horse racing's first Triple Crown winner since 1948. *September 20:* Billie Jean King defeats Bobby Riggs in the tennis "battle of the sexes" in Houston. *October 6:* Arab-Israeli Day of Atonement (Yom Kippur) war begins in the Middle East. *October 10:* Vice President Spiro Agnew resigns and pleads no contest to tax evasion charges; Gerald Ford assumes the office on December 6. *Debut:* American League's designated hitter.

40 years (1958). *May 31:* France names Charles de Gaulle premier. *September 29:* U.S. Supreme Court speeds up integration of schools in Little Rock, Arkansas, in *Cooper* v. *Aaron. Debuts:* United Church of Christ and United Presbyterian Church in United States; John Birch Society; U.S. Civil Rights Commission; American Express card; Sweet 'n' Low; Pizza Hut.

50 years (1948). *January 30:* Hindu extremists assassinate Mahatma Gandhi in India. *May 14:* The State of Israel is proclaimed. *August 22:* World Council of Churches is instituted in Amsterdam by representatives of churches in forty-four countries. *Debuts:* Transistor; phrase "cold war"; World Health Organization; comic strip "Pogo."

75 years (1923). *January 1:* Aimee Semple McPherson dedicates Angelus Temple in Los Angeles. *July 10:* Benito Mussolini dissolves Italy's nonfascist parties and begins to secure his fascist dictatorship. *September 1:* Earthquake and fire destroy Tokyo and Yokohama, killing 91,000. *Debuts:* Autogyro; *Time* magazine; Kahlil Gibran's *The Prophet;* Robert Frost's "Stopping by Woods on a Snowy Evening."

100 years (1898). *February 15:* Explosion that destroys the U.S. battleship *Maine* in Havana Harbor precipitates 112-day Spanish-American War beginning April 22. *Debuts:* Gideons association; Pepsi-Cola; George Gershwin.

Quotable Quotations

1. God gave burdens, also shoulders.—Yiddish Proverb

2. One of the proofs of the divinity of our gospel is the preaching it has survived.—Woodrow Wilson

3. Every artist was first an amateur.—Ralph Waldo Emerson

4. The giving of love is an education in itself.—Eleanor Roosevelt

5. Life is what happens to us while we are making other plans.—Thomas La Mance

6. A good example is the best sermon.—Thomas Fuller

7. A retired husband is often a wife's full-time job.—Ella Harris

8. I keep six honest serving-men (They taught me all I knew); Their names are What and Why and When and How and Where and Who.—Rudyard Kipling

9. No one is the whole of himself; his friends are the rest of him.—Harry Emerson Fosdick

10. People seem to enjoy things more when they know a lot of other people have been left out of the pleasure.—Russell Baker

11. A good book has no ending.—R. D. Cumming

12. I now perceive one immense omission in my *Psychology*—the deepest principle of human nature is *the craving to be appreciated.*—William James

13. The Providence that watches over the affairs of men works out their mistakes, at times, to a healthier issue than could have been accomplished by their wisest forethought.—James A. Proude

14. Never mistake motion for action.—Ernest Hemingway

15. Neighbor, n. One whom we are commanded to love as ourselves, and who does all he knows how to make us disobedient.—Ambrose Bierce, *The Devil's Dictionary*

16. Cleaning your house while your kids are still growing up is like shoveling the walk before it stops snowing.—Phyllis Diller

17. Anxiety is the dizziness of freedom.—Søren Kierkegaard

18. Perfectly to will what God wills, to want what He wants, is to have joy.—Meister Eckhart

19. This is the true joy in life, the being used for a purpose recognized by yourself as a mighty one.—George Bernard Shaw

20. If you want a place in the sun, prepare to put up with a few blisters.—Abigail Van Buren

21. You raise your voice when you should reinforce your argument.—Samuel Johnson

22. There is much to be said for failure. It is more interesting than success.—Max Beerbohm

23. There is nothing the body suffers which the soul may not profit by.—George Meredith

24. To speak of unforgivable sin is to impugn divine power.—St. Thomas Aquinas

25. We should all be concerned about the future because we will have to spend the rest of our lives there.—Charles F. Kettering

26. A God on the cross! That is all my theology.—Jean Lacordaire

27. Clean your finger before you point at my spots.—Benjamin Franklin

28. Without religion, morality becomes simply a matter of individual taste, of public opinion or majority vote.—Catholic Bishops of the United States, November 1952

29. I was gratified to be able to answer promptly. I said I don't know.—Mark Twain

30. The first sign of your becoming religious is that you are becoming cheerful.—Swami Vivekananda

31. If Christianity has never disturbed us, we have not yet learned what it is.—William Temple

32. Everything is funny as long as it is happening to somebody else.—Will Rogers

33. I've read the last page of the Bible. It's going to turn out all right.—Billy Graham

34. An individual religion can be as misleading and uninformed as an individual astronomy or an individual mathematics.—Fulton J. Sheen

35. It is easier to stay out than get out.—Mark Twain

36. The Bible is the Church's charter.—Hugh Pope

37. Dirt is matter out of place.—Oliver Lodge

38. God gave us memories so that we might have roses in December.—James M. Barrie

39. I once wanted to become an atheist, but I gave up—they have no holidays.—Henny Youngman

40. The place of the father in the modern suburban family is a very small one, particularly if he plays golf.—Bertrand Russell

41. I do not think the glory of God best promoted by a rigid abstinence from amusements.—John Keble

42. Seek the first possible opportunity to act on every good resolution you make.—William James

43. The God to whom little boys say their prayers has a face very like their mother's.—James M. Barrie

44. One man was so mad at me that he ended his letter: "Beware. You will never get out of this world alive."—John Steinbeck

45. Fanatics seldom laugh. They never laugh at themselves.—James M. Gillis

46. Superstition is to religion what astrology is to astronomy—the mad daughter of a wise mother.—Voltaire

47. The Holy Spirit is the living interiority of God.—Romano Guardini

48. Nowadays we know the price of everything and the value of nothing.—Oscar Wilde

49. I remember a friend of mine when growing up—he had every toy his father wanted.—James C. Humes

50. One of the most untruthful things possible . . . is a collection of facts, because they can be made to appear so many different ways.—Dr. Karl Menninger

51. The one thing we can never get enough of is love. And the one thing we never give enough is love.—Henry Miller

52. To be sure, it is a shocking thing, blowing smoke out of our mouths into other people's mouths, eyes, and noses, and having the same thing done to us.—Samuel Johnson

Questions of Life and Religion

These questions may be useful to prime homiletic pumps, as discussion starters, or for study and youth groups.

1. Are there absolutes, beliefs that are always true, that we can always rely on?

2. What are some of the features of the abundant life that Jesus came to give us?

3. How can we be sure that God accepts us?

4. Why is adultery wrong?

5. What special values does the season of Advent offer us?

6. When does adversity have positive results?

7. How does age affect our moral convictions?

8. Can the Bible help us make decisions about the use of alcoholic beverages?

9. Do we have personal angels to guide and protect us?

10. What can we say for and against anger?

11. Do we have a duty toward animals?

12. How can we handle anxiety?

13. Should we ever give up praying and hoping for the best for a particular "sinner"?

14. In what ways does the Apostle's Creed shore up our faith?

15. Can art be a servant of God?

16. What are the grounds of our assurance of salvation?

17. Why would anyone be an atheist?

18. What is the meaning of Christ's atonement?

19. How are our attitudes related to our character?

20. What are the sources of authority for a Christian?

21. What does baptism mean?

22. How much does one have to believe to be saved?

23. How are we to regard the Bible?

24. Can we bless people in such a way as to do them measurable good?

25. Do we have a moral obligation for the care of our body?

26. What can break the bondage of bad habits?

27. What are some of the books besides the Bible that contribute to spiritual growth?

28. How does God's call to special service come to an individual?

29. What are the pros and cons of capital punishment?

30. Is caring an inevitable attitude and activity for a true believer?

31. How do we distinguish between certainty and certitude?

32. Can human nature be changed?

33. What are the essential building blocks of solid character?

34. Why is cheating wrong?

35. What biblical standards should we apply in child rearing?

36. Is the test "What would Jesus do?" an adequate guide today?

37. Are there ways to observe Christmas more appropriately?

38. What is the Church and/or the church?

39. How does the gospel sometimes challenge tradition and custom?

40. What are the citizenship obligations of Christians?

41. According to John's Gospel, what are the several roles of the Comforter, the Holy Spirit?

42. To what do we commit ourselves when we make a profession of faith or experience confirmation?

43. What happens in Communion?
44. Is compromise un-Christian?
45. When is confession of our sins helpful?
46. How can conflict in Christian community be handled?
47. When is conscience a safe guide?
48. What are the sources of contentment?
49. How can we control our feelings and desires?
50. Is conversion once and for all or an ongoing process?
51. How are convictions formed?
52. What is courage?
53. When we call God "Creator," what do we mean?
54. How are cross and resurrection linked theologically?
55. What is a cult?
56. Death: friend or enemy?
57. Is depression a medical or a spiritual problem, or both?
58. How do we deny our Lord today?
59. Can disappointment become God's appointment?
60. How does God discipline his children?
61. What is divine providence?
62. Should divorce disqualify one for the service of God?
63. Is doubt a normal experience in the Christian pilgrimage?
64. What are our duties as good stewards of the earth?
65. When does eternal life begin?
66. How can we make responsible ethical decisions?
67. Why do we use such words as *the Lord's Supper, Communion,* and *Eucharist* to describe the memorial meal shared by Christians?
68. What are the various ways to do evangelism?
69. In what ways do we encounter evil in life?
70. What is faith?
71. How is family worship possible in our busy life today?
72. Can a faultfinding attitude be cured?
73. How can we master our fears?

74. Why is it difficult to forgive?
75. What does freedom in Christ mean?
76. What are the biblical guidelines for giving?
77. How can we practice the presence of God?
78. What is the gospel?
79. When do we experience the grace of God?
80. How does God guide us?
81. How can we "grow in the grace and knowledge of our Lord and Savior Jesus Christ"?
82. Can God use our handicaps in his service?
83. What is the difference between happiness and joy?
84. Why is hate self-defeating?
85. Does faith healing have a place in a church's ministry?
86. What does the Bible teach about heaven?
87. What is the role of the Holy Spirit in the life of a believer?
88. Does honesty require us to tell everything we know or feel?
89. How does hope function in the life of a Christian?
90. When is humility real?
91. What are some modern forms of idolatry?
92. In what ways are we made in the image of God?
93. Why did God come to us by incarnation, that is, in human form?
94. How does God speak to us today?
95. Does prayer for others do them good if they are not aware that we pray for them?
96. What does the humanity of Jesus imply?
97. When does judgment happen?
98. What is justification by faith?
99. Is there a necessary place for humor and laughter in the Christian life?
100. What is the purpose of Lenten observance?

Biblical Benedictions and Blessings

The Lord watch between me and thee when we are absent from one another.—Gen. 31:49

The Lord bless thee and keep thee; the Lord make his face to shine upon thee and be gracious unto thee; the Lord lift up his countenance upon thee and give thee peace.—Num. 6:24–26

The Lord our God be with us, as he was with our fathers; let him not leave us nor forsake us; that he may incline our hearts unto him, to walk in all his ways and to keep his commandments and his statutes and his judgments, which he commanded our fathers.—1 Kings 8: 57–58

Let the words of my mouth and the meditation of my heart be acceptable in thy sight, O Lord, my strength and my redeemer.—Ps. 19:14

Now the God of patience and consolation grant you to be like-minded one toward another according to Christ Jesus; that ye may with one mind and one mouth glorify God, even the Father of our Lord Jesus Christ. Now the God of hope fill you with all joy and peace in believing, that ye may abound in hope, through the power of the Holy Ghost. Now the God of peace be with you.—Rom. 15:5–6, 13, 33

Now to him that is of power to establish you according to my gospel and the teaching of Jesus Christ, according to the revelation of the mystery, which was kept secret since the world began, but now is manifest, and by the scriptures of the prophets, according to the commandment of the everlasting God, made known to all nations for the glory through Jesus Christ for ever.—Rom. 16:25–27

Grace be unto you, and peace, from God our Father, and from the Lord Jesus Christ.—1 Cor. 1:3

The grace of the Lord Jesus Christ and the love of God and the communion of the Holy Ghost be with you all.—2 Cor. 13:14

Peace be to the brethren, and love with faith, from God the Father and the Lord Jesus Christ. Grace be with all them that love our Lord Jesus Christ in sincerity.—Eph. 6:23–24

And the peace of God, which passeth all understanding, shall keep your hearts and minds through Christ Jesus. Finally, brethren, whatsoever things are true, whatsoever things are honest, whatsoever things are just; whatsoever things are pure, whatsoever things are lovely, whatsoever things are of good report; if there be any virtue, and if there by any praise, think on these things. Those things which ye have both learned and received, and heard and seen in me, do; and the God of peace shall be with you.—Phil. 4:7–9

Wherefore also we pray always for you, that our God would count you worthy of this calling and fulfill all the good pleasure of this goodness, and the work of faith with power; that the name of our Lord Jesus Christ may be glorified in you, and ye in him, according to the grace of our God and the Lord Jesus Christ.—2 Thess. 1:11–12

Now the Lord of peace himself give you peace always by all means. The Lord be with you all. The grace of our Lord Jesus Christ be with you all.—2 Thess. 3:16–18

Grace, mercy, and peace, from God our Father and Jesus Christ our Lord.—1 Tim. 1:2

Now the God of peace, that brought again from the dead our Lord Jesus, that great shepherd of the sheep, through the blood of the everlasting covenant, make you perfect in every good work to do his will, working in you that which is well-pleasing in his sight, through Jesus Christ, to whom be glory for ever and ever.—Heb. 13:20–21

The God of all grace, who hath called us unto his eternal glory by Christ Jesus, after that ye have suffered a while, make you perfect, establish, strengthen, settle you. To him be glory and dominion for ever and ever. Greet ye one another with a kiss of charity. Peace be with you all that are in Christ Jesus.—1 Pet. 3:10–11, 14

Grace be with you, mercy, and peace, from God the Father, and from the Lord Jesus Christ, the Son of the Father, in truth and love.—2 John 3

Now unto him that is able to keep you from falling, and to present you faultless before the presence of his glory with exceeding joy, to the only wise God our Savior, be glory and majesty, dominion and power, both now and ever.—Jude 24–25

Grace be unto you, and peace, from him which was, and which is to come; and from the seven Spirits which are before his throne; and from Jesus Christ, who is the faithful witness, and the first begotten of the dead, and the prince of the kings of the earth. Unto him that loved us, and washed us from our sins in his own blood, and hath made us kings and priests unto God and his Father, to him be glory and dominion for ever and ever.—Rev. 1:4–6

SECTION II.
Sermons and Homiletic and Worship Aids for Fifty-Two Sundays

SUNDAY: JANUARY FOURTH

Topic: Living in the Light
TEXT: John 1:1–18
Other Readings: Jer. 31:7–14; Ps. 147:12–20; Eph. 1:3–14

Fear of the dark is a real problem for some people. Often children, but adults too, are terrified of the dark. Yet a reverse twist on that subject is sometimes seen in the Scriptures. The suggestion is there that some people actually prefer darkness to the light because "their deeds are evil." The darkness can serve as a cover to hide from others that which is sinful, that which if seen in the light would harm one's reputation or cause others to view one as a hypocrite. John makes clear in the introduction to his Gospel that life needs to be lived in the light. One need not be afraid of the dark, and one need not cower in the darkness for fear of the light. In fact, the opening verses of the first chapter of the Gospel are dominated by the words *life* and *light*. And both of those words are attached to Jesus, for "in him was life, and that life was the light of men," and he is the One who is "the true light that gives light to every man." The good news is that not only that life *needs* to be lived in the light, but life *can* be lived in that light.

I. *The light challenges the darkness.* With the coming of Christ everything was turned upside down. Does darkness obscure the light? Not anymore, at least not for the person who walks by faith. In Christ's coming the darkness is challenged and can no longer maintain its power to dominate with

fear the lives of Jesus' followers. Martin Luther, the great Protestant reformer, often wrote, prior to his discovery of the magnificence of God's grace, of his fear that God would find him out as the worst of sinners and bring his wrath down upon him. Luther discovered, however, a God of love who brought the light of his grace in Christ to bear upon Luther and brought forgiveness to him even in the darkness of his sin. The darkness, while perhaps unable to understand it, cannot bear the challenge of "the true light." All the poets and the old gospel songs have it right: for those who believe, Christ does dispel the darkness. "He turns the night to day."

If darkness is the abode of fear, then this Gospel's call to life in the light provides a way of escape with the help of a word of confidence and joy. It is amazing how often the Bible has God saying to his children, "Do not be afraid." Remember Joshua at the time of Moses' death, when all the responsibilities of leadership for the people of Israel fell upon his shoulders? God more than once tells Joshua not to be afraid and to "be strong and very courageous." Likewise, the first words of the Resurrected Lord to the women in the garden that first Easter were, "Do not be afraid." Because the "true light" has come— because Jesus has come—we who believe need never be afraid of the dark or of anything, even death.

II. *Life in the light.* A concept such as never again having to be afraid suggests a special relationship to the Resurrected Christ, who alone is able to deliver us from the darkness of fear and to make possible life in the light. The first followers of Jesus came to understand their relationship to him in a variety of evolving ways. They initially understood themselves to be his "disciples," learners who received instruction from their teacher. Jesus' own ministry as modeled before his disciples was characterized and defined as a "servant" ministry. Yet Jesus came to the point of letting them see that while they were indeed to be his servants, they were more, much more. They were also his "friends."

But in the prologue to his Gospel, John speaks of another even more glorious dimension of that relationship that we experience as we live in the light. What joyous good news that "to all who received him, to those who believed in his name, he gave the right to become children of God"! Life in the light is fellowship in which one experiences the reality of God's presence, thus dispelling all fear. In that fellowship with Christ, and with others who know him too, we learn experientially the real meaning of life with all of the spiritual abundance that Christ promised. We come to know the real peace that he bequeathed to us and we experience the authentic joy of life that comes from the assurance of his love and grace. To live in the light of the reality of Christ's presence is to know oneself as a child of God.

III. *To live in the light is to reflect the light.* We also see in today's text that John the Baptist had the great responsibility for bearing witness to Christ the true light. Those of us who have accepted the call to live in the light are called to live in the tradition of John as well—that is, to bear our witness to Christ. If the Sermon on the Mount has validity for followers of Jesus today, then the words of Christ are as applicable to us now as they were to his original disciples. He said: "You are the light of the world. . . . Let your light shine before men that they may see your good deeds and praise your Father in heaven."

The call to discipleship—the call to live in the light—is a call to reflect the light of God's glory as revealed in Jesus Christ together with God's people in a community of faith. This call is at the core of the church's purpose. The church is called to reflect the light of God's love and grace in radical obedience. To reflect

that light is to be involved in God's redemptive mission in the world. That involvement signifies glorious privilege and awesome responsibility.—Dwight A. Honeycutt

Illustrations

THE COMING OF LIGHT.   Martin Luther is known to us as a person of great faith and self-confidence. Most often he is depicted standing his ground and proclaiming his convictions before the combined might and power of European religious and political institutions. At the mention of Luther's name our minds always leap to the solitary monk declaring before the Diet of Worms, "My soul is captive to the word of God. Here I stand. God help me."

Yet Martin Luther lived a significant portion of his life in fear: fear of his own death and fear of God. He grew up in a setting where death came often—too often to the young—and old age was something few people would live to see. And Luther grew up in an atmosphere where, because of his sin, he had come to believe that God was his enemy, not his friend. Years into his life as a reformer he would tell someone: "I was always told I ought to love God. But the truth is I did not love God. I hated God, because I believed God hated me." It took his famous "Tower Experience" to convince Luther that God loved him. As he struggled with Paul's Letter to the Romans, light broke for Luther; he found deliverance from his fear and the discovery of God's love in the truth that "the just shall live by faith."—D.A.H.

BECOMING CHILDREN OF GOD.   Leon Morris says of this marvelous potential of becoming children of God that John promises in the prologue to his Gospel: "It seems to me that John is simply piling up one expression on top of another to bring out his point that entrance into the heavenly family is not the result of anything human. It is not what we do nor where we stand in the human scale of importance that effects our entrance. We can do a good deal for ourselves and for one another in the here and now, but membership in God's family is quite another thing. . . . John is saying that no human effort of any sort will get us into the family of God. . . . Nothing human can bring it about."[1] Life in the family of God is gift.—D.A.H.

SERMON SUGGESTIONS

Topic: God's Endless Quest
TEXT: 2 Chron. 16:9
(1) One can take both pessimistic and optimistic views of humans. We hunger for God, and God hungers for us. (2) This endless quest of God for us is the central theme of the Bible. (3) God seeks us: through our daily experiences, through the beautiful lives of those about us, through our own individual needs, through the needs of others. (4) Why does God seek us? Not to cheat us but to enlarge us with the abundance of his blessings.[2]

Topic: Strength out of Weakness
TEXT: 2 Cor. 12:10
(1) *The Problem:* Weakness—physical and/or spiritual. (2) *The Potential:* (a) Does my life day by day witness to the power of the Gospel of Christ? (b) Does my faith in Christ affect the quality of my daily living? (c) Is there anything in my life that reminds people of the Master to whom I have pledged my allegiance? (d) Is there any discernible difference at all in my life as contrasted with the lives of those who have never acknowledged him? (e) Do I manifest in the midst of this fevered generation a serenity of spirit that reveals that the peace of God is dwelling in my heart? (3) *The Power:* The sufficiency of Christ's strength realized in surrender and self-mastery through Christ-mastery.[3]

Hymn Suggestions:
The Second Sunday After Christmas

1. "Of the Father's Begotten," Marcus A. Prudentius (4th century); "Divinum Mysterium" (Ancient plainsong)

[1]Leon Morris, *Reflections on the Gospel of John,* vol. 1: *The Word Was Made Flesh, John 1–5* (Grand Rapids: Baker Book House, 1986), 14–15.
[2]Adapted from Clovis G. Chappell, *God's Endless Quest.*
[3]Adapted from John Sutherland Bonnell, *Strength Out of Weakness.*

This ancient hymn admirably proclaims the truth of the prologue of the fourth Gospel. Its plainchant tune lends itself to antiphonal treatment.
2. "Praise to the Living God," medieval Jewish liturgy; "The God of Abraham Praise," Leoni, (17th-century Hebrew melody)
This hymn—words and music stemming from the Hebrew tradition—gathers up the notes of praise and thanksgiving for the blessings of the eternal God of Israel that are expressed in the Scripture selections from the prophet Jeremiah and the psalmist.
3. "You Satisfy the Hungry Heart," Omer Westendorf (1976); "Bicentennial," Robert E. Kreutz (1976)
Having for its refrain the thought expressed in Psalm 147:14b, this has become a popular hymn for use at communion.
4. "Holy, Holy," Jimmy Owens (1972)
The contemporary song "Holy, Holy" encompasses in its stanzas praise of the Trinity in the spirit of the Apostle Paul's message to the Ephesians (Eph. 1:3–14).—Hugh T. McElrath

Worship Aids

CALL TO WORSHIP. "Happy are those who do not follow the advice of the wicked, or take the path that sinners tread, or sit in the seat of scoffers; but their delight is in the law of the Lord, and on his law they meditate day and night" (Ps. 1:1–2 NRSV).

INVOCATION. Gracious Lord, as we make our way through this new year and through our entire lifetime, help us to see that for every type of temptation and testing there is a better way and a best way to respond. Give us the light that leads to your law, so that we can find our truest freedom and fulfillment.

OFFERTORY SENTENCE. "This is the thing which the Lord commanded, saying, Take ye from among you an offering unto the Lord: whosoever is of a willing heart, let him bring it, an offering of the Lord" (Exod. 35:4–5).

OFFERTORY PRAYER. We thank you, Lord, for making it possible for us to honor you with our offerings. Multiply them in their influence, so that your kingdom may grow, and we shall rejoice.

PRAYER.   Eternal Father, quest of ages, we never looked to meet thee in the stress of thought, the toil of life, or in the call of duty; we only knew that somehow life had lost for us all meaning, dignity, and beauty. How then shall we turn back again and see with eyes that fear has filmed? How can we be born again, now grown so old in fatal habit?

If we could see this life of ours in thee, its common days exalted, its circumstances made a throne, its bitterness, disappointment, and failure all redeemed, then our hearts might stir again, and these trembling hands lay hold on life forevermore.—W. E. Orchard

Sermon: Life Surrounded by God

TEXT: Ps. 125:2

This sermon begins with the rather commonplace observation that life cannot be understood apart from its surroundings. We are concerned, therefore, about the surroundings of life, and particularly on this first Sunday of the new year.

The spiritual leaders of the Hebrew people dared to believe that life is completely surrounded by God. "As the mountains are round about Jerusalem, so the Lord is round about his people from henceforth even for ever." This sermon, therefore, is the affirmation of the simple yet staggering fact that life is completely surrounded by God.

I. It is only fair, however, that we admit at the outset that there are attractive alternatives to that particular affirmation. Standing by the strict use of the word *alternative,* we can fairly say that in this instance there is only one alternative. There are others that sound plausible, but when you put them together, the only real alternative to the fact that life is completely surrounded by God is that life is surrounded by dust and darkness. Life—from blank to blank.

Columbia professor of philosophy Irwin Edman said, "Life is a brief bright moment between two oblivions of darkness. That lighted interval is ours to make the most of." This life we are living—a brief bright moment between two oblivions!

Such an alternative to the Bible affirmation has at least this much to be said for it: it is perfectly safe. Its sights are low. No one who accepts that alternative is in danger of being disappointed. It also puts a large premium on life and light. Saying that we have only this brief, bright moment between two dark oblivions does seem to imply that we had better make the most of the little sparks of life for the few moments that we have them. If you can take the kind of ultimate desperation that is implied in that assumption, then you are likely to have at least this much in your favor: you will lay hold on life and make something of it while you have it. From nothingness to nothingness, life surrounded by emptiness—that is the alternative.

II. But that alternative, attractive as it is, safe as it is, simply does not stand up when life is at its best.

a. For instance, when a baby is born. There is nothing much more mysterious in the world than that. There before you is a tiny bundle of human possibilities. All the human faculties are there, all the possibilities of the future stretch out before you in your imagination. Ask the father and mother what the baby's life is surround by. Do you think they would ever say by darkness, by sleep, by nothing? That baby is surrounded by their love. That baby comes from God and is on his way to God and all his life long will be surrounded by the embrace of the mind and the love that has conceived him. Nothing less will do at a time like that!

b. Likewise, when you listen to a Bach fugue. Is this surrounded by blankness? Does this great performance of sound come of the dark unconsciousness of sleep, and is it destined merely to be buried again in dust and darkness? That simply will not do. This fugue is surrounded by the mind of God.

c. So, even more so, when a great man appears upon the scene. One of the great men of all generations was Albert Schweitzer. You perhaps already know that he was the world's greatest exponent of Bach, and that he was one of the greatest Biblical scholars and writers of philosophy in the Western world. You may also know that he began, after all these other achievements, to study medicine. He went down into equatorial Africa, built a hospital, administered it, and took care of people there. When you come up against a man like that you cannot say that this great mind and spirit has come out of darkness and dust. There is too much dynamic, creative genius there. You can only say that this man has come from the mind of the Maker of all things and is destined ultimately to return to that same mind.

III. If it is true that life is surrounded by God, it makes a decided difference to us.

a. For one thing, if it is true, it makes the trials in transit more easily borne, more worth bearing. Some of us who are subject to seasickness would find our queasiness very difficult to bear if we were sailing from the shores of boredom to some place we cared not where. But if we are moving toward some place to which we wish to go and upon which our gaze is fastened, we can somehow bear with better grace the trials in transit.

b. Even more important, being surrounded by God takes the curse off the passing of time. I am not altogether sure how you feel on New Year's Day, whether you are among those who completely let themselves go in the frivolity that is characteristic of the celebration of that day. As for myself, I am occasionally in danger on New Year's Day of being depressed, because then more than at usually any other time during the year I am acutely aware of the fact that time is passing. One year less. What is more, I am one year nearer to that inevitable disintegration of all this physical makeup of mine. And I begin to ask myself, passing from what to what? And I think of some of the elderly people I see, breaking down after a long, glorious life, literally decomposing before my eyes, disintegrating, losing their personality many times, and their minds—is that what we are passing toward? Am I just drifting, idling, killing time to stave off that inevitable plunge into the darkness of oblivion? Then I try to remember the affirmation that we set before ourselves today and I think of some of the great elderly people that I have seen go through those torturous periods. I try to change the whole complex of my thought so that it goes something like this: here is a great soul not disintegrating but, sometimes in agony and with a good deal of transitional pain, heroically slipping loose from its moorings, preparing to launch out into the mystery of the great depths of God, the wonders of whose love we have never dared to conceive or fully imagine. Here is a soul going out into the unknown to meet its Maker face to face. And there is nothing grim about that.

c. Remember Jesus, and as you remember him, can you think of him surrounded by dust and darkness? Can you think of that life, streaming out of human existence like a comet, living his brief span and then dying on the cross to rise into newness of life—can you think of that life as surrounded completely by dust and darkness? Or do the words of John the Evangelist express it more truly and more adequately for you: "Jesus, knowing that he was come from God and went to God, took a towel and washed the disciples feet." Do you see how that affirmation lifts the whole of life up from oblivion toward the great horizons of reality and gives it depth and strength, gives it the power to reach down into the dust and wash our feet and perform the most menial service known to man?

d. That, then, is the affirmation I would like to leave you with at the beginning of a new year. Think of it when you are up against the trials and tribulations of a difficult crossing and say it over and over again to yourself, Life, my life, all life is surrounded by God.—Theodore Parker Ferris[4]

Illustrations

LORD AND FATHER. God is not only Father, he is also Lord. The whole world is his: he is King. Nature and history both come under his rule. Nevertheless, his rule is not yet fully exercised. The world is "in the power of the evil one." Man must look forward to a future when God's rule will be open and not hidden. In the meantime, God's rule is exercised through those who respond to his love and cooperate in his purposes. To them belongs a present responsibility and a future joy. Thus God's providence is both universal and particular. Because he is Lord, his active care is universal. Because he is Father, it is also particular. It is known by man especially in the forgiveness of his sins and his restoration to a right relationship with his God.—Peter Baelz[5]

THE SUMMING UP. Scarcely once in a year does anything really remarkable befall

---

[4] *Selected Sermons,* Vol. 2.
[5] *Prayer and Providence.*

us. If I were to begin and give an inventory of the things you do in a single day, your muscular motions, each of which is accomplished by a separate act of will, the objects you see, the words you utter, the contrivances you frame, your thoughts, passions, gratifications, and trials, many of you would not be able to hear it recited with sobriety. But 365 such days make up a year, and a year is a twentieth, fiftieth, or seventieth part of your life. And thus, with the exception of a few striking passages, or a few great and critical occasions, perhaps not more than five or six in all, your life is made up of common, and as men are wont to judge, unimportant things. But yet, at the end, you have done up an amazing work, and fixed an amazing result. You stand at the bar of God, and look back on a life made up of small things—yet a life, how momentous, for good or evil!—Horace Bushnell

SUNDAY: JANUARY ELEVENTH

LECTIONARY MESSAGE

Topic: What Are You Afraid Of?

TEXT: Matt. 2:1–12

Other Readings: Isa. 60:1–6; Ps. 72:1–7, 10–14; Eph. 3:1–12

In 1943 the German minister-theologian and ultimate martyr Dietrich Bonhoeffer was arrested by the Gestapo and imprisoned. Earlier that year he had become engaged to Maria von Wedemeyer. Alone in a prison cell, cut off from Maria, family, and friends, he composed a poem in the form of a prayer, which reads in part: "In me there is darkness. . . . I am lonely. . . . I am feeble in heart. . . . In me there is bitterness. . . . I do not understand your ways. . . ."[6] Bonhoeffer's world at that moment was a world of personal fear and anxiety. Admittedly, compared to our world Bonhoeffer's world was unique; and no one would wish to trivialize his experience by comparing it with our own dark moments of fear and anxiety. Yet if we are honest, we must admit that some degree of personal fear and anxiety is no stranger to us.

The Scriptures are intensely reflective of fear as a reality of human existence. For example, today's text from Matthew's Gospel reflects the presence of fear in that long ago age—a fear with which most of us today can identify. The word about a child who would be king did not bring joy to everyone. The main characters in the story all experienced fear.

I. *King Herod's fear was that the child would be found and that everything would be changed.* The narrative indicates that when Herod heard from the Magi about their search for one who recently had been born to be king of the Jews, "he was troubled and all Judea with him." King Herod on more than one occasion had put to death people who he feared posed a threat to his political status and power. Some of those he murdered or had executed had been members of his own family. Now the mission of the Magi in search of a new king generated new fear for Herod. His greatest fear was that the child would be found and Herod's world would be changed; everything would be upset. The trappings of his personal power would be lost. Everything would be changed.

Perhaps it is true that we, even those of us who claim to be the people of God, at times would prefer not to find him. We become fearful and anxious in knowing that an awareness of his presence would cause everything to change. What would we have to give up if we truly found him? What would his presence mean in terms of changed attitudes in the face of strained relationships? Would not finding him require of us a Christ-like response to the outcast, the hungry, the homeless? Certainly to really find him would cost us the comfort of our own selfishness and self-centeredness. Is that perhaps the real fear that at times dominates our lives: the fear that we will actually find him—or be found by him—and be confronted by the demands of that love that knows no boundaries, and that everything will be changed?

II. *The fear of the Magi was that they would not find him and nothing would be changed.* The

---

[6]Dietrich Bonhoeffer, *Letters and Papers from Prison* (New York: Collier Books, 1971), 139.

Magi, of course, are popularly known as the three wise men. We do not know how many there actually were in this particular group; early tradition suggested that there were twelve, while later tradition reduced their number to three. Likewise, we do not know the specific lands from which they came. But whoever they were, and however many there might have been, the point is that they had set out on a quest. They responded to the phenomenon of the star they had seen in the east. They came to the conclusion that a king was to be born, and now they were in Jerusalem seeking him. Yet he was not to be found in Jerusalem. How many doubts they must have had along the way! In Jerusalem they still had hope, but they must also have known fear—fear that they might not find him and that they would have to settle for things the way they had always been. But on the road to Bethlehem they saw the star again and were overjoyed. Their faith in moving toward the light overcame their fear and anxiety.

Fear and anxiety are powerful forces. Psychiatrists indicate that these forces can be so strong that they can even result in physical paralysis. Fear may result in an individual's being unable to move. Likewise, fear has the potential to make us spiritual and emotional paralytics. We surrender our hopes. We give up on our dreams. What happens if we set out to fulfill our hopes and they are never realized? What happens if we seek to make our dreams come true and it never happens? Are we sometimes characterized as those unwilling to take the risks of faith for fear that we will not find him and nothing will be changed?

III. *The Magi found him. They worshiped him. Everything was changed.* The Magi took the risk of faith. If we do that, we shall surely find him. Yet in finding him and truly worshiping him we likely will realize that we shall still have to live with some of our fears. Nevertheless, we will know with certainty that everything has changed. For in finding him and worshiping him we know that it is not a matter of giving gifts to Mary's son. It is rather a matter of giving our hearts to the Son of God. And then, everything is changed!

In the introduction to this meditation a portion of a poetic prayer of the imprisoned Dietrich Bonhoeffer was quoted. A few phrases were left out that now need to be included. For in the hurt of that experience he not only confessed his fear but also affirmed his faith in a loving God. Yes, he did pray, "In me there is darkness," yet he followed that with the declaration, "*but* with you there is light; I am lonely, *but* you do not leave me; I am feeble in heart, *but* with you there is help; I am restless, *but* with you there is peace; in me there is bitterness, *but* with you there is patience; I do not understand your ways, *but* you know the way for me." For us as for Bonhoeffer, even in the midst of our fear God desires to find us with his grace so that we in turn will be able to share the good news with a fearful world.—Dwight A. Honeycutt

Illustrations

THIS AGE.   The twentieth-century English poet W. H. Auden won a Pulitzer Prize in 1948, just three years after the death of Dietrich Bonhoeffer at the hands of the Nazi regime in Germany. Auden's prize-winning work was a poem entitled *The Age of Anxiety*. Paul Tillich, the native-born German theologian who himself had been dismissed from his professorship in a German university for his opposition to Hitler in the 1930s, said of *The Age of Anxiety* that Auden's poem "mirrored" perfectly the present age. And indeed it does, for the reflection of the work mirrors history generally. Every age is an "age of anxiety."[7]—D.A.H.

RESOURCES.   Anxiety and fear generate deeply personal and painful experiences. Yet Christianity claims to offer resources that counter the pain. The late Methodist bishop Bromley Oxnam, who was a minister in churches and a professor of theology in California before moving to the East Coast in 1927, on one occasion a few days before a particular Christmas wrote these words in his journal: "Yesterday a beautiful poinsettia was delivered to our home. No gift could be more meaningful to a Californian. It was sent by a young and highly gifted pastor. Three years ago I had appointed him to a nice

---

[7]Edward Callan, *Auden: A Carnival of Intellect* (New York: Oxford University Press, 1983), 212.

church. He was very happy. Then came news that his little son was seriously ill. It was cancer, and there was no hope. Death did not come swiftly. The little boy is still alive, perhaps to suffer a few weeks more. The minister and his lovely wife have carried on. He preaches; he ministers to his people. . . . [But] every night he is just a dad. He sits for hours holding his son in his arms. The pain seems less when the father holds him close. The father sleeps on a mattress on the floor beside his boy, so that he can take his son in his arms again whenever the boy cries out. He does not dwell on his sorrow. He prays. He serves. He sends poinsettias at Christmas. That is what happens when one bows before a manger and kneels before a cross."[8] Indeed the pain seems less when the Father holds us close.—D.A.H.

SERMON SUGGESTIONS

Topic: Personal Guidance or Pious Guess?
  TEXT: 1 Sam. 2:9
  God is concerned about every step I take as a sinner who wants to know more about him: (1) mostly through circumstances that afterwards I see to have been formed and shaped by his gracious hand; (2) through the clarifying of insights; God's guidance doesn't come at the expense of my mind, my best judgment, my clearest thinking; (3) through the deepening of conviction in the growing beliefs that arise in the stresses and strains, the calls and the refusals of our daily setting.—Elam Davies[9]

Topic: Highest Things
  TEXT: Matt. 3:13–17
  (1) The highest preacher, God. (2) The highest pulpit, the heavens. (3) The highest sermon: "This is my beloved Son, in whom I am well pleased."—Martin Luther

Hymn Suggestions: Epiphany Sunday

  1. "Jesus Shall Reign," Isaac Watts (1719); "Duke Street," John Hatton (c. 1790)

[8]"Manger and Mankind," in *Best Sermons, 1955,* ed. by G. Paul Butler (New York: McGraw-Hill, 1955), 117.
[9]*This Side of Eden.*

This, the earliest of missionary hymns in English, is Watts's free paraphrase or imitation of Psalm 72. He transformed the Hebrew psalm, with its prophecy of the glories of Solomon's reign, into a celebration of the conquests of Christ throughout the world.
  2. "As with Gladness Men of Old," William C. Dix (c. 1858); "Dix," Conrad Kocher (1838)
  The man who wrote the lyrics of this hymn, an insurance executive, was inspired during an illness, after reading the gospel story in Matthew 2.
  3. "O Morning Star, How Fair and Bright," Philipp Nicolai; "Wie Schön Leuchtet," Nicolai (1597)
  This classic chorale, known as "the Queen of Chorales," boldly addresses the Morning Star, symbolizing Christ, the "Light divine," which proclaimed to the kings from the East the hope and the blessing of the world.
  4. "Shine, Jesus, Shine," Graham Kendrick (1987); "Shine," Kendrick
  This song, made popular in youth evangelistic circles, voices the Epiphany theme of the light of Christ shining forth into a world of darkness, thus revealing the truth of the gospel to all people.

Worship Aids

CALL TO WORSHIP   "Salvation belongeth unto the Lord; thy blessing is upon thy people" (Ps. 3:8).

INVOCATION.
  Still us, Lord, we are restless.
  Quiet us, Lord, we are worried.
  Calm us, Lord, we are burdened.
  Then speak to us, Lord.
  For we need you every hour,
  And in this hour we seek your face.
                                  —E. Lee Phillips

OFFERTORY SENTENCE.   "The children of Israel brought a willing offering unto the Lord, every man and woman, whose heart made them willing to bring for all manner of work, which the Lord had commanded to be made by the hand of Moses" (Exod. 35:29).

OFFERTORY PRAYER.   Lord, we give today because we have first committed our lives to you. Take what we bring and use it to anchor others in the faith and joy of our Lord Jesus Christ.—E. Lee Phillips

PRAYER.   O God, we rejoice that today no burden of work will be upon us and that our body and soul are free to rest. We thank thee that of old this day was hallowed by thee for all who toil, and that from generation to generation the weary have found it a shelter and a breathing space. We pray for thy peace on all our brothers and sisters who are glad to cease from labor and to enjoy the comfort of their home and the companionship of those whom they love. Forbid that the pressure of covetousness or thoughtless love of pleasure rob any who are worn of their divine right of rest. Grant us wisdom and self-control that our pleasures may not be follies, lest our leisure drain us more than our work. Teach us that in the mystic unity of our nature our body cannot rest unless our soul has repose, that so we may walk this day in thy presence in tranquillity of spirit, taking each joy as thy gift, and on the morrow return to our labor refreshed and content.— Walter Rauschenbusch

Sermon: Speechless Wonder

TEXT: Gen. 1:1–8; Ps. 19:1–2

It was to be the culmination of the entire Youth Mission trip. It was to be a time for drawing things to a close—a time to be together and a time to enjoy God's amazing world.

Our goal was to see the Grand Canyon. The evening before we were finally to reach the Grand Canyon we all stood in a parking lot in Flagstaff, Arizona, and made our plans for the next day. And that's when I heard the question that gave me the direction for this sermon today. It was a question asked by one of our youth. The question was this, "Well, after we look at it, what do we do then?"

The doctrine of creation is one of the core doctrines of the Christian faith. It's not trivial, not insignificant, not optional. The doctrine of creation claims that this world—this entire world and everything in it—has been created by God. He's the source; he's the designer; he's the maker. Creation tells us a great deal about God—it tells us about his nature and his character and his power. But creation also tells us a great deal about our-

selves—it tells us about our source and our purpose, and it tells us about what God has in mind for us.

It has been the conviction from the earliest days of the Christian community that God created everything out of nothing. Our first reaction to that kind of picture is fairly predictable: Well, how exactly did that happen? What did it look like? When did it happen? And the Bible is consistent in calling us to go beyond questions such as these—and stand in awe before the Creator. According to the Bible, what is most important is not *how* God did it but *that* he did it.

God created everything out of nothing. If that's true, it means that God is radically, completely, totally different from everything else that exists. The doctrine of creation is the doctrine that reminds us that God is utterly transcendent, completely free, and absolutely sovereign. It is the doctrine of creation that reminds us that God is God. His ways are not our ways—and he can work in ways that are worlds beyond our understanding and comprehension. God can do what he chooses to do—because he's God.

But that same God—that same transcendent, free, and sovereign God—is also the One who calls us into intimate relationship. And that's part of the doctrine of creation as well. You see, this mighty creating God invites us to walk with him. He's the maker of all things—*and* he's also the One in whom we live and move and have our being. The One who spoke and called this world into being is also the One who cares about the hurts that scar our lives. And it is the doctrine of creation that forces us to hold these two truths in tension.

Which leads us right back to our question: "After we look at it, what do we do then?"

The words "he is my Creator" will always be followed by praise. The realization that he is Creator will always be followed by the realization that he is Lord. When we see that he has made us, we have no choice but to fall on our knees and worship that One who has given us life.

And that's what I learned at the Grand Canyon. God overwhelmed me with his distance and his nearness. He used a huge hole in the ground to remind me of his majesty and of my need to worship him. Do you ever notice how things change from season to season—but how things also seem to stay the same even as they change? This is God's creation—and when we see it as God's creation, we're moved to worship and praise.

This is our Father's world—and he's filled it with amazing wonders. He's filled it with pictures and parables of love and grace. And he's filled it with enough beauty to keep us speechless for a long, long time.

"After we look at it, what do we do then?" Well, if we really look at it, we'll know exactly what to do. We'll fall on our faces and we'll sing praise to the One who is the Creator.—Barry A. Stricker

Illustrations

CREATION.   I saw three properties: the first is that God made it; the second is that God loveth it; the third is that God keepeth it. But what beheld I therein? Verily the Maker, the Keeper, the Lover.—Julian of Norwich[10]

GOD'S ACTS.   What we say about God, whatever of praise and prayer is laid upon our lips, is an answer to his glorious and fearful acts. Therefore the preacher is charged with the task of understanding and retelling the story.—Kornelius M. Miskotte[11]

SUNDAY: JANUARY EIGHTEENTH

LECTIONARY MESSAGE

Topic: Sharing in Miracles
  TEXT: John 2:1–11
  Other Readings: Isa. 62:1–5; Ps. 36:5–10; 1 Cor. 12:1–11

Have you ever witnessed a miracle? "Perhaps," you respond, "depending on your definition." I doubt, however, that most of us would claim to have *performed* a miracle. Yet this interesting text for today seems to suggest that we can *share* in the miracles of our Lord. At the wedding at Cana in Galilee, Jesus turned the water into wine. Some of those present, though playing minor roles in the drama, assisted Christ on this occasion of his first sign of self-revelation. They shared in the miracle. If, as the chorus declares, he is still "a God of might and miracles, 'tis written in the skies," then Christ's disciples today should remain alert to opportunities to share in what he is doing in our world.

I. *The miraculous sign reveals Christ's glory.* John interprets that the changing of the water into wine does more than simply meet an emergency social need (v. 11). The original wine was gone, and there were still guests to be served. The miracle certainly saved the occasion from being a social disaster; it did make the host look very good. The real point, however, is one of tremendous theological significance. To read the first eleven chapters of the Gospel of John is to come across one sign after another. The signs signify some aspect of who Jesus is: the Savior sent from God. In the miraculous sign of

changing water to wine at the wedding, John stresses, and we dare not miss the point, that Christ "thus revealed his glory." Christ comes to us in glory through the pages of scripture. It is not just water that he changes, but the lives of those who seek him in faith. In a way that can only be described as miraculous, they come to apprehend his glory.

II. *A recognition of Christ's power enables one to share in his miracles.* Appearing in the story is Mary, the mother of our Lord and that wonderful prototype of what a Christian ought to be. It is encouraging that in John's narrative Mary is seen as a person like us; that is, she is seen as one who needs to grow in understanding of Christ and his redemptive mission. Nevertheless, she seems certain that Jesus has the power to deal with any situation. This is seen in her instructions to the servants, "Do whatever he tells you."

One challenge of living life as a follower of Jesus is to surrender ourselves to him as Lord in such a way that we respond to him in radical obedience. It is the challenge to live life with a committed mind-set, to do whatever he tells us. The commitment of our lives to Jesus in radical obedience, if it is to be authentic, will have its roots in the assurance of the availability of Christ's power to aid and sustain us. We will be able and we will be empowered to share with Jesus in his redemptive mission in the world: the mission

---

[10] *Revelations of Divine Love.*
[11] *When the Gods Are Silent.*

of helping people encounter Christ in such a way that they move from darkness to light, from death to life.

III. *Obedient servants share in God's miracles.* Those who followed the instructions and did what Jesus told them to do were the servants. They are often ignored in the biblical commentaries. They have minor roles in the story. They are bit players in the drama. Jesus told them to "fill the jars with water" and "they filled them to the brim." Then they faded into the background. Yet minor though it was, they did have a part to play.

Sometimes we followers of Christ, though called to be "the least" and "servants of all," seem to get mixed up, if our actions are any kind of indicator. We seem to need an overabundance of recognition and affirmation. More often than not we seem to want to be on center stage in the limelight. We would prefer to be the star of the show rather than relegated to playing a supporting role or bit part. If the truth were to be known, some of us would much prefer to turn the water into wine ourselves than to fill the jars with water. We would prefer to perform the miracle than simply to share in the miracle. However, we Christians are called to share in Christ's miraculous redemptive work rather than to be the miracle workers ourselves. We have the privilege at times of helping to prepare the way for God to do something absolutely breathtaking and wonderful, and yes, even miraculous. Like John we need to discern that the implications of living out our belief in Christ have to do with his glory, not ours. And in our following him, though it may mean that we receive little or no personal recognition, we are challenged to live in such a way that his glory is revealed.

What a privilege to be able to live a life sharing in the miracles of Christ! Where the church is gathered, there is Christ. He has called his people to mission. He has called them to tell a story—a story that reflects his revealed glory. There in the midst of his people his presence and power are made manifest. As God's people are faithful and obedient to the mission entrusted to them, as they exalt Christ in their actions and attitudes, his glory will be revealed. And just as John said of the disciples who were at that wedding so long ago and beheld that glory,

people today will likewise "put their faith in him."—Dwight A. Honeycutt

Illustrations

THE LESSON.   Herschel H. Hobbs, in reflection on the miracle at the wedding at Cana in Galilee, suggests: "Knowing the mystical nature of John, one cannot help but see the inferred lesson. The 'wine,' or way of life, which Jesus provides, is better than that which was available under the Law or under the Jewish system of religion. But John clearly states his primary purpose in recording this 'sign.' It was the first of many which revealed the glory of Christ. And the disciples, who already believed in Him, had their faith strengthened thereby."[12]—D.A.H.

Who did it? I once observed an individual who had received great accolades for several accomplishments express gratitude for those words of praise. His response was very ego-centered. He presented an outstanding litany of what *he* had done. I was aware, however, that this person had secured a number of volunteers to assist him in achieving his rather significant tasks. Yet in his response to the appreciation directed to him personally he made no mention of the many others who had labored long and hard in the background to make his success possible. Often we tend to forget those whose roles at times may seem minor but whose assistance is absolutely essential. If they share in the labor, should they not share in the reward?—D.A.H.

SERMON SUGGESTIONS

Topic: The Hand at the Helm
TEXT: Gen. 50:15–21, especially v. 20a
(1) The place of God, verses 18–19. (2) The provision of God, v. 20. (3) The peace of God—"fear not," verses 19 and 21.—Charles B. Bugg

Topic: Paul's Sure Cure for Care
TEXT: Phil. 4:6, 7
(1) A precept. (2) A prescription. (3) A promise.—H. L. Wayland

---

[12] *The Gospel of John: A Study Guide,* p. 19.

Hymn Suggestions

1. "Songs of Thanksgiving and Praise," Christopher Wordsworth (1863); "St. George's Windsor," George Elvey (1858)

Wordsworth, a gifted and respected clergyman of the Church of England and nephew of the poet William Wordsworth, wrote this hymn for the Epiphany season. In it he recalls the successive manifestations of Christ: at his birth, his baptism, in the wedding miracle of Cana, and in his future glorious appearance to judge the world.

2. "Glorious Things of Thee Are Spoken," John Newton (1779); "Austrian Hymn," Franz Joseph Haydn (1797)

Written by the author of "Amazing Grace, How Sweet the Sound," this great hymn is in praise of the church, emphasizing Isaiah's metaphor—Zion, the poetic name of Jerusalem.

3. "Thy Mercy and Thy Truth," The Psalter (1912); "Tallis' Ordinal," Thomas Tallis (1567)

This is a free paraphrase of the sure affirmations of Psalm 36, the Psalter reading for today.

4. "As Man and Woman We Were Made," Brian Wren (1973); "Sussex Carol," arranged by Ralph V. Williams (1906)

Set to a familiar carol melody, this new hymn by one of the most prolific of present-day hymnists celebrates the miracle at the Cana wedding and praises Christ's love that emanates not only from the marriage feast but from the communion table.—Hugh T. McElrath

Worship Aids

CALL TO WORSHIP.   "And let the beauty of the Lord our God be upon us; and establish thou the work of our hands upon us; yea, the work of our hands establish thou it" (Ps. 90:17).

INVOCATION.   Lord, our God, open us to the riches of the glory of your grace in Christ Jesus and lead us in the way everlasting by the power of the Holy Spirit.—E. Lee Phillips

OFFERTORY SENTENCE.   "Lay not up for yourselves treasures upon earth, where moth and rust doth corrupt, and where thieves break through and steal; but lay up for yourselves treasures in heaven, where neither moth nor rust doth corrupt, and where thieves do not break though and steal; for where your treasure is, there will your heart be also" (Matt. 6:19–21).

OFFERTORY PRAYER.   Gracious Lord, this offering is but a token of our love: make it more than we see, use it more than we know, multiply it beyond our telling, for to you all glory belongs, in heaven and on earth.—E.L.P.

PRAYER.   As the morning dew refreshed the dry and thirsty earth, so does your Word as a fountain spring forth into everlasting life, renewing our jaded spirits. For teaching and preaching that brings new perspective to old stories, challenging with a living word and calling to new life—the life of the Spirit—we praise you. How we thank you for fresh bread when there are so many who are put off with the stale, dry crusts of an orthodoxy, a literalism that kills!

We know now that he who makes all things new is among us, as your perennial Word. We sense that he who turns water into wine, the ordinary into the festive, the mundane into sacrament, is here among us ready with some miracle of the Spirit according to our need. He who draws life from the depths and satisfies with that drink indeed stands among us as the Messiah who has come to one and all. For the gift of metaphor in the Word becoming flesh, that can take the common prose of our every day and transform it into the rhythm and beauty of poetry, we are indeed grateful.

Love me, O God, until the poetry returns, until the song comes back, or until a new song possesses my heart—is formed on my lips. I do sense a new song stirring in my soul—the new song of grace, perennially new, for it knows no season but every season. Thank you, God, for your gift of grace in him who leads us from the winter of our discontent to the perennial spring of an eternal joy.

Through all of our days may there rise from our lips the song of your mighty deeds for our salvation and the salvation of all humankind.

We pray through the name of him who is our song and our salvation and teaches us

when we pray to pray together: "Our Father
. . ."—John Thompson

Sermon: Breakthroughs

TEXT: Exod. 3:4; Mark 9:7

We are still in the season of Epiphany, and
Epiphany is a season of manifestations, or
showings, or to use an even more current
word, *breakthroughs,* and the sermon today is
about breakthroughs, in season and out of
season.

I. The word *breakthrough* is relatively new.
It's a compound of two old words, a verb and
an adverb. The verb *to break* means "to divide
into parts," usually violently. *Through,* the
adverb, means "from one end to the other."

a. As far as I can discover, the two words
were first hyphenated and were used to
describe a military advance of decisive importance. More recently the word is occasionally
used to describe a different kind of movement—a movement not, so to speak, from
here to there, not initiated by man, but from
there to here, initiated by God and appreciated by man. It is this kind of breakthrough
that we remember in the season of Epiphany.

b. In the beginning, in the early Church,
and now in the Eastern churches, the event
that is remembered on the sixth of January is
the baptism of Jesus by John in the Jordan
river. It was God's breakthrough, so to speak,
into human life with all its agonies and
ecstasies.

It was not until the fifth century that the Western Church, and only the Western Church, con-
centrated on the story of the wise men. They
recalled that story because they felt that it told
how God broke through, not only to his own
people but also to the whole Gentile world.

II. Today, on the second Sunday after Epiphany, we read two passages from the Bible.
Both are about breakthroughs.

a. The first passage is a story from the Old
Testament about the way God broke through
to one man. That man was Moses. In the
story, Moses was in a bad way. In a fit of temper he had killed one of his own people and
had left the country and gone to a foreign
land called Midian. There he had fallen in
love, mercifully, with a nice young girl and
began to work for her father as the shepherd
of his sheep. When the story begins, he had
"led the flock to the backside of the desert."
Quite by chance, he looked at a small bush,

of which there are thousands in the desert—
little, scrubby bushes—and he noticed that it
was burning and yet it didn't burn up. He
said to himself, I had better stop and look at
this; this is very unusual. And he turned aside
to look at it. This is an essential part of the
story, for if he had passed by this uncommon
sight—a bush burning that was not being
burned up—because he was busy with the
sheep, nothing would have happened.

But as he stopped and looked at the bush,
he heard a voice, and the voice called him by
name: "Moses, Moses." He said, "Here am I."
And the substance of what the voice said was
this: "I have seen the affliction of my people,
I have heard their cry, I know their sufferings,
and I have come down to deliver them; and
you are the one who will do it." Imagine what
Moses must have thought when he heard
that he, the fugitive from justice, the person
who was not able to control his own temper,
was now being sent back to gather together a
handful of slaves and against all the opposition that the pharaoh of Egypt could rally
on his behalf, he was to lead them to the
Promised Land.

b. The second story, from the New Testament, was about the way God broke through
to three men, and this time not by way of a
natural phenomenon but a human one. The
men were Peter, James, and John. Jesus took
them up onto a high mountain. He had just
talked to them about the future, his future
and theirs, and it was a dark one, a future of
suffering and death. Once they were up on
the mountain, Jesus was transfigured. What
does that word mean? You have seen, I am
sure, as I have, faces that for a moment were
transfigured, radiant, not lit by a spotlight
shining on them from the outside, but lit, as
it were, from within. They glowed in a way
that you could not fully describe to anyone
else or wholly understand yourself.

Something like this was what happened
to Jesus. He glowed; he was radiant; he was
glorious in light; all the shadows disappeared. Again there was a voice, and this
time the voice came out of a cloud. It was
the voice of God saying, "This is my Son. Listen to him."

c. Those are the two stories. In both of
them something indescribable happened. It
is enough to say that in both there was light.
In both there was a voice, coming as it were

from the other side, yet somehow from the inside.

III. The breakthroughs of something to us from outside us continue in the season of Epiphany and out of the season.

a. God is constantly breaking through to people. Sometimes it happens by way of nature. Nathaniel Micklem, principal of Mansfield College in Oxford, has written a little book called *A Religion for Agnostics.* When he discusses the doctrine of the Incarnation, he goes out into his garden, which he obviously loves, and takes us to look at his roses. This is what he says: "I accept all that the physicists tells me of this rose that is breaking into bud; it is a system and collocation of electrons, a form of complicated energy; but when I see the rose I am directly conscious of the Power; the rose is to me an incarnation of the Power. . . . It is, I believe, an earnest or foretaste of the Word, that glory which I hope to know and experience hereafter. It points to the eternal glory."

b. Some people are more likely to see God in human nature. I had a call asking me to go see a lady in the hospital whom I had never seen before. When I went in she said, "Oh, I'm glad to see you." I listened for quite a long time, because it took a long time for her to tell me everything: how long she had been alone, how her husband had died years before. Finally I said, "What can we do for you?" "Well," she said, "there is only one thing I need, and that is a place to go when I leave here, where I can be relatively independent." I thought to myself, what a spirit! And then she said this, "You know, when I get to the point where I have done everything I can, I just say to God, 'You take over' and he does!"

It was not what she said that moved me so much as the look on her face—a beautiful expression of absolute serenity, confidence, and trust; a smile not at all sentimental, not in any way an effort to appeal to me or to please me. I thought to myself, this is a breakthrough to me, at a time when there is so much tension and bitterness in the world, when people are so afraid, so full of doubt and uncertainty. Here is God speaking to me through a human being.

IV. Breakthroughs like this usually come when we least expect them. Moses was on the backside of the desert, gloomy, with no future, no outlook. Peter, James, and John were baffled by what Jesus said about his future and theirs. It may be that a breakthrough comes at the moment when the outer crust is thinnest, when our defenses are down, when we are most reachable. It never comes to one who cannot stop to look or listen. Moses turned aside; Peter, James, and John went with Jesus up into the mountain.

So keep your eyes and ears open. God may be trying to get through to you now.—Theodore P. Ferris[13]

Illustrations

FACING UP TO FAILURE.   When circumstances or our own stupid follies involve us in uncertainty and difficulty; when we are completely fogged in and know not which way to turn; when we cannot see the way ahead at all, and do not know what to expect—why, there Christ is, at our side, going surely before us and saying, "Follow me!"—John Trevor Davies[14]

RIGHT OR WRONG?   Protestant ethics does not attempt to say legalistically what is right and wrong for every man. It is in the responsible spirit of love to God and our neighbor that we must decide concretely what is right or wrong. This is how we understand the moral radicalism that began in the greatest of the Hebrew prophets and has run through Christian ethics from the beginning. The prophets asserted the demand of the clean heart against all the specific requirements of the law. Jesus summed up all the law in the two commandments to love God and our neighbor. Paul put it radically when he said, "All things are lawful for me; but all things edify not." It is in the actual service of my neighbor's need and my own that the ultimate permission or prohibition of any action lies. St. Augustine put the Christian position most strikingly, "Love, and then do as you will."—Daniel Day Williams[15]

[13] *Selected Sermons, Vol. 1.*
[14] *Lord of All.*
[15] *God's Grace and Man's Hope.*

SUNDAY: JANUARY TWENTY-FIFTH

LECTIONARY MESSAGE

Topic: Engaging the World
TEXT: Luke 4:14–21

Other Readings: Neh. 8:1–3, 5–6, 8–10; Ps. 18; 1 Cor. 12:12–31a

When looking at our world I never cease to be amazed at its beauty and grandeur. Recently I was moved by the singing of small children in a choir, who pronounced ever so carefully the words to "God's *beau-ti-ful world,* God's *beau-ti-ful* world." In that same service of worship we sang the magnificent hymn "This Is My Father's World." There came to my mind an indelible image of a Vermont forest ablaze with colors during a fall season years ago. Both the singing of the children and the singing of the congregation reminded me that it indeed is a beautiful world, and that it is God's world.

While I affirm that "this is my Father's world," I also recognize that it is a world still in the process of being redeemed. For while this is a world of grandeur, magnificence, and beauty, it is also a world of ugliness, misery, sin, and need. It is also, after all, a world of pollution, crack cocaine, child abuse, murder, rape, war, terrorism, and so on. That is reality. Ours is a world of both magnificence and misery. Yet it was in just this type of paradoxical world that the gospel appeared. As the text for today reminds us, the world in Jesus' day, as in ours, was a world of poverty, prisons, blindness, oppression, and need. Into that world came Jesus, to preach good news to the poor; to proclaim freedom for the prisoners, recovery of sight to the blind, and release for the oppressed; and to proclaim the year of the Lord's favor (vv. 18–19). And just as Christ came to fulfill his redemptive mission in the world by engaging the world in the midst of its misery and magnificence, so the Church continues to face the challenge of redemptively engaging the same kind of world.

I. The Church's mission is to engage the world, recognizing all the while that it is a world that belongs to God. He possesses it by virtue of being its creator. Without him it was not, and without him it could not be. The world and all that is within it belongs to him.

God loves this world. We are called upon to involve ourselves in the world in such a way that people might know that the Christ depicted in this passage in Luke's Gospel came to engage the world at the point of its deepest hurts and greatest needs. In the Gospel of John there is the reminder that "God so loved the world that he sent his only Son." And we are shown that the Son weeps over the people of this world and shows compassion toward them. Christ has come into this world in which sinners have turned beauty into ugliness and magnificence into misery, and he is yet in the process of redeeming it. Make no mistake about that. He is redeeming it. He is setting it free. It is his world, and as the hymn declares: "Though the wrong seems oft so strong, God is the ruler yet."

II. This world that Christians are called upon to engage redemptively is a world desperately in need. The Church is to be about the tasks of preaching to, freeing, delivering, releasing, and helping people to recover. Followers of Christ are to be about the business of proclaiming good news, because the misery of this world is all about bad news. Too often it is news about pain and despair. Christians therefore are challenged to engage the people of this world in such a way that they will be able to recognize the reality of hope that is available in Christ. Christians are challenged to make the Church a center of hope. In the text Jesus interprets himself and his mission as one of hope to those whom this world considers hopeless.

III. This world that so desperately needs hope is likewise a world that followers of Christ need. Notice I did *not* state that it is a world that needs Christians—it is. But God is sovereign. He is in control. He will not abandon the world, whether followers of Christ respond to the challenge of engaging the world or not. Just as desperately as this world needs God, so you and I as Christians need this world.

Perhaps it sounds strange to say that Christians need the world. But it is true. Our involvement in and our engagement with the world as followers of Christ is mandated as we identify ourselves with Christ's redemptive mission. We do need the world, for it is the arena of God's activity, and it is the only context in which we can truly find ourselves. The world with its misery as well as its magnificence is the only adequate setting for self-discovery, and for finding out what Christian commitment is all about. Too often, in the face of overwhelming need the tendency is for Christians to withdraw from the world. We encounter the misery of this world's needs and experience the temptation toward disengagement, toward noninvolvement. As Christians we must resist that temptation.

Yes, we followers of Jesus need this world. We need a point on which we can focus our love and concern. We must be engaged with the world, taking the leap of faith that affirms belief in God's power expressed in Christ Jesus, namely, that hope can transform the hopeless ones: the poor, the prisoners, the blind, and the oppressed. As we seek to play our part in God's redemptive mission, we must engage the world, with confidence that the Spirit of the Lord is upon us, the followers of Christ who make up his Church today. We must engage the world with enthusiasm, proclaiming "the year of the Lord's favor." After all, it is still *God's* beautiful world.—Dwight A. Honeycutt

Illustrations

CENTERS OF HOPE.   In 1983 the South American country of Colombia was hard hit by the natural disaster of the eruption of Volcano Ruiz. The subsequent mud slide resulted in the deaths of more than 25,000 people. The tragedy created a situation of overwhelming need. To the credit of Christian communities and benevolent organizations in Colombia and around the world, response was immediate. One missionary organization near the affected area established places where persons could come for food, lodge in tents, and receive help in locating missing family members and friends. These places came to be known as *Centros de Esperanza* ("Centers of Hope"). And they were just that—bringing order out of chaos, and hope to those who were tempted to give up. Perhaps thought be given to posting on the sign of every church everywhere that the place where the people of God gather is a "Center of Hope."—D.A.H.

THEY CARED.   A church that takes seriously the potential to identify with Christ's mission as reflected in Luke 4:18–19 will inevitably become a "caring" church. In the book *Resident Aliens* by William Willimon the following vignette appears: "In the church where one of us was raised, Dorothy was a perpetual member of the third grade church school class. Every child in the church knew that, when you arrived at the third grade in the primary division of the Buncombe Street Church Sunday school, Dorothy would be in your class. She had even been in the class when some of our parents were in the third grade. Dorothy was in charge of handing out pencils, checking names in the roll book, and taking up pencils. We thought she was the teacher's assistant. It was much later, when we were nearly all grown up and adult, that the world told us that Dorothy was someone with Down's syndrome. At the church, we were under the impression that Dorothy was the teacher's assistant. When Dorothy died in her early fifties—a spectacularly long life for someone with Down's syndrome—the whole church turned out for her funeral. No one mentioned that Dorothy was retarded or afflicted. Many testified to how fortunate they had been to know her."[16]—D.A.H.

SERMON SUGGESTIONS

Topic: I Can Leap over a Wall
  TEXT: Ps. 18:29
  (1) Life closes in. (2) Life gets blocked. (3) Walls can be jumped over: cynicism; prejudice; hatred; fear.—Gerald Kennedy

Topic: To Whom Shall We Go?
  TEXT: John 6:66–68
  What Christ Jesus gave Simon Peter: (1) A new God. (2) A new relationship to God. (3) A new conception of humankind, and a new ideal of the riches of human fellowship. (4) An altogether adequate moral dynamic. (5) The light of eternal hope.—John H. Jowett

---

[16]Stanley Hauerwas and William H. Willimon, *Resident Aliens: Life in the Christian Colony* (Nashville, TN: Abingdon Press, 1989), 93.

Hymn Suggestions

1. "Hail to the Lord's Anointed," James Montgomery (1821); "Webb," George James Webb (1837)

Montgomery, a devout Moravian layman, based this hymn on the Messianic message of Psalm 72 as well as on Luke 4:18–19. In simple poetry and prayerful prophecy the hymn glorifies the redemptive function of the Christ we worship.

2. "I Love Thy Kingdom, Lord," Timothy Dwight (1801); "St. Thomas," Aaron Williams (1663)

The only hymn written in America before 1824 to survive in current use, this free paraphrase of parts of Psalm 117 expresses deep love for the Church, her worship, and "her heavenly ways."

3. "O God of Light, Thy Word, A Lamp Unfailing," Sarah B. Taylor (1952); "Ancient of Days," J. Albert Jeffrey (1886)

Authored by a twentieth-century American woman, this hymn magnifies the Epiphany ideal of God's Word being revealed to sinful mankind (see the Nehemiahan passage).

4. "We Are One in the Bond of Love," Otis Skillings (1971); "Bond of Love," Skillings (1971)

This "mini-hymn" affirms the unity in Christ of the body of believers that is delineated by the apostle Paul in the Corinthian passage.—Hugh T. McElrath

Worship Aids

CALL TO WORSHIP.   "Praise ye the Lord. I will praise the Lord with my whole heart, in the assembly of the upright, and in the congregation" (Ps. 111:1).

INVOCATION.   O God, as we enter your gates with thanksgiving and into your courts with praise, we but respond to your grace so freely given in Christ. In him we live and move and have our being. In him we discover the eternal Word of your meaning for every person, and we worship and adore you. For the opportunity of worship in this place and the experience of being at home with your people, we praise you. Through him who is our prayer and is becoming our song, we pray.—John Thompson

OFFERTORY SENTENCE.   "All nations whom thou hast made shall come and worship before thee, O Lord; and shall glorify thy name. For thou art great, and doest wondrous things; thou art God alone" (Ps. 86:9–10).

OFFERTORY PRAYER.   Bless this offering, Lord, beyond all we are able to do, that it may accomplish that which is the joy of your people and the hope of the world.—E. Lee Phillips

PRAYER.   We bless your name, O God, for calling us to be good stewards of the gospel of truth and grace. We are persons of privilege who have been entrusted with making known the unsearchable riches of Christ. Ours is a message of help and reconciliation to a world divided and in disarray.

We come into your presence today tempered with contrition and lamenting the way we have handled your gift of redeeming love. We have set it forth as a method of worldly success, as insurance against personal failure, and as a last resort when tragedy and crisis strike our families and homes. We confess we are more ready to use the gospel than to submit ourselves to what it requires of us or wants us to be. Each day we attempt to organize our faith in terms of getting out of it more than we put in, of sorting out from it recipes as solutions to our little problems, and of storing up a sum of merit for good works in the record books of heaven. Forgive us, Lord, for what we have made of your holy religion and the devices we have used to escape the need to walk humbly by your side. Hear our cry and so fill our hearts again with kindness and mercy that we shall live in justice and goodwill with men and women of every race and creed. Stagger our minds with the flame of truth in the life of Jesus Christ and in that light may each of us walk and serve until our traveling days are done.—Donald Macleod

Sermon: The Nearness of God

TEXT: Acts 17:16–34

We seldom realize how close God is to us. We often think, "Oh, if I only had the time or the energy I would go in search of God for my life. I would study the great books and listen to the great teachers, and I would learn to pray and discover God." But the truth is, we don't have to go anywhere and we don't have to study anything. God is as near to us as that block of silver was to the young man going through the gateway, only we don't realize it.

This is what Paul was trying to say to the men of Athens. He could see how close they were to discovering the presence of God. He had walked through their lovely city and seen all the evidence of their search for the eternal and the beautiful. He had seen the glistening temples raised to Diana and Apollo and Zeus and Poseidon. He had even seen a monument dedicated to "the Unknown God," as if, having turned over every other stone in their attempt to earn the favor of the gods, they did not want to miss this last one! How close they were to the secrets of everything! All those brilliant philosophers, from Empedocles and Socrates to Plato right on down to the men of Paul's own day! All the great artists, whose creations in stone and clay still draw students from all over the world to study their beauty! All the great dramatists, such as Aeschylus and Sophocles and Aristophanes, whose plays still form the basis for Western theater! All the poets and historians and statesmen and warriors! Theirs was a golden culture, perhaps the most shining society the world has ever known. If any people ever erected a ladder and threatened to scale the very heights of heaven itself, it was they.

But in spite of all of these efforts, their urge to find God had not been satisfied. They had looked everywhere, turned over every stone, and still had not found him.

Paul was filled with sympathy. He obviously liked the Athenians. His great heart was surely warmed by the beauty and symmetry of their city and the excitement of their intellectual life. But they had not had the advantage he had had, of meeting Christ on the Damascus road. They had not heard, as he had, the stories of the wondrous Galilean— of his wisdom, his insights, his parables. They had not dealt with the meaning of the cross and the Resurrection, which, simple as they were, confounded the Greek mind and its "scientific" way of viewing the world.

"You have done what God intended us to do," he said. "You have sought for God in all the places around us where he might be found. I am sorry you have not found him.

For the truth is, he is nearer than you thought. You have looked everywhere and missed him. He is not far from each one of us. In fact, it is in him that we live and move and have our being, as one of your own poets has guessed. You see, we are his offspring, his children. And he has told us this through Christ, whose resurrection is the proof of his love for us."

It was, Phillips Brooks once said of this passage, as if Paul had entered a room where a blind child sat and had held the child in his arms and stroked its hair and said, "Don't be afraid, my child, your father is here. You can't see him, but he is here nevertheless. He breathes in the very room with you. He loves you, and wants to take care of you. You don't have to worry any more, he is right here."

Are we any different from the Greeks? Ours too is a golden age: computers, space travel, techniques in medicine the world never dreamed of, engineering feats it never believed possible. We have our philosophers and artists and musicians. And we too are looking for ultimate value, for absolutes, for God. We try pleasure, drugs, business, everything—always looking, looking, looking for what will satisfy the God-shaped longing in our hearts. So near we could touch it, if we only knew, if we only realized.

"He is not far from each one of us," said Paul. No further than the bowing of our heads, the reaching forth of our hands, the muttered prayer of submission, the taste of bread and wine. God is here. He has always been here. He has always been here. He is always at our sides. In him we can't avoid him. We just haven't known.

What does this mean? It means that like the Greeks we ought to stop struggling for what we don't have. We ought to stop looking in faraway places for the joy and peace of life. It is here. It is now. It is in God, who wants to share his life and wisdom with us—who *has* shared them in Jesus Christ.

It means you are not alone with your problems and your pains. God is with you. He doesn't always take away your problems and pains. But he is with you in them, as he was with Christ in the Crucifixion. And that makes a world of difference in everything!

All you have to do is say "Yes, God," and live every day in the knowledge that he is present with you. It will transform your life, and you will see that the things you want most deeply in life all lie within your reach.—John Killinger

Illustrations

ACRES OF DIAMONDS. It is a fact of life that what we search for most eagerly often lies so close to us that we could reach out and touch it. Russell Conwell, whose famous speech "Acres of Diamonds" helped to build Temple University in Philadelphia, told the story of a boy he knew in Massachusetts who went to Yale College and became a mining engineer. He was a brilliant student, and during his senior year he was paid fifteen dollars a week as an assistant in his department. When he graduated they offered him forty-five dollars a week to remain an instructor. But by that time he had gotten the gold fever and wanted to be a wealthy man, so he persuaded his widowed mother to sell the family farm in Massachusetts and go west with him in search of gold. He never found gold, and the last Conwell heard of him he was working for a copper mining company in Minnesota for fifteen dollars a week. But not long after the new owner had taken possession of the farm in Massachusetts, he was harvesting the potatoes that lay almost on the surface of the ground. As he carried a bushel of potatoes through the narrow stone gateway, it caught on the posts, and he had to set it down and push it through. As he was doing so, his eye caught a particularly shiny stone that turned out to be a block of native silver worth more than a hundred thousand dollars! The young man had passed through that gate a dozen times a day, said Conwell, and his sleeve had brushed against that very block of silver. It was almost as if it had said to him, "Here is something of enormous value waiting for you to take it." But he never did. He went off looking for wealth in other places.—J.K.

DO YOU PREACH? There is an old story of a boy who joined the Franciscan Order longing to become a friar preacher. He was put to work in the kitchen for the first months and got more and more restive and impatient to get on with learning to preach. Finally Francis himself drew him by the arm one day and asked him if he would like to go into the village with him to preach. The boy's heart was full as they set out. They stopped on the way to see a man whose son needed work in the town, then to call on an old woman who was sick and lonely, and then to visit with a peasant at work in his fields. In the town they saw a merchant about a job for the son, begged some food for the Brothers at home, and talked with some people in the marketplace. Then Francis turned to the boy and gaily proposed that they return to the friary. "But when are we going to preach?" asked the boy in an anguish of concern. Francis slipped his arm about him and said, "Why, my brother, we've been preaching all the time."—Douglas V. Steere

SUNDAY: FEBRUARY FIRST

LECTIONARY MESSAGE

Topic: Choices Free God to Work
TEXT: Luke 4:21–30
Other Readings: Jer. 4:1–10; Ps. 71:1–6; 1 Cor. 13:1–13

Thank God for careful, clinical Luke! He alone of all the gospel writers solves the mystery of Nazareth. Matthew and Mark give only the briefest mention of Jesus' hometown, as if it were an embarrassment (Matt. 4:13; Mark 1:9). John supplies only an ambiguous epitaph, "He came to his own but his own received him not" (John 1:11). Why didn't Jesus make Nazareth his headquarters for his ministry? Why choose the seaside town of Capernaum, twenty-five miles northeast? What happened at Nazareth to make it unfit for the Messiah to mount his mission from his hometown? Luke tells us the answer and, in so doing, tells us how our responsiveness to Christ determines whether or not he will make our congregation his headquarters for a contemporary messianic mission.

Our choices free God to work supernaturally. God responds to our faith choices. Nazareth had no faith and no miracles. Capernaum had some faith and some miracles. God still seeks great faith to respond to with great miracles! Unbelief has ever frustrated God's mission in our midst. Without faith it is impossible to please and be rewarded by God.

I. Expect miracles in your church. Find fulfillment in Jesus. The only time we can ever find fulfillment is today. The only place to find fulfillment is in Christ. The only sure guide to fulfillment is the Scriptures. In this passage, Jesus has just read one of the best-known messianic prophecies from the scroll of Isaiah. It is the prophecy from which the very word *gospel* comes. Having read the passage, Jesus sits to render his interpretation. He announces what he had been meditating on since at least his bar mitzvah experience with the doctors in the Temple in Jerusalem some twenty years earlier. He announced what Mary had been pondering in her heart since the angel had announced that God would favor her with a child some thirty years earlier. This announcement of Jesus to his hometown congregation marks the initiation of the Messiah's earthly ministry. How Jesus must have longed to make Nazareth his ministry headquarters! But he could not.

II. Maturity means accepting unexpected realities. No one presumed that prophecies would be fulfilled at their feet. No one expected little Jesus of Joseph's carpenter shop to fill King David's royal sandals. Surely those shoes were much too big for anyone from Nazareth. But we forget that few towns know that one day they will be the site of a presidential library because their paperboy has grown up to become the president of the United States. We never look for senators in our backyards or Christ in the church nursery, but we should. No one in Nazareth was watching while young Jesus mastered the Hebrew Scriptures from Moses to the prophets. No one was watching as the young Nazarene learned to pray intimately to the Father— Abba. Because the reality of Jesus' announcement was so unexpected, his synagogue family refused to accept it. Just when the powerful words of his first sermon might have convinced them, they backed away from faith's invitation to follow by saying, "Wait a minute now. We know who you are. You're the carpenter's son. You make a good talk, but we will not commit to you as the Messiah." We will avoid the issue by pleading familiarity. Nazareth was guilty of letting familiarity breed unbelief. To God unbelief is always contemptuous. Unbelief frustrates God and causes him to move elsewhere and to find others to accomplish his mission.

III. Never presume upon grace. Grace is never obliged. God is sovereign over his grace. He will have compassion on whomever he chooses. God has no obligation to bless as he has blessed others. Yet Jesus' home congregation expected that God was so obliged. They resented him for giving their miracles to others. No doubt Jesus wanted to work wonders in this beloved place of cherished memories, but the key ingredient was missing: faith. Faith comes from hearing the Word of God spoken in the power of the Spirit. Jesus had just so spoken the Word, but his listeners did not respond with faith. These people had hardened their hearts with familiarity and stricken their minds with resentment.

IV. We force God to work elsewhere. As we all do, Jesus longed for acceptance among his own people. But no prophet before him had been welcomed in his own land, and neither would Jesus be welcomed. Jesus gave two forceful examples of the fact that God always has to go to outsiders to work wonders. He referred to the two wonder-working prophets of Hebrew history, Elijah and Elisha. God had sent Elijah to the Jordanian widow of Zarepath, despite the many needy widows who suffered from the famine in Israel. The leper cleansed by Elisha was not Judean but Syrian. In both instances it was the choices of the persons involved that freed God to work supernaturally. The widow gave her last cake and oil to Elijah, and proud Naaman bowed himself in the muddy Jordan at Elisha's instruction. No faith, no power; some faith, some power; all faith, all power. God will never respond to unbelief other than with judgment.

V. Grace withheld should not bring resentment. When confronted with the historical fact that unbelief had often forced God to work supernaturally next door, the Nazarenes sought to slay the messenger. The text says they expelled Jesus from the synagogue and the city. He was given a choice: either depart never to return, or be thrown from the well-known precipice on which the city sat. The question is not "Why was Jesus crucified?" but rather "Why was he not crucified sooner?" The passage ends with the phrase, "but passing through the midst of them he went on his way." As he would with the resurrection, Jesus passed through death that day. Resurrection is ever God's reversal of unbelieving attitudes and unreceiving anger.

VI. How many times has Christ passed through our midst without our lives being touched or changed? His way must be my way. No doubt Christ's first hope was to do a long work in his own home. Instead he relocated to Capernaum. Unbelief on our part means that Christ will not headquarter ministry in our midst. His work demands our participation by faith. Perhaps with some cynical chagrin laced with a tad of guilt they said, "Well, we sent that upstart packing," only to hear distressing reports that heaven had set up shop in Capernaum. We must struggle to receive our hometown prophets and prophetesses, lest we miss divinely intended miracles.—Rodrick K. Durst

Illustrations

MAKING LIGHT OF CHRIST.   To gain which world? That which we most highly value, we think we cannot buy too dear: Christ and salvation are freely given, and yet most men go without them because they cannot enjoy the world and them together. They are called but to part with that which would hinder them from Christ, and they will not do it. They are called but to give God his own, and to resign all to his will and let go of the profits and pleasures of this world, when they must let go either Christ or them, and they will not. They think this too dear a bargain, and say they cannot spare these things: they must hold their credit with men; they must look to their estates; how shall they live otherwise? They must have their pleasure, whatsoever becomes of Christ and salvation: as if they could live without Christ better than without these; as if they were afraid of being losers by Christ, or could make a saving match by losing their souls to gain the world.—Richard Baxter

THE COSTS OF GRACE.   I cannot love by being commanded to love. Commands only restrain me. But to obey, to rein in and stop, always means that I have to overcome, fight down something within myself. It is the base man, the old Adam within me, that is subject to commands, the old Adam of weari-

ness, of fear, of defiance. So when I merely obey commands I am never there as a whole person, but perhaps at most only with the better half of my self, while the other half remains in opposition. But when I love I am there as a *whole* person, for love is a movement of my *whole* heart; love is always an overflowing, limitless giving of one's self. Therefore it can never be commanded; it can only happen.

In other words, I can only give my whole heart when another whole heart gives itself to me. I can only love if love is shown to me.

And this is precisely the miracle that occurs when I stand before Jesus Christ.—Helmut Thielicke[1]

SERMON SUGGESTIONS

Topic: The Dissolving of Doubts
TEXT: Dan. 5:16
(1) Never be afraid of doubt. (2) Be afraid of all sophistries, tricks, and strifes of disingenuous argument. (3) Have it as a fixed principle also that getting into any scornful way is fatal. (4) Never settle upon anything as true, because it is safer to hold than not. (5) Have it as a law never to put force on the mind, or try to make it believe. (6) Never be in a hurry to believe. What seemed perfectly insoluble will clear itself in a wondrous revelation.—Horace Bushnell

Topic: Hearsay or Experience?
TEXT: John 18:34
(1) Some are quite content with a secondhand religion: it is "safer"; it is easier. (2) Why no sincere soul can rest satisfied with a secondhand religion: (a) there is always something *unreal* about a religion like that; (b) it is *insecure;* (c) it is *incomplete*. (3) The way to get to where Andrew, Peter, and those Samaritans were will be found by obeying three simple maxims: (a) keep following; (b) keep praying; (c) keep loving.—James S. Stewart

Hymn Suggestions

1. "O for a Thousand Tongues to Sing," Charles Wesley (1739); "Azmon," Carl F. Glaser (1828)

---

[1] *Life Can Begin Again.*

In this song written on the first anniversary of his conversion, Wesley pours out his soul in exuberant praise of Christ, the Redeemer.

2. "Gracious Spirit, Holy Ghost," Christopher Wordsworth (1862); "Anderson," Jane Marshall (1985)

Despite its first line, which would lead one to think that this is a hymn for Pentecost, it is in reality a free paraphrase of the Epistle reading for this day, 1 Corinthians 13.

3. "Lord of All Hopefulness," Jan Struther (1931); "Slane," traditional Irish melody, arranged by David Evans (1927)

Permeated by the hopeful theme of Psalm 71, this hymn portrays the cycle of life as well as that of the day.

4. "Though I May Speak with Bravest Fire," Hal H. Hopson (1972); "Gift of Love," traditional English melody, arranged by Hopson

The first stanza of this contemporary hymn paraphrases parts of 1 Corinthians 13. The final stanza becomes a prayer for the Holy Spirit to grant a wholesome fulfillment of love in the lives of the worshippers.—Hugh T. McElrath

Worship Aids

CALL TO WORSHIP. "I love the Lord, because he hath heard my voice and my supplications. Because he hath inclined his ear unto me, therefore will I call upon him as long as I live" (Ps. 116:1–2).

INVOCATION. Lord, we would be children of God today, eager to listen, willing to respond, trusting and hopeful. So fill us with truth that the Spirit will find us teachable and our worship obedient.—E. Lee Phillips

OFFERTORY SENTENCE. "As the Scripture says, 'the one who gathered much did not have too much, and the one who gathered little did not have too little" (2 Cor. 8:15 TEV).

OFFERTORY PRAYER. Lord, as we give our gifts today, merge them with the high purposes and great dreams of the gospel for every living soul. Allow them to bring home biblical truth in fresh ways to minds hungry and thirsty for the truth, through Christ, our Lord.—E.L.P.

PRAYER. We thank thee, our heavenly Father, that we are not come upon an errand of persuasion as unto one that is reluctant or unwilling to give. Our good is already the evidence of thy willingness that we should come. It is by thy Spirit that we are drawn. Thou art granting us the sense of spiritual need. From thee is that illumination by which we see things that are right, and see how far we deviate from them. The impugnings of our conscience spring from thy divine influence. Our yearnings for things better, and our reaching out toward them, are all of thee. Whatever there is of true light, whatever there is that would take hold upon nobler and nobler experiences, is the fruit of thy shining upon the soul. How waste and how barren is man, and how hopeless of culture would he be if it were not for thy divine influence! And when thou hast taken us in hand, and art Husbandman to us; when thou hast begun thy royal tillage in us, how slow are we in growing, how poor is the return which we make, and how poor is the fruit that hangs upon the bough!

We thank thee, thou that art patient in over-measure, beyond our comprehension— thou that dost dwell in an infinite mercy, and surround thyself with good works of kindness and love.

Grant thy blessing to rest upon every one in thy presence. Give wisdom to the conscience that is burdened. Give light to all that are darkened. Give to every one that needs confirmation the word of faith. Disclose thyself to those that look for thee and cannot find thee. Grant that those who are seeking the right way may be led by the very hand of God, and find the ways of wisdom. May those that are tempted be able to resist temptation. May those that are fallen not be destroyed. May they be lifted up by the mercy of God, and turn to better ways.—Henry Ward Beecher

Sermon: The Poor in Spirit

Text: Matt. 5:1–3

The Sermon on the Mount is perhaps the best known of all of Jesus' teachings. It's a sermon about love and relationships; it's a sermon about prayer and trust. And right at the beginning of the sermon are eight statements that we call the Beatitudes.

In these very short and (in some ways) very simple verses, Jesus is telling us what every

Christian ought to be. If we are genuine followers of Jesus, our lives will increasingly look like these eight statements.

I. As he begins his sermon, Jesus says that his people are blessed—at least that's how our modern translations interpret his word. It's actually a word of congratulation—it's a word of commendation. Congratulations to the poor in spirit!

a. The first Beatitude (quite simply) takes our breath away—because it's not at all what we expect to hear. "Blessed are the poor in spirit, for theirs is the kingdom of heaven." Are you poor in spirit today? You are if you've given yourself to Jesus Christ. I can be confident in making that statement because only the poor in spirit can give themselves to Jesus Christ. When we come to Christ, we come empty-handed—or we do not come at all. When we live each day with Christ, we live each day empty-handed—or we do not live with him at all.

b. Now, you might be thinking, "Well, wouldn't it be better to be rich in spirit?" Yes, maybe it would be better—but understand that the opposite of being poor in spirit is not being rich in spirit. The opposite of being poor in spirit is being proud in spirit—and that is a dangerous, dangerous thing!

If ever anyone had reason to be proud in spirit, it was the apostle Paul. In his own words, he "was circumcised on the eighth day, a member of the people of Israel, of the tribe of Benjamin, a Hebrew born of Hebrews; as to the law, a Pharisee; as to zeal, a persecutor of the church; as to righteousness under the law, blameless."

But writing to the Philippian Christians, Paul said, "All of that is rubbish; it's all worthless. None of that brought me into right relationship with God, none of that has kept me in right relationship with God, because right relationship with God is something that can happen only through God's grace."

Two words in the ancient Greek language were used to describe the poor. One word was used to describe a person who was required to work hard for a living. That kind of poor person was required to do manual labor to survive. But there is also a second word. It describes absolute and abject poverty. It describes the kind of poverty that has beaten a person down to the ground. This kind of person has nothing at all. And it is this second word that Jesus used in the first Beatitude. Blessed are those who are absolutely and completely destitute before God.

II. So what does it mean? Well, here's what it means: the one indispensable condition of enjoying God's gift of life is admitting our spiritual poverty. This admitting goes against everything we are as human beings. It is painful and belittling. It is our confession that we can't make it on our own. And it is the one indispensable condition of enjoying God's gift of life.

a. You see, the fact of the matter is that today we are each poor in spirit. The only question is whether we will in fact stand before God empty-handed and rely on God's mercy alone. Followers of Jesus are no poorer in spirit than anybody else. They're simply more aware of the depth of their poverty. Being poor in spirit means that we don't have to pretend anymore. We can stand before God just as we are!

b. Are you self-sufficient? Be careful—it's a trap. The only hope is to be Savior-sufficient. Congratulations to the poor in spirit, for theirs is the kingdom of heaven!—Barry A. Stricker

Illustrations

CHRISTIANITY IS DIFFERENT. The future tense of the Beatitudes resists all notions that Christianity is a "philosophy of life" designed to make people successful and calm today, in the present moment. Christianity is not a scheme to reduce stress, lose weight, advance in one's career, or preserve one from illness. Christian faith, instead, is a way of living based on the firm and sure hope that meekness is the way of God, that righteousness and peace will finally prevail, and that God's future will be a time of mercy and not cruelty. So, blessed are those who live this life now, even when such a life seems foolish, for they will, in the end, be vindicated by God.—*The New Interpreter's Bible*

FULFILLMENT NOW! The blessings pronounced by Jesus differ from their prototypes. No longer are there conditions to be met before someone can be called blessed. The question is not really raised as to who will receive blessings, but rather how it is with all those on this earth who are poor, who hunger, who weep. For all those poor enough to have ears to hear, Jesus promises blessings, and with an authority that establishes future fulfillment in the present.— Eduard Schweizer[2]

WHAT KIND OF POVERTY?   We must be careful not to think that his Beatitude calls actual material poverty a good thing. Poverty is not a good thing. Jesus would never have called blessed a state where people live in slums and do not have enough to eat, and where health rots because conditions are all against it. That kind of poverty it is the aim of the Christian gospel to remove. The poverty that is blessed is the poverty of spirit, the spirit that realizes its own utter lack of resources to meet life, and that finds its help and strength in God.—William Barclay[3]

SUNDAY: FEBRUARY EIGHTH

LECTIONARY MESSAGE

Topic: Fishing for Men
    TEXT: Luke 5:1–11
    Other Readings: Isa. 6:1–8(9–13); Ps. 138; 1 Cor. 15:1–11
    I. People always press to hear God's Word. When Jesus spoke, people heard God speak to them. We must speak the Word so that people might hear God speak to them (5:1). As the size of the crowds who came to hear the Word increased, Jesus had to find ever larger auditoriums. The local synagogue was no longer sufficient. Jesus was not about to let "the shoe tell the foot how big it could grow." He turned to open air preaching, using the natural slope of the land down to Lake Gennesaret as an amphitheater.
    II. Any pulpit will do. People pressed nearer and nearer to catch every word and perhaps to gain a touch from the teacher. Always sit as near your best teacher as possible. Press close to hear the Word. When Jesus felt the water of Galilee lapping at the back of his heels, he sought the best available pulpit. Any pulpit will do, must do, when there is opportunity to communicate the gospel. So Jesus asked to borrow the boats of the men, who as all good craftsmen do, were cleaning their tools before closing up shop.
    III. Obedience often feels like launching back out into the deep. As if to pay the owners of the boat with a catch of fish, Jesus told Peter to launch back out into the deep and put down the nets for a catch. Shallow efforts at response will never catch anything from the Lord. We must row into deeper waters until he no longer says, "Not deep enough."
    IV. Experience is no excuse for disobedience. Peter complained that they had not caught any fish despite a full night's try. And then Peter said and did something that changed his life forever. He decided to give Christ's words priority over personal experience. He said, "Nevertheless, at your word we will let down the nets." And let down the nets they did, to take in the catch of a lifetime. But catch those words again. "But at your word, I will. . . ." How pleased and interested God must be whenever we disregard our recent personal experience to be obedient to his words. The frustrated spouse might want to give up the marriage, but at Christ's word a hand is reached out once more to find reunion and renewal of romance. The Sunday school teacher so frustrated with lack of participation and response might want to resign, but at the Lord's encouragement she launches out in deep preparation and finds new excitement and growth in the students. The believer so disappointed with the lack of response to his witness to and prayers for his lost coworkers that despair is near, at Christ's Word shares one more witness and intercedes once more, with unexpected, incredible results. If we would have an incredible catch in Christian living and service, our faith must ever put experience second to Christ's words.
    V. Experiencing God involves confession of sin and confession of Christ. As Peter and his partners pulled in their incredible catch, the bottom of the boat quickly filled with fish. This experience of the overwhelming catch at the command of Jesus drove Peter

---

[2] *The Good News According to Matthew.*

[3] *The Gospel of Matthew, Vol. 1.*

down among the fish near the heart of Jesus. Peter had caught fish, but Christ had caught Peter and his partners. Peter confessed his condition of sinfulness: "Go away, for I am a sinful man, O Lord" (5:8b). We can see a process of conversion in Peter's life in this narrative. Peter moved from hearing Christ's message to experiencing God through obedience, to being aware of God's nearness and holiness through God's goodness in the catch, to confession of his own unworthiness, to receiving the cleansing word of a call to committed ministry. Commission is followed by training to make one who is called effective in service.

VI. To follow Christ is to fish for men. That day Peter and his partners found a new focus. They probably still went fishing as the opportunity arose, but now fishing was more avocation than vocation, more hobby than career. Their new call was to follow Christ and learn to draw men and women into the Kingdom. To follow Christ would be to fish for men. This was Christ's business and now he had brought some new men in as partners. We too can know we have been invited in as partners if we have that hunger for souls, to catch people for the Kingdom. The church ever needs to ask itself two vital questions: What's our business? and How's our business? Our business is to follow Christ's command to launch out into the deep and to let down our nets for a catch for the Kingdom. If we are going catchless, we may not be in deep enough waters or we may not be using the right bait. We may need to change our methods, but the call to follow and fish remains the same. Principles are few while methods are many. Principles never change but methods always do.—Rodrick K. Durst

Illustrations

CHRIST INCOGNITO. My old teacher, Professor E. L. Allen, a distinguished theologian and missionary, told me once that he never went into a village in China thinking that he was bringing Christ to the people for the first time. In a sense he was, for he preached the gospel in places where it had never been preached before. But he told me that he always arrived to find that Christ was there already, present by his Spirit in the hearts of all. I love the story of the old Hindu woman who said to a missionary from whom she first heard the gospel, "Thank you! I have always loved him and now you have told me his name."—R. Maurice Boyd[4]

BRIDGES. A bridge is something people walk on, but it leads from something to something. If you are to be a bridge between a man's indifference and his awakening, a bridge between groups and races, you will be walked on. Never mind; people may be getting somewhere when they walk on you. Judge Wilbur's son, a highly trained, gifted young doctor, went to China as a medical missionary. While attending typhus cases, he was stricken and ravaged by the disease. When he heard there was a coolie woman who would die if a caesarian section could not be performed, he bade them carry him into the operating room. They held him up, one on each side, as he operated and saved the life of the woman and her baby. But the shock was too much for him—in two days he was dead. He cared. Perhaps the coolie woman never knew and maybe did not care. He did—that is enough.—E. Stanley Jones[5]

SERMON SUGGESTIONS

Topic: Our Total Life and God
TEXT: Ps. 139:5
(1) Behind: All my yesterdays are covered. He saves me from my soiled past. (2) Before: All my tomorrows are anticipated. He is undertaking for my future. (3) Just here: In this very present he lays his hand upon me.—W. E. Sangster

Topic: When Opportunity Knocks
TEXT: Acts 9:10–19
(1) When opportunity knocks, are we in the spirit of prayer? (2) When the Word of the Lord comes, are we prepared to heed it? (3) When the command of the Lord is given, have we the courage to obey it? (4) When the leading of the Lord materializes, have we the grace to follow through as a true Christian?—Chalmer E. Faw

[4] *A Lover's Quarrel with the World.*
[5] *Abundant Living.*

Hymn Suggestions

1. "We Have a Gospel to Proclaim," Edward J. Burns (1968); "Germany," William Gardiner's Sacred Melodies (1815)

The first and last stanzas of Burns's hymn frame the gospel story—the birth, death, resurrection, and heavenly reign of Jesus Christ are set forth in the internal stanzas.

2. "God Himself Is with Us," Gerhardt Tersteegen (1729); "Arnsberg," Joachim Neander (1680)

This venerable hymn evokes the mystical spirit of Isaiah's vision in the Temple. Its theme of adoration incorporating the *Tersanctus* ("thrice-holy") of the heavenly creatures makes it an ideal hymn for a reverent opening to public worship.

3. "This Is the Threefold Truth," Fred Pratt Green (1980); "Acclamations," Jack Shrader (1980)

The refrain of this new hymn proclaims the central message of the Corinthian passage for the day—the threefold formula that characterized the early Christian creeds.

4. "Alleluia, Alleluia! Give Thanks," Donald Fishel (1971); "Alleluia No. 1," Fishel (1971)

This modern expression of praise focuses on the Resurrection of our Lord as proclaimed by the apostle Paul in 1 Corinthians 15.—Hugh T. McElrath

Worship Aids

CALL TO WORSHIP.   "Praise ye the Lord. Blessed is the man that feareth the Lord, that delighteth greatly in his commandments" (Ps. 112:1).

INVOCATION.   Eternal God, our judge and redeemer: we confess that we have tried to hide from thee, for we have done wrong. We have lived for ourselves. We have refused to shoulder the troubles of others, and turned from our neighbors. We have ignored the pain of the world, and passed by the hungry, the poor, and the oppressed. O God, in thy great mercy, forgive our sin and free us from selfishness, that we may choose thy will and obey thy commandments; through Jesus Christ our Lord.—*The Book of Common Worship*

OFFERTORY SENTENCE.   "Give unto the Lord the glory due unto his name: bring an offering, and come before him: worship the Lord in the beauty of holiness" (1 Chron. 16:29).

OFFERTORY PRAYER.   Loving Lord, let these offerings signal new hope for a life gone astray, redeeming grace for needy sinners, hope for all who trust in the Lord, now and always.—E. Lee Phillips

PRAYER.   "Wait for the Lord; take courage, be strong; wait for the Lord." What does it mean to wait upon you, O God, you who are holy and eternal?

It is surely to wait in reverence—to acknowledge who you are and to realize who we are. Yet we can come in confidence, for we are not groveling slaves but your sons and daughters. We have been adopted into your family, the household of faith, not because of our merit but because of your grace—your unmerited love. The spirit that we have received is not a spirit of slavery leading us back into a life of fear, but the spirit that makes us your children.

To wait on you is to be silent until all our striving ceases. It is to be still—so still—to know that you are God. It is to be so still that above the clamoring of self-will we may hear the still, small voice of your will.

To wait upon you, O God, is to wait upon one another. If we are really listening, we hear you saying: "Except your brother and your sister be with you, you shall not see my face." We do not see you except in the face of the other—whoever the other may be. Are we waiting upon our brother, our sister, listening to them, really listening, so that we can see life from their perspective, walking in their shoes? Do we conscientiously seek your living Word in open dialogue?

Let us wait in these moments with one another! In the face of family solidarity threatened by alienation, we pray for a persevering love so that reconciliation may come in the next few days. We pray for the ill among us. Where physical infirmity cannot be removed because of age or other disability, grant the strength of mind and of spirit that celebrates your wholeness even in the face of them. For those walking through the valley of the shadow of death we pray for the light of your countenance, for the strength of the ever-lasting arms. To wait upon you is to be over-taken by a peace that the world cannot give and that the world cannot take away.

Enlighten and encourage the leaders of nations and the United Nations with the ways of justice and peace.

To wait upon you is to come to know him who is full of your grace and truth. He is the way—may we follow him; he is the truth—may we trust him; he is the life—may we cel-ebrate with him.

We thank you, God, that you are always waiting—may we learn to wait before you.— John Thompson

Sermon: Putting Our Hearts at Christ's Disposal

TEXT: Matt. 5:21–42

In April 1963, Birmingham, Alabama, faced terrible turmoil. Martin Luther King Jr. initi-ated nonviolent action to desegregate the city's public facilities. King's followers en-countered threats, brutality, incarceration. King himself was imprisoned. And while he, as he later remarked, "rested in jail," he re-ceived a poignant letter from a group of min-isters, rabbis, and priests. Why, they wanted to know, must the country be exposed to these turbulent demonstrations now? Why couldn't the good citizens of Birmingham work in their own way, at their own pace, for the resolution of the racial problems? Why should laws be broken, the community dis-rupted, the social fabric tattered?

King's response to those questions, you will remember, proved to be one of the great documents of the twentieth century: "Letter from the Birmingham Jail." The letter is a majestic exposition of the human rights promised every American citizen. In his unique and peculiar way, King combines the promises of the Declaration of Indepen-dence, the Constitution, and the Bible into a description of a society where freedom and equality, liberty and justice exist in balance. "We will win our freedom," he writes, "be-cause the sacred heritage of our nation and the eternal will of God are echoed in our demands."

Dr. King's conflict with the Birmingham religious establishment is cut from cloth simi-lar to that pictured in our passage. Some pres-tigious religious folk accused Jesus of breaking the law. In offering a new social order, in rep-resenting and making possible a new quality of life in this world right now, the powers-that-be saw Jesus as a social radical, the breaker of community norms. Clergy types, magistrates, business people, and protectors of the public morals perceived in him a wrecker of the cur-rent order, a threat to community values. He broke Sabbatarian laws to feed hungry people. He healed others when he should have been in the synagogue. He said it was permissible for Christians to pay taxes but never to con-fuse their loyalties to God with their loyalties to Caesar. "Anarchist!" they cried. "Revolu-tionary!" they charged.

And our Lord's answer? How did he deal with these accusations of anarchy and revolu-tion? Well, like Dr. King, Jesus said, "I came to destroy nothing. Rather I came to build some-thing. I bear with my very being a community functioning not so much on constitutions, contracts, legal agreements, property rights, turf protection, jobs, titles, litigation, crime and punishment. No, I bring a beloved com-munity inaugurated with a new disposition of the human heart. I am harbinger of a social order in which personal security is rooted not in legal recourse but in simple trust; in which human relationships are grounded in the sure embrace of a God who sustains and undergirds us through everything life can throw at us. Anarchist, you say? You know not what true order is. Revolutionary, you cry? To be sure. But it means a revolution of values, an inverting of conventions to enable us to live not in fear, or to live in tolerance of one another at best, but in eager service, concern, care for, and trust of one another always.

I. For instance, Jesus continued, you as-semble a battery of legislation concerning murder. You define it as murder first degree, second degree, third degree. You design judi-cial systems, build prisons, set bail, debate punishments. (And the headlines in our morning papers just this week deal with laws for juveniles and adults, lethal injection or firing squad, the clamor for the death penalty in the current campaign—all of which drama-tizes a core pursuit of the human condition.)

But are these lawmaking, prison-building, gas chamber processes enough? Is a human community that guards itself against murder and devises complicated judicial procedures to detain or kill men or women convicted of murder the best of all possible worlds? Is it enough to say to one another, here in church, or in our various social settings, "I am not a murderer?"

Well, is it? "No," says Jesus. He knows we need to be healed of violent inner demons no less than we need tough laws against murder. He knows that murder arises from violence within. He knows that murder spills out in contempt for life, explodes from an inner rage, erupts from chaos, bursts from fury against our brothers, our sisters, our spouses, our neighbor.

And our Lord says that seeds of murder can be detected in what is accepted as our everyday routine—like name-calling. Yes, he says, "name-calling used to demean, diminish, destroy"—you know how it is. The crook ripping us off in the car repair shop; the boor making a left turn from the right-hand lane, driving his car like he plays hockey; the arrogant fool driving the Green Line car, pulling away from the station as we pound with futility on the front door; or the dweeb in the token booth engaged in some leisurely chat while we stand there freezing and seething. (Oh, what I'd give for a short fuse and a stick of dynamite when that happens!) And on it goes: the jerk stealing our parking space; the slob sliding seven items through at the six-item cash register at Star Market; the quack at the clinic robbing us blind and making us worse; the shyster writing our wills; the sanctimonious, hypocritically unctuous, mealy-mouthed, pharisaic, Tartuffean Elmer Gantry preaching this sermon. *Moron, stupid, scum,* and all their contemptuous and obscene cousins inappropriate for repeating in a family setting like this (as if I knew any of them, anyway)—the words themselves mean little, but the furious sentiment behind them, aimed at obliterating another human being, fills them with murderous content.

Do you remember saying to someone laying it on you when you were a kid, "Sticks and stones may break my bones. . . ." And names? Names can kill us.

Is murder, then, really our problem? My soul, murder surely is a terrible presence in our city and region as we assay the shocking filial and random homicides: babies, neighbors, live-in lovers, spouses, teenagers—murder is real. No joke! But I wonder if Jesus knows something about the depths of the issue—in some cases, environments breeding rage, frustration, fury. And perhaps right here in this room? Among us? Anger born of a father's humiliations, a mother's abandonment, an employer's scorn, a spouse's betrayal, a friend's denial, a job gone wrong, an accusation misplaced, a public assault? Murder, according to the New Testament, is a violent act of the heart gone haywire. We know how anger may have brutalized us and we know how we can brutalize others from the mayhem and fury within us. Anger wrecks community. Laws against murder are hardly enough. We need hearts surrendered to the love and patience of Jesus Christ.

II. And it is not only our anger that can be healed in this community of peace rooted in the grace of Christ; the skewed, injured, ruptured relationships triggered by our sexuality can be healed, too.

We do not have time this morning to review the particular dynamics of Jewish law regarding divorce and adultery that Jesus refers to. What he is saying, however, pictures in his reconciled and restored community the intimate ties we forge from our sexual identities. He promises that they can be truly heavenly—that we can be a flourishing, radiant, selfless community. We know that is possible. But we know as well that our sexuality can give rise to other elements that shatter community, smothering it, draining it, killing it. Adultery and divorce, Jesus says—as much as they represent estrangement, separation, and division—adultery and divorce are born of inner distortion, diverted loyalties, urgent desires, misplaced hearts gone cold as stone. The breaking of covenant between people begins—*begins!*—inside. The legal procedures attendant to divorce, the overt acts of estrangement endemic to adultery, mark the course of a long road of inner erosion and brokenness.

Oh friends, I am convinced that life in Christ enables us to live differently. It not only seals covenants, binds loyalties, and forges commitments, it enables us to live with one another on intimate and grace-filled terms.

III. Do you get the picture? Matthew tells us that what counts is the character of our inner life. Again, he insists that when we turn our lives over to Christ we illustrate an integrity that binds who we are to what we say. Our words, our deeds, our body language expose truth that is indivisible from the depths of our innermost being. Oaths, he says, are moot. They are irrelevant because being grounded in Christ is oath enough.

Heaven knows that relationships crumble, trust dissolves, community collapses when cynicism and self-interest subvert our integrity. Speaking under oath should be different from speaking without oath. The New Testament says it should make no difference. What we say, what we do, who we are in all circumstances coheres. Our "yes" means "yes." Our "no" means "no." Our loyalty to Christ makes of our very lives an oath.

IV. Lastly, as loyal followers of Christ we no longer engage in retaliation. It is no longer an eye for an eye, a tooth for a tooth. We are empowered to live through the worst demands others make on us and to respond in a creative transforming fashion.

Oh, I know it is hard when we are put down to avoid responding in kind. It is difficult to resist even just a touch of vengeance. "Don't get mad; get even."

There are the cheap shots, of course. Lady Astor, for instance, telling Winston Churchill if he were her husband she would put poison in his coffee. And Churchill responding, indeed, if she were his wife he would drink it.

It goes from there to the vengeful battles over family fortunes, payback among Democrats and Republicans on Capitol Hill, the vindictive scorching of Svrenica, the revenge-dripping IRA bomb in downtown London, the vendetta-driven genocidal slaughter in Rwanda.

Ah, sweet revenge. Can we beat it? As we approach Lincoln's birthday let me tell you one who did. After the bloodiest war in our history; the terrible division among families; the fierce and uncompromising battles, invasion, and massacres; after being mocked, laughed at, labeled a gorilla, a tyrant, a fool, and a satanic constitution-wrecker, Abraham Lincoln in one of the majestic addresses of all time—recognizing the violence, the hatred, the terrible cost of slavery and the war—Abraham Lincoln reaches out—remember?—he reaches out in his second inaugural address "with malice toward none, with charity for all, with firmness in the right as God gives us to see the right . . . to bind up the nation's wounds, to care for him who

shall have borne the battle, and for his widow and his orphan. . . ." It was an address aimed at all Americans, not just those in sympathy with the Union objectives. Retaliation must stop!

Here, friends, lies the mood described by Matthew alive and at work beyond laws and rules and quid pro quos to a bonding rooted beyond justice in forgiveness, beyond treaties in true peace; here we see a heart, if you will, put at the disposal of the grace of Christ.—James W. Crawford

Illustrations

WHAT KIND OF CROSS?   When the mainline clergy of Birmingham asked Martin Luther King Jr. to change the tempo of his struggle for justice from allegro to largo, to slow down, they were not speaking as though God had spoken to them. They had muted the words of eternal life and were echoing the voices of a society that had grown comfortable subjugating, embarrassing, ignoring, and denying persons on the basis of their color. They were pleading for an inhumane, unjust system to last a little longer, for the pain and hurt to continue until those who had grown callused to it were at last—whenever!—ready to allow it to subside. This is all the more confusing because these preachers talked and sang and prayed about the cross they seemed to recognize was the *gold* one dangling from a *gold* chain!—Samuel D. Proctor[6]

THE SOURCES OF OUR DEEDS.   All that is evil and all that is good comes from the intangible yet absolutely real center of man's nature. Sin exists as thought or motive or desire or covetousness before it becomes overt fact. The generous deed likewise arises from the generous heart. A man is defiled not by what someone does to him or fails to do to him but by the impurity of his basic motives. A man is essentially harmed neither by eating meat nor by failing to eat meat but by the lack of genuine, unselfish love in his inmost self. There is only one thing of prime importance in true religion and that is the new life of kinship with God which leads to love of his other children.—Elton Trueblood

[6] *"How Shall They Hear?"*

SUNDAY: FEBRUARY FIFTEENTH

LECTIONARY MESSAGE

Topic: The Level Truth, Hoping Skills, Truth on the Level

TEXT: Luke 6:17–26

Other Readings: Jer. 17:5–10; Ps.1; 1 Cor. 15:12–20

Matthew places this sermon on the mountain. For Luke, mountains are for praying and plains are for preaching. Luke's version of the sermon is on level ground, where all kinds of people can hear it. Both Matthew and Luke begin the sermon with eight pronouncements to the hearers. In Matthew, all eight are blesseds, but Luke again levels the field by making four of the pronouncements Beatitudes and four curses. Four hopes and four nopes. Jesus is the classic prophet who comforts the afflicted and afflicts the comfortable. The sermon is notable both for its inclusive scope of hearers and for its honesty about future hopefulness and future hopelessness. We need hope to navigate life effectively. Without hope we are becalmed, without wisdom and without wind.

I. *The hearing find healing.* Two elements have impressed doctor Luke about his research on this sermon event. He writes about the inclusiveness of the hearing and the inclusiveness of the healing. While Matthew aims the sermon at the disciples, Luke points out that Jesus took pains to include not only disciples but also Judeans, Galileans, Tyrites, and Gidonians among his congregation. The message of the Kingdom is for Jew and Gentile alike. Because suffering and sin show no partiality, the gospel ministry must show no partiality. Effective ministry needs to "come down" to the same level as that of the people, any people, who are in need. Luke is careful to keep hearing and healing in close and consecutive proximity. He seems to suggest that out of the hearing of Jesus comes the healing of Jesus. Both the diseased and the demonized found their cure in Christ. His was a healing touch "because power was coming from him," and power to heal is coming from him still. Healing will ever be in close proximity to hearing the gospel. Wherever and whenever sin and suffering abound, impartiality and grace abound more (Rom. 5:20).

II. What is heard gives people hope. Life on the plain is often full of pain. Hearing and healing will come as the preacher sees and feels the hurting. Whereas Matthew could be understood as spiritualizing his audience, Luke addresses four areas of human despair: poverty, hunger, grief, and religious hatred.

a. To those who suffer, Jesus offers an eschatological hope. Hope is the point of Christian eschatology, that is, the doctrine of last things or lasting things. Hope is the point of eschatology. Hope in God. Eschatology gives us hoping skills to cope with present circumstances. Hoping skills are the believer's coping skills. To the poor, who lack the necessities of enough, Jesus says, "Yours is the kingdom of God" (6:20). Note the present tense of the possession. Jesus is saying that based on your choosing to hope in the Messiah, your name is already on the title to heaven. If your name is on the title now, then present poverty is humbled by an undiminished hope. This hope by the poor must be accompanied, however, by an active remembering of the poor by the Church. Apostolic ministry is authenticated by a full preaching of the life, death, resurrection, and return of Christ, and by a remembering of the poor (Gal. 2:10). Not to remember the poor is to do much more than forget those whom God remembers. Not to remember the poor is to dismember them. This first hope proclaimed is a present experience of the assurance of salvation.

b. The second hope extended by Jesus is future satisfaction. The future is enough. To the hungry Jesus says, "You will be satisfied" (6:21). This hope is realized when Jesus feeds the five thousand in Luke 9:17, where it very pointedly says that "all ate and were satisfied"—with twelve baskets of "leftovers," no less! Where hunger can eat away at a person's spirit, Jesus says to choose hope in the Son of man. To the Church Jesus says, "Give them something to eat" (Luke 9:13)!

c. Have your laugh last. No one wants life to end in grief. Yet sometimes grief and depression are so present that the future holds no hope. To the weeping Jesus declares, "You will laugh" (6:21). This eschatological promise binds up our hurts so we can see a time beyond. Hope empowers personal detachment that mutes the grim with a glimpse of humor. We lose our sense of humor after we lose our sense of perspective. Hope restores both. This kind of humor is not a hysterical Toronto blessing but an honest hope that Christ keeps his promises. Leith Anderson told the story of visiting a church during a time when he was out of work. He said he felt alienated when the deacon prayed, "Thank you God for giving all of us good jobs." Leith said he felt like he did not belong, so he left. We must identify with the hurting among the hearing.

d. Verify your salvation. All humans experience hate and insult, but no such experience can be more discouraging than religious contempt. In the fourth Beatitude, Jesus both warns and encourages his "hopers." When we are personally attacked and ostracized "for the sake of the Son of man" (6:22), we can rejoice that we are walking with the prophets and that our names are as honored in heaven as they are dishonored by some people on earth. We hope through our poverty, hunger, and grief when we navigate by the Christ star.

III. Woe, woe, do not go. Rather than ask us to defend the hope that is in us, some people will launch a preemptive, personal strike. Why? Because our hope in Christ critiques their hope in mammon, freezers, IRAs, comfort zones, and being mentioned in society publications. Our hope in the Son of man illuminates the expiration dates stamped on their hopes and makes them admit a deep sense of hopelessness. Some prefer to hate rather than to find new hope. Some prefer to crucify rather than to follow the cross. To them Jesus says, "Woe, woe." Balanced with the four blessings are four corresponding curses.

a. Woe to those who refuse to look beyond their present abundance to see those in poverty. In Jesus' parable, the rich man went from banquet to brimstone because he refused to look beyond his pork roast to Lazarus dying on his porch (Luke 16:20–25). To hope in the Son of man is to choose God over mammon and to willingly sell all, give the proceeds to the poor, and then follow Christ. This woe is to the rich young ruler who was so near the kingdom yet fell dreadfully short because he found more comfort in his stuff than in the Savior.

b. Woe also to those who are so full of everything but God that they can see no need for God. All of us hate to go grocery shopping right after we have eaten. There is no motivation. Some have consistently chosen to garden the cares of the world in their souls and to feast off the resulting crop. We need to relearn the heavenly definition of a weed: anything in my life that God doesn't want there. When Americans consume the lion's share of the world's daily requirement of calories, surely it is not safe for us to camp too far from this second woe. We must support credible world hunger relief programs consistently and sacrificially. We must see that the protruding bones of the malnourished point in accusation at our apathy if not at our abundance. We must learn to live more simply that others may simply live.

c. Woe also to the entertained and the popular. Christ resents it when we make anything other than God our primary resource for comfort. Our spiritual idleness is idolatrous in his eyes. God has ever been hostile to idolatry in any form. Little wonder that Jesus warns his hearers against false comfort and false laughter. "Woe to you who laugh now" (6:25), for you shall have to weep at the last. Timing is everything. If we choose to laugh when the Messiah weeps over Jerusalem's waywardness, then how shall we laugh with the Messiah at the new Jerusalem's redemption (Luke 13:34; Rev. 22:2)? Intercessory tears was a qualification for the office of high priest. If we weep with and for the grieving, will not our tears be wiped away at Christ's return (Rev. 21:4)? If we choose the popular way, we walk with prophets too—false ones!

IV. He is no fool who gives up what he cannot keep in order to gain what he cannot lose. Jesus was confronting his hearers with a choice that day on the plain: present pain with future gain, or present gain with future pain. Our choice today to navigate by our hope in Christ sets our destination in eternity. Choose wisely and find the fair wind of Christ's Spirit.—Rodrick K. Durst

Illustrations

BLESSED BREAD. One Christian pastor refuses to call food left after the meal *leftovers*. He insists that they be called *blessed-overs*.

WHOLENESS. Many churches have the words "Do this in remembrance of me" engraved on the communion table. The word *remembrance* is usually understood to refer to the function of memory in a healthy mind. To remember is not to forget. However, to *re-member* means to put back together. Micro-surgery re-members the amputated limbs of persons who have been in accidents so that the body is whole again. Communion at the Lord's table is about the body of Christ being recon-ciled and re-membered into one fellowship for worship and mission together.—R.K.D.

SERMON SUGGESTIONS

Topic: Man Converted
TEXT: Ezek. 36:26

Two things are needed for salvation: (1) *The remission of sins.* Saving faith has God for its author, the Spirit for its agent, Christ for its object, grace for its root, holiness for its fruit, hope for its reward. (2) *The renovation of the soul,* as in 36:26. (a) It is a birth, John 3:3–6. (b) It is a resurrection, Rom. 6:4. (c) It is a great change, Ezek. 37:11–14.—Thomas Guthrie

Topic: Jesus Really Knows Us
TEXT: Matt. 21:18–22

(1) He knows our hypocrisy and con-demns it. (2) He knows our faith and blesses it.—Gerhard Aho

Hymn Suggestions

1. "Stand up and Bless the Lord," James Montgomery (1824); "Stuttgart," *Witt's Psalm-odia Sacra* (1715)

The stance of the righteous, "like a tree planted by streams of water" (Ps. 1:3), as well as the eighth Beatitude, "Blessed are those who are persecuted for righteousness' sake," are reflected in this strong hymn of worship.

2. "The One Is Blest Whom Fearing God," John H. Gower (1890); "St. Anne," William Croft (1708); the Psalter (1912)

This metrical paraphrase of Psalm 1 could well be sung in the place of the psalm read-ing for the day. Alternately, each stanza of the hymn could be sung following the reading of the corresponding verse of the psalm.

3. "Blest Are the Pure in Heart," John Keble (1819); "Franconia," Johann B. König (1738)

The four stanzas of this hymn were part of a much longer poem that Keble based on the Beatitudes given by Jesus as recorded in Luke 6 as well as Matthew 5. After three stanzas delineating the spiritual implications of the sixth Beatitude, the hymn becomes a prayer for spiritual purity.

4. "Christ Is Risen," Nicholas Martinez (1962); "Central," Pablo D. Sosa (1962)

The second stanza in particular of this contemporary hymn from Latin America takes up the argument of the apostle Paul in 1 Corinthians 15:12 concerning the truth of the Resurrection, and makes it sing!—Hugh T. McElrath

Worship Aids

CALL TO WORSHIP. "I will praise thee, O Lord, among the people; and I will sing praise unto thee among the nations. For thy mercy is great above the heavens; and thy truth reacheth unto the clouds" (Ps. 108:3–4).

INVOCATION. Without the assurance of your eternal presence, Father, we could not begin to manage life from day to day. So we come to express our gratitude for your guid-ance and love and to find again that sense of renewed nearness that fortifies us all along the journey. In the quiet moments of this worship may we truly be still and know that we are in the presence of God. In the singing moments may we genuinely utter praise to your name. In the thoughtful moments may we fix our minds and hearts on the truth that sets us free.—Henry Fields

OFFERTORY SENTENCE. "I am telling you the truth: whoever believes in me will do what I do—yes, he will do even greater things, because I am going to the Father. And I will do whatever you ask for in my name, so that the Father's glory will be shown through the Son. If you ask me for anything in my name, I will do it" (John 14:12–14 TEV).

OFFERTORY PRAYER. It is just a little wealth that we individually bring, Father; in light of the great needs we see, it is very small. But we place it in your hands, know-ing that you can use even the smallest bit in mighty ways. Let your blessing rest upon gift and giver and receiver, we pray in Jesus name.—H.F.

PRAYER.   Almighty and ever-living God, we gather in thy presence that our lives in time may feel the touch of thy life in eternity, and that the refreshment of heaven may fall upon our experiences on earth. We thank thee that thou dost give to us such a divine troubling of the Spirit that through life's difficulties we enter into life's deeper victories. May we this day learn the secret of that stronger faith that lies on the far side of discouragement. Grant that we may be able to find the ways of mastering our difficulties through the leading of thy Holy Spirit. May we learn from thee the secret of mastery in life.

We come to thee with eager and confident hearts, knowing that thou hast ever been dealing with us and for our good. Thou canst transform the strange and shadowed things of this life into the glories of thy holy and eternal Kingdom. So with confidence we put our faith and our prayers, our enterprise and our deep resolves in thy keeping, knowing that thou canst make use of us—all that we are and all that we are able to be and do—for the furthering of thy holy cause.

May thy blessing be upon all who are gathered together here. Bless our hearts and our homes. Bless the prayers spoken and unspoken that we lift to thee in faith. Quicken our understanding and strengthen our steps as we march forth in the ways of service and helpfulness. Make of us finer citizens in thy eternal city because we have been together in worship this day. Grant thy blessing upon thy people everywhere. Make them strong in faith, warm in spirit, one in purpose, unflagging in zeal. Bless all who have special responsibilities laid upon them in the ongoing life of this world, that they may walk in the light. And let thy Holy Spirit touch those who do not care about thy truth.

Grant that all people everywhere may learn to love the things they ought to love, to turn from the things that degrade life. Lead us according to thy infinite wisdom and according to thy wonderful love, in the ways that bring us inward satisfaction and peace and outward harmony with one another; and bind together the peoples of this world by the spirit of goodwill. We thank thee for our Savior Jesus Christ, in whom we rest our hope, whose life is our inspiration, and whose death reveals to us the deep mysteries of thy eternal and suffering love for us. We thank thee for his life, for his death, for his eternal victory, and for the hope that we repose in him. May we this day resolve more deeply to follow in his steps and to trust in his salvation.—Lowell M. Atkinson

Sermon: The Touch of Love
TEXT: Matt. 8:1–13 NRSV

The text reads, "there was a leper. . . . Jesus stretched out his hand and touched him, saying . . . Be made clean!" The touch of love— an appropriate topic as we begin this week when a lot of people are going to be thinking about love. I would point out first that:

I. We can reach out and touch people in love through physical contact.

a. Those with this dreaded skin disease were forced to live outside the city in leper camps because they were considered to be physically, socially, and religiously unclean. The Levitical law stated that a person with this dreaded disease "must wear torn clothes, leave his hair uncombed, cover the lower part of his face, and call out, 'Unclean! unclean!' to anyone who might approach him outside the city" (Lev. 13:45 TEV). Lepers were, no doubt, dirty, smelly, and unsightly.

Notice that the leper in our story did not ask to be healed. He asked to be made clean. He wanted to be made clean, as well as to be healed, so that he might return to society and no longer be considered an outcast.

b. Most of us don't know any lepers personally. But there are most certainly other members of our community who might be labeled unclean by society or who may feel unclean. Such persons desperately need the human touch of love.

The June 1994 issue of the *Mayo Clinic Health Letter* noted that "a small, but growing group of researchers is finding that touch has the subtle power to calm, nurture and help heal." The letter went on to note that touch is the first of our senses to develop and usually the last to diminish. Earlier in this century, pediatricians noticed that babies in orphanages and hospitals who were not held and cuddled failed to grow and often died.

Studies of long-term nursing home residents showed that those who were frequently touched when given their medication demonstrated a more positive attitude about themselves. Research has shown that a caring touch can possibly subdue heart irregularities, relieve depression, and lower blood pressure. We can reach out and touch someone's life for the better through physical contact.

II. We can extend a loving touch through the words we speak. In the case of the leper, Jesus spoke the words, "Be made clean." In the case of the centurion, Jesus spoke the words, "Go; let it be done for you according to your faith."

a. Let us not forget that in the person of Jesus, God reached out and spoke his Word to us by way of human flesh. Jesus was the Word of God incarnate. It was through Jesus that the healing, comforting, loving Word of God was manifested to humankind. Jesus, more than any other who has ever lived, served as a living revelation of God's nature, will, and Word for the world.

b. We, too, can touch people's lives through the affirming, uplifting, encouraging words that we speak. I often forget the potential power of the spoken word and sometimes have to apologize for words that I speak in haste without really thinking them through. We need to be reminded periodically that the words we speak to those around us, especially to the loved ones in our own homes, have the power to hurt or heal, to tear down or build up, to cause emotional pain or impart comfort. We can touch people's lives by the loving words we speak.

III. We can touch people through love by the way we listen. Jesus, in the scripture that we read, listened, especially in the case of the centurion. Jesus listened as the centurion shared his concern about his servant who was lying at home paralyzed and in terrible distress.

a. If you are like me, one of the things you want in a medical doctor is one who will take time to listen, because being able to share our concerns and have a medical profes-

sional listen to us is a vital part of the healing process.

Counselors tell us that the best way a lay church member can help someone who is struggling with problems is to listen—be a good, understanding, loving, and confidential listener.

b. Compassionate missionary, doctor, and humanitarian Albert Schweitzer said, "Open your eyes and seek another human being in need of a little time, a little friendliness, a little company, a little work. It may be a lonely, an embittered, a sick, or an awkward person for whom you can do something, to whom you can mean something."

We can, after the example of Jesus, change people's lives with the touch of love.—Randy Hammer

Illustrations

REACH OUT AND. . . ?   For a long, long time, a major telephone company used a beautiful and very moving slogan: "Reach out and touch someone." In other words, call somebody up and brighten his day; call somebody up and talk about old times; call somebody up and tell her some good news. In one commercial, a mother said to a father: "Joey called today." And the father replied, "Joey called! Are the kids sick? Is something wrong? Why did Joey call?" The mother answered, "I asked him the same thing. Joey said, 'I called just because I love you.'" Call somebody up and tell him you love him. Reach out and touch someone.—R.H.

HANDS UPON THE SICK.   The laying of hands upon the sick with love, faith, and prayer is an age-old practice, and it has documentable merit. No less a scientifically minded person than Dr. Morris Fishbein of the American Medical Association wrote pointedly of the value of this practice in the process of helping people back to health.

SUNDAY: FEBRUARY TWENTY-SECOND

LECTIONARY MESSAGE

Topic: Love Your Enemies
TEXT: Luke 6:27–38
Other Readings: Gen. 45:3–11, 15; Ps. 37:1–11, 39–40; 1 Cor. 15:35–38, 42–50

It's not "My way or the highway"; it's "My way is the high way." God's ways are not our ways. His way is higher than our ways like the sky is high above the earth. To walk in the Kingdom is to walk the high way. The high way is most clearly described in Luke

6:27–38. Now about this high way: we must acknowledge the reputed words of G. K. Chesterton, "It's not that Christianity has been tried and found wanting, but that it's been tried and found difficult." The high way will be difficult, but it's where God travels, and we will find much comfort with him as our companion.

I. *Four verbs.* Have you ever noticed that our Christianity is full of nouns whereas Jesus' Christianity is full of verbs? In verses 27–28, Jesus strings four verbs in a row: *love, do good, bless,* and *pray for.* And all these good actions are to be in response to hostility, evil treatment, cursing, and mistreatment. Christians are called to serve notice to the world that we are under divine management. We are different because the one we worship and adore is different. We love our enemies because he loves his enemies. We know this for a fact because we used to be his enemies (Rom. 5:10) and he loved us into a change of heart.

II. *Two examples.* The quadruple command to love the unlovely is followed by two examples of what Jesus expects. First, we are to turn the other cheek to the one who backhands us. If we are in Christ's service we cannot be focused on self-defense, self-justification, or personal acts of revenge. Vengeance is the Lord's, not ours. If we are in Christ's service we are not free to protect our person but only to promote the mission of his Kingdom: to evangelize God's enemies. Our experience of forgiveness transforms our hearts from the desire to get even to the desire to give kindness. Such a response is a sign of strength, not weakness.

Whereas the first example dealt with our person, the second example deals with our possessions.

Sometimes even our enemies need our help. The truest test of our Christianity is what we do when our enemies are in our hands and we have them just where we wanted them. They deserve justice but instead we give them mercy. They ask for a loan but we give it as a free gift. We must be careful not to disregard this passage as impossible idealism. Rather, it is the most practical realism when understood in the context of our personal enemies. Enemies are those who resent what we have that they feel they deserve. Enemies are those who want to be where we are. We are called to exert moral leadership. We are called to do to our enemies what we would like them to do to us, not what they do to us.

III. *Three arguments.* Jesus knows our hearts. He knew we would draw back from his command to love our enemies. He knew we would cheapen our distinctiveness from the world by declaring his way to be too ideal to practice in this present evil age. Jesus challenges our viewpoint in a very interesting manner. How can we expect a heavenly reward if we love only those who love us, do good only to those who are good to us, and lend only to those who return to us what was lent? The assumption of course is that we will also hate those who hate us, give evil to those who give us evil, and refuse to lend to those who are unlikely to return the loan. Even the sinner practices such negative reciprocity. If we respond to people exactly as the sinner responds, why in the world would the sinner be motivated to follow Christ? By our responses we are proving that Christ makes no difference. If this is our approach, we have actually become anti-evangelists. If we are to realize the heavenly reward of sonship and daughterhood, then we must practice love particularly with those who will not reciprocate it! We are called to practice a moral leadership of redemptive reciprocity. When we live in this way we look so much like the merciful Father that we are called his children. What an awesome reward! This ethic is powerfully evangelistic because it clearly shows the world how Christ makes a difference in our lives. It also makes room in the unbeliever's conscience for God to work.

IV. *Four results of redemptive reciprocity.* Even beyond this awesome reward of being declared as truly his children, Jesus specified four additional rewards. When we refuse to judge and condemn our enemies, God and others refuse to judge and condemn us. When we forgive our enemies, God and others are motivated to extend forgiveness to us. When we give even to our enemies, God and others give back to us a fully reciprocal gift, a gift that is not like the cereal boxes that explain their emptiness as a settling that occurred in shipping. In God's reciprocal giving, the box is preshaken and refilled before shipment! The practice of redemptive reciprocity restores the salty tang to life. It makes us the light of the world and calls even sinners to give thanks to our Father. Will you not become Jesus' brand of salt and light?—Rodrick K. Durst

Illustrations

LOVE DEFINED.   A definition of love that won a nationwide newspaper contest read: "Love is the doorway through which the human soul passes from selfishness to service and from solitude to kinship with all mankind."—Charles Wallis

I-THOU.   I follow the work of Jewish theologian Martin Buber in that I believe God gives us the model of the I-Thou relationship. God never sees us in terms of what we can do for him. He sees us in terms of how our relationship with him can enhance our growth. By that relationship he teaches us how to model our relationships with our spouses, our children, and our neighbors as I-Thou rather than on exploitative terms. We learn to relate to people with the goal of mutual growth, not with the goal of exploitation, advantage, or profit.—Harold Kushner[7]

SERMON SUGGESTIONS

Topic: A Gospel for the Defeated

TEXT: Gen. 49:19 KJV; 1 John 5:5

(1) These words contain a warning against expecting unbroken success in the spiritual life: "A troop shall overcome him." (2) These words contain a challenge to develop a spirit of stubborn endurance: "A troop shall overcome him, but. . . ." (3) These words contain a promise of ultimate victory: "But he shall overcome at the last."—John N. Gladstone[8]

Topic: Footnote on Freedom

TEXT: John 8:31, 36

(1) There is no absolute freedom. Freedom is always within a predestined structure. We are always both free and destined. (2) We know that we live in a polarity of freedom and destiny because we are made in the likeness and image of God. We see that image clearly in Christ: "If the Son makes you free. . . ." (3) So, what happens? (a) Pondering, even in small issues. (b) Purchases or choice. (c) Accountability. (4) No footnote on freedom can evade the fact of the abuse of freedom, of failure in responsibility. (5) Said Jesus: "If you continue in my word . . . you will know the truth"—not university information. "The truth will make you free." "If the Son makes you free, you will be free indeed." The Son is the disclosure of our destiny, the revelation of that realm from which we view our life, the mercy to overcome every failure in responsibility.—George A. Buttrick[9]

Hymn Suggestions

1. "Thine Is the Glory," Edmond L. Bailey (1884); "Maccabaeus," George F. Handel (1746)

A majestic hymn of praise glorifying the victory of Jesus in the Resurrection, it is appropriate to accompany a processional at the beginning of public worship.

2. "God Moves in a Mysterious Way," William Cowper (1774); "Dundee," Scottish Psalter (1615)

Cowper's famous hymn affirms God's gracious providence, which is assured in the reading from Psalm 37 and beautifully illustrated in Joseph's treatment of his brothers in the Genesis passage appointed for today's reading.

3. "If You Will Only Let God Guide You," Georg Neumark; "Neumark," Neumark (1657)

This strong German hymn reflects the spirit of the Psalter reading appointed for this day.

"Who trusts in God's unchanging love
Builds on the rock that naught can move."

4. "He's Got the Whole World in his Hands"; "Whole World," African American Spiritual

Few congregational singing expressions of the security and assurance of those who trust in God can match those of African American spirituals such as this one.—Hugh T. McElrath

Worship Aids

CALL TO WORSHIP.   "O give thanks to the Lord, call on his name, make known his deeds among the people" (Ps. 105:1 NRSV).

---

[7] *For the Love of God.*
[8] *The Valley of the Verdict.*

[9] *Sermons Preached in a University Church.*

INVOCATION.   Almighty God: you have commanded us to love our enemies, and to do good to those who hate us. May we never be content with affection for our friends, but reach out in love to all your children; through Jesus Christ our Lord.—*The Worshipbook*

OFFERTORY SENTENCE.   "My commandment is this: love one another, just as I love you. The greatest love a person can have for his friends is to give his life for them. And you are my friends if you do what I command you" (John 15:12–14 TEV).

OFFERTORY PRAYER.   Gracious God, as we give we are made whole; as we share we gain that which cannot be taken away; as we pray we learn the purpose of God for our lives; and with this offering we give and pray and believe all the more.—E. Lee Phillips

PRAYER.   We come to you this morning, Father, with a deep sense of need. So much happens in this life that we do not understand. People fail to live up to their word, and they break the hearts of others. Disease invades our bodies, even the most healthy of us, and life becomes a frightening journey. Folks who were once faithful allow small differences to become walls of separation that they will not demolish so that fellowship might be restored. Death storms into life at an inopportune time, creating havoc. We need your convicting and comforting spirit to move among us, opening our minds, hearts, and eyes so that we may manage difficulties after the fashion of Christ and learn in every circumstance to walk by faith, not by sight.

We need to experience conviction for our sins and cleansing from our sins, Father. This morning, renew a right spirit within us. Restore our wills that we may become resolute and steadfast in doing good. Bring us again into the drawing power of Christ. Enable us to live by the power of his Resurrection. May his virtues and graces appear in our lives as you heal us from all the separation that exists between us and others as well as between us and the Lord. Let our hearts become the citadel of your Kingdom, that through us your will may be done on earth with permanence and power.—Henry Fields

Sermon: The Journey of Faith

TEXT: Heb. 13:14; John 14:6

Two contrasting images form the basis of all biblical understanding. One is "the journey in the wilderness" and the other is "the city." The city of course is Jerusalem, in both the earthly and the heavenly versions. The earthly city failed; it became a symbol of pride, arrogance, and worldliness. Jesus wept over the earthly city, and pointed his disciples to another city "not made with hands, eternal in the heavens."

So it is the journey that remains the real metaphor for faith—the journey of the Israelites in the wilderness, searching for a promised land; the journey of the early Christians, seeking the eternal city; and the journey of all religious people since, looking for God.

Frederick Buechner called the first volume of his autobiography *The Sacred Journey,* for there is a sense in which every life is a holy pilgrimage, a journey into the heart of mystery. This has enormous implications for the nature of faith. Faith is not something static, settled, formed in concrete. It is not dogma, fundamentals, a particular way of looking at things. Faith is commitment to the journey, to discovery, to new ways of seeing. By faith, says the writer of Hebrews, people went out, took risks, were killed, wandered over deserts and mountains. He doesn't say they built temples and churches, recited creeds, and sang hymns. Perhaps they did these things, too. But it was the going out, the journeying, that was equated with faith.

Adventure, then, lies close to the heart of what it means to be a holy person. Not security, but danger, is our way. One does not become a disciple lightly. To begin is to risk everything, for we never know where the road will lead. One thing is certain: it always leads away from where we are. Our conservative friends who are forever talking about "getting back to the faith" are completely mistaken about where faith is or where it leads. Faith is not "back there." It is not in a set of propositions to which one assents or even in a mode of behavior to which one is pledged. Faith is a relationship with the fearless God who makes us fearless, too; who lets us snap our fingers at laws and codes and orthodoxies; who draws us on to new ways of being and seeing; and who says, "Fie upon security—that belongs to earthly cities; I show you insecurity—that will lead you in the *heavenly* way!"

We forget what risk takers the disciples of Jesus were. *Saint* Matthew, *Saint* Peter, *Saint* John, we call them, conjuring up images of stout traditionalists and monumental figures, like pious burgermeisters carved in stone. But they were men who broke all the rules, who had no idea of sainthood, nor even an aura of respectability. And Jesus himself was the very model of risk taker, defying the invincible orthodoxy of the scribes and Pharisees—defying it even in death. That is what the writer of Hebrews says: "So Jesus also suffered outside the gate in order to sanctify the people through his own blood." Outside the gate meant outside the perimeters of the holy city, and outside orthodoxy. "Therefore," he continues, "Let us go forth to him outside the camp, and bear the abuse he endured" (Heb. 13:12–13). You see? We too are expected to take risks, to defy the orthodox, to follow Jesus outside the city, even to die for what we come to believe.

Yes, *come to believe.* For that is the way it is in the journey of faith. We come to believe *along the way.* We don't start out with much. It is better that way. Then what we believe will be ours, not somebody else's. This is important. Kierkegaard understood. "There are many people," he wrote in his diary, "who reach their conclusions about life like schoolboys; they cheat their master by copying their answers out of a book without having worked out the sum for themselves." In real faith, there is no point in mimicking the answers of others. Either we make the journey for ourselves or we don't make it at all. In the end, it is what we ourselves have experienced that matters.

R. D. Laing, the psychoanalyst, says that we cannot experience the experience of others. We may think we do. We may read as though we do. We may read about the defection of Simon Peter and the conversion of Paul and think we have entered into what they felt or experienced. But we can't really enter in. All we can experience is our own experiences of reading or hearing about their experiences. We cannot really get inside their heads and have identically the same experiences they had. Therefore it is important to make our own journeys, to have our own experiences of God.

The real value of the Christian life lies in what one experiences along the way, not in being able to chat about theology and dogma and Christian history. There are professors of theology in many seminaries who can discourse brilliantly on doctrine but who abandoned their personal journeys of faith years ago. The important thing, in faith as in music, is to continue on our journeys, to continue to discover and learn and grow.

Even our own experiences remembered from years ago are not enough. We are inclined to try to make them enough—to assume that because we encountered the holy in a particular place or event back then, it will suffice to recall those experiences now. But it will not. The way of faith lies always forward, not backward.

It isn't always our bad experiences that stand in the way of our experiencing new things. Sometimes it is our good experiences as well.

Perhaps this is why Jesus never said, "Stay here with me." He always said, "Follow me."—John Killinger

Illustrations

POINT.   When I was a teenager, I had some remarkable religious experiences. During my twenties, I tried to repeat them by going to the kinds of meetings and doing the things that had produced the experiences before, but it didn't work. I began to think there was something wrong with me. Maybe God was letting me down. Maybe my earlier experiences had been mere illusions. Then I began to experience God in some new ways, and realized I had made a mistake. You cannot go back to the old places and expect to repeat the old experiences. God is always known in *new* experiences. The sacred journey moves forward, not backward. Jesus is not a stopping place, Jesus is a *way.* Here we have no lasting city; we must always seek the one that lies ahead. As the poet Chad Walsh has said, "We never step twice in the same redeeming river."—J.K.

COUNTERPOINT.   "In the convex driving mirror she could see," writes Jan Struther in *Mrs. Miniver,* "dwindling rapidly, the patch of road where they had stood; and she wondered why it had never occurred to her be-fore that you cannot successfully navigate the future unless you keep always framed beside it a small clear image of the past."—Charles Wallis

SUNDAY: MARCH FIRST

LECTIONARY MESSAGE

Topic: Temptation in the Wilderness
  TEXT: Luke 4:1–13
  Other Readings: Deut. 26:1–11; Ps. 91:1–2, 9–16; Rom. 10:8b-13

Jesus' baptism was his ordination for ministry. So it was with Paul and so it is with us (Acts 9:15–18; Eph. 2:9–10). But now the wilderness methodology for that messianic ministry must be confirmed. Integrity demands that the method of ministry match the morality of the message. The method must be tested against the motivation to which it appeals. Whatever is used to reach people must be continuously used to keep people. After all, any fool can gather a crowd with free food, bribes, or sensational public feats. The real test is whether the crowd can be transformed into a company of the committed. Methodology must follow theology, so methods must be tested. Methods are best tested in the wilderness before being implemented in the city. So Jesus followed the Spirit's leadership into forty days of sorting and searching in the desert. Those days were punctuated by Satanic attempts to distort the ministry by perverting the methodology.

Temptation is common to humanity. The incarnation of the Son of God meant that Jesus was tempted at all points as we are, yet he did not sin (Heb. 4:15). In the Lucan temptation narrative, Jesus is tempted but triumphant. His circumstance is instructive for our own temptations.

I. Fullness in Spirit is equipment for ministry. Ministry is effective as the minister follows the Spirit. The Spirit is as apt to lead into the wilderness as into green pastures. The Spirit-filled will follow the Spirit into the wilderness even if it means temptation and testing. Fullness should equate to fullness of following. The wilderness is the Spirit's seminary for learning to follow. Israel learned to follow the Spirit in the wilderness and so did Jesus. In the wilderness and in the Spirit, Jesus confirmed his method for ministry.

II. Isolated testing precedes public ministry. A time of isolation and clarification should precede any strategic new thrust of ministry. Note that the temptations consist of wrong approaches to good works, not appeals to do bad works. The first temptation, to turn a stone into a scone, was a good work but the timing and motive were wrong. The position and power granted Jesus were for the salvation of others not for his own. How many have lost ministry effectiveness because, like Eli and his sons, the ministry position became inseparable from preferential treatment (1 Sam. 2:12ff)! "The new man shall not live by bread alone, but by every word that comes from the mouth of God" (4:4; Deut. 8:3). Jesus received power and position as Messiah not for himself but for God's glory and our redemption. Use of such gifts for self quickly becomes addictive and easily erodes the influence. If Jesus were to be sustained by manna in the wilderness, it would be provided by the Father's command and not by his own. Much mishandling of manna would be eliminated if only we would wait for the Father's provision instead of taking things into our own hands.

III. The words of God are the sword of the Spirit. Anyone may minister effectively who shares the gospel of Christ in the empowerment of the Spirit. This eschatological promise of Joel 2:28 became a reality and ministry axiom in Acts 2. Messianic ministry always has the Word of God for its content, redemption for its intent, and the Spirit for its empowerment.

The apostle Paul developed his methodology of overcoming temptation from this temptation narrative (Eph. 6:17). In this narrative, we see the Spirit-directed Jesus using the right scriptural truth to parry each false thrust offered by the adversary. In times of threat, the Spirit searches our hearts for the right truth to rebuke even the intelligently twisted scriptures of the tempter. The Spirit fights with whatever Scripture we have hidden in our hearts. When we study and meditate on the scriptures, we are supplying the Spirit in advance with choice scriptures for effective combat against future temptation and discouragement.

IV. Ministry is more than meeting felt needs. Satan knew that free manna makes for quick messiahships. When people are hungry they feel it. They want to be fed. But appealing solely to the relevance of felt needs distracts from the recognition of real needs. Bread enables people to keep living, but the Word of God enables them to have a life worth living. Without bread, humanity cannot live at all; hunger must be a consistent concern for Christians. But without the word, people do not know why or how to live.

V. Ministry is more than sensation. The second temptation involves Satan prooftexting from Psalm 91:1–2. The quickest way to confirm messiahship would be to leap from the Temple pinnacle. According to Psalm 91, such a leap would force God to intervene and sensationally prevent injury to Jesus. Satan knows the Scriptures. But Scripture must be weighed against other Scripture if it is to be rightly applied. Requiring God to jump to our service is inappropriate to his majesty. The risks we take must be at his calculation, not ours. Appealing to the sensational does draw a crowd, but it does little to engender commitment. Jesus would later experience the crowd's capacity to shift rapidly from cheers to jeers, from crown to cross, and from following to fighting. Whatever method we use to gain a following must also be used to keep that following. So we must choose with wisdom.

VI. Ministry is more than power. The final appeal of Satan in the Lucan narrative was to acquire political or ecclesiastical power at any cost. Power is essential to doing great good. Would not such good ends justify any means? So, why not "bow down and worship me" and make all these thrones of power yours to use for good (4:9)? No doubt Satan could deliver some of these kingdoms. Having influence and recognition in the political and ecclesiastical power structures can do incredible

good, but not if it comes at the cost of the primary directive to worship God first. Humanity is for the glory, service, and enjoyment of God. Corruption occurs at the core of our humanity whenever we put anything or anyone ahead of God. Right-truthed, spirit-led worship is the engine of evangelism and effective ministry. Desiring the accumulation of influence and authority invites the acid of moral corruption. If the desire for power corrupts, then the desire for absolute power corrupted Satan absolutely, as it will us.

Now if power apart from God corrupts, then powerlessness in union with God redeems. History has well documented the corruptivity of power but given little note to the redemptivity of powerlessness. This latter reality is the chosen theme of the Bible. The incarnation of Christ is described as the conscious choice of God the Son to experience powerlessness as humanity, even to obedience unto death. The effect of such powerlessness is that his life and ours become perfect platforms for the display of God's omnipotence. Our willingness to be as one without authority allows and attracts God to exercise his power through us. Satan offered the royal stallion, Jesus chose the humble colt. Jesus shows us that the cross comes before the crown, or we end up ashamed, anxious, and accusing our loved ones for our own bad choices.

VII. Timing is everything. Jesus would later turn stones into bread a thousand times over and many would want to make him the Bread King. But Jesus would wait for the Father's timing and coronation at the Resurrection. He would cast himself down from the pinnacle of the cross and the Father would bear him up at Easter into heaven (Eph. 1:20). Jesus would get all authority and power on earth and in heaven, but by obedience to the Father, even unto death.

We discover the right timing as we submit ourselves to the Father. Satan flees when our resistance follows our submission to God. Satan abandons his temptation episode at Christ's command. He was unsuccessful with Jesus because Jesus refused to be distracted from the Father's face and to stray from the Spirit of the Scriptures. Jesus lived by every word that proceeded from the mouth of the Father. Luke is careful to identify this temptation episode as a battle but not the whole war. Satan "departed until an opportune time" (4:13). Jesus had experienced the faithfulness of the Father to match each temptation with a way of escape (1 Cor. 10:13). The Spirit had indeed placed the right Scripture as a sword in the Lord's mouth to counter each thrust of the evil one. With confidence and experience gained in the wilderness, Jesus turned his face to the world of ministry in Judea. With these time-tested resources to overcome temptation, Christ gives us confidence that our lives and service can overcome detours and dead ends.—Rodrick K. Durst

Illustrations

THE WAY OF ESCAPE. In John Bunyan's classic *Pilgrim's Progress*, Christian has finally learned not to get off the road for any reason. He has paid dearly to learn faithfulness to the path laid out in God's word. As he clears a high hill, he sees two large lions waiting on the road ahead. He moves forward down the road, repeating to himself, "Stay on the road, stay on the road," even as he wonders what he should do. As he stays on the road and draws closer to the lions, he discovers the way of escape. He sees that the lions are actually beside the road and chained so that if he walks in the middle of the road he will be safe. Pilgrim does pass safely beneath the lions' breath and goes on down the road to the Celestial City.—R.K.D.

THE SECRET OF PREACHING. Suppose we should dare to live the life? Already we have met more people than Jesus met. We have points of contact and means of influence denied to him. Suppose we came clean before God; suppose we were really ready to be killed for an inner something more dear than life; suppose we took our chance with Him! The secret of preaching is in the surrender of the preacher to Christ.—George A. Buttrick[1]

SERMON SUGGESTIONS

Topic: The Place of Recovery
TEXT: Gen. 13:3, 4
(1) Abraham's fall in Egypt and his way to recovery. (2) Our need. (a) We begin with an

[1] *Jesus Came Preaching.*

act of self-surrender to Christ, but we lapse. (b) We need to remember two things: something happened from the side of Christ that made it a covenant between him and us; our surrender is never complete, but there is nothing from which Christ cannot deliver us. (3) When we go back, let us remember the love to which we return.—James Reid

Topic: The Power of the Cross
Text: 1 Cor. 1:22
(1) We preach Christ crucified because it is the doctrine that incomparably preserves for us the sense of the holiness of God, (2) because it is the doctrine that incomparably creates and preserves the sense of the nature of sin, (3) because in experiencing this doctrine we incomparably discern the realities of grace, and (4) because it is the doctrine in whose heart we find ample resources for the attainment of moral and spiritual health.—John H. Jowett

Hymn Suggestions: First Sunday in Lent

1. "We Have Heard the Joyful Sound," Priscilla Owens (1887); "Jesus Saves," William J. Kirkpatrick (1882); "Limpsfield," Josiah Booth (1898)
An exuberant lyrical expression of the Epistle reading for the day, this gospel song with its insistent refrain "Jesus saves" possesses power when fervently sung.
2. "Forty Days and Forty Nights," George H. Smyttan (1856); "Aus der Tiefe Rufe Ich," Martin Herbst (1676)
This is one of three hymns by this author written for the Lenten season. The text is obviously based on the gospel reading on the temptation of Jesus in the wilderness. When sung with understanding, the hymn can be inspirational and devotional in contemplation of our Lord's supreme trial by Satan.
3. "As Men of Old Their First Fruits Brought," Frank von Christierson (1960); "Forest Green," adaptation by Ralph V. Williams (1906)
This stewardship hymn by a contemporary American author can serve admirably as a devotional response to Moses' instructions in the Old Testament reading for today. As the Israelites of old were told to remember their deliverance from Egyptian bondage by making thank offerings, so today's worshippers

are to bring their offerings of good and self in response to God's supreme offering in Christ Jesus.

4. "Christ Jesus Knew a Wilderness," Jane Parker Huber (1986); "St. Crispin," George Elvey (1862)

In this hymn based on the Lucan passage for the day, the writer, a contemporary Presbyterian woman, after contemplating Jesus' wilderness temptation, imaginatively affirms Jesus' presence in the wildernesses of the worshipper.—Hugh T. McElrath

Worship Aids

CALL TO WORSHIP. "Seek the Lord and his strength; seek his presence continually. Remember the wonderful works he has done" (Ps. 105:4–5a NRSV).

INVOCATION. Father of our Lord Jesus Christ, we approach thy throne in wonder and awe. We are great sinners and unclean. We seek the pure light of thy holiness that we may find our way in this world, to do good and love mercy and walk humbly with the God who never stops calling to us.—E. Lee Phillips

OFFERTORY SENTENCE. "Be ye therefore followers of God as dear children; and walk in love, as Christ also hath loved us, and hath given himself for us an offering and a sacrifice to God for a sweet-smelling savor" (Eph. 5:1–2).

OFFERTORY PRAYER. Our heavenly Father, who hast given everything unto us, what can we give unto thee except a grateful and happy heart, shown forth by our generous gifts of love. Bless these offerings to the glorification of thy holy name.—Lowell M. Atkinson

PRAYER. Turn to us, abiding God, through these days of self-examination and attentive contemplation, as we journey with our Lord toward the cross and crucifixion.

O God in Christ, Lamb of God who takes away the sins of the world, who takes away my sin, capture us in our anxious scurrying and call us to the way of the cross.

Tune our hearts to our own mortality that we may again begin to die to those things that keep us from living for you.

O crucified Lord, grant us fresh resolve and unflinching obedience to fully embrace the bidding of losing our lives for your sake, and in so losing, in thee to find life.

May you truly be our treasure.

Like our faithful Christ, as we seek your will in the wilderness, empower and inform us with the written Word, holy Scripture, spoken truth, the living Word, Holy Savior, Jesus Christ; the indwelling Word, Holy Spirit, Light Divine.

Grant us awareness of and openness to all voices that speak and reveal your truth.

Good Shepherd, who is always beside us to guide our steps and bless our journey, as we lean hard into hearing and accepting the call and the way of the cross, in these days of deep desire to know you better, to follow you more closely, to love you completely, cleanse us, purify us, renew us, that your will is done, your Kingdom comes. Through Christ, let it be, let it be.—William M. Johnson

Sermon: Religion as a Form and a Force
TEXT: 2 Tim. 3:5

I. The apostle speaks of "men who preserve the outward form of religion, but are a standing denial of its reality" (2 Tim. 3:5; NEB). This kind of statement makes sensitive, sincere Christians a bit anxious. We believe we want to take our religion seriously, to let it be more than a mere form in our lives, to allow it to make us more useful people in the world. But we can't be sure. We look at ourselves and see much that is either wrong or lacking. Sometimes we feel more like going fishing than going to church. And we may even at times feel more like cursing than praying.

But that is not what bothers us most of the time. Sooner of later we come to terms with our humanity. We recognize and accept our lack of perfection. We allow for our vagrant feelings. What bothers us most, or ought to bother us, is that the Church as a whole is making such a little dent in the armor plate of secularism and materialism. We have vast resources of personnel, of money, and of tradition, and yet we are weak. No group can beat us at the game of social commentary, analysis, and diagnosis. We even claim that we have the remedy for what ails the world. Yet many of the aims of Christians through the ages seem so far from realization: peace, justice, and personal righteousness. One pastor expressed his bitterness about a member of his church: "That man," the pastor said, "is so crooked that when he dies we won't bury him: we'll just twist him into the ground."

II. Perhaps that's good enough for the crooked man who has walked the last crooked mile. What about the rest of us? What is wrong with us? Let's try to keep matters in proper perspective. There has always been something wrong with the Church. Some of us keep hoping that we will break out of our bondage and be truly free. Perhaps that hope has kept the Church in business through the centuries. But we'll have to acknowledge that we've done more talking than doing; that we've kept our ecclesiastical machinery purring smoothly and haven't paid enough attention to what it is producing. We have brought people off the assembly line "who preserve the outward form of religion, but are a standing denial of its reality."

God knows that the world needs what religion has promised so beautifully or called for so insistently. But repeated disappointment has made some persons raise serious questions about the whole religious enterprise—whether to throw it away entirely or do some other drastic thing with it. What should we do?

III. We can go at the problem in one of several ways.

a. We might reject religion entirely. This is one possibility. But it is out of keeping with what seems to be a natural inclination of most of humankind. It goes against the traditions of our own nation. And it probably would be psychologically traumatic to us individually.

Yet it becomes easier and easier to get rid of religion—at least what is conventionally called religion—by soaking up arguments so freely disseminated today, by riding the crest of the wave of rebellion sweeping the modern world, or by assuming that something as old as religion can't be relevant and worthwhile. I would be really surprised not to find at least a few persons who are on the verge of tossing the old faith through the stained glass window.

One of the greatest preachers of America wrote his mother from college when he was a student, saying, "I'm going to clear God out of the universe, start all over, and see where I come out." It is easier than it once was to reject religion: you can find some social approval for your action, and you may be paid handsomely to speak or write on your views. Still you have to deal with yourself and with all that lies deep within you. For example, a client of psychologist Carl Rogers, trying to dismiss his guilt and the somatic symptoms that went along with it, said, "Intellectually I'm a pagan, but I'm a Puritan in my guts." To reject religion entirely is hard to do.

b. We might do something else. We might simply reject the form of religion. Some persons are unhappy that the church has become a political forum—a place for a lot of talk and little effective action. The church, they say, is trying to do things, even good things, that it is not always qualified to do. But mostly there is talk, diverse talk, and largely ineffectual action.

One newspaper columnist commented on pulpit preoccupation with politics: "Reason, restraint, and moderation too often are overwhelmed. The cacophony mounts; and the congregations decline."

But there's another side to this, too. Some people are staying away from our churches because they believe that what goes on in church never touches down where people live, never gets into the cracks where our communities are splitting apart, never makes any timely difference. We church people can be like Rip van Winkle, who slept through a revolution. But some persons have neither the talent nor the time for that sort of spiritual irresponsibility. So they go somewhere else where they think the action really is.

c. Now if we refuse to go so far as to reject religion entirely or even to reject the form of religion, what is left? What can we do if we are dissatisfied with religion as usual, with religion weighted down with an intolerable load of self-preoccupation?

I believe the answer is suggested in the words of the text: let the form of religion be infused with reality, with vitality. Give religion free rein. Let the knowledge of God cover the earth as the waters. Let this faith in God and this devotion to him take form and captivate our imaginations, engage our senses, and conquer our will.

IV. But let's not permit our enthusiasm to run away with us. The matter is not easily resolved.

For one thing, the form and the quality of religion may not be compatible. They may be like what English essayist Sydney Smith described: triangular bits of wood in square holes, oblong bits in triangular holes, and square bits in round holes. Let's look at the Free Church tradition. The form of that faith says that all persons are free to interpret the Bible for themselves; free to reach their own conclusions as they let the Holy Spirit guide them. A coerced faith is no faith at all. Yet some who give lip service to freedom deny with their deeds what their lips are saying. They call people heretics who disagree with them, mount misleading campaigns against them, and seek to ban their books. The trouble is that they preserve the outward form of freedom, make pronouncements on it, pass resolutions for it, but their works and their influence are a standing denial of honest belief in it.

On the other hand, a different tradition may openly deny the right of an individual to be wrong. It may use its own power or the power of government to control public expressions of independent religious opinion. This has been done, and persons like John Bunyan, Roger Williams, and Pierre Teilhard de Chardin have had heavy, unnecessary burdens laid upon them. In this case, the form of religion—intolerant bigotry—is bad, for it will not accommodate the burgeoning good within it, to say nothing of what is good outside it.

Jesus said, "No one sews a patch of unshrunk cloth to an old coat, for then the patch tears away from the coat and leaves a bigger hole. Neither do you put new wine into old wineskins; if you do, the skins burst, and then the wine runs out and the skins are spoilt. No, you put new wine into fresh skins; then both are preserved" (Matt. 9:16 NEB).

Our Lord said these words to justify his unorthodox approach to human need. Jesus came to do the will of God, and if the Temple stood in the way of God's will, then the Temple had to go; if a long-revered custom stood in the way, it had to go; if stubborn, close-minded individuals stood in the way, they had to change or be left behind.

Suppose Jesus had had to get office approval from the established religion of his time? How far do you think he would have gotten? To begin with, some people had certain suspicions about his parentage. Others tried to suppress his teaching, for many of his views differed from their own. If the officials had approved him, they would have swallowed him up with flattery or committee meetings, either of which can be lethal.

Jesus' religion was new wine, and it had to have new wineskins to contain it—skins flexible and resilient enough to expand with its new life and not break, durable enough to last in time of testing.

And that is what people in growing numbers are thinking about the Church. The Church as it is represented in some places is like an old wineskin; brittle, unresilient, unaccommodative to new, vital pressures within. So what happens to it? In some cases, the wineskin, the church, bursts dramatically, and the wine, the new life, is dissipated and lost in the explosion. In other cases, the wineskin, the church, springs a leak, and the wine, the new life, is lost gradually, almost unnoticed, while the old wineskin hangs intact, admired for sentimental reasons that have to do more with antiquity than with relevance.

There's nothing wrong with institutions per se. But there's plenty wrong with a fixed institutionalism that resists growth and change, that slays its prophets, and that denies its service to the modern world.

We love our institutions—home, school, nation, church. We sing of them: "Be it ever so humble, there's no place like home"; "Hail to thee, dear Alma Mater"; "My country, 'tis of thee."

I love thy church, O God!
Her walls before thee stand,
Dear as the apple of thine eye,
And graven on thy hand.
                    —Timothy Dwight (1752–1817)

And we should love all of them: home, school, nation, church. But we must not kill them or bury them alive by not helping them to reproduce their vitality and discover their adaptability.

The Chinese used to cripple their little girls for life by binding their feet in the name of beauty. Christians may cripple the church by wrapping it unwittingly in the grave clothes of an outlived tradition and placing it tenderly in a tomb of irrelevance in the name of authority and security. New life and fitting forms are what the times call for. And that may make astonishing demands upon all of us! It may not mean that our cherished institutions will be swept away. When Christianity burst upon the first-century world, the Temple of awesome beauty and haunting tradition went with the wind, but the synagogue, simple and functional, remained, though transformed into the shape of the earliest Christian churches. So all was not lost; the best was preserved. Religious life went on, though vastly changed.

V. Well, what do you think about it? What I have been saying is, I believe, not merely a private opinion but a judgment of history.

To reject vital religion will require nothing of us. Just let life, even religious life, go on as usual, and it will cease to be a vital force in you. You may argue for it; you may fight for it; you may even die for it; and it may hold no more value for you than allegiance to a political faction, to a family tradition, or to a mental quirk.

The apostle Paul could see that outward declarations of piety don't always jibe with what one really is. He said, "Men will love nothing but money and self; they will be arrogant, boastful, and abusive; with no respect of parents, no gratitude, no piety, no natural affection; they will be men who put pleasure in the place of God, men who preserve the outward form of religion, but are a standing denial of its reality" (2 Tim. 3:2–5 NEB).

To reject religion as a vital force in one's life can lead to such extremes. You don't have to be all hot and angry about it. Just let yourself go, and there are no depths to which you cannot sink. And all the while you may proudly wave a flag with the words inscribed, "Faith of Our Fathers." It is a sad fact that an individual or a nation can go to hell with all the banners waving, all the trumpets blowing, and all the church bells ringing. But to quote another New Testament writer dealing with similar matters: "Although we give these words of warning, we feel sure that you, whom we love, are capable of better things and will enjoy the full experience of salvation" (Heb. 6:8 PHILLIPS).

I said that to reject vital religion will require nothing of us. However, to allow faith to come alive does require something. We have to recapture a vision of God's will for the individual, for the Church, and for the world. Not what I want, not what the church wants, not what the world wants, but what God wants is all-important; this will continually call the Church to reformation; this will constantly call into being new forms of devotion and service and invest old forms with fresh vitality; this will take away some of the shame of our powerless religious institutions and give them a significance that far outweighs their present social prestige and political power.

We must remember that the symbol of the Church is not the life-extending apparatus of the geriatric ward but the cross. And the goal of the Church is not self-preservation but self-giving.—James W. Cox

Illustrations

TALK.   What a minister in New York said some years ago is still true: "In our time the Church's fault is not, as some would say, that she speaks too seldom. Rather, she speaks too often and on too many subjects. . . . Churchmen act as though they feel they have to pontificate on any problem and, having spoken, tend to assume that there is little more to be said. This is boorish behavior as well as bad theology. It leaves little alternative for those who disagree but to stay away. Thoughtful members of contemporary society are doing this in droves."—*Time*

TWO KINDS OF SAINTHOOD.   On the ancient minster at Basel are two sculptured groups: St. Martin cutting his cloak in two with his sword to clothe a beggar, and St. George spurring his horse against the dragon that devastated the country. Every Christian should embody both kinds of sainthood in his life.—Walter Rauschenbusch

SUNDAY: MARCH EIGHTH

LECTIONARY MESSAGE

Topic: The Fox and the Hen
  TEXT: Luke 13:31–35
  Other Readings: Gen. 15:1–12, 17–18; Ps. 27; Phil. 3:17–4:1

Foxes and hens do not get along well together. This bit of general wisdom and common sense is summed up in an old proverb that warns against letting foxes into chicken houses. It is interesting, therefore, to note that in the short space of five verses in the thirteenth chapter of Luke (vv. 31–35) there are pictures of both a fox and a hen.

I. *The fox* (vv. 31–33). Some Pharisees came to Jesus and warned him to leave the area governed by Herod Antipas. These Pharisees could have been in a temporary alliance with Herod in order to get the troublemaker, Jesus, out of the way. Ordinarily the Pharisees would not be friendly toward such a person as Herod, who ruled over them, but they would be interested in defeating a common enemy. It is also quite possible that these Pharisees were friends of Jesus and had his best interests in mind. Jesus did have friends among the Pharisees, such as Nicodemus and Joseph of Arimathea. Commentators are about equally divided on the question of whether the Pharisees who warned Jesus were his friends or his enemies, and absolute certainty is neither possible nor necessary. The important fact is that Jesus refused to be panicked by Herod's threat. Jesus describes Herod as a "fox," a fascinating choice. He might have compared Herod to a wolf because of Herod's cruelty and lack of moral conscience. If Herod had been a strong, domineering ruler, Jesus might have chosen the lion as an animal for comparison. But Jesus likened Herod to a fox, an animal noted for cunning, craftiness, and slyness. Perhaps Jesus also had in mind the fact that there were traits of indecision and weakness in Herod. At the trial of Jesus, Herod sent Jesus back to Pilate, refusing to make a final decision himself. Herod did, however, put to death John the Baptist, and it is unlikely that he would put to death another Jewish religious leader so soon after John's death.

Herod's threats did not end the mission of Jesus, and verses 32 and 33 present a compelling summary of his work. The verses are striking in that both verses use expressions relating to three days. There are idioms in the verses that would have been very clear to Jesus' hearers but are difficult for us to understand. The figure of speech relating to three days indicates the end of an uncertain but not too lengthy period of time. Jesus would work until his mission was accomplished, and no earthly ruler would dictate that length of time. The goal would be reached, even though death would be included. The reference to Jerusalem as the place where prophets die is rich in Old Testament symbolism. The emphasis is on accomplishment, not mere cessation of activity.

II. *The hen* (vv. 34–35). The protective, nurturing traits of God are likened in the Old Testament to the care given by a bird (see Deut. 32:11–12, Ps. 36:7, and Isa. 31:5). The Old Testament prophets dreamed of a time when the people of Israel would be gathered from all over the world (Isa. 60:4 and Zech. 10:6–10 are examples). Jerusalem would be the fitting place for such a gathering, with its Temple, its religious heritage, and its religious leaders. How strange that the City of Peace held so much contempt for God's messengers! Instead of a sanctuary for prophets, Jerusalem had become a killing place.

Matthew places this scene very near the crucifixion (23:37–39). The reasons for Luke's use of the words at this place in his account of our Lord's life are not known, but the contrast with Herod is obvious. The tender heart of Jesus yearns to gather the nation to himself, but the nation refuses the overtures of love and care. Now there is judgment, but in the last phrase of verse 35 there is the recognition that some day the people would recognize Jesus as the One sent from God. The time might be the Passover or the final triumph of God's Kingdom, but the time would surely come.

III. *The hen overcomes the fox.* Ordinarily a hen is no match for a fox, and as we noted at the beginning, a proverb warns against letting foxes in hen houses. But the conclusion of this account in Luke 13 is that the hen, Jesus, is ultimately victorious over the fox, Herod. This changing of expected roles is sometimes called the "Great Reversal" theme of the Gospels. In the Kingdom of God, those who were first according to the standards of the world become last. The strong and powerful in the world's eyes become weak, while the meek ones inherit the earth. The rich become poor if they trust only in their wealth, while the poor are welcomed and blessed. It is not surprising, therefore, that a hen could conquer a fox. Herod, the fox, lived and died. According to some estimates, he was the most capable ruler of the sons of Herod the Great. He built Tiberias and other cities. But for Christian historians, Herod's life is seen in relation to those blessed by God—John the Baptist and Jesus.

The fox lived, did a few memorable things, and died. The hen, Jesus, lived and died, but he rose from the dead and lives eternally. Herod's life can be summed up in a few sentences, but John reminds us that the whole world could not contain the books about Jesus if everything he said and did were recorded. Indeed, some of the greatest libraries in the world have taken as their purpose to collect materials about the life of Jesus of Nazareth. The point of reference is Jesus, not Herod.

The final triumph belongs to Jesus, not Herod. The fox was defeated and the hen was victorious. The last phrase of our text provides a fitting conclusion: "Blessed is he that cometh in the name of the Lord."—Paul Debusman

Illustrations

NAME CALLING. Our nation has witnessed another year of election campaigns (some would say we have *endured* another year). Mud slinging and name calling often seem to be the rule rather than the exception in political campaigns, and Christian ethicists and others interested in politics are calling for a return to basic civility in politics. Was Jesus a name caller? He called Herod a "fox" and referred to others as "hypocrites," "whitewashed tombs," a "generation of vipers," "false prophets," "ravening wolves in sheep's clothing," and "blind leaders of the blind." In the Sermon on the Mount, Jesus warned against the use of idle and destructive names (Matt. 5:22). Did Jesus fail to follow his own teaching about name calling? When Jesus referred to people with these descriptive names, he was stating facts, because he knew what was inside each person. The names described what was real and true. He did not use names lightly, and his harshest criticism was directed against those who abused and exploited others. Jesus "told it like it was."—P.D.

THOSE WHO ENDURE. The history of athletics is filled with accounts of persons who have endured inconvenience, distress, hardship, and pain for the sake of competition and the hope of winning. The Summer Olympic Games in Atlanta (remember Kerri Strug?) and the World Series of baseball provided examples of people who neglected their families, postponed needed surgery, and subjected their bodies to intensive training because they had a goal set before them of becoming the best. In a different yet similar way, Jesus would continue his mission until the will of God was accomplished in his life—and death. His redemptive mission was greater than any rejection or opposition.—P.D.

SERMON SUGGESTIONS

Topic: Turn Your Troubles into Treasures!
TEXT: Ps. 119:71

When we have troubles, (1) is evasion the answer? (2) or capitulation? (3) or constant rebellion? (4) or bravery? (5) or good sense plus daring? (6) By means of divine grace we can actually turn our troubles into positive helpfulness. If we learn to live deeply, we will make our own life another one of the lights of the world, to show others the way to the abiding values of time and eternity.—G. Ray Jordan

Topic: The Epiphany at Jacob's Well
TEXT: John 4:5-14

(1) He who was thirsty himself offered the most satisfying drink. (2) He who had nothing with which to draw gave water in abundance. (3) He who seemed less than Jacob revealed himself as infinitely greater. (4) He who gave drink made the drink itself a springing well.—R.C.H. Lenski

Hymn Suggestions: Second Sunday in Lent

1. "Thou Whose Almighty Word," John Marriott (1813); "Italian Hymn," Felice de Giardini (1713)

One of our earliest missionary hymns, "Thou Whose Almighty Word" is a work of art with its Trinitarian pattern and chorus line "Let there be light!" It would be appropriate either before or after the reading of the Psalter—Psalm 27.

2. "God Is My Strong Salvation," James Montgomery (1822); "Christus, der Ist Mein Leben," Melchior Vulpius (1609)

With Psalm 27 as the basis of this finely wrought hymn, James Montgomery, often claimed to be the greatest of lay hymn writers, has given us a strong expression of firm faith in God. Its stanzas could appropriately be used as responses interpolated in the reading of the verses of the psalm for the day.

3. "O Jesus Christ, May Grateful Hymns Be Rising," Bradford Gray Webster (1954); "Charterhouse," David Evans (1927)

Christian responsibility for the modern city is voiced in this hymn. Its third stanza invokes the vision of Christ's weeping over Jerusalem (Luke 13:31–35) as inspiration for the worshipers' concern and commitment to service.

4. "Be Strong in the Lord," Linda Lee Johnson (1979); "Strength," Tom Fettke (1979)

Reflecting the spirit of the apostle Paul's writing (Phil. 4:1; Eph. 6:10), this new song can invigorate a worshiping congregation for steadfast and courageous service.—Hugh T. McElrath

Worship Aids

CALL TO WORSHIP.   "The Lord is my light and my salvation; whom shall I fear? The Lord is the strength of my life; of whom shall I be afraid?" (Ps. 27:1).

INVOCATION.   Father, continue your loving kindness to us, we pray. We look to you as the Lord who is merciful and gracious, slow to anger and plenteous in mercy, who has not dealt with us after our sins, nor rewarded us according to our iniquities. Grant to us hearts filled with thankfulness and compassion like your own. Use us, marred and broken vessels that we are, as channels of your grace to bring mercy and joy and peace into the lives of our fellow pilgrims on this journey of life.—Henry Fields

OFFERTORY SENTENCE.   "Each one, as a good manager of God's different gifts, must use for the good of others the special gift he has received from God. Whoever preaches must preach God's messages; whoever serves must serve with the strength that God gives him, so that in all things praise may be given to God through Jesus Christ, to whom belong glory and power forever and ever. Amen" (1 Pet. 4:10–11).

OFFERTORY PRAYER.   Loving Lord, we give because we want to and we give in faith

that lives can be transformed by this gift through the unlimited power of the Holy Spirit. Let it be.—E. Lee Phillips

PRAYER.   O God, here we are, such as we are. So many times we are a disappointment to others and to ourselves, and surely to you. We are full of good intentions not lived out; we hold lofty ideals that never get translated in the market place; we champion all kinds of good causes from the back pew of the sanctuary, but we never brave the front line of the battlefield. We try so hard, at least we think we do, but we just seem to be spinning our wheels or going around in circles. We hunger and thirst, but it is not after righteousness. We would be building—but so often it is not your Kingdom but ours. It is not that we are not busy, but we seem to be getting nowhere fast. Are we lost?

There is only one thing worse than being lost and that is to be lost and not to know it. Could this be our predicament? In our more lucid moments, we confess that we have come here to find ourselves, for it is easy to get lost in the world.

O God, you are so patient with us; let us not give up on ourselves. Help us to be still and know you *are* God. We would see Jesus, for in his face we behold your glory, the glory of the fullness of your grace. This is our need, your perfection—the wholeness, the holiness, the fulfillment in Christ.

How we need the love, the trust, the commitment that we discover in him! Not in doing but in being; not in frantic effort but in loving reception; not in overachieving but in waiting on you is our salvation, the life that is life, the life that even death cannot diminish or destroy.

How we thank you for your Word of grace taught and preached through the ministry of this church.

We are grateful, too, for the beautiful people with whom our lives are set, who love us in spite of all our foibles, who understand even when we do not understand ourselves, who in their loving keep calling us to be and become.

We pray for members and friends who are our family of faith. As a family we pray for one another.

Through Him who is the Way, the Truth, and the Life, and among us teaching us to pray and live.—John Thompson

Sermon: God in the Desert

TEXT: Gen. 28:10–22

As the tiny airplane approached Mandera in northeast Kenya, I was busy looking out the window. I was trying to take in the strange sight. As I looked at the world below, I was looking for God.

You see, I had been told by the people who know that it would be very hard to see God in Mandera. Mandera is a place of oppressive darkness and spiritual captivity. A place of brokenness and pain. A place of heat and thirst. A place where people live enslaved to tradition and culture. So, I had been told, God might very well be in Mandera—but he would be very hard to find.

I searched the landscape for signs and symbols, for buildings and structures, for something—anything—that would point me to the presence of God. Something that would be evidence that God lived in Mandera. But from the plane I could find nothing that pointed to God.

Sometimes we feel that way even when we're not far from home. Sometimes we desperately look for God right in the middle of our familiar lives—and sometimes he's nowhere to be found.

In fact, more often than we care to admit, God's the last one we'd like to find.

But whether we're desperately looking for him or trying to avoid finding him at all cost, the bottom line is this: sometimes God is very hard to find.

Jacob knew that. Not that he was searching for God all that diligently. No, Jacob had done quite well without God, thank you very much. What that meant in his case was lying and cheating and stealing and conniving and doing whatever it took to get ahead—but still, he had done pretty well living that way. And he had done that—at least he thought he had done that—without God.

Things recently, however, had come to a point of crisis. Jacob had literally stolen the blessing that rightfully belonged to his brother Esau. And because of that, Jacob found it necessary to run for his life. He wasn't sorry about what he had done; he wasn't feeling guilty; he wasn't interested in repenting and making things right—no, he was just afraid that Esau would kill him, so Jacob ran for his life.

And that's when, according to the Bible, Jacob came to a certain place where he stayed for the night. Evidently he was far enough away from Esau to feel safe. He was exhausted and drained. He took a stone and used it as a pillow—and then he went to sleep. That's when he had a dream. Jacob dreamed of a ladder set on the earth that reached all the way to heaven. And on that ladder, angels (messengers of God) were ascending and descending. That's when Jacob heard the voice of God. And God said, "Jacob, I promised blessing to your grandfather Abraham and to your father Isaac—and I promise blessing to you as well. Your offspring will be so numerous that they cannot be counted—and Jacob, I will never leave you. Jacob, I am the Lord your God."

Well, that's quite a dream. That's especially quite a dream for somebody who's not even looking for God in the first place. Would you fall on your face before God and thank him for his grace and his mercy and his good favor? Isn't that what you would do? That's what I would do—I think. . . .

Jacob woke up and he said, "Surely the Lord is in this place. Surely the Lord is in this place—and I didn't even know it!" He said, "How awesome is this place. This is where God lives. This must be the house of God and this must be the very gate of heaven. And so here's what I'm going to do—I'm going to take that stone that I used as a pillow and make a shrine, a holy place. And I'll call this place Bethel—the house of God!" That's just what Jacob did.

And if we stop there, it's a fabulous story. It reminds us that God is here even when we cannot see him, that God is here even when we're not looking for him. It reminds us of the occasional joy we have when we actually see God. It reminds us that God can use people with bad character. It reminds us that God still chooses to use people who have made mistakes.

If we choose to read a little further, it's not a fabulous story at all. In fact, it's a rather troubling story. If we read it carefully we see that Jacob responds to his encounter with God with a bargain. God had assured Jacob of his love and blessing and the fulfillment of holy promise. And Jacob's answer to that holy encounter is a bargain.

Jacob deals with God just as he had dealt with everyone else in his life—with bargains, pride, and selfishness. And what's perhaps most unbelievable, God doesn't at this point take back his promise or change his mind or determine that he's going to have to find more suitable material to work with. No, God simply continues to work according to his plan—and continues, for some reason, to use even somebody like Jacob for his holy purposes.

This story is also a reminder that we are so very limited when we try to understand God's grace and God's choices and God's purposes. You see, this is a story about God using somebody who is unlovable and unworthy and not really the kind of person that we would ever choose to use—but this is a story about God using a person like that simply because God chooses to use a person like that.

Oh, Jacob eventually came around—at least a little. He eventually met God on God's terms; he eventually actually chose to walk with God. But even then, he continued to be Jacob. And God could work with even that— even in lives that are broken and sinful and inadequate and unworthy (even in lives like mine and yours). God continues to show up and serve up unmerited grace.—Barry A. Stricker

Illustrations

WHERE GOD LIVES.   Before I left, I did find God in Mandera. I didn't find him in a building or a structure or an institution. I found him living in the people who serve there. I found God living in the lives of a middle-aged couple named Bill and Kay who went to serve in Africa after their kids were grown. I found God living in the lives of two young nurses named Julie and Gena who surely never set out to live in a place like Mandera. I found God in Mandera living in the lives of these precious people who themselves feel they are unworthy and unqualified and sinful. They don't look anything like Jacob to me, but that's how they see themselves. But when God met them, Bill and Kay and Julie and Gena responded with reverence and humility and worship and obedience and awe and wonder and thankfulness. And through that response, they have learned the exact lesson that even Jacob eventually learned. And that is the lesson that God (through His grace) can use anybody.—B.A.S.

SURPRISING SURVIVAL.   I saw a delicate flower had grown up two feet high, between the horses' path and the wheeltrack. An inch more to right or left had sealed its fate, or an inch higher; and yet it lived to flourish as much as if it had a thousand acres of untrodden space around it and never knew the danger it incurred. It did not borrow trouble, nor invite an evil fate by apprehending it.— Henry David Thoreau

SUNDAY: MARCH FIFTEENTH

LECTIONARY MESSAGE

Topic: Taking Up Space
TEXT: Luke 13:1–9
Other Readings: Isa. 55:1–9; Ps. 63:1–8; 1 Cor. 10:1–13

I recently went through my library and removed the books that I had collected over a period of years that were just taking up space. Most libraries can be reduced to the few books that are quoted by everyone else. I found that was true with so many of my commentaries. A very good commentary takes years and years to write. In recent times, commentaries have been appearing at a very rapid pace. If you check the ones in your library, you will discover that one or two writers are quoted by all the rest. Thus, as hard as it is to give up books, occasionally one must do the task of sorting out the volumes on the shelves and keeping only the best.

In the realm of lives, we are happy that the good Lord does not see human lives as just taking up shelf space. From the Gospel of Luke we learn how important every soul is in the eyes of the Lord. Only Luke has a good Samaritan, a thief who repents on the cross, and a tax collector who is the hero of a story. In our lesson for the day, Jesus teaches the truth that the fruitless trees must be given chance after chance to produce. Even though the land in ancient Israel was very expensive and hard to till, the slave was told to continue to fertilize the tree until fruit appeared.

I. *A tree is a tree.* A tree that does not produce fruit is condemned in all cultures. The theme of "be fruitful and multiply" runs throughout the Bible. Christ looks through the person and sees the unique worth of the individual. He can see the potential in every person. Like a great sculptor he views a piece of granite and sees the great statue that will be brought forth by the artist. People who are dismissed by others merit worth in the view of Christ. Luke reports that Jesus healed the servant of the high priest whose ear was chopped off by some of the disciples. No other gospel writer records that event. It was enough for the other writers to say that the ear had been severed. Luke reported the moment of healing on the part of Jesus. No one is overlooked by Jesus because they are from the wrong side of the tracks or the lower end of town.

The owner of the fig tree looked at his tree and didn't see the missing fruit. He saw an otherwise green tree in leaf without fruit. There was something worth saving. He could not listen to his gardener who said to tear the tree up from the soil and plant something else. Even though the tree had been there three years, he still had hope. Maybe one last application of fertilizer would do it. Maybe next year would be the year of success. Some people look at a half cup of water and see a cup half empty; others see a cup half full. Some people get up in the morning and say, "Good morning, dear Lord"; others say, "Good Lord, it's morning!"

II. *A tree without fruit.* Every parable of Jesus contains a surprise. Some fact in the story makes a listener say, *"What?"* One should always look for this surprise element in a parable. Sometimes interpreters allegorize the parables to death and miss the one striking point that typifies a parable. Once in speaking to a group of housewives Jesus told of a woman who put leaven into a measure of wheat and according to the measure (three sata) would have ended up with a hundred pounds of bread. That is an astonishing amount—superabundance! The farmers standing around Jesus would have listened to this parable with their mouths open. They would have yanked the fruitless tree out long ago. It takes five years just to clear the fields and rid the soil of stone. Therefore, available land was very scare. One could not afford to risk any land to a crop that would not be successful at harvest time. Food preparation was

a struggle that consumed a family's total energy day to day. No supermarket beckoned with loaded shelves. In this grim society, fruitless trees did not exist. Thus the farmers would have said a great big *"What?"* when they first heard Jesus tell the parable.

Jesus told of a kingdom in which fruitless trees did exist and took up room waiting for a second chance. In our society today, one seldom gets a second chance. In Christ, the second door stands open. If you failed the first time, a door is not slammed in your face. The woman taken in adultery was not condemned to death by Jesus but told to "go and sin no more." We can be happy that the Kingdom of God is composed not of chopped-down forests but rather of forests that have been revitalized.

III. *Crooked trees.* Trees that spring back from near-death catastrophes have a crooked trunk, but they are alive! As the tree, the Lord accepts us with all our imperfections. The important thing for Luke is that we repent and take root in Christ. Sometimes waiting for a tree to bear fruit takes people who are willing to be spiritual gardeners. Sometimes it is hard not to give up on people when they make the same mistakes over and over again. One can imagine the good a bunch of perfect trees could be making to your property. In haste you want to chop down and start again. You would want to join the biblical gardener and point out how long the fruitless trees have been just taking up space. Yet the message of Christ comes over time, "Fertilize and work the soil yet again. I see something that you do not see just yet." Crooked trees can bear fruit also.—James L. Blevins

Illustrations

ALL SAINTS AND ALL SINNERS.   In the whole story of the ministry of Jesus, is there anything more extraordinary than the way in which he went to the most unlikely looking people, people who had made a mess of their lives, and spoke to them with a kind of supernatural hopefulness about what they could yet become? He thought not just of what they had once been in the innocence of childhood, and what they might have been if they had not gone wrong. How falsely sentimental that can become, that dwelling on the pathos of the "might have been," if there is nothing more. But with Jesus there was more. He looked at those people with the indefatigable faith that they could yet be made into sons and daughters of God.—D. M. Baillie

SOMEONE CARED.   D. L. Moody, famed evangelist, said that when as a youth he went to Chicago, where he became a shoe sales-man, he was the loneliest of creatures. He longed for someone to greet him on the crowded street, saying, "Well, young fellow, it is good to meet you. How are you getting along?" And one day such a person met him, greeted him warmly, and invited him to attend Sunday school and church. Moody's heart gave a joyous leap, and out of that chance meeting and a cheerful word came the young man's introduction to a glorious life of Christian activity. "A word fitly spoken is like apples of gold in pictures of silver."—Edgar DeWitt Jones

SERMON SUGGESTIONS

Topic: And Enoch Walked with God
    TEXT: Gen. 5:22–24
    (1) Enoch walked with God amid wicked surroundings. (2) Enoch walked with God in the ordinary walks of life. (3) Enoch walked with God amid lowly surroundings.—John A. Broadus

Topic: Temptation Is Everywhere!
    TEXT: 1 Cor. 10:13
    (1) Even the most dedicated Christians are tempted in matters of the flesh and in mat-ters of the spirit. (2) We can count on God's help in our trials. (a) We have the example of Christ. (b) We have the teachings of the Bible. (c) We are assured of our Lord's inter-cession for us. (d) We can be strengthened by the Holy Spirit. (3) The way of escape may not be easy, but it is *always there.*

Hymn Suggestions

1. "Guide Me, O Thou Great Jehovah," William Williams (1745); "Cwm Rhonda," John Hughes (1905)
    Rich in its symbolism of the Exodus expe-rience, this hymn goes appropriately with the Corinthian passage (1 Cor. 10:1–13) in which the apostle is reminding his readers of that experience in making his appeal for right-eous living. Williams, deservedly known as "the Welsh Watts," was the greatest hymn writer of the Welsh revivals of the eighteenth century. This, his best-known hymn in Eng-lish, breathes the valiant spirit of Christian pilgrimage, especially when sung to this strong Welsh tune.
    2. "Depth of Mercy," Charles Wesley (1740); "Seymour," Carl Maria von Weber (1825)
    Wesley's hymn of repentance would be a fitting response to the Lucan passage (Luke 13:1–9) with its searing theme "Except you repent, you will all likewise perish." It would be a good selection for an invitation hymn following a sermon on this theme.
    3. "O Lord, You Are My God," John G. Dunn (1983); "Alberta," William H. Harris (1930)
    This modern paraphrase of Psalm 63 ad-mirably expresses its predominating idea of utter dependence on God for strength and sustenance. Its tune, one of the finest to come out of the early twentieth century, aptly conveys the sense of urgency in the psalmist's prayer.
    4. "Seek the Lord," Fred Pratt Green (1986); "Geneva," George Henry Day (1940)
    Green has made a refreshing paraphrase of the Old Testament passage for this day (Isa. 55:1–9), concluding with a personal commentary that gives it a New Testament context.—Hugh T. McElrath

Worship Aids

CALL TO WORSHIP.   "Give ear to my words, O Lord; give heed to my sighing. Listen to the sound of my cry, my King and my God, for to you I pray. O Lord, in the morning you hear my voice; in the morning I plead my case to you, and watch" (Ps. 5:1–3 NRSV).

INVOCATION.   Enfold us, O Lord, in that fellowship of faith that only worship of God brings. Give us to know all over again the extraordinary grace that came our way. Show us what we need to do as we wait and sing and pray. In the name of Jesus.—E. Lee Phillips

OFFERTORY SENTENCE.   "The earth is the Lord's, and the fullness thereof; the world, and they that dwell therein" (Ps. 24:1).

OFFERTORY PRAYER. Creator God, who has made all things and entrusted us as stewards over a few, accept this offering of gratitude and sharing, so that many persons will find a closer walk with the Savior.—E.L.P.

PRAYER. Whom have we in heaven but You? And therein none we desire upon earth other than you. Our flesh and our heart fail; but you are the strength of our heart and our portion forever.

Great is your faithfulness. Hearing your Word proclaimed again on this occasion, we are assured that you are faithful according to all your promises. "Surely goodness and mercy shall follow us all the days of our lives."

From the beginning you call us by your Word of grace. With the freshness of each new day we are made conscious of the graciousness of your creation, from the Garden of Eden to the glory of this hour.

You did not forget your people in their bondage in Egypt but called a shepherd carefully schooled in the rigors of the wilderness to lead them out and through forty years of wandering in that same wilderness.

However the story of their deliverance may be told, it is the story of your grace.

For us living in these latter days, the fullness of your grace is present in the person, the life, the ministry, the passion, the living again of Jesus of Nazareth. And it is your grace in him as the Messiah that delivers us from the bondage of our Egypt. That this story of your grace has been shared with us by loving parents, faithful teachers, concerned ministers, caring friends, we praise you and give you thanks.

When we contemplate the magnitude of the universe, the worlds beyond the world, the galaxies without number, unlimited space, time without beginning and without end, we find ourselves exclaiming with the Hebrew poet: "What is man that you are mindful of him?" But on second thought, we rejoice that you are mindful not only of man but of people, of persons. That you are not only the great God and the great King above all gods, but you are the shepherd of every life. You are here as the Good Shepherd, calling us each by name. Your mighty deeds of old, of today, and in every tomorrow are for our salvation. The story of your grace intersects with our story at the cross as no other

place in human history, and we find ourselves praying—what else can we pray?—

Nothing in my hand I bring,
Simply to Thy cross I cling.

Through him who is the measure of the fullness of your grace and is becoming our prayer.—John Thompson

Sermon: Soul Food
TEXT: John 6:1–9

I. Now that crowd we read about a few minutes ago, what do they anticipate for lunch on their great outing? They follow Jesus across the lake with nary a brown bag in hand. And Jesus, noticing the paucity of food, detects hunger among them. He glances at Philip and asks how his small company might buy bread for so large a cohort—five thousand, and that isn't even counting women and children. Philip looks around. He sees no Pizza Hut on the beach of the Sea of Galilee. No sign of a Wendy's in Capernaum. A Whopper, a coke, some fries might solve the problem instantly, but sadly, no fast food, and even worse, no money. Jesus and his friends are broke, and as Philip sarcastically remarks, "Even a month's wages couldn't handle this gang." Things look bleak. This crowd, gathered for a massive testimonial, will roast in the sun. They will collapse without food and drink.

Then Andrew observes the littlest boy in the huge gathering with two barley loaves and five fish—just two biscuits and five little perch! For the disciples, with no money and that scrawny snack, it is hopeless. Nothing can be done. And for the five thousand, the shelf is bare. It is look elsewhere for lunch or go hungry.

Then the mood changes. Jesus invites the crowd to be seated. He takes the little tyke's bread and fish, offers prayers, feeds the crowd, and orders the ton of scraps left over picked up and crammed into a dozen large baskets. The crowd is replenished, renewed, restored.

II. Now of course we could try to figure out exactly what happened. The most popular speculation about this great event entails the little boy's generosity inspiring like generosity in thousands of others. Everyone possesses ample food, and the lad's initial offering triggers, among that vast horde, an eagerness to share.

I like that. The enthusiasm provoked by such generous motives needs always to be laid before us. Nonetheless, as inspiring as this perspective may be, I think John goes deeper. He makes this point and more. He tells truth beyond the facts of the narrative. Rather than offering us a biography of our Lord, John and his church reflect on the meaning of Christ. *Encyclopedia Britannica* and the *World Almanac* would never publish John's facts. The historic accuracy of those facts is essentially beside the point; their truth lies in their symbolic power. In the case this morning, John tells us that food filling our hungry stomachs can in no way match the satiating presence of the living Christ. John tells us that just as Jesus feeds that famished five thousand from his own hands, so the living Christ feeds us on Boylston Street, the Back Bay, the South End, Beacon Hill, Jamaica Plain, Brookline, Winchester, Andover, you name it.

And Jesus' food? His bread? His offering to us? You are loved! Hear that? You are loved! John tells us the generous love of Christ permeates, undergirds, creation itself; it is available as food nourishing us, carrying us through contingencies and crises, the tragedies and triumphs of our lives. John tells us what we see, what we know, what we bet on in Jesus Christ provides a staple for our lives more real, more vital, more sustaining, more life-giving than the staples keeping us alive every day: bread and water. Hear! Receive! Believe! You are loved! Now that's soul food!

Soul food! This food, more than the food sustaining and supporting us minute by minute, day by day—this sure and certain conviction that we are loved—this is the undying refuse-to-lose love that would not be crushed on Calvary. It promises that through whatever happens to us—yes, even amid those circumstances that appear most loveless—there resides behind this universe, with a magnitude as grand as the galaxies and an intimacy as close as the hairs on our heads, One who nourishes us with love and care, the true staple, the true bread of life, enabling us to forge new possibilities amid the tangles and meltdowns of our lives.

Our assurance of this undying, never failing, life-affirming love for us comes as we grapple, along with generations of Christians, with the meaning of the cross dominating our room. What do we see here? What

blazing message does it send? This empty cross proclaims that love can act through and transform even a bloody cross from an instrument of torture to a banner of hope. It testifies to power taking an apparatus for a violent execution and refashioning it into a sign of enduring, patient, persistent, and finally conquering reconciliation that grounds our life together, providing nourishment for our hearts, souls, and minds that even when bread is scarce bears us up and feeds our courage. This cross and its radiant meaning are the very source and root of our soul food. Here, if you will, right from the hands of the living Christ, we are offered the bread of life.

You see, John paints a picture of love's capacity to feed us what we starve for most. And what happens? How do we respond? The crowd in the passage blows it. They understand Jesus backwards and upside down. They clamor for a king! They recognize one who might provide what they think they crave most: charismatic political leadership. "Give us a king," they cry, and then seek to inaugurate him by acclamation. Remember how Jesus responds? He turns his back. He heads further up the mountain, shunning what we call these days "a draft."

III. Are we getting a message here, friends? Is John sending us a little reflection on Christianity and politics? Perhaps. It may run like this. Although politics is vital and exciting, although it shapes an enormous part of our lives, it does not provide the clue to our salvation.

No, what Jesus brings us are not the trappings and propaganda of political power, not the claims and triumphs of the monarch or president. On the contrary! In Christ Jesus we recognize one who takes risks saving those whom the politicians these days condemn. We find one who is not a xenophobe but rather breaks down the boundaries between nations and people and creeds and races. We see one known as the great physician whose whole life focuses on healing the emotionally distraught, the most physically ill, the deeply troubled. He brings life where it seems to dribble away; he disperses love where it gets tromped on; he radiates hope where cynicism reigns. The cross stands for all time as a judgment on our political opinions, it throws a revealing light on the interests of each one of us, our family, our friends, our crowd, and what we are willing to do to protect those interests. The cross reminds us that anyone pretentiously calling themselves a Christian coalition had better be careful, for when a crowd proposed a Christian coalition for the very first time on that Galilean mountainside, the Christ spurned it. They had gotten him wrong, and he withdrew to the mountains in solitude.

And John deflates not only our politics. He tackles our religion, too. When Jesus feeds the five thousand at Passover, he surpasses what John conceives as conventional religion. We encounter someone transcending our religious practice. In Christ, says the Gospel, someone grasps us who is more real than the sanctuary in which we gather, more alive than the liturgies we devise to transmit Christ. Do we have beautiful architecture here? Of course. Do we listen to glorious music here? Yes, we do. Do we speak of God, of Christ, of love for one another, of service to the world? Do we use the language of prayer? Are we moved to commune with God as well as to know an encounter with God? Yes, yes, and yes, again. But we dare not confuse these liturgical props, these dramatic symbols, these human constructs, these aesthetic masterpieces with the living, loving Christ.

These orders of worship, these great transepts, these glorious windows, this stunning cross, this ethereal music, these stumbling, mumbling sermons are simply pathetic efforts to point toward truth. They offer at best blurred mirrors of the divine love inspiring them; they prove broken lenses on the hope they seek to transmit. Bread really comes from the hands of the living Christ, the one whose invitation to you and to me and to this troubled world to walk in his way and live in his light lands him, for love's sake, on a cross, and urges us to a loyal and courageous discipleship.

In a few minutes, we will be leaving this place and many of us will be going to lunch. That is necessary, and I say, "Enjoy." But I pray that this day—this week—you may encounter in the gracious touch of a friend, the forgiveness of an adversary, the recovery of a child, the healing of a wound, in all of this and more, the nearness of a presence feeding, restoring, sustaining, nourishing— yes, blessing—you with soul food.—James W. Crawford

Illustrations

OUT OF THE DARKNESS. You can, if you will, accompany him on his ministry, witness his healing, and hear his intensely uttered truths. He is more intimately your companion in such an hour than any other person in your life. Such communication lies behind and within the healing ministry of Jesus that the pain and chaos in our lives is alleviated. We can keep a sane perspective upon them by contrasting them with his torture and betrayal. Out of his own conflict with the disrupted world of his day, Jesus taught us how to live.—David Seabury

DOES GOD CARE? Once a skilled physician about to perform a delicate operation on an ear said reassuringly to his patient, "I may hurt you, but I will not injure you." How often in connection with our suffering the great physician of our souls is saying something like that to us! "This may hurt you, but it will not injure you. It will bring you richer life, more abundant spiritual health." Dr. Arthur C. Benson has said, "The better we know the most afflicted lives, the more often does the conviction flash across us that the affliction is not a wanton outrage, but a delicately adjusted treatment."—John Calvin Reid

SUNDAY: MARCH TWENTY-SECOND

LECTIONARY MESSAGE

Topic: Prodigal Sons and Brothers
TEXT: Luke 15:1–3, 11b–32
Other Readings: Josh. 5:9–12; Ps. 32; 2 Cor. 5:16–21

Nothing men do prepares us to be fathers. We play ball, we fish, we work, but we don't play with dolls, and we don't fix bottles or change diapers! Being a father often requires us to redefine what it means to be a man.

One of the most profound stories about manhood in all human experience is the parable of the prodigal son, which we might better call "The Prodigal Son, the Waiting Father, and the Elder Brother." Here are three men and three male roles—men as prodigals, men as fathers, and men as elder brothers.

I. *The prodigal son.* The prodigal son succumbs to the allure of the "far country." The call of the far country is particularly strong when we are young and rebellious. The younger son had to contend with a successful father who had land, a house, fatted calves, and servants. He also had to compete with an elder brother who always worked hard, pleased his parents, and succeeded in everything he did. There was no future there for the prodigal.

When we are pushed to our limits, the far country always looks better than where we are: it can be just somewhere else, a new job, a new girlfriend. We want out, we want a new set of relationships. Rather than try to fix or reconcile our present relationships, we find it easier to demand what is ours, get some distance, and start over.

That is exactly what the younger son did. Without realizing it, the prodigal fell victim to one of the most pervasive of male myths— that he did not need anyone else, and that he could make it on his own. Rebellion and his need for independence led him to reject his family, his father, and his brother. How ironic that having rejected the laws of purity of his own people, he ended up in a pig pen feeding the swine!

Some level of rebellion is a natural and probably necessary stage in cutting the ties and achieving adult independence. On the other hand, maturity only comes when we can go home again, no longer as a child but as an adult, not bound by our family traditions but appreciating the identity they gave us.

Home never looks so good as when it is remembered from the far country. Remember how beautiful the earth looks in the photographs taken by the Apollo astronauts as they sped toward the moon? The journey home begins with coming to oneself. The younger son had to face himself in the swine pen of his own making before he could face his father on the road. For many of us, the struggle of the prodigal takes most of our adult lives. We are either on the road to the far country and finding that its allure was a mirage, or we are on the road home—and sometimes we go back and forth.

II. *The waiting father.* The second male role depicted in the parable is that of the father. The father's first decision came when the younger son asked him for his share of the inheritance. Absorbing the affront of the son's request, and probably suspecting what it would lead to, the father still gave the son what he asked for.

The father's second decision was a decision of the heart. He loved his younger son, and he would not let the son's separation from him cause him to withdraw his love for the son. No matter what the son did, he was still the father's son. The father did not need to hear the son's rehearsed speech. It was enough for him to see his son's familiar profile on the horizon. How long had he been waiting, hoping with all his being that his son would come home? His joy is conveyed in the report that he ran to meet him. Then he did not even let his son finish his speech. Instead, the father immediately received him as a son and called for the best robe, a ring, and shoes.

Just as the son needed to come home and to seek out his father, so the father needed his son. The father provided the male intimacy that the son needed. He embraced him, affirmed him, forgave him, and reestablished him in the family by lavishly giving him the best robe, the ring, and the shoes, and by killing the fatted calf. The bond is reestablished, and the story seems at an end.

III. *The elder brother.* But there is a third character and a third male role in this story. The elder brother has dutifully fulfilled his role, staying with the father and working hard while his younger brother was squandering his inheritance. We can feel the resentment in every phrase he speaks.

The elder brother is a male trapped in the system of merit and reward. For that reason, he may never have come to himself. Those who insist on living by merit can never know the joy of grace and unconditional love. The elder brother did not realize his father's unconditional love if he thought the father needed to give him a fatted calf for a party with his friends. How long had he harbored this resentment? He even refused to acknowledge his relationship to his brother, referring to him as "this son of yours" instead of as "my brother." Although he had never left his father, he too needed to come home. The father, on the other hand, was not satisfied just to receive back the younger brother; he wanted the boys to be reconciled also. He addressed the elder brother as "son," he affirmed that "all that is mine is yours," and he invited him to come in and join the celebration.

IV. *Conclusion.* The parable leaves us with the question of whether the elder brother joined the celebration. It ends there because that is the decision that each of us must make. This timeless parable depicts three male roles: the rebellious prodigal, the lonely father, and the resentful elder brother. They all need one another, but it is only the father's unfailing love that makes it possible for the sons to achieve the wholeness they both lack. No wonder God's love is so readily seen in the role of the father in this story. There are times when all of us need to go home, physically, emotionally, or in memory. We need to receive the father's embrace, and we need to learn that being a son also means being a brother.

Prodigal son, elder brother? The father is waiting. It is time to go home.—R. Alan Culpepper

Illustrations

HOMECOMING. The ultimate theme of this story is not the prodigal son but the Father who finds us. It is not the faithfulness of men but the faithfulness of God.

And this is also the reason why the joyful sound of festivity rings out from this story. Wherever forgiveness is proclaimed there is joy and festive garments. We must read and hear this gospel story as it was really meant to be: good news! News so good that we could never have imagined it. News that would stagger us if we were able to hear it for the first time as a message that everything about God is so completely different from what we thought or feared. News that he has sent his Son to us and is inviting us to share in an unspeakable joy.

The ultimate secret of this story is this: there is a homecoming for us all because there is a home.—Helmut Thielicke[2]

THE MEANING OF LIFE. God does not ask us to become blind to the mistakes and faults of others. If we are right in our criticism, why not utter it? If we have a better idea for solving problems, why not fight for it? There is one thing only that God demands from us: that we learn to love. I even think that this is the meaning of all life on earth, even of all suffering in it, that we learn to love: to love God, whose heart is waiting behind all our wild oats that we sow and who is burning with love. For if we learn this love, we are in—in the banquet hall of the father. And there we shall meet our younger brother who is, maybe, not quite so perfect as we are ourselves, perhaps not even by far.

But you see, if we have really learned what the love of the Father means, then it will be absolutely impossible for us to go on adding up all our righteous deeds and all the decisions in which we have been right. Then we learn to tell the story of our younger brother with loving hearts, just changing it a trifle, that decisive trifle, in his favor, because we have understood our younger generation and much of its unrest and its not-always-right ideas. Is it that we learn to love—to love God, and therefore also our sometimes strange younger brothers? I think, it is.—Eduard Schweizer[3]

SERMON SUGGESTIONS

Topic: A Significant Turning
TEXT: Ps. 37
(1) What we are: happy, forgiven. (2) What we were: miserable, guilty. (3) What we did: confessed our transgressions. (4) What we are counting on: the Lord's steadfast love and faithful counsel.

Topic: New Life in Christ
TEXT: 1 Cor. 5:16–21
(1) What we were: our old life outside of Christ. (2) What we are: our new life as re-created by God. (3) What we are to become and to do: Christ's ambassadors, reconciling the world to God.

Hymn Suggestions

1. "Rejoice, Ye Pure in Heart," Edward H. Plumptre (1965); "Marion," Arthur H. Messiter (1889)

---

[2] *The Waiting Father.*

[3] *Bible Studies.*

The last verse of the Psalter reading (Ps. 32:12) for this day could well have been the inspiration for the theme of this exciting hymn of rejoicing. Because the sins of true Christians have been forgiven, there is every reason to be thankful and glad in the Lord. The upright in heart cannot help but rejoice!

2. "Lord, I'm Coming Home," William J. Kirkpatrick (1892); "Coming Home," Kirkpatrick (1892)

Kirkpatrick's gospel song magnifies the confession of the prodigal as he repentantly returns home (Luke 15:1–31). After the reading of the gospel story, this song would be effective sung as a solo with the congregation joining in on the chorus.

3. "O Come and Dwell in Me," Charles Wesley (1762); "St. Michael," Genevan Psalter (1551).

Of the numerous hymns that incorporate the idea (2 Cor. 5:17) of one's becoming a new creation when old things have passed away is this fine one by the peerless Charles Wesley. It would make a suitable response to the reading of the Epistle for the day.

4. "Forgiven," Mark Blankenship (1983); "Ridgecrest," Buryl Red (1983)

This "mini-hymn" gathers together the theme of Psalm 32:1 and the gospel story in Luke 15. In a devotional service stressing repentance and forgiveness it could have meaningful use.—Hugh T. McElrath

Worship Aids

CALL TO WORSHIP.   "Listen! I am standing at the door, knocking; if you hear my voice and open the door, I will come in to you and eat with you, and you with me" (Rev. 3:20 NRSV).

INVOCATION.   Eternal God, who knows us as we are but who has made us for finer things, may our encounter with thee today set our sights on new levels of worship and service. Banish from our minds every wrong desire that competes with thy love for a place to reign. Claim us solely to be thine own and being possessed by thee may we be transformed from common flesh into children of strength and light. In thy holy name we pray.—Donald Macleod

OFFERTORY SENTENCE.   "You are so rich in all you have: in faith, speech, and knowledge, in your eagerness to help and in your love for us. And so we want you to be generous also in this service of love" (2 Cor. 8:7 TEV).

OFFERTORY PRAYER.   Gracious Lord, you opened your great heart to all of us in Jesus Christ and in all the provisions you have made for us. For our own good and in your love, you wish us to seek your Kingdom and your righteousness. You have blessed us in ways that we can easily see, but also in ways we will never know in this life. You have added blessing upon blessing. Now we pray, help us to love with forgiveness, care, and giving as you have loved us.

PRAYER.   Lord, let thy glory dwell among us, as here we would commune with thee. Let us hear thy voice of love, and let our hearts be filled with joy and peace. Help us to forget the noises of the outer world, and to enter into thy silence, where is healing for every wound, help for every weakness, consolation for every sorrow.

We pray for the strong, that they may abide in thee and in thee find renewal of their strength; for the weak and the tempted, that thine arm may work out for them a great salvation; for the disconsolate, that in thee their griefs may receive a noble consecration; for the bereaved, that they may have a vision of the world beyond, where there is no more death, nor crying, nor mourning, nor pain. Bless the poor, the homeless, the neglected, and the ignorant. Inspire our hearts with thy love, that we may be friends and companions to all thy children who need us. Have pity on all who foolishly trust in the false promises of sin, and awaken them from their deluding dreams to timely repentance. Succor all who are fighting against the dominion of evil habits. If they fall, help them to rise again; and put within them a faith and hope than cannot be quenched. Inspire all harassed and struggling souls with the assurance that all the forces of thy will are working for them, and are moving them on to peace and health and holiness.—Samuel McComb

Sermon: Live in the Present
TEXT: Phil. 3:12–16
There is a legend that says that the birds were gathered together one day many years

ago. They were all complaining that they had been burdened with wings. These seemingly useless appendages were heavy, bulky, and always got in the way. Besides, none of the other animals had been asked to bear them.

How surprised they were to learn that their wings were not burdens to be borne but blessings to allow them to soar above the earth and see things none of the other animals would ever be able to see. They had misunderstood a gift to be a burden.

How many times we have misunderstood a gift to be a burden? It is essential that we try to live in the present, that we not carry around unnecessary burdens from a yesterday we will not live again or a tomorrow that is not guaranteed.

Outward Bound is a challenging retreat to assist people in facing some difficulties in their lives. The participants are often given a little book of quotes. One of these quotes is by Storm Jameson: "I believe that only one person in a thousand knows the trick of really living in the present. Most of us spend 59 minutes an hour living in the past, with regret for lost joys or shame for things badly done (both utterly useless and weakening) or in a future which we either long for or dread. . . . There is only one minute in which you are alive, *this minute,* here and now. The only way to live is by accepting each minute as an unrepeatable minute. Which is exactly what it is—a miracle and unrepeatable."[4]

We should be able to say, "With God's help, I will release the past and live in the now." By accepting God's presence in our lives, we are able to release the past rather than relive it. The past cannot control our lives if we release it and don't relive it like an instant replay over and over again. Holding on to hurtful memories will take us down a road that leads nowhere. So it is up to us to choose a new direction. We should turn from a nowhere destination to live in the here and now. We should give prayerful attention to thinking positively and focusing on the present moment.

Robert Nathan once said, "There is no distance on this earth as far away as yesterday."

---

[4]Marian Wright Edelman, *The Measure of Our Success* (New York: HarperCollins, 1992), 66.

Today is a new day in which we can discard the baggage of old habits and limitations. We can start anew with God. Through divine guidance we can take control of our lives. We should be open and receptive to all the goodness that God has to offer us.

Have you ever experienced a loss and afterward thought that your world would end? After some time, however, you probably realized that you simply had not seen the whole picture. When Paul wrote the words of our Scripture passage, he wanted the readers to know that he too had not yet crossed the finish line in the Christian race. Paul wanted the Philippians to know that he had not achieved perfection. He was sure that Christ had taken hold of him and his life. But he had not reached the goal of life that had become a glorious possibility when Christ had seized him. He did not believe that he would obtain the glorious inheritance that lay before him.

In order to explain what he meant, Paul used the illustration of the athletic games. He was like a runner in a race. In races, the winner's prize, the laurel wreath of the victor, was often placed at the finish line as an added incentive to the contestant.

Like the runners in a race, Paul's attention was totally focused on the prize at the end. His concentration was complete. He did not glance back, for to do so could mean the lose of stride and speed. So he forgot what lay behind in order to "press on toward the goal." The prize was the crown of eternal life, toward which God had called him in Christ Jesus.

"Forgetting what lies behind" does not mean exactly what it says. Clearly Paul had not literally forgotten his past. In fact, in Philippians 3:4–6 he describes his former situation. His roots were completely Jewish. His religious affiliation had been with the most rigorous of Pharisees. He'd lived a legalistic life and had been instrumental in persecuting the church. Not just in this letter but also on other occasions, Paul remembered the persecution of the Body of Christ of which he had been the chief agent. Forget? No, he remembered—probably with tears.

He did not allow his past to shackle his future, however. That future was filled with Christ. His past was "forgotten" in the sense that it did not taint the spiritual reality of his present commitment to the gospel.

III. How often do we allow the sin of our past to impede us? We feel guilty. We feel shame. We feel embarrassment. We feel unworthy. We feel useless.

That is not Paul's way, nor the way of the gospel. Our sins are forgiven by the grace of God in Jesus Christ. We are freed from the guilt of our sins. In God's eyes we are beloved and worthy.

Let us say, "Yes, I have sinned, but God is greater than my sin. He calls me on, so on I will go until in the end I receive the prize—everlasting communion with God."

By living in the present, we forgo the burdens and painful memories of the past. The story is told of two Buddhist monks walking in a thunderstorm. They came to a swollen stream. A beautiful young Japanese woman in a kimono stood there wanting to cross to the other side but afraid of the currents.

One of the monks said, "Can I help you?"

"I need to cross this stream," replied the woman.

The monk picked her up, put her on his shoulder, carried her through the swirling waters, and put her down on the other side. He and his companion then went on to the monastery.

That night his companion said to him, "I have a bone to pick with you. As Buddhist monks, we have taken vows not to look on a woman, much less touch her body. Back there by the river you did both."

"My brother," answered the other monk, "I put that woman down on the other side of the river. You're still carrying her in your mind."

How easy it is to be obsessed with the past at the expense of the future. It is only too natural to dwell on the pain of what could have

been and not focus on the beauty of the moment.—Bobby J. Touchton

Illustrations

WHAT WAS AND WHAT IS.   Both the hummingbird and the vulture fly over our nation's deserts. All vultures see is rotting meat, because that is what they look for. They thrive on that diet.

But hummingbirds ignore the smelly flesh of dead animals. Instead, they look for the colorful blossoms of desert plants.

The vultures live on what was. They live on the past. They fill themselves with what is dead and gone. But hummingbirds live on what is. They seek new life. They fill themselves with freshness and life.

Each bird finds what it is looking for. We all do.—B.J.T.

LIFE IN CHRIST.   One thing is clear because Jesus himself said it: before we have even come to repentance, God has forgiven us. It is his prior forgiveness that awakens, or ought to awaken, our own sorrow for our wrongdoings. The logic of God's love is not a worldly logic, where often we must say we are sorry before others will forgive us. God always forgives—and without measure. Then it is our privilege as sharers in the life in Christ to make our glad response.

I can turn in repentance to the One who loves me, with utter confidence in his forgiveness, because already his "love unknown hath broken every barrier down," as the familiar hymn phrases it. Knowing this, I can make my own the refrain of each verse of that hymn, "O Lamb of God, I come." To come in repentance to God in Christ is to find renewed strength for life in him. This is the disciple's joy.—Norman Pittenger[5]

SUNDAY: MARCH TWENTY-NINTH

LECTIONARY MESSAGE

Topic: Seeing Beneath the Surface
TEXT: John 12:1–8
Other Readings: Isa. 43:16–21; Ps. 126; Phil. 3:4b–14
Looking inside something has become an everyday event. Security gates are set up at airports and X-ray machines peer into

bags that are carried onto a plane. Doctors and hospitals have machines that look within the human body to see abnormalities not visible to the naked eye. God's people need to use spiritual vision to ascertain what God is about.

[5] *Life in Christ.*

I. *Giving the best* (vv. 1–3). Jesus enjoyed sharing good times with his friends. One such occasion occurred in the home of Lazarus, whom Jesus had brought back from the dead. Jesus' disciples were also present. There was perhaps some tension, because all were aware that Jesus was not popular in Jerusalem. But such things could be forgotten in the midst of such a joyous occasion. It may have seemed an ordinary affair until Mary performed a most unusual act. While the guests were still at the table, she took a jar of very valuable perfume and used it to anoint the feet of Jesus. Did Mary perhaps see beneath the surface at what was going to happen in just a few days? We cannot be certain, but she expressed her love for Jesus by giving her most precious possession. It is hard for us to imagine the value of the perfume. It could have been sold for three hundred denarii, the wages of a working person for a year. It was an extravagant gift. But lest we forget, Mary was not the only one to give the best she had. Martha did this also. Her gift was that of serving, and she served the meal. She also gave the best that she had. It is tragic that many times God's people are satisfied to give the things they do not want or need rather than the best they have.

II. *A selfish protest* (vv. 4–6). When one looks only at the surface, extravagant gifts may appear foolish. But God often acts in most unexpected ways to teach us and to accomplish his purposes. This he did with Mary. Judas did not understand. He saw only the waste of something valuable. It could have been sold for a year's wages and the money used for good purposes. Of course, John reminds us that Judas was not interested in helping the poor; he was only interested in helping himself. We may not be dishonest, as apparently Judas was, but we often share his attitude. We see only the surface meaning; we cannot look beneath and see what God is doing. Isaiah reminded people about how God was doing a new thing for them (Isa. 43:19–21). Even the wild animals would see and understand, but did God's people have such a perspective? Neither did the disciples of Jesus, for we need not assume that the other persons at the meal had any better understanding than did Judas. They saw the pouring out of the perfume; they smelled the lovely aroma. But they did not understand

what was going to happen to Jesus. In spite of his repeated attempts to open their eyes, they preferred to remain blind.

III. *A deeper meaning* (vv. 7–8). Probably only Jesus understood the significance of what Mary had done. Because he knew of his approaching death, he saw her act as an anointing of his body for burial. According to the Synoptic Gospels, there was not sufficient time between his death and burial for this important ministry to take place. Mary's act of love and sacrifice would suffice for the anointing that would not be done. Jesus saw beneath the surface to the deeper meaning. What appeared on first glance to be a waste of valuable perfume actually was important in the work that God was about. And so it is in our day. Often we see someone act or hear someone speak and do not understand the deeper significance of the word or act. Yet it is these little, often unappreciated things that God uses to accomplish his deeper purposes. We must not selfishly criticize or oppose such acts and words. Rather, we need to open our eyes to see how God will use these things for his glory.

This event is also a reminder that we must use wisely every opportunity that is given to us, because the opportunity may not be repeated. Jesus was not indifferent to the situation of the poor (v. 8). He knew they needed all the help that could be given to them. But he also knew that there would be poor people after he gave his life on the cross. There would be opportunity to help them later. Assistance to him could only be shown in the present moment. But it took eyes of faith to see this. God's people need such eyes in our day to see beneath the surface and perceive what God is about in our time. Paul understood as he wrote to the Philippians that all the things that on the surface appeared important were nothing but refuse. What mattered was what could not be seen, to "gain Christ and be found in him" (Phil. 3:8–9).—Clayton Harrop

Illustrations

AS GOD SEES. It is easy to form our opinion of people on first impressions. I think of a man I went to school with who I would never have assumed God could use in any significant way. What a refreshing thing it was to learn a few years ago that God saw more beneath the surface than I could see. He has used this man in a marvelous way to do the work of his Kingdom. A man whom I would have written off as of little value God saw as a precious instrument.—C.H.

PRECIOUS TREASURES.   The rock and gem show held annually at Quartzite, Arizona, is an amazing sight. Almost anything one might wish to see is there. Among the items for sale are some rocks that look quite ordinary and of little value. Surface appearances, however, are totally deceiving. When they are cut open, they are found to be lined with precious amethysts.—C.H.

SERMON SUGGESTIONS

Topic: The God of the Impossible
    TEXT: Isa. 43:16–21
    (1) Life presents us with many dead-end situations. (2) Understandably, we sometimes react with (a) anger, (b) depression, (c) despair. (3) God can change things: (a) sometimes by eliminating the problem; (b) always by assuring us of his creative presence as we face the problem, solve it, or go forward in spite of all, glorifying God in every case.

Topic: Knowing Jesus Christ
    TEXT: Phil. 3b–14
    (1) It is better than any human achievements, honors, or possessions. (2) It is always ahead of us, something to strive toward. (3) We press on because we belong to Jesus Christ.

Hymn Suggestions

1. "Awake, My Soul, Stretch Every Nerve," Philip Doddridge (1755); "Christmas," George F. Handel
    Doddridge wrote this hymn to be sung following his sermon based on Philippians 3:12–14. It was given the title "Pressing on in the Christian Race." It has been described as "a matchless challenge—ringing like a trumpeter's note to start the athletes."
2. "Come Down, O Love Divine," Bianco da Siena (c. 1430); transcribed by Richard Vaughan Williams (1906)
    Not particularly related to any of the readings for this day, this venerable hymn is traditionally used during Lent as an exquisite

expression of devout yearning for the presence of God's loving spirit. It could appropriately be used as a sung invocation.
    3. "When God Delivered Israel," Michael A. Saward (1973); "Sheaves," Norman L. Warren (1973)
    This contemporary paraphrase of Psalm 126 in both words and music gives a fresh view of the truth that those who go out weeping but sowing seed will return with sheaves rejoicing. Alternation in reading the psalm verses with the three stanzas of the song would contribute to freshness of meaning.
    4. "O God Who Gives Us Life and Breath," Carl P. Daw (1990); "Shepherd's Pipe," Annabeth M. Gay (1952)
    This modern hymn pulls together many of the themes from the Lenten reading from the Old Testament, including the first reading for today from Isaiah. It is suitable when expressing the truth that God is doing a new thing that it be couched both in a new text and a new tune.—Hugh T. McElrath

Worship Aids

CALL TO WORSHIP.   "Bless the Lord, O my soul; and all that is within me, bless his holy name. Bless the Lord, O my soul, and forget not all his benefits" (Ps. 103:1–2).

INVOCATION. We would enter into your gates with thanksgiving and into your courts with praise. O God, we praise you for the Church, the churches and this church. For the loving—the caring and sharing—that we experience in the life of this congregation, we give you thanks. For the privilege of being together in fellowship to celebrate your Word of grace in worship, we are grateful. We pray for any bereft, the lonely, for the one who has lost his or her way, for any who are discouraged because of illness or infirmity, for the one estranged, that each may hear his or her need addressed by that Word of grace in Christ Jesus that saves to the uttermost. Praise be to You, Father, Son, and Holy Spirit.—John Thompson

OFFERTORY SENTENCE.   "Be ye steadfast, unmoveable, always abounding in the word of the Lord, for as much as ye know that your labor is not in vain in the Lord" (1 Cor. 15:58).

OFFERTORY PRAYER. Lord, as we dedicate this offering may we dedicate ourselves, that as this offering is spent we too might be spent in the service of our Savior, Jesus Christ.—E. Lee Phillips

PRAYER.

Grant us, O Lord, to know what
  is worth knowing,
to love what is worth loving,
to praise what delights you most,
to value what is precious in your sight,
to hate what is offensive to you.
Do not let us judge by what we see,
nor pass sentence according to what
  we hear,
but to judge rightly between things
  that differ
and above all to search out and to do
  what pleases you,
through Jesus Christ our Lord.[6]

Sermon: To Shoot Through Darkness with Unexpected Light

TEXT: John 9:1–8

When we confront that blind man at the side of the road and witness his healing we find ourselves tempted to ask some up-to-date questions. Do we witness here the first corneal transplant? Is this a actually a case of some psychosomatic condition, with Christ present as a skillful psychiatrist dissolving a psychological smoke screen and releasing the man to integrated wholeness?

I. Well, the answer is none of these! The roadside blind man is no simple individual craving sight. As a person blind from birth, he is the symbol of a divisive and virulent synagogue struggle between the Jews who confess Jesus as Messiah and those who don't. But more, John understands that man blind from birth as you, as me, as our churches, our nation, our world—blind from birth apart from Christ. Jesus understands our natural existence as blindness. Within his own time, John attacked his orthodox antagonists as blind and the world without Christ as blind, but his accusation reaches all of us who seek to build our lives apart from grace, magnanimity, generosity, love. Looking out on our world today, John understands the obsessive pursuit of profit, the aggressive clamoring to be number one, the

eagerness to manipulate others for sexual, commercial, or narcissistic advantage as blindness! He perceives communities fragmented by national arrogance, religious exclusivity, ideological rigidities, class aggrandizement, and egregious economic disparity as the natural world—a world blind from birth.

And as our world sits figuratively at the side of the road crippled by blindness, John sees Christ healing our blindness: Christ dissolving the barriers we build to wall out others; the love of Christ wiping out distinctions of language, nation, race, religion, and the sexual orientations we use to assault one another. Christ, says John, pours into our lives and subverts all claims to status based on title, seniority, political muscle, property rights, bank balance, or bloodlines—any of the human claims we use to identify ourselves, to find our niches, to put others in their place. Christ reorients us, offering an identity rooted simply in the solidarity of human community. When John describes Jesus daubing earth soaked by his spittle into the eyes of the man blind from birth, and then sending that man to bathe in the pool called "Sent," John offers us not only a figure who gains sight but a figure who embodies a new creation. He becomes a new community bound by love, a domain that in a dark world can only be described as light, which in a blind world illustrates dramatic and true sight.

II. How shall we describe this light? How do we grasp the dimensions of this promised sight? Well, let me illustrate with a word from Helen Keller, blind and deaf, truly one of the great spirits of our century. In a little reflection by Rufus Jones, we learn of Helen Keller attending a Quaker Meeting. It was her first Friends meeting, says Jones, and in addition to the delight in this unique manner of worship, Helen Keller commended the Friends over their stance during World War One and their relief work "in the long period of agony following the war." The thing that touched her most, writes Rufus Jones, was the Friends' persistent pursuit of love and community, the new way of life and spirit of reconciliation. And Jones continues, "With extraordinary effect, but with uttermost simplicity, she referred to her own life as an illustration. Once there was a little girl, she said, who was shut up in utter darkness and unbroken silence with no real life, no world, no hope, no future. Then someone came who with

6Adapted from Thomas à Kempis.

patience and tenderness brought her into contact with the world out there beyond her, and opened in her undreamed of capacities of intercourse with that new world of life and thought. Even with closed eyes she learned how to look out on a world full of beauty, hope, and possibility. "So you," she continued, addressing the Friends' Meeting, "so you have had the privilege of helping men, women, and children to discover a richer life and a deeper love and sympathy than they knew before. They have found through you a world before unknown. You have shot through their darkness with an unexpected light."

"You have shot through darkness with an unexpected light." That is the way Helen Keller described the impact that Annie Sullivan, her patient and tender teacher, had on her life. And even more vividly, that is the way she describes the impact of the Friends on the terrible human catastrophe of the First World War. And I wonder, isn't that the way John describes the impact of Jesus' presence on that blind man wasting away by the roadside? Isn't that what we are called to do, as the Gospel affirms, "while it is still day?" Are we who claim discipleship called to a ministry no less dramatic—to shoot through the darkness with an unexpected light?

III. I think so. And what brings light to this world more than any other source is the manner in which we choose to treat each other. To be light to the world is a matter of ethics and service. To shoot the darkness with unexpected light means taking the case for those who do not vote. It means joining in the struggle with those who bear stigma, those who have no friends in high places, those who get the short end of the stick, those who live in fear. And this Lenten season reminds us especially that it means doing it at risk—risk of failure, risk of foolishness, risk of rejection. In this season of the cross, one of the cross's most courageous twentieth-century witnesses, South Africa's Archbishop Desmond Tutu, insists that he is not kidding, that "the heart of the Christian Gospel is precisely that God the all Holy One, the all powerful One is also the One full of mercy and compassion. This God is not a neutral God inhabiting some inaccessible Mount Olympus. This is a God who cares about his children and cares enormously for the weak, the poor, the naked, the downtrodden, the de-

spised. This God takes their side not because they are good, since many of them are demonstrably not so. God takes their side because God is that kind of God and they have no one else to champion them."

In this shadowed world, friends, where the politics of the nineties is filled with contempt, rejection, and punishment for the downtrodden and despised, where walls get built almost daily between "them" and "us," this mission of justice and reconciliation would be, in our world, "to shoot through the darkness with unexpected light." As the Gospel ordains, I pray we work the works of One who sends us into the world while it is still day. I pray that you, I, this church, amid the darkness, may be luminous, splendent, radiant lights in this world. Yes, God grant it may be so.—James W. Crawford

Illustrations

TO GLORIFY GOD.   It is said that St. John likes to heighten the miraculous element in his narrative. But if he does, it is not from any love of the marvelous. It is not the wonder but the symbolism of the acts of the Lord that he would emphasize. The works are for him not primarily miracles but signs. The man blind from birth is every man. For it is a part of that sin of the world that the Lamb of God beareth away that by nature we are blind, until our eyes are opened by Christ the Light of the world. It is in bearing away that sin of the world that the Son is glorified, and God is glorified in Him. The vitally important question is not "Who is responsible?"—this man or his parents?—but "How can this fact be turned to the glory of God?" All things exist for that glory; even sin, and every form of evil, is compelled to minister to that glory; and the opportunity of glorifying God is the ultimate moral factor in every situation.—William Temple[7]

SELF-CRITICISM.   It is not at all certain but it is quite possible that the reappearance of Christ at the close of the drama was not solely for the purpose of confirming and vindicating his followers. There seems also to be a warning to his disciples in the words to the

[7]*Readings in St. John's Gospel.*

Pharisees: "If you were blind, you would have no guilt; but now that you say, 'We see,' your guilt remains" (v. 41). To become self-assured, to close the mind to any further word from God, to be the possessors of the final truth with no need to listen to prophets, to build institutions without the means and occasions of self-criticism would be to write into the script "disciples" instead of "Pharisees" and "church" instead of "synagogue."—Fred B. Craddock[8]

SUNDAY: APRIL FIFTH

LECTIONARY MESSAGE

Topic: The Thin Place
TEXT: Luke 22:14–23:56
Other Readings: Isa. 50:4–9a; Ps. 31:9–16; Phil. 2:5–11

Sometime during the seventh or the ninth century, St. Angus came to Balquhidder, a beautiful valley surrounded by forested hills at the eastern end of Loch Voil in the Scottish highlands. Centuries later the Scottish rebel Rob Roy MacGregor would be buried there. Moved by its beauty, St. Angus said it was "a thin place"—a place where the separation between heaven and earth was very thin—so he settled there and built a church that has survived to this day.

Like St. Angus, many of us spend our lives searching for a thin place—a place where heaven is opened and God is especially close to us.

The Gospel of Luke implies that the death of Jesus is a thin place. Indeed, Luke tells us that when Jesus died, in the heavens there was darkness and on earth the veil in the Temple was rent. So thin was the separation that God was near enough for Jesus to talk to God from the cross, and those who heard his prayers were moved to confession and contrition. The one who was hailed by a chorus of angels at his birth committed his spirit to God as he died. Paradise is just a step away from the place called "The Skull."

I. Each gospel tells the story in a different way. In Luke we stand with the crowd of people watching while Jesus is crucified by those who taunt him with mock pleas that he save himself and others. Jesus' death confirms who he has been throughout his ministry. The authorities have pronounced him innocent. The taunts derisively hail him as the Messiah, God's Chosen One, and the king of the Jews, but Jesus prays for forgiveness for those who have rejected and crucified him.

He assures the penitent thief of blessing in paradise, and he dies with the prayer of one who trusts God even in death. Jesus faithfully undertook the work of redemption—lifting up the lowly (Luke 1:52) and preaching good news to the poor (Luke 4:18)—and it cost him his life.

Luke's account of the events surrounding the death of Jesus unfolds in a series of five scenes. First, Simon of Cyrene is compelled to carry Jesus' cross, and Jesus warns the "daughters of Jerusalem" about the terrors that are to come. Second, the actual Crucifixion is reported, with attention to the place, the two who were crucified with Jesus, the dividing of his garments, the mockery of him, and the inscription placed over him. Third, the penitent thief defends Jesus, and Jesus assures him that he will be with Jesus that day in paradise. Fourth, from noon until three in the afternoon there is darkness, but when the centurion hears Jesus' dying prayer, he too affirms Jesus' innocence while the crowds beat their breasts. Fifth, the series of scenes ends with an account of Joseph of Arimathea's role in the burial of Jesus, and the women's preparations for the anointing of his body.

The people leave The Skull beating their breasts. How terrible that God has sent the Savior and we crucified him on a hill outside the city! At Jesus' death even a hardened soldier was moved to confess that he was innocent—a just man. If we have rejected the Savior, God's only son, what hope is there? "What then will the owner of the vineyard do to them" (Luke 20:15)?

II. Perhaps it is well not to dispel the darkness of Jesus' death too quickly. We naturally move on to try to make some sense of the cross. The early church interpreted Jesus'

[8]*John.*

death as God's triumph over Satan—the Christus Victor theory—or that Christ was the ransom paid to the devil for us—the ransom theory. Anselm maintained that it was a satisfaction that God required—the satisfaction theory. Abelard, who I think was closest to the truth, said that Christ died on the cross in order to reveal God's love and thereby arouse in us an answering love—the moral influence theory. John Calvin said that the death of Jesus was a sacrifice and penal substitute for the debt we owe for our sins—the penal substitution theory. But let us not move so quickly to some rational explanation. Wonder at the love of God revealed in the death of Jesus. Part of the power of the gospel is that it calls us to tarry at the cross and then return home beating our breasts with those whose hopes seemed to have died there. Only by witnessing the darkness of Jesus' death and the despair of the loss of hope can we fully appreciate the joy of the resurrection.

III. Jesus came "to give light to those who sit in darkness and in the shadow of death" (Luke 1:79). So, when we sit in darkness, we can hold to the hope that the light will come. We can join those at the cross who confessed Jesus, beat their breasts in grief and contrition, and then went away to serve as witnesses that they had been at the thin place, where the design of the God of the heavens was revealed on earth.

Through the centuries, human beings have looked for thin places in many ways. Some have climbed mountain tops, others have observed cultic rituals, some have searched religious lores, and others have looked within through prayer and meditation. Where is God to be found in human experience? Where can we see God revealed through the veil that surrounds us? Who would have thought that The Skull would be the thin place? At such a place we can only confess our wretched unworthiness of such love as this.

Let us go to the thin place, therefore, as the people of Jerusalem went out to The Skull. Let us hear the story again, and then let us tarry there, reflecting in the silence and the shadows on the sin of humanity and the love of God that led Jesus to the cross. And perhaps this will become the thin place for us also.—R. Alan Culpepper

Illustrations

GRACE AND THE CROSS.   The grace of God is no simple solution to the plight of man. The Christian faith does not offer solutions in the utilitarian sense of that term. It offers new life, and power, and faith. The rediscovery of the meaning of grace has come to our time through the way of agony and despair. It remains for evangelical Christianity to state again with power the faith that grace is present, victorious over evil. We must show how we rightly understand our human history, when we see the sign of the cross in all of it and over all of it.—Daniel Day Williams[1]

LIKE JESUS.   We can never be the same again after having once clearly seen the "light of the knowledge of the glory of God in the face of Christ." We shall always be different. If indeed we invest our faith in him, we shall be like him, for we shall see him as he is.—Wayne E. Oates[2]

SERMON SUGGESTIONS

Topic: One Who Speaks for God
TEXT: Isa. 50:4–9a
(1) Has a divine call. (2) Listens for a message from God. (3) Suffers for faithfulness. (4) Receives God's vindication.

Topic: The Model for Christian Service
TEXT: Phil. 2:1–11
(1) Because Christ was in the form of God, it might be assumed that he was incurably exalted. (2) Yet he did the unthinkable thing and accepted the humiliations, limitations, and sufferings of a slave, dying on a cross. (3) However, God honored him with an exaltation he did not seek. (4) Therefore, "Put yourself aside, and help others get ahead. Don't be obsessed with getting your own advantage. Forget yourselves long enough to lend a helping hand."—*The Message*[3]

[1] *God's Grace and Man's Hope.*
[2] *The Revelation of God in Human Suffering.*
[3] *The Message: The New Testament in Contemporary English.*

Hymn Suggestions: Passion Sunday

1. "At the Name of Jesus," Caroline M. Noel (1870); "King's Weston," Ralph V. Williams (1925)

"At the Name of Jesus" was included in a collection of hymns written during a time of illness and suffering in the life of Miss Noel, daughter and niece of Anglican clergymen who were also hymnists. It is based on the Epistle reading for the day (Phil. 2:5–11).

2. "All Glory, Laud, and Honor," Theodulph of Orleans (eighth to ninth century); "St. Theodulph," Melchior Teschner (1615)

One of the best depictions in hymnody of Jesus' triumphal entry into Jerusalem, this hymn is quite suitable for accompanying a processional with palm branches.

3. "All Praise to Thee, for Thou, O King Divine," F. Bland Tucker (1938); "Sine Nomine," Ralph V. Williams (1906)

Tucker's free paraphrase of Philippians 2:5–11 is an excellent version of this summons to possess the self-denying mind of Christ. It could well be substituted for the oral reading of this passage in worship.

4. "I Come with Joy," Brian Wren (1977); "Dove of Peace," arranged by Austin Lovelace (1977); "Land of Rest," arranged by Annabel M. Buchanan (1938)

This contemporary expression of feeling toward the Last Supper is one of many that could be used for the communion service. Other possibilities include "Now Let Us from This Table Rise," Fred Kaan (1964); "Deus Tuorum Militum," Grenoble Antiphoner (1753); "Now to Your Table Spread," Shirley Erena Murray (1987); and "Love Unknown," John Ireland (1966).—Hugh T. McElrath

Worship Aids

CALL TO WORSHIP.   "Worthy is the Lamb that was slaughtered to receive power and wealth and wisdom and might and honor and glory and blessing" (Rev. 5:12 NRSV).

INVOCATION.   We raise our voices to you, O God, praising you in song, sermon, and supplication, for your great gifts to us, especially the gift of your Son, your Lamb slain for our redemption. Your daily providences

encourage us, and your desire for our prayers also heartens us. May what we do here today be acceptable to you.

OFFERTORY SENTENCE.   "You know the grace of our Lord Jesus Christ; rich as he was, he made himself poor for your sake, in order to make you rich by means of his poverty" (2 Cor. 8:8 TEV).

OFFERTORY PRAYER.   These few coins and bills we lay before you, Father, knowing that in and of themselves they can do little to make a difference for Christ in this world. Yet in your power they can be multiplied until they travel to hearts and needs across the world. So we give them and commit them to you.—Henry Fields

PRAYER.   Designer, Creator, most provident God, whose greatness is beyond our understanding, we praise you that morning has broken, for the glory of the rising sun, and that we may rejoice in the goodness of this Lord's day. Creator God, creating still, create within us this day, clean hearts, fresh spirits, a renewed humanity to serve your Kingdom and your will. Wondrous God, slow to anger, quick to forgive, in this holy season of pilgrimage with our Lord to Jerusalem and to the cross, many of us walk with uncertain steps. Often there is a hole in our resolve, our faith wavers, we stumble by the wayside, detours flash their glamorous appeal, and we desert you, though our intentions are noble. Forgive us and strengthen our walk, our every step. God of endless arms and boundless embrace, who loves everyone of the world as much as you love each one of us, we pray for our fragile and often broken world; for those who in the name of you harm others and wreak havoc with goodwill and efforts for accords of peace. We pray for persons torn from their homeland, those ripped away from family. We pray for children brutalized by war and the terror of endless fighting. Comforting and surrounding Presence, we pray for our community of faith, for those deeply grieving the death of a life partner, a loved one, a member of the family. We pray for those who are desperately yet valiantly fighting diseases, and we pray for their families who faithfully support and care for them. O

God, we pray for the call to be church and faith community in this community. During this season of contemplation and baptismal renewal, help us to be true to our calling, honest with our name, and faithful with the gift, Jesus Christ our Lord.—William M. Johnson

Sermon: The Jesus We Want

TEXT: Matt. 21:1–11

This is Palm Sunday—that day that opens the door for what we Christians call Holy Week.

This event of Jesus' entering Jerusalem is as crucial to us today as it was on the first Palm Sunday long ago. That's true because this story is about how people understand Jesus; it's about what people expect of Jesus; it's about what people want Jesus to do and to be.

I. From the first day of Jesus' earthly ministry, people began to ask the question: Just who is this?

a. Sometimes when they saw him act in some dramatic way, the question was given words and spoken out loud. He stilled the storm and his disciples spoke to one another: "Who is this—who is this that even the wind and the sea obey him?" Sometimes the question was unspoken, but still there—just beneath the surface. Sometimes Jesus himself asked the question: "What are people saying about me? Who do people say that I am?"

"Well, Jesus, some people think you're John the Baptist—and some think you're Elijah. Well, many people think you're a prophet."

"And what about you—what do you think about me? Who do you say that I am?"

The disciples all shuffled their feet and looked around at the ground and prayed that somebody would say something. But they knew that Peter was in the group—so they wouldn't have to wait long. And sure enough, Peter spoke: "Jesus, you're the Christ, the Son of God."

b. That's it! It's a good answer. But even as they sighed with relief, the disciples wondered what it meant. Jesus congratulated Peter and then went on to explain the answer. He explained that it meant suffering and rejection and persecution and ultimately death. And hearing all that, Peter "corrected" Jesus. "Jesus, it can't mean that—because that's not what I want it to mean."

II. That same kind of intellectual and emotional struggle continued as Jesus made his way into Jerusalem that first Palm Sunday.

a. The struggle continued for the disciples. Who is this? What does this mean? And the struggle continued for the crowds. Who is this? And the struggle continues even today for you and me. Just who is this Jesus? We know who we want him to be—but is that who he really is?

b. That's why the symbols of today's story are so important. The crowds call Jesus "King." They sing "Hosanna" to him. They call him "the son of David." They confess that he's coming in the name of God. If they had anything at all to say about it, they would take him physically—right now—and they would make him king! This day is a coronation, an inauguration, an installation. It's all that—but it's not that at all. Do you notice? Jesus is not riding a white stallion. He's on the back of a donkey colt.

He's marching into Jerusalem—to die. And that is a scandal. Even as the palm branches are waved and even as the songs are sung, the cross stands in the distance (and not too far away at that).

III. But that's not who we want him to be. That's not who the crowd wanted him to be. And that's certainly not who we want him to be today.

a. We want a Jesus who will take away our pain.

We want a Jesus who will change the system.

We want a Jesus who will crush the people who don't treat us fairly.

We want a Jesus who will give us just what we want—a Jesus who will give us just what we think we need.

But Jesus reminds us that we don't even really know what we need. Jesus tells us that he's the only One who knows what we need.

b. Just like all those people standing along the streets in Jerusalem that day, we know exactly who we want Jesus to be. We want a king—a king who will do what we want. We want a savior—a savior to rescue us from what we can't stand. But we neglect to notice that he's on a donkey. Sure, he's the King—but not the kind of king we have in mind. So he rides into Jerusalem and marches straight to the cross. And he actually expects us to follow him there. That's not who we want him to be. But that is exactly who he is.

IV. Who do you want Jesus to be today? Maybe it's an interesting question—but it really doesn't matter. What's important is not who we want Jesus to be. What's important—the only thing that's important—is who Jesus really is. Lamb of God crucified for your sin and mine. He is God in the flesh. He's the One willing to pour out his life as a ransom for many. He's the One who is King—just not the kind of king we were expecting. And ultimately, Jesus is just who Thomas said he was: "My Lord and my God."—Barry Stricker

Illustrations

THE SCANDAL OF THE CROSS.   Do you remember when Jimmy Carter insisted on walking in his inauguration parade? Do you remember what an embarrassment and a scandal that was? What Jesus is doing here is absurdly scandalous because it's Jesus' public announcement that he's the suffering servant—the One who is going to give his life as a ransom for many—the one who is going to die. Willingly. He's not a conquering hero in any conventional sense.—B.S.

OUR SIN AND GOD'S REDEMPTION.   Precisely because they really do thus threaten our deepest good, we may by God's grace so repent of our sins and so bear our sufferings that they become elements within something else—namely, our reconciliation with God and our growth into the finite likeness of our Maker. We thus have to say, on the basis of our present experience, that evil is really evil, really malevolent and deadly, and also, on the basis of faith, that it will in the end be defeated and made to serve God's good purposes. From the point of view of that future completion, it will not have been merely evil, for it will have been used in the creation of infinite good. This duality and paradox is expressed by a sentence which the Christian Church has always cherished even when it has been unable to assimilate it into the prevailing theological framework: *O felix culpa quae talem ac tantum meruit habere redemptore* (Oh fortunate crime which merited such and so great a redeemer). In their far-reaching implications, these words are the heart of Christian theodicy.—John Hick[4]

SUNDAY: APRIL TWELFTH

LECTIONARY MESSAGE

Topic: Too Good to Be True
TEXT: John 20:1–18
Other Readings: Isa. 65:17–25; Ps. 118:1–2, 14–24; Acts 10:34–43 or 1 Cor. 15:19–26
"It seems too good to be true." How often we hear these words, or even say them ourselves. There are certain things that we simply do not expect to happen. And if they do, we cannot believe our senses. The first followers of Jesus must have felt just this way on the first Easter morning.
I. *An empty tomb* (vv. 1–7). Jesus' followers were people of their day. They accepted most of the ideas that prevailed. One such belief was that when a person died, that person stayed dead. They could hope in a resurrection on the last day, God's judgment day, but there was no hope for the present. This must have been their feeling with regard to Jesus. He had died on a Roman cross. Some women had seen his body placed in a tomb. He was dead. Their great hopes had been shattered.

This one who they had hoped would redeem Israel (Luke 24:21) had failed and been executed. And the events of Easter morning were just too good to be true.
All of the gospels tell us about that morning. Women, including Mary Magdalene, went to the tomb early, while it was still dark. John tells the experience of Mary. She found the stone rolled away from the opening of the tomb. Not knowing what might have happened, she ran to inform two of the disciples of this amazing sight. Peter and the beloved disciple ran to the tomb. They were not expecting Jesus to be raised from the dead, in spite of his repeated efforts to prepare them for his death and Resurrection. He had told them that he must die. But he had also told them that he would be raised on the third day. They had not believed his words. So it was a shock to discover the tomb was empty. Well, not quite empty. Jesus' body

[4]*Evil and the God of Love.*

was missing, but the burial cloths were still in the tomb. Could he be alive? It was too good to be true.

II. *A newfound faith* (vv. 8–10). When one does not believe something can happen, it is hard to accept when it does take place. So, at first the two disciples did not understand or believe. We can imagine Peter's amazement when he rushed into the tomb and found only the burial cloths. But the other disciple was able to overcome his shock. He saw and believed (v. 8). It was a great leap of faith to believe that Jesus had been raised and that he was alive, to realize that the power of God was not limited. He could do what he had promised. It was as the prophet of old had come to realize. God promised wonderful things to his people: new heavens, a new earth, a new Jerusalem, long lives, answers to prayer, and peaceful relations in all of creation (Isa. 65). It was too good to believe, and many did not. So the idea that Jesus was alive was too good to believe and many did not believe. They had to see the risen Lord before faith could be born.

We are so much creatures of our age that we find it difficult to believe that God can do what he has promised. He has promised to answer prayer; he has promised to give new life. But we prefer things we can see, touch, handle, control. We see an empty tomb, and it is easier to believe in grave robbers than in a resurrection from the dead. It is easier to believe in chance or physical cause than to see the hand of God working in our lives. But it is not too good to be true. The tomb is empty and Jesus is alive.

III. *Personal experience* (vv. 11–18). God understands our weakness and our needs. Some could see the empty tomb and believe. Others, like Mary, needed something more. When the two disciples left, Mary remained outside the tomb. She was deeply grieved. Her Master was dead. She looked again into the tomb and saw two angels. This must have given her hope that God was present and at work. She turned around and saw a man standing. It was the risen Lord, but Mary did not recognize him until he spoke her name. Jesus had said that the good shepherd calls his own sheep by name and they hear and follow him (John 10:3). The risen Lord is the good shepherd and he called Mary by name. She was convinced that her Lord was alive, and she

sought to obey him. When he commanded her to tell the disciples, she went to them and said, "I have seen the Lord" (v. 18). It took an appearance of the risen Lord to convince Mary that it was not too good to be true.

Easter is a celebration that says *Jesus is alive, he is risen*. We believe this because the tomb was empty and because he appeared to his followers on many separate occasions. But even more, we believe it because we, like Mary, have experienced him. He is alive, and because he lives, we live and will live forever.—Clayton Harrop

Illustrations

PERSONAL EXPERIENCE.   Some things can only be learned by personal experience. I may read manuals and other books about how to work on a computer. I may master the language and know in my mind all the things required to operate it. That is all good, but it is not enough. The only way I can learn how to use a computer is to sit down and operate it with my own hands. Books and words of others are never enough. Personal experience is required.—C.H.

REALITY DISPELS DOUBT.   In May 1945, I had been transferred to Fort Meade, Maryland, to be sent to the European theater of operations. I was an officer in the infantry. The prospects were not very encouraging. Three days later the word was flashed around the world that Germany had surrendered. The war in Europe was over. I did not have to go to that area of the world to fight and risk my life. It seemed too good to be true. But indeed the war in Europe was over. What seemed beyond the wildest dream was reality. My doubts and fears were overcome because what seemed too good to be true was actually true.—C.H.

SERMON SUGGESTIONS

Topic: The Easter Miracle in Its Blessedness
    TEXT: Matt. 28:1–10
    (1) There's an open tomb. (2) There's a shining angel. (3) There's a blessed announcement. (4) There's an inspiring duty. (5) There's the living Savior himself.—R.C.H. Lenski

Topic: The Triumphant Adequacy of Christ
TEXT: Rom. 15:29
(1) "I am coming to you *with Christ*." (2) "I am coming to you *with the gospel* of Christ." (3) "I am coming to you *with the blessing* of the gospel of Christ." (4) "I am coming to you *with the fullness* of the blessing of the gospel of Christ."—James S. Stewart

Hymn Suggestions

1. Christ the Lord Is Risen Today," Charles Wesley (1739); "Easter Hymn," Lyra Davidica (1708)
For the past two centuries and a half this has been the standard opening hymn for Easter worship. The florid alleluias give vent to joyful feelings and added exuberance to singing worship.
2. "Come, Ye Faithful, Raise the Strain," John of Damascus (eighth century); "St. Kevan," A. S. Sullivan (1872)
This jubilant hymn draws upon the symbolism of both the deliverance of the Israelites at the Red Sea and the coming of spring, when the warm sun returns, to celebrate the Easter triumph.
3. "This Joyful Eastertide," George R. Woodward (1894); "Vruechten," Dutch melody (1885)
This exciting Easter carol captures the Easter joy in an exceptionally effective way. The seventeenth-century tune enhances the joyful mood of the text.
4. "Open Now the Gates of Beauty," Benjamin Schmolck (1732); "Unser Herrscher," Joachim Neander (1630)
This classic chorale for the opening of worship quotes directly from Psalm 118:19. It could appropriately introduce the Psalter reading for the day.
5. "Alleluia, Alleluia! Give Thanks," Donald Fishel (1973); "Alleluia No. 1," Fishel (1973)
This relatively new "mini-hymn" in both words and music came as a sudden inspiration to its author and composer. It reflects the spirit to be found in the Old Testament readings as well as the Epistle for the day.—Hugh T. McElrath

Worship Aids

CALL TO WORSHIP. "Ye seek Jesus of Nazareth, which was crucified; he is risen"; "The Lord is risen indeed" (Mark 16:6; Luke 24:34).

INVOCATION. You have conquered, O living Christ, and you have brought life and light into our dark world and into the dark places of our personal lives. Continue to shine upon us today, and banish the lingering shadows of guilt and fear and unbelief that may still haunt our hearts.

OFFERTORY SENTENCE. "All shall give as they are able, according to the blessing of the Lord your God that he has given you" (Deut. 16:17 NRSV).

OFFERTORY PRAYER. Lord, we who have much now share with those who have less, mindful that your Spirit can multiply any gift for the furtherance of that kingdom that knows no end. In Jesus name.—E. Lee Phillips

PRAYER. Redeemer God, Victorious Christ, Triumphant Spirit, the words of our mouths and the whisperings of our hearts this glorious day are *alleluias!* Our unborrowed language is praise and adoration, because all that we have longed and hoped for, all that we have waited and prayed for, has come true: Jesus Christ our Lord Is risen, thanks be to God!
All creation does join to say alleluia. Dogwoods, brilliant and splendid in bloom, wave and nod their hosannas. Coveys of birds voice their predawn chant of praise and melody. Easter lilies trumpet fanfares of rejoicing. Tulips and azaleas, ablaze with color and magnificent beauty, add their reply. Luscious, deep green lawns carpeting the good earth join the chorus. All nature sings to the King of Kings. And we, your redeemed children, lift our voices to love's redeeming work.
Resurrected Lord, come into our gathered presence this Easter Sunday. As you did with Mary, speak our names that we may turn and know you and reply, "Teacher." As you did with Thomas, show us your side and hands that we might truly believe and proclaim, "My Lord and My God." As you did with Peter, forgive our weakness and denial, and empower us and send us forth to feed your sheep.

Speak peace to us and take away our doubts and fears. May your words burn within us with joyful fire. May our worship this day of days of the Lord of Lords guide us forth into all the world, telling and living the good news: Jesus Christ is risen! He is risen and shall reign victoriously forever and ever. O for a thousand tongues to sing: thanks be to God, thanks be to God!— William M. Johnson

Sermon: We Are Surrounded

TEXT: Heb. 11:14–16, 39–12:2

We gather today as a people of faith in a room full of lilies to celebrate the resurrection of Christ. Barbara Brown Taylor notes that Easter is the only Christian festival set by the phases of the moon—it is the first Sunday after the first full moon of the spring equinox, obviously set to coincide with the re-birth of life that erupts from an ugly bulb planted in the winter ground, representing a message of hope from nature. Or perhaps we hear the word of Christ in the Sermon on the Mount (Matt. 6:28–30): "Consider the lilies of the field. . . . But if God so clothes the grass of the field, which is alive today and tomorrow is thrown into the oven, will he not much more clothe you—you of little faith?" If a lily can bloom by the power of God, what can be the destiny of the people made in the divine image? Rabbits, eggs, and butterflies abound as symbols of fertility and the rebirth of nature; but nature cannot begin to approximate the Christian hope. Our hope is fulfilled not in the cycles of the seasons but on an empty cross and in an empty tomb. The man Jesus who was crucified and buried under the authority of Pontius Pilate was raised to life on Easter morning by the power and authority of God.

The Resurrection of Christ is the center of the Christian faith. We are not restricted to-day to a repetition of the Easter narratives in the gospels. The entire New Testament flows from faith in the risen Christ. The Christian hope hinges on this one moment in time, and the entire gospel is viewed through the window of Easter.

I. Have you been to the tomb? We have been to the woods and the gardens and have seen the glories of the world that God has created. Many of us have also been to the hospital and to the cemetery. Along with Abraham, Sarah, Isaac, and Moses, the tombs cry out, "All of these died in faith without having received the promises." Lilies, chickens, and rabbits do not speak of the people we have given up in death. How can they represent the Christian hope? No blooming lily, hatching egg, or breeding rabbit has the power to turn tears into joy. Some of us more than others understand the dam of emotions that broke before the empty tomb on Easter morning. If you have never been to the place where you said your final good-bye, the place where you were sup-posed to bring closure to a relationship with a person you love, you cannot begin to com-prehend Mary's tears as she visited the place where Christ was buried.

II. Death continues to be a part of life. I was about fifteen when I first sang with the Union Baptist Association choir on Easter morning at the Forest Park Cemetery in Houston. We were up at four to get to the cemetery an hour before sunrise. There we sang "Lift Up Your Heads, O Ye Gates" and "God of Our Fathers," and we heard again the message of Easter by one of the local pas-tors. The early morning venture, the beauty of sunrise over the duck pond, and breakfast with the choir made a statement in my faith pilgrimage: "This Sunday is special." Yet the cemetery seemed to be a strange place to cel-ebrate the Resurrection. Under the direction of the cemetery association, it had a com-mercial flavor. Evidently a sunrise service made good advertising for the sale of ceme-tery lots. One of the wealthiest residents of Houston was buried right outside the chapel where we sang. The grave was intact when we finished. We always checked. Our singing may have disturbed the residents of Forest Park, but it did not produce miracles. We went to the tombs of Easter morning as a reenactment of Easter, but this ritual did not produce magic.

The reality of death did not change be-cause we gathered on the first Sunday after the first full moon following the spring equinox, but maybe this was not such a strange place to celebrate the resurrection of Christ after all. I have since realized that some of the visitors on the lawn were there for personal reasons. They had been there before and, I suspect, often. They came to the place where they had left a child, a parent, or a spouse. Like Mary, they were seeking the Christ, grasping for hope. Grief does not go away on Easter morning. These tombs were not empty. They represented loss beyond words, unfinished hopes and dreams. The sting of death and the apparent victory of the grave can overpower all sense of hope.

The Bible never pretends that we have disposed of death, not even for the Christ. Even today as we celebrate the risen Christ, death continues to plunder and destroy. Apart from the cross, there is no Resurrection. Good Friday comes before Easter Sunday. Hebrews deals in realities: "Yet all these, though they were commended for their faith, did not receive what was promised." But there is the spark of hope: "God had provided something better so that they would not, apart from us, be made perfect."

III. We are surrounded. If we can lift our eyes above our own personal dreams and losses to the larger vision of the Kingdom of God, we will begin to grasp the hope we celebrate today. The sinking of the *Titanic* was a cameo of human nature, revealing the best and the worst of us. The personal stories tend to reveal two kinds of people. There were people of courage and there were the cowards willing to do anything to save their own skin. The cross of Christ was a cameo of the humanity of the disciples, revealing the best and the worst in them. The very moment we begin to lock onto the personal survival of me and mine, we have completely missed Christ. Easter gave birth to a new community of faith, which we call the Church—the Body of Christ on earth. Christ is the pioneer who has gone ahead, but God in Christ has not finished. If death is about unfinished lives, how much more is Easter about the unfinished work of God? We celebrate the Resurrection of one man, while we live toward the fulfillment of the promise of life eternal.

We are not Lone Rangers here. We are a communion of saints. We are surrounded by a cloud of witness who have gone ahead of us and opened the pathway, and we are bound together as a community of faith. In this room full of lilies, the strong word of hope is that we have come together by faith in Christ. —Larry Dipboye

Illustrations

MORE THAN VALIDITY.   We joyfully celebrate this great mystery of Christ's life, his Resurrection from the dead. And should I put the question, "Why did Jesus so rise from the sepulcher?" perhaps you could give no better answer than this: "In rising from the dead, Christ proved himself God; his Resurrection stamped all his teaching with approval of God; it established the validity of his claim to be truly God. It is a pledge of our future resurrection." But Christ's Resurrection should give us more than this. It should give us something of great and special import spiritually. Our rising from the dead must, in a spiritual sense, be accomplished after the pattern of Christ's while we are still on earth. And it is to this that we must direct all our efforts. Self must die in order that God may reign in undisputed sway in us. In that lies the whole explanation of suffering in life. The cross is the way or the means to the Resurrection. Without the one, we cannot have the other.—John Mark Gannon

LUTHER ON GOD'S LOVE.   Christ, says Luther, is described as the Word of God; and a word is the best means of signifying what is in the speaker's heart. God's revelation of himself in Christ therefore enables us to know "what is going on in the Supreme Majesty." This is a far greater thing than if God had revealed how he created heaven and earth, for here he discloses his inmost self, his very essence or substance.

If we ask what precisely the "substance" of God is, Luther can answer very simply: "What," he says, "will you find in Christ that does not breathe mere love?" It was out of mere love that Christ undertook his whole redeeming work; and the love that is in him is none other than God's own. He could not have shown love to us, "except the will of God by his eternal love had so appointed."—Philip S. Watson[5]

[5]*Let God Be God.*

SUNDAY: APRIL NINETEENTH

LECTIONARY MESSAGE

Topic: Meeting the Risen Lord
TEXT: John 20:19–31
Other Readings: Acts 5:27–32; Ps. 118:14–29; Rev. 1:4–8

One event can change history. It may be on a grand scale such as D-Day in World War II. Or it may affect only one single person: a new home, a new job, marriage, illness, the loss of a loved one. But nothing has more impact than meeting the risen Lord. This event changed lives in the first century and continues to do so today.

I. *Peace for the troubled* (vv. 19–21a). The first Easter day was filled with troubling tales. Women reported that Jesus' tomb was empty. Some of them claimed that the risen Lord had appeared to them. Cleopas and another disciple had returned to Jerusalem telling how the risen Lord had made himself known to them at Emmaus. The Lord had appeared to Peter. What was going to happen next?

In this situation, the disciples of Jesus gathered together. There was comfort in the presence of friends. But the comfort was shattered when Jesus suddenly appeared in their midst. They were so afraid of the religious and political authorities that they were meeting in a room with the doors and windows closed. Yet Jesus entered that room. His sudden appearance must have shocked them. Jesus spoke words of assurance: "Peace be with you" (v. 19). They needed exactly this Word. He showed them his wounds, the nailprints in his hands, and the place in his side that had been pierced by the spear.

In these events, we see how God can work in our lives. He understands our needs and our fears. And he comes to speak the right words and to do the things that will enable us to rise up from our despair. We meet the risen Lord and we, too, are given peace to ease our troubled minds.

II. *A task to be done* (vv. 21b–23). It is not enough to have peace of mind. Such a feeling is fine, but God requires more. Jesus commissioned his followers to a task. He had been sent by the Father. In turn, he was sending them forth. The world needed to be confronted with the good news of what God had done in Jesus, and these people were the ones being commissioned to take that word to the world. To do that, they needed power. So Jesus "breathed on them, and said to them, 'Receive the Holy Spirit'" (v. 22). They were equipped for the task. When God calls men and women to serve him, he always gives the power necessary for the task.

The Gospel of John contains many promises concerning the work of the Spirit, the Paraclete (14:16–17, 25–26; 15:26; 16:7–11, 13–15). The promise has been fulfilled. The Spirit came in power upon these people so that they could go into the world with the message of Jesus, the promise of forgiveness of sins to those who turned to Jesus, and the warning that sins would not be forgiven those who did not turn to Jesus. The message is the same today. The same Spirit is present to empower people. Believers are commissioned and sent.

III. *The great confession* (vv. 24–31). Thomas was not present with the other disciples that first night when Jesus appeared to them. He refused to believe that Jesus was alive. He demanded more than words. He needed to see the risen Lord himself. He wanted to put his finger in the nail holes in Jesus' hands, and to put his hand in the hole in Jesus' side. Only then would he believe. Actually, Thomas had no more doubts than the other disciples. His problem was that he had not been present when Jesus first appeared to them. Doubts are always difficult to dispel, especially when they relate to something that goes beyond normal experience. But God can take care of even the deepest doubt.

John tells us that the disciples were gathered again a week later, and this time Thomas was present. Once more Jesus suddenly appeared in their midst, speaking the same words that he had spoken on the previous occasion. Then he turned to Thomas and challenged him. He was encouraged to touch the scars in Jesus' hands and side. There is no indication that Thomas did so. To see Jesus was enough. And Thomas spoke the greatest confession found in the New Testament: "My Lord and my God" (v. 28). Thomas had come to believe that Jesus was alive; even more, that Jesus was divine. He was God. There is no deeper understanding than to realize that this One who had become flesh and lived among other human beings was not only human but shared the same nature as the Father himself. Meeting the risen Lord enabled Thomas to make this confession. And this is the confession that all people need to make.

Jesus commended Thomas for his confession, but he knew that people in future generations would not have the same privilege of seeing the risen Lord with physical eyes. Others would have to believe without seeing. And God makes it possible for people to meet the risen Lord in other ways than seeing him with their physical eyes. And in meeting him, their troubled souls are quieted, they are commissioned to a work, and they confess, with Thomas, "My Lord and my God."—Clayton Harrop

Illustrations

A COMFORTING PRESENCE. I had been in the army less than two months. I was only eighteen years old; I had never been away from home before. Everything was different. Many things were deeply troubling. And it was my luck to draw guard duty on Christmas Eve and Christmas Day. This seemed to make matters worse. But in the quiet of the hours walking alone, there came the deep realization that Christ would give peace, even in the most unusual circumstances. My troubles seemed to disappear in the presence of Christ with me.—C.H.

AN ESSENTIAL TASK. Through the centuries, God has stirred the minds and hearts of selected people to work in special ways to carry out his purposes. One such man was William Carey. He lived in a time when people had no interest in taking the gospel to other parts of the world. But God had impressed Carey that this needed to be done, and that he was the man God wanted to use to convince others and even to go, himself, to India. In 1792, Carey inspired others to form the Baptist Society for Propagating the Gospel among the Heathen. He became its first missionary in India. He knew that to be a Christian carried with it a task to be done.[6]

[6]Williston Walker, *A History of the Christian Church* (New York: Scribner, 1949), 522–23.

SERMON SUGGESTIONS

Topic: Authorities in Conflict
TEXT: Acts 5:29
(1) Human authority: killed Jesus; tried to silence his followers. (2) Divine authority: exalted the slain Jesus; made bold witnesses of Jesus' threatened followers.

Topic: The Doubt of Thomas
TEXT: John 20:29
(1) The naturalness of the doubts of Thomas, which partly excuses them. (2) The evidences of the Christian Resurrection: (a) the evidence of the senses—"Thomas, because thou hast seen me, thou hast believed"; (b) the evidence of the spirit—"Blessed are they that have not seen, and yet have believed."— Frederick W. Robertson

Hymn Suggestions: Easter Two

1. "This Is the Day the Lord Hath Made," Isaac Watts (1719); "Arlington," Thomas Arne (1762); (1719)
This is a fine hymn for the beginning of worship, its first lines being based directly on Psalm 118:24. Indeed, "This Is the Day the Lord Hath Made" constitutes the last four stanzas of Watts's twenty-stanza paraphrase of Psalm 118 and therefore could be substituted (in part, at least) for the Psalter reading.
2. "Lo, He Comes with Clouds Descending," Charles Wesley (1758); "Helmsley," traditional English melody, arranged by T. Olivers (1765)
This hymn takes up the Second Coming theme of the passage in Revelation, especially verse 7. Its tune is the one Wesley himself selected for this text.
3. "Breathe on Me, Breath of God," Edwin Hatch (1878); "Trentham," Robert Jackson (1888)
Taking his inspiration from the passage in John's Gospel that describes Jesus' appearance to the disciples, this hymn focuses particularly on John 20:22. Hatch, a prominent British scholar, expresses here simple and heart-felt longing for the Spirit of God to dwell in his entire being.
4. "This Is the Day," words and music by Les Garrett (1967)
This is a scriptural song coming out of New Zealand that was given by sudden inspiration

to its author/composer. Based on Psalm 118:24, it lends itself to informal antiphonal or responsorial singing.—Hugh T. McElrath

Worship Aids

CALL TO WORSHIP. "O sing unto the Lord a new song; for he hath done marvelous things: his right hand, and his holy arm, hath gotten him the victory. The Lord hath made known his salvation" (Ps. 98:1–2a).

INVOCATION. Omniscient, omnipotent, omnipresent God: Dare we invoke your name and invite your presence on any occasion? Is that our prerogative? We're not sure. . . . But God, we seek your attention. We request your presence. We desire an encounter with you. So we invoke your name. . . . We are eager to meet you, O God. Or to be met by you. Hear, then, our invocation. Out of your grace, come to us. . . .—Adapted from C. Welton Gaddy[7]

OFFERTORY SENTENCE. "God is able to make all grace abound toward you; that ye, always having all sufficiency in all things, may abound to every good work" (2 Cor. 9:8).

OFFERTORY PRAYER. Because of your love toward us, we are never without means to bless others. It may not be that we always have the money, but we always have the love that you have put into our hearts to do something worthy and helpful. So we pray that in whatever way we are able that we shall be good stewards of what we have received.

PRAYER. We praise you, O God, that you are the great God and the great King above all gods. You have been our dwelling place in all generations. Before the mountains were brought forth or you had formed the earth and the world, even from everlasting to everlasting, you are God.

That at the dawn of history you covenanted with Abraham that through him and his seed all people should be blessed, we praise you.

You are not only a covenant-making but a covenant-keeping God, for in the fullness of

time—when all things were ready—you came in person to this planet in one of us—Jesus of Nazareth—that through his life, ministry, passion, and living again we should know the fullness of your love that even death cannot vanquish.

We praise you for the Church founded upon the rock of Peter's faith and confession and upon all of those who confess Jesus as the Christ, and that the gates of hell shall not prevail against it.

We praise you for your "Yes," spoken so decisively in Christ's Resurrection that we know assuredly now that you are faithful concerning all your promises.

We praise you that we have been entrusted with the gospel of reconciliation. May we be faithful to this high calling in all of our relationships, that we may hear the Master's blessing spoken to us and to all others: "Peace be unto you!"

O You who in your creative and redemptive love claim all of life, we pray for this congregation and for the great Church in which its life is set. May we affirm those things that unite us, that your people may dwell together in the unity of the Spirit and the bond of peace, calling the nations of the world and the peoples of the earth to reconciliation in Christ.

Be with all those who are our fellow voyagers, for we realize that "no person is an island, but each is a part of the main," and that what distresses one distresses all. Be with those suffering distress of mind or body or spirit. Grant to them a quiet confidence in you whose grace alone heals.

We praise you for him who though crucified is not dead but alive forevermore and present among us as risen Lord, and for your eternal Word teaching us to pray and live: "Our Father. . . ."—John Thompson

Sermon: A Child's Eye View of God

TEXT: Isa. 43

Have you ever heard God speak? Have you ever seen God? What is God like? These are important questions, because what we believe about God will determine everything else about our lives.

I found a passage of Scripture to use for our text that gives us an interesting picture of God. This message about God comes from Isaiah, one of God's greatest prophets. The passage I want us to look at is Isaiah 43.

[7]*Prayers: From Adoration to Zeal.*

In these verses, Isaiah tells us six very important facts about God.

I. First, Isaiah says that God is our creator.

a. Look around at the world in which we live. See the people with their different shapes and sizes and colors. See the animals, both small and large. See the plants, which range in size from the smallest blade of grass to the largest tree. Then expand your mind as far as you can and think of all the parts of our universe. And then hear this message from God's Word: God created it all. Everything that is, God made. He is our Creator.

b. Now what does that mean? If God made everything, then he is greater than everything and everybody. And he alone is worthy of our ultimate devotion. If God made everything, then everything and everybody is worth something, because God doesn't make junk! Who is God? He is our creator, the maker of all things.

II. Second, Isaiah says that God is our redeemer.

a. In verse 1, God speaks through his prophet: "Do not fear, for I have redeemed you." Don't let that big word throw you. To redeem simply means to set free. God is our liberator. He is a let-my-people-go kind of God.

b. God sets us free from the bondage of our sin and our selfishness and our hatred and our bad habits. God is a let-my-people-go kind of God. He sent Moses to Egypt to set the Hebrew people free. He sent judges and kings and prophets from time to time to set Israel free. Finally, he sent his Son to die on the cross for our sins so that all who would believe in him could be free forever. Who is God? He is our redeemer, the one who wants to set us free.

III. Third, Isaiah tells us that God is involved.

a. Still in verse 1, God says through his prophet, "I have called you by name, you are mine!"

b. Some of you might be thinking, "If God is involved in my life and in this world, why can't I see him?" God cannot be seen with the physical eye. You cannot see God, but you can know he is involved in your life and in the world because you can feel him and because you can see what he does in the world. God did not make the world and then set us free, leaving us to make it through life on our own. Instead, God chose to be involved in life with us.

IV. That leads to the fourth thing to remember about God.

a. Notice the way God put it in verse 2 of our text: "When you pass through the waters, I will be with you. When you walk through the fire, you will not be scorched."

b. The "waters" and "fire" referred to in verse 2 are symbols of all the difficulties and dilemmas that Israel had encountered along the way, and those that were still before her. Problems come into the life of every child of God, but we have this assurance: we will never have to face those problems alone. God will be with us, and God will deliver us.

Sometimes God will deliver us from our problems as he did when he brought Israel out of Egypt. At other times he will deliver us through our problems as he did Christ on the cross. In either case, the promise is for real. God will deliver us because of his presence in our lives.

V. Notice the fifth fact about God that Isaiah mentions. Isaiah refers to God as "the holy one of Israel."

a. What does it mean to call God holy? When the Bible calls God holy, it means that God is different from us, that he is separate from us. This does not contradict the rest of what I have said. Rather, it helps us to keep all of the other facts in proper perspective.

b. God did create us, and he does want to set us free, and he is involved in our lives, and he is present with us. But God is not just like us. He is different. He looks at things differently. He acts differently. He approaches things differently. He is different. He is a holy God.

VI. One more idea is here in our text. Listen to the way Isaiah expresses God's thoughts in verses 10–11: "Before me there was no God formed, and there will be none after me. I, even I, am the Lord; and there is no Savior besides me."

a. The Jews have an old legend about Abraham, one of the greatest men of the Old Testament. According to this legend, when Abraham was a young man he was hidden in a cave to be saved from Nimrod, who wanted to kill him. When Abraham came out of the cave for the first time, he stood looking across the face of the desert. The sun rose in all of its glory and Abraham said, "Surely the sun is

God, the creator!" So he knelt down and worshiped the sun. But when evening came, the sun sank in the west, and Abraham said, "No! The author of creation cannot set!" So the moon arose in the west and the stars came out. Then Abraham said, "The moon must indeed be God, and the stars are his host!" So he knelt down and adored the moon. But after the night was passed, the moon disappeared and the sun rose again. Then Abraham said, "Truly, these heavenly bodies are not gods, for they obey law. I will worship the God who imposed the law upon them."

b. As you grow up, as you go through life, many suns and moons will arise over the horizon and call for your allegiance and for your worship. But remember this, all people and all powers and all purposes are under the control of the God who made them. No one person or thing in all the world is as great as God.

c. That is the message of Easter. God is so great that even death cannot stop him, even death cannot thwart his purpose, even death cannot defeat him. This great God has put us on this earth and has given us every second of every minute of every hour of every day of every week of every month of every year to answer one question. It is a question so simple that the youngest child could answer it. It is so important that no one needs to leave here without answering it. The question is, "Will you love me and trust me and let me have your life?" Will you answer that question? Will you say yes to God?—Brian L. Harbour

Illustrations

WHERE GOD LIVES.   A little girl who had just moved went with her family to their new church for the first time. The church was just a block from their house. On the way back from church she said, "Boy, we sure are lucky to live in the same neighborhood as God." The Bible tells us something even better. We not only live in the same neighborhood as God, we live in the same house as God. For he is present in each of our lives. And as Christians, we never have to face any experience alone.—B.L.H.

WHAT "GOD" MEANS.   Professor D. M. Baillie has written, "It requires all the training of a religious home, all the fellowship of religious people, all the worship of the church, woven into life itself, to show what the word 'God' means."

SUNDAY: APRIL TWENTY-SIXTH

LECTIONARY MESSAGE

Topic: A Second Chance
    TEXT: John 21:1–19
    Other Readings: Acts 9:1–6 (7–20); Ps. 30; Rev. 5:11–14

It has been said that the only person who does not fail in anything is the one who never attempts anything. There is much truth in that, in both the physical and the spiritual realms. It seems strange that we often judge failures more harshly in spiritual matters. Someone makes a mistake, often foolish and tragic, and it is never forgiven or forgotten by other people. Fortunately, God is more merciful.

I. *Success through obedience* (vv. 1–8). Complete obedience to God is always difficult. The early disciples were no different from us in this respect. They had seen the risen Lord on more than one occasion. Yet Peter returned to his fishing boat on the Sea of Galilee. Six of the other disciples joined him. Was this simply a night of recreation, a trip to catch fish to fulfill hunger, or a return to the old style of life before becoming followers of Jesus? True, Jesus had been raised, but he had not yet established the earthly kingdom they were expecting. Whatever the reason, they toiled all night without success. All who are fishers can sympathize with these men.

But things were about to change. As dawn broke, they saw someone standing on the shore. This man inquired how successful they had been. When they admitted that they had caught nothing, he called to them to cast their net on the right side of the boat. When they did, they caught so many fish that they could not drag the net onto the boat. The beloved disciple recognized that the man on the shore was the Lord. Peter acted in typical fashion. When he learned it was the Lord, he put on his clothes and swam to shore, leaving the other six to bring the boat and the fish to shore. The lesson is clear. No matter how hard one may work, success is always in the hands of the Lord. Only when people obey him do their efforts have beneficial results. While his directions may not be so explicit today, it is nevertheless only as people obey him that success comes.

II. *Ample provision* (vv. 9–14). We live in a day of diminishing physical resources. People worry about what will happen when natural earthly supplies run out. There are only finite amounts of the things we use to make life comfortable. But there are no such limits with God. Just as Jesus took five loaves of bread and fed five thousand, so God can supply the needs of his own today. The disciples discovered that Jesus had already made provision for their breakfast. He had fish and bread available. No one dared to ask him where they came from. They had learned that he could supply whatever was needed.

Although this is true, God also makes use of what people can do. The net full of fish was still in the water, and Jesus instructed the disciples to bring some of the fish they had caught to supplement the breakfast menu. God gives his people strength, ability, and opportunity. He expects us to make use of what we achieve through his help. He never promised to supply our needs without our cooperation.

III. *Challenge and victory* (vv. 15–19). The climax of this story comes in the conversation of Jesus with Peter. Here was a man who had denied three times that he even knew who Jesus was, let alone that he was one of Jesus' disciples. Although Peter did deny his Lord, as Jesus had foretold, the other disciples, with the exception of the beloved disciple, had gone into hiding. They did not have the courage to follow along to see what might happen to Jesus. And this must have been at least as serious as the denials of Peter.

Peter probably felt much as we do when we fail. There is a sense of sin, of guilt, of being unworthy and not deserving another chance. Although Peter had seen the risen Lord on at least four occasions, his doubts must have continued as he thought about his relation to Jesus and his place in God's work. Jesus acted to dispel Peter's doubts and restore him to his place of leadership among the apostles. Peter had denied his Master three times, and three times Jesus asked him whether he loved him. Each time Peter answered, "Yes." The third time must have brought back all the shameful memories of his denials, and he was grieved because Jesus insisted on asking him the question the third time (v. 17). But this was necessary so that Peter might realize forgiveness and restoration.

Each time Peter affirmed his love, Jesus gave him a commission: "Feed my lambs" (v. 15); "Tend my sheep" (v. 16); "Feed my sheep" (v. 17). Three denials, three questions, three answers, three commissions. We see in this something of the mercy of God. We might say that Peter did not deserve another chance. But God saw differently. The same is true for us. We do not deserve a second chance, but God gives it, and more. We fail many times, and many times we receive God's forgiveness and restoration.

The close of the story was not such a happy one for Peter. Yes, he had been restored, but the future was not bright. Jesus pointed out to him that he was to die a martyr in service for Christ. Peter had no option. Jesus said, "Follow me" (v. 19). So it is with every believer. We fail. God gives us a new chance and we are restored. Then we are called to follow Jesus. The future may not be spelled out so clearly to us as it was to Peter, but we are called to follow whatever the future may hold. Only then is life worth the living.—Clayton Harrop

Illustrations

READ THE INSTRUCTIONS! All of us have had the experience of seeking to assemble something we have bought, whether it was a child's toy or a piece of furniture. Perhaps you have done as I sometimes do. I think I know how to do it and I begin, only to discover that I do not know how. But when I read the instructions and follow the diagrams, I can put it together. I am able to succeed when I obey the instructions.—C.H.

A FATHER'S OPPORTUNITY. It was the first service of the revival meeting. A teenage girl made a profession of faith. That afternoon the pastor and I visited the girl's home to talk with the parents. The mother was a Christian but the father was not. We witnessed to him, but he refused to accept Christ, using as an excuse a person who claimed to be a believer but whose life was not a good witness. There appeared to be little hope that this man would change his position. But the last night of the revival, the daughter was baptized. The father came to watch. God gave him a second chance, and when the invitation was given, he came forward to give his life to Christ.—C.H.

SERMON SUGGESTIONS

Topic: How to Stand Up and Take It

(1) A man like Ezekiel certainly started by tackling himself. (2) He saw that a difficult situation can positively call out a man's powers. (3) He saw that when God made him, God put into him some qualities that were meant for just such difficult occasions. (4) Ezekiel believed that whatever happened, God was not dead. (5) This thing that happened to him was not so much something he did as something that was done in him.—Harry Emerson Fosdick

Topic: The Causes and Cure of Talebearing

TEXT: Phil. 4:8; Luke 6:3; 1 John 3:14; in IIb

(1) Diagnosis. (a) Symptoms: faultfinding; the raised eyebrow; slanderous remarks. (b) Causes: irritability; carelessness; insecurity; jealousy; and envy. (2) Remedy. (a) Theory: patience; thoughtfulness; self-examination. (b) Method of treatment: looking for the good (Phil. 4:8); living by the golden rule (Luke 6:31); conversion (1 John 3:14).—James W. Cox

Hymn Suggestions: Easter Three

1. "The Strife Is O'er, the Battle Done," Latin (c. 1695); translated by Francis Pott (1861); "Victory," G. P. da Palestrina (1591); adapted by William H. Monk (1861)

One of the simplest yet most impressive hymns dealing with the Easter victory, the alleluia refrain of this hymn is most effective when sung only before stanza one and after the last stanza.

2. "More Love to Thee, O Christ," Elizabeth P. Prentiss (1856); "More Love to Thee," William H. Doane (1870)

This simple devotional hymn magnifies the confession of Peter related in the gospel reading for the day. Its one theme is the aspiration, more than for earthly joy, peace, or rest, to love Christ even unto death.

3. "See the Morning Sun Ascending," Charles Parkin (1953); "Unser Herrscher," Joachim Neander (1680)

A comparatively new hymn, this one is based on Revelation 5:11–14. It would be eminently appropriate for the start of worship on this particular day. The German chorale melody is associated in the minds of many with the opening of worship.

4. "Worthy Is the Lamb," words and music by Stephen Leddy (1967)

Inspired by the title of a book on Revelation, Leddy composed both text and tune of this contemporary song in his dormitory room while a university student. Created within an hour, its repeated refrain is based on Revelation 5:12. The remainder of its four stanzas is made up of the personal reflections of the hymnist.—Hugh T. McElrath

Worship Aids

CALL TO WORSHIP.   "Make a joyful noise unto the Lord, all ye lands. Serve the Lord with gladness; come before his presence with singing. Know ye that the Lord he is God; it is he that hath made us and not we ourselves; we are his people, and the sheep of his pasture. Enter into his gates with thanksgiving, and into his courts with praise; be thankful unto him and bless his name. For the Lord is good; his mercy is everlasting; and his truth endureth to all generations" (Ps. 100).

INVOCATION.   Holy, holy, holy, Lord God of Hosts, we adore thee, we magnify thee, we wait before thee in humility and openness. Speak to us that we may hear, and give us the joy that divine fellowship alone can bring.—E. Lee Phillips

OFFERTORY SENTENCE.   "If ye be risen with Christ, seek those things which are above where Christ sitteth on the right hand of God. Set your affection on things above, not on things on the earth" (Col. 3:1–2).

OFFERTORY PRAYER.   Gracious God, grant that our living and our giving will more and more reflect the reality and joy of our true home.

PRAYER. Almighty God, our heavenly Father, we look to thee with happy hearts because of thy goodness. We look to thee with trustful spirits because of the adequacy and strength of thy character. We look to thee with eager and expectant hearts, for we can hardly know the good things that thou hast yet to break forth out of the treasury of thy grace. As we turn to thee in confident hope, grant that we may, from the depths of our hearts, give worthy praise to thy holy name.

We come into thy presence with deep humility, recognizing our inadequacy when we are with thee in the great holy moments of worship. Thy thoughts are above our thoughts and thy ways above our ways, yet thou hast invited us graciously to come to thee. But we are not unmindful of our own unworthiness. Grant us thy forgiveness for all that is limited, inadequate, evil, selfish, and wrong in our lives. Grant us thy cleansing and strengthening forgiveness. Give us the renewal of thy indwelling spirit, that we may grow in grace and evermore forward on the upward way in the pilgrimage of this our spiritual life.— Lowell M. Atkinson

Sermon: Keeping Going When God Is Silent
TEXT: Ps. 94:17, 18

"My soul had almost dwelt in silence." Whoever wrote this psalm had experienced the silence of God. The psalm opens with a familiar complaint: life is unfair. The psalmist is in a mood of despair and impatience with the ways of God: "Lord, how long shall the wicked, how long shall the wicked triumph?"

I. We have to remember that when this was written the people of God, to whom the promise had been given that he would shield and protect them, were at the mercy of imperial powers that scorned their God and threatened to destroy them.

a. What brings the psalm very close to us is the throbbing note of near despair, the realism with which the writer protests the unfairness of life and rejects any conventional consolations. We know the resentment caused by the spectacle of organized crime filling the coffers of the wicked while millions of decent people live in varying degrees of poverty. We know what it is to see tragedy strike some of the finest people we know—a highway accident, a cancer, a business failure, unemployment—while others prosper who seem to care little for either God or their neighbors. And we all go through periods of depression that cannot be shaken off by either a quick pill or a Bible text.

b. We've just celebrated the most glorious and uplifting moment in the Christian year. The joy and hope of the Easter season radiates from the churches and lifts the spirits of even the least religious among us. Then we wonder why the God we lauded with our praises on Easter morning seems to have withdrawn into the shadows, and there is a silence in our souls. Why does the song of the Risen Christ not sound continually through the dull days, the difficult days, the worrisome days? Above all, why does God often seem to be most silent just when we need him most?

c. To me, it is immensely reassuring to find such questions raised in the Bible itself. Here is the book to which we turn for news about the living God. We call it the Word of God, and what can that mean but a communication from him to us? When I use words, as I am doing now, I am not just trying to pass a series of thoughts from my mind to yours. Something far more vital, far more mysterious, is happening. We are communicating, person to person. The Word of God is like that. When I say "Hear the Word of God" before reading from the Scriptures in church, I mean, "Let's be ready now to meet our God who is revealing himself to us through the stories, the adventure, the vision, the inspiration of these records of his people, which culminate in the supreme story of Jesus Christ in whom the Word was made flesh and dwelt among us." And it is wonderful to find that among these records is the voice of this psalm complaining of the very fact that God often seems to fall silent, as if the revelation had stopped.

II. So the Bible reckons with the silence of God as well as with his communication. In spite of the constant refrain of the prophets, "Thus saith the Lord," there are those other recorded moments when the cry was, "Is there no Word from the Lord?"

a. There are times—usually the times of deepest distress, when we most need to hear from God—when the silence seems to be absolute. The Bible reveals such moments, and gives no promise that we shall be spared this baffling and heartbreaking experience. Was there ever a more total silence in the heavens, a more apparently unresponsive God, than when Jesus called out from his cross: "My God! My God! Why hast thou forsaken me?"

b. Just because the Bible is honest about this experience of God not coming near to speak just when we need him most, we can learn from it the secret of keeping going when silence falls and the lights go out. We begin to understand that faith is not some mental gymnastic by which we convince ourselves that all is well when obviously it isn't. We learn to hear the drumbeats of God's grace that sound through the silence, those muffled yet certain assurances that God is indeed alive, has not withdrawn his presence, and will bring us through.

III. True faith knows that, no matter how we feel in a moment of deep despair, the silence has not extinguished the voice of the living God. Those who keep going learn to disregard their feelings and hold to the promises of God that fill the universe with his grace. They know, like the psalmist, that "the Lord is my defense; and my God is the rock of my refuge," just as we all know today that the silence of the air around us, the muteness of the atmosphere in which we move, is an illusion, for it is really filled with a million sounds. So the total silence of God is an illusion, for the drumbeats of his grace are sounding everywhere.

a. We are not living in a silent universe. The faith that keeps us going is tuned, despite all slipping and falling, despite all moments of despair, to the eternal drumbeats of God's grace.

This is the tough and resilient faith that has carried Christians through their times of near surrender to the powers of unbelief. This is another powerful witness that speaks in the Bible and in the experience of the saints from then until now. "When I said, 'My foot slippeth,' thy mercy, O Lord, held me up." That's the divine hindsight that reveals the truth and strengthens us for the next time. "My God," says St. Paul, "shall supply all your needs according to his riches in glory by Christ Jesus."

b. We hear a lot about safety nets these days. As I read the Bible, and as I reflect on my own ups and downs of faith, I become more and more convinced that in spite of all our slipping and all our experience of the silence of God, there is a safety net through which we cannot fall. It is woven of the grace of our Lord Jesus Christ, the love of God, and the communion of the Holy Spirit. Whatever else may let you down, this never will. "My soul had almost dwelt in silence—unless the Lord had been my help." "When I said, 'My foot slippeth,' thy mercy, O Lord, held me up."—David H. C. Read

Illustrations

THE ANSWER.   In her book *Turn Over Any Stone,* Edna Hong told the story of her reaction when she learned that her three-month-old granddaughter was brain-damaged. The news threw her into a crisis of faith: What kind of God would do this? She asked, "What are you—Creator or Father? If Creator, are *they* your image? . . . If Father, then what happened to all the fatherly virtues: tenderness, protectiveness, affection, solicitude? Answer me, you who claim to be both Creator and Father. Answer! But all I got was silence. I scolded him like a shrew. . . . I insulted him. . . . But he was silent, and I remembered a verse in a psalm and found it: *"Is he deaf, the God who planted the ear?"* At last, the words of Isaiah spoke pointedly to her: "But they who wait for the Lord shall renew their strength; they shall mount up with wings like eagles."

PERSEVERANCE.   On the rock near the top of Mt. Washington there is a marker on the trail to show the spot where a woman climber lay down and died. On a clear day her action looks ridiculous. There is the top, so close that you can almost hit it with a stone. One hundred steps more and she would have reached the hut at the summit, the shelter she sought. But this she did not know. She was disheartened by the storm that beat on her body and reached at her courage. She could not measure how far she had to go. She died one hundred steps from her goal. A battle, so the strategists say, is won by the army that can hold out minutes longer than the foe. A man cannot do everything, but he can keep going. He has energy for one step more. He has a bit of resource left, even when he thinks all is spent.—Allan Knight Chalmers[8]

[8] *The Constant Fire.*

SUNDAY: MAY THIRD

LECTIONARY MESSAGE

Topic: Plain Speaking
   TEXT: John 10:22–30
   Other Readings: Acts 9:36–43; Ps. 23; Rev. 7:9–17

Growing up, I was always told by my parents the importance of being nice to people—especially anyone older than I. Living in the South, an important part of our culture was hiding your true thoughts and always being nice to people. Very few persons want to hear plain speaking today. In the world of religion, sometimes we want to hear things only in nice terms. Jesus was always quite plainspoken. We never allow the real force of Jesus' words to be heard. Jesus had shown his opponents, the religious leaders of his day, the true teachings of his Father, but they did not want to hear them. What plain truths did he teach?

I. He taught the unity of himself and his Father. The leaders thought that he was committing blasphemy whenever he made such assertions. The crime of blasphemy was one of the most severe in Judaism. It consisted of any human being claiming any quality of God for himself. In verse 24, the leaders want to be told plainly whether Jesus is the Messiah. In reality they did not want to hear the truth. They were waiting for an opportunity to charge him with blasphemy. Often we say that we want to hear the plain truth but in reality we are very fearful of hearing it. If the leaders really heard that Jesus was the Messiah, certain reactions would have been required. Some type of response would have had to be made to that revelation. Often, to condemn and charge are easier responses than commitment.

II. Plain speaking is sometimes most plain in works rather than words. Jesus' works had been done clearly before the leaders, but they could not perceive the truth in them. Jesus had done mighty miracles before their eyes, but they were so blinded by the religious rules he might be breaking that they missed the truth. Some people will look at an event and perceive the facts quite differently than another group. Many see exactly what they want to see and nothing else. Some looked at Jesus and saw another false teacher,

a threat to the kind of religion they had been teaching. Others looked at Jesus and perceived that he was indeed the Son of God. Some people cannot follow a map even though you drew as plainly as possible. They still wind up getting lost. Jesus had drawn a very graphic picture in the works that he had accomplished.

He had come to the very headquarters of Judaism, the Jerusalem Temple, to observe the Feast of the Dedication. Perhaps he expected the religious leaders to observe his mighty deeds in the Temple. He expected the very house of God to be a "house of prayer for all people." Instead he found large walls of division separating people. The Gentiles were cordoned off in the outside court, where they saw nothing but the greed of the money changers. The women were not permitted to mingle with the male worshipers in the inner courts. The laymen were not allowed into the court of the priests. Finally, only one man, the high priest, could enter into the presence of God. In such a place, the works of Jesus could not be seen because of the high wall of exclusion.

III. The greatest of these plain points of speaking had to be Jesus' assertion that the sheep always recognize the voice of the shepherd (v. 27). The Great Shepherd was right in the midst of the undershepherds of the Temple, and they did not recognize him. They could not hear the plain truth that he and the Father were one. For the religious leaders, the walls of division blocked their views. They were more concerned about keeping unclean people away from God than about recognizing God's Son right in their midst. This was a tragedy then, but we still do the same. At times, those preaching the text have a most difficult time hearing the plain message of the text. Often we have to set aside a prepared sermon and allow its plain truth to grip our hearts and confront us with its basic demand. Then we are able to preach the sermon on Sunday morning to other Christians. We must always be ready to hear the voice of the Shepherd.

The passage ends as the religious leaders desire a chance to charge Jesus with blasphemy. Some hear the plain words of Jesus and hear only blasphemy. Others hear the plain words and allow those words to confront their lives with the wonderful message of hope. We are truly in the hand of the Great Shepherd and will be guided into the green pasture where walls will not divide according to the rules set down by humans.—James L. Blevins

Illustrations

A MODERN PARABLE.   I do about fifty biblical characters in monologue. I was to do John on Patmos for a church whose morning worship was televised. The minister told me to go around to the front of the building and enter the sanctuary so the television camera would pick me up better. I went around to the front door, but the church ushers would not let me in. They took one look at my biblical robe and beard and decided I was a street person there to cause problems.—J.L.B.

DELIBERATE BLINDNESS.   Jonathan Swift (1667–1745) put it well in one of his works: "There is none so blind as they that won't see."[1]

SERMON SUGGESTIONS

Topic: The Voice from Heaven That Speaks Today
TEXT: Jer. 1:9b–10
(1) God has always spoken to our world: through prophets, especially Jesus Christ, his Son; through the Church. (2) What is our task, as those who presume to speak for God? It is both a work of judgment and a work of grace. (3) How do we do this work? We call people to repentance; to faith; to personal and corporate righteousness; to service to others.

Topic: The Things That Strengthen Faith
(1) Our faith will be strengthened if we exercise patience (Ps. 37:7). (2) Our faith will be strengthened if we practice obedience (John 7:17). (3) Our faith will be strengthened if we live by the law of love (1 John 4:18).

[1] *Polite Conversation.*

Hymn Suggestions: Easter Four

1. "O Thou in Whose Presence," Joseph Swain (1791); Davis, Wyeth's Repository of Sacred Music, Part Second (1813)
Drawing together the various motifs of the Shepherd Psalm with the theme of deliverance and strength in tribulation found in the Revelation passage, this hymn with its lovely folk hymn tune setting is particularly appropriate to accompany this day's lectionary.
2. "Savior, Like a Shepherd Lead Us," Dorothy A. Thrupp (1836); "Bradbury," William B. Bradbury (1859)
This simple poetic rendering of the ideas contained in Psalm 23 as well as in the gospel and Revelation readings, together with its tune, was intended largely for children's use. Addressed to "blessed Jesus," it is a prayer that we, God's children, will turn early to him, and hear him, who has brought us and whose grace will cleanse, defend, and empower us.
3. "My Shepherd Will Supply My Need," Isaac Watts (1719); "Resignation," William Walker's Southern Harmony (1835)
One of the oldest but still most appealing paraphrases of Psalm 23, this Watts hymn also attracts with its lovely folk hymn setting from the Southern shape-note tradition.
4. "See the Morning Sun Ascending," Charles Parkin (1953)
This recent hymn is based on Revelation 7:11–12, and incorporates the words of the anthem sung by the angelic choir. Stanza 4 is an almost direct quotation from the text in verse 12.—Hugh T. McElrath

Worship Aids

CALL TO WORSHIP.   "Sing a new song to the Lord! Sing to the Lord, all the world! Sing to the Lord, and praise him! Proclaim every day the good news that he has saved us. Proclaim his glory to the nations, his mighty acts to all peoples" (Ps. 96:1–3 TEV).

INVOCATION.   Master of our souls, as we sing the songs of Zion today, pray the prayers of the faithful, and listen for the still small voice, come to us as never before and transform us from within to give witness without to the mighty power of God.—E. Lee Phillips

OFFERTORY SENTENCE. "For every beast of the forest is mine, and the cattle upon a thousand hills" (Ps. 50:10).

OFFERTORY PRAYER. Lord, we give, mindful that all we have or hope to have comes from you; thus do we pray that the portion we give today will be blessed by your Spirit for all time, and all that remains with us may be equally blessed.—E. Lee Phillips

PRAYER. Wake us up, Father! It's time that we became fully awake and alive to the gift of life and the beauty of your creation! Time is passing, the seasons are changing, our children are growing up, we are growing older, and we sometimes fear that before we know it—certainly, before we are ready—the opportunities to live and to enjoy the relationships that enrich our lives will all be gone! Wake us up, Father! We want to live every moment to its fullest!

There are some among us who are deeply troubled today because they are forced to look at your world of beauty and love through the eyes of those who know they must prepare to leave it. Comfort them, we pray, with the presence that makes all life one—life in your Son, Jesus, both in this world and in the world to come.

Others are dissatisfied with life because they don't own enough of the world—their ambitions are unfulfilled, their desires unmet. Help them, we ask, to discover the joy of little things and the excitement of sharing with others.

Some can't see the beauty of life because they are bound with pain, or poverty, or imprisonment of one kind or another. Meet their needs, we pray through the ministry of this church and the means we provide the church to do its work.

Help us, Father, to devote this entire day to pondering the gifts that are ours from your hand. And help us to discover life abundant and eternal, both now and in the Kingdom of God, through your Son, Jesus Christ. —Gary C. Redding

Sermon: Have You Begun to Live Yet?

TEXT: John 10:10

Let me share three basic truths that I hope will help you begin to live again—if somehow or somewhere along the way you have lost your song and your enthusiasm for life. And if you feel that you have never really lived before, it's my prayer that these truths will ultimately point you to Jesus, whose whole purpose in life was to empower you and me to really live!

I. The first truth is simply this: life is meant to be lived—even the ordinary, uneventful, and undramatic moments.

Someone once said that one of the greatest tragedies of the human experience is that many people spend the better part of their life getting ready to live it. Fathers wait until other obligations are less demanding to become acquainted with their sons. Mothers sincerely intend to spend more time with their daughters. Husbands and wives are going to be kinder and more understanding with each other. When in the world are we going to begin to live as if we understand that this is life today—here and now? This is our time, our day—and it is passing. What on earth are we waiting for? Perhaps one of our greatest needs is not to be so concerned that one day our life shall come to an end, but to understand that unless something profoundly changes, our life may never really begin.

Even if you have been paralyzed by tragedy, overcome by obstacles, discouraged by unfulfilled dreams and expectations, devastated by loss, surrounded and threatened by intimidating circumstances, or even betrayed and wounded by the selfishness of someone in whom you sincerely believed and upon whom you heavily depended, you must not ever give up on life!

Listen! We're here for a purpose and our life is headed somewhere. But if we don't change our direction, we're likely to wind up exactly where we're headed—wherever that is!

II. The second truth is this: life is designed to have meaning! But then, you have already discovered that for yourself, haven't you? You've been able to make enough progress in your profession to realize that even if you make it all the way to the top, it will likely not be far enough: something will still be missing. Even when you know that your friends, neighbors, peers, and in-laws envy you, you're smart enough to understand already that it's not enough to give you lasting contentment and peace of mind, aren't you?

At Callaway Gardens, Georgia, the Cecil Day family has funded a butterfly exhibit and research center. If you go, you will be introduced to the moth with no mouth. It's a species of caterpillar that lays its eggs and then changes into a moth that has no digestive system—no way of taking in food, so it starves to death in a matter of hours. Once it has fulfilled its reproductive function, it dies.

We aren't like that, are we? We're more than a moth that lives for a few hours and then disappears, aren't we? There is something more to being alive than just eating, sleeping, going to school, working, having children, and growing old, isn't there? There must be a purpose to our existence beyond simply existing. It must make some difference that we have lived! Our souls are starved for meaning, for the sense that we have figured out how to live so that our life matters. Day after day, life goes on. We may be successful or unsuccessful, filled with worry or pleasure. But the question that haunts us is this: Does our life have any significance? Does it mean anything?

Tell me, what does being a Christian mean to you? To some it means a stiff, upright, inflexible way of life—colorless and unbending. For others it describes a surprise-filled adventure, moments and hours and days lived on tiptoe, at the very edge of expectation. For me, it means that I've chosen to believe that Jesus is who he said he is. I've chosen to believe that Jesus can and will do what he said he could and would do! And I believe that if we rely upon the Bible for our information, there is simply no way to avoid the conclusion that God intends for the Christian to be full of life—a person given to singing and dancing, leaping and living, dreaming and daring!

Imagine what kind of impact we Christians—and our Lord—could have upon our world if we would quit sitting on our perches, staring off into eternity! Imagine what kind of impact we could have if we truly come alive through his power. It's difficult to be indifferent to a wide-awake, real-live person of God. And it's even more difficult to be indifferent to a church full of Christians like that! The world may hate us or love us, but one thing is certain: they will never be able to ignore us!—Gary C. Redding

Illustrations

THE MOST IMPORTANT THING.   Bob Buford is a Texas businessman whose family has made and multiplied millions of dollars in the cable television industry. Nearly five years ago, his only son and three companions, on a hunting trip in the southwestern part of the state, drowned while trying to swim the Rio Grande River. Last month I heard Bob Buford talk about the devastating impact of that loss upon his and his wife's life. I also heard him describe how, through his personal faith in Jesus, hope had come out of his utter despair, life had overcome death, and purpose had emerged from the senseless tragedy. He described the five years since his only son's death as "a time of transition from success to significance." He said, "There was a time when my Christian faith was only one item on the buffet of the many good things I was doing with my life. But now, my relationship with God through his Son is the single most important thing in my life!"—G.C.R.

THE GIFT OF LIFE.   Thornton Wilder's Pulitzer Prize–winning play *Our Town* focuses on life in the small ordinary town of Grover's Corners. It could be the story of any one of us. The setting could very well be our town. With profound brilliance, Wilder underscores the wonder of everyday life—a fact that many of us fail to recognize until it's entirely too late.

No one can read or see the play without pausing for just a moment to thank God again for the gift of life.—G.C.R.

SUNDAY: MAY TENTH

LECTIONARY MESSAGE

Topic: Can Love Be Commanded?
TEXT: John 13:31–35
Other Readings: Acts 11:1–18; Rev. 21:1–6

When you were young you thought of laws and commandments as dreary and negative. Christianity was often designed as a series of "thou shalt nots." Some people even today are turned off to Christianity because of these negative and repressive commandments. Yet the fact that Christ calls his followers and commands them to love one another demonstrates the positive nature of his message. Love is a new commandment that was very hard for the legalistic religious leaders of his day to grasp. Disciples find it far easier to follow a list of rules that ensure that if you keep them you will be an excellent Christian. Jesus chose the difficult way by stating that authentic believers will love one another. Such action is harder to determine or assess. The positive way is fraught with danger. One finds it much more difficult to determine an excellent way. People write to advice columnists in the newspapers seeking ten commandments for being a good father or mother, wife or husband. By taking the ten steps, they can pronounce themselves perfect. Jesus took the more difficult way, defining the good Christian in terms of love. That approach is very difficult to measure.

I. *Christ is love.* Jesus based the new commandment on his own person. The standard of love is the very same love that Christ demonstrated for his followers. All of the New Testament shouts the universal principle of God's love for his people. The greatest evidence of this love is God's giving of his Son for the sins of the world. No greater love can persons possess than to give up their lives for their friends. Jesus lived up to his own words. He demonstrated that this was not a negative rule that a Christian had to fulfill. The commandment sprang from the very roots of the faith. Love identified the very person of Jesus. The ancient people feared their gods. The Greeks saw them as vengeful deities always plotting woes for human beings. The Bible presents God as the very essence of love.

Very few gods of world history have been characterized by the word *love.* Raw power seemed always to exclude love. A powerful god by his very nature would not possess such weak traits as love. Some societies even viewed love as a feminine trait that true males would not portray. Truly strong gods would lead the nation to war and show very little empathy for human weakness. What a surprise when Jesus indicated that his father was characterized by love!

II. *Disciples must love.* Thus Christ places upon us the injunction to love as a commandment. During Holy Week, we observe Maundy Thursday. *Maundy* comes from the Latin term *mandamus est,* which refers to the commandment to love one another. The commandment defines the very nature of Holy Week, which leads up to the death of Jesus on the cross. Jesus' disciples must be willing to take on the commandment to love even as our Lord did. His great love led him to Golgotha. Our love must also lead to sacrifices. We find it easier to like people than to love them. Love is unconditional. Jesus did not demand that we be at a certain level of keeping rules before he would love us. Jesus did not love sin, but he did love sinners and called them to repentance. Jesus said that the physician's duty is to go not to the well and healthy but to the sick. The love of Christ constrains us to go to all people who need the gospel.

III. *Glory and love are related.* The glory of Christ grew out of his love for people. In fact, he was fulfilling the very charge of the Father. That is why he had come into the world. The religious leaders of Judea would have disagreed. They charged him with breaking the religious commandments of the Sabbath and other commandments. He could not possibly radiate the glory of God! Jesus pronounced the truth that he was glorified because he had identified the very love of God. This glory had been right in their midst and they had missed it. Sometimes the greatest truths are missed because we do not recognize them. In a world characterized by blood and war, sometimes we cannot see love or even hear Jesus' command because of the din of violence.

The world of that time would never have defined glory in terms of love and goodwill. Kings were not glorified in that way in the Roman empire. Money and the size of armies were more likely to be the measuring rods. Hatred of enemies was more likely the rule than genuine love of enemy. Jesus' words were most shocking to his opponents. When a general won a battle in the Roman world, the glory came as he paraded his victims back into Rome with the captured loot in a gigantic victory parade. Jesus talked about a victory parade in which there would be love even for the victors by the ones vanquished.— James L. Blevins

Illustrations

WHAT SHOCKS US.   The churches are justifiably shocked when the glamour of a film actress is assessed by the number of her love affairs and divorces; they are less shocked when the glamour of a man, or a work of art, is headlined in dollars. They are shocked when unfortunates are reduced to selling their bodies; they are less shocked when journalists are reduced to selling their souls. They are shocked when good food is wasted by riotous living; they are less shocked when good crops are wasted and destroyed because of overproduction and underconsumption. Something has gone wrong with the emphasis; and it is becoming very evident that until that emphasis is readjusted, the economic balance sheet of the world will have to be written in blood.—Dorothy L. Sayers[2]

OUR DEBT OF LOVE.   To be in debt! Should this be difficult? Nothing, indeed, is easier than to be in debt! And then also that it should be one's task to be in debt! Usually we think the task is to get out of debt, whatever the debt is, a money debt, a debt of honour, a debt involving a promise—in short, whatever the debt is, the task is always rather to get out of debt, the sooner the better. But here it should be the task, therefore an honour, to be in debt!—Søren Kierkegaard[3]

SERMON SUGGESTIONS

Topic: In the Hand of God
TEXT: Jer. 18:6
(1) What may be marred: our nation, forgetting its finest heritage; the Church, becoming insular and self-serving; the individual, being content with an inner piety that neglects the needs of the neighbor. (2) How what is marred can be refashioned: by listening to the prophetic voices, whether in Scripture or otherwise; by allowing our attitudes to be changed; by personal commitment and corporate action to change what can be changed; by looking to God for guidance and empowerment.

[2] *The Whimsical Christian.*
[3] *Works of Love.*

Topic: Walking with Jesus
TEXT: John 6:67–69
(1) We, too, are tempted to go away from Christ: because of the lure of the crowd; because of the shattering of our personal hopes and expectations. (2) In spite of powerful and persistent temptations to go away from Christ, some are persuaded to stay: because of simple, stubborn refusal to follow the crowd; because of sheer loyalty to a commitment; because of a settled conviction of the rightness of staying with Christ.

Hymn Suggestions: Easter Five

1. "Praise the Lord, Ye Heavens, Adore Him," Anonymous, The Foundling Hospital Collection (1796); "Hyfrydol," Rowland H. Pritchard (1855)
This excellent hymn expressing praise for the wonderful works of God's creation is a paraphrase of the Psalter reading—Psalm 148. Very likely it was first sung by children. Its source is a book of hymns used in the chapel services of a London orphanage.
2. "All Creatures of Our God and King," Francis of Assisi (1225); "Lasst uns erfreuen," Geistliche Kirchengesange (1623)
Francis of Assisi's famous "Canticle of the Sun," of which this text is an English translation, makes an admirable companion to the reading of Psalm 148. Grand indeed is the adoration of the inanimate world—sun, moon, mountains, water—and of every animal—cattle, birds, beasts of the field; but how much more grandly can redeemed humanity join in God's praises—*alleluia*!
3. "Walk in the Light! So Shalt Thou Know," Bernard Barton (c. 1840); "Manoah," Greatorex's Collection of Church Music (1851)
Taking up the theme of the gospel reading, this hymn is an exhortation to walk in the light of God's love. Its author, known as the "Quaker poet" of England, spent his entire career not as a clergyman but in the position of a bank clerk.
4. "Spirit of the Living God," Daniel Iverson (1935); "Living God," Iverson (1935)
The reading in Acts concerning the free spirit of God that is extended to all—Gentile as well as Jew—could well be followed by this simple prayer for God's Spirit to fall fresh on all the worshipers.—Hugh T. McElrath

Worship Aids

CALL TO WORSHIP.   "It is a good thing to give thanks unto the Lord, and to sing praises unto thy name, O Most High; to show forth thy loving kindness in the morning, and thy faithfulness every night" (Ps. 92:1–2).

INVOCATION.   Holy God, we bow before you in penitence and openness. It is through worship that we learn the deep lessons of life and are armed for the battles of every day. We honor you, God, and we await that moving of the Spirit that makes the truth of Christ so real to us.—E. Lee Phillips

OFFERTORY SENTENCE.   "I have showed you all things, how that so laboring ye ought to support the weak, and to remember the words of the Lord Jesus, how he said, It is more blessed to give than to receive" (Acts 20:35).

OFFERTORY PRAYER.   O God, in these special moments of stewardship and commitment, remind us that the Church exists by mission as fire exists by burning. Because your love is so great, the Church's mission is worldwide. The field is the world, as Jesus said.

Transform these moneys into daily bread and the Bread of Life for many here to the far reaches of your love.—John Thompson

PRAYER.   O Thou heavenly Parent, who out of the imagination and creativity of your great love has ordained the family for the being and well-being of humankind, we thank you for the family that has given us life—for the family of which we are a part today—for the family of faith to which we are called through this church.

We praise you for all generations that you have made sacred the family in your advent through the home of Mary and Joseph. We thank you for Jesus, born of woman, whom you anointed to be the Messiah whose touch of grace makes our eyes to see and our ears to hear, who strengthens us to do the truth, and delivers us from the power of death. How the meaning of this life, ministry, passion, and living among us has confronted us in the strong Word proclaimed in this hour! To follow him is never easy, but it is the way to life. May the promise of life that this Lord's Day has awakened in us be fulfilled in the daily.

For all of our relationships, may we be open to your love in Christ—the love that looks for ways of being constructive, even to dying on a cross, that is patient in understanding, that is not judgmental but forgives to the uttermost, that never gives up but perseveres through every estrangement.

As we thank you for this household of faith, we are grateful for the love and caring among us as brothers and sisters that make us a family.

Blessed be the tie that binds our hearts in Christian love, the fellowship of kindred minds is like to that above! For our sisters and brothers among us who suffer any brokenness, we pray for a faith, a love, a trust, that the healing of your amazing grace may make whole. We thank you for the healings among us. We thank you that where physical disease or infirmity is not to be removed, there is the miracle of the Spirit winning victory upon victory. For those among us passing through the valley of the shadow of death, sensing the weakness of our own finiteness, may we know the strength of your everlasting arms.

We pray, too, for the human family—for families that today are the victims of hostility and war, displaced persons, without homeland or home, living daily with the tenuousness and uncertainties of existence as refugees. We pray for the oppressed, and the oppressor, that those energies squandered through hatreds and fears may be disciplined to construct that order of justice upon which the foundations of peace must rest.—J.T.

Sermon: What Being a Parent Sometimes Means

TEXT: Exod. 1:15–2:10; Acts 7:17–22; Heb. 11:23

"The Lord gives good many things twice over; but he don't give ye a mother but once." So says Tom in Harriet Beecher Stowe's *Uncle Tom's Cabin*. Today is the day that has been set aside annually to pay tribute to motherhood, a sometimes thankless, and sometimes difficult, job. No one has ever said that being a mother, or being a parent in general for that matter, is easy. Such is evident from the scripture passage that was read from Exodus.

I. *Being a parent sometimes means making difficult choices.* Let us consider the mother of Moses and the difficult choice she had to make. The Hebrews had fallen into slavery down in Egypt. They began to be fruitful and multiply. Afraid that the Hebrews might grow strong enough to rise up and rebel, as the story goes, the king of Egypt decreed that all male Hebrew children born should be killed. Now, this is a heart-wrenching story. To really appreciate the plight of Moses' mother, we need to read between the lines. Pharaoh instructed his officials to find all the baby boys born to the Hebrews and throw them into the Nile River. Can you imagine what agony, what apprehension, what turmoil these Hebrew parents must have suffered as it neared time for their babies to be delivered? This is one of the few instances in the ancient world, I am sorry to say, when the parents hoped and prayed for a girl. Usually they were more interested in the male gender.

But then when the baby Moses was born, it was evident that he was a fine baby. So his mother "hid him for three months" (Exod. 2:2). Imagine what this family must have endured these three months, living in fear that the child would cry out and be discovered. How they must have pampered him, and covered his mouth to try to muffle his crying! Someone from Pharaoh's court could pass by their dwelling at any time and discover their secret.

As we look closer into the scriptures (Acts 7:17–22), we find that some parents were forced to abandon their infant sons rather than have them taken from them by force, in hopes, perhaps, that someone would discover them and take pity on them. And so it was that the mother of Moses had to make the difficult decision to abandon her own child. I am sure that having to make this decision broke her heart. But she felt she had no choice. And so, when it was impossible for her to hide him any longer, the child's mother secured a basket, plastered it so it would not leak, gently tucked the boy inside, and placed the basket on the bank of the river. It was a difficult decision, but a decision she felt forced to make.

And you know, parents are still making difficult decisions today. It has always been that way, and it always will be. Parents are often called upon to make tough decisions regarding discipline, medical or dental care, education, getting involved in their children's relationships, and so on.

II. *Being a parent requires wisdom and savvy.* The mother of Moses didn't just abandon her son; she demonstrated a certain amount of wisdom and savvy in the process. Moses' sister, Miriam, was instructed to stand back at a distance to see what would become of her little brother. The implication is that her mother had given her instructions about what to do should the child be discovered. So when Pharoah's daughter saw the basket, opened it, and found a baby inside, Miriam said she should go find a Hebrew nursemaid to care for it. When Miriam returned with her own mother, the woman showed wisdom and restraint as she agreed to care for the child. She would even be paid wages for it!

Today's parents also need wisdom and savvy. We need wisdom to know when to say "yes" and when to say "no"; when to head for the hospital or try to doctor at home; when to go to the school and talk to the principal or wait it out and see what happens; when to give a little more freedom or tighten up restraints; when to rejoice over a new relationship or friendship or call it to a halt; when a child is really being truthful or testing our powers of observation; when to buy those designer labels and when to go for something less expensive; and what to say when our children come to us with those difficult questions about life.

III. *Being a parent means trusting God's providence.* The mother of Moses must have trusted the providence of God when she placed him in that basket by the river. She again showed her trust in God's providence as she took Moses, once he had grown up, to Pharaoh's daughter and entrusted her own flesh and blood to a stranger's care.

The writer of the book of Exodus rightly saw the events surrounding the life of Moses to be providential. He was born with a destiny, to lead God's people out of Egyptian bondage, and to be the greatest lawgiver the world has ever known. It was providential that Moses was conceived and born. It was providential that Moses grew up in Pharaoh's palace, where he could be educated and made ready for the great tasks that lay before him (Acts 7:22). It was providential that Moses later fled to the wilderness, where he encountered Divinity in a burning bush while tending his father-in-law's sheep. The mother of Moses was a woman of great faith who believed in Yahweh and entrusted her son to divine providence (Heb. 11:23).

There comes a time when all parents have to trust their children to God's providence. As much as we would like to, we cannot always go with our children out into the world. In her diary, Anne Frank wrote, "Parents can only give good advice or put them [their children] on the right paths, but the final forming of a person's character lies in their own hands." There is certainly a lot of truth in that statement. But as Christians we can go further and say that we believe our children's futures are also to some extent in God's hands.

Most Christian parents are quite familiar with praying for their children and entrusting them to God's care and safekeeping. If I have prayed once, I have prayed a hundred times for God to bless my children, to keep them safe from danger and harm, to guard them from trouble and evil. And I am sure that those of you who are parents have done the same. You see, when we present our children for baptism, we are calling upon God to bless them, to be at work in their lives, to guard them from evil and temptation. In baptizing our children, we are claiming the godly providence of God.

Yes, being a parent is no easy thing. But it is a joyous experience, the most rewarding experience life has to offer. For you see, in being parents we have the possibility, we have the potential, we have the opportunity, to raise a wonderful child who can make a mark on the world. Think of how different the world might be had Moses' parents not been the parents of faith they were.

Again, being a parent sometimes means making difficult choices, it always requires wisdom and savvy, and it means trusting our children to the providence and goodness of God. But think of the possibilities!—Randy Hammer

Illustrations

AGAINST THE CULT OF HAPPINESS.   We must defy with our faith the cult of happiness that has no regard for holiness. We must start meaning the prayers we pray in the marriage service, and start translating those devotions into disciplines that witness, that transform and redeem society.—William Fredrick Dunkle Jr.

LIFE *IS* SUCCESS.   When we were in Agra, India, we fell into conversation with an American medical missionary and his wife in the hotel lobby. He had left a successful, lucrative practice in the United States to come to India to take over a hospital.

But he was discouraged and disillusioned! In America he had been a success. Here he seemed a failure. All his efforts to teach sanitation had been ignored, and his attempts to teach Christ had fallen on deaf ears. He felt frustrated and ready to give up. His work didn't seem worthwhile.

His plaint drew the group of us into earnest discussion. And out of it came the realization that it wasn't so much what one did (though, of course, it counted) or how successful one was in terms of tangible results, but it was the quality of the love poured into it—that, as Jesus said, a cup of cold water given in love and compassion was rewardingly effective, because it released that much love to touch the life of the recipient and provided a means for God's spirit to get through and speak. That was what counted!—Clayton E. Williams

SUNDAY: MAY SEVENTEENTH

LECTIONARY MESSAGE

Topic: Joy in the Midst of Sorrow
    TEXT: John 14:23–29
    Other Readings: Acts 16:9–15; Ps. 67; Rev. 21:10; 22–22:5
    Sooner or later everyone experiences sor-

row in life. It may be the loss of a loved one, the fear of what tomorrow holds, or a multitude of other events. But God desires better for his children, even in the most tragic experiences of life.

    I. *Obedient love* (vv. 23–24). Jesus' last night with his disciples before his death was filled with uncertainty and concern. He talked about things the disciples could not or would not accept. He was going to leave them, but he would not leave them as orphans, helpless. He had given them commandments, and the evidence of their professed love for him would be obedience to him. It is easy to talk about love. Especially, we find it easy to talk about loving God and loving Jesus. There seem to be no standards by which we can measure such love. If we are not careful, it can be love in word only. But Jesus reminds us that this cannot be. Love for him requires that we obey him. He goes on to promise that those who show love by obedience have the assurance of the presence of Jesus and the Father: "We will come to them and make our home with them" (v. 23). In the face of the uncertainties that lay before these men, they could rest in the assurance that God would be with them no matter what might come. For those who live in an uncertain world, and that includes all of us, this promise gives hope and confidence. We claim to love God. We claim to love Jesus. We are called to show that love in obedience to his words. And he has promised that if we do this, he will make his home with us. One should not ask for more. We can face the future with assurance because we know he is with us.

II. *The promised Spirit* (vv. 25–26). We find it difficult to believe things we cannot test with our physical senses. Perhaps the early disciples were the same way. Jesus had said he was leaving them. How could he make his home with them if he had gone to the Father? The answer, of course, is that his presence remains in the person of the Holy Spirit, who he promised the Father would send upon them.

Chapters 14 to 16 of this gospel have many references to the coming and work of the Spirit, who is often referred to as another counselor or advocate. The same word is used in 1 John 2:1 to refer to Jesus. The Spirit continues the work that Jesus began during his earthly ministry. Many things are said about the work of the Spirit in this chapter. In these verses, two things are stated. First, the Spirit will teach us all things. He is the great teacher, the interpreter of Jesus' work and words. While we may learn much from others, from study,

and from the reading of books, it is the Spirit who gives us the final truth. Second, that which he teaches is always God's truth and draws us closer to God. The Spirit will also remind us of all that Jesus said. This was of great value to the early disciples as they went about preaching and teaching Jesus to people who had never heard him. The Spirit can work in our lives in the same way, giving us the right words to speak when we are faced with questions from people who are concerned about their relationship to God. In the midst of the trials and uncertainties of life, the promised Spirit is our constant companion, teacher, and guide.

III. *Peace and joy* (vv. 27–29). Jesus knew his followers were troubled. They had not accepted that he would die, even though he had repeatedly taught them he would. They had built up in their minds certain dreams that they thought he would fulfill, but he had not done so. The future was dim. So Jesus promised them peace. This is more than the absence of warfare or strife. Peace speaks of the wholeness of life. It concerns one's relationship to God as well as one's relationship to other people. Jesus promised that peace would characterize his followers of every generation. The world cannot give this peace. It can only come through Jesus. With this peace, one will not be troubled even when difficult times arise. One will not fear even when faced with the dangers of existence in a sinful world. God's Spirit is present.

It was only natural that the disciples would be sorrowful and afraid when Jesus told them that he would leave them and go to the Father. But this should have instead brought joy to their hearts. Love for Jesus should have meant that they could see beyond the present tearful moment and realize that he had completed the task for which the Father had sent him. They should have rejoiced because he had won for them the victory over all the trials that the world could throw against them. Jesus never said that sorrows would not come. But he did say that in the midst of the tears and sorrow there can be joy because he has won the victory over sin and evil. God is in control, and we share the victory with him. If we love him, we will rejoice even in the darkest hours of life.—Clayton Harrop

Illustrations

JOY AND SORROW.   I do not remember the details of many funerals. But one is vivid in my mind. The man had been a faithful pastor, professor, and administrator. He was deeply loved by family and friends. The funeral was a celebration. The songs were uplifting, the prayers were encouraging, and the speakers expressed joy. Yes, there was, and should have been, sorrow, but in the midst of this there was deep joy because the loved one had lived faithfully and was now at home with the Lord. A few years ago, the church of which I was a member was forced to disband. The members were sorry that this had to take place. But there was also joy. Money from the sale of the property was made available for mission work around the world. God took the tragedy of the moment to bring joy to multitudes of people.—C.H.

THE COIN WE PAY.   Egocentricity always defeats happiness. That is why Kunkel makes so much of the suffering which is necessary to overcome egocentricity as a prelude to happiness. From *yes* through *no* to *in spite of* is a thorny and tortuous path for most people. But the suffering by which we learn is the simple coin we pay for joy; we should never know happiness had we not the capacity for unhappiness, and our spirits could not know joy had they not been sensitized by suffering.—Rollo May[4]

SERMON SUGGESTIONS

Topic: Living Hopefully
    TEXT: Jer. 32
    (1) If we live hopefully in these times, our faith must be in Almighty God. (2) If we have unshaken confidence that God's gracious purpose for his people will win out, our faith will kindle faith in the hearts of others. (3) If we can experience a faith so radiant that the lives of others about us can be illuminated, we ought to find small ways, as well as perhaps great ways, to express that transforming faith.

[4]*Springs of Creative Living.*

Topic: The Transformed Life
    TEXT: Rom. 12:1–2
    (1) There are strong pressures upon us to conform to the world about us. (2) Superior strength is available to overcome temptations to harmful conformity.

Hymn Suggestions: Easter Six

1. "God of Mercy, God of Grace," Henry F. Lyte (1834); "Dix," Conrad Kocher (1838)
    Lyle's paraphrase of Psalm 67 could well by sung in place of the Psalter reading of the day. The Dix tune also makes it suitable for antiphonal singing.
2. "Come Down, O Love Divine," Bianco da Siena (c. 1420), translated by R. F. Littledale (1867); "Down Ampney," R. V. Williams (1906)
    This fifteenth-century Italian hymn gathers up the spirit of the gospel lesson, especially John 14:23. The hymn tune by R. V. Williams fits appropriately the introspective character of the text.
3. "O Holy City, Seen of John," Walter Russell Bowie (1909); "Morning Song," Wyeth's Repository of Sacred Music, Part Second (1913)
    The underlying imagery of this twentieth-century hymn comes from the apostle John's vision of the Holy City on the isle of Patmos (Rev. 21–22). But against the idealism of that heavenly city is pitted the realism of earthly cities where lust and greed prevail. So the hymn in its latter stanzas becomes both a challenge and a prayer for strength to build the city of love and brotherhood.
4. "Send the Light," Charles H. Gabriel (1890); "McCabe," Gabriel (1890)
    Gabriel's gospel song was inspired by the story of the apostle Paul's vision of the Macedonian call in Acts 16. It can be used as a suitable response to the New Testament reading for this day.—Hugh T. McElrath

Worship Aids

CALL TO WORSHIP.   "O come, let us sing unto the Lord: let us make a joyful noise to the rock of our salvation. Let us come before his presence with thanksgiving, and make a joyful noise unto him with psalms" (Ps. 95:1–2).

INVOCATION.   How can anyone appear before you, O God, except in the spirit of praise and thanksgiving? Your mercies have been ever of old, and your grace is present in the breath and heartbeat of this moment.

For the privilege of being among your people and sharing the heritage of the faith and celebrating your livingness in the gift of this new day, we are thankful.

For your Word present in the beginning, creating all that is, we praise you. For your Word present in these latter days in Jesus of Nazareth, leading us to know you as heavenly present and our true destiny as your children, we are grateful.

Lost in wonder, love, and praise, we worship and adore you.—John Thompson

OFFERTORY SENTENCE.   "Let love be genuine; hate what is evil, hold fast to what is good; love one another with mutual affection; outdo one another in showing honor. Do not lag in zeal, be ardent in spirit, serve the Lord. Rejoice in hope, be patient in suffering, persevere in prayer. Contribute to the needs of the saints; extend hospitality to strangers" (Rom. 12:9–13 NRSV).

OFFERTORY PRAYER.   In these moments, O God, re-call us to mission. As the Church, once again, may we hear the Master's commissioning: you are the salt of the earth; you are the light of the world. In response to your abounding grace may our giving be generous and joyous. Through your love, translate the gifts that we bring, that they may become the bread and the Bread of Life for those near and those far. Through him who said: the field is the world.—John Thompson

PRAYER.   Ours is just a simple prayer, Father. The vast complications of the world befuddle us, and while we know they are there, we just can't seem to get a personal handle on them so we can talk to you about all the complicated issues of the times. Maybe the best thing we can do is tell you that we realize they are there and then leave them in hands bigger than ours, hands like yours, which are so capable of managing the circumstances and events we do not understand. So that is what we do in all good faith this morning and turn our expression to you toward the things we can feel and see and experience in a personal way that matters deeply to us.

We understand sickness, Father. It has happened to almost all of us. We know about the fear that some sickness brings because there are no cures for it. We know about the pain that accompanies disease. We know about the terror that comes with the whispered announcements like "The baby won't live" or "The tests are positive, it is cancer." Help us to manage the sickness of others as well as our own. We need your steadying presence in our sickrooms, Father, and we invite you to be the ever-present physician for us in our struggles with illness.

We understand loss, too, Father. Death, divorce, job failure, business setback, children not measuring up. We know about those things. But we need help in managing them. Our wisdom isn't enough because our feelings rule in these areas too often and we need a wiser, steadying, and hopeful presence. We need you, Father, when loss hits hard and we don't know how to handle it. Be the sustaining friend for us when loss is hard on life, we pray.

We understand happiness, too, Father. And there are many things that bring it to us. First love, newborn children, opportunities in work, joy in others. Giver of every good and perfect gift, teach us how to celebrate happiness so that we glorify you even as we make the happy moments cameos to which we return again for renewed joy. Be the present celebrant in our happiness as we worship now in Jesus name.—Henry Fields

Sermon: "It Is Too Good Not to Be True"
TEXT: Gen. 18:9–15; Rom. 5:1–8

The passage that has been read from the New Testament is one of the great portions of Christian Scripture. So I walked with that passage this week. Wherever I went, it went. I thought about what it says to us. But my journey took a very sudden turn. It was Thursday and I had a call from the hospital from parents whose teenage daughter had died. When a young person dies, no matter who we are, even if we don't know that person or that family, there is something that catches us up short. That experience made me think of many others in this congregation: those who are battling life-threatening illnesses, those who are going through dark and difficult days. I was reminded that we do not have a lock on tomorrow, no matter what our circumstance. We either deny that or find some way to deal with it.

I. Then I went again to this Scripture, and I saw not an answer to those specific whys, an answer that we will never know: why this person, why this time, why this illness, why this accident? But what we are thrown on again is the mercy of God and the desire for "How?" How do we get through this? How do we go out into a world that has these kinds of difficulties, surprises, and turns in the road? How?

a. You know, I have been in and out of the cancer center so many times I didn't notice that right there at the entrance are two big banners. They read: "Celebrate Life." In the midst of life, we deal with death. But there must be a greater message, a greater hope, that in the midst of death there is life. And I believe that is the great theme of this passage of Scripture in Romans 5.

b. Indeed, as I thought about it some more, I realized how this congregation has helped me. There is a song that we sing that has become the signature of this congregation. That little song that talks about "Go now in peace, in faith, in love" has made a difference to us. Even if the sermon is a real yawner that Sunday, going out with those simple but profound words, "Go now in peace, and faith, and love" has made a difference. This has taken me back to this passage, because these are the great themes of Romans 5.

II. If you will look above Romans 5:1, you will hear that Jesus' death and resurrection happened so that we might be justified to God. *Justified* means to be set right. The outcome is described in the beginning of chapter 5: "that we have peace with God." Peace. The word *justified* shows up in verse 10 as "reconciled." Don't we live in a world that needs to be reconciled? You can hear the news and know the violence and turmoil that come from not being reconciled to one another and to God. In verse 11, that same word shows up and can be translated as "atonement," at-one-ment with God.

a. Someone has said, "Blessed are the peacemakers for they will never run out of work." But woe to us if we try to be peacemakers and have not received the peace of God. Our political ideology will run out. Our altruism will run out. What we need is the deep-down peace that comes from God's reconciliation through Jesus Christ.

b. We also sing "Go now in faith." Paul is very clear in this passage that the peace that comes to us is not something that we earn or manufacture. It is based on the grace of God. We do not know the future, but we know who holds the future. Put your hand in the hand of the one who is better than a known way and better than a lighted path. That is faith not in ourselves but as verse 1 says, in our Lord Jesus Christ.

c. We are to go from this place in love. That is the culmination of all that Paul is saying here. The word *love* can be used in so many ways. Here in Romans 5 it says that God poured his love on us so that while we were yet sinners Christ died for us. That's the kind of love we are talking about. It is the love that moves to us before we have things straightened up.

III. Sarah, in the Old Testament Scripture, laughed because she couldn't believe that God would be that good to her. Later, it was a laugh of recognition. It is too good not to be true! God gives us peace and faith. God gives us love so that we may be instruments of peace, faith, and love. Go now in peace. Go now in faith. Go now in love.— Gary D. Stratman

Illustrations

WAYS BEYOND WORDS. I sat with a family overwhelmed with grief. They spoke of how people had responded in so many loving ways, and so many of those ways go beyond words. This brought to mind my mother when I was a teenager. I couldn't understand why she did silly, simple things like baking a loaf of bread in a coffee can, taking the bread out, putting a bow on it, and delivering it to a family who had a lost loved one. Often not saying a thing, she would hug the person, give the bread, and go. It is only now that I realize there are some times when words cannot come, and should not come. —G.D.S.

ON THE JOURNEY. So, says the psalmist, let me tell you about the valley of the shadow of death, when God is present:

There, on the journey, we are comforted by God's protective rod and staff, instruments of guidance. We are not on our own, but guided—guided by God's presence and God's Torah, safe from all that would rob us of life.

There, on the journey, we thought there were no resources, but in the very presence of need, fear, and hunger, God sets a table of generous food. It is like coming around the corner of deep threat, and there in the middle of the road is a lavish table of marvelous food, water from the rock, bread from heaven.

There, on the journey, where we thought there was only scarcity, the God of generosity pours out precious oil on our heads, into our cup. Our lives brim over because of God's inexplicable generosity, just when we thought God had no gifts to give.

The journey, with the power and purpose of God, changes the circumstances in which we live. Wilderness becomes home, isolation becomes companionship, scarcity becomes generosity.—Walter Brueggeman[5]

SUNDAY: MAY TWENTY-FOURTH

LECTIONARY MESSAGE

Topic: Truth Has Many Faces
TEXT: John 17:20–26
Other Readings: Acts 16:16–34; Ps. 22:12–14; Rev. 22:12–14, 16–17, 20–21

I. *Truth sets you apart.* In verse 17, Jesus indicated that truth has its origin in sanctification. The Greek word behind sanctify means "set apart for a special purpose." Jesus prayed in the great high priestly prayer that those who are his would be sanctified to truth. Truth must be the goal of the believer's constitution. Truth must be the goal of our lives.

Truth never exists in a vacuum. It must be the key element in the midst of a busy life. Jesus came into the world to bring truth. We can be as sure of that truth as any facts of life. We accept certain facts of the scientific world and do not even question them because they are scientific truth. Jesus taught spiritual truth about God, which also is just as certain. Truth demands a dedication of life and commitment. We usually think of sanctification as involving the world of holiness. Jesus placed it right in the middle of the world of truth. You cannot really achieve the goal that God has for your life unless you make truth the center of your life.

Some think that truth cannot exist in our present evil world. In the din of lies one cannot even hear the truth. Jesus told us the opposite words: truth is the most powerful force in our present world. The people around us cannot always comprehend it. Believers must, however, dedicate themselves to it. No other choice lies before us.

II. *Truth brings unity.* People sanctified in truth achieve a unity of purpose. One of the main focuses of Jesus' prayer was for the unity of his people. The basis of Christian unity is the model of Christ and his Father. They were one. Jesus' followers should also be one. Christianity today is splintered into many groups and churches. Jesus indicated that the unity for which he prayed would be achieved in spirit and in deed. Super organizations do not necessarily promote unity. Christians who see the essence of unity in the savior find the longed-for unity. Christians need to learn to work with and not against each other. Christ demonstrated the kind of love for one another that is needed. The unity of the faith binds believers into a band presenting the truth of God.

We live in a world with so much sham. It is difficult to see truth as the cement that brings believers together around a common truth. Persons cannot be accepted on their word any longer. False claims and promises are made every day. Many Christians find it very hard to accept the truth of the Lord and the unity that it brings among his followers.

III. *Truth: a face-to-face encounter.* Those who devote their lives to the truth of Christ will be with him in eternity. Jesus desired a permanent relationship with his disciples. Truth has an eternal aspect. Truth unites us with our Lord, and this relationship will be eternal. We will be with Christ. In him we see the very face of God and see it filled with love and truth. We discover that when we meet

[5] *The Threat of Life.*

Christ we see the very face of God. The ministry of Jesus becomes very important. He spent his brief time on earth telling us about the Father. Truth was the most important mission of our Lord. Many people rejected his truth and sought the way of lies. The gospel writer John uses great themes, such as light and darkness, to present the ministry of Jesus.

The Synoptic writers tell the life of Jesus by relation events. John introduces his gospel with a hymn to the Logos. The themes introduced in the hymn, like themes in a great symphony, are taken up later in his gospel to paint the face of Jesus. Truth is one of these great themes. We have the story of the important events in the ministry of Jesus, but we also have the paint brush of the great themes to define Jesus. "The truth shall make you free" (John 8:32). That theme, like an aria, echoes through the Gospel of John.—James L. Blevins

Illustrations

SHAM.   An Indian woman who lived on a reservation out west walked one day into the nearby town and stalked into the local beauty parlor. The lady in charge said, "May I help you today?"

"Yes," the Indian woman said, "I would like a real-poo!"

"You mean shampoo, don't you?" the proprietor said.

"No," the Indian woman said angrily, "I have had enough sham on this reservation to last me a while."—J.L.B.

TRUTH SPELLED OUT.   I went to my Greek class to give a final exam. I entered the room and found no one. I thought I was becoming the absentminded professor. Suddenly the doors of the classroom swung open and my class of thirty students came striding into the room. They were carrying a large cake. I knew it was not my birthday. They set the cake on my desk. I looked down at the cake. Written in beautifully lettered Greek was the term *eleos*, "mercy." I sat and ate the cake while the class took the Greek exam. Sometimes truth has to be spelled out before it can register in our hearts.—J.L.B.

SERMON SUGGESTIONS

Topic: From Gloom to Glory

TEXT: Isa. 6:1–7; 1 John 1:9

How do we explain a life of surpassing usefulness to God and humankind—Isaiah's actual experience and our potential experience?

(1) Isaiah was shaken by catastrophe: his familiar world had collapsed. When some great crisis comes, we may find ourselves where Isaiah was. (2) Isaiah was further shaken by meeting God face to face: now the seeking Isaiah was confronted by a seeking God. The mighty One who "plants his footprints in the sea and rides upon the storm" comes not to destroy but to redeem. (3) The sight of God led Isaiah to confess his sinfulness: he acknowledged his own sin and the sin of the community for which he shared responsibility. When God enters our lives it is with a dual purpose: "to forgive us our sins, and to cleanse us from all unrighteousness."

Topic: Beyond Suffering

TEXT: 1 Pet. 5:10

(1) Beyond suffering is wholeness: "God will restore you." (2) Beyond suffering is maturity of faith: "God will establish you." (3) Beyond suffering is spiritual power: "God will strengthen you."

Hymn Suggestions: Easter Seven

1. "Sing Praise to God Who Reigns Above," Johann J. Schutz (1675); "Mit Freuden Zart," Bohemian Brethren's Kirchengesange (1566)

Coming from the strong singing tradition of the Bohemian Brethren, this hymn carries the spirit of Psalm 97 with its assertions that God reigns (stanzas 1 and 2) and that every idol is to be cast out (stanza 4). It lends itself to antiphonal singing, with the whole congregation joining together on the rousing refrain: "To God all praise and glory!"

2. "Christ Is the World's True Light," George W. Briggs (1931); "Darmstadt," Ahasueus Fritsch (1679)

This hymn takes its initial inspiration from Rev. 22:16, with its proclamation that Christ is the bright and morning star. It then resolves into a prayer that Christ will bring racial harmony, healing, and peace to the world. In its third-stanza plea for Christian unity, it also echoes Jesus' prayer that all his followers may be one (John 17:20–26).

3. "And Can It Be That I Should Gain," Charles Wesley (1739); "Sagina," Thomas Campbell (1835)

Wesley, the great humanist, draws upon the Philippian jail deliverance of Paul and Silas as a metaphor for his own deliverance from the prison house of sin in this testimony to God's amazing love.

4. There are several fine hymns that incorporate the claim of Christ to be the alpha and the omega (Rev. 22:13), including the following:

- "Of the Father's Love Begotten," Marcus A. C. Prudentius (fifth century), translated by John M. Neale (1854)
- "Love Divine, All Loves Excelling," Charles Wesley (1747); "Beecher," John Zundel (1870)—Hugh T. McElrath

Worship Aids

CALL TO WORSHIP.   "Lord, thou hast been our dwelling place in all generations. Before the mountains were brought forth, or ever thou hadst formed the earth and the world, even from everlasting to everlasting, thou art God" (Ps. 90:1–2).

INVOCATION.   You are always there, here, and everywhere, O Lord, and we would seek to find you and be found by you here today in worship and wherever we are, always.

OFFERTORY SENTENCE.   "Why do you pass judgment on your brother or sister? Or you, why do you despise your brother or sister? For we will all stand before the judgment seat of God. For it is written, 'As I live, says the Lord, every knee shall bow to me and every tongue shall give praise to God.' So then, each of us will be accountable to God" (Rom. 14:10–12 NRSV).

OFFERTORY PRAYER.   Help us even now, O God, to be truthful about our stewardship and not measure ourselves by others. You know our abilities and our limitations: you are the God of truth. Even now we can rejoice in your love and forgiveness and so order our total life in terms of truth.

PRAYER.   How can we appear before you, O God, except in awe-full reverence, for you are the great God and the great King above all gods. You break the spear asunder and cause war to cease to the ends of the earth.

In this holy place we would worship you in the beauty of holiness, but who among us is not haunted by scenes of the tragic, perplexed by the brokenness in us and in the world, and plagued by our own doubts and fears?

We confess our need for a renewed vision of your grace and glory, to see you high and lifted up, King Eternal, to sense your presence in all of life—in the darkness as well as the light.

In the light of your Word, so faithfully proclaimed, may we see light.

Help us to see, O God, how we neglect those things that make for peace, when we are not evenhanded in our foreign policy but prejudicial in seeking our own national interest, when we isolate rather than seek to engage in dialogue, when we parade our power rather than lifting up the weak.

May many bridges be built along the highway of international understanding so that in the spirit of sisterhood and brotherhood we may live on this fantastic planet as the one family you have created us to be.

Grant us the faith, O God, to believe in our better moments, in spite of all that contradicts them.—John Thompson

Sermon: My Cup Runneth Over
TEXT: Ps. 23

Next to the Lord's Prayer, the twenty-third Psalm is probably the best-known passage in the Bible. It is a stream of clear waters, but they run deep. One never really drinks of those living waters that spring up into everlasting life until one draws a drink from the depths of this well. Where can the hot, weary traveler find refreshment for his parched throat and renewal for his lagging spirit like at this oasis? Where can one starting out on life's journey discover the assurance of adequate resources for the way as in the promise of this psalm?

I. It begins: "The Lord is my shepherd, I shall not want."

a. To appreciate the meaning of this initial affirmation, one needs to understand that Eastern shepherds often house their flocks in a common fold at night. In the morning, at the voice of a particular shepherd you can see the sheep here and there nose their way through the others toward the gate. No sheep of another flock moves. Each knows its shepherd, and it will follow him and no other. When a person says, "The Lord is *my* shepherd," he can be confident that he "shall not want."

b. As the Bible witnesses in many different contexts, to have God is to have all. And the converse of this is equally true: you can have everything else and, not having God, have nothing. It is in having him that our deepest needs are satisfied. The God-led man is not more secure materially, for he does not move through life under skies that are always sunny; but he knows who he is.

In this conclusive affirmation, "I shall not want," everything depends on what we mean by "I." If we mean the real self, the enduring self, the words stand. One who has arrived at such a self-understanding and trusts in the Good Shepherd can say meaningfully, *"I shall not want!"*

II. The rest of this psalm is actually an amplification of the first verse. The second stanza explains why we do not want when the Lord is our shepherd. "He leads me in the green pastures and beside the still waters."

a. I do not believe that I am overdrawing the portrait of the "still waters" by describing them as a symbol of the peace that God gives. His peace is one of the greatest resources of life. Who has not experienced God's tranquility in following some stream until it becomes a quiet pool under the shade of an overhanging oak or willow? Such a resting place is not only for our bodies; it is for our minds and spirits as well. This line of thinking will be helpful even if it only reminds us of our need to seek quiet in this noise-rocked world.

b. Have you contemplated the meaning of the next line: "He restores my soul"? The feeding in the green pasture, the drinking at the quiet pools, and the rest in the shade of some oak are not ends in themselves; they have the purpose of renewing us as persons so that we may resume our pilgrimage. It is not to salve our conscience for another week, nor is it to fulfill our religious duty for one more day; surely we congregate to celebrate the wholeness of life.

c. "He leads me in the paths of righteousness for his name's sake." God, as the shepherd of our lives, leads us in the way where there is life. He does not lead us down a dead-end street or lose us on a detour; his paths are direct and righteous altogether.

d. "He leads me in the paths of righteousness for his name's sake." This is the assurance that God is not going to betray himself. It is in keeping with his name—the Holy One; he is God and there is none other. We do not make these paths right; they are right because they are so ordained from the very beginning.

III. This psalm may have endured the wear and tear of the centuries merely to preserve the fourth stanza: "Yea, though I walk through the valley of the shadow of death, I will fear no evil; for thou art with me. Thy rod and thy staff, they comfort me."

a. "I will fear no evil." Why? "For *thou* art with me"! The divine companionship is not limited; even in the valley of death we can count on the presence of the living God. Where he is, there is love; therefore we need not fear. Life and death both are kept in his hands.

We pass *through* the valley of the shadow of death. But are there not those who try to avoid it—to detour around it—by denying its reality? We try to camouflage it with pretty flowers. We try not to talk about it. But God's love and grace are experienced not in denying death's reality but even in the very presence of it.

b. He does not leave us there; instead, he leads us through. Life goes on. Sometimes, perhaps, it would seem easier if it didn't. How can *we* go on? Because he is with us. "I will not leave you without strength."

IV. This strengthening—this encouragement—of the eternal God who is the Shepherd of our lives is expressed in the final phrase of this amazing fourth stanza: "Thy rod and thy staff, they comfort me." They comfort, for they are *his* rod and *his* staff.

a. "Thou preparest a table before me in the presence of my enemies." With this verse, the scene changes. The psalmist now uses the metaphor of the host to express the graciousness and the hospitality of the eternal Father. That a table would be spread in the presence of our friends, we might expect; but that one is made ready in the face of our enemies, we experience the ultimate graciousness of our divine host.

b. "Thou anointest my head with oil." Such an anointing indicates sonship. This is our heritage. "Now are we the sons of God," exclaims a New Testament writer, "and it does not yet appear what we shall be."

c. This amazing psalm rises to a climax in the joyous outcry of thanksgiving: "My cup runneth over." Our host does not hand us a cup that is full, but one that is running over. When the writer of the fourth gospel describes Jesus' mission in terms of the Good Shepherd, he records: "I have come that men may have life, and have it in all its fullness." This abundant life is symbolized in the cup that is running over.

d. "Surely goodness and mercy shall follow me all the days of my life, and I will dwell in the house of the Lord forever," the Psalm concludes. Here it appears that the images of shepherd and host are blended. "Surely goodness and mercy shall follow me all the days of my life" suggests continued shepherding. "To dwell in the house of the Lord forever" promises the everlasting hospitality of the divine host.

Goodness and mercy are not something that we can strive for or earn; they come to us as gifts. David was right when, in another context, he assured: "For as the heaven is high above the earth; so, great is his mercy toward them that fear him." How high is heaven? Without limit! So is God's love!

To appreciate the grace-full-ness of life is the beginning of a relationship in which we know God as shepherd and as divine host. We need not wait on God's goodness and mercy, for they are not in some far-off place; they are right here.

Is life gracious to you? Do you find a cup that is not only full but running over? Do you experience goodness and mercy following you all your days? Are you determined to make your home in the household of God? Do you *know* the shepherd?—John Thompson

Illustrations

"ALL I WANT!"   One Sunday, an eight-year-old girl was learning the twenty-third psalm in her church school class. Instead of the right words, she said: "The Lord is my shepherd, That's *all* I want." Although she got the words wrong, she caught the real meaning. Are there not those among us who are so anxious about the gifts of God that we miss God himself?—J.T.

THE HOUSE OF THE LORD.   A friend of mine described his experience in walking to work one morning recently: "The air is so refreshing; when I go to work at six o'clock each morning, it has a special crispness about it. The mockingbirds serenade me along the way. The variety of Florida flowers in bloom is thrilling. I am so grateful that my senses are awake to this amazing wonder and glory of life." As I talked with this friend, I knew the Lord was his shepherd. He finds his home in the household of God.—J.T.

SUNDAY: MAY THIRTY-FIRST

LECTIONARY MESSAGE

Topic: Christian Memories
TEXT: John 14:8–17, 25–27
Other Readings: Acts 2:1–21 or Gen. 11:1–9; Ps. 104:24–34, 35b; Rom. 8:14–17

I. *Memories can be dull.* Believers do not always have sharp memories. Philip, one of the twelve disciples, did not remember well. Jesus had told him along with the other twelve that he and the Father were one. Jesus was almost exasperated that Philip did not know that truth, for he had asked Jesus to show him the Father. Jesus asked him, "Have

I been with you so long and you still don't know the answer to that question?" It is interesting that persons can hear the truth but *not* hear it. Philip had been with Jesus for some months and had heard the truth on many occasions. Yet he did not perceive the truth. He had forgotten the truth if he had learned it. Many teachers despair when they spend hours teaching students only to hear the same question asked again. They want to scream out, "Don't you ever learn?"

Memories can easily become dull. After the crucifixion, the disciples were in despair because their spiritual leader had been killed.

They had trouble remembering Jesus' words that he would be resurrected. The resurrection appearances of Jesus came as quite a shock. If they had listened, the empty tomb on that first Easter morn would not have been so surprising. Teachers constantly have to hold review sessions in the midst of lesson plans. Jesus indicated that his disciples would need to have their memories awakened.

II. *The Holy Spirit awakened memories.* In verse 26, Jesus indicated that one of the duties of the Paraclete, or Holy Spirit, was to bring to remembrance "all that I said to you." Comfort comes to the Christian from knowing the will of the Father. That is why services of renewal have been important to Christian congregations. Each new generation is confronted with the word of God in a vital dynamic way. We read about the great awakening movements in British history and early American life. God continues to use his Spirit to refresh spiritual hearts. Each new generation provides a fresh occasion to enliven the spirit of believers. The Church needs to be reminded of the reason for its existence. The words of our Lord have to remain powerful and active in the lives of people.

The exciting thing about the Christian faith is that it is just as real and exciting now as it was two thousand years ago. God raises up women and men in each generation to herald the truth of Christ. Someone has said that we are always just one generation away from the demise of Christianity. If one generation failed to pass on the faith, there would be no faith in Christ anymore.

The word *paraclete* in Greek comes from a root meaning "to call by to render aid." In the great Gospel of John, Jesus makes five statements about the Paraclete. The activity of "jogging our memory" is just one of the Paraclete's very important activities. Looking at Philip's question gives all of today's believers some reason to hope. Someone who walked with Jesus had difficulty in perceiving Jesus' ministry. We are grateful that God gave the Paraclete to keep in front of our memories the demanding words of Jesus. We are happy that no generation will go by without being reminded of Jesus' basic message.

III. *Memories that call to obedience.* Each time the memory of Christ is evoked by the Paraclete, one hears a summons to radical obedience. "If you love me, you will keep my commandments," Jesus said. A test of faith always involves action. I am so happy that the book of James is in our Christian canon. One can talk forever about problems in a church and never do anything about them. Many people in our modern society like to talk about religion or theology. Few want to hear the challenge to concrete action. Jesus always talked in blunt terms. "Let the dead bury the dead," he would say. "Don't put your hand to the plow and then turn back." He always discouraged people from running up to him in a fit of excitement wanting to be his disciple. He always reminded them of the cost of discipleship. He was not afraid to tell the rich that it is as difficult for them to get into the Kingdom as for a camel to go through the eye of a needle.

He always stressed the difficulties of the way into the Kingdom. The path leading into the Kingdom is always cross-shaped. One has to suffer and live a life of denial. Jesus did not preach a message of grow rich and drive a big car because one is true to Jesus. Radical obedience demands that we put others first. We must show the love of Jesus, even as he loved us and gave up his life for us. In the modern world it is too easy to join a church. All you need to do is get your name on the membership list. Sometimes no expectations or obligations are stressed. In some places it is easier to join a church than a social organization or lodge. True Christian memories bring to mind a harsher demand left to his disciples by Christ.—James L. Blevins

Illustrations

DISCUSSION, NOT ACTION. A church had set aside an evening for the discussion of its budget for the next year. Open discussion took place about the individual items of the yearly budget. Some noticed that the amount for local missions in the community had been lowered. Much argument ensued. Finally an old man in the back row arose and said to the young man discussing the point, "Young man, don't you know that we come to this church to talk about our problems, not to do anything about them?"—J.L.B.

A TEACHER WHO REMINDS US. The gospels make it clear to us that the disciples often did not understand what Jesus was saying or doing. They were people of little faith, yes, but they also did not have the proper perspective to be able to grasp the significance of all that was unfolding before their very eyes. Only after the Resurrection could they put the pieces of Jesus' teaching and acts together and make sense of it all. This is reflected in Jesus' words in the fourth gospel: "I have said these things to you while I am still with you. But the Advocate, the Holy Spirit, whom the Father will send in my name, will teach you everything, and remind you of all that I have said to you" (John 14:25–26 NRSV).—James W. Cox

SERMON SUGGESTIONS

Topic: "A Call for Volunteers"
TEXT: Isa. 6:8
(1) The divine call: it comes to those with spiritual qualifications, though they may be conscious of personal shortcomings and unworthiness; it comes ordinarily in a quiet manner, though sometimes with dramatic features. (2) The human response: when God's call is sure, we ought to ask God no questions, though we will ask questions; when God's call is sure, our response should be immediate; when God's call is sure, the opportunity of special service should be considered a privilege.

Topic: Winning God's Favor
TEXT: Eph. 2:8–10
(1) We may try the way of good works: it is a popular way; it is a way of frustration; it is the wrong way (Gal. 2:21). (2) We may try the way of presumption: that God expects a little; that because God is merciful we can forget about our sins; or that the rules don't apply to us. (3) However, the right way is the way of grace with works: it takes into account all the facts; it pays God the highest honor; it has the highest motivation; it is really the means of our fulfilling the divine purpose.

Hymn Suggestions: Pentecost

1. "Come, Holy Spirit, Heavenly Dove," Isaac Watts (1707); "St. Agnes," John B. Dykes (1866)
This classic hymn by the "Father of English Hymnody" is an invocation for the coming of God's spirit to inspire and enable genuine worship. It would be excellent as a call to worship.
2. "Holy Spirit, Light Divine," Andrew Reed (1817); "Mercy," Louis M. Gottschalk (c. 1888)
Focusing attention on the work of the Holy Spirit, this hymn's four stanzas itemize that work as "light shining," "power cleansing," "joy cheering," and "divine dwelling." It could well be sung either preceding or following any of the readings of the day.
3. "Wind Who Makes All Winds That Blow," Thomas H. Troeger (1983); "Aberystwyth," Joseph Parry (1879)
Based on the Pentecostal event in Acts 2, this splendid contemporary hymn is a mind-stretching petition for the powerful visitation of the Spirit on today's church. Employing the metaphors of wind and flame, the author has given contemporary worshipers a finely-wrought meditation on the Holy Spirit's work.
4. "Like the Murmur of the Dove's Song," Carl P. Daw, Jr. (1982); "Bridegroom," Peter Cutts (1969)
This recently written hymn could appropriately accompany the gospel reading of the day with its message that the Spirit of God, the Counselor, brings a sense of peace. The first stanza imaginatively reflects on the *how* of the Spirit's coming—as a dove cooing; the second stanza contemplates the *where* of the Spirit's coming—to the whole church; and the final stanza dwells on the *why* of the Spirit's coming—for prayerful reconciliation, divine power, and quiet peace.—Hugh T. McElrath

Worship Aids

CALL TO WORSHIP.   "I will sing of the mercies of the Lord forever: with my mouth will I make known thy faithfulness to all generations" (Ps. 89:1).

INVOCATION.   Eternal Father, before whom generations rise and generations fall, we consciously pause in your presence this morning, seeking strength, guidance, and grace. We do not ask that you come to us. Rather, we seek your Spirit's power as that Spirit comes to people of faith.—Henry Fields

OFFERTORY SENTENCE.   "Our first duty is to be faithful to the one we work for" (1 Cor. 4:2 CEV).

OFFERTORY PRAYER. May these gifts exemplify our steadfastness in following Christ, our determination to serve him, and our loyalty to good stewardship.—H.F.

PRAYER. O God, how often your words call us to remember. As you spoke of old through Moses to his generation, so you speak to every generation: "Beware that you forget not the Lord your God." May we not neglect the call of this Memorial Day Sunday: "Remember! Remember! Remember!"

> Lord, thou hast been our dwelling place in all generations,
> Before the mountains were brought forth,
> Or ever thou hadst formed the earth and the world,
> From everlasting to everlasting thou art God.

Often we think that hope comes from looking to the future, but actually the springs of hope are in the past. There are memories we need to keep green. Memory can give perspective for the present and direction for the future. The past is prologue. "Surely goodness and mercy shall follow us all the days of our lives." From your faithfulness in the past we can take hope for our every tomorrow. Help us to comprehend that only as one cherishes great memories will one be able to entertain great hopes.

May we not forget from whence we have come, lest we forget who we are. In the beginning you created the heavens and the earth. You took dust from the ground and fashioned us in your image and breathed into our nostrils the breath of life. In the fullness of time you sent forth your only Son. We are indeed children of grace—sons and daughters of your amazing grace. May we not forget the givenness of life: "We have brought nothing into this world and it is certain that we shall carry nothing out."

The intimations of your abounding grace are everywhere: in the first cry of birth, in every breath we draw, in each heartbeat, in the last gasp for breath in death. There are memories we need to keep green: your goodness to us and to all people, your mighty deeds through your people Israel, the fullness of your grace in Christ.

In keeping memories green, let us remember, too, those who have lived and died for us—some who have sacrificed supremely—that their living and their dying may not have been in vain, and that their fondest hopes and cherished dreams may not be neglected in the agenda of our living and dying.

You who watched over the destiny of men and of nations, we pray that our leaders may have the memory and wisdom to heed the lessons of history, lest we but repeat the mistakes of the past. We pray for our president and all world leaders, that they fail not the dreams and hopes of the human family for peace and life for all.—John Thompson

Sermon: Do You Know How to Really Enjoy God?

TEXT: John 15:11

Anyone who reads the New Testament will discover that Jesus didn't mind at all being with prostitutes and other "left out" people. The publicans and sinners loved him precisely because he didn't seem to be embarrassed by them. The lepers of society—the "pushed out people"—loved him because he would sit down and eat and drink with them. He didn't even mind touching them. It's true that the pious couldn't relate to him and his crowd, but all the lonely people who usually didn't get invited to big dinner parties or to birthday parties took to him with wonderful excitement.

It seems to me that one of the rarest species of living creatures on the face of the earth may soon become extinct without anyone even noticing. I'm talking about those few human beings who have learned how to really enjoy God and his grace, who have learned how to enjoy life and every twenty-four hours they are given, people who really know how to spread their joy around!

You and I were created for joy, you know. It's our destiny! If we miss it, we miss the whole reason for our existence. But even more than that, the reason Jesus lived and died was to give us back the joy taken from us by our sin and separation from God. That's what he told us in the text.

So why do we have such a ridiculously hard time doing the very thing for which we were created and redeemed? What do we think is wrong with wanting to enjoy life a little? Why is it that every once in a while we meet a Christian who feels that it would betray his or her calling to ever enjoy anything—including

God? What's our problem? I want to help you discover joy by helping you define this dimension of new life in Jesus Christ, and then I want to help you identify some of the things that keep us from it.

I. So, what is this joy that Jesus came to give us? At the outset you need to understand that it is a misconception to conclude that a Christian is supposed to be happy and smiling all the time. Christian joy is not gushiness, mushiness, or jolliness in spite of the circumstances and conditions under which you or others are living. Some argue rather forcefully that joy is hardly ever appropriate for Christians in the kind of world in which we live. With so much pain and suffering, and so many tragic and harmful consequences of sin, with so much work for the Christian yet to do, how could a serious and sensitive Christian even think about joy? But joy is not a false, phony, naive, and blind cheerleader kind of excitement toward life. In fact, the New Testament teaches that the real test of joy's integrity is its compatibility with pain and tragedy.

The writer of Hebrews described our Lord as one "who for the joy set before him endured the cross" (12:2). The fact is, the closer Jesus drew toward his own painful suffering, the more he talked with his disciples about joy. And that attitude reproduces itself in his followers. The New Testament is full of it. The more the apostles Peter, James, and Paul suffered, the more their letters focused upon joy. Joy was their choice!

Joy is not in spite of painful and tragic circumstances; it is instead the confidence that pain and tragedy will not have the last word. Joy is the confidence that no matter what happens, this is still my Father's world. When you come down to it, joy is a feeling that everything will be all right with us and with our world, even when everything seems wrong, simply because God is still on his throne!

II. So what keeps us from having this joy? Part of the problem is that most of us spend a good part of our lives practicing being unhappy. A lot of people are simply unimpressed with life. It's not that they're necessarily desperate, but they are vaguely dissatisfied—either with significant segments of their life or with the whole thing. Listen to them talk. Nothing is ever right. Everything is always all wrong. Nothing ever completely pleases them. No one ever fully lives up to their expectations. They seldom are cheerful, pleasant, or happy. Their attitude is only rarely optimistic, upbeat, or positive. They are lethargic and half-hearted in everything they do. They spend their days and night practicing being unhappy—complaining about how disappointing the whole experience of living has been for them. They have no joy because they are forever rehearsing their unhappiness.

Think of the impact these people have on us. Someone said, "Some folks bring joy wherever they go, but others bring it only when they go." Some people invigorate and energize us whenever we're around them. When they leave, we're full of resolve, inspiration, new ideas, and wonderful new attitudes. We can't wait to see them again. Others, however, simply exhaust us whenever we're around them. They drain every ounce of energy from us. When they leave, the only thing we're ready to do is take a very long nap. They literally kill our joy!

While the attitude and influence of others can do that, probably the greatest detriment to our own joy is our lack of personal faith and confidence in God. For some, every problem is a major catastrophe. Every pain in the chest is the heart attack you've been expecting. Every case of the flu is probably deadly pneumonia. Every unexpected repair of the car or an appliance is the expenditure that will break your financial back and plunge you into certain insolvency and bankruptcy. Every argument with your mate signals the end of the marriage. Every attempt by your teenager to exercise a little independence means that he or she must be on drugs. When you begin to think like that, it affects your spiritual life as well. Even the smallest mistakes become spiritual catastrophes. Suddenly, any sin calls into question your salvation—but most of all, it calls God into question. How could you do that if he had really saved you?

Don't you see it? The absence of joy means that you have lost confidence in God. Nehemiah understood the connection when he called his people to hope. "The joy of the Lord is your strength," he said (8:10). It implies that as you choose a millimeter of joy, God will give you an inch of strength and the capacity to choose more joy. But without confidence in God, there is no reserve of strength on which you can draw to endure the difficult days and nights, the long, lonely, and dark seasons of winter.

Jesus came to increase your joy, to restore your confidence, to remind you that God is still in control, to give you back your joy—and not just a little dose of it but to fill you with it! But the choice is entirely yours. If you choose him, you will choose joy. And when you have joy, you will have the strength to go on.

What do you say?—Gary C. Redding

Illustrations

SONGS IN THE NIGHT.   It is strange that when God gives his children mercies, they generally set their hearts more on the mercies than on the giver of them; but when the night comes and he sweeps all the mercies away, then at once they say, "Now, my God, I have nothing to sing of but thee; I must come to thee; and to thee only."—C. H. Spurgeon[6]

DON'T LOOK BACK.   In a Sunday school class for children, the teacher reminded her children that Lot's wife turned into a pillar of salt when she looked back toward Sodom and Gomorrah. "That's nothing," said a young boy. "My mother turned into a telephone pole when she was driving and looked back."—Jerry Hayner[7]

SUNDAY: JUNE SEVENTH

LECTIONARY MESSAGE

Topic: Unbearable Words
    TEXT: John 16:12–15
    Other Readings: Prov. 8:1–4, 22–31; Ps. 8; Rom. 5:1–5

I. *Complete words.* Sometimes a complete story is too overwhelming to bear. Little did the twelve disciples know what would be in store for them. The cross would be at the center point of the way of Jesus. Most of those listening that day to Jesus' words about the Paraclete would soon endure martyrs deaths.

At times we can only deal with the part of the story immediately before us. Many times we can look back at our lives to see the way God has been leading and guiding our pathways; the Holy Spirit then enables us to see the whole story. But when events happen, it is difficult to discern the hand of God on our lives. When we face a problem, it is best to take one step at a time. The whole sometimes seems too immense to handle.

The blessing of being a disciple is that the Lord never gives burdens too heavy to carry. He provides the courage to deal with the whole problem as we encounter each part. It is a blessing that we cannot perceive all the problems to come in our lives. We can deal with them one by one. The disciples present when Jesus delivered this message dealt with events as they happened. God gave to them the courage to face the situation head on and to give an account of their activity.

II. *Words disclosed.* One role of the Paraclete is to reveal the Word of the Lord at the proper time. The work of the Spirit is always very timely. If we are in tune with his will, his plan will be made clear to us. Many disciples of years past were surprised that they reacted to events of their day with the right words for the time. People who were afraid to speak did speak. Persons afraid of death looked death in the eye and went on and accomplished what God would have them do.

These five statements about the Paraclete in John's Gospel are most important for the working out of the Christian gospel. They teach how God continues his activity among us. We are not alone. Even like the first disciples, we may be afraid of what the future will bring, but through the indwelling power of the Holy Spirit, believers receive the strength to encounter the events of the world around them.

True glory is found in the disclosed Word of Christ. He completed his work on earth and has not left us without a comforter. The word *paraclete* does not indicate a comforter who makes the believer comfortable. The word paints a strong image of a person coming to stand by your side to render all the help you will need to make you a dynamic person.

[6] *Great Pulpit Masters: Charles H. Spurgeon.*
[7] *Yes, God Can.*

III. *Words to reach fulfillment.* The words of Christ stand on his promise that we shall be with him in eternity. The statements about the Paraclete end with the promise of the glorious future. Believers will see their Lord again. The Greek word *arrabon* as used in Eph. 1:14 is employed by modern Greeks to mean "engagement ring." The Spirit is thus the pledge of things to come. The Spirit reminds us that the message of Christ is wrapped in eternity. The best is yet to be. We cannot be slack when we realize the future aspect of the words of Jesus. There is more to the events than meets the eye. Christ has directed the past and present, and will be the leader of the future. Such encouraging words need to be heard in the midst of the struggle. The Holy Spirit ultimately paints the large picture of which we are just a tiny part.

So often the present event seems enormous. When viewed against the future and the past, the present seems very small. When the history of humans is viewed against the clock of history, we are just a fraction of a second in the course of time. Yet God has intervened to bring meaning to that time. He has planned that we see our lives against the clock of history and post-history. We are that important to God.—James L. Blevins

Illustrations

A SMALL MATTER.   The newspaper reporter John Toland tells that Adolf Hitler's father was born illegitimately and bore the name of his mother, who was a Schicklgruber. When the boy was a teenager, his father appeared one day and adopted him and changed his name to Hitler. Toland indicated that the whole of World War II would have been changed if Germans would have had to say "Heil Schicklgruber." One little event changed the course of world history. Sometimes we are not able to see the forest because of the numerous trees.—J.L.B.

PEACE AND JOY.   As one notices that a current is in the wire when the light bulb becomes bright with the snapping on of the switch, so one notices that the Holy Spirit is there when a joy goes through one with the naming of God's name. "Peace and joy in the Holy Spirit," says Paul. It does not always have to happen with the receiving of the Holy Spirit as strikingly as on the first Pentecost. There do not always have to be flames of fire and speaking in tongues. It can happen quite silently and unstrikingly; quite softly the door to God can open, and when it opens, his light flows in without a sound and yet powerfully. Peace with God—that is the first opening of the door; joy in God—that means that it has opened wide so that, as the poet says, "your room becomes full of sun." And this opening of the door to God is indeed what alone matters in this life.—Emil Brunner

SERMON SUGGESTIONS

Topic: A Strange Kind of Success
TEXT: Isa. 6:9–13
(1) When we begin consciously to work for God, we set out with high hopes. (2) However, even the Word of God may not achieve what we anticipate for it (6:9). (3) Nevertheless, we are sustained by the faith that through us, in spite of failure, the purpose of God is being worked out.

Topic: The Blind and the Seeing
TEXT: John 9
(1) Everyone experiences what it is to be spiritually blind. Godliness is not a native talent, though it has been said that there is a God-shaped void in each of us. (2) It is heartening, however, to know that we may receive our sight. Christ wants to give us sight "that the works of God might be made manifest in us."

Hymn Suggestions: Trinity Sunday

1. "Holy, Holy, Holy," Reginald Heber (1827); "Nicaea," John B. Dykes (1861)
A hymn of great dignity and uplifting power, this hymn was written for Trinity Sunday. No more appropriate expression of God's threefold being as Father, Son, and Holy Spirit could be suggested for this day.
2. "Lord, Our Lord, Your Glorious Name," Psalter (1912); "Chautauqua," William F. Sherwin (1877)
This poetic version of Psalm 8 could appropriately follow the Psalter reading of the day. The more familiar refrain of "Day Is Dying in the West," with its quotation of the Sanctus ("Holy, Holy, Holy"), could well be

alternated with singing the refrain of this paraphrase.

3. "Come, Thou Almighty King," Anonymous (eighteenth century); "Italian Hymn," Felice de Giardini (1769)

Of the many hymns built on a Trinitarian pattern, this one is undoubtedly the most beloved. After invoking the presence of each aspect of the Godhead—"Almighty King," "Incarnate Word," and "Holy Comforter"—in the first three stanzas, the final stanza gathers up the worshipers' praises directed to the "Great One in Three."

4. "How Majestic Is Your Name," Michael W. Smith (1981); "How Majestic," Smith (1981)

Here is a modern mini-hymn that paraphrases in popular fashion the first verse of Psalm 8. It would be suitable used as an antiphon sung between the reading of the various verses and at the end of the psalm.—Hugh T. McElrath

Worship Aids

CALL TO WORSHIP. "Teach me thy way, O Lord; I will walk in thy truth: unite my heart to fear thy name. I will praise thee, O Lord my God, with all my heart: and I will glorify they name forevermore" (Ps. 86:11–12).

INVOCATION. Lord, we have come into your house from different places, bringing with us different experiences and having different needs. Just about the only thing that holds us together is the love of Christ. We ask you to take that love today, Lord, and cover over all the differences among us. Make us over into one body of Christ, so that we can worship you as he would want us to.—James M. King

OFFERTORY SENTENCE. "And whatsoever ye do, do it heartily, as to the Lord, and not unto men; knowing that of the Lord ye shall receive the reward of the inheritance: for ye serve the Lord Christ" (Col. 3:23–24).

OFFERTORY PRAYER. O Lord, thou has given us the power to work, to earn, to save, to spend, to share; may we share, knowing that all is of thee. And may we ever be found faithful as Christ Jesus was faithful to do thy holy will.—E. Lee Phillips

PRAYER. O God, wilt thou bless the praise that we lift up to thee, the thanksgiving, the joyous adoration? Wilt thou also bless the humble prayers of penitence and confession and contrition as each one, in his or her own heart, honestly confesses to thee all that is wrong within? We seek thy cleansing, we seek thy renewal. Grant that we may be finer, stronger, better persons because of this experience of worship. We lift our prayers not only for ourselves. We pray for others. We ask that thou wilt be with all who are sick and those who are shut-in, with all who have particular problems, distresses, or pressures. Grant thy holy grace, which is more than sufficient for our every human need.—Lowell M. Atkinson

Sermon: Picking Pronouns

TEXT: Acts 4:32–37

The time written about in this story may be the only time in history that one could write about the Church that the whole body of believers "were of one heart and soul." I am more accustomed to another description of the Church: "Where two Baptists come together, there will be at least three opinions." Luke's picture of early Christians is idealistic, even for the New Testament. The experiment in communal living is never associated with any other expression of the Church in the New Testament. That fact, along with the story of the cheaters Ananias and Sapphira in the next chapter, suggests that this particular kind of idealism may have been abandoned in short order.

I. Is church unity too idealistic? Perfect attendance, the physical ideal of gathering the whole congregation at the same place and time, is close to impossible in every church that I have ever served or known. The fiscal ideal of depositing all membership wealth in one bank account is beyond comprehension. No wonder this idealistic venture of the early church has been treated as an experiment rather than as a model for the proper organization of the church. A few exceptions should be noted: some of the Roman Catholic religious orders, some Anabaptist bodies of the Reformation, the Shakers of American origin, and no less than Clarence Jordan's Koinonia Farm started in 1942.

Jordan was a Baptist preacher/scholar and a missionary (and he was called a few other things). Accused of being a liberal and a communist, he was mostly guilty of taking the Bible seriously, if not literally. Koinonia Farm was modeled after the idealistic experience of the early church, in which no one claimed private ownership of wealth and all property was jointly owned. The people of the community described in Acts were believers in Christ who were willing to share everything so that all deprivation and need disappeared from the Christian community. Barnabas, a man of means who sold a field to bring the cash to the apostles, was a showcase example of the trust and generosity that marked this congregation. Jordon took some exception to the Acts experiment. He was more likely to call the wealthy to follow the command of Jesus to the young ruler, to sell what they had, give it to the poor, and follow Jesus with nothing but themselves. By now you know that this advice is the seed that prompted Millard Fuller to start Habitat for Humanity. Getting people together across lines of race and social class is somewhat controversial; the very idea of bringing people together under one budget had a way of raising hackles and suggesting heresy even if it was right out of the Bible.

II. The Church is a gathered people. Forgive my repetition of the obvious. The church is not the accumulation of wealth or property. The issue has never been money, and it never will be. We pick our pronouns for the Church out of either mindless habit or a deliberate ideology. In religion, the choice of gender is often implied in the choice of pronouns. Why do we typically call God "he"? Certainly it is not because of some correlation between God and the male gender. Early in Christian history the Church was identified as "she." The language was only figurative, but the common way of thinking was of Father God and Mother Church. If we personify the Church, the personal pronoun is much more appropriate than the neuter "it." The Jewish theologian Martin Buber pressed Christians as well as Jews to give thought to the pronouns for our relationship with God in his book *I and Thou*. He suggested that God is not an "it" but "The Eternal Thou." God calls us aside from the world of things to a personal worship of the personal God.

The Acts experiment is less about property than about community. Here people from all walks of life came together with a commitment to one another. The lonely individuals, the isolated islands of humanity, became family. "I" became "we." "Me" and "mine" became "ours." The dynamic of this Church that led to communal property was a unity of spirit. Maybe the idea is not so far-fetched as we may assume. Joe Priest Williams was pastor of the Tabernacle Baptist Church in Louisville for three decades after the white suburban community became predominantly black and economically depressed. He and his church were committed to witnessing to the grace of God where they lived. I once heard Joe observe the difference between the churched poor and the unchurched poor. People who have a church family survive. Folks who are totally dependent on community resources are often at risk. The "me-ism" common to the past two decades is not the child of need. Crisis brings people together. Strangely enough, crisis is often the catalyst for community while material independence is the major barrier.

Which comes first? Shall we pool our wealth and depend on each other? Or shall we pool our hearts and souls and give our possessions a lower place in the hierarchy of values?

III. What brings us together? We are always looking for the right recipe for success. Our shelves are full of formula books and periodicals on "how to" win a life. We don't want to think about it. We could care less about the philosophy or the rationale behind a solution. All we really want is results.

One of the publications that have come across my desk during the past year is *Net Results*. It is full of practical advice on how to fix the broken church, how to make an old church grow, how to get more money for the building program, or how to reach young adults—"Generation X"—or the "Baby Boomers." It even contains regular articles by one of my mentors, Lyle Schaler. And I share the contents with leaders of the church in hopes that they will see something that I miss or come to understand something about which I am far from expert.

The early church is a limited success story. By current measures, the story may be more about the church's failures and struggles than about its expansion and success. We must take note of the power behind this church. This is the church born of Pentecost. It is the church driven much more by the Spirit of God within than by the appeal of success without. William Willimon noticed that this passage has often been the focus of worship on the Sunday after Easter. The dynamic of the church that brings people together has never been a new gimmick of structure or organization. The power is within us now as it was within them then. We come together as family, as church, in the unity of the Spirit and the bond of love. So it was then, it is now, and ever shall be.—Larry Dipboye

Illustrations

BELONGING.   Thus the doctrine of the Trinity, though it adumbrates a mystery, is not incongruous with the whole mystery of man's life. It answers human need. We worship God in his creation as our Father; we worship God in his Incarnation in Christ, and claim his pardon; we worship God in the Holy Spirit, rejoicing that instead of our being bereaved by the exaltation of Christ, we are indwelt by his presence. The mystics have sometimes dared to speak of "The Family of the Godhead." They know and are blessed, while others who captiously speak of the "hairsplitting of theologians" still move in shallowness. Why not launch out into the mighty deep of faith? There is life in the adoring "Holy, Holy, Holy" of the doctrine of the Trinity.—George A. Buttrick[1]

CURE FOR LONELINESS.   The only way to put an end to our cravings and combats and to heal our loneliness is to come back to the fellowship for which we were created—the fellowship of love in the Kingdom of God made manifest in his Church. We shall then see that neither individual nor state nor any social structure nor any denominational structure can be an end in itself; that no life reaches its truest and highest fulfillment until it shares in honest and open relationships with all other men whom God has created. "For none of us liveth to himself, and no man dieth to himself" (Rom. 14:7). We live unto Christ and there is only one place where we may live in the fellowship of Christ and that is where all others in that fellowship live.— Charles A. Trentham

SUNDAY: JUNE FOURTEENTH

LECTIONARY MESSAGE

Topic: Debts Canceled Here
    TEXT: Luke 7:36–8:3
    Other Readings: 1 Kings 21:1–10 (11–14), 15–21a; Ps. 5:1–8; Gal. 2:15–21
    America has become a nation of debtors. Our government's national budget deficit is approximately five trillion dollars. Most people find it impossible to own a home or a car without taking out a loan. Credit card offers flood the mailboxes and the television screens of the American public. Nearly one million people will file personal bankruptcy this year because of their inability to pay back their debts. Wouldn't it be wonderful if someone would tell us that our debts had all been canceled and present us with a perfect credit record? That is what this story is about.
    Jesus was a dinner guest at the home of Simon the Pharisee. It was common for a teacher to be invited to a meal to discuss the-

ology, and it would have been acceptable for people who had not been invited to dine to come and go during the meal to listen to Jesus speak. Yet Simon was obviously disconcerted at the presence and actions of this sinful woman. Her reputation was known. Probably she was a prostitute. Bursting on the scene, she did not fade into the background to listen but became the focal point of Jesus' message. As Jesus reclined toward the banquet table, she stood behind him, covering his feet with tears and kisses and ointment.
    Simon assumed that Jesus must not be a prophet, for by Simon's moral code no one who knew this woman's reputation would allow himself to be touched by her. Jesus showed that he not only knew who this woman was but he knew Simon's heart as well. He told the parable of the two debtors—both of whom

[1] *So We Believe, So We Pray.*

were unable to pay even though their debts are of different sizes. The woman was reassured that her sins were forgiven because of her faith. Simon was left to ponder whether or not he wanted to be forgiven.

I. *Jesus offers forgiveness to all.* Earlier in Luke 7 (v. 34) we are told that Jesus was a friend to tax collectors and sinners. In accepting the woman's actions, Jesus was once again inviting the "outsiders" into God's Kingdom. Often we see Jesus at odds with the Pharisees. Here he was dining with them. His invitation was to them as well, if they would accept it. There is room in God's kingdom for everyone.

II. *Gratitude follows forgiveness.* Simon had not been a rude host, but neither had he been overly gracious and hospitable. Jesus' feet would have been dusty from wearing sandals on the roads of Palestine; having a servant wash Jesus' feet would have been a welcome gesture of hospitality. A kiss or a drop of olive oil on the head would have been a sign of welcome and honor. Simon was full of his own self-righteousness and felt no need for humility toward Jesus or actions of gratitude.

The woman, however, was conscious only of her need for forgiveness. She was unashamed and focused solely on Christ. We are not told any details, but she obviously had some prior contact with Jesus or his message. She had repented from her life of sin and felt God's forgiveness. She came to Simon's house to anoint Jesus with her ointment, probably intending to anoint his head, but as she stood at Jesus' feet she was overcome with emotion. Her heart overflowed with gratitude toward Jesus for his acceptance and forgiveness of her and she began weeping on his feet. Her natural reaction was to dry the tears off with the only thing she had available—her hair. Respectable Jewish women only let their hair down before their husbands. This immodest act no doubt caused Simon more discomfort. The woman had already broken a number of social codes in her effort to express her gratitude toward Jesus. Here she was, a woman and a sinner, in the home of a Pharisee who had invited guests for a theological discussion, a discussion open only to men in first-century Judaism.

Simon had shown only self-satisfaction. The woman showed humility. Only a servant would wash someone's feet. Kisses and anointing were usually bestowed on the head as a sign of respect. The woman bestowed them on Jesus' feet as a sign of her humility and thankfulness.

Finally, the woman's action showed gratitude in its lavishness. Alabaster was a costly stone and was usually reserved for the most costly ointments or perfumes, the kind that would be used to anoint the body of a loved one before his or her burial. This may have been the most valuable thing that this woman owned.

In our worship of the Lord we should stand with the woman and not with Simon. God is less concerned with social forms and proprieties than with honest expressions of gratitude and love in our worship. Along with the woman, we owe our salvation to Jesus. What is to be our response?

III. *"Who is this who even forgives sins?"* Simon's guests were amazed when Jesus reassured the woman that her sins were forgiven. This story, along with the rest of the chapter, shows that Jesus does indeed have the power to forgive sins. Previously in chapter 7 he healed the centurion's slave with just a word and raised the widow's son from the dead. Jesus answered the questions of John the Baptist's disciples by reminding them of all the miracles that he had performed. Finally, in dealing with this sinful woman, he showed his power to forgive the debt of sin and completely change a life.—Mary Beth McCloy

Illustrations

WHY WE LOVE. A little girl was playing with her doll in a room where her mother was busily engaged in some literary work. When the mother had finished her writing she said, "You can come now, Alice, I have done all I want to do this morning." The child ran to her mother, exclaiming, "I am so glad, for I wanted to love you so much."

"But I thought you were very happy with dolly."

"Yes, mother, I was, but I soon get tired of loving her, for she cannot love me back."

The mother's eyes filled with tears as she whispered, "And is that why you love me—because I can love you back?"

We love Him because he first loved us.—C. H. Spurgeon

HOW GOD LOVES. There is that in the heart of God that enables him to know us altogether, to sympathize with us. He is the all-knowing and the all-loving. But this comfort that is offered to the anguished soul is not based on the knowledge of God as a kind of isolated phenomenon but rooted in Jesus Christ. It is in him that the God who knows all and yet loves, confronts us. It is on the just and faithful God whom he revealed that we rest our hope—that is, on the constant and infinite goodwill of God in Christ.—W. D. Davies[2]

SERMON SUGGESTIONS

Topic: How Great Is Your God?
TEXT: Isa. 44:9–20; Gen. 31:34a
(1) All of us are into God-making at some time in our life—a little god who flutters about to give us everything we want; a little god who is the prisoner of our special group; a little god who excuses everything. (2) All of us must find our little gods inadequate. Why? The human mind grows; the human spirit yearns; the stresses of life require a greater God. (3) Our security lies in our openness to the future—with the true and living God.

Topic: An Open Door
TEXT: Rev. 3:6
(1) The Church has apparent liabilities: "You have but little power." (2) The Church also has positive assets: "You have kept my word." (3) The Church is given unlimited opportunities: "I have set before you an open door."

Hymn Suggestions: First Sunday After Trinity

1. "My God, How Wonderful Thou Art," Frederick W. Faber (1849); "Windsor," William Damon (1591)
Appropriate as a response to the gospel reading (Luke 7:38–8:3), this hymn magnifies the tenderness and compassion of Christ in forgiving those who are truly penitent in spite of their waywardness and sin.
2. "Alleluia, Alleluia! Give Thanks," Donald Fissile (1973); "Alleluia no. 1," Fissile (1973)

[2] *The New Creation.*

This recently created hymn makes clear references to the singers being crucified with Christ—the theme of the Epistle reading for this day (Gal. 2:15–21). It would be a good call to worship.
3. "As Morning Dawns," Fred R. Anderson (1986); "Wareham," William Knapp (1738)
A modern paraphrase of the psalm for this day (Ps. 5), this hymn could be alternated stanza by stanza with the read verses of the psalm.
4. "Lead Us, Heavenly Father, Lead Us," James Edmeston (1821); "Regent Square," Henry T. Smart (1867)
A Trinitarian hymn written by a devoted layman, "Lead Us, Heavenly Father, Lead Us" reflects the message of the Psalter reading, especially Psalm 5:8. Its second stanza also relates to the forgiveness theme of the Gospel lesson (Luke 7:36–50).—Hugh T. McElrath

Worship Aids

CALL TO WORSHIP. "And all the angels stood round about the throne, and about the elders and the four beasts, and fell before the throne on their faces, and worshiped God, saying, Amen: Blessing, and glory, and wisdom, and thanksgiving, and honor, and power, and might, be unto our God forever and ever" (Rev. 7:11–12).

INVOCATION. Holy God, give us to see today the light that never fades, the hope that never wavers, the love that never lets us go. Then let us worship and praise our God with exceedingly great joy and humble adoration.—E. Lee Phillips

OFFERTORY SENTENCE. "And whatsoever ye do in word or deed, do all in the name of the Lord Jesus, giving thanks to God and the Father by him" (Col. 3:17).

OFFERTORY PRAYER. Lord, as we see the shadow of the cross fall across the centuries, lead us to give for the proclamation of the gospel of our resurrected Savior.—E. Lee Phillips

PRAYER. Eternal Father, before all, in all, and beyond all, we gather in this sacred place to worship you in spirit and in truth. Enlarge our thoughts of you, we pray. In our limited abilities we cannot fully understand all that you are. We can only stand in hushed silence before your presence and power and know that if we lived a thousand lifetimes, we could never comprehend all that you are or fathom the heights and depths of your mighty power. With awe and wonder we enter your presence in praise and adoration, asking that some light from you fall upon our souls today. Indeed we come praying, "Search us, O God, and know our hearts. Try us and know our thoughts. See if there be some wicked way in us, and lead us in a way everlasting."

Some of our need we know well, Father, as we gather before you. We know that we need help with the inner relationships of our lives. We ask your guidance in our dealing with ourselves. Give us sincerity, honesty, and candor as we manage our lives. Save us from the folly of self-defeat and give us the grace to see ourselves as we really are, hating that which is evil in us and rightly appraising those powers that are ours that can be used best in the service of God and neighbor.—Henry Fields

Sermon: Turning Aside

TEXT: Exod. 3:1–12

Somewhere I came across one of those sayings that have a way of sticking in your mind and becoming part of your experience. When under pressure from the demands of every day, I find myself repeating the words, "Life is not hurrying. Holy ground is all around." If I listen to myself as that saying runs through my mind, I feel a calm and a relaxation of the pressure of the moment. "Life is not hurrying. Holy ground is all around."

God's servant, Moses, discovered that reality in a dramatic confrontation with God in the Sinai desert. To Bible readers, this is a familiar story. He was a herdsman, Moses was, before he became the great prophet and leader of the Hebrew people, caring for his father-in-law's flock of sheep in the wilderness area of the Sinai Peninsula. Moses one day suddenly and unexpectedly came upon a bush blazing with flame. The bush burned but was not consumed.

No wonder Moses stared at this isolated fire and then said to himself, "I must turn aside and look at this great sight and see why the bush is not burned up." His curiosity led to an even more startling experience as the very voice of God was heard calling out from that site. "Moses, Moses!" called the voice. Tremulously he answered, "Here I am." "Come no closer!" was the next Word, followed by the command, "Remove the sandals from your feet, for the place on which you are standing is holy ground."

Overcome with awe, Moses hid his face from God and then listened to an astonishing commission. God in that encounter claimed Moses for a monumental task—to rescue his fellow Israelites from the oppression of the Egyptian Pharaoh. There in the presence of God, standing on holy ground, this seemingly ordinary herdsman found himself set apart and empowered by God for a unique, divinely appointed destiny.

None of us may ever remotely approach Moses' experience, but all of us can become sensitive to sacred moments and holy ground. Quite possibly, there already are places that you and I invest with spiritual meaning—places where God has been real; where life-changing decisions have been made; where we have felt wonder and reverence and the blessings of God. This church sanctuary, the Moore Prayer Chapel, or the Francis Chapel may hold these meanings for some of us. For others, there may be outdoor settings of particular inspiration, or a special room at home. Holy ground can be of infinite variety and description. Above all, it is essential that it exist for each of us in some form or another.

I. *Regaining our spiritual moorings.* Human beings almost instinctively search for the holy. Often that search is directed outward; just as often, people look inward. The California naturalist John Muir once said, "I only went out for a walk, and finally concluded to stay out till sundown, for going out, I found, was really going in." Nature's outdoor splendor led Muir to think introspectively, in personal terms; going out became a process of going in. We need to be willing, as Moses was, to turn aside. God then may be found in new and unexpected places.

Accenting prayer and anticipating a course of action, as this devotional indicates, both belong to our experience of the holy. And here, especially, is where we need to insist that life is not hurrying.

In one of the Old Testament psalms we are counseled to "wait on the Lord: be of good courage [we read] and he shall strengthen your heart: wait, I say, on the Lord." We cannot improve on that timeless counsel!

II. *Finding our way to church.* Faithfulness in attending the services of the church becomes for most of us a meaningful way to search for the holy. Each person here today has come by choice; an intentional turning aside from other involvements is represented by your presence at worship.

That simple invitation, one observer noted, states the real reason for going to church. You and I are here because we believe there really is a "central peace subsisting at the heart of endless agitation." We believe that by turning aside we shall meet God, and by God's grace the buried life, the potential and power within us, shall be released. We gather here to worship, to pray, and to think about the things of God so that we might experience life in all its fullness and brightness and meaning. The more sensitive we are, the more we look with wonder at that which is before us—just as Moses did. Reverence in the face of lofty mysteries—mysteries truly felt even though imperfectly understood—becomes our fitting response. In this setting we stoutly affirm that life is not hurrying; no, for us holy ground is all around.

Moses was commanded to remove his sandals at that sacred place where the bush burned but was not consumed. The religion of Islam requires the same when a person enters an established worship area. Christian practice is not that, but there rightfully is meant to be a symbolic casting off of whatever impedes our receptivity to the presence of God. I bid you, think of that, and take time each day to turn aside, all in anticipation of the great things God will do. The scriptural promise we may claim is this (from Psalm 66): "God will not reject our prayers, nor ever remove his steadfast love from us."—John H. Townsend

Illustrations

WHAT IS WORSHIP? This world can be saved from political chaos and collapse by one thing only, and that is worship. For to worship is to quicken the conscience by the holiness of God, to feed the mind with the truth of God, to purge the imagination by the beauty of God, to open up the heart to the love of God, to devote the will to the purpose of God.—William Temple

WHAT HAPPENS IN WORSHIP? As Christians assemble they rehearse life within the unitive purposes of God. In coming together, being gathered and gathering, they not only acknowledge but also enact a vision of reality. They have been convened, given the privilege and function, gift and task, to be pioneers in what God wills for the world. Their gatherings, their life together, their congregations, are called to model the meaning of life as social, revealed in Jesus as the Christ. They come together, are brought together, in order to risk, explore, and share graced reality. In their ways of gathering, styles of leadership, and patterns of worship they all receive from each other, as means of grace, so that what they are and do and become together expresses the reality of God among them.—John E. Burkhart[3]

SUNDAY: JUNE TWENTY-FIRST

LECTIONARY MESSAGE

Topic: The Power of God to Transform
TEXT: Luke 8:26–39
Other Readings: 1 Kings 19:1–4 (5–7), 8:15a; Ps. 42; Gal. 3:23–39

Jesus was always aware of his mission on earth. He came to seek and to save that which was lost. He was always sensitive to the needs of those around him. He worked *with* individuals and not *on* them as on an automobile. In this chapter of Luke, Jesus teaches and practices his divine power. Jesus and his disciples pass through a storm on the lake, then go ashore to find a man with a tremendous storm going on in his life. Throughout his life Christ was confronted by the devil and his angels. Now Jesus was to confront the power of evil and the selfishness of individuals who place a greater importance on material things than on a human being.

[3]*Worship.*

I. *The power of evil* (vv. 26–30). Why was this man in such a horrible condition? Sin comes in many forms, and it seems that this man was totally controlled by the power of evil spirits. Myron Madden, in his book entitled *Raise the Dead,* suggested that the state of this man was due to his inability to handle unresolved grief. Perhaps he was not able to work through the death of a loved one who was buried in the cemetery where he now lived. Others have suggested that this man at one time lived a normal life in the village and slowly went insane. The reality and relevance of this man show us how miserable we can be when Satan is in control of our lives for whatever reason. Jesus first listened and then responded to the unique needs of this man. Understanding those we seek to help is of prime importance before we decide what needs to be done in each situation. To the world this man seemed hopeless and a nuisance to society. He was not at peace within and with others. However, somehow he knew that Jesus could help, and he left the cemetery to go down to the shore to meet the boat. This man represents the horrible state of the sinner. Battles take place in each of us and, if we do not seek the help of God, can escalate into a similar situation.

II. *Christ was in control* (vv. 31–33). This was not the first time that the devil and his legion had experienced Jesus. They recognized him and acknowledged him as the Son of the Most High God. He did not call down a band of angels, or use strong force to overcome the evil spirits. He commanded and a miracle took place in a most unusual way. When Christ comes into our lives he cleanses us from all sin. The all-powerful God who casts out evil spirits will not force us to change. We must seek and ask if we want to be made anew.

III. *Complete deliverance* (vv. 31–33). The evil spirits knew that Christ had power to send them to an eternal abiding place in hell and begged that they be put in the swine on the hill. We have available to us, as Christians today, this same power in the presence of the Holy Spirit. We do not know why Christ responded to the request of the evil spirits. It certainly was a strong confirmation to the man that he had been restored to a normal way of life.

IV. *Self-interest* (vv. 34–37). It was one thing for a former resident of their town to be restored to wholeness, but another when it meant a loss of material things. Jesus had performed a miracle in the life of this man who had been a deep concern of the community. But some of the town's people lost material possessions when the swine rushed into the water, and now others did not want Jesus around as a threat to their well-being. The world often sees that it is too great a sacrifice to be associated with Christ.

V. *Redeemed to tell others* (vv. 38–39). Jesus makes a difference in our lives, both in the present and in the future. The man experienced a physical, emotional, and spiritual change of great magnitude. He did not want to be separated from the one who had given him new hope. Christ does not always want us to leave home to serve him; sometimes he wants us to grow and witness where we know the culture and the people. His witness of the power of God to transform was without question in this community. We are responsible to witness in the world where God places us. It may not be as exciting to stay at home, but it is just as important as going to the end of the world.

God makes all things new when his power enters our lives.—William P. Cubine

Illustrations

A WISE FATHER.   There is a story, quite possibly apocryphal, about the philosopher John Dewey walking with his little boy on a wet, cold, windy day. The youngster had no rubbers on his feet and was splashing around in a puddle. A friend coming by said, "You had better get that boy out of the water. He will get pneumonia."

"I know it," the philosopher replied, "but I am trying to find a way to make him want to get out of the water."—Gerald Kennedy

WHAT CHILDREN DO.   A prominent wealthy family of Chicago was horrified when the daughter, sixteen years of age, became a victim of the dope habit. When she was committed to an institution so that the habit might be broken, she said, "My parents gave me everything—everything but themselves." They had in their busy lives committed her to a nurse when she was a baby, to a baby-sitter when she was a child, and to a paid companion when she grew older. They had sought to rear her by remote control. They gave her everything that she needed but themselves.—Gaston Foote

SERMON SUGGESTIONS

Topic: Our Sin and God's Love

TEXT: Isa. 53:6

This text is a verse in one of the "servant passages" in the book of Isaiah, interpreted in the New Testament as describing the sufferings of Christ. Jesus understood his mission in terms of these passages (Matt. 3:17; Isa. 42:1). (1) We have sinned: "We . . . have gone astray." (2) God has made possible our salvation: "The Lord hath laid on him the iniquity of us all."

Topic: May I Help You?

TEXT: Gal. 6:1–5

(1) Personal responsibility (v. 5). (2) Duty toward others (v. 2). (3) The right approach: (a) We must radiate a spirit of goodwill and helpfulness. (b) People who have achieved a measure of spiritual victory themselves are those who should try to help the fallen, weak, or inexperienced. (c) This delicate task should be performed with genuine humility and in a gentle manner.

Hymn Suggestions: Second Sunday After Trinity

1. "Dear Lord and Father of Mankind," John G. Whittier, (1872); "Rest," Frederick C. Maker (1887)

Among the many scriptural allusions in this well-known hymn by the American Quaker poet are those of the "earthquake, wind, and fire" of Elijah's experience in the Old Testament passage and the "still, small voice of calm" that spoke to the prophet on Mount Horeb.

2. "As Pants the Hart for Cooling Streams," Nahum Tate and Nicholas Brady (1696); "Martyrdom," Hugh Wilson (1827)

This venerable paraphrase of the psalm for this day is one of the few to survive from the "New Version" of the psalms by Tate and Brady. It could be sung to any of many common meter tunes available. A more modern version also available is "As Deer for the Streams" by Christopher Webber (1986).

3. "Baptized in Water," Michael A. Saward (1981); "Bunessan," Gaelic melody (1888)

Written by a contemporary British clergyman, this new song focuses on the truth of Gal. 3:27–29, that those who have been "baptized into Christ have put on Christ."

4. "Thine Arm, O Lord, in Days of Old," Edward H. Plumptre (1864); "St. Matthew," Supplement to Tate and Brady (1708)

One of the finest hymns on the healing ministry of Jesus, this hymn would be a good selection to accompany the gospel reading concerning the healing of the Gerasene demoniac.—Hugh T. McElrath

Worship Aids

CALL TO WORSHIP.   "I will praise the Lord according to his righteousness; and will sing praise to the name of the Lord most high" (Ps. 7:17).

INVOCATION.   Stir in our hearts this hour, O Lord, waking us from the sleep of indifference and the boredom of routine. Rouse us to be children of faith who see the possibilities and set forth to touch the world with the power of the living God.—E. Lee Phillips

OFFERTORY SENTENCE.   "There was a certain man in Caesarea called Cornelius, a centurion of the band called the Italian band, a devout man, and one that feared God with all his house, which gave much alms to the people and prayed to God always. He saw in a vision, evidently about the ninth hour of the day, an angel of God coming in to him, and saying unto him, 'Cornelius.' And when he looked on him, he was afraid, and said, 'What is it, Lord?' And he said unto him, 'Thy prayers and thine alms are come up for a memorial before God'" (Acts 10:1–4).

OFFERTORY PRAYER.   Lord, as these gifts are but the outward manifestation of the inner person, let them be filled with faith, endowed with the power of God, used to accomplish holy ends, for Jesus' sake.—E. Lee Phillips

PRAYER.   Almighty God, our heavenly Father, bless this time of worship and all gathered together in this congregation. Wilt thou bless the deep consecration of the hearts of all thy people—thy holy purposes to which they are committed, the deep affection with which they regard their Savior? Grant thy holy blessings here. Give us grace, confidence, assurance, and peace.

We would lift our prayer for all thy people, here and everywhere. Grant that the Kingdom of Christ may be growing in depth of faith and in the quality of compassionate love in the strength of this victorious loyalty and competent allegiance to the Savior. We would pray especially for those who have special need of thy grace this day. Attend with thy holy presence those who are in sorrow; be a friend to the friendless and a companion to the lonely. Give inner robustness and strength to those who feel the outward pressures of life in the world, in the strains and tensions of their various relationships, in the circumstances that batter and beat and bruise. Grant us that inner strength that will enable us to withstand, and having done all, to stand in strength. Wilt thou hearten us on our way? Give us a gladness of spirit, a victorious joy, a perennial sense of triumphant overcoming, so that all the vicissitudes and difficulties of this, our life, may be transfigured and transformed by the redemptive quality of that spirit that is given of thee.

Wilt thou bless this church in all that it does and endeavors in thy name and in thy spirit? Bless us deeply in our souls that we may be linked to thee in faith, in love, and in loyalty, and that we may receive from thee the high commission to work, to serve, to sacrifice, and to help in the Spirit of Jesus Christ.—Lowell M. Atkinson

Sermon: Dad, the Tender Commander

TEXT: Luke 7:1–10

If I should ask you to define the qualities of a good father, chances are we would agree on a number of factors. Whereas we might stress qualities we feel are quite noble and expected, our offspring might cite a few that we would put at the bottom of the list.

We turn to Jesus. It is not only what he says that gives us our clues but what he does. We are familiar with the setting: it is Capernaum. Here is where Peter and Andrew, James and John had their fishing businesses. It is where Zebedee lived, and it is nearby to countless places in which great events of the New Testament took place.

We know the characters also in this episode. Jesus, of course, is the focus of the story—and yet others play important roles. There is a sick slave we know little about, except that his master thought of him dearly. There is also the centurion, the owner of the slave. A Roman officer, the commander of a hundred men, he is not a Jew. To Jews this man ordinarily would be anathema. He was a Gentile, and Jews did not associate with Gentiles. Yet this Gentile was different. He was sensitive to Jewish customs, which we can see by the fact that he did not go to Jesus himself but sent Jewish friends. This centurion, however, had embraced their faith as much as a Gentile could. He even built their synagogue, and therefore was known to be an exceedingly generous man. He belonged to a people who believed in many gods and ate unclean food and did unclean acts. But this Roman was held in high esteem, because he was not like the rest.

He was a tender commander, and thereby offers himself as a model for all Christians—but in a particular way to Christian fathers.

Luke says that when the centurion heard about Jesus, he did not hesitate to send for him. His slave was ill, one for whom he had more than an owner's interest. In many Roman households, slaves were treated as members of the family—within certain limits, of course. Others saw slaves only as tools, but many saw them as important adjunct members of the household.

Yet the centurion did not tread on Jesus' Jewishness. He did not approach the Lord himself. He got help from Jewish men who knew him, and they approached Jesus. They gave the centurion high marks.

Jesus did not hesitate either. He left immediately for the centurion's home. The Lord never let Jewish ritual law stand in the way of ministry. But as he neared the house, more friends of the centurion greeted Jesus and said, "Lord, do not trouble yourself." They quoted the centurion, who had sent them with the message, "I am not worthy to have you come under my roof; therefore I did not presume to come to you. But only speak the word, and let my servant be healed. For I also am a man set under authority, with soldiers under me; and I say to one, 'Go,' and he goes, and to another, 'Come,' and he comes, and to my slave, 'Do this,' and he does it."

If tenderhearted, he is nevertheless very much a military commander who gives orders and expects them to be carried out. But he is also something more. He is a faithful believer. He knows little more about Jesus than that he is an able rabbi with a history of healings and miracles behind him. To the centurion, that was enough. He trusted Jesus. He did not let doubt impale opportunity.

And Jesus responded to the man's faith and the slave's grave condition with healing power that left the slave in good health.

Now if today's dads can learn anything helpful from the centurion, it might be that they too will find themselves to be tender commanders. It is obvious that this tender commander had friends. It is plain that this tender commander did not practice miserliness but generosity. It is evident that he applied what he had learned of faith to life. Here is one who knew how to go to Jesus unhesitatingly and publicly, and we would all do well to emulate him.

But why should we go to Jesus? Is it merely because he performed miracles? Not at all. There was more than magic in the hands of Jesus. In his words, the people found love. In his actions, they saw compassion. In his death upon the cross and in his Resurrection triumph they discovered the promises of the long-awaited Messiah fulfilled. We discover that he comes to heal and to help, to encourage and befriend, to save and redeem.—Richard Andersen

Illustrations

THE ANGUISH OF GOD.   There are images of God in the Bible that suggest a God totally immersed in our struggles and emotions and messy, frustrated lives.

And perhaps the clearest picture of this God is in the eleventh chapter of Hosea. It's really a fantastic picture. First it pictures God with all the tenderness of a father thinking back to the childhood of his son: "When Israel was a child, I loved him. . . . It was I who taught Ephraim to walk, I took them up in my arms." And then, thinking back about the rebellion and disobedience of his son, his anger flares: "The sword shall rage against their cities, consume the bars of their gates and devour them in their fortresses." But the mood changes again from anger to compassion for his child: "How can I give you up, Oh Ephraim! . . . My heart recoils within me, my compassion grows warm and tender, I will not execute my fierce anger . . . for I am God and not man, the Holy One in your midst, and I will not come to destroy."—Edmund A. Steimle[4]

THE DISCIPLINE OF LIFE.   Probably the thing that made Paul great was his longing for people in their afflictions. There in the Mamertine Prison at Rome he lay shivering because he could not afford to buy a cloak but had to wait for someone to bring him the one he had left at Troas. There in miniature is his greatness. He was forced to feel how hard it is to be poor, and he thought first of Jesus, who for our sakes became poor; and he thought of other people and their needs. So because in his poverty he permitted God to straighten him, he who once was the most compassionate of men. "Remember," he said, "the Lord Jesus Christ, how he said it is more blessed to give than to receive." That became the refrain of his life's song.—Frederick Keller Stamm[5]

SUNDAY: JUNE TWENTY-EIGHTH

LECTIONARY MESSAGE

Topic: Charting a Course for the Kingdom
TEXT: Luke 9:51–62
Other Readings: 2 Kings 2:1–2, 6–14; Ps. 77:1–2, 11–20; Gal. 5:1, 13–25.

The navigators of ships and airplanes always try to chart a course directly for their destination. They understand that detours consume more fuel and increase costs. In the text for today, Jesus challenged his hearers to chart a course leading to the Kingdom of God. Christians should focus their attention on the Kingdom of God and avoid all routes that would divert them from their course.

Jesus emphasized the Kingdom of God in his teaching and preaching. In fact, there are more than one hundred references to the

[4]*From Death to Birth.*
[5]*Seeing the Multitudes.*

Kingdom of God and the kingdom of heaven in the first three gospels. The Kingdom of God is simply defined as the "rule of God" or "the reign of God." Jesus taught his disciples that the Kingdom of God is both present and future. The Kingdom is present because Jesus has come and inaugurated it, yet the Kingdom of God is still future because Christ has not yet returned to establish his rule over the new heaven and the new earth.

I. *Jesus set the example* (v. 51). When the time drew near for his Passion and Ascension, Jesus "set his face to go to Jerusalem." He knew he had a divine appointment in Jerusalem, and he determined to go there. The parallel passage in Matthew 20:17 indicates that Jesus understood exactly what awaited him in Jerusalem. He knew he would be arrested, tried, convicted, and crucified. Even so, he "set his face to go to Jerusalem." One can only wonder: What prompted Jesus to set his course for certain destruction? What navigator would chart a course that would take his ship to destruction on a reef?

Jesus was determined to go to Jerusalem because his suffering was essential to the establishment of God's Kingdom. He knew he would have to suffer on the cross, but he also knew he would rise from the grave. Both his suffering and his triumph were required. Jesus placed the welfare of the Kingdom over his own feelings and comfort.

Jesus was determined to go to Jerusalem because obedience demanded it. God had a plan for human redemption, and Jesus had to play his role in that drama. In the Garden of Gethsemane, Jesus prayed: "Let this cup pass from me," but God did not grant his request. Paul declared that Jesus was "obedient unto death" (Phil. 2:8).

Christians today must follow Jesus' example. Like Jesus, Christians have a role to play in God's Kingdom. God gives each believer spiritual gifts to use in edifying the Church. Christians should unselfishly place a higher priority on Kingdom matters than on personal concerns and comforts. Similarly, Christians should be obedient in all things. Like Jesus, Christians must focus on the Kingdom of God, and not allow the cares of this world to distract them from the course God has charted for them.

II. *Jesus challenged his disciples* (vv. 57–60). As Jesus and his disciples traveled toward Jeru-salem, they encountered three men who wanted to become followers of Jesus. Jesus challenged each one of them to count the cost of discipleship. The first man said, "I will follow you wherever you go." Jesus replied, "Foxes have holes and birds of the air have nests; but the Son of man has nowhere to lay his head." By saying this, Jesus challenged the man to count the cost of discipleship. Jesus did not have a permanent home. He moved about constantly teaching, preaching, and healing.

It is interesting to note that Jesus did not invite the man to join his band of disciples. This man possessed superficial enthusiasm, but he had not truly counted the cost of following Jesus. Jesus asked him if he was really willing to forsake the comforts of home. Apparently the answer was no. This man did not follow Jesus; it cost too much.

Jesus invited the second man to follow him. This man replied, "Lord, let me first go and bury my father." Modern readers are inclined to think the man wanted to attend his father's funeral and then follow Jesus. Actually, the man was saying, "Let me wait until my father dies, and then I'll follow you." He declined to follow Jesus because of family obligations.

Jesus' response seems strange. He said, "Leave the dead to bury their own dead; but as for you, go and proclaim the Kingdom of God." Jesus meant that the man should join the apostolic band and let the spiritually dead bury the physically dead. Apparently, Jesus saw potential in this man, but the man put family concerns before Kingdom concerns.

In this conversation, Jesus was not instructing his disciples to neglect their parents' care. Jesus' concern for his own mother as he hung on the cross shows that such is not the case. Rather, Jesus challenged the man to commit himself to the Kingdom and to trust God to provide for his family's welfare.

III. *Jesus warned his disciples* (vv. 61–62). In the third encounter a man said, "I will follow you, Lord; but let me first say farewell to those at my home." Again, one might think the man just wanted to dash home and say good-bye. However, the man was really saying, "Let me go home and put all my affairs in order; then, at a later time, I will follow you." In reply, Jesus gave a stern warning to this man and to all who would follow him.

He declared, "No one who puts his hand to the plow and looks back is fit for the Kingdom of God."

In his answer, Jesus took a familiar proverb and gave it a new meaning. Obviously a farmer must look ahead or he cannot plow a straight furrow. Jesus applied this imagery to the Kingdom of God. No one who continually looks back to the things left behind can serve effectively in the Kingdom of God. Effective service in God's Kingdom requires undivided attention. Only those who are able and willing to give that attention are fit to serve the Lord.—John Mark Terry

Illustrations

LOOKING BACK.   Once two veteran missionaries inspected a missionary house with a new missionary couple to whom the house had been assigned. The couple asked that many improvements be made in the house. One of the veterans said, "I don't know if the mission can afford all these things or not," to which the new missionary replied, "You don't know what we left behind." "That's the problem," said the veteran missionary. "You didn't leave it behind."—J.M.T.

CURIOUS ALCHEMY.   I can see that Jesus drew men and women into the Kingdom by promising them two things: first, trouble—hardship, danger—and second, joy. But what curious alchemy is this that he can make even danger and hardship seem joyous? He understands things about human nature that we grasp only dimly: few of us are really challenged by the promise of soft living, by an emphasis on me first, or by a life of easy compromise.—Catherine Marshall[6]

SERMON SUGGESTIONS

Topic: Guarding the Springs
TEXT: Prov. 4:23

(1) Our actions spring from our thoughts and feelings, with some exceptions, such as the instinctive and the learned and the automatic. (2) The wellsprings of action may be poisoned, because of our inclination to sin or because we are poorly taught. (3) Yet the

springs of action can be purified, through repentance, whether as a revolutionary change or a never-ending adventure.

Topic: The Life and Fortunes of the Critic
TEXT: Matt. 7:1–5

(1) Chronic faultfinders are likely to be blind to their own faults. (2) Chronic faultfinders fail to show the goodwill and faith that create achievement and character. (3) Chronic faultfinders are, sooner or later, themselves judged.

Hymn Suggestions: Third Sunday After Trinity

1. "God of the Prophets, Bless the Prophet's Heirs," Dennis Wortman (1884); "Toulon," Louis Bourgeois (1551)

The first stanza of this hymn, with its reference to "Elijah's mantle o'er Elisha cast," makes it ideal to precede or follow the reading from 2 Kings. This hymn is also appropriate for ordinations or seminary commencement programs.

2. "Spirit of God, Descend upon My Heart," George Croly (1884); "Morecambe," Frederick C. Atkinson (1870)

"If we live by the Spirit, let us also walk by the Spirit" (Gal. 5:25). As a response to the reading of the Epistle for the day, this prayer hymn would be a natural choice.

3. "Of All the Spirit's Gifts to Me," Fred Pratt Green (1979); "Threefold Gifts," Austin C. Lovelace (1987)

This contemporary hymn was inspired by Galatians 5:22, in which the first fruits of the Spirit mentioned are love, joy, and peace. The first four stanzas, cast in the first person singular, could appropriately be sung by a soloist with the congregation joining in on stanza 5.

4. "Footsteps of Jesus," Mrs. Mary B. C. Slade (1871); "Footsteps," Asa B. Everett (1871)

As an accompaniment to the Lucan reading concerning the cost of following Jesus, this gospel hymn could inspire the congregation's response and give voice to their aspirations.—Hugh T. McElrath

Worship Aids

CALL TO WORSHIP.   "And the Spirit and the bride said, Come. And let him that heareth

[6]*A Closer Walk.*

say, Come. And let him that is athirst come. And whosoever will, let him take the water of life freely" (Rev. 22:17).

INVOCATION.   Lord, draw us to the throne of God today, that kneeling before the Lord, our Maker, our hearts will be strangely warmed, our minds will see new light, our souls will cry out for joy, as our faith is gloriously renewed!—E. Lee Phillips

OFFERTORY SENTENCE.   "And Jesus sat over against the treasury, and beheld how the people cast money into the treasury" (Mark 12:41).

OFFERTORY PRAYER.   You know our hearts, Lord Christ, and we cannot deceive you with our pretensions, if we would. Make us your willing partners, even if some sacrifices are required of us, for our own sakes, but especially for the blessing and support of your cause.

PRAYER.   Now wilt thou make use of us as instruments of thy will. May our lives become channels of thy grace. May our deeds build strong the city of thy truth. May all of us know that our life counts for something in making this a better world for thee and according to the pattern of thy will. To that end we seek that thou wilt bless this time of worship and bless all who are gathered together here with earnest hearts. Make our lives the better, our wills the stronger, our spirits the more fervent because we have worshiped together today.

Grant especially to all who have sorrow or distress the blessings and consolation of thy presence. Grant us the experience of victory in all of life's vicissitudes, and may we be more than conquerors through him who loved us and gave himself for us.—Lowell M. Atkinson

Sermon: Not in My Life

TEXT: Rom. 7:13–25

Paul has attempted to describe his understanding of how grace comes into our lives and changes us. God has offered us the gift of grace in Jesus Christ. God has promised to make us acceptable by the gift of grace. We accept that gift, we are filled with a joy, a relief, a happiness, which so delights that we find ourselves changed. We are changed from the kingdom of the damned to the kingdom of grace. We are freed from the slavery to sin and we become slaves to righteousness. We are ruled by the kindness of God. That is the way it is written in the manual.

Now, Paul says that when it comes to application of that process, it is not as easy as it may seem. "I know that my selfish desires won't let me do anything that is good. Even when I want to do right, I cannot. Instead of doing what I know is right, I do wrong. . . . The sin that lives in me is what does them." Paul confesses that even in his own life the transformation process is not as simple as it sounds when he describes it—even for Paul, with his dramatic conversion, with all of the great new zeal for God's grace, even with his experiences of God's abiding grace in the midst of his troubles. Paul still says that the old Adam has not vanished. This transfer from the slavery of sin to the slavery of righteousness is not immediate and it is not total. It is not easy. And for most of us that is a great relief to hear.

It is not that we don't want what Paul has described to happen to us. It is just that we are afraid that it has not happened to us. We have accepted Jesus Christ as our Lord and Savior. We come to church. But we are not sure we have seen all that changing in us. We don't necessarily feel like we have become that different. Often we begin to think that conversion was not that big a deal. Maybe there is nothing to this Jesus stuff. We tried God and it did not work for us. We wanted God to make us better, take away our bad habits, and the bad habits did not seem to be fading away.

Oh, maybe in the first flush of enthusiasm when we got baptized, or when we first became a disciple on our own decision, our faith changed our lives. We had regular devotions, read our Bible, came to worship, but ever so slowly we began to dip into the old habits and old ways.

Maybe we have seen and heard of what Paul talks about in the testimonies and witnesses given by other people. Theirs always seem so dramatic and so solid. From some sordid life of wickedness, in the moment of conversion, their old lives drop away and they become celebrities on the Trinity Broadcasting Network. What Paul says about the joy of grace transforming our lives—well, we have heard people talk about it from their lives, we have seen it change our lives a little for a while, and we have had a chance to talk with some of the senior saints of our congregations, who tell of little changes, small conversions, decisions made over and over, day after day, rededication, reaffirmations, who now look back and see how far they have changed from who they thought they were and where they thought they would have ended up.

But it is such a blessing to have Paul stop here and confess that even for him the conversion was not instant, complete, or total. Even for him, the struggle with the old self, the old powers, the old ways continues. The switch from the slavery of sin to the slavery of righteousness is not as easy or as immediate as it sounds in the manual.

For evil is more extensive and more pervasive than we ever like to admit. The evil of racism is so much wider and deeper than most of us like to confess. The evil of hatred of others is most often ignored. We push it under cover. Jesus told his disciples to pray for those who hated them and persecuted them. Yet when you ask Christian people, who do you hate and who hates you—I have yet to meet a Christian who will acknowledge hating anyone or that anyone hates them. Evil continues to spread the myth that all we have to do to get rid of evil is to make a few simple choices, to pray a few minutes each day, and to modify a few habits in our lives— and then we are surprised when evil is not gone. The Christian faith takes evil so seriously that it says that nothing short of death or God could free us from the power of evil. So it is no surprise to Christians that to free our lives from the power of evil, to make the transition from being the servant of evil to being the servant of God's holiness, will be a major struggle. As Paul reminds us, that struggle will not be quickly or easily won. The Crowder House next door has changed ownership, but even if we wanted to free it from the powers of decay, rot, and collapse, even if we wanted to restore the house to its nature as a house, that struggle would be massive and difficult. Paul says that the powers of evil, rot, and decay are still at work in his life, but he is now under new management that is focused on restoration of his life. Just because we do not become immediately changed by our acceptance of God's promise in Jesus does not mean we ought to begin to think that God is not at work restoring us.

Now that we are slaves to the righteousness of God, the places where evil still abides in our lives trouble us. The more we are focused on becoming servants to the holiness, justice, truth, and mercy of God, the more we are aware of the places where we fall short. The more we want to keep our sheet of paper clean, the more we worry about the smudges and the pencil marks that get on the paper. The higher our expectations, the more we are disappointed when we do not meet them. In this year when the Olympics are all we hear about, we are reminded that the higher the level of competition, the more we worry about the little mistakes that are marked off. It is part of that new desire we have to be slaves to the righteousness of God that we are still disappointed and disturbed by the presence of evil in our lives. The struggle Paul describes is a struggle that stays with us all our lives. Just because we are still having that struggle does not mean that we have failed or been abandoned by God in our growth in faith. Strangely enough, all of the great Christian saints and witnesses have, even at the end of their lives, called themselves chief among sinners, still beset by temptations and evil. The closer we get to the likeness of Jesus Christ who is our Lord, the more we still notice the forces in our lives that still oppose the goodness of God.

The grace of God comes into our lives and transfers us from the slavery to evil to the slavery of righteousness. Ah, but that process of sanctification in our lives surely takes a much longer and more difficult time than is described in the first part of Paul's manual. In fact, the Christian faith has always said that the process may not be completed in this lifetime. That is why the Roman Catholic Church has worked out the whole notion of Purgatory. That is where you go to finish the process of sanctification before going to heaven. The Protestants of the Westminster Confession acknowledge that the process is not completed in this life, but it is kind of fast forwarded at the time of death by the grace of God. "The souls of the righteous, being then made perfect in holiness, are received into highest heaven, where they behold the face of God in light and glory."—Rick Brand

Illustrations

THE CHOICE IS OURS.   Our God, the New Testament insists, "desires all men and women to be saved" (1 Tim. 2:4). Our hope is the God-man Jesus Christ, who clothed himself in our flesh and carried it to a bloody cross not simply for the "nice guys"—his mother and most of the apostles, Teresa of Avila and Teresa of Calcutta, the Irish Republic and the Blue Army, Holy Trinity parishioners and holy Hoyas. God's compassion reaches out to sinners—and you know, that means everybody. Even a three-point homilist. Even those who stretch God's compassion to the breaking point—the proud men and women who, like the Pharisee in the temple, thank God that they are "not like the rest of humankind" (Luke 18:11), who "have it made," have the world by the tail, don't need God after conception or implantation—even these God loves. There is a breaking point, yes; but it is not really God who reaches it. Only I—if and when I say a final no to God: "I know who you are, and I choose of my own free will to reject your love."—Walter J. Burghardt, S.J.[7]

A STUDY IN CONTRASTS.   On one side, Clarence Darrow, a good man with an eminent career, says as he reaches life's conclusion, "The outstanding fact that cannot be dodged by thoughtful men is the futility of it all," while another good man, Robert Louis Stevenson, long familiar with hardship, says, "Sick and well, I have had a splendid life of it, grudge nothing, regret very little." What a difference between two kinds of good men!—Harry Emerson Fosdick[8]

SUNDAY: JULY FIFTH

LECTIONARY MESSAGE

Topic: Radical Trust
   TEXT: Luke 10:1–11, 16–20
   Other Readings: 2 Kings 5:1–14; Ps. 30; Gal. 6:(1–6)7–16
   The story Luke is telling us does not begin in chapter 10. As with all of our gospels, the story begins in the presence of God. Let's use our imaginations to visualize the scene.
   I. Picture this:
   God decides that it is time to send his Son on a mission to earth. He explains this to his Son.
   CHRIST: Which of the angels should I take?
   GOD: Sorry, no angels.
   CHRIST: How big/glorious should I appear?
   GOD: Sorry, you begin as a baby and remain in human form.
   CHRIST: Which of my mental powers will I have?
   GOD: You'll be an intelligent, sensitive human, but sorry, no foreknowledge.
   CHRIST: How about a halo?
   GOD: You'll have only yourself as a vehicle for my word.
   CHRIST: Can't I carry anything?
   GOD: Only a cross! *Trust me.*
   Thirty years later, we find Jesus instructing some disciples (Luke 10:1–16).

   II. Let's use our imaginations to visualize the heart of the scene. Picture this:
   Christ decides to send seventy disciples on a mission. He explains this to his disciples.
   THE DISCIPLES: How much money should we take?
   CHRIST: Sorry, no money—not even a purse.
   THE DISCIPLES: We'll just get our staffs.
   CHRIST: Sorry, nothing for protection.
   THE DISCIPLES: We'll get our shoes.
   CHRIST: Sorry, no shoes.
   THE DISCIPLES: Well, how about a coat?
   CHRIST: Sorry, no extra clothing.
   THE DISCIPLES: We'll certainly need begging bags!
   CHRIST: Sorry, no bags either.
   THE DISCIPLES: You mean we go empty-handed?
   CHRIST: You have only yourselves and my word.
   THE DISCIPLES: Can't we carry anything?
   CHRIST: Only a cross! *Trust me.*
   III. The story, of course, doesn't end there. [*Read verses 17–20.*] Can you catch their excitement?

[7] *Grace on Crutches.*
[8] *On Being Fit to Live With.*

"It was scary, but you told us to trust you and we did. And *wow!*"

Triumph results from radical trust.

IV. This account of Jesus and his seventy disciples is no isolated incident. Do you remember hearing Paul's description of his life story?

"May I never boast of anything except the cross of our Lord Jesus Christ, by which the world has been crucified to me and I to the world" (Gal. 6:14).

And what did Paul carry with him? In his own words, "I carry the marks of Jesus branded on my body" (Gal. 6:17).

Triumph results from radical trust.

V. Can you imagine one more scene? Picture this:

Christ decides he needs people for a special mission. He calls us and explains what he needs us to do right here at home.

Us: Is there a budget item for that?

CHRIST: Just trust.

Us: Where will the money come from?

CHRIST: Just trust.

Us: Who's going to help?

CHRIST: Just trust.

Us: Where do I get the training?

CHRIST: Just trust.

Us: You mean we go empty-handed?

CHRIST: You have my word.

Us: Can't we carry anything?

CHRIST: Only a cross. *Trust me.*

VI. The rest of this story is still ahead of us, but one thing is certain:

In an economy obsessed with financial security, in a culture centered on possessions and power, we Christians should hear the real message of Christ's commission—only radical trust in God will bring us to the ultimate triumph; *triumph results from radical trust.*—Bruce E. Shields

Illustrations

FOR DRAMATIC EFFECT. The dramatic impact of this sermon could be increased by the preacher's changing position from section to section. The conversation between God and Christ could be done from behind and facing the pulpit; the conversation between Jesus and the disciples could be done in front of and looking at the pulpit; and the final scene could be done among the congregation and facing the pulpit. The beginning, and end transitions could be spoken from behind the pulpit.—B.E.S.

FOR A FOCAL POINT. A large cross behind the pulpit makes an effective focal point for the whole sermon.—B.E.S.

SERMON SUGGESTIONS

Topic: A Comprehensive Blessing

TEXT: Num. 6:22–27

(1) God's vigilant keeping. (2) God's unrelenting friendship. (3) God's gift of total well-being.

Topic: The Peace That Christ Gives

TEXT: John 14:27

(1) We wish for peace: among the nations, in the family, within our inner self. (2) Christ offers us a special kind of peace: in the midst of conflict, through trust in God, by submission to the will of God, and under the tutelage of the Holy Spirit.

Hymn Suggestions: Fourth Sunday After Trinity

1. "In the Cross of Christ I Glory," John Bowring (1825); "Rathbun," Ithamar Conkey (1849)

Inspired by Galatians 6:14, this familiar hymn could well follow the reading of the Epistle.

2. "Come Sing to God," Fred R. Anderson (1986); "Ellacombe," Gesangbuch, Wittemberg (1784)

This modern paraphrase of Psalm 30 could be sung stanza by stanza in alternation with the reading of the Psalm of the day.

3. "When I Survey the Wondrous Cross," Isaac Watts (1707); "Hamburg," Lowell Mason (1824)

Often considered the greatest hymn in the English language, this hymn was also inspired by Galatians 6:14. Frequently the third stanza is sung in the parallel minor key to reflect the pathos of its words and to effect a contrast (in the return to the major key) to the climactic final stanza.

4. "Hark, the Voice of Jesus Calling," Daniel March (1868); "Ellesdie," Anonymous; attributed to Mozart (1830)

This clarion call to witness and service would appropriately follow the gospel reading having to do with the commissioning of the seventy followers of Jesus. It would be ideal as a hymn of invitation after a sermon based on the Lucan passage.—Hugh T. McElrath

Worship Aids

CALL TO WORSHIP. "I bless the Lord who gives me counsel; in the night also my heart instructs me. I keep the Lord always before me; because he is at my right hand, I shall not be moved" (Ps. 16:7–8 NRSV).

INVOCATION. Now in the quiet of this hour, O Lord, beckon to us, speak to us, fill us with those powerful thoughts that attune our souls to the Creator. We long for this, we pray for this. We wait and say again: Lord Jesus, show us the Father. All glory to God!—E. Lee Phillips

OFFERTORY SENTENCE. "Give, and it shall be given unto you; good measure, pressed down, and shaken together, and running over, shall men give into your bosom. For with the same measure that ye mete withal it shall be measured to you again" (Luke 6:38 KJV).

OFFERTORY PRAYER. Our Heavenly Father, who hast come among us to give thy supreme gift in Jesus Christ, now we would come into thy presence to give our gifts of love and devotion. Grant that they may represent a worthy spirit of sacrificial praise and may build strong thy Kingdom. We pray in the name of Christ our Savior.—Lowell M. Atkinson

PRAYER. O God, our heavenly Father, we are gathered together in the spirit of praise, rejoicing in the good tidings that thou art ever making known to us out of thy Holy Word. We would ask thy blessing upon our worship so that our minds may be kindled and our hearts duly stirred, our spirits made deeply sensitive, our wills made strong and resilient. Refresh and refurbish us new persons for having been here in thy holy presence, and send us into our life of this week with fresh purpose, finer faith, stronger devotion, and a closer sense of thy loving presence.

We come into this place of worship with eager hearts and expectant spirits, knowing that thou art a God of grace and graciousness, that thy love is beyond our comprehension and far beyond anything we merit or deserve. Our hearts are full of wonder and awe at the thought of thy goodness. Our spirits are humble as we confront the stark facts of our egotism, our pride, our unworthiness in thy sight. Grant us a due sense of reverence and gratitude in all the experiences in this, our life, and may our thoughts be completely in thee.

May we be the means of channeling thy grace into the life of our community, to make a better spirit; into the life of our nation, to create a finer wisdom; and into the life of our world, to make a deeper brotherhood.

May our living in this world in the Spirit of Christ make a difference for good. Because of us, may thy will be done and thy Kingdom come in the lives of men. Grant us thy grace within our hearts, grant us thy grace in our deeds. May we count it our highest honor, privilege, and joy to be instruments of thy holy will. For this we pray as we seek to follow in the steps of the Master, even our Savior, Jesus Christ.—Lowell M. Atkinson

Sermon: Citizens of Two Kingdoms

TEXT: Matt. 22:15–22

With one clear statement, Jesus made the astounding point that his people are citizens of two kingdoms. What does it mean to belong to an earthly kingdom? And what then does it mean to belong to a heavenly kingdom? And what does it means to belong to these two kingdoms at exactly the same time?

I. Jesus' words here in Matthew 22 give us some guidance. His words came in response to a clever plot hatched by some very unlikely allies. The Pharisees were part of the plot. They hated the Roman government of their day and they bristled at the thought of paying a tax to an earthly king. People known as the Herodians were also part of the plot. Normally, the Pharisees and the Herodians hated each other. But evidently they each despised Jews more than they hated each other. So they got together to ask Jesus a question—a question that was just bound to get him into trouble.

a. They began with flattery: "Teacher, we know that you're true and sincere, and we know that you teach the ways of God, and we know that you don't give in to the opinions of others. So tell us what you think—Is it right to pay a tax to the Roman emperor?"

b. Now, if Jesus says yes, he'll be delivered to the Jews. They'll say, "Ah, we knew that he wouldn't have the courage to stand up to Rome. He's just playing it safe." But if he says no, he'll be charged with treason by the Romans. The gospel writer is aware of the malice of the questioners, and the Bible tells us that Jesus refuses to be swept into their trap. He answers the question with an astounding statement: "Yes, you do have an obligation to support the government. But the authority of the state has its limits, because there is also a duty to God's Kingdom—and that Kingdom claims an even higher citizenship. So, pay your tax to the emperor. It belongs to him. But give to God the things that are his— things like obedience, service, praise, honor, and love."

II. So, where exactly does that leave us today? Well, it leave us as citizens of two kingdoms.

a. First, we pledge allegiance to the flag of our earthly land. We admit and recognize the responsibilities we have to support our government, to vote, to be subject to those with political authority, to obey the laws, to pray for public officials. These are important responsibilities to remember on a holiday set aside to celebrate independence. As God's people, we must be faithful with those responsibilities. We are citizens of an earthly kingdom—and we need to be good citizens of that kingdom.

b. So we do pledge allegiance to the flag — but we also give unto God those things that belong to God. What Jesus is telling us is that the state, the nation, the government, the culture, the society is never supreme. God alone is supreme. What Jesus is telling us is that there are limits to our civil responsibility—even if we have a heritage that is as glorious and as worthy of celebration as ours.

III. I understand that culture and conformity can be deadly when they come into conflict with what God has in mind.

a. Those Old Testament heroes named Shadrach, Meshach, and Abednego were ordered by their earthly authorities to bow down before a false god, an image of the king. And they said, "We can't. We won't."

The apostles were ordered by their earthly authorities to stop preaching about Jesus. And they said, "We can't stop. We won't stop." Reformers five hundred years ago were told by their authorities to keep quiet about their new ideas. And they said, "We can't be quiet. We won't be quiet." Thomas Helwys, in the early 1600s, told the King of England that only God was God. He was told to change his mind or face severe persecution. And he said, "I can't change that conviction. I won't change that conviction." Civil rights leaders in the 1960s were ordered to stop in the name of the law. And they said, "We can't. We won't."

b. You see, for us there's an authority even higher than the authority of our government and even higher than our culture. And even on a day of freedom such as this day—maybe, especially on a day of freedom such as this day—God's people need to be reminded of that. Let's live with that holy tension and let's refuse to confuse our allegiance to country with our devotion to God. What is demanded of God's people is a faithful spirit, a discerning mind, a courageous heart, and a vigilant will.

IV. Let's thank God for our freedom. And as we thank God for that freedom—as we celebrate Independence Day and enjoy our glorious heritage—let us at the same time remember that we are citizens of two kingdoms. When our earthly kingdom and the heavenly kingdom are in agreement, let us thank God for that as well. But sometimes there is conflict. When that is the case, we have no choice but to serve God. If our two kingdoms ever force us to choose, that choice is an easy one. We answer to a higher authority—and God alone is our God.—Barry A. Stricker

Illustrations

A GLORIOUS HERITAGE.   What a history America has as a nation! What freedom and what opportunities we have today because of the costly sacrifices of people who gave and who give everything so that we can be free. I'll always remember my days at Harvard, but around July Fourth I remember them even more deeply than usual. I gained so much from classes and friendships and school activities at Harvard—but I perhaps gained even more by simply being in that part of the world. Many times I followed the Freedom Trail through Boston. The patriots met in that building; there's the Old North Church; that's where Paul Revere stood; here's where the battles were fought. I was an American history major in the land of American history. And we are all beneficiaries of that heritage.—B.A.S.

THE MUSIC OF ETERNITY.   It was Martin Luther King Jr. who said, "We need, today,

people like Shadrach, Meshach, and Abednego, who when ordered by the king to bow down before the golden image, said, 'We will not serve other gods.'. . . Christians must continually make a choice. Will we continue to march to the drumbeat of conformity and respectability, or will we, listening to the beat of a more distant drum, move to its echoing sounds? Will we march only to the music of time, or will we, risking criticism and abuse, march to the soul-saving music of eternity?" —B.A.S.

SUNDAY: JULY TWELFTH

LECTIONARY MESSAGE

Topic: Wake Up
TEXT: Luke 10:25–37
Other Readings: Amos 7:7–17; Ps. 82; Col. 1:1–14

I. How would you like to wake up battered and bleeding to look into the face of a stranger—a stranger whose dress and accent indicate that he is one of "them"? Who are "they"? Northerners, Southerners, Iraqis, Palestinians, Jews—people of different color, different religion, different values? "They" are the people we love to hate, people we detest from a distance. Your first reaction upon waking up close to one of "them" might be to get away as far as possible—and fast. But you are injured and can't escape. The stranger gives you first aid, gets you to a hospital, and pays for your care. This does not compute. "They" are supposed to be bad people, but this one treats you like a friend. What can you make of it?

That's how the story reported in our text must have affected the people who heard Jesus tell it. We almost automatically attach the word *good* to the word *Samaritan*, but that Jewish audience would not have made the same connection. Quite the contrary—they would more likely have attached to the term *Samaritan* adjectives like unclean, mongrel, or heretic. And even worse, Jesus tells the story in response to the question, "Who is my neighbor?" Even more difficult for his hearers than calling a Samaritan "good" would have been calling a Samaritan "neighbor." Jews kept their distance from Samaria and from Samaritans if possible. They certainly

would not want one of "them" living in their neighborhood.

II. Who is this who tells such a story? This is Jesus, the one who asked a Samaritan woman for water. This is Jesus, the one who invited himself home to the house of Zacchaeus, the hated tax collector. This is Jesus, the one who permitted his feet to be washed by a prostitute. This teller of shocking stories is one who lived the stories, allowing himself to be served by the outcasts of his society. He is the one who demonstrated that life lived upside down is really right side up. He is also the one who told us that we should "go and do likewise."

III. Do likewise? Like whom? Who is the example in this story—the Samaritan or the man who fell into the hands of robbers? Maybe both? Let's start with the Samaritan. That is the most obvious application of the parable. The Samaritan saw the need of a fellow human being and went out of his way to help the man. That is a good example for anybody, and it is certainly the loving, neighborly thing to do. Jesus would want his followers to act as the Samaritan in the story did.

IV. But why would I even suggest that we could somehow be like the other man? Would Jesus want us to take a trip and be injured? Of course not. But on the other hand, there are many instances in life in which we find ourselves totally helpless. It might be because of disease, as was the case with Naaman the leper (2 Kings 5). Naaman was told by the prophet to dip himself seven times in the dirty Jordan river. He at first refused because it sounded so absurd; but later he followed the instructions, since he had nothing to lose. It was only then that he was healed by God's power. Nothing to lose—perhaps that went through the mind of the injured man on the Jericho road. "I might as well let this Samaritan help me; I have nothing to lose."

Your situation of helplessness might be a spiritual problem or an emotional problem, or perhaps a problem with a relationship. You find that you have nothing to lose, so you turn to God and God's people to help. Sooner or later we all find ourselves in the nothing-to-lose category, and all too often we realize then for the first time that that's our category every day of our lives. Then we begin to recognize people and events bringing us the grace of God. Then we begin to understand what true love of God and neighbor is all about. Then we begin to be able to be neighbor to others in need. Then this is possible because we have finally seen ourselves as people who are lying helpless by the roadside, needing anybody who can offer us healing. And then we can heal them.

V. Is the parable of the good Samaritan really a parable of the grace of God? For centuries preachers interpreted it that way, but we have been told more recently that we should not allegorize. So we have settled on the understanding that the story is a good example. Instead of allegorizing, we moralize it. Even though I am not comfortable with a complete allegory of the story, I suggest that we can see the grace of God in it. Only by seeing ourselves as helpless as a result of the attack of sin can we begin to appreciate what it means to be served and saved by a gracious Other. And only when we have grown to appreciate the God whose grace has pulled us out of the ditch can we freely serve others after the example of the good Samaritan. Only when we wake up to God can we be truly awake to the needs of others.—Bruce E. Shields

Illustrations

UNDERSTANDING "SAMARITAN." "Good Samaritan" stories often appear in our local newspapers. A recent one would make a good illustration for our modern understanding of *Samaritan*. Some localities even have "Good Samaritan Laws" to protect people who help others from being sued.—B.E.S.

A NEW PERSPECTIVE. A man I had known for some time was stricken with cancer. He had before that had little time for God. From his hospital bed he told me, "Sometimes we must be flat on our backs before we can look God in the face."—B.E.S.

SERMON SUGGESTIONS

Topic: When We See God Best
TEXT: Isa. 6:1–13 REB
(1) When outward circumstances challenge our faith. (2) When personal guilt and unworthiness overwhelm us. (3) When God changes everything: by forgiving our sinfulness; by giving us significant work to do for him; by giving us confidence in the ultimate success of his plan: "Its stump is a holy seed" (v. 13).

Topic: Life as a Battle
TEXT: Eph. 6:10–18
(1) In this life we are up against overwhelming odds: powerful instinctual desires; societal pressures to conform; satanic forces, both visible and invisible. (2) However, there are strategies for victory: alertness to danger; trust in the mighty power of the Lord; putting on "the full armour provided by God" (NEB); stubborn refusal to give in; constant prayer.

Hymn Suggestions: Fifth Sunday After Trinity

1. "The Lord Will Come and Not Be Slow," John Milton (1648); "St. Magnus," Jeremiah Clark (1707)
This paraphrase of Psalm 82 (as well as Psalms 85 and 86) is a plea for God to put an end to injustices under which the nations suffer. It could be used as a response to the Psalter reading.
2. "Jesu, Jesu, Fill Us with Your Love," Tom Colvin (1969); "Chereponi," Ghana Folk Song (1969)
This Ghanian folk song beautifully expresses the unprejudiced love and care of neighbor that is the heart of the teaching of the parable of the Good Samaritan (Luke 10:25–37). It lends itself admirably to solo singing on the stanzas and response by the entire worshiping group.
3. "O Day of God, Draw Nigh," R.B.Y. Scott (1937); "St. Michael," Genevan (1551)

A hymn that calls on God to mete out judgment and bring justice, "O Day of God, Draw Nigh" could appropriately be used in connection both with the Amos prophecy and the Psalter reading.

4. "Lord, Dismiss Us with Thy Blessing," John Fawcett (1773); "Sicilian Mariners," Sicilian Melody (1792)

Following a sermon based on the Epistle (Col. 1:1–14) in which the apostle Paul is praying that the Colossians may bear the fruits of the gospel, this hymn for the closing of worship would be suitable, especially its second stanza.—Hugh T. McElrath

Worship Aids

CALL TO WORSHIP.   "How amiable are thy tabernacles, O Lord of hosts! My soul longeth, yea, even fainteth for the courts of the Lord; my heart and my flesh crieth out for the living God" (Ps. 84:1–2).

INVOCATION.   O God, satisfy the faintest or the deepest yearnings among us, as our hearts reach out toward you. Draw us into your purposes for us in this service now, and lead us as we seek to do your will in the wider world.

OFFERTORY SENTENCE.   "If you are eager to give, God will accept your gift on the basis of what you have to give, not on what you don't have" (2 Cor. 8:12 TEV).

OFFERTORY PRAYER.   We know that you can do without what we bring, Father, but we can't do without bringing it. Use these offerings for your glory, in Jesus name.—Henry Fields

PRAYER.   O God, you have not left yourself without witnesses in this world; you are continually seeking to break through to us. Help us in these moments so to center that we may hear "deep speaking unto deep." Your Word is not far from any one of us, for in you we do live and move and have our being.

Your Word is in us, in the very fact of our incompleteness without you; your Word is about us, in the beauty of the flowers at the altar, in the song of the mockingbird that awakened us this morning; your Word is above us, in that it is given, breaking in upon us through the voice of the prophet—and supremely through Christ, your Word eternal. We praise you that wherever your Word is spoken, it is the Word of an amazing grace.

We rejoice in that great cloud of witnesses in the stands cheering us on as we run the race of your high calling in Jesus. As the torch has been passed to us, may we run with perseverance the race that is set before us, looking unto him who is the pioneer and inspiration of our faith. We are indebted to all of those who have gone this way before us and all of those who today are our fellow pilgrims encouraging us along the way. It is of your grace that when we have slipped and stumbled and fallen there has always been some guiding angel who has picked us up, dusted us off, and set us on our way again.—John Thompson

Sermon: A Few Good Men
TEXT: Judg. 7:2–8
I. This was the time of vigilante law, the period between the conquest of the Promised Land and the establishment of a king over Israel. I suspect that most of the stories of the Judges were preserved to prove the necessity of a monarchy. Bernhard Anderson calls this period, "The Struggle Between Faith and Culture." A cycle is repeated throughout the book. Each Judge arose after the people had sold out to the religious culture of their neighbors. The Judge, primarily a military champion, would lead the people to repentance and reestablish control of the Land. The moral influence and corruption of Israel's neighbors was a continuing threat to its faith long after the rise of the monarchy. The Judges were historical points of reference for later failures and hopes. Times change, but the ways of God are always the same.

Gideon was among the more admirable military rulers of the time, and his story illustrates a major theme in the faith of Israel: not by my hand but by the hand of God. Gideon's military leadership was rooted in his own family. He pulled down the altar of Baal that belonged to his father Joash and replaced it with a bit of wisdom that was to reappear in future generations: "If he is a god, let him contend for himself." A real god ought to be able to act in defense of his own altar. Gideon then sounded the trumpet, calling out 32,000 soldiers. Immediately Gideon released 22,000 who were afraid. Then he was led by God to choose 300 of the remaining soldiers for the war with Midian. Selecting these soldiers according to the manner in which they chose to drink water from a stream was a reasonable way to determine the most cautious soldiers. However, the downsizing of the army of Gideon was not about military strategy. It was about Israel's dependence on God. With trumpets and jars Gideon's 300 routed the Midianites. The message of Gideon: a select minority in the power of God are a majority in the battle with moral corruption.

II.a. *God prefers minorities.* The plot is repeated with Elijah at Mt. Carmel and frequently returns throughout the Bible in the struggle with overwhelming odds against the Kingdom of God. The God of the Bible seems to prefer minorities. Israel is a tiny nation compared to the great Empires of Persia, Greece, and Rome. A visit to modern Israel is a shocking encounter with geographical reality. The size of the territory is inconsistent with the size of the impact of Israel on world history. It seems that Israel was much more at risk of total failure when she enjoyed international recognition and military success than when she became a political football for the military games of the Mediterranean. Throughout history, Israel has always been a minority power. The grandiose ideas of world dominance were never politically realistic. A message that is often unnoticed in the Old Testament is that God prefers a few good men to the masses. Jesus attracted the masses, but he chose the Twelve. Elijah whimpered that he was the only faithful servant of God left in Israel, and he was nearly right, but God does not play the numbers game so popular in the human imagination.

I have been a witness to social movements in my lifetime that have identified almost everyone with a minority. We moved from racial and ethnic conflict to a generation gap. Then we moved into the era of the gender wars, in which men and women were set against one another in competition for the leadership of every institution in our culture except the family. Now men have been declared to be an oppressed minority. The "Men's Movement" is under way, character-

ized by male bonding and the attempt to redefine masculinity. The famous evangelist Billy Sunday expressed the accepted wisdom of his time when he said, "Give a child a good mother and any old stick will do for a dad." Men have been ruled null and void, inadequate, and invisible by changing roles. If it were not so serious and if we were not all so involved, we might sit on the sidelines laughing at the politicians who appeal to the oppressed male, reverse discrimination, and the loss of masculine identity. Both the Promise Keepers and Louis Farrakhan have appealed to the flex of muscle and the show of strength in the gathering of masses. It seems that if men will form large armies beating their chests and raising their fists, they again can come to dominate the culture and win the war.

b. *Culture changes through commitment.* Gideon was engaged in a culture war with the Canaanite neighbors of Israel. The Jews had surrendered to the influence of pagan religion without a struggle. They simply swallowed the garbage of the prevailing morality and the dominant religion. Sound familiar? That is the way culture changes. I once heard a seminary teacher suggest that we need fewer "enlargement" campaigns and more "ensmallment" campaigns in our churches. What in the world did he mean? Does the church need to be smaller? That is arch heresy in the Baptist culture with which I am familiar. Where I come from, big and powerful is good. Small and weak is bad. But nothing is quite so simple. A nation or a church can be big, powerful, and spiritually weak. In the economy of God, numerical weakness is meaningless. A people has always been measured in the mind of God by the size of the commitment, not by the size of the armies.

If gathering with a mass of males in a football stadium is what you need to help you grow to spiritual maturity, go to it. But I suspect that what counts is how we act in the smaller contexts of life. A man is measured not by the force he can muster to dominate others, but by the faithfulness he demonstrates to the people who rely on him. A man is measured by the depth of his soul, not by the size of his biceps. "Culture war" is largely a battle over authority. We are not going to solve our problems by deciding who's boss. Israel won many battles but recycled their mindless submission to the thinking of the prevailing culture. We will not create a Christian culture through the power of commitment. God is still seeking a few good men to do the work of the Kingdom, and our God will choose three hundred committed men any day over 32,000 macho males who are out to rule the world.—Larry Dipboye

Illustrations

THE HOPE OF THE WORLD IN ITS MINORITIES.   When the Master in Palestine began calling out his first disciples from the mass of their countrymen, he was interested not in quantity but in quality—in seed, though but a few kernels, which if carefully sown might multiply itself. He was thinking not primarily of the 98 percent but of a germinal 2 percent. To use his own figure in the thirteenth chapter of Matthew's Gospel: "The kingdom of heaven is like unto leaven, which a woman took, and hid in three measures of meal, till it was all leavened." Quantitatively small, vitally active leaven—that is a true simile of the method of Christianity's transformation of the world.—Harry Emerson Fosdick[1]

THE NEW LOVE.   When the New Life takes hold of a person it means, among other things, that one image takes precedence over all the others. It does not, of course, do what we wish it would; it does not immediately wipe all the others out, all the other poor ones, that is. But if we give it a chance, gradually, little by little, it exercises dominion over them! It is the image of a man, a strange man, strange to us in many ways. He usually first comes to us as a young man with a beard, in a long white robe, out of an entirely different world, living by an entirely different pattern of life. But this strangeness is superficial. The real strangeness goes far deeper than that. He is a man with no money; he gave up his job to undertake a mission for no pay, and the mission was a failure. Yet paradoxically, he himself as we look at him is the only really successful one among us.—Theodore Parker Ferris

SUNDAY: JULY NINETEENTH

LECTIONARY MESSAGE

Topic: Listen Up
TEXT: Luke 10:38–42
Other Readings: Amos 8:1–12; Ps. 52; Col. 1:15–28

I. *We celebrate Martha.* Who gets the honor in our society—the doer or the thinker? Even our institutions of higher education have been forced to justify their programs in terms of higher earnings and job placement. Have you ever heard of a guidance counselor suggesting that somebody attend a school so as to become a better person? In most cases a counselor will say that a person has the gifts to do this or that kind of work and should therefore go where he or she can be best prepared to do it and most likely find a job after the preparation.

Who gets elected to high office in our society—the doer or the thinker? We rarely hear anybody say, "Let's elect her; she really understands the situation." We are more likely to hear, "Let's elect him, he gets things done." Do you remember the definition of WORK taught in high school? As I recall, it was, "Work is moving an object from one place to another." Rodin's statue "The Thinker" has no place in a world driven by such an attitude.

Who gets called to minister to the big churches—the doer or the thinker? Even in the church we tend to quantify work. Rarely if ever does a search committee or a bishop ask to see a prospect's seminary transcript. What we look for is a proven track record. We look for success in the activities of ministry. Has the congregation grown? Has the budget increased? Even doctrinal questions are slipping farther and farther down the priority list. It is of little importance to know what a person thinks, only what the person can get done. We celebrate Martha.

II. *We denigrate Mary.* Jesus clearly disagrees with our priorities. He tells Martha that only one activity is important—the one Mary is involved in. Martha is "worried and

[1] *The Hope of the World.*

distracted by many things. . . . Mary has chosen the better part, which will not be taken away from her." And what is it that Mary is doing? The description is simple: "Mary . . . sat at the Lord's feet and listened to what he was saying." She put herself in the position of a learner and listened. The better activity is listening to Jesus.

This accolade for the listener should not surprise us. The primary activity of the religion of Israel is contained in the Shema, which begins: "Hear, O Israel" (Deut. 6:4). Jesus fended off his first temptation from Satan by quoting Deuteronomy 8:3: "One does not live by bread alone, but by every word that comes from the mouth of God" (Matt. 4:4). The apostle Paul wrote: "So faith comes from what is heard, and what is heard comes through the word of Christ" (Rom. 10:17). The whole Bible undergirds Jesus' teaching that the one important activity is listening to God.

Yet we denigrate listening. We throw around our cute sayings like "Actions speak louder than words" or "A picture is worth a thousand words." We quote the poem that begins, "I'd rather see a sermon any day than hear one." We have developed proverbs like, "Talk is cheap." The older proverb, "A man's word is his bond," seems downright ancient, doesn't it? The work of speaking and listening is not even honored in education today. Students are encouraged to discover knowledge for themselves. Hands-on education is honored above lecture-style learning. Our society has thrown listening on the garbage heap of old-fashioned methods. We denigrate Mary, the listener, and we elevate Martha, the doer.

But we can't escape Jesus' accolade in our text. "Mary has chosen the better part," and even our modern society cannot take that away from her. We need to shake ourselves and begin to criticize our priorities. It is high time that we begin to hear again. Hear the Word of God. Listen to Jesus.

III. *We listen to Jesus.* To follow Mary's example we must first assume a particular position. Mary seated herself at Jesus' feet. This is more than just a description of a physical position. To sit at a person's feet in Mary's society meant to put oneself in the role of a pupil in the presence of a master teacher. I once heard a European university professor

say that when he was teaching at Harvard he had the feeling that his barber considered a professor somebody who couldn't make it in business. I fear that this is all too accurate. Perhaps if we begin with the Son of God it will be a bit easier for us to honor his role as teacher. Jesus knows something that we need to attend to. He has insights into human life that we need to hear. Let's put away the distracting activities of our busy lives and for a time seat ourselves humbly at his feet. Let's assume the posture of the learner.

Then, once Mary was seated at Jesus' feet, she "listened to what he was saying." Listening is an art that we should cultivate. We must discipline ourselves to pay attention. There are many distractions. Even in a service of worship we are surrounded by people and objects that can easily lead us away from the words of Jesus. It is too easy to allow our minds to wander. We owe it to God and to ourselves to do whatever it takes to set our minds on a regular schedule for a specific time on the Word of God. One thing you might try is reading the Bible aloud. The Bible was written to be pronounced. We can read to our spouses, our children, our friends. But we can also read to ourselves. Listen, hear, O Christian. Let your faith grow out of your hearing the Word of Christ.—Bruce E. Shields

Illustrations

THINKER AND DOER.   Adlai Stevenson, the thinking politician, had little chance to win his race for the presidency of the United States; he was running against Dwight D. Eisenhower, the proven doer.—B.E.S.

DISCIPLINE.   Learning is not a passive activity. The concentration necessary for listening in order to learn saps energy. It takes real discipline, a word that comes from the same root as *disciple.*—B.E.S.

SERMON SUGGESTIONS

Topic: A Study in Contrasts
TEXT: Ps. 1

(1) The way of the righteous. (2) The way of the wicked. (3) The role of the Lord.

Topic: Confidence That Changes Everything
TEXT: Rom. 8:38–39

(1) The sheer fact and grace of our human existence—we are here! (2) The daily little blessings and occasional surprises that brighten our lives—we have seen! (3) The testimony of the Scripture on providence and miracle, forgiveness, and promises—we have heard! (4) The personal decision to go with God in Christ—we have believed!

Hymn Suggestions

1. "Jesus, the Very Thought of Thee," twelfth-century Latin, translated by Edward Caswall (1849); "St. Agnes," John B. Dykes (1866)

A hymn expressing supreme devotion to Christ, "Jesus, the Very Thought of Thee" can reflect the mood of Mary in the Gospel reading for this day.

2. "Before Thy Throne, O God, We Kneel," William B. Carpenter (1925); "St. Petersburg," Dimitri S. Bortnianski (1825)

This hymn of repentance pleads for Christian responsibility in the face of God's judgment. It is therefore appropriate for use in connection both with the Old Testament reading in Amos and with the Psalter reading (52).

3. "Mighty Mortal, Boasting Evil," Helen Otte (1985); "Madill," Aubrey L. Butler (1971)

A new version of Psalm 52, this hymn with its militant tune conveys the anger against the enemies of God that dominates the message of the psalm.

4. "How Clear Is Our Vocation, Lord," Fred Pratt Green (1981); "Repton," C. Hubert H. Parry (1888)

Should the worship and homily focus on the Epistle reading in Galatians, this recently created hymn on Christian vocation would be quite appropriate.—Hugh T. McElrath

Worship Aids

CALL TO WORSHIP.   "O come, let us worship and bow down; let us kneel before the Lord our Maker. For he is our God; and we are the people of his pasture, and the sheep of his hand" (Ps. 95:6–7a).

INVOCATION.   Lord of life, bring the reconciling power of God to bear on our hearts this day, so that we will gladly right wrongs, forgive others, repent of our sins, and worship God with clean hands and pure hearts. —E. Lee Phillips

OFFERTORY SENTENCE.   "For unto whomsoever much is given, of him shall be much required; and to whom men have committed much, of him they will ask the more" (Luke 12:48b).

OFFERTORY PRAYER.   Lord, let our priorities be kingdom priorities, our goals the goals of God, our desires the wishes of Christ for every person, our giving the means to those ends through the power of thy Holy Spirit. —E. Lee Phillips

PRAYER.   We are indeed a part of every person we have ever met. No person lives or dies unto herself or to himself. When we contemplate the interrelatedness of life we are amazed at all of those who contribute to our well-being in our every day. How grateful we are for those who hold up our arms lest we become weary and drop the torch that has been passed to us. For all of those who have been patient, understanding, loving, and encouraging, we thank you. May we never take others for granted but always think of them with gratitude.

What a blessing good health is! How often we never appreciate it until it is threatened. May we not take our health for granted but pursue those disciplines that are so essential to well-being. For those ill among us, we pray for the miracle of your healing grace. Where there are physical limitations that must be lived with, we pray for a wholeness of mind and spirit that transcends the brokenness of body. For any of us passing through the valley of the shadow of grief we pray for the light of your presence. For the tasks of today, and every day, may we experience the power mediated to us in Christ's Resurrection.

We pray for the family that is our home! We pray for our faith family! We pray for the family of the nations, we pray for the family of humankind, that all may experience the joy of peace.

Through him who teaches us to pray as a family, with all peoples: "Our Father. . . ." —John Thompson

Sermon: How to Hold Up Your Head When You're Feeling Down

TEXT: Lam. 3:1–25; 1 John 3:1a NRSV

Have you ever been in a situation where you felt really low, so low that you were tempted to give up and call it quits? So low that you despaired of life? So low that you didn't care if you lived or died? If you have, you should not be ashamed. It is a common experience of all humanity.

We have read the account of one who was at the point of despair. The Lamentations, traditionally attributed to the prophet Jeremiah, are communal laments that were written after the destruction of Jerusalem by the Babylonians in 587 B.C. The Lamentations are mournful dirges over the loss of their beloved holy city. The speakers could not understand how God could let such a thing happen to Jerusalem and its people. There was devastation, hunger, personal loss, and loss of self-esteem and confidence. The people were about as low as one can get.

Yet, as we read the Lamentations, we see some biblical principles that, if remembered, can help us hold up our heads when we are feeling down.

I. *Remember that you are loved.* One of the first things we begin to think when we are feeling down is "nobody loves me." I have thought it, perhaps you have thought it, and I am sure the composers of the Lamentations thought it. Though we may not be able to see it because of the dark clouds that obscure our lives, there are always people in our families, in our church, in our community who love us.

In spite of his depression and discouragement, the writer of this lamentation was able to assure us, "The steadfast love of the Lord never ceases" (3:22). When you can count on little else in life, you can still count on the steadfast love of God. As the apostle John put it, "See what love the Father has given us, that we should be called the children of God; and that is what we are" (1 John 3:1). If we can only remember when we are feeling down that we are loved, we will have already begun the process of picking ourselves back up again.

II. *Remember that you are not alone.* In the early part of this lamentation, the author feels all alone. He says, "Against me alone he [God] turns his hand" (3:3). You see, the writer feels that through the destruction of Jerusalem, God is punishing him personally. He felt all alone in his suffering.

And that is often the way it is with us. When trouble comes, we may immediately ask, "Why is God punishing me?" And then we may feel that we are all alone in our suffering. People suffering terminal illness or diseases that carry social stigma often feel isolated or alone. And that is why the human touch—a squeeze of the hand, a pat on the shoulder—is so important to one who is hospitalized. The psalmist in Psalm 25 said, "I am lonely and afflicted" (25:16). In the 102nd Psalm, he lamented, "I am like a lonely bird on the housetop" (102:7).

But the truth is we are never alone. There is always a family member, a friend, a neighbor, a coworker to stand beside us. And God is always there, too, to hold us up with his invisible presence. As put so beautifully in Deuteronomy, "The eternal God is your dwelling place, and underneath are the everlasting arms" (33:27 RSV). Remember that you are never alone.

III. *Remember that things often seem worse than they really are.* I am sure that the author of this lament felt that things would never turn around, that the devastation would last forever, that Jerusalem would never rise again, and that things would never be any better than they were right then.

I am reminded of the prophet Elijah, who contended against the evil queen Jezebel and the prophets of Baal. Elijah saw things to be much worse than they really were. He, too, felt all alone and saw little hope for positive change. The prophet Elijah lamented, "The Israelites have thrown down your altars, and killed your prophets with the sword. I alone am left, and they are seeking my life, to take it away" (1 Kings 19:10, 14).

And yet God revealed to Elijah that there were thousands in Israel who had not bowed the knee to Baal and who were in the same boat he was in (1 Kings 19:18). Things were not as bad as Elijah had perceived them to be.

And so it often is with us. Things often appear much worse to us than they really are. We may feel that we are left alone to deal with unsolvable problems, that nobody knows what we are going through, that things cannot possibly get any better than they are right now. But things often seem worse than they really are.

IV. *Remember that there is always hope.* "This I call to mind, and therefore I have hope: [God's] mercies never come to an end; they are new every morning" (Lam. 3:21–23). Great is God's faithfulness! You have heard the old saying that "the darkest hour is just before the dawn." What that means is "morning comes." Just when we think our world cannot get any darker, we see the glow of light on the horizon. God usually sends some sort of angel of hope to us, as he sent an angel of help to Elijah in the wilderness.

In reading Elizabeth Brown Pryor's biography of Clara Barton, we learn that Barton, professional angel of the battlefield and organizer of the American Red Cross Society, was plagued with depression off and on throughout her life. A nervous breakdown incapacitated her for a two-year period. At another time she was so depressed that she despaired of life. During this dark time of depression Barton wrote in her diary, I "have done . . . with my efforts on behalf of others. I must take the little remnant of my life, that may remain in me, as my own special property, and appropriate it accordingly." Later she confessed to her diary, "Have been sad all day. I cannot raise my spirits, the old temptation to go from all the world. I think it will come to that some day, it is a struggle to keep in society at all. I want to leave it all."[2] Her biographer states that Clara Barton at this point was considering suicide. What is so surprising about all this is that this dark period when she contemplated suicide occurred before she founded the Red Cross. At this point in her life Barton felt there was no hope. Yet her greatest work, her greatest happiness, and her greatest contribution to the world was yet to come. There is always hope!

Unless you are some kind of super human, the time will come, no doubt, when you will feel as low as low can be. It is the common experience of all humanity. But these four biblical principles, if you can remember them, will help you hold up your head when you begin to feel down. Remember that (1) you are loved, (2) you are not alone, (3) things often seem worse than they really are, and (4) there is always hope!—Randy Hammer

Illustrations

DEPRESSED.   The person caught in this unhappy experience needs to do several things. From a religious standpoint his most important need is to realize that even in the deepest spiritual darkness, God is with him in the dark. Though there may be no awareness of God's presence, God has not forsaken him. Though one's prayer may seem to have no answer, God is answering it by imparting the faith and the strength by which to go on.—Georgia Harkness[3]

GOD'S WILL.   That "resignation" or acceptance of God's will is what Kierkegaard explored in *Fear and Trembling*—not a surrender of personal initiative, not an apathy, not a descent into gloom or despair, but a thoughtful acknowledgment of what can and cannot be done. For Kierkegaard such resignation was a believer's step: I await what the Lord decides.—Robert Coles[4]

SUNDAY: JULY TWENTY-SIXTH

LECTIONARY MESSAGE

Topic: Speak Up
    TEXT: Luke 11:1–13
    Other Readings: Hos. 1:2–10; Ps. 85; Col. 2:6–15 (16–19)
    I. *Jesus' prayer life.* Jesus must have had an impressive prayer life. We see mention of his praying in many parts of the gospels. We are given details of prayers in John 17 and in the depictions of the Garden of Gethsemane scene. Then, in our gospel text for today, we have the only incidence of somebody requesting his teaching on a specific topic—and the topic is prayer.

After they had observed Jesus praying, the disciples asked him, "Lord, teach us to pray." Whether this is a request for a group prayer or for basic instruction in individual prayer is

2 *Clara Barton: Professional Angel,* p. 124.

3 *Prayer and the Common Life.*
4 *The Call of Service.*

not clear. The disciples might not have seen a distinction between the two. What is clear is that Jesus had such an impressive discipline of prayer that his disciples wanted to know how to pray that way.

II. *Jesus' model prayer.* Jesus began by wording for them a model prayer. The words Luke records as being given to the disciples are a bit different from those recorded by Matthew as given to the crowd on the mountain (Matt. 6:9–13). It is Matthew's version that Christians usually memorize and pray together, but Luke's version is interesting in its own right. Let's pray it together as it is printed in your bulletin:

Father,
hallowed be your name.
Your kingdom come.
Give us each day our daily bread.
And forgive us our sins,
for we ourselves forgive
everyone indebted to us.
And do not bring us to the time of trial.

III. *Pray directly and simply.* Even more obviously than Matthew's version, this one is a bare-bones model of a prayer. It has a certain poetry to it, but the abrupt ending would make it difficult to use in corporate worship. Without going into a detailed analysis of the prayer, we can recognize that it first addresses God as Father; it then requests that God be glorified and that God's reign be actualized; it then offers petitions for daily necessities, for forgiveness, and for the guidance and power necessary to keep us from succumbing to temptation. Perhaps most important, we should note the very simple and direct manner in which this prayer speaks with God. It seems always to have been a problem (and it seems to be for us today) that we humans want to make our religious speech somehow more exalted in style than normal speech. The motivation for this is understandable and laudable, but it appears from Jesus' teaching that it is misguided.

One reason we pray less than we should—either in private or in public—is probably that we think we should pray like a professional. Or maybe we think we need some special language to make prayer acceptable. Jesus shows that our prayers can be very simple and very direct. As Rosalind Rinker has put it, prayer is "conversing with God." God understands not only our words but also our hearts. Therefore we should feel free to speak to him in our normal voices and words.

IV. *Pray persistently.* Jesus was not finished teaching them to pray when he gave them the model. He went on to tell them a brief story about going to a friend at midnight to ask for some bread to feed a surprise visitor. Even though we might have to ask several times, the friend will give the bread if for no other reason than our persistence. God, of course, is not to be compared with an exasperated human friend; but Jesus thus makes the point that we should persist in prayer. One commentator wrote, "Go on praying because God responds graciously to the needs of his children."[5] Our prayers should be both direct and persistent.

V. *Pray expectantly.* And then we find the familiar words of Jesus, "Ask, and it will be given you; search, and you will find; knock, and the door will be opened for you." He follows this with the example of the kind response of the earthly father to his child. The father would not give a snake if asked for a fish, nor a scorpion if asked for an egg. So we can pray to the heavenly Father expecting that he, even more than earthly parents, will respond with kindness. In fact, the conclusion of Jesus here is rather surprising. God is seen giving not just what we ask but "the Holy Spirit to those who ask him!" This God who responds to our prayers does so with surprises that go beyond "all we can ask or imagine" (Eph. 3:20). In this knowledge, we are encouraged to pray expectantly.

How then shall we pray? We should pray simply and directly, knowing that God reads our hearts as well as understands our words. We should pray persistently, knowing that the gracious God wants to respond with what is best for us. We should pray expectantly, trusting that God will pour out gifts far beyond our dreams.—Bruce E. Shields

Illustrations

DIRECT PRAYER.   It would be appropriate for the preacher to give some simple instruction to the congregation in direct prayer.

[5]I. H. Marshall, *Commentary on Luke* (Grand Rapids, Michigan: Eerdmans, 1978), 462.

Rosalind Rinker's approach in her book *Prayer: Conversing with God*[6] has proved helpful. The steps in her method are: Jesus is here; Thank you, Lord; Help me; Help my brother/sister.—B.E.S.

KINDNESS. The preacher should be able to find an example of an unlikely father who treats his child with kindness even when he treats others meanly.—B.E.S.

SERMON SUGGESTIONS

Topic: Getting to the Heart of Things
TEXT: Prov. 4:23
(1) The source of our actions: imagination, affection, anger, decision. (2) The consequences of our actions: sometimes harmful to self and to others, sometimes all to the good. (3) What makes the difference: (a) seeking the will of God in Scripture, prayer, and public worship; (b) living by the law of love.

Topic: Real Love
TEXT: Rom. 12:9
(1) Its source: Christ, who loved us and gave himself for us. (2) Its reflexive expression: the members of the body of Christ (a) share each other's lot, (b) bear each other's burdens, (c) share each other's joy.—After Anders Nygren[7]

Hymn Suggestions: Seventh Sunday After Trinity

1. "Great Is Thy Faithfulness," Thomas O. Chisolm (1923); "Faithfulness," William M. Runyan (1923)
This favorite of singing congregations exalts the steadfastness and faithfulness of God that is a basic theme in Psalm 85.
2. "Great Redeemer, We Adore Thee," John Roy Harris (1934); "Redentore," Paolo Conte (1930)
Hosea's life—an incarnation of God's redeeming love—should call forth praise for the Great Redeemer, which is the theme of this hymn of adoration.
3. "Awake, My Heart, with Gladness," Paul

[6]Grand Rapids: Zondervan, 1959, and later editions.
[7]*Commentary on Romans.*

Gerhardt, translated by John Kelly (1867); "Auf, Auf, Mein Herz," Johann Cruger (1648)
This venerable Easter hymn is quite appropriate as an accompaniment to the Epistle reading in which the triumph of Christ over the powers of evil is realized in the fullness of life given to those who have received Christ. Those stanzas that refer specifically to the Resurrection (stanza 2, for example) could well be omitted, if desired, in order to focus more generally on the joy and hope of those who are rooted and grounded in Christ.
4. "Our Father God, Who Art in Heaven," Adoniram Judson (1825); "Morning Song," traditional American melody (1820)
"Our Father, Which Art in Heaven," Cleveland and Nix (1988); "West Indian," folk tune, arranged by C. Young (1981)
"The Lord's Prayer," Matt. 6:9–14; "Malotte," Albert Hay Malotte (1935)
These are three widely varied settings of the Lord's Prayer from among the many that are available. Luke 11:2–4 is an abbreviated version, the reading of which could be replaced by singing one of these settings. The second version is in a call and response pattern, in which a soloist or choir could sing the phrases and the congregation could respond with the "Hallowed Be Thy Name" refrain.—Hugh T. McElrath

Worship Aids

CALL TO WORSHIP. "Cast thy burden upon the Lord, and he shall sustain thee: he shall never suffer the righteous to be moved" (Ps. 55:22).

INVOCATION. We are grateful for the privilege of prayer, O God, and we have come here to pray. Teach us again how to pray and find strength to do your will as you reveal to us what you would have us do.

OFFERTORY SENTENCE. "Our brothers, we want you to know what God's grace has accomplished in the churches in Macedonia. They have been severely tested by the troubles they went through; but their joy was so great that they were extremely generous in their giving, even though they are very poor. I can assure you that they gave as much as they could, and even more than they could. Of their own free will they begged us and pleaded for the privilege of having a part in helping God's people in Judea. It was more than we could have hoped for! First they gave themselves to the Lord; and then, by God's will they gave themselves to us as well" (2 Cor. 8:1–5 TEV).

OFFERTORY PRAYER.   Loving Lord, our God, bless the mission enterprise of the church through our gifts today, build up the saints, carry the gospel into new places, and let Jesus reign.—E. Lee Phillips

PRAYER.   O God, guide us through the dark places in life. Grant that we may not fear the loss of thee, knowing that thou art always by our side, and that life will renew itself in us if we give it time and are willing to wait. And as we rise out of the low places through which we sometimes must walk, help us to be thankful for them, because through them and by them we may be able to help someone else through the darkness into light.—Theodore Parker Ferris

Sermon: Hearts to God
TEXT: John 15:1–11

I. One of the most vivid symbols Jesus ever gave his followers was that of the vine and the branches. It was something everyone could understand—an image of unmistakable meaning and significance. "I am the vine," said Jesus, "and you are the branches." He then spoke of how a vine, through its branches, produces fruit—but only, of course, if that branch remains attached to its source of life and nourishment, which is the vine.

So clear is this symbol, and so important, that Christian art and architecture through the ages have reproduced it, in all sorts of ways. All around us, if we stop to look, are representations of Jesus' teaching when he said, "I am the vine, you are the branches."

The connection is crucial. Jesus said, "Anyone who does not remain in me is like a branch that has been thrown away—he withers." Only in linkage and relationship can there be an abundant flowering of life; only as our lives "make their home" in Christ and remain in him can there be fruitful results. It is always through the branches that the vine bears, whether the subject is agriculture or the spiritual life. By ourselves, no sustained productivity is possible. In company with

Christ, there is an overflowing harvest. Said Jesus, "It is the person who shares my life and whose life I share who proves fruitful." He added, "The plain fact is that apart from me you can do nothing at all." Summing it up, preacher Roger Fredrikson writes, "This fruit that the disciples bear is not what they do, but the life of Jesus in them. It is his character reproduced within them and shared with others in love. This cannot come to pass without the disciple abiding in Jesus, making his home in him as Jesus makes his home in the disciple. His life is shared with the disciples as their life is given to him."

It becomes a matter of where one's loyalties lie. Enormous competition exists for the allegiance of each man, woman, youth, and child among us. The merit of all the competing causes before us ranges from low to lofty; all too easily, the low is chosen and the lofty remains unrealized. Jesus, of course, beckons us to the highest possibilities.

II. *Our unique offering.* An intriguing way of expressing the loyalty we give to Christ and the life we commit to him is found in the meditative writings of Thomas Merton. Struggling to clarify the meaning of his own life, Merton concluded that he and every person has "a special, peculiar destiny which no one else ever has had or ever will have. . . . My own individual destiny," he writes, "is a meeting, an encounter with God destined for me alone." Then Merton says, "God's glory will be to receive from me something God can never receive from anyone else." Without defining what he uniquely will be able to offer to God, Merton nevertheless sees this as an exciting, fulfilling experience—the whole point of his life, the whole reason for his existence.

One's commitment has consequences, in other words. Abiding in Christ does not signify a cozy, private companionship separated from responsible living and serving in Christ's name. The description offered by Thomas Merton is appropriate, indeed; his point is that each individual has a special contribution to make as the outcome of his or her encounter with God. "God's glory will be to receive from me something God can never receive from anyone else."

III. *The promised outcome.* To all the rest of us comes the same expectation. We in our places, in our activities, are also called to bear fruit and go give God glory. That certainly is the agenda for each person. Loyalty and allegiance given to our Lord combined with acts of loving service both glorify God and produce fruits worthy of God. Such is our Christian calling—as students, graduates, persons of every age and circumstance—to give hearts to God, hands to work.

Most of us will be taking one step at a time in doing these things, in offering ourselves and our service to God. At some point an unusual opportunity may present itself. Much of the time, however, we shall be engaged in ordinary tasks; to them, to those tasks, we have the privilege of bringing blessings beyond the ordinary as we live out our Christian commitment. God will honor each effort and enable us to produce even more fruit than we dare to imagine.

We, you and I, give ourselves to God—hearts to God—and ask him to make productive persons of us. We want to glorify God and become disciples of his calling. The promised outcome of such commitment is in this concluding statement from the lips of Jesus: "I have said these things to you so that my joy [my perfect happiness] may be in you, and that your joy may be complete."—John H. Townsend

Illustrations

COMMITMENT.   As General William Booth, founder of the Salvation Army, lay dying, one of his associates asked, "Tell us General, before you go, what has been the secret of your wonderful life?"

"If there has been any secret," the aged man whispered, "it has been that God has had all that there was of me." There was absolutely no doubt about William Booth's loyalty and allegiance. God had the fullness of his commitment, the totality of his life. As he said, "God has had all that there was of me."—J.H.T.

YIELDING ALL.   Perhaps we can put ourselves in the situation of a little boy who Corrie ten Boom heard about. A mother she met told her that one day her little boy was sitting in the corner of the room saying, "A-B-C-D-E-F-G. . . ."

"What are you doing?" asked the mother.

The boy answered, "Mom, you told me I should pray, but I have never prayed in my life and I don't know how. So I gave God the whole alphabet and asked him to make a good prayer of it."—J.H.T.

SUNDAY: AUGUST SECOND

LECTIONARY MESSAGE

Topic: Our Stewardship of God's Providence
TEXT: Luke 12:13–21
Other Readings: Hos. 11:1–11; Ps. 107:1–9, 43; Col. 3:1–11

I. *The fruitfulness of God's earth.* Jesus here gives us stories of two men who had connection with an abundance of goods and of the principles governing the disposition of their wealth. In relation to the first man, let us ask, Where did the "abundance of the things he possesses" come from? No doubt many will say from the providence of God.

a. Natural law without humanity is a mere barbaric, fruitless force; but natural law with mankind is a power of civilization. A pastor visiting a parishioner at his large and beautiful farm was expounding on the beauty and fruitfulness of the fields God had given, and on the plentifulness and richness of the harvests God had provided. After a thoughtful moment, the farmer replied, "Yes, but you should have seen it when he had it all to himself." The farmer had brought stumps and stones under control so that God could exercise the laws of growth where seeds were sown.

b. Natural laws are fruitful and beneficial only when they have been touched by the power of the human mind and spirit. Can you picture the Earth without humanity, with every vestige of human life removed? Within a few short years it would become uninhabitable even for the beasts—the globe would soon become as empty as the moon. It would still be following all the natural tendencies of the forces that have been discovered and elucidated by science—gravity, magnetism, electrostatic charges, light, heat, pneumatics, and hydraulics—everything that causes the seasons to change.

c. But such impersonal forces of God's creation leave only a barren wilderness unless guided by the caring intelligence of humanity. All that makes time and the world of any value would perish. God could not stand the world without his presence in the form of mankind. And for mankind God especially provides.

II. *The burden of fruitfulness.* Now, what happens when humans use their higher powers for their own self-centered indulgence?

a. After converting the void, vulgar, coarse, hard, bestial forces of nature into servants of mankind, we employ them for the glory of mankind—so much so that one person gets the idea of saving it all for himself, of hoarding the best fruits of the ground in storage facilities—not just for tomorrow's needs, as the man in the second story sees it, "for many years," but for personal gratification as well. What then? Just as human mentality can harness, employ, translate, convert, and even reverse the actions of the natural laws discovered by science, so the human spirit can control the laws of the human body and its forces.

b. Isn't most of our destructiveness from selfish origin? Whenever one sees any part of life as a force to be exploited or betrayed, disaster results. Consider the financial cost—much more, the human cost—of such individual exploitation. God has guided the intelligence of humans to discover natural elements that will alleviate all kinds of suffering, but when used to destroy ordinary sensations and to obliterate society and conscience, these substances become unbearably costly to individual, family, community, and national life. Alcohol, drugs, tobacco, hemp, and poppies may be used to provide temporary isolation of the individual from the duties and burdens of normal life, to violate intelligence, and even to destroy human life and possessions.

How dare those who destroy their own bodies and consciences by one of these substances attempt to pass the cost to society by suing their providers? How dare the rich man in our parable plan to tear down his barns and build more and larger ones to store his wealth? God claims the life of each one of us as his own. If we put ourselves or our possessions ahead of him, who enabled us to enhance our portion of life, he will take it all away from us. "This night your soul will be required of you." Is that not what is happening to our civilization? God's providence

in no way acts to relieve mankind of the responsibility for its outcomes, but he will hold us to account for our use of it, individually and collectively.—John R. Rodman

Illustrations

ECOLOGICAL SANITY.   Piety is deepest practicality, for it properly relates use and enjoyment. And a world sacramentally received in joy is a world sanely used. There is an economics of use only; it moves toward the destruction of both use and joy. And there is an economics of joy; it moves toward the intelligence of use and the enhancement of joy. That this vision involves a radical new understanding of the clean and fruitful Earth is certainly so. But this vision, deeply religious in its genesis, is not so very absurd now that natural damnation is in orbit, and man's befouling of his ancient home has spread his death and dirt among the stars.—Joseph Sittler[1]

THREE MANDATES.   Throughout the Hebrew Scriptures runs a promise of a messianic time when "kindness and truth shall meet; justice and peace shall kiss" (Ps. 85:11). Then justice will be "secure" and peace without end (see Isa. 9:6–7). Meanwhile, the covenant places urgent "within history" responsibilities upon its adherents. The classic summary of what Yahweh asks in covenant of all humankind is found in Micah 6:8; a passage that King refers to as "the Magna Carta of prophetic religion." God asked "only this, to act justly, to love tenderly and to walk humbly with your God" (Mic. 6:8 JB). The three mandates cannot be separated; as people do justice with loving kindness, their faith as right relationship with God is realized.—Thomas H. Groome[2]

WAKING UP.   Even as we celebrated the twentieth anniversary of Earth Day on 22 April 1990, it became clear that we weren't just celebrating the past; we were anticipating the future. For more and more people from

[1] *The Care of the Earth.*
[2] *Sharing Faith.*

all walks of life—young and old, Republican and Democrat, in the United States and worldwide—are hearing an urgent environmental wake-up call from the twenty-first century. It is, in fact, an ultimatum: clean up our act or pay the consequences—possibly the breakdown of the very systems that support planetary life as we have known it. I believe that at maximum we have ten to fifteen years to begin reversing the trends of environmental degradation—or suffer the consequences. —Tom Sine[3]

SERMON SUGGESTIONS

Topic: Test for Those Who Claim to Speak for God

TEXT: Jer. 23; Matt. 7:15–23

(1) Ethical/moral test (Jer. 23:9–12; Matt. 7:15, 21–23). (2) Test of vain hopes (Jer. 23:16–17). (3) Test of effectiveness (Jer. 23:29, 32; Matt. 7:16–20). (4) Test of integrity/responsibility (Jer. 23:18–22, 25–28, 30, 31–32; Matt. 7:21a). (5) Test of vitality (Jer. 23:33, 36).—Ron Blankenship

Topic: The Love of God

TEXT: John 3:16

The love of God: (1) is needed; (2) is provided; (3) is experienced; (4) is consummated.

Hymn Suggestions: Eighth Sunday After Trinity

1. "O Love That Wilt Not Let Me Go," George Mattheson (1882); "St. Margaret," Albert L. Peace (1884)

The first phrase of this hymn that was born out of tragic experience sums up the message of Hosea: God in loving patience refuses to give up on his rebellious and disobedient children.

2. "Sing Praise to God Who Reigns Above," Johann J. Schutz, translated by Frances E. Cox (1864); "Mit Freuden Zart," Bohemian Brethren Kirchengesange (1566)

This great German hymn gathers up the themes of praise and thankfulness for "the God of love," which is the burden of the Psalmist's song in this day's Psalter reading.

3. "God of Grace and God of Glory," Harry E. Fosdick (1930); "Cwm Rhondda," John Hughes (1907)

Fosdick's great hymn, written for the dedication of Riverside Church in New York City, is a prayer for wisdom and courage to be responsible as Christians. It is an admirable response to the Lucan parable of the man who was "rich in things but poor in soul" (stanza 3).

4. "I'm Pressing on the Upward Way," Johnson Oatman Jr. (1892); "Higher Ground," Charles H. Gabriel (1892)

As a response to the exhortation of the apostle Paul (Col. 3:1–11) to put off the old nature and set his mind on things above, this gospel song of aspiration can be useful.

Worship Aids

TO WORSHIP.   "I will praise thee, O Lord, with my whole heart; I will shew forth all thy marvelous works. I will be glad and rejoice in thee: I will sing praise to thy name, O thou most High" (Ps. 9:1–2).

INVOCATION.
Lord of our days,
Give to our worship substance,
To our prayer resonance,
To our resolve grace,
That we may be made strong through worship,
Wise in prayer,
And dedicated in service,
Through our Lord Jesus Christ.—E. Lee Phillips

OFFERTORY SENTENCE.   "But this I say, He which soweth sparingly shall reap also sparingly; and he which soweth bountifully shall reap also bountifully" (2 Cor. 9:6).

OFFERTORY PRAYER.   Lord, please take these offerings, small and great, and multiply them by your power so that they may do mighty things in your name across the vastness of this world.—Henry Fields

PRAYER.   God, we thank thee for this universe, our great home—for its vastness and its riches, and for the manifoldness of the life that teems upon it and of which we are part.

[3] *Wild Hope.*

We praise thee for the arching sky and the blessed winds, for the driving clouds and the constellations on high. We praise thee for the salt sea and the running water, for the everlasting hills, for the trees, and for the grass under our feet. We thank thee for our senses, by which we can see the splendor of the morning and hear the jubilant songs of love and smell the breath of the springtime. Grant us, we pray thee, a heart wide open to all this joy and beauty, and save our souls from being so steeped in care or so darkened by passion that we pass heedless and unseeing when even the thornbush by the wayside is aflame with the glory of God.

Enlarge within us the sense of fellowship with all the living things, our little brothers, to whom thou hast given this earth as their home in common with us. We remember with shame that in the past we have exercised the high dominion of man with ruthless cruelty, so that the voice of the Earth, which should have gone up to thee in song, has been a groan of travail. May we realize that they live not for us alone but for themselves and for thee, and that they love the sweetness of life even as we, and serve thee in their place better than we in ours.

When our use of this world is over and we make room for others, may we not leave anything ravished by our greed or spoiled by our ignorance, but may we hand on our common heritage fairer and sweeter through our use of it, undiminished in fertility and joy, that so our bodies may return in peace to the great mother who nourished them and our spirits may round the circle of a perfect life in thee.—Walter Rauschenbusch

Sermon: Life's Detours

TEXT: Rom. 8:18–28; James 1:2

When we plan a trip, we study a road map and make sure that we have chosen the best roads to our destination. How perturbed we are when we set out on our tour and discover that some of the routes we have chosen have long and rough detours. Even the signs, "Excuse Our Progress," do little to quell our anger.

So, on life's journey, we encounter detours. Life does not move in a straight line for any of us. There are curves that take some maneuvering; there can be long and difficult detours, trying our patience; there are tunnels in which we cannot see the light of day. No matter how carefully we lay our plans, in life we do not move directly to our goal; sometimes we may all but lose sight of it.

I. It is man's response to life's detours that James is talking about in our text when he writes: "When all kinds of trials come your way, do not resent them as intruders but welcome them as friends."

a. Detours can be opportunities to learn some of life's most strategic lessons. On a detour, we sometimes discover that we were not really going where we thought we were, at all. We thought we were headed for the Promised Land, but then when there is time for retrospection, we discover that we were going down a dead-end street.

b. On detours we can learn some of life's most important secrets. In fact, God can use the crises in life to bring us down to earth—to confront us with reality. A person confessed to me recently that out of her religious experience she had become high and mighty; she was quite sure that she knew God's will for everyone else's life; she found herself more judgmental than loving toward others. If not actually playing God, she was quite sure she had a direct line to the Almighty. After flying high for several months, her life suddenly seemed to go into a tailspin that has brought her down to earth. The hopefulness of this woman's experience is that she is not resenting these seeming adverse experiences as intruders but is thanking God for them because she is becoming more humble and realistic.

II. In this message I am not intending to speak so much of suffering as a universal necessity but rather in more personal terms—as something demanded by our own personal destiny.

a. In difficulty and suffering we can learn that life has a spiritual meaning above its material fact. This lesson we might not otherwise comprehend, and many only learn it when they are confronted with circumstances that shake their lives to the very foundations. It was only through suffering that the apostle Paul shared with the Corinthian Christians and, in turn, with us the insight: "We live not by the things which are seen but by the things which are not seen, for the things which are seen are passing, but the things which are not seen are eternal."

b. As Jesus states this same insight: "Man shall not live by bread alone, but by every Word that comes from the mouth of God." Life is more than bread. The material, no matter how high the pile, can never satisfy the deepest hungers and thirsts of the human spirit.

III. Life's detours force us to reassess our values but also offer opportunity for unparalleled growth. Have you gone through periods of difficulty and sensed that you were growing in spirit like you can hear corn grow in Iowa on a hot, muggy night in July?

a. Life's crises can develop capacities in us, qualities of character, depths of spirit, that probably cannot be developed otherwise. Sorrow makes possible great joy. The psalmist reports such an experience: "I called upon the Lord in distress: the Lord answered me, and set me in a large place" (Ps. 118:25).

b. There is no doubt that God yearns to keep us from doing things that hurt us or hurt others; but if we do err, he can use our mistakes for his own glory and for our growth. Is this not something of the meaning of our text from James?

"When all kinds of trials and temptations crowd into your lives, my brothers, don't resent them as intruders, but welcome them as friends! Realize that they come to test your faith and to produce in you the quality of endurance; but let the process go on until that endurance is fully developed, and you will find you have become men of mature character with the right sort of independence" (James 1:2–4 JBP).

IV. Life's detours afford opportunity to trace the rainbow through the rain—to discern God's purpose at work even in the most untoward circumstances.

a. As many of you know from visiting there, Hawaii is a fantastically beautiful place. One of the sights that impressed me most was the exquisite rainbows with their vivid colors. As depicted in Genesis, the rainbow is a symbol of hope for men in every generation.

b. In tracing the rainbow through the rain, perhaps there is no passage of Scripture that is so helpful as the apostle Paul's statement in the eighth chapter of Romans: "We know that all things work together for good to those who love God, to those who are called according to his purpose." Those who are participating in God's purpose can turn evil days

into positive, constructive good. When the world does its worst, the followers of Christ are challenged to do their best. When the world turns out lights, Christ's disciples are to turn them on. Christ can turn a man's failure into stepping-stones. As one's Savior, Christ can take a dream than has failed, a plan that has gone wrong, a sin that has haunted, and by his forgiving, healing, restoring grace, fashion them into a new life.

V. Suffering is not just to be endured; we are not just to grin and bear it. Suffering can be converted into a sacrament bringing us into the very presence of God. We need not be victim; we can be *victor* in the strife.

Paul tells us how, in the text, "We know that all things work together for good to those who love God." There is nothing in the constitution of the universe that ensures the easy optimism that all things will automatically work out to the satisfaction of good people. What Paul affirms in our text is that God cooperates wherever he has a chance. But he only has a chance with those who are open to him in love. Loving him, "the sufferings of this present time" can be transformed into a blessing. This is no sentimental attempt to persuade ourselves that evil things are good. Far be it from that! They remain what they are, but though bad in themselves, they have lost their power to defeat us. No matter how difficult circumstances may be, we can discover God's cooperation in them. Often it is in things that seem most to dent his goodness that we discover him most indubitably present. Man's disappointments can very well be God's appointments.—John Thompson

Illustrations

TEACHABLE MOMENTS.   Howard Thurman speaks of life's crises as "teachable moments." A disappointment, some failure, a difficulty can make a crack in our armor through which God can get into our life.— J.T.

WHAT MATTERS MOST.   In one of the classes I taught at Drake Divinity School a student was absent for several days. When one morning he appeared, I inquired as to the reason for his absence and he told me the story of the illness of his parents. They had both been at the point of death. He commented in words that I have not forgotten: "When it is a matter of life and death, there are not many things that really matter." This young man had been forced to sort out his values when he was sidetracked for a while from his main objective. He learned things more fundamental on this detour than he would have ever learned in the several class sessions that he had missed.—J.T.

SUNDAY: AUGUST NINTH

LECTIONARY MESSAGE

Topic: Preparing for a Great Surprise
TEXT: Luke 12:32–40
Other Readings: Isa. 1:1, 10–20; Ps. 50:1–8, 22–23; Heb. 11:1–3, 8–16

The days in which we live are fateful: they definitely affect our future destiny, and that destiny may be full of either death and disaster or fame and fortune. It is a shock to anyone's mental balance to realize how swiftly the course of a life may be changed by an accidental occurrence on the road or in the air, by the sudden onset of an illness, or by a natural catastrophe. Likewise, good fortune may smile on one and crowd his life with good friends, pleasant experiences, career advancement, or loving relationships.

The advice of our text is that we should *be ready.* How can anyone prepare for what he cannot anticipate? How can we always be ready when we know not what is coming?

I. We can, first of all, divest ourselves of the excess baggage of this life. Of some things we can be sure—"all these things shall be dissolved" (2 Peter 3:11); and as Luke advises us in verse 40, "The Son of Man is coming at an unexpected hour" (NRSV). In other words, we must at all times expect the world's greatest surprise. Our wisest (and most blessed) course is to follow the advice of verse 33, "Sell your possessions, and give alms."

a. Mentally, we should seek to find truth to dispel the error and myth that surround us. One does not need to be a brain surgeon to know, as one church notice board reminds passersby, "It is never a mistake to trust an unknown future to a known God." The more we can learn of God's Word and his plan for our godly living, the less we have to worry about the charlatans of ideas seeking to ensnare us in their webs of deceit and self-aggrandizement.

b. Physical property and possessions, besides contributing to our comfort, safety, good health, and pleasure, can become liabilities in the manner of being all-consuming ends in themselves. Do we need to sell, give away, or divest ourselves of all our possessions in order to get right with God? Perhaps we only need to rid ourselves of those that have become millstones around our necks. Sometimes it can be very satisfying to have a good yard sale, in order to realize how few things we really need to make us happy and help us be easy to get along with.

c. Spiritually, we must get the picture of ourselves in our stark, open souls, before God. The truths we have heard often but never experienced can suddenly clothe us in glory and joy when faith leads to practice and love leads to service.

II. We can, then, strengthen our spiritual purpose by discipline.

a. Let us look again at the malady of our society. It is now of soul size. These are critical times, possibly resulting in either danger or opportunity for the best possible experiences. Luke advises us (verse 35), "Let your loins be girded and your lamps be burning." The New Revised Standard Version puts it, "Be dressed for action." Girding our spiritual condition means supplying what is missing, adapting some materials to replace others, as wartime plastics development replaced metals, and petroleum and corn produced butyl and butadiene to replace rubber. Right now, public and private honor and morality—not to mention plain courtesy—are in extremely short supply. We have too little spiritual inventiveness to solve our problems of social dislocation.

b. What girding, or furnishing, of mind and spirit can meet our needs? One can think of qualities that will take us a great way toward the goal: sympathy, tolerance, appreciation, good will, patience, and encouragement. We could also return to the practice of plain and simple honesty.

III. We can watch and wait for the Lord's

promised return. That is, we can expect and anticipate while we daily practice our faith.

a. We can be resourceful in planning and working for the common welfare. We can do our utmost in feeding the hungry, housing the homeless, healing the sick, caring for infants and the aged infirm, and giving solace to the injured. We can make a society in which single working parents can both enjoy their children and develop their own lives, by providing care and relieving them of some responsibilities.

b. Along with having faith in God, we can promote faithfulness among our associates by being faithful and trustworthy ourselves. We must help children learn to be trustworthy by being restorers of social trust. We are told to *be ready*. Remember how Hamlet refused to kill Claudius, the murderer of his father, while Claudius was praying, lest Hamlet send him to heaven instead of to eternal punishment. That is a rather simplistic concept of being ready to meet God. We ought to practice the genuine article in all that we do.—John R. Rodman

Illustrations

READY.   I am convinced that some of us will never really know the Christ of the New Testament until we follow him from the safety of the sanctuary into the dangers of daily discipleship, where faith is costly and external rewards are few or nonexistent. We *will* know him, however, if we follow him, go where he goes, and do what he wills.

If you imagine that life cannot be different for you, then you have not reckoned on God, for with his invincible grace God can overcome the worst that life can do to us, "for the Lord God omnipotent reigneth" (Rev. 19:6). —James W. Cox

CONFIDENT.   When Dr. D. E. King, a well-known African American preacher, was asked why the Christians in the black churches have always been so joyful in their worship, even when things were going very badly for them everywhere else, he said, "We rejoice in what we are going to have." Indeed, regardless of what is happening around us, regardless of our discouragements, our crises, and the grim fact of death itself, we can rejoice—not because of our troubles, but because of

what we are going to have. We can enjoy the confident assurance that we shall share the glory of God. This glorious assurance is ours for the taking.—James W. Cox

SERMON SUGGESTIONS

Topic: The Making of a Prophet
TEXT: Jer. 1:5–10 NRSV
God says: (1) "I knew you." (2) "I formed you." (3) "I consecrated you." (4) "I appointed you." (5) "I have put my words in your mouth." (6) "I am with you." (7) "Today I appoint you . . . to pluck up and to pull down . . . to build and to plant."—Suggested by Kyle M. Yates

Topic: The Conversion of Public Enemy Number One
TEXT: Acts 9:1–18
(1) A meeting with Christ (vv. 1–9). (2) A prayer for light (v. 11). (3) An interview with a believer (vv. 10–16). (4) A leading of the Holy Spirit (vv. 17–18).—Andrew W. Blackwood

Hymn Suggestions: Ninth Sunday After Trinity

1. "Awake, Awake, for Night Is Flying," Philipp Nicolai, translated by Catherine Winkworth (1858); "Sleepers, Wake! A Voice Astounds Us," translated by Carl P. Dew Jr. (1985)
This chorale, one of the great classics of German song, conveys with vigor the necessity for watchfulness as expressed by Jesus in the gospel reading (Luke 12:35–40).
2. "The Mighty God and Sovereign Lord," The Psalter (1912); "St. Petersburg," Dimitri S. Bortnianski (1825)
The first three and the last stanzas of this metrical paraphrase of Psalm 50 are the ones that parallel the verses selected for this day's reading. This version is so close to the Bible that it could well be sung in place of having the Psalm read.
3. "Come, Let Us Reason," text and tune by Ken Medema (1972)
This contemporary scripture song quotes directly from Isaiah 1:18 and thus would be suitable as a response to the reading of the Isaiah passage.
4. "On Jordan's Stormy Banks I Stand,"

Samuel Stennett (1787); "Promised Land," Southern Harmony (1835)

This favorite hymn gives expression to the longing for the heavenly country that is the result of profound faith, as expressed by the writer of Hebrews (11:16).—Hugh T. McElrath

Worship Aids

CALL TO WORSHIP. "He that dwelleth in the secret place of the Most High shall abide under the shadow of the Almighty. I will say of the Lord, he is my refuge and my fortress, my God; in him will I trust" (Ps. 91:1–2).

INVOCATION. Almighty Father, infinite in wisdom, creator of all things; we come before you, worshiping with praise him who holds the sun and stars and planets in their courses and yet is rich in mercy, loving us with an everlasting love. Expand our finite minds to think large thoughts. Enlarge our hearts to embrace with love the world larger than our own. Spur our souls that we may be quick to identify with godly missions and things eternal. In all that we say and do, help us to show forth your grace.—Henry Fields

OFFERTORY SENTENCE. "Offer the right sacrifices to the Lord, and put your trust in him" (Ps. 4:5 TEV).

OFFERTORY PRAYER. O God, thou art and thou hast so loved the world that we accept it all and give up doing alone and working alone and bearing alone, and we accept thine offered partnership in our life, through Jesus Christ.—Frank W. Gunsaulus

PRAYER. Merciful Father, bless us in our dealings with our fellows. Quicken our hearts that we may be swift to hear our brother's cry from the pit of humiliation or of need. Give us the forgiving spirit, else how should we know ourselves forgiven by thee? If any have wronged us, grant that we may bring to them thy charity and win them to a better mind. If any are in disgrace or shame, outcasts from the world, make us thy messengers of mercy, that we may share the pain, and by our love, which is also thine, lead them back to thy home and fellowship. May we be to all men thy revealers and interpreters, bearing thy

appeal to the sinning, the sorrowful, and the despairing. And this we would be and do, through Jesus Christ our Lord.—Samuel McComb

Sermon: Bridging the Gaps

TEXT: Acts 10:1–7

Controversy and conflict have been creative inspirations for the Church since its birth. They have humbled the holiest churches. They serve to remind us that the church is human, weak, and oftentimes imperfect. Some people never understand this. Some people spend a lifetime looking for the perfect church.

The perfect church does not exist. In fact, someone has said, "If you find the perfect church and join it, it won't be perfect anymore." How true!

In the first century, the church was not perfect either. A controversy arose that threatened to divide and split this young church. It was a Jew/Gentile controversy. Should a predominantly Jewish, Christian church welcome Gentile Christians into its membership?

The meeting between Cornelius and Peter was an example of how this controversy played itself out many times in various fellowships. This conflict would ripple throughout the whole church at multiple levels. Let's introduce the characters of our story.

The writer, Luke, introduces Cornelius as "a centurion of the Italian Cohort and a devout man who feared God." By profession, Cornelius was a leader in the most powerful military organization of his time. He was stationed in Caesarea, the headquarters of the government of Palestine. Since he was a centurion, a position he held over a number of men, we could assume that he was used to being treated with respect, honor, and fear.

Cornelius was also very religious. Luke made special note of this when he wrote, "He . . . feared God with all his household; he gave alms generously to the people and prayed constantly with God." His faith was more than a shallow belief or passing idea. It was meaningful, active, and consistent. His devotion began in private prayer, spilled into his household, and flowed into his community.

In this instance, his main concern seems to be for an opportunity to learn more about Christianity. Maybe he heard about it through family or friends or on the street. Being a spiritually sensitive individual, he probably wanted to learn more about this new religion. Maybe he asked: How is it like the faith that I have? How can I become a Christian? The questions raced through his mind.

He could have heard the gospel proclaimed through Peter on the Day of Pentecost: "Everyone who calls on the name of the Lord shall be saved." He understood the good news to mean that God's love, mercy, and forgiveness were open to everyone (Jew or Gentile) through Christ. Somewhere along the way, he trusted God's promise. He called on the name of the Lord. He experienced God's forgiveness. Now he wanted to know what to do next?

Peter was well known in the area as a prominent Christian leader. He had enjoyed the privileges of being one of the first disciples, following Jesus throughout his ministry, and preaching on the Day of Pentecost. Peter was in Joppa, about a day's journey from Caesarea, when Cornelius heard God say, "Your prayers and your alms have ascended as a memorial before God. Now send men to Joppa for a certain Simon who is called Peter; he is lodging with Simon, a tanner, whose house is by the seaside."

Peter probably represented the views of the majority within the church on this matter: the Gentiles were uncircumcised, immoral, idolatrous, and unclean. The Old Testament declared it, and Jesus had even said, "I was only sent to the lost sheep of Israel." God was Jewish. God spoke Hebrew. No one was going to tell them anything different.

While Peter was praying, with three attempts God tried to speak to him. Peter could or would not listen. It was not until God appeared to him in the form of Cornelius that he understood. (Jesus did say he could come in the form of a stranger.)

At this meeting, Peter saw God in a way he had not seen before. He saw that God was with Cornelius, a Gentile. When he began to understand this, the myths and stereotypes began to fade. Cornelius was moral, not unmoral like Peter had been taught. Cornelius was righteous, not unclean like he'd been told. Cornelius believed in one God. He was not idolatrous like Peter had assumed. Cornelius was probably uncircumcised, but who cared?

Cornelius had a family. Peter had a family.

Cornelius worried about the education of his child. Peter worried about his children. Cornelius gave alms to the poor because he was concerned about the welfare of his community. Peter healed the sick and gave to the poor because he was concerned about the same. Cornelius struggled to be a good leader in his profession. Peter struggled to be a good leader in the church. Cornelius hurt in pain and rejoiced in happiness. Peter did the same.

As Peter sat in this Gentile's home, sharing food, fun, and faith, he finally understood what God was trying to say to him. He said out loud, "I truly understand that God shows no partiality, but in every nation anyone who fears him and does what is right is acceptable to him."

Traditionally, we see this as the time when Cornelius became a Christian. I wonder if it wasn't Peter who truly became a Christian at this meeting? For Peter, the gap between Jew and Gentile was closed through a relationship.

As we race towards 2000, I wonder what other kinds of Corneliuses God will send our way. Will they be Korean, African American, Latino, Caucasian, homosexual, or baby boomer? Hopefully we can remember the lesson Peter learned: *God shows no partiality*.

Unfortunately, what often happens is that we forget Peter's lesson and miss the opportunity to see God in a way we haven't before. We miss God because we miss one another.— Daniel N. Alejandro

Illustrations

THE LESS WE GET TOGETHER. There's a story about a minister who returned to visit a church he had once served. He ran into Bill, who had been an elder and leader in the church but who wasn't around anymore. The pastor asked, "Bill, what happened? You used to be there every time the doors opened."

"Well, Pastor," said Bill, "a difference of opinion arose in the church. Some of us couldn't accept the final decision, and we established a church of our own."

"Is that where you worship now?" asked the pastor.

"No," answered Bill, "we found that there, too, the people were not faithful, and a small group of us began meeting in a rented hall at night."

"Has that proven satisfactory?" asked the minister.

"No, I can't say that it has." Bill responded. "Satan was active even in that fellowship, so my wife and I withdrew and began to worship on Sunday at home by ourselves."

"Then at last you're found inner peace?" asked the pastor.

"No, I'm afraid we haven't," said Bill. "Even my wife began to develop ideas I was not comfortable with, so now she worships in the northwest corner of the living room, and I am in the southwest."—D.N.A.

THE TRIUMPH OF LOVE. The love for equals is a human thing—of friend for friend, brother for brother. It is to love what is loving and lovely. The world smiles.

The love for the less fortunate is a beautiful thing—the love for those who suffer, for those who are poor, the sick, the failures, the unlovely. This is compassion, and it touches the heart of the world.

The love for the more fortunate is a rare thing—to love those who succeed where we fail; to rejoice without envy with those who rejoice; the love of the poor for the rich, of the black man for the white man. The world is always bewildered by its saints.

And then there is the love for the enemy—love for the one who does not love you but mocks, threatens, and inflicts pain. The tortured's love for the torturer. This is God's love. It conquers the world.—Frederick Buechner[4]

SUNDAY: AUGUST SIXTEENTH

LECTIONARY MESSAGE

Topic: What Christ Brings to Our Lives

Text: Luke 12:49–56

Other Readings: Isa. 5:1–7; Ps. 80:1–2, 8–19; Heb. 11:29–12:2

The passage in which these verses occur is a set of instructions and warnings to Jesus' disciples. He is preparing to send them out to teach the people of the land, but in a sense he is also preparing them to carry his saving truth to all the world after his death and Resurrection.

The disciples are ready to believe that Jesus is the culmination of the long-developing messianic hope of Israel, but they no doubt expect too much too soon. They may look from the mountain top of Jesus' life to the bright and shining mountain top of humanity in its heaven-kissed glory, but they are being told to take account of the valley that lies in their way, full of rocky terrain, swollen rivers, burning sand, and animal and human predators.

I. The symbols Jesus gives are symbols of danger and personal suffering.

a. The fire of which he speaks is for the world's purification, and he is anxious that it not be delayed. It is part of the fulfillment of the purpose of history, to burn away the impurities by its judgment and to reveal the character of honor and morality developing in history by the furnace's tempering heat.

b. The baptism that Jesus anticipates is the final one, a baptism of hell that he knew was before him, that was to be the great stressful constraint of his life and his death before his Resurrection would seal the world's salvation. This is the baptism of which he speaks in Mark 10:38, asking the disciples if they can share his baptism and promising them that they would be part of it. In the meantime, he outlines more of his program through the divisions of humanity and the understanding of history's unfolding.

II. The divisions that Jesus said he was bringing are all those that are already present naturally.

a. He intended to show that his disciples should not expect peace in even the closest, dearest human relationships without at first instituting the course of the gospel among men and women by their preaching and teaching. He knew that if the disciples preached loving family harmony, parents and children would react with squabbles and jealousy. Discord is present; it must be overcome by spiritual and moral maturity blessed by God.

b. Would we choose, if we could, to have the end of our desires without the means? Yes. As an example, surely the knowledge and understanding gained in college are great,

[4]*The Magnificent Defeat.*

but first come the work and the many painful steps to get that knowledge and understanding. One college student came to his room at 9:30 each evening, after spending the four hours after his last class at his job. He grabbed a sandwich at the campus diner, and then he sat down to study the next day's class assignments, often until midnight or later. When he heard the other guys of the rooming house coming back from their bowling or pool playing or club meetings, he would gladly have exchanged places. He would have liked to have his expenses paid by his family so that he could really study and really enjoy college life. Most of us would enjoy having income without the hard work. We would like to have a house to fit our special ideas of comfort and security without the labor, mess, and expense of building it. But in God's plan the sequence is learning and work, then income; strife, then rest; fishing and baking, then enjoying the loaves and fishes; first the battle, then the victory; first planting and cultivating, then the fruit. The best things come after they are earned. So Jesus is telling his disciples (us?) that the way will be hard and converts must be won by faithfully living and serving in his name. The earth badly needs the evidence of moral and spiritual faithfulness. Its people succumb to false promises because their way sounds so easy. Believers in Christ need to show the fruits of spiritual maturity in order to win them.

III. The hypocritical failure to recognize signs is a failing still with us.

a. The signs of the times were really evidence, according to Jesus, that history was being fulfilled by the events of his ministry, that the things he did pointed to God's suffering reclamation of the goodness that he had created in all his people, rather than an aggrandizement of one family or nation over all others. Jesus criticizes the kind of heart-corrupted hypocrisy that claims righteous positions but practices selfish superiority toward others.

b. Anyone who asks for visible proof must recognize the affirmation of God's purpose in what can be seen, rather than demanding instant personal gratification or replicable scientific confirmation of what are, rather, spiritual conditions and events.

c. Those who attempt to apply scientific methods to social, personal, and political aspects of human activity are misconstruing the true nature of human reality. The social construct of communism, for example, could not possibly come to pass, depending as it did on aspects of humanity simply not natural or real. To attempt to apply objectivity to moral and spiritual areas of life as truly to posit a uniformity that flies in the face of human nature, which God truly deals with only in the ministry and death of his Son.—John R. Rodman

Illustrations

DIVISIONS.   His coming would inevitably mean divisions. In point of fact it did. That was one of the great reasons why the Romans hated Christianity—because it tore families in two. Over and over again a man had to decide whether he loved his kith and kin or Christ better. The essence of Christianity is that loyalty to Christ has to take precedence over the dearest loyalties of this earth. A man must be prepared to count all things but loss for the excellence of Jesus Christ.—William Barclay[5]

FIREBRANDS.   Jesus does not bring the peace and quiet that we would expect, but in the ultimate and deepest sense he is "our peace" (Eph. 2:14). Nothing is said of vicarious suffering on the part of Jesus. . . . But Jesus does go his way to the baptism of death in order that others following him may be granted something of his burning heart, to make them firebrands of a difficult and sometimes violent but amazingly helpful love for humankind.—Eduard Schweizer[6]

SERMON SUGGESTIONS

Topic: The Fear of the Lord
TEXT: Prov. 1:7

(1) The fear of the Lord: (a) Is it terror? No. (b) Is it chronic anxiety? No. (c) Is it suspicion and distrust? No. (2) What is the fear of the Lord? (a) It is awe. (b) It is obedience. (c) It is proper relationship to God. (Compare "Proverbs: Introduction" in *The Harper-Collins Study Bible*.)

[5] *The Gospel of Luke.*
[6] *The Good News According to Luke.*

Topic: Who Is Really Wise?

TEXT: James 3:13–18 NRSV

The truly wise person: (1) Is not the envious and selfishly ambitious person. (2) Rather, one who is single-minded, peaceable, gentle, agreeable, compassionate, practically helpful, impartial, and genuine. (3) The latter type is a peacemaker who plants seeds of peace and harvests justice.

Hymn Suggestions: Tenth Sunday After Trinity

1. "Awake, My Soul, Stretch Every Nerve," Philip Doddridge (1755); "Christmas," George F. Handel (1728)

Although Doddridge wrote this hymn to cap his sermon preached on Philippians 3:12–14, he paraphrased the passage in Hebrews 12:1–2 as well. Set to the vibrant Handel tune, this is an urgent call to press on with vigor in the race set before us, seeing that we are surrounded by such a cloud of faithful witnesses.

2. "Hear Us, O Shepherd of Your Chosen Race," Bert Polman (1985); "Yorkshire," John Wainwright (1750)

This modern paraphrase of Psalm 80 can be sung in the place of the Psalter reading for the day. Stanza two may be omitted to parallel the exact verses selected for reading. Special emphasis should be placed on the biblical refrain: "Restore us, Lord, your saving power release; make your face shine on us and give us peace."

3. "O God of Earth and Altar," Gilbert K. Chesterton (1908); "Llangloffan," Welsh folk melody (1865)

The evils bringing God's judgment described in both the Old Testament and gospel readings for this day are mentioned in more modern terms in this early twentieth-century hymn.

4. "Faith of Our Fathers," Frederick Faber (1849); "St. Catherine," Henri F. Hemy (1864)

The account of the faithful fathers and mothers listed in Hebrews 11 should prompt the fervent singing of the aspiration to be true to their faith till death.—Hugh T. McElrath

Worship Aids

CALL TO WORSHIP. "I am Alpha and Omega, the beginning and the ending, saith the Lord, which is, and which was, and which is to come, the Almighty" (Rev. 1:8).

INVOCATION. Because of your love, O God, your love that never changes, we trust ourselves to you completely. We love you and worship you. Grant through your grace such courage and strength that what we think, say, and do shall honor and glorify you.

OFFERTORY SENTENCE. "Then he said to them all, 'If any want to become my followers, let them deny themselves and take up their cross daily and follow me. For those who want to save their life will lose it, and those who love their life for my sake will save it. What does it profit them if they gain the whole world, but lose or forfeit themselves'" (Luke 9:23–25 TEV).

OFFERTORY PRAYER. Heavenly Father, if the cross seems too demanding and painful to bear, help us to remember our Lord, who for the joy that was set before him endured the cross, despising the shame, and has sat down at your right hand.

PRAYER. All the Church doth worship thee, O God; every heart renewed by grace takes a delight in adoring thee, and we, among the rest, though least and meanest of them all, yet would bow as heartily as any worshiping, loving, praising, in our soul, being silent unto God because our joy in him is altogether inexpressible.

Lord help us to worship thee in life as well as lip. May our whole being be taken up with thee. As when the fire fell down on Elijah's sacrifice of old and licked up even the water that was in the trenches, so may the consuming fire of the Divine Spirit use up all our nature, and even that which might seem to hinder, even out of that may God get glory by the removal of it. Thus would we adore.— Charles H. Spurgeon

Sermon: A Powerful Prayer

TEXT: Eph. 3:14–21

Perhaps you have seen the cartoon that depicted a man chatting with a salesperson. In the beautiful showroom were cars that glittered with elegance. In the caption, the salesperson is saying to the customer, "Sir, if you have to ask how much they are, they are too expensive for you!" No believer ever has to worry about having inadequate resources to meet the demands of life. Paul's prayer in Ephesians 3:14–21 is a prayer for spiritual power in the life of believers.

I. Paul expresses a prayer that grows out his awareness of all that God is doing in believers. It is an expression of confidence in God's ableness. Paul kneels before God, indicating a sense of urgency. Paul addresses his prayer to God as Father, following the words of Jesus (see Matt. 6:9–10). God's divine fatherhood points to the truth that he is a personal God, a loving Heavenly Father, whom we can approach in genuine humility, confidence, and devotion.

First Paul prays for inner power, that is, power through the Holy Spirit in the inner being. This power is not of ourselves but comes through faith. Faith in this context points to self-distrust. It is the result of Christ dwelling in our hearts, taking permanent residence so as to be completely at home. The apostle prays that Christ will not just be present in our lives, but that he will be resident and preeminent.

II. Second, he combines metaphors to ask that believers be "rooted" and "established" in love with all the believers. Paul here does not refer to individualistic Christianity but to his concern for the believing corporate community. He prays for believers to understand how wide, how long, how high, and how deep is Christ's great love for his people. It is a wide as all humanity and bridges the gap between all cultural and ethnic divisions, including that between Jew and Gentile. Christ's love is as long as all eternity. It is a love that is completely sufficient and inexhaustible in all its ways. It is as high as the heavens and as deep as our darkest sin. At the cross of Jesus Christ, the love of God brings the height of heaven and the depth of sin into reconciliation. Jesus Christ's life and death exemplified divine love by his ultimate sacrifice. This incomprehensibly valuable redemption delivered sinners from enslavement and reconciled us from our estrangement into full fellowship and inheritance in the household of God.

III. Third, he wants believers to be filled to the measure of the fullness of God, with all the energies and powers of God. We can draw on the infiniteness of God. Believers can be filled with the Godhead and with the fullness of God's love. Paul's prayer reminds us of Jesus' words recorded in John 7, "We can drink of this water and never thirst."

Paul requests of God that the inner person might have inner strength that will in turn lead to a deeper experience with Christ. This deeper experience will enable us to apprehend and take hold of Christ's great love, which will result in being filled with the fullness of God. So then Paul prays for apprehension of God's strength, depth, and fullness. In one sense the believing community already has attained these lofty petitions since we have been made full in Christ (see Col. 2:9–10). In our standing before Christ, we are complete in him, but practically and experientially we enjoy these spiritual graces only to the degree that we apprehend them by faith. The resources are ours. Paul prays that we will accept them and enjoy them and use them for understanding what it means to be a part of the community of faith in service to the Lord Jesus Christ.

IV. After considering such marvelous spiritual truths, Paul bursts into a grand doxology concerning the ableness of God. He prays with assurance of the indwelling strength of God the Spirit, made accessible to us through God the Son. He prays that believers will be able to do much more abundantly than they can ever think or imagine. These wonderful thoughts help us to think more loftily about the love and grace that has been given to us. Incredibly, God can do immeasurably more than we can think of or ask for. He is able to do this because he is neither an idle nor an inactive God. But he is a loving, caring, infinite, all-wise, all-knowing God who never runs out of energy. He is able to do more than all, for his expectations are higher than our own. He is able to do much more abundantly than all, because he does not give his grace in insufficient measure. He is able to do vastly more than more, because he is an infinite God of superabundance and immeasurable grace.

God is able to do whatever he will and do it the way he wills it. Yet he never chooses to do anything contrary to his nature. He generally works through the obedience of men and women or their permitted disobedience. His eternal purposes are not frustrated and we can petition our loving, gracious, infinite, and omnipotent God to hear and answer our prayers. Paul's confidence in the ableness of God represents a boldness that we must claim.

Finally, Paul ascribes glory to God, who alone is worthy. The ultimate goal of our existence is God's glory. God has called the Church to an extraordinary position and vocation. The God to whom Paul makes these requests has the capacity that exceeds our capacity for asking or even imagining. Paul piles synonym on top of synonym to emphasize an eternity of glorifying God. In our eternal state we will keep on expanding in our capacity to bring glory to him for all eternity. What we do here and now will glorify Christ forever and ever.—David Dockery

Illustrations

THE SPIRIT'S OPERATIONS. The great events of crucifixion and resurrection may be decades or almost two thousand years removed, when the Ephesians (or we) read Paul's Epistle. But neither the godless nor the pious are left without witness that God is ruling and that he rules through Christ. The Spirit's operations on earth are proof to us that God's work of salvation is still going on, and is not a past, completed "fact" of history or mythology. It is by this very same continuing action and self-communication that the perfection of God's work is revealed most clearly.—Markus Barth[7]

A SPECIAL FACE.   Lady Tennyson had a lovely face. Even the scornful housemaid who contemptuously referred to her master, the poet, as "only a public writer," said of her mistress, "Oh, she is an angel." Tennyson himself remarked one night to a friend, after his wife had gone to bed, "It is a tender, spiritual face." Her looks matched her spirit, and her sanctity was outstanding even in an age of formal goodness. She knew the use of imagination in prayer. She told her husband once: "When I pray, I see the face of God smiling upon me."—W. E. Sangster[8]

SUNDAY: AUGUST TWENTY-THIRD

LECTIONARY MESSAGE

Topic: The Right Time for Good Deeds
TEXT: Luke 13:10–17
Other Readings: Jer. 1:4–10; Ps. 71:1–6; Heb. 12:18–29

Christians are often faced with problems of priorities and hardly ever have time to do all the good things they would like to do. One principle that will serve us well is to do as Jesus did—act on the presentation of an opportunity and deal with the present need. What Jesus did, as told in this passage, is an illustration of the principle that there is never a wrong time to do the right thing, just as there is never a right time to do the wrong thing.

I. *The woman's infirmity.* While teaching on the Sabbath day in a synagogue, Jesus looked up and beheld a suffering woman, a woman bent double and unable to straighten herself up. As Jesus usually did, he at once associated her bodily condition with the status of her soul, saying to the crowd later that Satan had bound her.

a. The body of each one of us human be-ings is a home for the soul and can't help being a reflection of it. If the spirit is in bondage, the body will be handicapped or weakened. Many of us have hampering habits we'd love to break, habits that deplete our bodies' resources against illness and pain. Dr. Louis H. Evans Sr. used to say that we can't tell where the body ends and the soul begins, but we know that they are so close that they catch each other's diseases.

b. Even though she was bent so badly that she could not look up and see Jesus, she was in the right place. She was in the synagogue when Jesus came, and glory of glories, he saw her and immediately responded to her plight.

II. *The mercy of Jesus' healing.* It is interesting to note that this is not a case of possession by a demon but an example of spiritual and bodily illness, and that Jesus therefore dealt directly with the woman's ailment. He healed both her soul and her body. If we need evidence of instrumentality, he healed

[7] *The Broken Wall.*
[8] *He Is Able.*

her soul first by his Word and then her body by his touch. Remember that his word is God's word, carrying all the creative power and healing strength of God.

a. The debilitating habits of a lifetime are not broken easily—not by wishing, often not by long and serious diligence. The presence of friends gives us the fellowship of sympathetic caring, but Jesus brings the Word and touch of true therapeutics. If that implies the necessity of loosing the bonds of sin, he can do that.

b. Also, we are encouraged and healed by noting that Jesus addressed this one woman personally. He called her to him. Everyone is an individual person to him, and he finds each one who needs him in the midst of his surroundings, to heal, not with a panacea but with specifically pointed, uniquely suited therapy of soul and body.

III. *Why Jesus seemed to violate the Sabbath.* Jesus' description of the woman is based on a contrast with the accepted practice of Sabbath help for livestock. He points out that Jewish law permits doing what is necessary for health or safety. He knew that whatever affected a life permitted the setting aside of Sabbath restrictions. He then describes the woman as one of God's own, calling her a daughter of Abraham, one of the true people of God's heart, of much more worth than an animal. And he pointed out that her affliction had gone on for eighteen years, not just overnight, and that the bondage of her affliction was not to be compared to an animal's chains.

a. Jesus' principle of action was that not to do a good thing is to do an evil thing. Good is the opposite of evil, and if Jesus had not healed the woman he would have been the agent of prolonging her suffering. Even though perhaps one more day would not have been serious after eighteen years, not to heal her then was unthinkable.

b. When the ruler of the synagogue berated Jesus for healing on the Sabbath, Jesus called him a hypocrite, as he did others who thought the same way as the ruler. Jesus was always a Sabbath observer and never broke any law, ceremonial or otherwise. The ruler's only purpose was to shame Jesus, thus using the Sabbath not for its benefit for workers but for its potential to help him get rid of Jesus. This may raise the question of how many of us cite laws, appeal to traditions, and quote requirements and rules only when it suits our purposes and when we think we can further our cause by using them. We find rules convenient to use against others, but find it easy to excuse ourselves from following those rules. We should always obey the Fourth Commandment, remembering that God made the Sabbath for our good.—John R. Rodman

Illustrations

AN *A FORTIORI* ARGUMENT.   Though some have criticized the logic of the retort of Jesus, its cogency is irrefutable, which asserts that if the Sabbath rest may be broken to minister to the needs of beasts, how much more may this be done in order to minister to the needs of man.—H.D.A. Major[9]

A NEW STATUS.   Several features of the story suggest that the woman's condition may be seen as indicative of her diminished status as a woman; her condition is attributed to "a spirit of weakness." This weakness has left her bent over and unable to stand straight. Jesus addresses her with the general term "Woman" and Jesus answers the leader of the synagogue by contrasting what one would do for an animal with what he has done for the woman. In the end, Jesus confers on the woman a status of dignity: She is a "daughter of Abraham" (see 16:22–31; 19:9). Jesus is in the process of releasing the captive, freeing the oppressed (4:18), and raising up children to Abraham (3:8). As in other scenes in Luke in which Jesus responds to the needs of a woman, this scene points to a new status for women in the kingdom of God.—R. Alan Culpepper[10]

SERMON SUGGESTIONS

Topic: River of Life
    TEXT: Ezek. 47:9
    Here was Ezekiel in Babylon, dreaming of his fatherland across the desert. From the mass of symbolism in the prophet's vision: (1) The river came down from the heights— God alone can give the power to make a bet-

[9] *Incidents in the Life of Jesus.*
[10] *The New Interpreter's Bible,* Vol. IX.

ter world. (2) The river issued from the Temple—its source was beneath the altar; it came out from the courts of the Lord's house. (3) Ezekiel's river deepened—there is something wrong with our religious experience if it is not an ever-deepening tide. (4) "Everything shall live whither the river cometh"—so marvelous is the power of God's Spirit to heal and bless that wherever that Spirit comes all things are possible.[11]

Topic: The Christian Secret of Courage
TEXT: Acts 4:1–22
(1) The Christian meaning of courage: (a) Standing up for Christ in Jerusalem. (b) Speaking out for him before his slayers. (c) Facing death for Christ and his Church. (2) The Christian secret of courage: (a) Being in the School of Christ. (b) Being at the Cross of Christ. (c) Being filled with his Spirit.—Andrew W. Blackwood[12]

Hymn Suggestions: Eleventh Sunday After Trinity

1. "Lord, Speak to Me That I May Speak," Frances Havergal (1872); "Canonbury," Robert Schumann (1839)
Jeremiah's reluctance to speak was answered by God's putting words into his mouth and assuring him of the divine presence. This is the basic message of this hymn of commitment and consecration.
2. "All My Hope on God Is Founded," Joachim Neander (1680), translated by Robert Bridges (1899); "All My Hope Is Firmly Grounded," translated by Fred Pratt Green (1986); "Michael," Herbert Howells (1930)
These translations of a venerable German hymn give voice to the firm hope expressed by the psalmist (Ps. 71:1–6).
3. "Heal Us, Emmanuel, Hear Our Prayer," William Cowper (1779); "Grafenburg," Johann Cruger (1647)
This prayer hymn asking for God to touch us and others in healing ministry could be sung after the gospel reading on Jesus' healing of the woman with an infirmity.
4. "Sent Forth by God's Blessing," Omer

Westendorf (1964); "The Ash Grove," Welsh folk tune (eighteenth century)
Intended for the close of worship, this contemporary hymn expresses praise and thanksgiving—themes found both in the Psalter reading and in the passage from Hebrews (12:28).—Hugh T. McElrath

Worship Aids

CALL TO WORSHIP.   "Let the people praise thee, O God, let all the people praise thee. Then shall the earth yield her increase; and God, even our own God, shall bless us. God shall bless us; and all the ends of the earth shall fear him" (Ps. 67:5–7).

INVOCATION.   Lift us above the things of this world, Lord, that the power and majesty of God will be glimpsed, that something of the mystery and omnipotence of God will be pondered, and that the love of God will overpower us.—E. Lee Phillips

OFFERTORY SENTENCE.   "Offer unto God thanksgiving; and pay thy vows unto the Most High" (Ps. 50:14).

OFFERTORY PRAYER.   Lord of life, let this offering serve as a seed of the gospel planted in fertile soil, that germinates, takes root, and blossoms in hearts of faith committed to Jesus Christ our Savior.—E. Lee Phillips

PRAYER.   O source of life and strength! Many of thy mercies do we plainly see, and we believe in a boundless store behind. No morning stars that sing together can have deeper call than we for grateful joy. Thou hast given us a life of high vocation, and thine own breathing in our hearts interprets for us its sacred opportunities. Thou hast cheered the way with many dear affections and glimpses of solemn beauty and everlasting truth. Not a cloud of sorrow, but thou hast touched with glory; not a dusty atmosphere of care, but thy light shines through! And lest our spirits should fail before thine unattainable perfections, thou hast set us in the train of thy saints who have learned to take up the cross of sacrifice. Let the time past suffice to have wrought our own will,

[11]Adapted from James S. Stewart, *River of Life*.
[12]*Expository Preaching for Today*.

and now make us consecrate to thine.—James Martineau[13]

Sermon: Is It OK to Question God?

TEXT: Job 42:1–6

Have you ever wrestled with the axiom, "Faith does not question 'Why?'" As a pastor I have encountered many Christians who have been taught that a person of faith never raises any questions with God about the circumstances of his life. In my experience, those believers either suffered in silence and carried guilt about their unvoiced questions, or verbalized their inquiries with great difficulty, reprimanding themselves for their audacity and their lack of faith.

With a sincere desire to minister to persons caught in this web of misunderstanding, I have raised the question, "Is it OK to question God?"

In my judgment, there is ample evidence within and outside the biblical record that questions have been raised with God at perplexing, burdensome points in the human situation. I do not see God reprimanding an individual who questions with a right motive, so please explore with me the question, "Is it OK to question God?"

I. Situations that prompt questions are real.

a. The statement sounds rather obvious, but let me get the matter before us. Let's face it: there are those situations that are a part of the warp and woof of life that are beyond our ability to understand.

A person becomes ill. Doctors say the illness is terminal. Suffering is prolonged. Death does eventually come. But there wells up within us a "Why?"

We pray in the name of Jesus, with all that that implies, exercising faith. God undoubtedly hears, but we see no evidence of any action on his part. He apparently is delaying. We wonder why. We ask, "Why?"

b. At other times, life gets blocked. We are cut off from fulfilling some aspiration of our hearts because of personal failure, obligation, or circumstances beyond our control. We want to ask "Why, Lord?" or "Why me, Lord?"

The truth is that life is often more than we

[13]*Prayers Ancient and Modern.*

can handle. In fact, it is *always* more than we can handle without divine resources. Faced with that reality, we often have questions.

II. Precedents that seem to provide us with permission to raise questions with God do exist.

a. First I refer you to Job. Job raised many questions with God that arose out of the perplexity of physical and emotional struggle. But I want you to know that God did not reprimand Job for asking questions.

God did not deal with Job's sufferings or their cause. He only dealt with the limits of Job's knowledge. He wanted Job to know that no man could bring charges against God about his operation of the universe because man does not have all the facts. Man is finite. His knowledge is limited. After hearing God speak, Job gave way to confessions and repented of any foolish things he may have said about his own goodness and God's justice. Then he lost himself in the will of God. He became aware of and certain of God's care for him. Answers to questions no longer mattered. But God did not reprimand him for having asked!

b. Look at Moses. I remind you that he questioned the Lord about the calling that came to him. God did not slap his hands. He only used the occasion to remind Moses of God's far superior understanding and of his adequacy to supplement Moses' every inadequacy, if Moses would only be available and obedient to the call.

c. Consider the prophet Habakkuk. He saw that a sinful, oppressive situation existed among God's people. God seemed unaware and inactive. The prophet asked, "How long, O Lord, will I call for help, and thou wilt not hear? Why dost thou make me see iniquity, and cause me to look on wickedness?" (Heb. 1:2–3 NASB). Then God showed Habakkuk that he was busily engaged in raising up a nation—Chaldea—that would be used to punish God's wicked people. When Habakkuk heard that, he was astonished that God would use a heathen nation to punish his own people. Out of his bewilderment he questioned God again. Three times in verses 13 and 14 of chapter 1 he asked God, "Why?" Then God answered that the just in all nations shall live by faith and the faithless wicked shall perish. Having heard the Lord speak, Habakkuk grew to a pinnacle of personal faith that led him to admit that he did not understand all of God's ways but he would be teachable and faithful. He rejoiced in God's presence and strength, not in his own imperfect understanding of God's ways.

d. Best of all, consider Jesus. As he hung on the cross he cried, "My God, why hast thou forsaken me?" (Matt. 27:46). In the midst of a great tide of suffering that threatened to overwhelm him, he was tempted to lose nerve and to feel utterly defeated. But he was without sin even then and affirmed his faith with the cry, "My God."

I believe that cry reveals his true humanity—his depression, his agony of mind and spirit. Actually, the Father was never closer than then, for "God was in Christ reconciling the world to Himself" (2 Cor. 5:19 NASB). In accomplishing reconciliation for us as sinners, Jesus experienced the real significance of sin, which is separation from God. He cried out, "Why?" God did not reprimand his Son for asking a question. He reaffirmed his presence so that Jesus died crying out, "It is finished!" and praying, "Father, into thy hands I commend my spirit."

III. Pointers that prove helpful need to be observed.

a. *Watch your attitude.* Are your questions coming from a spirit of rebellion or from a desire to cooperate with the Lord? From a heart that desires to be full of praise or from a murmuring, complaining spirit? Questioning can even be beneficial if it springs from a quiet, reverent spirit that is committed to obeying God and his purposes.

b. *Do not demand answers.* Asking questions in a spirit of reverent humility is one thing, but demanding of God in a spirit of arrogance and haughtiness is quite another. He is Creator; I am creature. For me as a Christian, he is Lord, and I am subject. Who am I to come demanding anything of him?

c. *Be cautious about always expecting answers* or about expecting to attain so much understanding at once. Sometimes God chooses not to answer at all. At other times he answers directly. He answered Habakkuk's questions quite specifically. But he never explained to Job the why of his suffering.

We are free to question God! Done in the right spirit, the questioning can bring a new experience of God and spiritual growth to us. But God does not always choose to answer our questions.

d. *Listen for divine guidance and truth.* While you are asking questions and seeking answers, concentrate on looking for God's guidance in the situation. Listen with an ear to learning and obeying! The important thing is not that you get answers but that you meet God in your circumstances.

He can show us that we are not self-sufficient.

In our questioning situations God can teach us that life is more than we can handle.

He can teach us that he is present and that we need not fear.

He can show us that through the discipline our trying circumstance requires, we can choose to grow.

He can teach us the value of waiting for him to do what only he can do instead of rushing in to pick up the ball and run in our own way with our own strength.

He can show us that he is conforming his children to his image and that cooperation with him and progress in that direction take priority over everything else.

He may show us a new direction for our lives in the midst of our turmoil and perplexity.

He can teach that having answers does not matter!

e. *Maintain faith in God.* Remember, God is not finished yet. Because all his paths are loving-kindness and truth, you can hold onto him in faith.

IV. *Conclusion.* Through a personal faith in Jesus Christ that relates us to God as Father, we are as free to ask questions of our heavenly Father as our own children are free to ask questions of us. But we are also free to live by the truth that grief, perplexity, alienation, or whatever may be prompting your questions does not have the last word.—C. Ferris Jordan[14]

Illustrations

SKEPTICISM. Before we are too hard on ourselves, before we place ourselves in the company of Voltaire, Paine, and Ingersoll, we ought to face one undeniable fact: the Bible itself is not only a book of faith, it is also a book of skepticism. The Bible is too honest to cover up the weaknesses and faults even of

[14]*Award-Winning Sermons,* Vol. 4.

its best men and women. Though the heroes of the Bible scaled great heights of courage and daring and demonstrated amazing faith in God, these same heroes sometimes fell into chilling depths of doubt and hopelessness.—James W. Cox[15]

MEETING TROUBLE. As free moral agents made in the image of God, we are allowed to make choices which, if they are foolish and selfish, will bring dire consequences. And since millions of us live together in an inter-dependent world, it frequently comes about that the mistakes of others bring innocent men and women into the greatest difficulties. When trouble comes, no matter what the cause, there are just two ways to meet it. We may face it quietly and hopefully with the sure faith that God will give us the strength and wisdom to see it through and to emerge stronger than ever; or we may stand before it without faith or hope—and go down to defeat.—Lewis L. Dunnington[16]

SUNDAY: AUGUST THIRTIETH

LECTIONARY MESSAGE

Topic: Spiritual Etiquette for Guest and Host
TEXT: Luke 14:1, 7–14

Other Readings: Jer. 22:4–13; Ps. 81:1, 10–16; Heb. 13:1–8, 15–16

In verse 7, our text calls Jesus' words a parable. Seminary students study the parables of Jesus quite seriously, because they are his dramatic, multimedia communications of truth. Almost all students hear the succinct definition that a parable is "an earthly story with a heavenly meaning." One aspect of the parables is that they usually cloak the spiritual, heavenly meaning in a veil of symbolism, so they do need interpretation, which Jesus himself provides in some instances. That there is difficulty, however, shows up in one student's answer to a test question: "A parable is a heavenly story with no earthly meaning."

I. *It is hard to compare one parable with another.* This one is not the usual kind of story about certain characters, but rather is a set of instructions in guest etiquette.

a. Jesus noticed the propensity of the guests at this particular Sabbath-day meal to take the preferred seats. He gave them advice ostensibly to prepare them for disappointment and to prevent their feeling shame when asked to yield, to give up a seat at the head table to a VIP with higher status.

b. Jesus could also have given this advice not only to help prevent shame but also to discourage violence. Some people place such extreme value on social status that they might react with resentment and even belligerence when asked to give up a good seat. It might be observed that those given the best seats are often the ones who arrive late, making an effective entrance, just in time for the aperitif. They remind us of those who hold tickets for the front-row seats at a game or a show. No first-come, first-served rules apply, and others already seated are forced to move or maybe even to stand, to give up a good seat to a reserved-ticket holder. We do feel embarrassed by the event.

c. The lesson of humility is even more difficult to learn than that of courtesy. Therefore, this is a true parable—a supposed situation in which a hearer may picture himself as the protagonist, experiencing the described events, and gaining spiritual insight for his benefit both now and in the life to come. We can for a moment become the person going right to the head table, or at least the one nearest to it, only to end up feeling belittled and shamed by having to pick up our hat and maybe even the water glass we have already used to go to another place. Fortunately, human beings *can* learn from the experience of others. It is not necessary for each of us to give it a try at the next dinner to which we are invited. We can accept Jesus' words at face value and perhaps have the pleasant experience he holds out as a possibility—being drawn closer to the host

[15] *Surprised by God.*

[16] *Handles of Power.*

after all. Fortunately, with Jesus as our savior, the sin of pride may be conquered by grace and not send us to outer darkness.

II. *The host also must learn true hospitality.*

a. True hospitality forbids attempts at bribery, flattery, or undue influence over those invited. Self-promotion is a sin for the host as well as for the guest. Those who entertain politicians or contribute to campaigns must not seek preference in return. They might improve their spiritual and moral health by taking Jesus' words to heart and not inviting only those who can do them favors. Jesus elsewhere urges hosts to seek those to eat their food who have nothing to trade in exchange, no way to make the invitation worth more to the host than an opportunity to extend a kindness to another child of God.

b. The standards of social behavior urge us to consider others before ourselves, to prefer especially those who are less powerful, poorer, weaker, or otherwise unequal in the struggle for place in the world. We would do better in all the paths of life if we would recognize that we are engaged in a brief opportunity to prepare ourselves for eternity, and that, as Jesus was described as thinking, equality with God is not a thing to be grasped after. The truth we must realize is that human values will undergo a spiritual alteration between this life and the life to come.

c. The lesson of this parable is to enforce all the truth of Christian living. The achievements of the redeemed are truly traded in for a higher reward; as Jesus promised, "You will be repaid at the Resurrection." The children of God serve others rather than themselves. Believers accept the fact that greed and selfishness are traits of the lost, whereas the glory of God attends the ways of those who are kind to all, who without neglecting the love of friends and family search out those who are lonely or grieving; while not failing to honor those to whom honor is due, they find the lost and helpless, sick and mistreated, to share with them the glow of faithfulness and the richness of their heavenly Father's gifts.—John R. Rodman

Illustrations

THE LITTLE TASK. The great flowing rivers represent only a small part of all the water that is necessary to nourish and sustain the earth. Besides the flowing river, there is the water in the earth—the subterranean water—and there are the little streams which continually enter the river and feed it and prevent it from sinking into the earth. Without these other waters—the silent, hidden, subterranean water and the trickling streams—the great river could no longer flow. Thus it is with the little tasks to be fulfilled by us all.—Albert Schweitzer[17]

THE ULTIMATE SEAL. Viktor Frankl,[18] the founder of the school of logotherapy, wrote of his own discovery of this truth. After describing the wretched existence of life in a concentration camp and the suicidal despair that destroyed so many inmates, Frankl turned to describe the reason for his own survival. One morning, Frankl and other inmates were being taken under heavy guard to their work site. Stumbling in the darkness, with swollen, broken flesh on feet further tortured by huge stones, icy water, and frigid winds, the man next to him humorously said, "If our wives could see us now!" Frankl's mind turned to thoughts of his own wife, now in another camp—dead or alive he did not know. Her image appeared in his mind, and he heard her talking with him, smiling and encouraging him. "A thought," he said, "transfixed me: for the first time in my life I saw the truth . . . that love is the ultimate and the highest goal to which man can aspire." It was in that moment that Frankl came to see that great secret he had never really understood before: "The salvation of man is through love and in love."—Paul D. Simmons

SERMON SUGGESTIONS

Topic: Religion as a Burden
TEXT: Isa. 46

(1) Religion is a burden, and necessarily so, when it becomes selfish, idolatrous, and ultimately sinful. (2) The religion of the true and living God is not something that we carry, but a faith and a God that carry us, bearing us up in even the most difficult circumstances.

[17]Quoted in *For Example.*
[18] *Man's Search for Meaning.*

Topic: "Into Christ's Likeness"

TEXT: 2 Cor. 3:18

(1) The method of being changed into Christ's likeness is by "beholding his glory"—his character. (2) There are various means of beholding the glory of Jesus Christ—that is, of fixing a steady gaze upon his character: (a) Parents, teachers, and friends help us to keep our sights on Christ. (b) So does the Church. (c) So does the Bible. (d) So does regular, personal prayer time. (3) Being changed into the likeness of Christ is a gradual process. In the end, it is the work of the Spirit.

Hymn Suggestions: Twelfth Sunday After Trinity

1. "All My Hope on God Is Founded," Joachim Neander (1680), translated by Robert S. Bridges (1899); "Michael," Herbert Howells (1930)

The writer of Hebrews (13:15) invites us to offer a "sacrifice of praise to God, that is, the fruit of lips that acknowledge his name." This hymn, using the same metaphor, "sacrifice of praise" (stanza 5), gives the congregation a worthy means of doing just that, that is, offering the fruit of lips as well as heart and mind, to acknowledge the name of the great God we worship.

2. "How Firm a Foundation," "K" in Rippon's *A Selection of Hymns* (1787); "Foundation," *Sacred Harp* (1844)

Embodying (especially in its final stanza) the promise that God will never fail nor forsake us (Heb. 13:5), this sturdy hymn of faith is also appropriate for use in connection with the Epistle reading for this day.

3. "Sing a Psalm of Joy," Marie J. Post (1984); "Genevan" 81, *Genevan Psalter* (1562)

Stanzas 1, 5, 6, and 7 in this metrical version parallel the selected verses in the reading from Psalm 81. This modern paraphrase captures the truths of the original psalm; its stanzas, as indicated, could therefore be used profitably in alternation with the verses of the Psalter reading.

4. "Our God Has Made Us One," Niles Borop (1984); "Old 134th," *Genevan Psalter* (1551)

This recently written hymn reflects the spirit of this day's gospel lesson: "The one who humbles himself shall be exalted." The words of stanza 2—"As we build each other

up, our love becomes his praise"—especially express the Christian virtue of "in honor preferring one another."—Hugh T. McElrath

Worship Aids

CALL TO WORSHIP.   "Thou hast a mighty arm; strong is thy hand, and high is thy right hand. Justice and judgment are the habitation of thy throne: mercy and truth shall go before thy face. Blessed is the people that know the joyful sound: they shall walk, O Lord, in the light of thy countenance" (Ps. 89:13–15).

INVOCATION.   We come into your presence, Father, awed that you have placed in our hands the material out of which life is to be fashioned. Yet we are made confident that with your presence and leadership we can use the material given to create works of art. This morning we ask that you give us understanding of what you have for us to do. When we are tempted to follow the foolish desires of our own hearts and minds, draw us back upon the course which is our God-given destiny for life. When our choices become difficult, empower us with wisdom and insight so that we may not miss the way.—Henry Fields

OFFERTORY SENTENCE.   "Bear ye one another's burdens and so fulfill the law of Christ" (Gal. 6:2).

OFFERTORY PRAYER.   O God, we know that the law of Christ is the law of love. We acknowledge that law as the proper rule of life for those who have been redeemed by Christ's love. So we bring our offerings to you as an expression of our love and in the expectation that we shall bless one another as well as people beyond this fellowship by what we give.

PRAYER.   Our heavenly Father, we thank thee for this privilege of coming into thy presence at thine own invitation to worship and praise thy holy name. We come with humble hearts, knowing that the place where we worship thee is holy ground. Here we would humbly bow in contrition, knowing the inadequacy and frailty and sinfulness of our lives, not only of our nature but also of our deeds. We would come asking that thou wouldst accept our praise and thanksgiving and gather us the more closely to thee in fellowship and in service. We thank thee that thou hast filled life with meaning in times past by the wonder of thy presence. Wilt thou keep our souls awake? Wilt thou give us clear vision for the eyes of faith that we may ever see thee and find life's wonder in the wonder of thy character? Teach us in the hour of prayer to speak to thee as one speaks to a friend, to hear and to heed thy word, to live our life every day in thy presence.—Lowell M. Atkinson

Sermon: Confessions of a Clay Pot
TEXT: Exodus 4:1–12
I. The first thing that should be said, I suppose, is that Moses was right. His concerns were entirely legitimate. His excuses were valid. There was, in fact, no reason for anyone to listen to Moses.

a. Moses could see that clearly—and that's exactly what he told God. "God, it's a wonderful thing to be called; it's wonderful to be sent; I'm sincerely flattered that you would want to use me—but you've got the wrong person. Nobody will listen to me. It's a nice idea, but it's just not practical."

b. And we learn as we read this story that God's not all that interested in being practical:
"Moses, that staff in your hand. Throw it on the ground. Moses, I can use even that staff to accomplish my purposes."
"Moses, your hand, place it inside your cloak and watch what happens. Moses, you need to understand that even your own hand belongs to me."
"Moses, who made your mouth? I know all about your speech, Moses, and it's time for you to understand our respective responsibilities. It's your responsibility to obey—and it's my responsibility to be God. It's that simple."

II. You and I need to hear those words today. We need to hear those words and make them our own. We need to stand with Moses and hear God's thundering voice: "Who made you? Who made your mouth? Who made your hands?" To borrow the words of the psalmist, you and I are fearfully and wonderfully made—and that means that in the hands of the Creator, no purpose is impractical or absurd or impossible, not because of who we are but because of who our Creator is.

a. This theme is at the very heart of Scripture; it is repeated over and over again. God took the prophet Jeremiah down to the potter's house and said, "Let me draw you a picture. Let me explain who you are—and who I am." The same image was used by Isaiah, and by Paul in his letter to the Romans. It is the very same image that God revealed to Moses. It's a very simple image really: we're the clay pots, and God is the potter.

b. In this picture of clay pots and potters, there's a word for everyone. Within this image, there's a word for all those people who want to be God, for all those people who feel worthless and hopeless, for all those people who seem to think a little too much of themselves, and for all those people who are afraid to act and speak and live.

III. Our goal and our need is to find some kind of balance—to live with the knowledge that we have been fearfully and wonderfully made, and with the knowledge that we're just clay pots.

a. So one message today is, "I'm just a clay pot." And the other message today is, "Oh, what a wondrous clay pot I am." Both messages are true and they are both part of the gospel. The tragedy is that we usually pick the wrong message to hear. The people who are captive to pride often hear only the part about the wonder. And the broken, hurting people often hear only the part about the clay pot. Today let's be careful to hear the right message. Some of us need to be brought down—and some of us need to be built up. And the picture of the potter and the clay can do both of those things.

b. Some days I need to be reminded that I'm just a clay pot. And God has many ways of reminding me of that. I seem to go back and forth. I suppose it would be a mark of maturity to live between those extremes. "I'm just a clay pot—but what a marvelous, God-created, God-empowered clay pot I am!"

c. That's at least part of what Moses was facing when God called him to return to Egypt to challenge the children of Israel to see the activity of God. Moses evidently knew full well that he was just a clay pot—but he seems to have forgotten the wonder of being a clay pot. God responded to Moses' excuses one by one. He reminded Moses that even clay pots can be used by the potter. God reminded Moses that because of the power and grace of the potter, no purpose is impractical or absurd or impossible. Running out of excuses, Moses went off to be a clay pot—a clay pot to be used by God. And that was exactly what God wanted. "Some calling!" you might be thinking. "Called to be a clay pot." But a clay pot in the hands of the Creator is able to be used in marvelous and magnificent ways. What a joy it is to have a realistic view of how greatly God can use clay pots.—Barry A. Stricker

Illustrations

A COMICAL PICTURE.　I know that dishes dance and sing in Walt Disney movies, but it's still a comical picture to imagine a clay pot lecturing the potter about what needs to be done and lecturing the potter about how the crafting should be completed. Imagine that lump of clay on the potter's wheel informing the potter that this or that was not being done correctly. Or imagine that lump of clay stubbornly refusing to be used after the crafting has been finished. It's comical because we understand that potters shape the clay

and mold the clay and then use the clay pot that has been made. The clay pot is not a debate partner but an instrument to be used. As sobering as it is, we need to remember that God is the potter and that we are the clay pots.—B.A.S.

CHRIST'S MESSAGE TO THE WEAK.　Jesus Christ will see to the certain salvation of the least little Christian as well as the greatest, because He does the saving. Oh, precious truth, most glorious doctrine, salvation is by grace. The least saint in His kingdom will be as certainly saved as the greatest, because the salvation of both is by grace. "By grace are ye saved, through faith, and that not of yourselves; it is the gift of God, not of works, lest any man should boast." And so that little, timid, shrinking Christian, daring hardly to venture the public confession that he believes on Christ, yet if he does really believe on Him, he is as thoroughly saved as the mighty Christian who shouts, "I know that my Redeemer liveth," because Jesus does the saving of them both.—George W. Truett[19]

SUNDAY: SEPTEMBER SIXTH

LECTIONARY MESSAGE

Topic: No Yard-Sale Disciples Need Apply
TEXT: Luke 14:25–33
Other Readings: Jer. 18:1–11; Ps. 139:1–6; Philem. 1–21
Introduction. In early first-century Palestine, news about Jesus of Nazareth was on the home page of every hamlet in Judah and Israel. Jesus' growing reputation as a healer and teacher of great power commanded wide respect. People wanted to hear him. They must have been overjoyed that he offered his words freely, without tuition or the collection of tithes. Many frequently passed idle days listening to his wonderfully powerful brand of the Hebrew faith.

On this day recorded by Luke, Jesus' teaching was not so gentle. His tone was crisply demanding. Tenderness was put aside and the more obligatory face of his teachings was seen. He spoke directly, without equivocation.

"If you want to be a disciple of mine, plan on investing your entire life." Christianity cannot be purchased on a trip through a flea

market or yard sale. Christians must pay full price. Discipleship is costly. It requires a total commitment of life and a sacrificial lifestyle.

I. The first ingredient of costly discipleship, Jesus said, is commitment to pay whatever price is necessary in your generation. His shift in subject matter was quite radical and riveted his listeners to full attention. Look carefully, he said, to your own commitments: your fathers, your mothers, your wives, your children, your brothers, your sisters. You must lower them a notch in your priorities. And your own selfishness must go. Look at the unreserved way you lavish emotional, physical, and religious resources on yourself. Discipleship requires you to "hate" yourself, to "hate" your families, or at least to "love me more than you love them" (see Matt. 10:34ff) if you wish to be my disciple.

What a stunning blow to all the listeners, the wealthy and the poor alike. For many in the audience, the only true wealth they possessed

[19] *We Should See Jesus.*

was the value of their accumulated relationships. In this medium of value, all were equally chastised, equally challenged.

The enthusiasm among the fainthearted in the crowd was surely dampened, but zealots present were sure to have been encouraged. Then, leaving the abstract, Jesus turned to some ways to consider how such discipleship is possible.

II. "Bear your own cross," Jesus continued. That ugly form of execution in Jesus' day was reserved for murderers and felons, those guilty of crimes against neighbor and state. My disciples are already dead to themselves, Jesus had said on other occasions. As soldiers enter their battles as if they were already dead, you must enter discipleship only to fight for me and my cause.

This is as death-defying an invitation to become a Christian disciple as one can get. Surely the task of cross-bearing requires interpretation. It means at least (a) to consider serving God as a higher priority than serving self, family, or neighbors; (b) to consider spirituality as the highest or deepest level of commitment in life; (c) to expect suffering as a way of life for those truly committed to Christ; (d) to resist all man-made forms of repressive governance in family, political, or ecclesiastical life; and (e) to assert the priority of God's core teachings in Holy Scripture, especially those of the prophets, against all human misinterpretations. To do these things half-heartedly is to miss the point of the redemptive suffering of God in the person of Jesus Christ. Jesus invited those who would be his disciples to join him in a pilgrimage of suffering for the redemption of all.

III. It was as if Jesus had also said, "Why do you suppose I tell you these things about being a Christian?" Such a statement would be an easy transition to the next two examples in this text. Does a builder just grab hammer and nails and go to his building site poorly prepared? Certainly not. Builders go prepared. They plan for materials and funds to pay the workers; they consider foundation, walls, and observation deck. A builder does not set himself up for ridicule because he is unable to accomplish what he set out to do.

None of my disciples, Jesus implied, are to begin following me without knowing the cost of being a Christian. My disciples know that discipleship will require total commitment of personal resources. It will necessitate maximum willingness to make strategic decisions from time to time about how to invest those resources, and the resources are to be invested according to my teachings.

This brand of Christianity is not for weak souls.

IV. Our enemies in this battle are the contemporary incarnations of the powers of evil. In this interpretation, they are serving Satan, who always seems, according to human standards, to have twice the firepower of the forces for God. Do you want to fight in such a battle? Or are you more likely to prefer to sue for peace from a distance?

Jesus Christ does not mince words with this illustration. If you are not ready to commit yourself to fight evil in any arena, however ill-equipped you may be, then you had better negotiate yourself out of being a Christian. Jesus instructed his disciples to walk past the billboard message "Danger, do not follow Jesus unless you are willing to pay the price" and go forth under the banner "Wherever, whenever, until as long as it takes, here am I; send me."

Conclusion. There are no short cuts to Christian discipleship, no discounts available for those who would bargain for places in the Kingdom of God at less than the full price. Following Jesus is not for the fainthearted or for intellectually lazy persons who glean their most soul-searching ideas from the yard sales of life.

"Lift up your hearts." The God and father of our Lord Jesus is rich in encouragement to all who believe and follow the Christ. The human fellowship of sisters and brothers who are members of the ongoing band of Christian disciples provide a human bond of mutuality and endurance based on that encouragement. Both are available today, and a chief source continues to be the unity we find as we gather to worship God in Jesus' name. For wounded disciples, Christ provides healing; for the discouraged and downhearted, God provides presence and comfort. The original goal of Christian discipleship has not faded in the heart and mind of God. That goal continues to be that the kingdoms of this world shall become the Kingdom of our God and his Christ, and he shall reign forever and ever. Amen.—Walter P. Jackson

Illustrations

NOT THE REAL THING.   In a seminary class, a brilliant young student began his sermon with this illustration: You all know what this object is [*holds it up*]. It is a standard Ritz cracker made with wheat flower, sugar, salt, leavening, vegetable oil, not to mention preservatives and flavor enhancers. It has been toasted to perfection. It is not only robust and delicious, it is the favorite of generations of American chicken soup lovers. Here is another one [*holds it up*]. It looks like the real McCoy! Not! It is lower in calories, lower in fat, lower in salt, and is less pleasant to the taste. It is not as robust as the first one. Actually, its food value is about 40 percent less than the original. I believe you know my sermon today is not about Ritz crackers, but I make this comparison only to make a point. This sermon has to do with believers masquerading as true Christians, when they really are anemic versions of the first disciples of Jesus Christ.—Ben McGinnis, on 2 Cor. 5:17

WATER AND SALT—GOOD AND BAD.   Water fit for the Christian disciple comes from the pure springs of the gospel of Jesus Christ; salt for the preservation of the fellowship comes directly from the purest forms in creation. Many there are who attempt to find both in streams like the Dead Sea, whose water is brackish and whose mineral deposits are so mixed with contaminants that the salt found there is impure and tasteless. Christian baptism is in the Jordan River, before it becomes part of the Dead Sea.—W.P.J.

SERMON SUGGESTIONS

Topic: We Do It to Ourselves
  TEXT: Prov. 5:22
  (1) If we do wrong, we tend to shift the blame: to circumstances, to someone else, to natural human weakness. (2) However, God has given us the power of choice about what to do with the problem. (3) We seal our own destiny with that choice. But God makes a way of escape.

Topic: What Is the Good Word?
  TEXT: Various
  (1) The word of regeneration (James 1:18). (2) The word of spiritual nourishment (1 Pet. 2:2). (3) The word of ethical instruction (Titus 2:1–5)

Hymn Suggestions: Thirteenth Sunday After Trinity

  1. "Have Thine Own Way, Lord," Adelaide A. Pollard (1902); "Adelaide," George C. Stebbins (1907)
  The allegory of the potter and the clay in Jeremiah may be appropriately accompanied by the singing of this hymn of submission and sanctifying grace.
  2. "My God, How Wonderful Thou Art," Frederick W. Faber (1849); "Windsor," William Damon (1591)
  Faber's hymn echoes the praise of the psalmist in today's reading, especially as found in Psalm 139:14. It may best be used after the Psalter reading as a worshipful meditation in contemplation of the attributes of an all-merciful God.
  3. "Take Up Your Cross, the Savior Said," Charles W. Everest (1933); "Bourbon," Freeman Lewis (1825)
  This hymn, with its opening refrain carrying Jesus' demand that to be his disciple one must take up one's cross and follow him faithfully, would be eminently suitable to introduce the gospel reading of the day.
  4. "Lord, You Have Searched My Life and Know," Calvin Seerveld (1985); "Leicester," John Bishop (1711)
  The first and third stanzas of this contemporary paraphrase of Psalm 139 relate particularly to the selected verses in today's Psalter reading.—Hugh T. McElrath

Worship Aids

CALL TO WORSHIP.   "Let anyone who has an ear listen to what the Spirit is saying to the churches. To everyone who conquers, I will give permission to eat from the tree of life that is in the paradise of God" (Rev. 2:7 NRSV).

INVOCATION.   Again we come as a congregation into your presence, Father. Some of us come reluctantly, having been buffeted by life's circumstances, to the point of wondering if faith makes any difference. Renew our hearts and minds so that reluctance may give way to eagerness to seek you early and often as we try to manage daily life.—Henry Fields

OFFERTORY SENTENCE. "And he said unto them, Take heed what ye hear: with what measure ye mete, it shall be measured to you: and unto you that hear shall more be given. For he that hath, to him shall be given: and he that hath not, from him shall be taken even that which he hath" (Mark 4:24–25).

OFFERTORY PRAYER. Father, knowing that we all shall give an account of ourselves unto the Lord, inspire us to give our money as well as our very selves, as we have been instructed to do. Bless gift and giver to your glory, we pray.—Henry Fields

PRAYER. Our heavenly Father, we praise thee for the way thou dost fill our daily life with strength. We know our inadequacy and our frailty and we turn to thee asking for that grace that alone can make our lives sufficient. We have tasted of thy strength and we have known the happiness of doing deeds in thy name. To thee we give all the glory, for thou dost inspire the good thoughts that come into our minds, the good intentions that are welcomed in our spirits, the good deeds that are given us to do in thy service. Thou art ever encouraging and strengthening us in the good way.

We would praise thee that thou dost fill life with the happiness and the strength of goodness. We would praise thee this day for the gift of thyself. Thou hast come into our world, touching our mortal life with eternal splendor, lighting earth with the glory of heaven. Thou hast flung a rainbow against the storm clouds to give hope to human hearts. Thou hast come personally to live among us in Jesus Christ and hast fastened forever to the earth the rainbow of our eternal hope that binds earth to heaven. For all the wonders of thy dealings with us, we would praise thee.—Lowell M. Atkinson

Sermon: What Makes You Angry

TEXT: Jonah 4:1–11; Matt. 5:21–24; 21:12–13; Eph. 4:26

Anger is very natural. It is simply a part of being a human being. Anger is as much a part of our human nature as becoming tired

or getting hungry. But we have to make a distinction between anger that is uncontrolled and anger that is healthy and normal.

I. Let me mention a few examples of destructive anger.

a. We might call the first example the "blazing" kind of anger. This type represents an individual who lets his anger explode. This person goes all to pieces. Whatever he or she feels is dumped on you or anybody nearby. Unfortunately, some individuals let their anger blaze at anybody who gets in their path.

b. The second type of anger I would mention is the "blistering" kind. This type of anger is directed in a bit more subtle way. Sarcasm is one of its chief weapons. People who express this type of anger are not as direct as the blazing kind, but in a sarcastic way they cut, dig, and try to hurt the persons at whom they are venting their feelings.

c. Another type is the "brooding" kind of anger. These individuals may carry inside of them a great deal of anger about what is happening on their job or at home or at some other place like school or church. These persons want to appear as "Mr. Nice Guy" and not "make waves," so they are unable to verbalize their real feelings. So they push it down inside and brood on those angry feelings and let them fester within them. Many of us carry throughout our lives a slush fund of anger that is brooding in our subconscious, waiting for someplace where it can be vented. Withholding affection toward a spouse is one way some people express the anger that is brooding deep within them.

d. Another kind of anger is the "bullying" kind. Individuals who experience this kind of anger try to dominate those around them with anger. They can't change someone else with intellect, so they try to do it with anger. They can't do it with persuasion, so they attempt to do it with red-faced heat.

II. Paul, writing to the Ephesians, said, "Be angry but sin not." All of us will be angry at some time or another, because some anger is normal. But let's be careful that our anger does not become uncontrollable and sinful. May I offer some suggestions on how to try to avoid letting your anger become sinful?

a. The first thing I would suggest is not to let your emotions control you. Don't be a victim of your moods. Don't be mastered by your emotions, but master them.

That is a difficult lesson to learn. Studies indicate that uncontrolled anger can affect our blood pressure, our heart, and other organs of the body. Psychosomatic medicine has clearly indicated the affect of our emotions on our body. Because we have difficulty controlling our emotions, we often let others control us by our reaction to them. The first step in dealing with anger is not to let your emotions control you completely.

b. Second, I am convinced that uncontrolled anger is a sign of immaturity. Destructive anger is transmitted by a person who demonstrates that he or she is not in command of himself or herself. Sometimes this anger may be set off by the most trivial or insignificant things. In some ways anger is nature's defense weapon. Somebody may hurt your feelings. You may have been intimidated, frustrated, threatened, humiliated, or manipulated, so you respond with overt anger. Sometimes the most immature thing persons can do is to give in immediately to feelings of anger and respond in a hostile way.

c. Third, find some avenue of release for your anger. It is unbelievable how many people have buried within them old grudges, mistakes, sins, hurts, or resentments. These feelings of hostility have festered below the surface for years.

To be unwilling to forgive others is to say in essence that you really do not accept the grace of God. Jesus told his disciples they were to pray, "Forgive us our trespasses as we forgive those who have trespassed against us." In our Scripture text for today from Matthew's Gospel, Jesus says: "If when you are bringing your gift to the altar you suddenly remember that your brother has a grievance against you, leave your gift where it is before the altar. First go and make your peace with your brother, and only then come back and offer your gift" (Matt. 5:23–24 NEB). Hanging onto grudges, hurts, and mistakes from the past and being unwilling to forgive and forget is totally destructive and unchristian.

d. Fourth, find some relief from your anger, if possible. You may not be able to direct all of your anger toward the source that should receive it. If you are angry at your boss, you may or may not be able to talk with him about certain things. What do you do then? Well, you do a lot of jogging, tennis, or some other form of exercise. You learn to laugh. You try to find some kind of diversion. You may hit a punching bag or play golf or racquetball. You may want to talk to a friend or a professional counselor. Whatever you do, find some way to keep from burying your feelings inside of you. If your problem is severe or very personal, you may need to confess it to your pastor or a trained counselor.

III. The final suggestion I would make this morning is that we need to follow the example of our Lord Jesus Christ. If there were ever an individual who was in control of himself it was our Lord. But there were times Jesus expressed anger. One of these occasions was when he entered the Temple to worship. He saw what the money changers were doing in the temple, and his anger was kindled. His anger was not over a personal hurt or a wrong somebody had done to him. He was upset by the exploitation of others.

a. There are times that you should be angry. Not to be angry at some times or in certain situations is a sin. If you and I can be surrounded by poverty, disease, hunger, racism, crime, and other abuses and not be angry enough to want to change these conditions, then something is wrong with us. This anger is not over some personal or petty concern but about someone else's needs. This kind of anger can express love and genuine concern.

The Church cannot be silent in the face of world problems; it has a responsibility and a commission to be the transforming element within the world. The Church is to be the salt, the light, the leaven to change mankind.

b. Some voices are saying that the Church has become too tame and comfortable to challenge the evils of our society. If the Church, however, can recapture its birthright, it will sense the creative and redemptive power within its body.

Religious history rings with those who cared enough to be angry at the right time. Moses was angry at the enslavement of the children of Israel in Egypt. Elijah was angry at the prophets of Baal and the idolatry they practiced in Israel. John the Baptist was angry at the distortion of religion by the Jewish leaders. Paul was angry at those who wanted to confine the gospel to the Jews. Luther was angry at the corruption in the established church. John Wesley was angry at the practices of religion in the Church of England.

There are times when anger needs to be directed toward particular situations or problems if we are to find a solution.

c. Anger needs to be directed in a positive way. The apostle Paul has said, "Be angry and sin not." Phillips has translated that verse, "Never go to bed angry—don't give the devil that sort of foothold."

What makes you angry? There should be some things that do. But on other occasions, you need to keep your anger under control. You are measured by what makes you angry. —William Powell Tuck

Illustrations

THE REAL CULPRIT. All eyes in the grocery store suddenly turned to look at the shopper at the cash register. As I listened to that man, I realized that he was completely out of control. The veins were standing out on his neck. His face was blood-red. He was screaming at the cashier at the top of his voice. He thought the clerk had charged him twice for an item. He was demanding that every item be rechecked. He poured out his fury on the cashier until finally she called for the manager. While they rechecked each item, the man continued to pour out his anger. When the items were rechecked, they found that there was no discrepancy at all. As the man stormed out the door of the store, his face still filled with anger, he declared: "I will never come back to this place to shop again!" Those of us who had stood behind him said to ourselves, "We hope not!"—W.P.T.

WHO'S IN CONTROL? I like the story about the old Quaker who had an encounter in a store one day with a man who unloaded all of his anger on him. As they walked out of the store, the Quaker man's friend asked him, "Why didn't you zap him back?"

"Friend," the Quaker responded, "I have learned not to let the behavior of others determine my own behavior."—W.P.T.

SUNDAY: SEPTEMBER THIRTEENTH

Topic: Reclaiming the Throw-Away People
TEXT: Luke 15:1–10
Other Readings: Jer. 4:11–12, 22–28; Ps. 14; 1 Tim. 1:12–17

Introduction. According to the religious leaders of his day, Jesus, the teacher from Nazareth, had an exasperating habit. He spoke to every person as if they were of equal value before God. For that reason, if for no other, status-conscious people have forever had difficulty with the religious faith he taught. People who prefer society to be divided into the good and the bad, the beautiful and the ugly, are often angry, or at least uncomfortable, whenever anyone teaches that each person is in some way equal in God's eyes.

The Pharisees in the time of Jesus were first-class examples of people like that. They organized their lives around what was necessary to be good. They fastidiously kept the religious rules and regulations they designed. They loudly proclaimed that they were "good." At the same time, they despised anyone not like themselves. They had a simple category for such people. They called them "sinners." So repulsed were they by "sinners," they taught that they should be avoided, excluded from the good society so the good could remain good, separate, and apart, and the bad could be with and contaminate only each other.

In the text for today, this sort of exclusionary thinking forms the backdrop for the narrative. The leading Pharisees and the scribes denigrated Jesus because he insisted on associating with people they classed as sinners.

As Jesus taught, healed, and spoke of God's love and grace in inclusive terms, sinners of all kinds—even tax collectors, the worst kind of sinners—gathered to hear him gladly. True to form, the Pharisees and their scribes chastised Jesus for associating with these sinners: they are worthless; such people are not the kind who promote your organization; they are among life's "throw-away" people. Anyone wanting to get ahead in the religion game should avoid people who would give their group such a bad name.

In response, Jesus told a series of stories for the express purpose of highlighting the hidden value of things and persons otherwise considered worthless.

I. His first example was about a shepherd and the way a shepherd may value each sheep. Gone among the Israelites were the days when shepherds were valued role models. The rugged, almost comfortless way of life lived by a shepherd was spurned for the preferred life of a city dweller. Sheep were important, but they were not a great wealth-producing commodity in their modern society. Sheep were dirty, ugly, and unmanageable, and their stench frequently created unpleasant odors in the marketplaces, the homes of the poor, the shops, and even in the Temple. The occupation of shepherd may have launched David to royal prominence, but a shepherd could not have even wished for a life of leadership in the Roman Empire. A shepherd also could not keep the kosher rules or the other requirements of the law. A shepherd was forcefully rejected by the synagogue's religious parties, but was carefully chosen by Jesus as the hero of an otherwise throw-away vocation. Using a shepherd, Jesus made his lesson all the more clear.

Jesus' shepherd lavished affection and care upon his nearly worthless charges. With a hundred animals to lose, he squandered his time, energy, and heroics on one, stray, stubborn sheep. The irony of the narrative is clear. Jesus knew the city-slicker rabbis would view the story as much ado about nothing. Their "take" on the story was not only that a shepherd had chosen his profession poorly, but that such lower-class priorities were destined to trap him in less-desirable social circumstances for life.

Then Jesus added the community—townspeople who valued shepherds, sheep, and their kind of economic values. What kind of group would rejoice if a single lost sheep were found? That is a question the Pharisees would have asked. What kind of society could be satisfied to be friendly and neighborly in such a drama? To this unspoken question Jesus gave a stirring answer.

Just as the shepherd and his neighbors rejoice over the found sheep, even so the occupants of heaven rejoice over a single sinner who repents. The joy of God is attached both to the ninety-nine who were safe and to the Pharisee-labeled throw-away stray now safely returned to the fold.

That interpretation surely captured the Pharisees' attention.

II. The second parable, with its melody on the same theme, followed quickly after the first. Women were mostly powerless in first-century Palestine and were important only as pawns in alliances for and with their families of origin. A woman who lived in a hut that needed a lamp for light in the daytime was poor indeed, especially if she spent a whole day looking for a coin worth about twenty-five cents. Jesus defined her as desperately poor, and thereby considered worthless as a person by the Pharisees, even if she possessed ten such coins. If they carried their point to its logical conclusion, the Pharisees certainly wondered who would tell a heroic story about a woman who was that poor? And what kind of friends and neighbors would celebrate the finding of a quarter?

Again, the point of the parable series is thrust home with precision. The Pharisees and community leaders knew the relationship between money and religion: wealth, and wealth alone, enables a person to practice religious philanthropy. Only independent capital could release a person from arduous labor and enable that person to follow the teachings of great men of the faith. But if one really wanted to get ahead in the field of religion, poverty could only prove the most serious handicap. Wasting time on the poor is such a foolish activity if one is really interested in discovering the work of God in any era. In a world like theirs, only big bucks, not silver coins, were considered the proper foci for religious attention.

Jesus again makes his point with clarity and power: poverty does not destroy the value of a person to God. Wealth may set a person above his or her neighbors by human standards; but a poor person, even a poor woman, may be a heroine in the eyes of God. In the context of this series of parables, Jesus forces his interpretation of the value of the otherwise throw-away item. No person is valueless to God—especially to the God whose bands of angels celebrate when one of the least among human sinners finds a way to be reconciled with God. Even sinners, poor sinners, are value-specific to God.

III. The third parable clearly focuses the theme in the human dimension. Elder brothers who obey their fathers are really not of more value than younger brothers who waste their substance on loose living. The issue here seems to be that neither of these two sons fits into any human category of throwaway persons.

a. The sin of wastefulness and disobedience does not in the end destroy a person's value to God. Being God's child gives even a prodigal an equal chance before the lovingkindness of the covenant God of Israel, the "Abba" of Jesus.

b. Obedience, even lifelong obedience, does not tip the scales of value to the elder brother. Prejudice like the kind demonstrated by the elder brother toward his sinful sibling is also not eternally condemning behavior. The elder brother's harsh judgment of his prodigal brother, as well as his exclusionary behavior, is not necessarily a sin that removes him from the grace and love of God. Neither son is vulnerable to damnation only because of such behavior. Neither one of these children of their father is relegated by God to a throw-away category. Both are eligible for the salvation of the God who was so clearly introduced by Jesus of Nazareth.

Conclusion. All of us can say quickly with whom we would prefer to share dinner, faith, or any other intimate or social relationship. Little wonder that even in the most charitable of religious faiths, categories of exclusion are to be found. The poor, the uneducated, the ugly, the diseased, the disfigured, and the mentally retarded are often shunned. The most intense shunning is usually reserved for those who believe nearly as much as the judges but who differ in what is termed a "significant deviation." Even some of the brilliant contributors to society are excluded if those making the categories of judgment use human standards rather than God's standards as taught by Jesus Christ.

Every generation is filled with its own specific brand of sinners. They can be found everywhere. Some are incorrigible. They never repent and they never change. Jesus applies his "equal before God" doctrine even to them, but implies they too must turn to God in order to find peace.

We frequently spend all our time creating definitions of sin and miss one of the main points of Jesus as he told these three parables: every person has equal access to God. All have equal opportunity to turn to God, to confess their sins and repent, to come into the peace of God's grace.

Those who are intent to pass themselves off as sinless would not dare do anything like that. It is only the self-aware sinners who know that "all have sinned and have fallen short of the glory of God" (Rom. 3:23). They are those who can move into the truth of Jesus' great message. They are not throwaway people, but people who continue to be loved by the God who hopes beyond hope for their repentance and return to faith. The proper task of those who minister in the name of Jesus is to reach out with the mindshattering truth that Jesus is the loving, forgiving, saving Son of God for everyone. Those who embrace him, "sinner" or "humanly righteous," are the true believers. Thank God for the "people savers." May they forever outnumber those who see others as throw-away people.—Walter C. Jackson

Illustrations

WHERE THE LORD IS. Jesus came to power by dying for the truth of God's all-embracing reconciliation. A church that is not ready to die will die without resurrection, will become a ruin which is nothing more than a few walls of stone open to sightseeing tourist groups for not much more than a tip, and the guide may still cry, "This is the temple of the Lord who was worshiped here in 100 or 1900 A.D., this is the temple of the Lord, this is the temple of the Lord." The Lord, however, is not to be found in the ruins; he is going just now, step by step, beside his disciple who refuses to hate; who attacks all churchly or worldly self-conceitedness; who opens the doors for all the gentiles.—Eduard Schweizer[1]

"IT'S ME, O LORD." I must therefore begin with myself and my own guilt whenever there is anything to be said about the world's guilt. I cannot simply look out the window and be morally indignant over the great Babylon that lies spread out before me in all its godless darkness. No, what I see out there in global proportions must only remind me of my own "Babylonian heart" (Francis Thompson). And quite involuntarily I will be reminded of the prophet Nathan's hard rebuke to David: "Thou art the man!" I am the

[1] *Bible Studies.*

one who needs forgiveness, and the sanitation of the world must begin with me.—Helmut Thielicke[2]

SERMON SUGGESTIONS

Topic: When Things Get Worse

Text: Jer. 12:1–6; Rom. 8:18–30

(1) We can be honest with God about our fears and our feelings, as Jeremiah was—and Jesus. (2) We can learn in our suffering: (a) that creation and redemption are in process but not completed; (b) that patience is imperative; (c) that the Spirit's help is at work; (d) that the goal of it all is that we shall "be conformed to the image of his Son."

Topic: Uncluttering Our Past

Text: 1 John 1:5–10

The past cannot be changed, but God can give us the resources to gain a victory over the past. (1) We may not sin deliberately, but we sin inevitably. (2) We find complete forgiveness when we confess our sins to God. (3) Constant victory can be ours if we live consciously in the presence and example of Christ.

Hymn Suggestions: Fourteenth Sunday After Trinity

1. "Immortal, Invisible, God Only Wise," Walter C. Smith (1867); "St. Denio," John Roberts (1839)

The last verse of the Epistle lesson (1 Tim. 1:17) is the basis for this hymn of pure praise. It would be effective sung phrase by phrase antiphonally by choir and congregation.

2. "The Foolish in Their Hearts Deny," Marie J. Post (1983); "Maple Avenue," Richard L. Van Oss (1984)

This modern paraphrase includes every idea in the original psalm, a lament over the unrighteous. The singing of this version of Psalm 14 could be enhanced by the prior reading of that portion of the Scripture that parallels each stanza, as follows: Ps. 14:1–2 read; stanza 1 of the hymn sung; verses 3–4 read; stanza 2 sung; verses 5–7 read; stanza 3 sung.

3. "Christ Receiveth Sinful Men," Erd-

mann Neumeister (1718), translated by Emma F. Bevan (1858); "Neumeister," James McGranahan (1883)

Neumeister, an eloquent German preacher, wrote the original of this gospel song to follow his sermon on the parables of today's gospel reading. The author takes the complaint of the scribes and Pharisees in Luke 15:2 and makes it the theme of a singing witness and an invitation to accept the gospel.

4. "My Lord, What a Morning," African American Spiritual

In some versions of this spiritual, the fifth word is spelled "mourning," thus conveying the idea that God will bring a day of mourning and judgment in a manner not unlike that described in the reading from Jeremiah. The anonymous slave-poet who created this song, while viewing judgment as terrifying destruction for the wicked, considered it a happy event for the survivors—the righteous.—Hugh T. McElrath

Worship Aids

CALL TO WORSHIP.   "Sing praise to the Lord, O you his faithful one, and give thanks to his holy name. For his anger is but for a moment; his favor is for a lifetime. Weeping may linger for the night, but joy comes with the morning" (Ps. 29:4–5 NRSV).

INVOCATION.   Today, Father, grant us the wisdom to submit our lives completely to you, that we may join the vast company of those who through the years have made a difference in the world because they were known as the followers of Jesus.—Henry Fields

OFFERTORY SENTENCE.   "But my God shall supply all your needs according to his riches in glory by Christ Jesus" (Phil. 4:19).

OFFERTORY PRAYER.   Lord, let this act of stewardship redound to the glory of God because the risk of faith is in it and the joy of sacrifice for the Christ as well.—E. Lee Phillips

PRAYER.   God of all helpfulness, who has called us to intercede for others and to make those petitions for ourselves for things most needed for our fulfilling of your will, we pray for all followers or disciples who are not

[2] *Our Heavenly Father.*

ashamed to own you as Redeemer and Lord. Make us always to test our lives by yours and to be strong not for our own gain but for the Master's sake. May we restrain ourselves from becoming too much a part of the noise and clangor of our day that we cannot hear his voice saying, "Follow me." Show us how to bear stoutheartedly the yoke he lays upon us, and with firm and steady steps may we carry forward the frontiers of his Kingdom. Bind together in common loyalty to him and to themselves each company of Christian disciples in every community, and in their efforts to be obedient servants may they sow the seeds of love and peace.—Donald Macleod

Sermon: The Easy Yoke

TEXT: Matt. 11:28–30

"Come to me, all you that are weary and are carrying heavy burdens." Does that sound like you? I think that our weariness, our feeling that life is almost more than we can take and that our problems are lots bigger than we'd like them to be, is almost universal in our society. We are all weary, we all feel burdened, we all wish life were easier.

But the rest of Jesus' quote sounds like advertising hype. "Come to me, all you that are weary"—that's right on the money. But "Take my yoke upon you and learn from me, for my yoke is easy and my burden is light" sounds like package labeling to me. You know how you look at the package and it says "lite" or "lo-cal" and then you read the label and it is nothing of the sort? How can there be an easy yoke or a light burden? A yoke, to remind us, is a big piece of wood curved in such a way that it fits over the neck of a draft animal. It is used to hook an animal up to something too heavy for a human to drag—a plow or wagon. A yoke implies work. You yoke an animal up in order to make it pull something. A yoke implies submission. You yoke an animal up so that you can control it more easily. Wearing a yoke means that you give up your freedom to go where you like and do what you like. Why would anybody choose a yoke over freedom?

Our culture has a different answer. Do you feel burdened and weary? It is because you are expecting too much for yourself. You are trying to live up to standard that other people set. Learn to accept yourself and don't worry about it. It's not your fault; you shouldn't feel

guilty; don't worry, be happy, be gentle with yourself.

Imagine, if you will, a whole community full of those who might join a church if it made them feel better about themselves, but as soon as any sort of demand was made that they felt pressured them, they would opt out. They might undertake a charitable project, if it made them feel better about themselves. Doing things for other people can make you feel better about yourself, if the others are grateful and praise you for it. But if the persons receiving the charity don't express gratitude, then you will opt out—no sense in doing something if people are going to be negative about it; life is too short to lay that sort of guilt on us. Opting out, in fact, makes real community impossible.

Our culture gives us other options as well. Is your life hard? Are your problems too great for you to bear? Then make your life easier with this gadget. Buy a new car; you'll feel better about yourself. Take a long vacation in the Bahamas; go to Disney World and you'll feel your burdens lifted. Get a new house; get a new, better-paying job; get a new, more exciting spouse and family. If your life is hard, if your burdens are too heavy, you can feel better by acquiring more things or different things. You can narcotize yourself with better things.

I don't really have to prove this one, or even illustrate it. The American definition of humans as consumers is so pervasive, so ever-present, that it seems as natural to us as air and water. Everything about our world is sold, advertised, and packaged as new, improved, and better, and we are taught from infancy to believe that we are successful to the degree that we acquire more new, improved, and better things. We are taught that things set us free, that things make life easier, that new things make life better.

Our culture does a soft-sell number on us, advertising "be good to yourself" and "buy something new" as freedom. But as ways of life, they are just another yoke.

"Be gentle with yourself, be good to yourself" is a yoke. You can be a slave to yourself and your own pleasure as much as to anything else in this world. People who opt out of relationships because they don't want any pressure, people who opt out of common values because they don't want to feel guilty—

people like that lose the ability to give themselves to anyone else and lose the ability to trust anyone else. The cult of self is a very heavy yoke that in the end crushes the self it purports to worship.

And materialism is a yoke, not a freedom. Once you acquire things, you become their slave. This is not a new idea, but it is one that seems hard for us to learn. Materialism drives us to be slaves to our jobs; it ruins families; it causes us to do wretched things to our world in order to gain a profit. Materialism is a very heavy yoke indeed, crushing the self under the weight of lifeless things.

Listen again to Jesus, then: "Take my yoke upon you and learn of me, for my yoke is easy and my burden is light." The choice is not between Jesus' yoke and freedom. We have a choice of yokes, and that is all. On another occasion Jesus said, "You cannot serve God and mammon"—or God and culture, as we'd put it. The corollary to that is that you must serve one or the other. Our choice is a choice between yokes. We come back, then, to the question we began with: How can the yoke Jesus offers be considered "easy" or "light"?

It is certainly not easy in the sense of being simple to wear. Jesus' yoke demands a very high standard of conduct. We are to love our enemies, to forgive those who persecute us— pretty much the exact opposite of "be gentle with yourself." Jesus teaches us to reach toward those who cause us pain, to try to heal their pain with God's love. We are to put God ahead of everything and to put others on a par with ourselves—pretty much the exact opposite of materialism. Materialism teaches us to accumulate things and to enrich ourselves above everyone else. Jesus teaches us to divest ourselves of things, because they stand between us and God; he teaches us to use what we do own to enrich others. Jesus' yoke is not simple to perform. It is tough; it takes discipline; it takes lots of practice; and it takes the constant support of a whole group of people who are all committed to living under that yoke.

This yoke is not simple, but compared to the alternatives, it sits easy on our necks. Our choice in life comes down to giving ourselves to God and to others under Jesus' yoke, or giving ourselves to culture in some form. Culture's alternatives will crush us in the end, will destroy our values, will make true community impossible, will ruin our families. When we think of the way that Jesus lived and of the way he called us to live, the words *easy* and *light* would not be what came first to mind. But compared to the alternatives, his yoke is easy. This is the gospel.—Richard B. Vinson

Illustrations

A YOKE THAT FITS.   Jesus says, "My yoke is easy." The word *easy* is in Greek *chréstos,* which can mean *well-fitting.* In Palestine, ox-yokes were made of wood; the ox was brought and the measurements were taken. The yoke was then roughed out and the ox was brought back to have the yoke tried on. The yoke was then carefully adjusted so that it would fit well and would not gall the neck of the patient beast. The yoke was tailor-made to fit the ox. Now there is a legend that Jesus made the best ox-yokes in all Galilee, and that from all over the country men came to Him to the carpenter's shop to buy the best yokes that skill could make.—William Barclay[3]

SHEILAISM.   Several years ago a sociologist of religion named Robert Bellah wrote a classic book called *Habits of the Heart,* which was a study of American religious behavior. He gave us the unforgettable picture of "Sheilaism" after interviewing a young woman named Sheila Larson, who told him that her faith was really in herself. "My faith has carried me a long way. It's Sheilaism. Just my own little voice. It's just try to love yourself and be gentle with yourself."[4] According to Sheilaism, moral standards are bad, because when you fail to meet them, you feel guilty. Your only standard is yourself and feeling good about yourself; whatever makes you feel good about yourself is the right thing to do.—R.B.V.

---

[3] *The Gospel of Matthew.*
[4] *Habits of the Heart.*

SUNDAY: SEPTEMBER TWENTIETH

LECTIONARY MESSAGE

Topic: A Clever Man's Lesson
Text: Luke 16:1–13
Other Readings: Jer. 8:18–22; Ps. 79; 1 Tim. 2:1–7

Introduction. In the passage following the story of the prodigal son, Jesus focused again on the subject of discipleship. How intensely is one to invest in the religious quest? Where can we turn to find an example of intense commitment sufficient to illustrate the way Jesus intended his disciples to give themselves to God?

One behavior seems sufficiently powerful in every generation to serve as a model, and that is human devotion to money and commitment to its use. Surely money provides just such a universal example of single-minded dedication.

Of all the changeless characteristics of humans from generation to generation, the love affair men have with money is a single most unchangeable subject. Nothing in human history has ever been able to interrupt the love affair the children of Adam have with money. Every method available to assist a man to accumulate and/or control money has been used by believer and unbeliever alike throughout the ages. The truth of the matter is, the more clever a man has become, the more clever are the ways for that man to deal with money.

This text, then, is actually not about money itself but about the single-minded intensity of men to accumulate and use it for their own ends. Jesus clearly used the clever steward's passion for money as an example of the kind of ardor he would like to engender among men in the matter of religious faith.

Jesus' listeners were probably not so puzzled by this story as are some modern readers. As Jesus unfolded the narrative, the progress and methodology of the key character easily claimed the central attention. The primary focus was on the process of a man's activity related to money rather than on the money itself. Jesus' clear labeling of the man as dishonest (v. 8) signals hearers about his negative judgment on the steward's behavior. However, that judgment contrasts with Jesus' lavish praise for this rogues's single-minded devotion. Whereas a child of darkness would be devoted to his own personal welfare, a child of the light would be devoted with similar energy and focused goal to doing the will of God.

Actually, Jesus was so blatantly obvious as he told the story that the listening religious leaders saw themselves being panned as children of darkness. They could not disguise their preoccupation with money. Jesus clearly told the parable "against" their preoccupation with money under the guise of following God's laws. But Jesus was reaching for an obvious conclusion he had carefully observed: (1) men involved in *both* religious and secular vocations are intense in their commitment to monetary profit, but (2) neither religious or secular men can generate a fervor of commitment toward God with the same intensity they display toward money.

Through the ages, no religion seems to have made a significant inroad to the preoccupation of men with money. Indeed, money frequently is, in every generation, the target of almost everyone's obsession. And that has been true both before and since the time Jesus told this story.

When this story was told, its message was not received well by the religious leaders of Jesus' day. Ordinary people also found it a confronting message. Both rich and poor would have been glad to have avoided hearing this story altogether.

I. *The background of the story.* A more finely crafted story would be hard to find. In it, Jesus described a rich man who had so much wealth that he employed one or more high-level employees, called stewards, to oversee his many investments. The stewards operated their master's business much like trust officers in a bank. The rich man apparently placed almost blind trust in his stewards. It seems he was not intimately acquainted with the daily operations of his fortune. He unbelievably gave his managers free reign with his resources.

Jesus then sketched the villain in his story in skillful detail. With somewhat unlimited resources at his command, one of the stewards got into the habit of offering special favors to his master's creditors. The entice-ment to abuse his authority had been too great for him. Having the power over so much wealth tempted him to succumb to a rather cavalier lifestyle. He began to behave as if his master's wealth was of no consequence, and so he wasted it.

Waste, whether of time, talent, or money, is not always a pattern reserved for the af-fluent. Many among us are practiced in the art of waste. Whether the wealth is in the twenty-five-cent category, as the woman who lost a coin, or the twenty-five-dollar category of a slightly more well-funded neighbor, lack of care in the use of money (or other commodity) is a practice well known to most of us.

II. *The main story line.* Informed by rumor, the rich man called his steward to give an accounting. Then an unusual series of events took place. The steward knew he was guilty. He also knew he would be discovered and fired. With doomsday facing him, the stew-ard began wasting his master's goods with even more blatant waste, only this time the steward had a clearly ulterior motive. With a "measure" of olive oil being somewhere near 9 gallons, he reduced the first debtor's oblig-ation by about 360 gallons; with a measure of wheat being between 10 and 12 bushels, he reduced the second debtor's obligation by at least 440 bushels. While we know little about the terms of the contract, 50 percent of the first bill or even 40 percent of the second bill seems quite excessive, and a significant loss to the creditor. But again, the quantity of the wealth was not the main point.

If, the crafty steward conjectured, he could make friends with some wealthy people, they just might come to his aid when he lost his current position. In fact, the steward in ques-tion promoted just such a trade-off to feather his own nest and to increase the possibility that he would be reemployed by a grateful benefactor after being dismissed from his current position.

III. *The surprise ending.* Under all the cur-rent laws of finance and money management, this steward would have been fired, possibly fined, and perhaps imprisoned for his inex-cusable conduct.

But the wealthy master, as Jesus told the story, passed a compliment to his rogue stew-ard. He complimented him on his clever use

of power and position to feather his own nest. He admired the radical manner in which the steward moved to secure his future employ-ability. Some commentators conjecture that the wealthy owner may himself have mastered the art of shrewd self-survival. His admiration for a man skillful enough to make such a maneuver as his employee had made might well have prompted the compliment. Perhaps the fear that his steward might do him more harm if he were to join the management staff of a competitor may also have drawn the words of guarded praise. While we do not know if Jesus concluded the parable with the master's verdict, "This man is guilty, but so clever, I must forever keep him in my busi-ness," such an outcome would not do vio-lence to the story as presented by Luke.

IV. *Jesus' application of his own story.* What seems clear in the story is that Jesus praised (1) the ability of the rogue steward to make clear decisions, (2) the clarity of purpose of the shrewd manager to follow his decision with decisive action, and (3) the powerful motivation and commitment of this child of darkness to follow through boldly with his self-survival plans.

This steward did not hold himself out to be a religious man. He had accepted no code of ethics, had given no bond of security, and had lived in an openly secular manner. He had clearly chosen to serve mammon and not God.

The key teaching of Jesus seems forcefully presented in verse 13: "No servant can serve two masters. Either he will hate the one and love the other, or he will be devoted to the one and despise the other. You cannot serve both God and money."

The recorded sneers of the Pharisees sig-nal the truth that Jesus' parable, like a skilled archer's arrow, had struck the center of the target. Our own hearts may be similarly pierced as we search out our own motives and objec-tives in the processes of our lives. Disciple-ship to Jesus Christ in the Kingdom of God is not to be sealed off in a separate compart-ment. Our wealth, our energy, our deeds, our influence, our time commitments, and all that we are or ever will be are called to exhibit the lesson we may yet learn from the clever man in Jesus' parable. Passionate, single-minded devotion to God is the hallmark of the true child of God.—Walter C. Jackson

Illustrations

TO BE CHRIST'S. Jesus said, "Man shall not live by bread alone, but by every word that proceeds from the mouth of God," and in the end every word that proceeds from the mouth of God is the same word, and the word is Christ himself. And in the end that is the vocation, the calling of all of us, the calling to be Christ's. To be Christ's in whatever way we are able to be. To be Christ's with whatever gladness we have and in whatever place, among whatever brothers we are called to. That is the vocation, the destiny to which we were all called even before the foundations of the world.—Frederick Buechner[5]

THE KEY WORD. I keep staring at him on his cross; and to save my soul I can't help feeling that here is a great key word that unlocks the secret of all the suffering and defeat we know anything about; one answer anyhow, may be the full answer, to the immense enigma of pain: a Love which stands so squarely in the center of things that it can "afford to lose" like that without ever for a single moment "risking its own chances of victory!"—Paul Scherer[6]

SERMON SUGGESTIONS

Topic: A Surprising Encounter

TEXT: Exod. 3:1–12

You may find yourself on "holy ground" where and when you least expect it. (1) Like Moses, you may be singled out and assigned to an unusual task by none other than God himself. (2) Just as significantly, your holy ground may be your home, your community, or your chance meeting with someone who needs you.

Topic: Don't Misunderstand Jesus

Text: Matt. 5:17–20

(1) Jesus' all-embracing love can be misinterpreted to mean that he is soft on sin. (2) In his teaching and example, Jesus fulfilled or brought to completion the intent of the ancient law by carrying out its spirit.

[5] *The Hungering Dark.*
[6] *The Place Where Thou Standest.*

Hymn Suggestions: Fifteenth Sunday After Trinity

1. "There Is a Balm in Gilead," African American Spiritual

The answer to the plaintive question in Jeremiah 8:22 is that there indeed *is* a balm in Gilead. It provides the typical answer of hope and encouragement. In keeping with the origin of these spirituals in a call-and-response pattern, a soloist can sing the stanzas, with the worshiping group joining in on the refrain.

2. "In Your Heritage the Nations," *Psalter* (1912); "O Mein Jesu," *Geistliche Volkslieder Paderborn* (1850)

One of the few paraphrases of Psalm 79 available, this hymn can easily be sung in biblical fashion, that is, antiphonally by two groups: choir and congregation or two sections of the congregation.

3. "Jesus Paid It All," Elvina M. Hall (1885); "All to Christ," John T. Grape (1864)

This gospel song gives expression to the apostle Paul's assertion in his first letter to Timothy that there is only one mediator between God and humankind, the man Jesus Christ, who gave himself as a ransom for all (1 Tim. 2:5b–6a).

4. "Come, All Christians, Be Committed," Eva B. Lloyd (1963); "Beach Spring," *The Sacred Harp* (1844), arranged by James H. Wood (1958)

Appropriate for use with the gospel reading for this day, this hymn of commitment, especially in its second stanza, is a call to faithfulness in stewardship.—Hugh T. McElrath

Worship Aids

CALL TO WORSHIP. "Show me thy ways, O Lord, teach me thy paths. Lead me in thy truth, and teach me for thou art the God of my salvation; on thee do I wait all the day" (Ps. 25:4–5).

INVOCATION. Where else are we so well known, where else can we come and find the words that endure, where else can our parched souls find the sustenance that never fails, but in thee, O Lord? Accept our worship, for we were created for such praise and through such activity we are indeed found.—E. Lee Phillips

OFFERTORY SENTENCE. "Bring the full tithe into the storehouse, so that there may be food in my house, and thus put me to the test, says the Lord of hosts; see if I will not open the windows of heaven for you and pour down for you an overflowing blessing" (Mal. 3:10 NRSV).

OFFERTORY PRAYER. Lord God, bless what we bring and what we wish we could bring today, that both deed and motive might magnify the name of Jesus and bring many to saving faith.—E. Lee Phillips

PRAYER. Father of our Lord Jesus Christ, we come into this service today from a world that beckons us to be elsewhere. The enticements to abandon the practice of faithful worship in the congregation are plentiful and strong. The allurements of entertainment are everywhere, the glitter of man-created enjoyments contrasts strongly with the steady ways of the Church. We see the exciting creations of human hands and think that we are gods unto ourselves. Bring us to ourselves. Help us to realize that we are but temporary sojourners on this Earth and that life is more than what we see and feel and taste and experience as human pilgrims.

Remind us of what the world cannot give us and that our lives and spirits gain eternal joy by the indwelling of your holy spirit in us. So we bring our lives to you polluted as they are by sins of greed, anger, and mistrust; darkened by fear, anxiety, and indifference; hurt by sickness, disease, and death; defeated by doubt and misgivings. We bring our lives because we have been promised forgiveness of sins, light in the place of darkness, strength to bear the hurts, and victory over all defeat. Here in this sacred place, we ask for the fulfillment of these promises. As we today submit our lives to the working of the Spirit, may we go from this service fortified daily to manage life after your fashion and will.—Henry Fields

Sermon: Christ's Compelling Love

TEXT: 2 Cor. 5:14–17

"For the love of Christ urges us on." That's the declaration made by the apostle Paul: "The love of Christ urges us on." And quite frankly, there are numerous occasions when we require something to urge us on in this ministry—only because the several tasks to which Christ calls us can be, and often are, terribly demanding.

I. I'm certain that most of us would agree that love can be an extremely compelling force. Think, for instance, of those relationships in which we've witnessed love to be the singular source of empowerment for commitment, constancy, compassion, and genuine care.

a. A father spends hours tending to the needs of his ailing child—and it is love urging him on. A single-mother of four devotes herself, in body and soul, to the well-being of her children—and it is love urging her on. A spouse remains vulnerable and available to the one who has had an affair—and it is love urging him, or her, on.

b. Likewise, says Paul, there is this far more powerful and persuasive "love of Christ [which] urges us on" in our respective avenues of service to the Savior—which seems to imply that, with Paul, there can be no more compelling force in the Christian life. And that's why he encourages each of us, and all of us, to recognize that particular love as the fuel that feeds the fires of all faithful service. Sustained commitment is the consequence of Christ's compelling love, Paul seems to say.

c. In other words, this "love of Christ that urges us on" has a power all its own, one with which the world is unfamiliar, one that cannot be measured in terms of ordinary strength and force. One writer has rightly confessed, it is only Christ's love—with us, for us, and within us—that "enables the martyrs to endure!"

II. To which we could add more, couldn't we? Paul introduces us to the deepest truth of this towering love, and then he gives voices to what is "both the greatest act and his own deepest conviction," that is, "Christ died for all!"

a. "The love of Christ urges us on" he declares, "because we are convinced that one has died for all." This may or may not be the consensus belief among Christians in the contemporary Church—so contemporary, in fact, that in many sectors of her life the concept of what has rightly been called "substitutionary atonement" is no longer embraced enthusiastically.

b. This, then, is the unaltered declaration of God's own apostle: "The love of Christ urges us on, because we are convinced that one has died for all." I find this altogether amazing—not the truth of Paul's assertion but rather the unqualified confidence with which he speaks that truth. Rarely in my own life have I have been able to speak of anything with such ringing conviction as I hear him speak with!

c. When I consider the opportunities I've had to give witness to the wonder that is Christ, I recall speaking in fits and starts, stuttering and stammering my way through some witnessing word, tripping over my tongue in the effort to compromise the conflicting nature of God's gospel. Yet here we have the apostle Paul, facing the firing squads of stonings, beatings, and rejections, and he speaks with stunning conviction. "We are convinced" he cries; "We are convinced!"

III. But are we? Admittedly, in our own day it's tough to remain convinced about anything for long. Family life, the workplace, global politics, religious beliefs and practices—everything seems to be suspended in the fluids of constant change. It's unsettling, isn't it? And just when we lock onto something certain, we discover that it too is founded on the shifting sands of perpetual change.

a. Under such circumstances, it's hard to remain convinced about anything. However, here we have Paul, and he steps forward to say something like, "Yes, well, be that as it may, always remember this one unshakable, unalterable truth: that one has died for all!" And "therefore, all [Christians] have died."

b. The apostle Paul roots the Christian life in a very unique soil, doesn't he? He grounds the life of faith in the granite we call "Calvary." Accordingly, there is no Christian life that hasn't been created through that splintered cross and by the power of the Savior with nail-scarred hands and feet.

Paul points to Calvary and to the glory of that first Easter dawn and says, "This changes everything!" So, "from now on . . . we regard no one from a human point of view."

Because, you see, we tend to treat others with compassion and care as a fulfillment of obligation, or as a favor seeking some refund, or as a deed for which we look to receive recognition.

c. Paul shatters all such motives, saying, in effect, that when we engage in this ministry of service, doing deeds of mercy, kindness, and generous goodwill, we do so for one rea-

son only: because Christ "died and was raised for them!" Make note of it. Ministry in service to our nail-scarred Savior is not about personal power or charisma or character of any kind. None of that will help when the tasks become burdensome. Then there's only one source of strength: "the love of Christ [which] urges us on!"—Albert J. D. Walsh

Illustrations

GOD'S LOVE AND OURS.   God not only loves us more and better than we can ever love ourselves—but God loved us before we loved, or could love, him. God's love of us rendered possible and actual our love of God.—Friedrich Von Hügel[7]

SERVICE.   And why should we even care to serve others? Paul encourages us to do it because Christ "died and was raised for them." In other words, they are precious in Christ's eyes. They are his children, purchased at so great a cost, claimed in the hard timbers of a timeless cross. That's the truth we disciples should always bear in mind. And so is this: Paul points to the outcome of what he has thus far proclaimed when he writes that "from now on . . . we regard no one from a human point of view."

He says "from now on" as if to imply some intrusion into the passing of time, the infusion of some new beginning.

Here we have a husband and wife sitting before their pastor. There's been some painful breach in their marriage. Nevertheless, they've committed themselves to reconciliation and to the renewal of their covenant vows, "from now on."

Here's a teenager, constantly in trouble with the law. Mom and Dad are at their wits' end. Then, under the sensitive care of a school counselor, the child's attitude and actions begin to improve. He promises his parents that he will try harder, "from now on."

In both cases, there was a point at which some significant change was marked. Paul says "from now on" while pointing a bony finger to the cross of Calvary and the rocky garden of Resurrection.—A.J.D.W.

---

[7]*Essays and Addresses* (2nd series).

SUNDAY: SEPTEMBER TWENTY-SEVENTH

LECTIONARY MESSAGE

Topic: Neglect—A Gross Sin of Our Time
TEXT: Luke 16:19–31

Other Readings: Jer. 32:1–3a, 6–15; Ps. 91:1–6, 14–16; 1 Tim. 6:6–19

Introduction. The lectionary text for today reads like the synopsis of a play. The first act depicts a setting on Earth easy for modern readers to understand. This is so because the rich and the poor seem ever to be with us.

In the first scene of act one, a rich man is observed enjoying his supper, a meal that is always a banquet. He is comfortable and healthy, is dressed in the latest fashion, is well cared for, and appears quite well nourished. He lacks nothing. Tradition records his name as Dives.

The second scene of the first act sketches a poor man whose name is Lazarus. He is uncomfortable and sick, is clothed only in hand-me-down rags, has no one to care for him, and appears near starvation. He is easily observed to be the subject of neglect. He is abused even by the neighborhood dogs.

The second act reverses the easily drawn portrait of the first act. In the transition to the next life, Dives has arrived in hell, his eternal residence. He is in torment. No one is permitted to alleviate his suffering.

Lazarus, however, has been transported to heaven and pictured as being comforted in the bosom of Abraham. The circumstances of each man have been reversed.

Cries for mercy from Dives are rejected. Pleas for warnings to his brothers are likewise disallowed. The only benefit permitted the rich man in hell is the opportunity to hold a conversation with Abraham in order to plead his case. Alas, his arguments for himself are rebuffed; those for his brothers, although belatedly compassionate, are turned aside.

I. *The plain teaching of the parable.* The wealthy man's sin is almost too obvious to mention: his failure to share his wealth with the poor man is his crime against humanity and God. Neglect in the exercise of one's personal gifts is here characterized as sin. Garden-variety Hebrew theology grants extra religious credit to anyone feeding the poor and hungry. Dives apparently represented a person who rejected the current teachings of Judaism and its leaders.

In addition, the most ancient of Jewish traditions require hospitality both to a stranger and to the poor. Gleanings were to be available in the fields for the poor (see the book of Ruth), and it was a common practice to invite the poor, the handicapped, and the hungry to eat the leftovers of banquets. Dives did not do this. He is also represented as a person who rejected the teachings and ethical requirements of the most ancient of the Jewish traditions. His neglect of the needs of others was deeply embedded in his personality.

Jesus has continued the theme reported in Luke's previous chapter: wealth can destroy faith. It can replace true spirituality. It can preoccupy a person's mind, heart, and soul with self-interest. It can deflect a person's attention from the task of good stewardship in the form of self-giving. It can function as a barrier in a person's life in the achievement of the goal to participate in the Kingdom of God.

A good thing to notice here is that wealth itself is not necessarily depicted as sinful. This man's sin, however clothed in pious living, was neglect. The way in which he indulged himself without sharing with the poor man was the seat of his error.

Actually, Dives' neglect of the poor man competes energetically with his activity of self-indulgence. The misuse of wealth as self-indulgence and the practice of selfishness graphically illustrates the theme in this part of the Gospel of Luke. Jesus here teaches that one must choose between God and mammon. With power Jesus proclaimed, "anyone who follows mammon is incapable of following God."

If the Kingdom of God has arrived, and Jesus proclaimed that it had done so with great force, the law itself has "in him" been replaced by the gospel as the primary way to relate to God. But that does not excuse believers from carrying forth the spirit of the law. Jesus came to fulfill it, not to destroy it. The spirit and works of compassion are to be available from the hands of Christians for anyone abused or neglected, the poor, the halt, the lame, the blind—all for whom Jesus himself showed compassion in his earthly life.

II. *An ethical teaching of the parable.* The Jewish law is clearly an ethical institution. Strict obedience and proper conduct are requirements, if the teachings of the Pharisees and their scribes are taken as the norm. Compassion for the poor, then, is not an option—it is a requirement. Neglect is also a Hebrew sin. The very law of Moses and the lengthy traditions of the scholarly rabbis testify to that end. In a clearly transparent way, however, the Hebrews through the ages and each of us from all times and places seem to have learned, as if from a single script, ways to live luxuriously without letting the ethical teachings of our various faith expressions interfere in any but minor ways.

Americans are no exception to this practice. Self-indulgent consumerism is seen as routine by secular as well as Christian citizens. The truth of the matter is that most secular as well as Christian citizens in the United States have developed a general sense of pious caring for the underdog, pity for the helpless, and concern for the poor. There seems to be little difference between these two groups.

While Christian ethical behavior is externally similar to the ethical behavior of non-Christians—Christians do perform compassionate acts, even "random acts of senseless kindness"—they are to avoid being swept away with every sentimental whim of the general population. Christians are to be compassionate in ways consistent with the vision and purpose of God's Kingdom plans. They are not to use their compassionate responses as substitutes for holistic ethical behavior. They are to choose the ways they will express their charitable gifts, and to do so within the will of God, and not to substitute sentimentality for ethical practice.

In the coming of Jesus, the actual door of the Kingdom of God has been opened. Since the coming of Jesus, one enters the Kingdom of God by behavior directed by a personal faith decision in Jesus Christ. Priorities are discovered within that faith. Acting on those priorities is the way of being Christian. The law still exists, but its purpose is to call attention to the inbreaking of the good news of God in Jesus Christ; the law itself has been replaced by "the way" of faith.

The radical demands of personal commitment in faith call each Christian to the kind of lifestyle that includes both belief and com-

passionate behavior. This text proclaims such a message with force and power. In such faith, neglect of a neighbor's need is no longer an optional way to behave.

III. *A contemporary application of the parable.* In some circles of Christians, compassion is not only encouraged, it has become a way of life. Compassion itself can be used as an act of defiance in the face of the teaching of this text.

In some Christian places, compassion has surfaced as a "new legalism." Here one can see compassion exercised in extremely aggressive ways. This new legalism was seen in some nineteenth-century modernistic teachings that Christians are generally to "do good" to all. Today, in a covert evangelical way, compassion is portrayed as a pious way to become the compassion of God himself. If one is really a "spiritual" Christian, many of our contemporary faith interpretations insist, the primary expression of that spirituality is to become a committed "rescuer" who functions as a helper whether the person in apparent need wants to be helped or not.

Actually, this form of compassion is but a subtle form of control. Even worse, it becomes a way for the helper to gain religious credit or even to gain otherwise unavailable self-esteem by overpowering others with their compassion. When discovered to exist in this fashion, such "help" is easily seen as what has come to be called codependent behavior.

Truly Christian compassion, as indicated by this parable of Jesus, is the activity of discovering those who cannot help themselves. Christians next attempt to eliminate the temporary pains and agonies wherever possible. Finally, they assist the needy to help themselves.

Codependent helping attempts to force a dependent role upon those who are being helped, keeping them forever attached, forever helpless, forever in a state of guilty gratitude to the helper. True Christian compassion seeks to help individuals, but also to eliminate the conditions that caused the neglect or abuse in the first place. Such Christian activity is fearless in the face of oppression, openly vocal in confronting injustice, and bold in acting out the truth of this parable of Jesus.

Conclusion. What then are Christians to do? They are to use their resources in the

direction of God's Kingdom work as directed
by the teachings of Jesus. This means, at least,
(1) to seek places of legitimate need, (2) to
provide from their own money and reservoir
of time some program of assistance, and (3)
to search out and change any condition or
system that creates the conditions that
engender poverty, denigrate persons and
groups, and perpetuate personal and community neglect of the needs. Abuse is both a
sin and a crime in twentieth-century America, but neglect has become a subtle and
destructive abuse in its own right. As such,
neglect itself is a sin.—Walter C. Jackson

Illustrations

MOBILIZING POSSIBILITIES.   One of the
most difficult of all fields of pastoral work is
that of giving aid to prisoners, both those still
in prison and those who have been dis-
charged. In this work, it is necessary to guard
not only against credulity and sentimentality—nowhere will you see more conversions
than in prison, but very few of them last
more than a few weeks after release—but
also against the fatalism which simply believes that no more good can be expected of
a man with "previous convictions." The right
approach is to take the man in question as he
is, not to expect more than he can perform
at any given moment, but at the same time to
recognize "what God meant him to be," what
possibilities lie dormant in him, and how
they can be mobilized.—Theodor Bovet[8]

THE CHURCH AT ITS BEST.   The church at
its best has a record of humanitarianism, of
social service and action, of meeting the
needs of the hungry, the poor, the disinher-
ited, that can stand the closest scrutiny. In his
Gifford Lectures, Arnold Toynbee claimed
that a big factor in the incredible success of
the early church was its capacity for care.
More than the government or the municipal
authorities, the Christians cared in the Name
of Christ for the despised and the destitute.
So it has continued to do through such revolutionary movements as the Salvation Army
and such noble women as Mother Teresa of
Calcutta. "Christianity," wrote Baron Van

Hugel, "taught us to care. Caring is the greatest thing. Caring matters most."—John N.
Gladstone[9]

SERMON SUGGESTIONS

Topic: Why Praise the Lord?
(1) Because of God's worthiness in himself. (2) Because of God's many benefits that
we receive.

Topic: Justified!
TEXT: Rom. 5:1–5
Our being justified means: (1) We can
enjoy peace with God. (2) We have something to lawfully boast about: (a) the assurance of future salvation; (b) the significance
of the sometimes painful process that produces this hope; (c) the experience, through
the Holy Spirit, of God's love.

**Hymn Suggestions: Sixteenth Sunday After
Trinity**

1. "Praise to the Lord, the Almighty," Joachim Neander (1680), translated by Catherine Winkworth (1863); "Lobe den Herren,"
Stralsund Gesangbuch (1665)
This majestic hymn of praise echoes the
spirit of hope found in Psalm 91 that God
will protect his faithful ones from evil. Stanzas 2 and 3 are particularly appropriate in
their specificity: God shelters us under his
wings (Ps. 91:4), and God will be with us to
prosper and defend us (Ps. 91:14–15).
2. "May Choirs of Angels Lead You,"
Latin, translated by F. Bland Tucker (1978);
"Christus, der Ist Mein Leben," Melchior
Vulpius (1609)
Suitable for use at funerals and memorial
services, this metrical translation from the
Book of Common Prayer burial liturgy makes
reference to the heavenly comfort and peace
of the poor man, Lazarus, as related in the
Gospel story for this day.
3. "On Eagle's Wings," Michael Joncas
(1978); "On Eagle's Wings," Joncas (1978)
This mini-hymn originally was the refrain
of a longer hymn used by its author/com-
poser at a memorial service for a friend's
father. It is a free interpretation of Psalm 91:4

[8]*That They May Have Life.*   [9]*Living with Style.*

and could effectively be used as an "anti-phon" in alternation with the verses of the Psalter reading.

4. "God Moves in a Mysterious Way," William Cowper (1773); "St. Anne," William Croft (1708)

The prophet Jeremiah's confidence in the future of Judah, as illustrated by his purchase of a field, is reflected in the hopeful outlook of Cowper's hymn. It could appropriately be sung as a response to the Old Testament reading of Jeremiah's prophecy.—Hugh T. McElrath

Worship Aids

CALL TO WORSHIP.   "One thing have I desired of the Lord, that will I seek after; that I may dwell in the house of the Lord all the days of my life, to behold the beauty of the Lord, and to enquire in his temple" (Ps. 27:4).

INVOCATION.   Our God and Father, draw us to thyself by thy Spirit, and may the few minutes that we spend in prayer be full of the true spirit of supplication. Grant that none of us with closed eyes may yet be looking abroad over the fields of vanity, but may our eyes be really shut to everything else now but that which is spiritual and divine. May we have communion with God in the secret of our hearts, and find him to be to us as a little sanctuary.—C. H. Spurgeon

OFFERTORY SENTENCE.   "For this service you perform not only meets the needs of God's people, but also produces an outpouring of grateful thanks to God" (2 Cor. 9:12 TEV).

OFFERTORY PRAYER.   We rejoice, O God, to take part in this special act of worship, and we thank you that you have made it possible to share the good gifts of your providence for your glory and the blessing of others.

PRAYER.   O blessed Lord, our true and only God, whose visions of the higher way and better life have come to us so clearly through Jesus Christ, your Son, we worship you in the fullest way we can by offering ourselves in reverent devotion and service. You are the fountain of life and in your light alone can we see light. Through your providence we make our way in the world and by the nurture of your Spirit are we kept whole in body and mind. We thank you for the critical and decisive moments of our spiritual journey when a word from you drives us out of our complacency or the routineness of religious habits and upon strange ventures and risks for causes not our own. We recall with joy those turning points when by your grace we said no to self and yes to Jesus Christ. We thank you that ever afterwards our feeble hearts grew stronger and our story was marked by true things truly done each day. We live and move now at the right hand of him whose name is above every name, and humbly we boast that we are his disciples.—Donald Macleod

Sermon: RSVP

TEXT: Ps. 22:23–31; Rom. 10:5–13

More of the New Testament is written in letter form than in any other form. There is a reason for that. A letter is a very tangible form of being addressed; it has our name on it. It is not to folks in general. It is a way of saying, "I speak to you."

Paul used many different styles of letters that he inherited from his culture. There were letters of friendship, letters of business, letters of comfort, and letters of advocacy. There was yet another style of letter that Paul used in Romans, chapters 3 through 11. It was called *protreptic*. It was a way of writing a letter of invitation—an invitation to new life—and it was a time-honored tradition by the time Paul came along.

I. First of all, this kind of letter of invitation did not use flattery. A letter of invitation in the protreptic tradition was too honest to employ an appeal to one's vanity to coerce a decision. So Paul wanted a positive response to his invitation, but he would not sacrifice the truth.

a. In this form, the writer of the letter would often speak as if he were answering questions that he assumed the reader was asking. This was a letter that included an RSVP; it calls for a response. Paul was not shy about the invitation. He began in the very first verse of chapter 10 saying, "my heart's desire and prayer to God for them is that they may be saved." He used the words *saved* or *salvation* again in verses 9, 10, and 13. At first we wonder if there is much dialogue in this invitation to salvation.

b. Unfortunately, we have all kinds of filters at work when we hear that word. We remember some people that tried to push us into a corner saying, "Are you saved?" We think of other people who seem to be more intent on numbers than who we are as a person. To them, "being saved" seems only a notch to be carved; to be saved means to be rescued. There are habits, addictions, and fears that have so gotten ahold of our life that we cannot live freely and joyfully now and with hope of all that is to come.

II. We are overwhelmed with something that has happened in our life, something that we can't get on top of, that we don't have the answer to, and so we try holding onto anything that might save us. It seems natural to look to God and cry for help, but when the answer is to let go of what we are trusting in, we don't want to let go. I have heard folks in the throes of addiction say that they are afraid to let go because they are afraid there won't be anyone to catch them. They are afraid to believe the promise that there is a better life for them. This need to let go and trust God's promise is as true for those of us who do not seem to be hanging by a thread. The word *salvation* means wholeness, completeness, health. God wants us to be healthy for time and eternity. The invitation is extended to us, but we've got to let go of what we are holding onto first.

a. Just as the ancient writers did in the protreptic letters, Paul began talking to someone who seemed to be asking questions. He anticipated their questions, yet one part of the passage raises more questions than it answers. What does it mean to say, Who will ascend into heaven? Who will descend into the abyss? Who can attain to God's holiness and righteousness? Who would say that we are perfect? Who can bring God down from heaven? No one. Who can sacrifice in such a way that sin and death are defeated? Only Christ. Here is the point. He had already done it. We don't have to strain and try. He has bridged the gap. All that remains is to RSVP. Respond because it is already accomplished in Christ. This is the message of invitation.

b. The last part of this passage is as clear as we want it to be. Paul says, "If you will confess with your lips that Jesus is Lord and if you will believe in your heart that God has raised Christ from the dead, you will be saved." In this confessing and believing, we will be saved. Now, we've heard that over and over again. Yet the invitation needs to be proclaimed today because there may be some who have heard it many times but have never responded. This is not my invitation, not this church's invitation, but the invitation of God in Christ.

III. There is something more about this invitation. We forget that if the invitation and need for response is true at the beginning of our faith, it is true all the way through. Right now some of us are struggling with some heavy issues, but we want to keep holding onto that bush. We don't want to let go. The same grace that saved us keeps saving us. When we let go, God is able to rescue us and put our feet on a firm foundation. This is the heart of Paul's letter. It's an invitation that always includes an RSVP.

Finally, this invitation is to be at the center of the Church. It was meant to be there from the beginning, and it is there now. Let us hear the invitation that comes to us. God has already moved to us in Jesus Christ; if we let go, if we confess with our lips that Jesus is Lord (the manager of our lives) and believe in our hearts we will be saved, we will continue to be saved, and ultimately will know his salvation in body, mind, and spirit.—Gary D. Stratman

Illustrations

DECISION. The Danish philosopher Søren Kierkegaard wrote a book entitled *Either/Or* to puncture this illusion of neutrality. He demonstrated that while we can put off making up our minds, we can't put off making up our lives. Indecision is decision—the wrong way! He told of a ship's captain who approached a harbor and was undecided whether to pull in or not. What he failed to take into consideration was the motion of the boat while he dithered. After a certain point he didn't have to decide; the boat decided for him by drifting past the harbor. We can decide, and, in fact, we do decide.—John N. Gladstone[10]

[10] *The Valley of the Verdict.*

TO TAKE A STAND. H. H. Farmer remembered the Sunday morning when, as a young man, he was preaching on the love of God. There was in the congregation an old Polish Jew who had been converted to the Christian faith. At the close of the service he came up to Farmer and said: "You have no right to speak of the love of God until you have seen, as I have seen, the blood of your dearest friends running in the gutters on a gray, winter morning." Farmer later asked him how it was that, having seen such a massacre, he had come to believe in the love of God. The answer the man gave, in effect, was that the Christian gospel first began to lay hold on him because it bade him see God in those bloodstained streets on that gray morning. It pointed him to the love of God—not somewhere else, but in the midst of that sort of thing, in the blood and agony of Calvary. He did at least know that this was a message that grappled with the facts. Then he went on to relate something, the sense of which Farmer said he would always remember although he had forgotten the exact words. It was, in effect, "As I looked at that man upon the cross I knew I must make up my mind once and for all and either take my stand beside him and share in his undefeated faith in God or else fall finally into a bottomless pit of bitterness, hatred, and unutterable despair."—Chevis F. Horne[11]

SUNDAY: OCTOBER FOURTH

LECTIONARY MESSAGE

Topic: Please Lord, Increase Our Faith
TEXT: Luke 17: 5–10
Other Readings: Lam. 1:1–6; Ps. 137; 2 Tim. 1:1–14

Introduction. Have you ever seen or heard something you just didn't want to believe? Do you remember a time when you understood something you just didn't want to be true, but you knew it was true all the same? This was a routine experience for many would-be disciples of Jesus Christ as he taught and preached in the days of his earthly life.

Believing is often an easier task for a person of faith than living out those beliefs in behavior. Behaving like a Christian is not easy. Today's preachers of an easy Christianity have misread the gospels, or they misrepresent Jesus' message. Signs and wonders, healings and miracles abound in the gospels. The good news of the break-in of God's kingdom is joyous to the maximum degree. Many stimulants to faith and ongoing strength for belief fill the pages of the New Testament. But all miracles aside: to follow Jesus' teachings as a way of life requires a stalwart commitment and an iron will.

When Jesus unfolded his ethical teachings for his most-beloved disciples on the day recorded by this morning's text, they could scarcely believe their ears.

I. *The plain text.* Our text begins with a plaintive cry by the disciples, "Lord, increase our faith" (v. 5). Hearing only this cry, one could get the simple thought that the disciples wanted to grow in faith in nonspecific ways. However, the disciples plea closely followed one of the most demanding of Jesus' teachings.

Let's suppose, Jesus taught, that one of your real-life brothers sinned against you, hurt you quite badly, and then repented of his sin and begged your pardon. What would you do? In the face of confession of wrongdoing, Jesus directed his disciples to *forgive*. If the violator really is your brother—and that might mean any Hebrew—and he sins against you repeatedly on the same day and repents each time, even seven times a day, Jesus directs his disciples to forgive.

In any society and at any time, this would be a difficult teaching to follow.

In Jesus' day, the rabbis instructed believers to forgive persons who had sinned against them if those persons repented. More generous rabbis implied that a true believer could forgive a single trespasser as many as three such times in a lifetime. But here, Jesus instructed his own disciples to forgive seven times each day for an unlimited number of days.

"How is this possible?" the disciples must have asked. "Who can have such faith?"

Between the lines of the text, the disciples

[11]*Preaching the Great Themes of the Bible.*

added this command to the many previous ones Jesus made to his disciples. They were to carry a cross with and on behalf of Jesus; they were to seek the lost; they were to use their time, talents, and money for God; they were to care for the poor; they were to manage everything in harmony with God's Kingdom wishes; and now they were to forgive trespasses and sins with a frequency beyond the capacity of ordinary men.

It is no wonder they wanted to know how the faith to do these things could be found.

II. *The plain, central meaning of the text.* How can our faith be strengthened? "Forgive, as I have just instructed," Jesus may have said. The act of forgiving is a schoolhouse of faith development. Forgiveness is no idle teaching, but active and imperative! If you have faith in Jesus Christ and wish to live according to his "way," forgiveness, to the level of unmerited grace and unconditional love, is to be offered by you to all, especially your brothers.

This important teaching about forgiveness is not to be automatic, however. It is couched within two important directives.

a. *"If your brother sins, rebuke him"* (v. 3a). Christianity is not a religion of "anything goes." Sin is to be identified and rebuked with plain, forthright, and face-to-face methods. Honesty and openness about all sin is to be the basic part of the "way" of Jesus (Matthew 18:15–17).

b. *"If he repents, forgive him"* (v. 3b). A true disciple of Jesus Christ listens for repentance on the part of the confronted sinner. Forgiveness is conditioned upon repentance. Perhaps you remember your own profession of faith—and your own repentance. Remember that Jesus insisted, just as John the Baptist had, on the need for believers to "repent, for the Kingdom of God is at hand." Indeed, in Jesus it had already come.

Forgiveness as a human activity is different than love. Love is unconditional, but forgiveness is a special relationship ingredient that follows a person's repentance from sin. "If we confess [or "keep on confessing"] our sin, he is faithful and just to forgive [or "keep on forgiving"] us our sin, and to wash us clean from all unrighteousness" (1 John 1:9). Nowhere in the New Testament does one find forgiveness as a universal requirement imposed on all Christians. God's pattern of forgiveness requires voluntary repentance. A Christian who forgives any offense with an automatic, knee-jerk response is practicing a universalism that is foreign to the Christian faith. That would not be consistent with the activity of divine forgiveness, which requires repentance. But in this context, each act of forgiveness following repentance is an opportunity for a Christian to increase his or her personal faith.

III. *The plain truth of the text.* Christian faith is never a static, once-and-for-all act.

a. Faith can grow and develop throughout life. Even if it begins in minuscule quantity, the size of a mustard seed, it can grow (v. 6). Even the smallest amount of faith can produce miraculous spiritual consequences. It is the exercise of even the smallest part of faith that enables faith to grow. To rest on the laurels of yesterday's faith is to cause it to atrophy and grow weak. The answer of Jesus is powerfully direct. If you really want to achieve the goal of increased faith, then exercise vigorously the faith you do have. Forgiveness is a case in point, but previous directives to feed the poor, to love one's neighbor as one's self, and to live peaceably with all are also activities destined to increase the faith of any disciple, especially if the disciple is faithful in practicing them.

b. Jesus taught that faith grows and develops as a disciple practices true servanthood (vv. 7–10). And here is one of the stumbling blocks of the gospel: Christians are, as Martin Luther proclaimed, "true servants of all, and lords of none." Our duty is to serve our master, the God and Father of our Lord Jesus Christ. We do not do so for gain or reward. None has been offered; none will be given. We do so because we have learned the humility of servanthood from Jesus Christ, and in his name, before God, we live.

IV. *Conclusion.* So many troublesome events that challenge our faith occur in life; events that arise in the living of our appointed days on the earth usually stretch whatever faith we have. No Christian life ever lived has possessed sufficient faith, because true Christian faith is ever growing, ever increasing, ever discovering how small "mustard seed faith" really is at every stage of its growth. The person with faith must be ever striving to become more like Christ. In the face of any challenge to faith, such as abuse, neglect, illness, injury, sin, crime, suffering, or death, you may have prayed like the disciples, "Lord, increase our faith." The message of this text is as difficult as teaching believers in any age to forgive the same person seven times on the same day.

Exercise the faith you have, for you will discover its great power as you exercise it. Remember, as a believer in Jesus Christ, you are at your best when you function as a servant. True Christian disciples leave the lofty places in their minds where they have assumed the roles of judge and jury of the events before them. They are reminded that if Christ really is their Lord, they are to play the role of servant. Perhaps, then, all of us will learn the truth that one great Christian has wisely spoken: "It is not until you discover faith in Jesus Christ is all you have, that you will learn the truth that Jesus Christ is enough."—Walter C. Jackson

Illustrations

LIFE'S DEMANDS.   Life's demands are so draining. Surely God did not install enough faith power in a single human believer to sustain her constant belief in the face of multiple tragedies. Leukemia took the life of her child at age six; an intoxicated driver caused an accident that killed her sister and severely injured the other three members of her sister's vacationing family; a gunman's stray bullet disabled a young athlete—her brother's boy—on a football field in another state; and then, her dad's heart attack last month surely will shorten his life. All this happened within ten months. Even the most powerful prayer warrior can feel the pain bursting through her tears. Lord, she weeps. Give her more faith.—W.C.J.

FAITH TO PERSEVERE.   Many are beset by the agonies of dysfunctional families. Brothers and sisters sin against each other as a routine way of life; parents intentionally interfere in their children's lives in destructive ways; and members of extended families constantly behave in ways that cast doubt on the integrity and value of everyone in the clan. Abuse, neglect, and gross manipulation of the weaker members of the family continue overtly and covertly as a matter of course. These things have existed for so many generations that cure seems bewilderingly beyond any person who has such experiences. Faith in

the face of such a history, faith enough to persevere, seems beyond the reach of anyone interested in possessing it.—W.C.J.

SERMON SUGGESTIONS

Topic: Why I Am a Christian
TEXT: 1 Pet. 3:15b
The occasion of Communion is a time of a self-examination, a restatement of our faith in Jesus Christ, a celebration of our oneness in Christ, and an opportunity to recommit ourselves to Christ. For me to do any or all of these things, it should be helpful to reflect on why I am a Christian: (1) because my parents were Christians; (2) because being a Christian meets certain needs of mine: (a) the need for a sense of purpose for my existence; (b) the need to worship; (c) the need to recognize my kinship with all humankind; (3) because being a Christian opens the way of service to humankind (Luke 4:18–19); (4) because of Jesus himself and the way Jesus portrays God—in his humanity, by his example, through his presence; (6) because of the indirect as well as the direct influences of people around me.—James W. Cox

Topic: On Being an Honorary Jew
TEXT: Deut. 6:4–5
The late Pope Pius XII observed that spiritually we are all Semites. (1) We proudly proclaim that ours is a Jewish faith because we believe in one God. (2) I proudly proclaim that we are Jews because we affirm that this one God has revealed himself in history, concretely in events. (3) I proudly proclaim that I am a Jew not only because I believe in one God encountered in human events, but because I belong to a community, called apart for service, a chosen people.—R. Benjamin Garrison

Hymn Suggestions: Seventeenth Sunday After Trinity

1. "O Thou Who Camest from Above," Charles Wesley (1769); "Hereford," S. S. Wesley (1872)
In the sacrificial imagery of this hymn, the writer asks God to kindle the flame of love in his heart, much as the apostle Paul reminds the young Timothy to "rekindle the gift of God that is within you" (2 Tim. 1:6a). The

power of this earnest prayer hymn by Charles Wesley is enhanced by the flowing grace of its tune composed by his grandson.

2. "O, for a Faith That Will Not Shrink," William H. Bathurst (1831); "Arlington," Thomas A. Arne (1762)

This hymn voices the plea of the apostles for increased faith (Luke 17:5). The thoughtful singing by the congregation about those qualities of life and action that real faith brings can reinforce the gospel lesson that obedience is a requirement, not an occasion for reward.

3. "I Know Whom I Have Believed," Daniel W. Whittle (1883); "El Nathan," James McGranahan (1883)

This gospel song, with its refrain quoting the apostle Paul's assertion in today's Epistle reading (2 Tim. 1:12), would be suitably sung following that reading.

4. "Babylon Streams Received Our Tears," Calvin Seerveld (1982); "LLEF," Griffith Hugh Jones (1890)

The doleful mood of today's imprecatory psalm (Ps. 137) is captured in this modern paraphrase as well as by its minor tune.—Hugh T. McElrath

Worship Aids

CALL TO WORSHIP.   "Rejoice the soul of thy servant: for unto thee, O Lord, do I lift up my soul. For thou, O Lord, do I lift up my soul. For thou, Lord, art good, and ready to forgive; and plenteous in mercy unto all them that call upon thee" (Ps. 86:4–5).

INVOCATION.   Father, as we approach the Lord's Table, make us truly worthy to celebrate the supper that has been given to us. Cast from our lives any taint of sin that would prevent us from worshiping with clean hearts. Above all, give us the kind of love that would make us want to share with all the world the good news that is ours.—James M. King

OFFERTORY SENTENCE.   "He will always make you rich enough to be generous at all times, so that many will thank God for your gifts which they receive from us. For this service you perform not only meets the needs of God's people, but also produces an outpouring of grateful thanks to God" (2 Cor. 9:11–12 TEV).

OFFERTORY PRAYER.   Almighty God, whose loving hand has given us all that we possess: grant us grace that we may honor you with our substance, and remembering the account which we must one day give, may we be faithful stewards of your bounty, through Jesus Christ our Lord.—*Book of Common Prayer*

PRAYER.   For the hospitality of your house, for the bread which is bread indeed and the drink which is drink indeed by which life is sustained and we live, for the companionship of the Way that we have experienced around your table, for the Communion not limited by time or space, we give you thanks.

May your Word of grace mediated to us in Christ be real to us, that it may be real through us to minister wholeness in the face of any brokenness. Lest the Word becoming flesh in Christ, we turn into mere words again; grant us faith, grant us courage for the living of these days.

> Love Divine, all loves excelling,
> Joy of heaven, to earth come down,
> Fix in us thy humble dwelling,
> All thy faithful mercies crown! (Charles
>   Wesley, 1707–1788)
>   —John Thompson

Sermon: Coming to Remember
TEXT: 1 Cor. 11:23–26

One of the greatest gifts of God, and one of the dearest joys in life, is the capacity to remember. Memories constitute some of our most prized possessions: memories of loved ones no longer with us; memories of family vacations and other fun times shared together; memories of special days like the birth of a child, a wedding, a graduation, and so on. We thank God for the ability to remember.

Today we come to this place to remember. I am sure that you have taken note of the inscription across the front of almost every communion table: "In Remembrance of Me." These are, of course, the words of Jesus spoken on the night of his arrest as he shared the Last Supper with his disciples. As he broke the bread and passed the cup, he said, "Do this in remembrance of me." We come to remember.

I. *We come to remember with joy.* Coming to the Lord's Table is a joyous occasion. This is why we often announce a Sunday in advance that next Sunday we will "celebrate" the Lord's Supper or Holy Communion. The Lord's Day was a day of celebration for the early Christians. On every Sunday they would come together to rejoice in Jesus' life, death, and resurrection. The disciples of Jesus soon adopted the day as a day of worship and celebration. That is why we worship on Sunday, the first day of the week.

When they came together on Sunday, or the Lord's Day, they would read and expound upon the Old Testament scriptures that they believed spoke of Jesus. They would also have a meal together, and then conclude by sharing the bread and the cup as they recited the words of Jesus in the upper room. Much like the Sundays when we have a potluck fellowship dinner, it was a time of celebration and rejoicing.

So it is, after the early Christians' example, that we come to remember with joy and celebration.

II. *We come to remember with thanksgiving.* In fact, some churches refer to Holy Communion as the *Eucharist,* a word that means thanksgiving. As we gather around this table, we give thanks for the life that Jesus lived and for the great teaching that he left us. We give thanks that in Jesus we see the purest manifestation of God the world has ever known. We give thanks for the sacrificial death of Jesus and the fact that he died for what he believed in and for the principles he held dear. In the death of Jesus we hear the Word that God forgives our sins, in Jesus' uttering while on the cross, "Father, forgive them, for they know not what they do" (Luke 23:34).

But above all, as we gather around this table, we give thanks that Jesus did not stay dead. Death could not hold him. On the third day, the Lord's Day, he arose again. And his presence is with us always, even to the end of the world. Therefore many believe in what is called the "spiritual presence of Christ" at the Lord's table. As Christians we believe that God is present everywhere. And we are just as certain that in every place where Communion is truly observed, Christ keeps his promise and is spiritually present.

So for all these reasons and more, we come to the Lord's Table to remember with thanksgiving.

III. *We come to remember with dedication.* Further down in the chapter from which we read, the apostle speaks of the need for self-examination before we partake of the Lord's Supper so that we do not partake of the sacrament unworthily. "Examine yourselves," Paul says, "and only then eat of the bread and drink of the cup" (1 Cor. 11:28). The Lord's Supper calls us to examine our lives and correct any waywardness or shortcomings. We are called to confess our sins, to seek and embrace God's forgiveness. Coming to the Lord's Table should serve as a new beginning for us as we are pardoned.

The apostle warns us against coming to the Lord's Table irreverently. We are not to look upon this ordinance lightly because we are remembering one who died an agonizing death. We are not to eat the bread and the cup nonchalantly or carelessly.

But also, as we depart from the Lord's Table, we depart with a commission to share the good news of what God has done in Christ with the world. "As often as you eat this bread and drink the cup, you proclaim the Lord's death until he comes," Paul says. Through our words, deeds, and lives we become living testimonies to the world of our faith in the crucified and resurrected Christ. The Lord's Supper calls us to rededicate our lives anew to Christian discipleship and service in the world.—Randy Hammer

Illustrations

THE LORD'S PRESENCE. In the Middle Ages, a popular preacher announced an evening sermon on the love of God. The congregation gathered early. Evening shadows lengthened. The last sunlight faded from the stained-glass windows.

The preacher entered the church carrying a large candle. He walked to a life-sized figure of Christ on the cross. The preacher silently held the light beneath the wounds in the Lord's feet; next, his hands, his side, and his thorn-pierced brow. Then he went out. The silent sermon left some worshipers weeping at the love of God which is beyond words.—Alton H. McEachern[1]

---

[1] *The Lord's Presence.*

MEMORY AND THE PRESENT.   In Christian corporate worship there is an element of memory—the recollection of God's mighty deeds on His people's behalf—but memory is merely a prelude to His present fellowship with them. In the Supper of the Lord this factor of memory is basic: "This do in remembrance of Me." The broken loaf, the outpoured wine, derive their meaning from a momentous event in ancient Jerusalem. It is an occurrence in the stream of human history: He "suffered under Pontius Pilate, was crucified, dead, and buried. The third day He rose again." And in the community of believers brought into being by that occurrence of a distant past, the memory of these happenings in history becomes the vehicle in the present for God's manifestation of Himself to His believing people. He continues to be known of them in "the breaking of the bread."—Henry Sloane Coffin[2]

SUNDAY: OCTOBER ELEVENTH

LECTIONARY MESSAGE

Topic: Gratitude
   TEXT: Luke 17:11–19
   Other Readings: Jer. 29:1, 4–7; 2 Tim. 2:6–15
   One must note carefully the total context of this reading, because the healing it tells about occasions a "living word" about salvation in a total sense. With such a rich menu, the preacher is tempted to belabor ingratitude and make gratitude another burden for the overburdened believer. One must place gratitude in the context of a faith response.

This healing story comes at a change point as Jesus moves toward Jerusalem (Luke 9:51–19:28). Following this move is the actual ministry in Jerusalem (Luke 19:29–21:38). The healing event takes place "between" Samaria and Galilee. This location points to the introduction of the Samaritan in verse 16. Jesus is located close to home, where he is accepted, and far from Jerusalem, where the issues of conflict, rejection, and possibly execution would be raised.

As Jesus goes toward Jerusalem, Luke relates a healing story. Note in Luke 17:13 and 18:38 where the people cry, "Jesus, have mercy!" and then in Luke 17:19 and 18:42, Jesus' response, "Your faith has made you well." Luke wants us to understand healing and total salvation. He is concerned not only with the physical aspects of healing but with faith as well.

There is a hint of fulfillment with this healing, as it refers back to the healing of Naaman the leper in 2 Kings 5:8–19a and is mentioned by Luke in 4:27 and 7:22. The healing of lepers fulfills the expectation that salvation is for all people. Luke's favorite group, the marginalized, allows for an existential hero, a grateful and "completely" healed Samaritan leper. Typically, lepers grouped together irrespective of racial, religious, or ethnic divisions. On the one hand, according to Leviticus 1:3–14, they were required to stand apart and announce their location by shouting "unclean" when anyone approached. Yet, on the other hand, they had to be close enough to people to seek food and help. They were to wear torn garments and cover their mouths, and the only community open to them was with other lepers. The degree to which they were shut out of normal relationships deepened the need for total healing. They were a helpless and hopeless lot. (One cannot but see the analogy with AIDS. People with AIDS need medical help; yet despite information to the contrary, many people find the sickness of people with AIDS repulsive and abhorrent, and therefore many people with AIDS feel isolated.) In Luke's portrayal of the pathos of the lepers who approached Jesus, they "cry out" (from a respectful distance) for healing. Their cry does not go unheard by Luke's Jesus. Luke constantly nudges us to understand that the most unlikely people recognize the offer of divine healing, and respond. Luke, in both his Gospel and in Acts, reminds us of the faith of foreigners (see Luke 7:9 and 10:25–37, and Acts 10:1–11). Again, this healing anticipates Jesus' rejection by the Jews, and his enthusiastic reception by foreigners in Acts 10:11.

   I. The human cry "Jesus, Master, have pity on us" is a good summary of the human situ-

[2] *Communion Through Preaching.*

ation. Humankind is truly in a state of separation and isolation. In this story, the lepers stand in for all of us as they stand "at a distance." All humans stand at a distance when placed against the inescapable presence of the God whom Jesus was revealing. The human condition reflects a situation that is much worse than leprosy—alienation from God and isolation from other people. Humankind is in need of healing and community. Therefore, the cry to Jesus is for both healing and salvation. The cry of the lepers hints more of submission than of a request for an intimate relationship.

II. The lepers hoped for healing and salvation, and in response to their first cry came the immediate assurance, "Go and show yourselves to the priests." One is always challenged by hope. The immediate physical healing from leprosy came wrapped in the immediate hope of reunion with family, friends, and community. So it is with the full salvation that Christ promises. Salvation is truly a changed life "in Christ." The hope for healing and salvation rests solely on the authority of Jesus. One can guess that at least nine of the lepers knew the law about the healing of lepers and their integration back into society. In any case, their faith was implicit in their cry and is confirmed in the hope found in the words, "and as they went they were cleansed." Their faith cry is confirmed in their obedient trust. So the church has sounded forth, "Trust and obey for there is no other way."

III. *The total response of faith.* The divine Word in this reading tells us about "seeing." In the initial meeting, the lepers undoubtedly "saw" Jesus. But there is a hint that Jesus did not "see" them until they cried out. When Jesus "saw" them, he responded. Their situation was defined by the distance between them and Jesus, and between them and others as the law specified. However, when one of the lepers "saw" that (his body) was healed, he turned back, praising God with a loud voice, and fell on his face at the feet of Jesus, giving thanks. The distance is closed and the lepers are brought near. We do not know how the distance was closed. One would like to believe that Jesus closed the distance, for that is the case with Jesus. His movement toward the lepers ratifies what Jesus represented: "The God who comes." This coming of God requires a total response of faith with praise and thanks, worship and submission (kneeling?). The action by this leper is noted, "Now he was a Samaritan."

The final questions by Jesus confirm the divine Word: "Were not ten cleansed? Where are the nine? Was no one found to return and give praise to God except this foreigner?" Somewhere in these questions is the paradox of the Church regarding those who identify with Christ and yet do not enjoy the fullness of salvation. Real gratitude is confirmed in worship and holy obedience.—Dave Hunsicker

Illustrations

SAYING "THANK YOU." A four-year-old actress was appearing in a movie with an aging, crotchety star. One day the star came on the set made up to the nines, and the little girl said to her, "Gee, you look so nice." The actress made a pouty face and spoke: "What am I supposed to say to that?" The little girl immediately replied, "You're supposed to say thank you."—Leonard and Thelma Spinrad[3]

WELLSPRINGS OF GRATITUDE. Walter M. Horton, in *Our Christian Faith*, tells the story of a pious deacon who, "goaded apparently beyond endurance by the persistent malice of an enemy, publicly vowed to kill him." The enemy heard of his vow and laughed to his friend over what the "good, harmless old fool would do." What the deacon did, to the astonishment of everyone, was to take every opportunity to do his enemy good. At first it was a source of merriment and then of annoyance; but in the end, after the deacon had risked his life in saving the man's wife from drowning, "the deadlock between the two of them was broken and a new relationship set up. 'All right,' said the man, 'You've done what you said you'd do, and I admit it. You've killed me—or at least you've killed the man that I was. Now, what can I do for you?'"—Lance Webb, *Conquering the Seven Deadly Sins.*

[3]*Speaker's Lifetime Library.*

SERMON SUGGESTIONS

Topic: Be Strong—and Work!

TEXT: Hag. 2:4

(1) The need revealed by the command to "work." (2) The responsibility that rested on the people in view of the need. (3) The encouragement given to them to take up that responsibility and meet that need. The need was to build the house of God. The responsibility was that they should be strong and work. The encouragement was the promise and covenant that God made with them: "I am with you, saith the Lord of hosts."—G. Campbell Morgan

Topic: A Preacher's Prayer

TEXT: Phil. 1:9–11

(1) Paul prayed about their love life. (2) Paul prayed that they might approve things that are excellent. (3) Paul prayed that they might be sincere and without offense until the day of Christ. (4) Paul prayed that they might be "filled with the fruits of righteousness, which are by Jesus Christ."—Perry F. Webb

Hymn Suggestions: Eighteenth Sunday After Trinity

1. "The Head That Once Was Crowned with Thorns," Thomas Kelly (1820); "St. Magnus," Jeremiah Clark (1707)

The message of the early Christian hymn fragment quoted by the apostle in 2 Timothy 2:11–12 is reflected in this classic hymn on the ascension and reign of Christ. The basic truth is that the way of Christ is the way of discipleship: if one bears the cross of suffering for Christ, one will also share in his glory and reign.

2. "Your Hands, O Lord, in Days of Old," Edward H. Plumptre (1866); "St. Michael's," in Gawler's *Hymns and Psalms* (1789)

The gospel story of the ten lepers who were healed and the one who returned to thank Jesus can be appropriately accompanied by this hymn recounting Jesus' healing ministry and praying for God's continued healing that all may praise and thank him eternally.

3. "Come, Everyone, and Join with Us," Marie J. Post (1985); "Eleanoe," Dale Grotenhuis (1985)

The first three stanzas of this contemporary paraphrase of Psalm 66 parallel the selected verses for the Psalter reading. Alternate reading and singing could follow this plan: Psalm 66:1–3 read, stanza sung; verses 4–7 read, stanza 2 sung; verses 8–12 read, stanza 3 sung.

4. "Song of Hope," Alvin Schutmaat (1984); "Argentina," Argentinean Folk Melody

This simple religious folk song from Argentina gives joyful expression to the kind of hope for future justice and peace that is expressed in the Old Testament reading from Jeremiah (29:11). It would be in keeping with its origin and spirit to have it accompanied by guitar.—Hugh T. McElrath

Worship Aids

CALL TO WORSHIP. "Wait on the Lord: be of good courage, and he shall strengthen thine heart; wait, I say, on the Lord" (Ps. 27:14).

INVOCATION. Deal mightily with us today, our God. Show us as we have never seen before the divine economy in human affairs. Allow us to envision the providential purposes of suffering and success. Help us to plumb the depths of your will, which to know is the joy of every Christian and our overriding desire, through Christ our Lord.—E. Lee Phillips

OFFERTORY SENTENCE. "Every man according as he purposeth in his heart, so let him give; not grudgingly, or of necessity; for God loveth a cheerful giver" (2 Cor. 9:7).

OFFERTORY PRAYER. May we give wisely today, our Lord, so that the things that most need to be done are done and so that the priorities of the great commission may be fulfilled and Jesus glorified.—E. Lee Phillips

PRAYER. We thank thee, Lord, for the love without beginning that chose us before the earth was; for the love without measure that entered into covenant for our redemption; for the love without failure that in due time appeared in the person of Christ and wrought out our redemption; for the love that has never changed though we have wandered; for the love that abideth faithful even when we are unfaithful.

O God, we praise thee for keeping us till this day, and for the full assurance that thou wilt never let us go. Some can say, "He restoreth my soul." They had wandered, wandered sadly, but thou hast brought them back again. Lord keep us from wandering; then will we sing "unto him that is able to keep us from stumbling and to present us faultless before his presence with exceeding joy." Bless the Lord, our inmost soul, bless the Lord. Blessed be the Father, the Son, and the Holy Spirit, the Triune; blessed be the Lord for every office sustained by each divine person, and for the divine blessing that has come streaming down to us through each one of those condescending titles worn by the Father, Son, and the Holy Spirit.[4]

Sermon: The Advantages of Trouble

TEXT: Ps. 119:65–72

Few people making a mental review of their blessings would include their troubles in the list. In fact, we construct all kinds of philosophical systems for explaining them. The psalmist, of course, is an exception to the rule. He is far more sensitive and mature than the average person—and his maturity likely came through trial itself. So his attitude is strange to us at first, for in one swift sentence the psalmist frames his faith when he looks back and says, "It was good, O Lord, that I had trouble."

May I suggest that we gather up our troubles and travel along with the psalmist to discover the advantages of trouble?

I. *Trouble can mature our faith.*

a. *Some people learn obedience in suffering.* Hear these words of the psalmist: "Before I was afflicted I went astray: but now I have kept thy word" (v. 67). The writer of the Psalms knew that God was working out obedience through the lives of his children. The psalmist was committed to the Father's wisdom in permitting his affliction and was able finally to say, "It is good for me that I have been afflicted; that I might learn thy statutes; I know, O Lord, that thy judgments are right" (vv. 71, 75). David could have written these lines out of his experience of affliction at its severest point—the loss of a child. Into David's life was woven the crimson thread of

[4]*C. H. Spurgeon's Prayers.*

obedience. All affliction can be counted worthwhile if we learn the lesson of obedience.

b. *Other people suffer and their relationship to God is refined.* The finer graces of the Christian life are often attained in an hour of trial. Prayer often becomes more real; faith usually becomes stronger; attitudes are purified. Study the experiences of Job. Job trusted God, and his relationship was refined so that he could say, "But he knoweth the way that I take: when he hath tried me, I shall come forth as gold" (23:10).

c. *Still others suffer that they may bring glory to God.* If in our trouble our faces are turned toward God, he can receive glory from our experience. We can agree with the writer, "Call upon me in the day of trouble. I will deliver thee, and thou shalt glorify me" (Ps. 50:15).

The apostle Paul was matured by a thorn in the flesh that God refused to remove. The wife of C. F. Weigle came home one evening and told him that she was tired of being a preacher's wife and was leaving never to return. He sat down at the piano and, out of a heart matured by Christian commitment and the experience of disappointment, wrote, "No One Ever Cared for Me Like Jesus." Trouble can serve to mature us.

II. *Trouble can increase our understanding.*

a. Jesus always understood why people were as they were. It was not a matter of being a psychologist and analytically probing their past, but it was a sincere desire to love individuals no matter what they had done. Like Christ, we must develop the ability to see beyond the public sins of an individual to the possibilities of his redemption to a better way of life.

b. Personal trial carries with it the possibility of enlarging our understanding. The apostle Paul admonishes us to "rejoice with them that do rejoice, and weep with them that weep" (Rom. 12:15). His own personal trial matured him so that he could write, "Blessed be God, even the Father of our Lord Jesus Christ . . . who comforteth us in all our tribulation, that we may be able to comfort them which are in trouble" (2 Cor. 1:3–4). Paul had experienced rejection, misunderstanding, and personal ill will, along with physical trial. Perhaps the deepest hurt came from being falsely accused. It is tribulation such as this, however, that has "forged the steel" in many strong Christians.

III. *Trouble can strengthen our commitment.*

a. Many preachers have pounced upon the phrase, "It was good, O Lord, that I had trouble," in a tenacious defense of God for afflicting the psalmist. Yet the psalmist never ascribed his affliction to God. The psalmist did see, however, that in the permissive will of God, good can come out of any experience. That's what Paul said: "And we know that all things work together for good to them that love God, to them who are the called according to his purpose" (Rom. 8:28).

b. Trouble can strengthen or crush us. It carries with it the possibility for either outcome. The question is, How shall we face our trouble? There are those who face it cynically. They decide that nothing is and can be right with the world. Cynics always question the motivation of any person who has hope. They believe that everything anyone does, every aspiration, every attitude, is directed toward self-interest. It is human pessimism that denies the most basic need of persons for hope.

Some persons face trouble by adopting a stoical attitude toward life. They set their jaws and become indifferent. They act as if nothing matters. They become impassive and merely exist through life. Remember the British cockney who often quoted his favorite Bible verse, "Grin and bear it." Stoicism is where the rigor mortis of resignation has set in on a walking corpse. Endurance becomes the goal.

No doubt there were times when the psalmist was discouraged by his trouble, times when it must have seemed very dark and dismal. Yet beyond the darkness there was the light of eternal purpose, and that sufficed.—Allen F. Harrod[5]

Illustrations

FREEDOM.   The great motif of Christianity is freedom—redemption at a price and for a purpose, the liberation of mankind. In the synagogue at Nazareth, Christ announced Himself as "the opener of prisons," and throughout Galilee He proclaimed the truth that makes men free. As the dominating figure of the Old Testament is Moses the Liberator, leading men out of Egyptian slavery into the freedom of the promised land, so the dominating figure of the New Testament is Christ the Son, who makes men "free indeed."—Reginald E. O. White[6]

CENTRAL MEANING OF THE CROSS.   For me, the meaning of the grace of God is the compassionate, forgiving stoop of God, turning everything, including my sin, to good and fruitful account, making my prison and chains of my own building and forging my crippled manhood and winged life, my wounds and my weakness, all ministering spirits and agencies, teaching me sympathy, humility, lowly trust, and so turning my self-created poverty into treasure-trove.—A. E. Whitham[7]

SUNDAY: OCTOBER EIGHTEENTH

LECTIONARY MESSAGE

Topic: Persistence and Vindication in Prayer
    TEXT: Luke 18:1–8
    Other Readings: Jer. 31:27–34; 2 Tim. 3:14–4:5

The command to "pray without ceasing" has been a tremendous challenge to believers throughout the centuries. Persistence in prayer is highlighted in this parable. Jesus is on his way to Jerusalem, telling his followers that they "ought always to pray and not lose heart." In typical Lucan style we are presented with a two-level story, from the lesser to the greater. We are told of a widow who represents herself before an earthly "unright-

eous" judge, and of the possibility of representation before God, a righteous judge. Implied throughout this reading is the issue of future fulfillment and the vindication of God's persistent "chosen ones . . . and soon." Jesus sets this story firmly in a context of pleading, as in a legal situation.

Prayer and the *parousia* are dominant themes as Jesus moves toward Jerusalem. The question of whether there will be faith "on the earth" at the parousia further embell-

---

[5] *Award Winning Sermons 3.*
[6] *A Relevant Salvation.*
[7] *The Discipline and Culture of the Spiritual Life.*

ishes the parable. If believers are as persistent as this widow, the Kingdom will be advanced. If in the end an uncaring human judge can be worn down by persistent pleading by a defenseless widowed woman, to the point of granting her legal relief, how much more will God, a loving Father, grant his children what they need? God, and only God, knows the long-term needs of his people. God will vindicate his people, and in a timely manner, as was the case with this widowed woman.

I. *A contrast in judges.* The uncaring judge is presented as concerned only with his verdict, which gives him a "black eye." In the time of Jesus, certain corrupt judges were called "robber judges," because their chief modus operandi was extortion. Since a widowed woman had nothing to extort, this evil judge was only concerned with his public image. Clearly this judge, while he didn't care for people, was concerned for his reputation. He was afraid that he just might get a female fist in his eye from this persistent woman. We are not told what the case was about. However, we are told that it was a case presented to the judge by a helpless and powerless widowed woman who has an "adversary." We do not know if the adversary was present. Her continuous pleading, nagging, bugging, wearying, whining, and bothering won her vindication. The arbitrary judgment by this uncaring judge is contrasted with God's justice for his chosen ones who plead or "cry out" to him persistently. The judgment by God will favor their long-term interests, and God will make his verdict of vindication at the earliest possible moment. God's vindication of his people is always at just the right time, because all time belongs to God.

II. *A delayed response.* Unanswered prayer does not exist. Jesus teaches us to pray and to "not lose heart." He is the Lord of prayer, because he is the one who intercedes, pleads, and petitions the Father. He teaches us the reality of "Thy will be done." Praying as Jesus taught may involve just waiting patiently for a delayed answer. Such praying raises the question of doubt. Losing heart and failing to be persistent in prayer may show the character of one's faith. The type of faith-induced praying that Jesus exemplified was unto the end, "Thy will be done." The actual timing of God's answer may be delayed. So it is with God's vindication of his elect. God's vindica-

tion will come soon enough. The contrast is between human calculations of time and God's righteous timetable, "the parousia." Waiting for God's answer calls for persistence. The widow in this parable exemplifies the type of Kingdom praying that will always be vindicated. So Jesus' followers, or God's elect, pray continuously, "maranatha," or "Our Lord, come!" Our Lord's coming will be a rebuke to human calculations. In Mark we are told, "No one knows the time." In Luke we are nudged to be persistent in prayer, because the wrong type of faith may result in not being vindicated.

III. *A proper faith.* We are encouraged by the parable to "not lose heart." The delay of the parousia is at stake in this parable. Praying is integral to the anticipation of the parousia. These words from Luke are set within a context regarding "end times." The delay of the verdict of the unrighteous judge raises the parallel issue of the delayed parousia. How does one behave when the vindication is delayed? Calculating the time of vindication is a risky business, and Jesus warns his disciples about this error. Besides, the issue of how one should behave because of the delay of the end is also suggested here. In the preceding section, 17:20–37, the issue of a proper faith is also addressed. A faith that is equal to God's timetable is at issue here. As it was with the early Church, so it is today. There can be neither anxious waiting or comfortable relaxation. Finally, Jesus encourages us regarding God's response, with the words "soon" or "speedily." The Church throughout the ages has found great encouragement in the words "How much more!" God is not bound by the type of concerns modeled by the unrighteous judge, but by the reality of a timetable that the followers of Jesus must anticipate and expect. It was unusual for a question to follow a parable, but here Luke gives us a unique piece of critique: "When the Son of Man comes, will he find faith on the earth?" A faithful, patient, and persistent prayer encourages and strengthens one to confront an uncaring world. Vindication will come through persistent prayer, "maranatha."—Dave Hunsicker

Illustrations

PRAYING WHEN YOU DO NOT FEEL LIKE IT. It is often assumed that because feeling is a part of prayer, therefore you cannot pray without your feelings. This is rather like the assumption that because petition is a part of prayer, all prayer is petition. It is to mistake the part for the whole. Yet this mistake is widespread, and is usually expressed like this: "I pray only when I feel like it; otherwise it would not be genuine and real." One has only to apply this to other aspects of life to see how absurd it is. On Monday at six o'clock in the morning a bus driver is lying in bed, listening to the horrid noise of his alarm clock. He is due on duty at 7:15 A.M. The morning is cold and foggy, so instead of getting up, he turns over in bed, saying to himself, "I don't think I'll go to work today, I don't exactly feel like it!" Because he is "on duty," he goes irrespective of his feelings.—Stephen F. Winward[8]

HOW WE PRAY.   Notice how graciously prayer has been designed. To pray is nothing more involved than to let Jesus employ His powers in the alleviation of our distress. To pray is to let Jesus glorify His name in the midst of our needs.—O. Hallesby[9]

SERMON SUGGESTIONS

Topic: Frontiers of Danger
TEXT: John 17:9–19

Every life that catches a vision of God's purpose for him in this world must catch fire in an "I-thou" experience—a personal encounter with God. (1) His time and ours (Gal. 4:4). (2) His world and ours (John 16:33). (3) His mission and ours (John 17:18). (4) His commitment and ours (John 17:19).—H. Guy Moore[10]

Topic: How to Face Failure
TEXT: John 21:1–6

Christians need to face failure remembering that (1) no failure is final until we quit; (2) success is much closer than we realize; (3) failure may be necessary to sensitize us to the will of God.—J. Alfred Smith Sr.

[8] *Teach Yourself to Pray.*
[9] *Prayer.*
[10] *Christ for the World.*

Hymn Suggestions: Nineteenth Sunday After Trinity

1. "Lord, Keep Us Steadfast in Your Word," Martin Luther (1542), translated by Catherine Winkworth (1863); "Erhalt Uns, Herr," J. Klug, *Geistliche Lieder* (1543)

Of the many hymns exalting the Word of God and our responsibility to be faithful to its teachings by right living and diligent proclamation, possibly none is more powerful than this one by Martin Luther. It would be a natural component of a service focused on Paul's exhortations concerning the Word to the young Timothy (2 Tim. 3:14–4:5).

2. "I Am the Lord Your God," Helen Otte (1895); "Russia," Alexey Lvov (1833)

Based on the reading in Jeremiah 31, this hymn—especially stanza 3—reinforces the truth concerning the covenant that the Lord writes on the hearts of his people, promising grace and forgiveness. It would be effective sung in response to the Old Testament reading.

3. "Lord, Teach Us How to Pray Aright," James Montgomery (1823); "Richmond," Thomas Haweis (1792)

In connection with Jesus' exhortation when relating the parable of the importunate widow—that one must always pray and not lose heart (Luke 18:1–8)—the singing of this hymn would be appropriate.

4. "Teach Me, Lord, Your Way of Truth," *Psalter* (1912); "St. Crispin," George J. Elvey (1862)

Though based specifically on the verses in this day's Psalter reading, this hymn paraphrases other verses from Psalm 119 that reflect its basic theme of love for and fidelity to the law (commandments, precepts, testimonies, and so on) of God. It could be used as a prayer following the Psalter reading.—Hugh T. McElrath

Worship Aids

CALL TO WORSHIP.   "Sing praise to the Lord, all his faithful people! Remember what the Holy One has done, and give him thanks! His anger lasts only a moment, his goodness for a lifetime. Tears may flow in the night, but joy comes in the morning" (Ps. 30:4–5 TEV).

INVOCATION.   Gracious Lord, we confess that we sometimes doubt you when things go wrong, but again and again you show us your love. Let these moments of worship be a time of honest examination of ourselves, and of trusting commitment to your mercies, O God of the cross and resurrection.

OFFERTORY SENTENCE.   "What you are doing is much more than a service that supplies God's people with what they need. It is something that will make many others thank God" (2 Cor. 9:12 CEV).

OFFERTORY PRAYER.   Help us, O God, to realize anew that our tithes and offerings are being put into the service of your providence, and that there is no way of knowing the abundance of blessings that will come not only to us who worship here but also to others in many parts of the world that you love, the world for which Christ died.

PRAYER.   Almighty God, we praise you for the gift of grace and victory in Jesus Christ. So fill us with your Holy Spirit that our faith will stand sure and firm in the war we must wage against evil, and bring us, at last, into the glory of your great Kingdom—where fear and death and despair will be no more. We pray this in the name of him who teaches us to pray, saying, "Our Father. . . ."—Albert J. D. Walsh

SERMON

Topic: Because the Days are Evil
TEXT: Eph. 5:15–20
I. Rather ominous, isn't it? I mean the language with which the apostle Paul describes the human condition. He says, "the days are evil." And, you know, I can imagine members of the Ephesian congregation nodding their heads in agreement with Paul's assessment.

How so? Well, frankly, I'm not certain. I have no direct knowledge of what life was like in the city of Ephesus.

(a) But maybe when the Christians at Ephesus heard Paul's words—"the days are evil"—they thought, almost immediately, of the temple to Artemis, the Greek goddess of fertility. Or perhaps they were at once conscious of the pervasive immorality; the sick-

ness of a society gone mad with the pursuit of sensual pleasures.

The apostle's words strike a chord in us as well, don't they? It's all around us and within us. And there are times when it really frightens us too. "Because the days are evil."

(b) Now, some have suggested that when the apostle Paul said, "the days are evil" he was speaking symbolically. In other words, Paul was using a kind of "code language" which only other Christians could comprehend.

So, you see, with this line of argument, Paul was referring to something other than the immediate present. He was, rather, talking about the great and terrible "tribulation" said to precede the return of Christ in glory. But I'm not convinced of that.

(c) No. I believe the apostle Paul was writing with a much broader perspective. I think Paul refers to the time between Christ's coming and return as a time for guarded optimism. And more important, as a time to become reliant upon God's grace, because evil still has sufficient energy and enticement to wage all-out war against the wonder of Christ's church! And the present evil, which so often plagues our lives, is but a foretaste of what will one day be a terrible tribulation.

II. And so we have the apostle Paul to remind us—as if we needed a reminder!—that "the days are evil." Evil. The very word runs cold in our veins, doesn't it? We know it when we see it.

(a) Do you recall what the Lord God said to Noah subsequent to the great flood? I assure you, for a number of reasons, they're words well worth remembering. God, I would suppose, looked with compassion on his creatures—cowering from the devastation they'd seen. And he said:

"I will never again curse the ground because of humankind, for the inclination of the human heart is evil from youth; nor will I ever again destroy every living creature as I have done."

(b) I can almost feel the pain in God's voice as he says, "the inclination of the human heart is evil from youth."

I speak of God's pain because the human heart wasn't created to be contaminated by evil! It was created as the seat of a divine compassion, as the center of a divine compassion, as the center of all covenant commitments, as the focal point of all true freedom and faith. So evil bears down upon the human heart with a vengeance all its own. And God painfully acknowledges the pervasiveness of evil. Even in the human heart "the inclination of the human heart is evil from youth."

(c) This thing called "evil" runs deep, doesn't it? We know it, because we've so often seen it. And we've felt its icy tentacles laying hold of our own hearts. The sheer agony of it. The awesome power of it. It's a terror that lays hold of your soul, and then whispers its hideous warning: "I won't let go! I'll never let go!"

III. Now, when he said that "evil is easy," what he meant was—evil is effortless. Have you ever noticed that? Have you ever noticed how truly and terribly simple it is to be sinful? Beyond that, have you ever observed the infinite number of ways we can be so wicked? Wasting time trifling with temptations?

(a) Life is never quite good enough. We want more, and we'll have more. I've counseled a good many people whose sole problem seemed to be a basic dissatisfaction with day-to-day living. And, almost to the person, they were searching for more. All too often, that search became the incentive for sin. We want more, and we'll have more. But at what cost?

(b) Perhaps the present days are evil because of the moral decay which seems to abound in every avenue of life. Speaking as a representative of us all, Paul once cried out, saying, "I am of the flesh, and sold into slavery under sin." Good Lord! He could have been reading this morning's paper when he made that observation!

(c) When Paul says, "be careful then how you live . . . because the days are evil," he really wants us to wake up and smell the coffee. He's warning us that we underestimate the pervasiveness of evil only—and always— at great risk to ourselves—our souls!

IV. Here's something more. Their world, like ours, was willing to provide a number of different pathways to such security. Religious cults, with some pretty bizarre ritual practices, abounded throughout the ancient world. Ephesus was no exception!

(a) So, when the apostle Paul admonished the Christians of Ephesus—"do not get drunk with wine"—he's not merely offering some friendly advice on behalf of the local chapter of Alcoholics Anonymous!

His concern runs much deeper than the issue of chemical dependency. Paul's regard is for the seduction of the human spirit. You see, some of the cultic sects actually used alcohol in order to induce an experience of ecstasy. And then—while drunk—people believed God would speak to—or through— them. That was just one of several forms of bad faith.

(b) And now? Today? Now we have our "New Age" of spiritual enlightenment. We have gurus, living in multi-million dollar mansions and driving gold Mercedes-Benz cars. We have the practice of using peyote— a hallucinogenic—by Uppies seeking a "spiritual high."

Haven't you seen it? People today are "drunk" with everything and anything promising some form of spiritual delight. Actually, what they're searching for—even though they may not know it!—is some form of release, some refreshment, some form of redemption. "Because the days are evil."

V. Let's cut to the chase! Do we desire to discover some way to deal with all those terribly destructive elements in our world? Do we yearn—and are we longing—for something more than mere answers to the apprehensions and agonies of life?

(a) Here's my best advice. Let every disciple etch the admonition of the apostle Paul deep in his or her heart. Paul said: "Be careful how you live, not as unwise people but as wise, making the most of the time . . . be filled with the Spirit, as you sing psalms and hymns and spiritual songs among yourselves, singing and making melody to the Lord in your hearts, giving thanks to God the Father at all times and for everything in the name of our Lord Jesus Christ."

(b) The apostle Paul said, "be filled with the Spirit."—That is to say, "be filled with" the power of Christ's presence and promise. In other words, if we would find the "wisdom" to conquer evil, we must first—and through the eyes of faith—look to Christ.

Someone has said that "the truest (human) of all (humanity) was the 'Man of Sorrows.'" But if that is so—why is it so? Maybe because this "Man of Sorrows" revealed to us, for all time and eternity, that genuine wisdom is borne in the bosom of a sacred and sacrificial love.

(c) We're not speaking here of a self-serving sorrow. Not sorrow that surges up from the depths of self-pity. But a sorrow that comes as the consequences of having confronted and challenged evil whenever and wherever it was to be found.

A sorrow that comes from sharing in the pains and problems and perplexities of others. A sorrow hammered out on the hard steel of a self-sacrificial love. In fact, a Savior's love for his suffering and struggling humanity.

VI. You finally see, don't you? Paul exhorts the saints to accept with manifest gratitude—with great joy!—all that we receive and are called to do or to suffer for Christ our Savior. Under all conditions, God is to be praised. "Giving thanks to God the Father at all times and for everything" is exactly how Paul said it. And believe me—he meant every word of it!

(a) Why would the apostle Paul and these others encourage us to "sing God's praises" while we—and those we love—suffer the "slings and arrows" of evil?

Because the character of Christian witness is far from bitter, gloomy, or desperate—despite the evil days of the present. Christian testimony is full of emotion, and energy, and a joy that continually breaks out into jubilation! Together, the saints form a celebrating community, consisting of free men and women—filled with the power of Christ—living and acting graciously and courageously

under the promise of God to one day eradicate all evil from the face of the earth!

(b) The wisdom to live by the promises of God, and not by the fear that all forms of evil are final. The wisdom to sing God's praise, while the rest of the world wonders if, in fact, evil will ever be eradicated. And the wisdom that knows that "the only thing necessary for the triumph of evil is for (Christians) to do—nothing!"—Albert J.D. Walsh

Illustrations

EVIL DESCRIBED.   Somewhere in the story *Moby Dick* there's a description of evil. An attempt to capture evil in all its complexity and its calamitous conditions. Here evil is described as "all that most maddens and torments; all that stirs up the less of things; all truth with malice in it; all that cracks the sinews and cakes the brain; all the subtle demonisms of life and thought . . . all general rage and hate felt . . . from Adam's down." That's pretty much it, wouldn't you say?—A.J.D.W.

FEAR AND DEATH.   For all of his foolishness and balderdash, perhaps the atheistic philosopher, Bertrand Russell, was right when he said that "to conquer fear is the beginning of wisdom." Because, you know, the polar opposite of faith is not doubt—but fear!—A.J.D.W.

SUNDAY: OCTOBER TWENTY-FIFTH

LECTIONARY MESSAGE

Topic: Two in Need
    TEXT: Luke 18:9–14
    Other Readings: Joel 2:23–32; Ps. 65; 2 Tim. 4:6–8, 16–18
This parable is not about false humility. Neither is it a simple contrast between two extremes of Jewish society—Pharisees and tax collectors. Rather, it is a graphic picture of "the great reversal"—from works-righteousness to faith alone. It is about free grace! The grace of God, as shown by Jesus, cannot be measured or accounted by any human standard. This was Israel's toughest lesson, and appears to be the toughest lesson for Christians as well.

Jesus gave the parable for those who "trusted in themselves." With this target firmly in mind, he taught about propriety, prayer, and piety. This reading goes right to the heart of the spiritual problem. No human could ever come up with a scheme to put himself or herself right with God. Interestingly, the parable is given as Jesus tells the disciples, for the third time, that he shall die. Jesus had in mind the radical gospel, which teaches about a God who puts humans right with himself through death and resurrection. No one had ever seen that type of justification, and Jesus anticipates that reality here.

To get at the problem, Jesus overstates the case. He presents us with two types of losers. The first, "a Pharisee," is presented as one who can be easily identified in our world. Here is a real do-gooder of the worst sort. Christianity has been punctuated with this kind of person since its beginning. Many a church has had the services of this type. He (or she) is a good person, a faithful spouse and parent; he or she is active in the community, holds a good reputation, and is generous with tithes and offerings. Piety and scrupulous attention to behavior is the hallmark of this person. From a strictly human frame of reference, this is a good person. Such a person would have been a candidate for leadership in any ecclesiastical system.

By contrast, this one is surely better than the other loser, the publican. This must be the most despicable person one could describe. He is a true carpetbagger, one who would have worked for the Nazi regime. This one worked for Rome, although he was a Jew. One could not be a tax collector and be anything but suspect. Tax collectors were Jews recruited by Rome to collect taxes from their own people. In the minds of the Jewish establishment, they collaborated with the enemy. Such a person would be the classic "wheeler and dealer." His lifestyle and attitude would have been difficult to deal with. According to the Pharisee, he was a "robber/swindler." We are told that fraud and dishonesty were common vices of tax collectors. Publicans were so despised by the Jews, that they were prevented from being witnesses in court. They were grouped with the worst sort. Their character would have been well understood by Jesus' audience.

I. *Propriety.* Jesus tells us about "a Pharisee." Possibly Jesus had a particular one in mind. The Pharisee characterized in this reading can be contrasted with other Pharisees Jesus encountered during his ministry who were not so self-righteous. By his own evaluation, this Pharisee is proper, correct, and fit in every way. His self-identity is one of being "unlike" swindlers, robbers, adulterers, and the unrighteous. All these characterizations are set over against the tax collector. By the standard of public propriety, the picture is accurate. Although the Pharisee may not have had firsthand evidence, his generalization about the tax collector fits all the known descriptions, including that of "adulterer." But the tax collector is presented as publicly humble, as "standing far off." The fact that the Temple had restricted areas gives a clue to the meaning of these words. This tax collector, despite his occupation, comes to the Temple seeking God. Yet he must seek God in the right location, with the other marginalized people: the women, the gentiles, and the "unclean ones."

II. *Prayer.* The prayer of the Pharisee tells us about a negative aspect of thanksgiving. An integral part of praying for a devout Jew, according to the best of Jewish tradition, is thanksgiving. However, and unfortunately, this Pharisee's prayer of thanksgiving is shortsighted and misses the mark because it is framed as a self-congratulating indictment of others.

Now, the prayer of the tax collector comes from a different perspective. His prayer is couched in humility and self-abasement: (literally) "O God, have mercy on me, a sinner." His body language is telling; he "stood afar off." This distance is akin to that of the other marginalized people in his society, whom Luke seems to favor. Social and religious isolation are revealed in the prayer of the tax collector.

III. *Piety.* Regarding prayer, Jesus spoke of piety. In the Sermon on the Mount (Matt. 6:5–8), he had in mind the prayers of certain "hypocrites." Real piety is built on the firm foundation of reverence, truth, and honesty. Self-righteousness is the real target of Jesus in this parable. Although the lesson is set in a context of social comparison, the truth of the parable would, of necessity, apply to any type of self-righteousness. The piety of the tax collector is underscored not only by his location in the Temple but also by his body language: "not lifting up his eyes to heaven," and "he continued beating his chest." The beating of the chest was, and is now, a well-known act of contrition among pious Jews. The tax collector's posture was reflective of his inner attitude of seeking mercy. One is reminded of the sincere penitence of Psalm 51. The behavior and words of this tax collector are more congruent with the penitential psalms than are those of the Pharisee. The baseline of this parable is reflected in the summary words of Jesus: "This man went down to his house justified rather than the other, for everyone who exalts himself will be humbled, but he who humbles himself will be exalted." The most painful part of the meaning of this parable is that all humans have a Pharisee and a tax collector within them.—Dave Hunsicker

Illustrations

EVIL MIXED WITH GOOD.   As soon as we investigate the motivation of our thoughts and actions we see that the best and the worst are as inextricably mixed together as are the oxygen and the nitrogen in the air we breathe. I have seen many people quite overwhelmed by this discovery, as their experience of life or psychological analysis brought them to maturity, so that they looked back with a certain nostalgia to the simplicity of their childhood, when good and evil were clearly distinguishable from each other.

The fact is that evil is everywhere mixed with good. The Bible proclaims the fact and our experience confirms it.—Paul Tournier[11]

THE WAY THROUGH THE CRISIS.   We live in a jail which we call our castle; a foreign soldier breaks through the doors, come to free us by blasting the walls of our castle—and we fight him with the last might of our broken Ego, calling him scoundrel, knave and devil, until we are exhausted, overwhelmed and disarmed. Then looking at the victor with disinterested objectivity we recognize him: St. Michael smilingly sheathes his sword.

The power which brought about the fight was grace. The "evil" which caused our anxiety was, in the last analysis, grace. And even the real scoundrels, our competitors in egocentricity who betrayed us and wounded us so unjustly, even they, as we discover now, were already working unknowingly and unwillingly in the service of the superhuman strategy of grace. This fact is no excuse for their evil doing; but it shows the transcendent power and wisdom of the coming kingdom of heaven. And above all it shows that the kingdom is there already and is working in spite of and even through the errors and felonies of its prospective citizens.—Fritz Kunkel[12]

SERMON SUGGESTIONS

Topic: Freedom—Society and the Individual
TEXT: Eph. 4:25
(1) The New Testament never thinks of the individual and society in isolation from each other. (2) The New Testament gives us a view of the nature of man upon which our conceptions of society and of liberty must be based. (3) The New Testament gives the key to the solution of the problem of freedom and control, which is one of the most vexing questions in this modern world.—Leslie J. Tizard[13]

Topic: Tests for Teachers
TEXT: Matt. 7:15–23
(1) Do they live by what they teach? (2) Do they teach only to give their hearers what they wish to hear? (3) Does their teaching reflect the purposes and message of Christ? (4) Are their hearers better and happier people?

Hymn Suggestions: Twentieth Sunday After Trinity

1. "Fight the Good Fight with All Thy Might," John Monsell (1863); "Pentecost," William Boyd (1864)
The reading of the Epistle lesson could well furnish the motivation and inspiration for singing this call to action through the strength that Christ supplies.
2. "Praise Is Your Right, O God, in Zion," Stanley Wiersma (1987); "Genevan 65," Louis Bourgeois (1543)
This new version of Psalm 65 is sufficiently close to the thought and progression of ideas of the original psalm to justify its use in place of the Psalter reading.
3. "O God of Vision," Jane Parker Huber (1981); "Lobe den Herren," *Stralsund Gesangbuch* (1665)
Joel 2:28–29, in which the prophet asserts that God's Spirit will be poured out indiscriminately on women and men, young and old, is the scriptural basis for this contemporary prayer hymn.
4. "No, Not Despairingly," Horatius Bonar (1866); "Kedrow," Ann B. Spratt (1866)
The humble mood and penitent spirit of this hymn expand on the prayer for mercy of the publican in Jesus' parable of the Pharisee

---

[11] *Creative Suffering.*
[12] *Fritz Kunkel: Selected Writings.*

[13] Leslie J. Tizard, *Facing Life and Death.*

210 THE MINISTERS MANUAL FOR 1998

and the publican (Luke 18:9–14). Singing it with sincerity and feeling will reinforce the lesson in humility that Jesus was teaching.—Hugh T. McElrath

Worship Aids

CALL TO WORSHIP.   "Blessed are the people who know the joyful sound! They walk, O Lord, in the light of Your countenance. In Your name they rejoice all day long, and in Your righteousness they are exalted" (Ps. 89:15–16 NKJV).

INVOCATION.   We have reason to rejoice, O Lord, for you are our faithful God. Grant us such faith that even the dark hours may be cheered by the illumination of your presence and promises.

OFFERTORY SENTENCE.   "Give unto the Lord, O ye kindreds of the people, give unto the Lord glory and strength. Give unto the Lord glory due unto his name; bring an offering and come into his courts" (Ps. 96:7–8).

OFFERTORY PRAYER.   Lord, if in giving a small part we are left with less than expected, or if in giving a large part we are still comfortable, teach us the equalization that faith brings by blessing every gift and giver through the power of the living Christ.—E. Lee Phillips

PRAYER.   Eternal God, creator of life, and our life, we pause this day to bring to you the houses of our lives. We acknowledge that they are constantly in need of repair. Go down into the damp basements of our lives and bring to us the brightness of your love and grace.

Enter the cluttered attic of our lives and discard those things from the past that hold us back from following you into the future. Come into the den, the living room, the kitchen, the bedroom, all of the rooms of our lives, and fill them with your presence. May we have such an awareness of your love and your guidance that we will constantly seek to make the repairs that will enable us to live more closely with you and to walk more like you.

Bless us as we come to this place that is set apart to hallow your name. May we glorify you, learn more how to serve you, and go forth into the world to let our lives reflect the love and grace that we have experienced through Jesus Christ, our Lord, in whose name we pray.—William Powell Tuck

Sermon: Bearing Your Own Cross
TEXT: Gen. 13:1–13; Luke 9:23–25

I. Look at the story of Abraham and Lot found in Genesis 13:1–13. They both were wealthy men in their day. In fact, each of them had such large flocks that they could not graze their flocks in the same area. Quarrels were breaking out among the herdsmen, and they realized that they needed to separate.

a. Abraham gave Lot the first choice of land on which to settle. On one side was the Jordan Valley with its fertile green grass and flowing streams. On the other side was the rough mountain terrain, which was not barren like the wilderness nearby but was not as choice as the Jordan Valley. Lot chose the lush, green valley, which was the easier way. Abraham was left with the mountains, which would be a rough and difficult existence. Notice that the text states that after Lot settled in the valley, he pitched his tent toward Sodom.

b. It is usually true that those who choose the easy, comfortable style of life often pitch their tents toward Sodom, and pleasure soon becomes the chief end in the choice between two ways of life. One way is represented by Lot, who chose the comfortable and easy way. The other way of life is the more adventuresome style of living, which Abraham chose. Note what is involved in these two choices.

c. Lot's choice was based on a self-centered approach to living. It also represented a more comfortable, easier lifestyle. In choosing his pathway, Lot also indicated that he was indifferent to what Abraham did.

d. Abraham chose the more adventuresome way—the way of faith. He chose the way that showed he was willing to take risks, to be a pioneer. He had gone out searching for God's city, which was without foundation. He began by taking a journey of faith. Now, rather than taking the easy path into the fertile valley, he climbed again to the mountain peaks and labored strenuously for God. I don't think God always calls us to the most comfortable places. I don't understand God's ways. Who among us doesn't want ease and comfort?

II. Sometimes God calls us to difficult places with hardships and burdens. These may be places where no one else wants to go. Jesus calls us to a way that is radically different from the way of the world. The cross is not just an inconvenience in our faith; it is a way of life. Let's see if we can understand what that means.

a. Jesus said, "If any person will come after me, let him or her get their priorities right." When you get your priorities right, then you will find a pattern for life. Jesus states that our pattern for life is "to take up our cross." He has called us to a different way of living—the crosslike way. It is a call to live sacrificially in ministry for him.

b. If you are willing to "take up your cross," then Jesus calls you to discipleship with his words, "Follow me." He issues us a call to obedience. You are not called to see what you can get out of life or how happy you can be, but to follow the way of Jesus. Jesus himself was soon going to lay down his life. He was calling his disciples to "come follow me" and be willing to do the same.

III. The call to follow Jesus is a demand for daily self-denial. How can you die daily for Christ? Jesus' call is to a sacrificial way of living. It is a summons to a continuous denial of self-centeredness. The call to follow him is not just a one-time call to commitment. You do not make a single commitment to Christ in a moment and it is all over. "I'm a Christian! Isn't that wonderful!" you say. Christ's summons to discipleship is a call to begin living the Christlike way of life everyday. To take up your cross daily.

a. Jesus Christ has called us to a way of life that demands sacrificial living, and when we begin to realize that the cross is supposed to be a way of life, it is even more offensive to us today than it was to the people of Jesus' day. Few people really live a sacrificial kind of life. But Jesus has called us to the crosslike way of life.

b. In the twentieth century, Albert Schweitzer has exemplified sacrificial dedication. Although he was acclaimed as a noted philosopher, theologian, organist, musicologist, minister, and professor, he believed something was missing from his life. The void in his life was filled when he prepared himself to go as a medical missionary to Lambarene, Africa. In his autobiography he states that he was stabbed awake one morning with the realization that "I must not accept this happiness as a matter of course, but must give something in return for it. . . . I tried to settle what meaning lay hidden for me in the saying of Jesus: 'Whosoever would save his life shall lose it, and whosoever shall lose his life for my sake and the Gospels shall save it.'. . . In addition to the outward, I now had inward happiness."[14]

c. "The paradoxical thing is," Jesus said, "that you find your life by losing it." You find it by losing it in service. You save your life by giving it up, by spending it in service. As you die to selfishness, you find rebirth. In ministering to others, you find what real life really is.

If we have met the Master face to face, he has called us to walk in the Christlike way. We are to take up our cross and follow him. It is a call to discipleship. Let us hear that call and follow.—William Powell Tuck

Illustrations

THE ROAD NOT TAKEN.   Alfred Adler tells a story about two men who met in a railway station in Austria. One of the men was a wino who was begging for money for his next drink. The stranger asked the man who was begging, "How did you get into such a condition? You seem like a man who has fine gifts."

"Ah," the beggar said, "you don't understand. The cards have always been stacked against me in life. My mother died when I was very young. My father beat me up a great deal. In the war I was separated from my family and I never saw them again."

"That's strange," the other man said. "My background was very similar to yours. My mother died when I was very young. My father also was brutal to me, and I was separated from my family in the war. Because of my adverse circumstances I thought I should try to do the best I could to make something of myself." As the two men continued to talk, they discovered that they were brothers! One of them had become an alcoholic and spent

[14]Albert Schweitzer, *Out of My Life and Thought* (Austin, Tex.: Holt, Rinehart and Winston, 1961), 85.

his life wandering from one place to another begging for money to get a drink. The other had risen to a significant place in society. Both came out of the same kind of circumstances.—W.P.T.

INDIFFERENCE. Indifference is a horrid sin. C. S. Lewis addresses this sin in his *Screwtape Letters*. He depicts the Devil briefing his nephew, Wormwood, on how to tempt human beings. The goal that you need to establish, he advises him, is not wickedness but indifference. You don't need to persuade people to do evil itself, but always keep them busy doing nothing. The important thing is to keep your patient comfortable. Let nothing upset or disturb him. If he becomes the least bit concerned with anything vitally important, keep him thinking about something else that might give him indigestion. "I, the Devil," he states, "will always see to it that there are bad people. Your job, my dear Wormwood, is to provide me with people who do not care."—W.P.T.

SUNDAY: NOVEMBER FIRST

Topic: A Changed Life
TEXT: Luke 19:1–10
Other Readings: Heb. 1:1–4, 2:1–4; Ps. 119:137–144; 2 Thess. 1:1–4, 11–12

As the song says, "He climbed into the Sycamore tree, for the Lord he wanted to see." Zaccheus, the hero of short (small stature) people, was confronted by Jesus, and a changed life resulted. For Jesus came "to seek and to save the lost." That is the outline of the reading—but it isn't that simple. A changed life is never that simple; much life and living is presupposed when Jesus confronts a Zaccheus or a Mary Magdalene. Repentance is the operative word in this story of a changed life, and repentance is never easy. Feeling sorry is easy. Feeling sorry that one has been "found out" is easy. Repentance is costly grace. Most surgery calls for removing some good tissue and bad.

Conversion is the foundation on which the connectives "repent" and "believe" ("be baptized") are built. Conversion deals with a new orientation of the deeper self: the Biblical "heart," and not just the ego. Augustine, John Wesley, General Booth, and others experienced what psychologist William James called "the divided self." Converted persons, however, witness to a new kind of self, which has unity and peace. It is growth oriented and reaches out toward "more." To some, the change comes suddenly, and to others it comes slowly. Christians through the ages have been either once or twice born. The Russian writer Dostoyevsky says that in his conversion he was born "not as a child, but out of a white hot crucible of doubt."

I. *The person.* In this reading, the particular candidate for conversion is a chief tax collector—but not just an ordinary tax collector, as in the story of the Pharisee and the tax collector in the Temple. This tax collector was a "chief" tax collector. He was a notch above the average tax collector. We do not know if Jesus had prior knowledge of him. Zaccheus might well have had a wide reputation as the chief tax collector at Jericho, a major highway and trade junction. He functioned at the county seat. He was, by description, "of small stature," but in his role he was a "big cheese."

Somehow Zaccheus had built up a curiosity about Jesus, because he felt he must climb into a tree to see him. It is entirely possible that Zaccheus had known about John the Baptist and his cry for repentance. Additionally, as a leading citizen, Zaccheus may have known of Jesus and his ongoing confrontations with the authorities. He may have known the rising drama of Jesus going to Jerusalem. And he may have heard about Jesus' teachings on riches. Such teachings must have touched Zaccheus. For a chief tax collector to have grasped what Jesus taught about riches strongly suggests that he was interested in and open to a changed life.

II. *The confrontation.* Because he was small of stature and despite his prestige, Zaccheus located himself in a tree so that he could "check out" Jesus. Against all propriety, Jesus not only identified Zaccheus but also invited him to take a meal with him. The invitation not only startled Zaccheus, it startled Jesus' followers and the larger audience as well. Such a move could only have served to add another charge against Jesus: "He has gone in to be a guest of a man who is a sinner."

Sometime before, during, or after that meal, Zaccheus showed his heart. "Behold, Lord, the half of my goods I give to the poor; and if I have defrauded anyone of anything, I restore it fourfold." There it is! Zaccheus, one of the marginalized children of Abraham, had grasped the deep teaching of Jesus regarding riches. The implication is that Zaccheus "took a stand" against his public self. Such a stand was radical, at the least. Implied also is the matter of repentance, a real change of heart, as Zaccheus had undoubtedly experienced conversion. His desire to make restitution fulfilled the intent of the Law found in Leviticus 6:5 and Numbers 5:7. In the case of robbery, one was also compelled to repay, as in Exodus 22:1, 3b–4. Jesus' response confirmed the changed life of Zaccheus (and his household!) as demonstrated by his practical and proper actions.

III. *The rest of the story.* Jesus confirmed the changed life of Zaccheus: "Today salvation has come to this household, since he also is a son of Abraham. For the Son of man came to seek and save the lost." The word *lost* implies that something is out of place. The real and vital conversion of Zaccheus had all the essential elements of a changed life. Zaccheus experienced a "psychic enthronement" of Jesus Christ. So impressive was the change that Jesus indicated that it included his household. Such a total conversion must of necessity involve all of one's life. No disassociation here. No splitting of the self. No double-mindedness. Zaccheus found his right place regarding riches, his most essential temptation. No more fraud or immoral practices for this converted Son of Abraham.

In this regard, Jesus confirmed his role of "ministering to the sons of Abraham." So, does God love drug dealers, prostitutes, murderers, and the most despicable characters of our world? Yes! His love was and is extended to all: Hitler, Stalin, Capone, Ted Bundy, Jeffrey Dahmer, Richard Speck, Charlie Manson, and all of us. When Moses asked God who he was, the answer came back, "Mercy and compassion." So it is with Jesus, for he came to seek all who were not in the right place, and to show mercy and compassion. The church is the extension of this ministry to all who are not in the right place. Thank God, Jesus represented to the world a loving Father who comes, and comes, and comes . . . seeking the lost.—Dave Hunsicker

Illustrations

WORTH OF INDIVIDUALS.   Here shines forth the glory of Jesus' ministry. Jesus dealt with people as individuals. Certainly the multitudes thronged about him. He did not drive the crowds away. But he sought out individuals within the crowd. He had love for these persons; he had time for them; he had a message tailored to their uniqueness. Some of the yearning faces that looked up at him were the lean faces of the poor; some were the twisted faces of the suffering. Some of the eyes that sought him out were the frightened eyes of the persecuted and exploited; some were the old, calculating eyes of the proud and hardhearted. But Jesus read again and again the story told by the lines in those faces and by the looks in those eyes, and he went after the individuals they represented and helped them one by one.—James W. Cox[1]

EVANGELISM.   In this incident was Jesus' philosophy of evangelism. Here Jesus showed us by what he did, what we ought to do. If we do not seek out the rejected, the morally homeless of this world, and if we do not see them as individual souls made for God, then we may discover that even in our "churchiness" we are working for ourselves, not Jesus Christ; that custom and convention mean more to us than does the kingdom of God. Jesus declared that the "Son of man came to seek and to save the lost" (Luke 19:10 RSV). As those who represent him today, we have no greater task ourselves.—James W. Cox[2]

SERMON SUGGESTIONS

Topic: From Trouble to Praise
   Text: Ps. 50:15
   (1) Our unavoidable challenge—the day of trouble. (2) Our appropriate response—to call upon God. (3) Our heartfelt confidence—that God will deliver us. (4) Our inevitable service—praise, honor, glorifica-

[1] *Surprised by God.*
[2] *Surprised by God.*

tion of God, and all that this implies in life and service.

Topic: On Standing Alone

Text: Eph. 5

(1) We must develop some convictions about what pleases the Lord. (2) We need to be informed about current issues. (3) We must take appropriate action. (4) We need the guidance of the Holy Spirit.—Dan Baumann

Hymn Suggestions: Twenty-First Sunday After Trinity

1. "All Hail the Power of Jesus' Name," Edward Perronet (1779); "Coronation," Oliver Holden (1792)

To reflect the prayer of the apostle Paul in the Epistle reading that the name of Jesus might be glorified, there is no finer hymn than this. Either of the other popular tunes for this exuberant hymn ("Miles Lame" or "Diaden") could be used in place of "Coronation."

2. "O Word of God Incarnate," William W. How (1807); "Munich," *Gesangbuch Meiningen* (1693)

Any hymn that exalts Holy Scripture would be appropriate to accompany the Psalter reading (119:137–144). This classic hymn that uses the metaphors of lantern, sacred vessel, banner, chart, and compass to describe the Bible's value and use is one of the best known and loved.

3. "My Lord, I Did Not Choose You," Josiah Conder (1843); "Whitfield," Anonymous (1811)

This hymn with its simple confession that Christ takes the initiative in offering us salvation can be used as a meaningful response to the Gospel reading (Luke 19:1–10). Though Zaccheus climbed into a tree to see Jesus, he did not invite Jesus to be a guest in his house; rather, Jesus sought out Zaccheus and invited himself to his home in order to save him.

4. "Fret Not for Those Who Do Wrong Things," Christopher Webber (1986); "Culross," *Scottish Psalter* (1635)

The passages in Habakkuk in which the prophet, in the presence of violence, trouble, and destruction, first questions whether God may be unjust (1:1–4), but then takes his stand to wait patiently for the Lord's answer

(2:1–4), are reminiscent of the psalmist's thought in Psalm 37, of which this hymn is a contemporary paraphrase.—Hugh T. McElrath

Worship Aids

CALL TO WORSHIP. "Thou art worthy, O Lord, to receive glory and honor and power: for thou hast created all things, and for thy pleasure they are and were created" (Rev. 4:11).

INVOCATION. O God, show us how to glorify and honor you, how to acknowledge your power, and so worship you by what we say and what we do. Let this meeting of your people help all of us to do better what we attempt from time to time, so that little by little, more and more, we may magnify your wonderful name.

OFFERTORY SENTENCE. "Seek ye first the kingdom of God, and his righteousness, and all these things shall be added unto you" (Matt. 6:33).

OFFERTORY PRAYER. Our loving Father, you have given us so much, and even our best giving is so little, yet you have multiplied our small gifts and through them spread the Good News and blessed your Kingdom causes throughout the world. In all things make us good stewards of what we receive from your gracious hand.

PRAYER. O God, you have been our refuge all the days of our lives. You have blessed and kept us until this hour. Even when we thought our ways were hidden from you, you were with us to bring us back to an awareness of your comforting presence. Our faith leads us to thank you for the painful reminder of our willfulness, our foolishness, our sinfulness. The strange ways of your love have brought us to see again the wisdom of your will and the loyalty of your love. May we not forget that your every command is for our good and happiness.

Sermon: Remember This!

TEXT: Deut. 6:4–9; Matt. 11:28–30

A good case can be made for saying that *faith* is a matter of remembering. When we remember, we call back to mind events and experiences that somehow have influenced us. We bring to the forefront of our thought things that have meaning and application to our individual lives. When these remembrances are positive, they lift our spirits; they are helpful and motivational.

Faith is a matter of remembering the great things that God has done. Our memory evokes images of divine blessings experienced in days gone by. We recall the teachings that have shaped us and the good gifts that have come our way. Even if one's past has been clouded by troubles or burdened by grief, some evidence of the mercy and grace of God has flashed somewhere across that past. A recollection of that evidence, plus an affirmation of it, is what is meant by faith. Faith begins as we remember the movement of God in our personal lives and in the life of the world. Such recollection is positive. It truly lifts our spirits, proving to be helpful and motivational.

Very early in their religious pilgrimage, the people of Israel—the Hebrew followers of God—discerned the relationship of faith and remembering. They recognized that their understanding of God would be lost without constant reflection and repetition. The wisdom, the morality, the devotion that belonged to their lives because of the acts of God prompted them to devise patterns of remembrance. The Hebrews knew that their faith depended upon remembering the great things God had done. They left nothing to chance; they insisted upon varieties of remembrances—of memoranda—so that the great things of God would not be forgotten. As a result, their faith, and ours, relies heavily upon remembering. Memory preserves and perpetuates all that we know and have experienced of the workings of God. Faith becomes, then, a matter of remembering.

I. *Jesus' invitation.* What are sermons or Sunday School lessons or religious discussion groups all about? Is not their purpose to elicit our remembrance of the great things God has done, and then to enlarge that field of memory so that we may live ever more completely in the knowledge and grace of God? We gather to study and worship on a regular basis so that faith may inspire our lives—so that what we recall of God's ways may guide our ways. While we come to church to enjoy fellowship and to offer service, we also come to respond to that call from Deuteronomy, "Remember this!"

Jesus himself has invited us to this kind of experience. Often in our worship time, as we unite here in prayer, Jesus' words are spoken, including his invitation, "Come to me, all who labor and are heavy-laden, and I will give you rest. Take my yoke upon you and learn from me; for I am gentle and lowly in heart, and you will find rest for your souls." Those words constitute a meaningful call to prayer, as they tell us that our burdens can be lifted and our spirits given peace by the power of Jesus' presence. Jesus went on to say that his yoke is easy and the load he puts on us is light. Appropriately, we repeat his statement as we enter into prayer.

Another dimension attaches to these words as well. It relates to our emphasis on faith as an act of remembering. Jesus said, "Come . . . take my yoke upon you." Knowing the human need for purpose and significance in life, Jesus in essence said, "Come, accept my challenge." His yoke can be understood as the sum of his teaching and example. In other words, "Take these things upon you; accept them as a challenge, thus giving your life purpose and significance." Jesus went on to say in that same invitation, "Learn from me." To learn means to fix something in our minds. When Jesus' message is fixed in our minds, we have resources to draw upon, giving us needed content for faith. And then Jesus concluded, "You will find rest for your souls." He told us that the outcome of accepting his challenge and fixing his message firmly in our minds is an experience of the full blessings of life. "Rest for our souls" signifies fulfillment and enrichment of an order that only the Lord can provide. Coming to Jesus, receiving his message, and learning from him lead to a completing or rounding out of human life, and this, surely, is what all of us desire.

II. *Remembering, human and divine.* When the Scriptures call us to "Remember this!" they are doing us a marvelous service. They are helping us to hold fast, by means of memory, to the witness of Jesus, and to the wisdom of prophets, teachers, and a vast host of ordinary people of faith. As we remember, we are enabled to live and serve well, as others have done before us.

One final point remains. It is the recognition that while you and I invoke memory to increase our faith, God invokes his own memory to deal with his people. God remembers persons, to show mercy, to protect, to deliver them. God remembers the prayers of the faithful, to answer them. God remembers the sin of his people, to judge them. God remembers the promises he has made, to fulfill them. The remembrance of God is at one with the divine action in judgment and salvation. Memory is power; it has purposes; it truly is of God. In the words of Scripture, "Remember this! Remember this!"—John H. Townsend

Illustrations

MEMORANDA.   I have always delighted in that quip from the fantasy *Alice in Wonderland,* by Lewis Carroll. Said the king to the queen, "The horror of that moment, I shall never, never forget!"

"You will, though," the Queen said, "if you don't make a memorandum of it."[3]—J.H.T.

RECOLLECTION.   Preacher Halford Luccock called memory and our capacity for remembering "a great gift, vastly worth cultivating." Dr. Luccock suggested that memory makes it possible for time to be used more than once. "Think," he said, "how many times people have been refreshed and fortified by memories of some shining hour in the past. It is a wise way of living to store the mind with high and lovely things to remember—and to call them often to mind." That becomes a good description of how faith is fostered: our recollections of valued spiritual experiences and learnings refresh and fortify our current journey. We recall the past to empower the present.—J.H.T.

SUNDAY: NOVEMBER EIGHTH

LECTIONARY MESSAGE

Topic: On Being Wrong-Headed
TEXT: Luke 20:27–38
Other Readings: Hag. 1:15b–2:9; 2 Thess. 2:1–5, 13–17

In Luke's beautiful tapestry of Jesus' confrontation with the religious establishment, the weaving now involves the Sadducees. Jesus was in Jerusalem and engaged by his detractors. In this reading, the Sadducees were prompted by one of their most closely held "wrong-headed" beliefs: their denial of the Resurrection. They used this bias to discredit Jesus' teachings. Being wrong-headed is a combination of prejudice, stubbornness, and being just plain "closed." We have seen this attitude in ourselves, our families, at the workplace, and in religion. We throw up our hands at such a posture in others, and yet with ourselves we rationalize the problem.

Being wrong-headed about the Resurrection is the issue here. Jesus had a continuing discussion with the Pharisees, and they were more open to his teachings. But there seemed to be a greater theological distance between the Sadducees and Jesus. They were more biased than the Pharisees, and less likely to depend on all the scriptures in formulating their beliefs. The Pharisees believed in fate, that a person's life was planned and designed by God. The Sadducees believed in unrestricted free will. The Pharisees were committed to an anticipation of the messiah, while the Sadducees took the position that the coming of a messiah would disturb their well-ordered lives. The Pharisees believed in spirits and angels, the Sadducees did not.

In Acts 23:8 Luke tells us about the Sadducees' denial of the Resurrection. (One Sunday school teacher taught, "Because the Sadducees did not believe in the Resurrection, they were sad, you see!") What really got their attention and troubled them was Jesus' view of the Resurrection. The subject raised their hackles, and their bias was revealed. They had difficulty finding a basis in the Torah for believing in the Resurrection. So they put a question to Jesus, aimed clearly at tripping him up. They had a whole arsenal of such questions, which they were constantly putting to their friends the Pharisees. The impetus for this present riddle was the tradi-

[3]Lewis Carroll, *Alice in Wonderland.*

tional belief in what was called the "Leverite marriage." This was the provision in the Law of Moses (Deut. 25:5–61) for a childless woman to be taken in by her brother-in-law in order to guarantee support and an inheritance. This was also the problem addressed in the story of Ruth. The Sadducees used this well-known provision to trap Jesus. The trap did not work, and the response of Jesus is a sweeping indictment of their being wrong-headed. Jesus gave them a broadside that attacked their position on two levels: (1) their understanding of the Torah was faulty regarding a continuing relationship with God; and (2) their estimate of the power of God was limited. Their prejudice and bias did not allow them to read the Scriptures, other than the Torah, with imagination and creativity. As noted, their position was quite different from that held by the Pharisees. They believed that soul and body perished at death. Their sole authority in these matters was the Torah, and that is precisely where Jesus attacked their wrong-headed position.

I. *Being wrong-headed about a continuing relationship.* The logic used by the Sadducees was limited, because it did not grasp the reality of a continuing relationship with God. A question often posed by the rabbis was, "How is resurrection derived from the Torah?" So Jesus' rebuttal was based on the Torah, where Moses called the Lord "the God of Abraham, Isaac, and Jacob." More important, Jesus argued from a position of life: the God of the Resurrection is a God of life and not death. Jesus would affirm the question of Job: "If a man dies, will he live again?" Significantly, Jesus' answer was not so much an affirmation of Plato as of Job. However, even an argument based on Moses did not influence the Sadducees and their bias. Jesus spoke about a spiritual reality that was integral with his own death, burial, Resurrection, and *parousia.* It was a continuing, life-producing reality—a gift from God.

II. *Being wrong-headed about life.* Jesus also responded to the Sadducees that God is a God of life and living and not a God of the dead. Clearly the Sadducees did not grasp the basics regarding the power of God and eternal life. Jesus insisted that God's power is based on his being. God is eternal love, is faithful to his people, and keeps his covenant. Jesus said, "For in him, all are alive."

Now, such a statement would, of necessity, fly in the face of the Sadducees' wrong-headed position. They were continually posing riddles about the Resurrection, much to the dismay of the Pharisees. One of their riddles was that Resurrection was impossible because it implies that one had come into contact with a corpse, and thus one was ritually unclean. Their stubbornness on the matter of resurrection was in direct conflict with the concluding statement by Jesus: "He is not the God of the dead, but of the living, for in him all are alive." In this statement we find the real basis for the Resurrection. God, as Jesus taught and as established by his victory over death, is a life-giving reality, by the power of the Holy Spirit. The Holy Spirit recapitulates the Resurrected life of Christ in the believer. Such a life is a gift of God to be received by faith, and is available to everyone. Stated simply, resurrection is not immortality, but eternal life through Jesus Christ.—Dave Hunsicker

Illustrations

THE MATTER OF MERIT.   No one can read the Bible with a clear eye—a "single eye"—and proceed to make the Devil a "whipping boy" for his own sin. A Christian profession which ignores ethical values is no *Christian* profession at all. At the same time, the moral life which we live and the moral values we achieve are no occasion for merit-making on our part. They are made secure for us because it is *in Him* we possess them, and not in our own virtue or conceit; it is *His* glory we seek, and not our own.—William Robinson[4]

GROWING AS A CHRISTIAN.   I am sure you have all heard of Stanley Jones, that great missionary to Africa. In his book *The Christ of Every Road* he speaks very personally: "I find myself better or worse as I pray more or less. It works with almost mathematical precision." I have found this to be true in my own life also. Communion with God through prayer and Bible reading is a tremendous source of strength and power.

Basically, the ultimate experience of God is to surrender your cares, your sins, your life, your ego, and say, "Here I am, Lord. Take me

[4] *The Devil and God.*

with all my shortcomings and love me and care for me." And He will surely do so.— Bryan M. Kirkland[5]

SERMON SUGGESTIONS

Topic: The Only Way out of the Dark
TEXT: Ps. 119:105

Why does the Bible, which contains the Word of God, have such vitality, such potency, such explosive power? (1) The Bible is a *God-centered* book. When it is opened, we come immediately face to face with God. (2) The Bible is *man-centered*. It is man in whom God is interested and for whom he gives his Son.—Hugh T. Kerr

Topic: Why Must God's Children Suffer?
TEXT: 2 Cor. 7:10–11

(1) God does not send suffering or pain. (2) But does God not allow suffering? The answer must be yes. (3) Much of the suffering endured by good persons, by Christians as well as sincerely religious persons of other faiths, is mysterious. (4) Suffering is sometimes punitive: "What a man sows, he also reaps." (5) Suffering may be remedied. (6) Suffering can be so accepted that it becomes redemptive.—David A. MacLennon

Hymn Suggestions: Twenty-Second Sunday After Trinity

1. "Come, Thou Long-Expected Jesus," Charles Wesley (1744); "Stuttgart," Witt's *Psalmodia Sacra* (1715)

Although the season of Advent is still a few weeks away, the Haggai passage and the Epistle reading both deal with the coming of Christ and the calamitous events that will precede it. Therefore, a great Advent hymn such as this one by the peerless hymnist, Wesley, is not inappropriate.

2. "Easter People, Raise Your Voices," William M. James (1979); "Regent Square," Henry T. Smart (1874)

Although Easter is far removed from this season, the Gospel reading (Luke 20:27–38) concerns relationships in the resurrected life; therefore, this hymn celebrating that life is suggested. After all, for the Christian every

[5] *A Pattern for Faith.*

Sunday is Easter, as indeed this hymn declares in stanza 3.

3. "I Will Extol You, O My God," *Psalter* (1912); "Noel," Arthur S. Sullivan (1874)

This paraphrase parallels the first verses of Psalm 145 and thus is an appropriate accompaniment to the Psalter reading.

4. "Great Is the Lord," Michael W. Smith and Deborah D. Smith; "Great Is the Lord," Smith and Smith (1982)

This mini-hymn—a paraphrase of Psalm 145:3—could be used as an antiphon interpolated among the various verses of the Psalter reading for this day.—Hugh T. McElrath

Worship Aids

CALL TO WORSHIP.   "Those who hope in the Lord will renew their strength. They will soar on wings like eagles; they will run and not grow weary; they will walk and not be faint" (Isa. 40:32 NIV).

INVOCATION.   Almighty God, heavenly Father, as we confess our weakness, grant us a new vision of what your imparted strength can do in and through us, precisely where we live and serve.

OFFERTORY SENTENCE.   "It is more blessed to give than to receive" (Acts 20:35).

OFFERTORY PRAYER.   Lord, we have found it blessed to receive, even as you have given us salvation and provision for our needs. Now help us to find those other blessings of sharing what we have received.

PRAYER.   Send forth your light, O God, that we may see and know your truth, and that we may by our witness shine that light into the dark places of this world. We often feel that we are engulfed in darkness, even where the name of Christ is known, for the powers of evil are at work everywhere. We pray that your Word and searching judgment may penetrate every aspect of our society, and that your redeeming grace may bring forgiveness and cleansing. Help us to be faithful to you wherever we live and work, and to uphold your standards in all circumstances. Grant a special measure of your mercy to those who struggle with temptations that some of us have never known, and give them strength and patience and faith to survive their difficulties and even be more than conquerors through the One who loves us all and who gave himself for us.

Sermon: Who You Are and What You Do When No One's Looking

TEXT: Luke 21:1–4

Most of try to look our best, be our best, and be on our best behavior when we know that someone is watching us! But what are we like when no one's looking? This story from Luke's gospel reminds us how really important are those issues to God!

I. The Bible repeatedly reminds us that the most important things we do in life are often neither dramatic nor memorable—and certainly not public! In fact, on Judgment Day Jesus will reward a lot of people who can hardly remember the significant things for which they will be honored (Matt. 20:39, 44).

a. One day Jesus was watching people. Quite by accident he noticed something that would have gone completely unnoticed had he not been there. But because he saw it, it became one of the most memorable events of human history. Who hasn't heard—or ever spoken—of the widow's mite?

The world in which Jesus and this widow lived was not so different from our own. For some, religion provided plenty of opportunities to "show off." But for many more—including this widow—faith remained something substantial and full of meaning. They would never allow the shameful behavior of a few to rob them of a faith that sustained them and made a difficult life more bearable!

b. In comparison to the offerings of others, this widow's gift—totaling less than one eighth of one cent in today's currency—was nothing at all! So many had given much more. So why, do you suppose, had she even bothered to give it at all? What motivated her? Do you suppose that anyone would have missed her gift had she kept it for herself? And why, if a person cannot afford to give a substantial gift, should they bother to give anything at all? I think some of you struggle with questions like that—at least once a year, at budget and personal stewardship emphasis time. I want to try to help you find a good and satisfying answer.

II. Jesus drew the contrast between her gift and the others given that day. "All these people gave . . . out of their wealth," he said, "but she out of her poverty put in all she had to live on" (v. 4). The most important difference in what they gave was not the amount but the degree of their response to the generosity of God.

a. No doubt many of them felt that they deserved the blessings of God—the wealth and comfort they enjoyed. After all, they had worked hard for it, and for the most part were "pretty good people." That's a fairly common assumption even today: everything I have is mine, I earned it, and I ought to be able to do with it whatever I want. Yet that assumption is only partially true—and therefore partially a lie.

The truth is in the second half. You can do what you want with what you have. Your time, your strength, your health, your mind, your relationships, your money, your freedom, and your opportunities. You can do with them whatever you want. You can use them or abuse them. You can squander or you can save them. It's entirely up to you. That's the truth.

b. The lie is the front end: the assumption that everything we have is ours, that we earned it and deserve it. Both the Bible and human experience tell us that that is a lie! We brought nothing into this world and we will take nothing from it. Look as hard as you wish: you won't find luggage racks in delivery rooms and you can't hook a U-Haul to a hearse. Everything we have is on loan to us from a gracious, generous God.

The widow knew that. She knew that she had received infinitely more than she ever deserved, and she responded in extravagant gratitude. In spite of the sad and tragic conditions of her life, even in the face of her own cruel poverty, she chose not to protest life's unfairness, but instead to celebrate God's goodness!

III. It's a choice we all make. And it's a debt that hangs over each of our heads—this debt of love. God's grace comes into our time and into our tired, sinful, and broken lives. He doesn't always shape life into our liking, cure all our cancers, transform all our kids into winners, or send us soaring into the upper regions of success and affluence. But his grace always enables us to look life squarely in the face, and in spite of what we may see, he makes us capable of praising and thanking him—if we choose!

a. How can we ever pay it all back—all that God has done for us? The truth is: God doesn't really expect us to pay it all back. It's just that we ought to feel that we owe a debt toward God. Even though we can never pay it back, we are committed to pay on it for as long as we live. It's just one of the ways we choose to express our gratitude!

b. I know—it is a deeply personal matter. And that's also one of the more obvious lessons of this text. What we give should always be confidential, between us and God only. The biblical record clearly indicates that God does not want us to put our giving on public display. There are simply too many dangers inherent in that. There is the danger of pride and a sense of superiority if we are fortunate enough to be able to give a large amount. On the other hand, if our gift is small, there is the danger of shame and a sense of unworthiness.

But that we give is another issue entirely! God clearly expects us all to do that. When we refuse to give at all, we resist his grace and are guilty of the sin of ingratitude and self-sufficiency. It is a sin that the Bible teaches God judges with extreme harshness.

IV. It's time that we become more serious about our giving—about the debt of love each of us owes. It's increasingly difficult for churches to raise money these days. Some sincerely feel that their gifts are so small and insignificant that the church could not possibly benefit from them. The fact is, no one of us could possibly support the total ministry of this church—and God doesn't really expect just a few folks to do so either. Every gift is important toward accomplishing the mission God has given this church in this community and around the world.—Gary C. Redding

Illustrations

THIS LITTLE ACT.   Sending a card to someone who is a bit down and needs a lift—reminding them that you care and are praying for them; visiting a shut-in who is lonely—or taking them for an afternoon drive in the country to see the autumn leaves in full color; placing a crisp twenty-dollar bill in an unmarked envelope—with no note attached, nor any other clue about its origin—and leaving it on a student's windshield or tucked in the inside cover of one of their textbooks; calling someone on the phone to let them know that they have not been forgotten; or, giving a cup of cold water in the name of Jesus—these are the kinds of things we won't even remember doing a few weeks after doing them. Still, the people we do them for are occasionally changed by our acts, and Jesus will never forget them!—G.C.R.

MORE HELP AVAILABLE.   Not long ago, a little boy was trying his best to move a huge rock from its place in the backyard. His father watched for a few minutes before he asked, "Son, are you using all your strength?"

"Yes, sir!" said the boy, with confident exhaustion. "I sure am."

But the father disagreed. "No, you're not, son. You haven't asked me to help you."—G.C.R.

SUNDAY: NOVEMBER FIFTEENTH

LECTIONARY MESSAGE

Topic: Standing Firm: It Is a Matter of Life or Death

TEXT: Luke 21:5–19

Other Readings: Isa. 65:17–25; Isa. 12; 2 Thess. 3:6–13

The entire facade of the Temple was covered with gold plating while the upper parts were pure white, probably marble. It was so brilliant that the reflection from the rising sun caused people to look away, the same as if they had tried to look directly at the sun itself. Recent archeological studies of the Temple Mount retaining wall discovered an area equivalent to approximately thirty-five football fields on which stood the three outer courts and the Temple. No wonder the Jews had such great pride in their Temple and marveled at its outward beauty and adornment.

One day, Jesus and his disciples were at the Temple. The disciples were in awe, especially noting the beauty of the stones, and made mention of this to Jesus. So imagine their shock when Jesus responded that there would come a day when those huge stones, so carefully cut and placed upon one another, would be so utterly torn down that not one would be left upon another (vv. 5–6). The day was coming when the Temple of God was going to be totally destroyed.

Stunned, the disciples wanted to know when this catastrophic event would take place (v. 7). Jesus warned them not to be deceived by the claims of false messiahs, not to be alarmed when they heard reports of wars and revolutions, and to expect natural disasters such as earthquakes and famines (vv. 8–11). But Jesus then stated that before all of these other signs took place, the disciples would first face persecution and they would need to stand firm if they were to gain life (vv. 12–19). Thus, while the text begins by focusing on the Temple and the signs of its coming destruction, it shifts the focus to Jesus' warning of the potential destruction, both physically and spiritually, of the disciples themselves and their need to stand firm.

I.   *The early disciples were called to stand firm* (vv. 12–19). Jesus made it clear that to be one of his disciples was to invite persecution (Matt. 10:17–42). He warned them that they would be arrested and taken before the authorities for questioning. Ironically, this persecution would present the disciples with the opportunity to witness to their persecutors. And most important of all, God would not be far away. God would be there, through his Spirit, giving them the words to say.

Later, Peter and John found themselves in just such a position. Arrested and forced to stand before the Sanhedrin to answer questions, Peter and John served as witnesses to the power of Jesus and proclaimed that he was indeed the Messiah, crucified yet raised from the dead (Acts 4). When commanded to stop speaking of Jesus and to forsake their faith in him, they spoke defiantly, "Judge for yourselves whether it is right in God's sight to obey you rather than God. For we cannot help speaking about what we have seen and heard" (Acts 4:19–20; see also 5–7, 13–14, 16–28).

II.   *Contemporary disciples are still called to stand firm.* The apostle Paul wrote to Timothy saying, "In fact, everyone who wants to live a godly life in Christ Jesus will be persecuted" (2 Tim. 3:12). What was true in Paul's day still holds true today. Contemporary disciples will face various kinds of persecution if they seek to live a godly life.

For example, sometimes new converts can alienate family and friends because of changes in their attitudes and behavior. They may try to witness to family members who don't want to hear, or they may lose friends because they no longer want to party with drugs or alcohol. Christians who take unpopular social stances are often ridiculed, held up for public contempt, and sometimes assaulted or killed.

In the face of persecution, we are still called to stand firm. Why? Because it is a matter of life or death.

III.   *It is a matter of life or death.* Ironically, in the same breath that Jesus warned his disciples of persecution even to the point of death, he also promised that not even a hair on their head would perish and that if they stood firm they would "gain life" (vv. 16–19). But how can that be? Was he promising us all good hair days or did he mean something else?

Stephen stood firm and was stoned to death (which definitely resulted in a bad hair day). And what about James, whom King Herod killed by the sword (Acts 12:2)? In fact, Church tradition has it that nearly all of the original twelve apostles were violently killed by enemies of the faith.

So, is there a contradiction here? No, not at all. For Jesus, in another text, clearly taught that some would die by persecution but that wasn't all there was to death. The disciples were *not* to fear those who could *only* kill the body but not the soul. Instead, Jesus told them to fear God, who could destroy both the body and the soul in hell (Luke 12:4–5). He then reassured them that God cared for them. They were not to be afraid, for if they acknowledged Jesus before their persecutors, Jesus would acknowledge them as his faithful followers and they would have eternal life. In other words, they would "gain life." But (and this is a huge conditional statement), if they disowned (renounced, denounced, denied) Jesus to their persecutors, then, though they might save their physical bodies from death, Jesus would disown them as his disciples and they would die spiritually (Luke 12:8–9; John 12:25). It will be as Jesus said: "Whoever finds his life will lose it, and whoever loses his life for my sake will find it" (Matt. 10:39).

Standing firm really is a matter of life or death—yours!—Michael M. Jones

Illustrations

PERSECUTION TODAY. A total of five Christians were executed by crucifixion from July through September 1994 in Sudan. One was an Anglican priest and two were believers from Akon. The persecutors used six-inch nails to crucify the Christians. "There is no clear reason, except that they are Christians," the Sudanese Anglican bishop Daniel Zindo said. "The government is persecuting those who are Christian leaders, because they want the people to all become Muslims."—M.M.J.[6]

IT MAY COME TO THIS, AT LEAST. I made a public confession of Christ and was baptized when I was nineteen years old. At the time, I had a good friend named Ricky. We were both students and worked as cooks in a restaurant. Before my conversion, we use to tell dirty jokes. Not long after coming to Christ I realized that Jesus wouldn't do that, nor would he take pleasure in such jokes, so I decided I wouldn't either. After a while, the jokes just weren't funny anymore. One day, frustrated and confused with my change in behavior, Ricky lashed out, "What's wrong with you Mike? You're no fun anymore!" I had tried to share my faith and explain why I felt differently about things, but Ricky wasn't interested. Because I no longer laughed at dirty jokes, I had somehow, in Ricky's eyes, become a religious fanatic. Unfortunately, our friendship steadily declined after that.—M.J.J.

SERMON SUGGESTIONS

Topic: Pageantry of the Woods
TEXT: Isa. 64:6

Most persons preaching from this text find in it only a vein of sadness. I find that I have two strings to this gospel harp: a string of sadness and a string of joy infinite. We all do

fade as a leaf. (1) Like the foliage, we fade gradually. (2) Like the leaf we fade; it makes room for others. (3) As with the leaves, we fade amid myriads of others. (4) As the leaves depart with a variety of appearance, so do we. (5) As the leaves fade and fall only to rise, so do we. All this golden shower of the woods is making the ground richer, and in the juice and sap and life of the tree the leaves will come again.—T. DeWitt Talmage

Topic: Beyond Death—Are You Curious?
TEXT: Job 14:4; John 14:2

The thought of immortality first arises in the Bible as a wistful question, a question that is echoed in every society on earth and in every age right to the present. How do we find our way among all the competing voices that offer directions about life after death? Some guidelines: (1) We should beware of those who claim to know too much. (2) We waste our time asking how. (3) Our convictions about the reality of life after death come to us, and grow in us, as we relate to our God here and now.—David H. C. Read

Hymn Suggestions: Twenty-Third Sunday After Trinity

1. "O for a Thousand Tongues to Sing," Charles Wesley (1739); "Azmon," Carl G. Glaser, arranged by Lowell Mason (1839)

This grand hymn by the sweet singer of Methodism reflects the spirit of the song of praise quoted by the prophet Isaiah (especially 12:4) and could well be sung as a response to the reading of that Scripture.

2. "Lord Christ, When First Thou Camest to Earth," Walter Bowie, (1928); "Mit Freuden Zart," Bohemian Brethren *Kirchengesänge* (1561)

A twentieth-century hymn of cruel contemporaneity, this prayer of penitence in the face of the fearful signs of the end of the age described in the Gospel lesson (especially Luke 21:6) would make an appropriate response to the gospel reading.

3. "Awake, My Soul, and with the Sun," Thomas Ken (1695); "Morning Hymn," Francois H. Barthêlêmon (1785)

Ken's morning prayer suitably reflects the exhortations against idleness made by the apostle Paul in the reading from 2 Thessalonians.

---

[6]*Word & Way*, Missouri Southern Baptist State paper, Sept. 22, 1994, p. 12.

4. "Surely It Is God Who Saves Me," Carl P. Daw Jr. (1982); "Lord, Revive Us," early American tune, harmony by Dale Grotenhuis (1985)

This modern paraphrase of Isaiah 12 could well be sung in the place of the reading. Its American folk tune could easily be sung in antiphonal fashion.—Hugh T. McElrath

Worship Aids

CALL TO WORSHIP.   "Blessed are they that do his commandments, that they may have right to the tree of light, and may enter it through the gates into the city" (Rev. 22:14).

INVOCATION.   Embolden us, O God, for the doing of your holy will in a world where evil often seems to have the upper hand in our personal lives and in the world at large. May what we do here today open our minds and hearts and hands to what you would have us do in our everyday living.

OFFERTORY SENTENCE.   "Don't get tired of helping others. You will be rewarded when the time is right, if you don't give up" (Gal. 6:9 CEV).

OFFERTORY PRAYER.   Lord, we confess that we like to be thanked and appreciated for the right things that we do, but we pray that you will help us to see that the greatest reward comes when lives are changed, families strengthened, and our world made better. To that end, grant us a willingness and strength to continue in the good stewardship of our opportunities, to share our material possessions and whatever else would make this a better world.

PRAYER.   O Lord, our Lord, Majestic God, indeed how lovely is thy dwelling place. Surely you have dwelt among us in this glorious and extended autumn season. Each day is an added and unexpected treasure of beauty and wonder. We give you thanks. Surely this sacred space of worship is your dwelling place, too. Our hearts and lives, our worship and praise, know it is true. You share presence with us here, and we are graced and made glad and whole again. O God of dwelling presence, we give you thanks.

As we worship this hour, embracing God,

hold us close to you and nearer to each other. Help us to be comfortable with our self and willing to receive your love and care, your forgiveness and hope. In trembling wonder, we lift to you our brokenness.

God, who touches earth with beauty, make us lovely by dwelling within us. We live in an unlovely world, not because of your touches but rather because of our ugliness and harm. As a country we have turned anger and meanness into an art form. We glory in our ability to put down, to humiliate one another—sadly, often in your name. O God, O God, forgive us and redeem us.

Today we pray for those caught in the crossfire of hard business deals, of buyouts and takeovers. We pray for those suddenly without job or security or hope. Generous and giving God, on this day, as we contemplate our generosity and giving, help us to look to you and the cross for a model, and not just to our sister or brother in Christ. And most of all, O Christ in God, clear our hearts and our minds to ponder hard the treasure of our life. And more and more may it be the Christ in whom we pray.—William M. Johnson

Sermon: Here's Mud in Your Eye
TEXT: Ps. 23; John 9:1–41
In the New Testament lesson for this morning, Jesus heals a man who was born blind. The text says that he took some dirt, spat on it, and thus made mud, or clay. Then he spread it on the man's eyes. I wonder if Jesus then said, "Here's mud in your eye."

Jesus walks down a road, sees a man blind from birth. He heals the man, and then goes away. This story is about a man who has to explain what has happened to him. His listeners can't see Jesus. Jesus isn't here anymore. All they can see is the man. He has to explain what happened to him.

He is harassed by his neighbors, who aren't sure they like this changed person. They turn him over to the authorities, who question him and challenge his story. The authorities call in his parents. They wash their hands of him, saying, "He's an adult, talk to him. We don't have responsibility for him anymore."

They bring the poor guy back again to the authorities for more interrogation. This time they tell him that if it was Jesus who healed him, they know that Jesus is a sinner. Besides that, they now have evidence that this healing took place on the Sabbath. Therefore, the healing itself is in violation of the law.

The story ends with Jesus returning, which is what we believe he will do. He will return, claim his Kingdom, come in glory. It concludes with a parting salvo over the bow of the Pharisees: "You are really the blind people in this world."

I. You can expect three things, according to this story.

a. First, your friends won't recognize you. You will be different. You'll look the same, as ugly as ever, but you won't act the same. They don't know quite what it is that has come over you. They can't quite put their finger on it, but they know it is something. Something must be wrong with you.

b. The authorities, those who have power in this world, will suspect something sinister has happened to you because you don't conform anymore to their image of what a religious person should look like. So you must be lying, or else possessed by demonic forces of some kind. So they question your family. What's come over her? We don't know. She has just changed. We are not responsible for her. Go talk to her.

c. Then the verdict comes. Given the evidence, this couldn't be of God. Then comes the man's wonderful response, "All I know is that once I was blind, but now I see."

So the first lesson from the story told to John's audience, and to us, is don't believe those preachers who say if you become a Christian that your life will all of a sudden be a wonderful success and you will have no more sorrow, worry, or pain. The fact is, it may get worse.

II. But there is a more powerful lesson in this story. It is the definition of a Christian. That is really what this story is all about. It says a Christian is a person who once was blind but now can see.

a. The Gospel of John uses darkness as a metaphor for the human condition. He begins his gospel by announcing the birth of Jesus in this way: the light has come into the darkness of this world, and the darkness has not been able to overcome it. It is in John's Gospel that Jesus says in several places, including this text, "I am the light of the world." In John's Gospel, and in the other gospels, Jesus heals people who cannot see. It

happens so often that there must be something more here than just reporting a miracle. This is what it means: to be Christian is to have your eyes opened.

b. Look more closely to what happened to the man. John loves to see symbols, and there are wonderful symbols in this story. Jesus takes a handful of dirt, he spits on it, and he makes clay. The last time that happened in the Bible was in the book of Genesis, when God created human beings. So what we are witnessing here is a new creation, a salvation, a person being reborn.

c. And look at this. He places the mud on the man's eyes, then sends him to the pool at Siloam. He tells him, "Go, wash in the water." Everyone in the Church in the first or second century listening to this story would think immediately, "baptism!" It is like he is baptized. Listen to John's description: he went and washed, he came back and he could see.

III. Someone has made a study of genius and written a book about it. He studied a thousand or more geniuses to see if there were common threads in their stories. I was happy to discover in reading a review of that book that having a high IQ is not necessarily a requirement for being a genius.

a. There are evidently two characteristics of genius, two common threads that he was able to find. The first is *imagination*. Imagination is the ability to make mental images. Scientists call them *paradigms*. A paradigm will change the way we see the world. Poets call them *metaphors*. You know what the Bible calls them? *Parables*. Jesus taught with parables. That is how Jesus opened eyes, with parables. The purpose of his teaching was to enable us to see the world in a new way. He took the stuff, the data, the information of everyday life, what was common to everyone, and with imagination, saw it in a way that would open our eyes to see a new way of living in this world.

b. The second characteristic of genius is *childlikeness*. The author says that geniuses are childlike in what they do—which means they never lose their childlike wonder. Which is why Jesus said, "Unless you become like a child, you will never see the Kingdom of God." Unless you can ask, Why are things this way? Why can't they be different? you are trapped right where you are.

c. *Imagination and wonder.* That is what

characterizes genius, and the Christian life. Geniuses change the world. I mean radically change the world. They change history. They can take the same data, the information, the colors, the notes, the words everyone else works with, and create something new, and surprising, and breathtakingly beautiful.

IV. We have been working our way through the Gospel of John. We find ourselves repeatedly going back to the story of Nicodemus and that phrase, The spirit blows where it wills, and you hear the sound of it but you do not know where it comes from, nor do you know where it is going. So it is with everyone born of the Spirit.

That is exactly consistent with what geniuses say happened at that moment of creation. They confess that is what happened to them. Oh, they did some work, some of them did research for years, but one day, by accident, or serendipity, or in a dream even, everything just fell into place, and they could see what they couldn't see before. They can't explain it. It just happened. It is like, once they were blind but now they see.—Mark Trotter

Illustrations

JESUS AND OUR SEEING.   Joyce Cary, who wrote *The Horse's Mouth*, has a character in that book say of Matisse, the artist, "He peeled my eyes."[7] The story of the healing of the blind man will do the same thing for you. It is not only a story of how Jesus opened a man's eyes; it is also there so Jesus can open your eyes.—M.T.

LIFE FOR A REAL CHRISTIAN.   It was Teresa of Avila who prayed, "O Lord Jesus, if this is the way you treat your friends, it is no wonder you have so few of them." That is the first lesson communicated by this story: your life isn't necessarily going to get easier when you become a Christian.—M.T.

SUNDAY: NOVEMBER TWENTY-SECOND

LECTIONARY MESSAGE

Topic: Christ the King Crucified
  TEXT: Luke 23:33–43
  Other Readings: Jer. 23:1–6; Luke 1:68–79; Col. 1:11–20
  "Two others," "they," "people," "the rulers," "the soldiers," "the Jews." These words paint a distressful picture—Jesus was not alone when he was crucified. In fact, he was surrounded by onlookers, bystanders, role players, and directors. Still, Christ died for each one of them, as well as for you and me. In fact, he was crucified for the sins of all mankind—past, present, and future.

Where were you? Where were you when Christ, your redeemer, your Savior, was crucified? Were you . . .

I. *In front of him?* It's in front of the Savior that we find the prevailing people and the reigning rulers. People watched Jesus' every move, scrutinized his every breath, and continually canvassed the heavens in defiant expectation of Elijah—another savior (Matt. 27:49). People percolated with false self-righteousness, misguided innocence, and the self-appointed title "protectors of the faith." Peo-

ple sneered scornful expressions of anger and contempt while ridiculing his divine call.

Those standing in front of the crucified Christ today are no different. They watch him move in and out of their communities; they challenge his claims and his witnesses. They misunderstand his offer of salvation, and often look for others ways to accomplish what only he can give. They are filled with pride and false innocence, and remain indifferent to the Church. Were you standing in front of Christ when he was crucified? Are you right now? Perhaps you were . . .

II. *Behind him?* It's behind our dear Jesus that the soldiers stood. Mocking and taunting the Savior, they inflicted painful blows, spoke cruel commonalties and repugnant antagonisms, and displayed distasteful sensibilities. From behind the Savior, out of the sight of almost everyone else, they carried on the dastardly deed of dividing his garments and gambling for his belongings (Mark 15:24b, John 19:24). And it was from behind the crucified Son of God that these men

---

[7] *The Horse's Mouth.*

"came up" to make an offering—not a self-giving, sacrificial offering, but the foul offering of discontent and wine vinegar.

Out of the sight of others, in a low voice and under a growing cloud of darkness, many today stand behind the crucified Lord. Their actions appear socially acceptable, routine and commonplace, but are all the while morally damaging as well. Were you behind Jesus that day he was crucified? No! Then maybe you were . . .

III. *Beside him*—to his right or to his left? "By his side" and "my right-hand man" are endearing terms of status and allegiance reserved for loyal followers and privileged aides. And while one might think that such a place—at the side of Jesus—would be an ideal place to be, such is not necessarily the case.

On one side of the Savior hung a blasphemer—a desperate, despicable example of a man whose only true commonality with our dear Lord Jesus was the fact that he too was dying on a cool, dry, wooden cross. In agonizing pain, moments from his own death, the blasphemer was understandably desperate to be removed from the torment of such a cruel death. In anger he hurled insults intended to win his release. Unfortunately, seldom does anger improve our situation—even when the reason for it is clear.

On the other side of Jesus there was another criminal—a common thief, a local renegade, a social degenerate, a man who, according to Matthew (27:44), was not totally innocent himself. Convicted and sentenced to death like the blasphemer, the man on the other side of Jesus had lived the same sinful life as his counterpart. But at the critical moment, this criminal rose above his life of illegality and looked to Jesus in repentance, for forgiveness, and with confession on his lips. He received all that he asked for and more—including the promise of paradise!—a promise received by all who profess Jesus as Lord.

The promise of paradise is only one way of knowing where you were when Christ was crucified. Another is by knowing where you were not—for only Jesus was . . .

IV. *In the middle!* The middle is not a place for us carnal, sinful humans. Many may claim to stand in front of the Savior; some may hide themselves behind the Lord; multitudes may stand on the side of the angry, blasphe-

mous criminal; countless others may in fact stand with the repentant, redeemed, and promised one. But only Jesus stands in the middle! That position, the middle position, is reserved for he who is the King of Kings and Lord of Lords, the suffering one, the sacrificial lamb, the mighty one, the begotten one, the great judge, the Emmanuel—the God with us. For only he is God!

The sign above Jesus' head acknowledged his place in the middle. The marks on his back paid the price for him to be there. The nails in his hands and feet secured him there. And those around the cross, those like you and me, mandated his being there. Yes, Jesus is the only one who could and the only one since who has stood on the high, middle ground; and he remains symbolically there today—symbolically because the cross of Calvary is now empty but Jesus remains in the middle of our life of contradictions.

When your walk contradicts your talk and when your presence in church contradicts your presence on the golf course, Jesus is in the middle to listen and to hear. When your lifestyle contradicts what you can afford, when your wedding vows contradict your desires, and when your prayer time contradicts your sleep time, Jesus is in the middle to forgive. When your faith is contradicted by your doubts, when your security is contradicted by your fears, and when who you are in public is a contradiction of who you are at home, Jesus is in the middle still, to promise, to save, and to give eternal life.

Where were you on that bloodstained day when Jesus the Christ was crucified? Dear friend, you were where you've always been—in need of his grace, his love, and his forgiveness.—Charles J. Williams Jr.

Illustrations

ON HIS MIND.   Several years ago the Florida Boys answered the question of where believers were when Jesus was crucified with their pop song, "When He Was on the Cross, I Was on His Mind." Indeed, as a just and loving God, Jesus died for all people regardless of the year, the circumstances, or the situation.—C.J.W.Jr.

AS CHRIST PARDONS.   Alexander H. Stephens served as vice president of the Confederacy. Unfortunately, he was crippled and died shortly after becoming governor of Georgia. When it became known that he was soon to die and the physicians had no hope of prolonging his life, many great men of state crowded his bedroom and besought him to sign many important documents.

Stephens, however, waved each away and called for his private secretary—telling him to bring out of his desk an old, faded paper. The secretary found it. It was the petition of an old humble woman back in the hills seeking the pardon of her sinful son in the penitentiary.

With the great state officials begging Stephens to lay the petition aside and take up weightier matters, he replied: "No! I am going to sign this. The great matters of state will take care of themselves."

Propped on his pillow, Governor Stephens took the yellow, faded appeal of the heartbroken mother who had no other intercessor at the governor's mansion. He dipped his pen in ink, and across the appeal he wrote "P-A-R-D-O-N-E-D." Underneath he scrawled his name, "Alexander H. Stephens, Governor." Then he dropped back upon his pillow—dead.—Robert G. Lee[8]

SERMON SUGGESTIONS

Topic: The Whereabouts of God

TEXT: Ps. 139:7–12

The question of God is an ever-present one. Where is God in this life of ours? (1) God is everywhere—present in the restraint of evil, present in active goodness. (2) God is a personal presence.—Peter H. Pleune

Topic: First Sunday in Advent

TEXT: Eph. 4:13

If a stranger were to come today into our service and watch it as it moves along from step to step, one thing would become evident to him in it all. He would see that we were beginning something. (1) The *Advent*—Jesus came into a world that had been prepared for him. (2) The *Nativity*—a visible fact with all its possibilities. (3) The *Epiphany*—which celebrates the manifestation of Christ to those entirely outside his life and all its asso-

ciations. (4) *Lent*—with its preparation for and culmination in *Good Friday,* opening suddenly into the glorious light of *Easter Day.* (5) *Whitsunday*—the day of the giving of the Holy Spirit.—Phillips Brooks

Hymn Suggestions: Feast of Christ the King— The Sunday Before Advent

1. "Blessed Be the God of Israel," James Quinn (1982); "Forest Green," English folk song arranged by Ralph Vaughan Williams (1903)

The Song of Zechariah—one of the Evangelical Canticles in Luke—has been metricized numerous times, but never more skillfully than by contemporary Scottish clergyman James Quinn. This sung version could well be used in place of the reading of the *Benedictus Dominus Deus Israel* (Luke 1:68–79).

2. "Prepare the Way," Frans M. Franzen (1819), adapted by Charles P. Price (1982); "Bereden Väg För Herran," *Then Swenska Psalmboken* (1697)

This newly adapted old Swedish hymn captures the spirit of Zechariah's song in its anticipation of the coming of the King who will rule in peace and freedom. It could be used as a response to the reading in Luke.

3. "Rejoice, the Lord Is King," Charles Wesley (1746); "Darwall's 148th," John Darwall (1770)

This great Wesleyan hymn exalts Christ, the Lord and King, who comes to rule in righteousness. It could be a natural accompaniment to the Epistle reading in Colossians.

4. "He Is King of Kings," African American spiritual, arranged by J. T. Jones (1961); "He Is King," adapted by Melva W. Costen (1989)

This spiritual would be quite suitable on this Christ the King Sunday, to be sung in the call-and-response manner so typical of this genre's performance practice.—Hugh T. McElrath

Worship Aids

CALL TO WORSHIP.   "Lord God Almighty, true and righteous are thy judgments" (Rev. 16:7b).

INVOCATION.   We trust your true and righteous judgments, O God, even when we

[8]*Sermonic Library.*

do not understand your ways. Grant that we may never fail to see the cross of our Lord Jesus Christ or our own cross except in the light of the Resurrection.

OFFERTORY SENTENCE.   "How gladly will I offer you sacrifice, and praise your name, for it is good" (Ps. 54:6 JB).

OFFERTORY PRAYER.   O Lord, let our tithes and offerings be one more way of praising you for your many-splendored goodness, and may what we do be worthy of your glorious name.

PRAYER.   Almighty and ever-living God, who hast called us to labor, but not outside the area of thy love; who hast laid upon us the obligations and duties of life, but not without the help of thy Holy Spirit—we gather together to praise thy Name. We thank thee for the way thou dost give a lift to life, for the strength thou dost impart when we recognize our own weakness, for thy heartening presence that dispels the tragedy of loneliness.

In this Thanksgiving season especially, we would count our blessings, for they come from thee. All that is good in life came from thy hand, and from thee we receive nothing that is not good. Let us not take for granted the good things that we enjoy. Rather, let us lift our prayer of thanksgiving lest we forget from whom all blessings flow. Beyond all other blessings, we rejoice in thyself and thy character of outgoing love and the goodness and overflowing mercy offered to us in the great salvation through Jesus Christ. We take joy in him who gathers together all the threads of our life's experience and weaves them into one glowing pattern wherein we can read of faith and hope and love and joy and victory. We thank thee for his living presence, for the call to serve him, for the happiness we have when we give ourselves in loyalty to our Savior. Thou who hast touched life with glowing meaning, thou who hast given to every dark experience an aspect of brightness, wilt thou teach us to look upon the Godward side of life and in all things see thy character and thy gracious purpose? So may our hearts perpetually be giving thanks to thee, as we truly understand how all things work together for good if we love thee.

Wilt thou this day bless all who have particular needs? Wilt thou grant thy grace to fulfill all that is good in our life and to chastise and correct and redeem all that is wrong? Grant that our constant prayer may be that thy will may be done in our lives. May our best thanksgiving be the kind of life that we live in loyalty to thee.

Wilt thou bless thy Church? Grant to it thy peace and thy power. Give to it the spirit of enterprise and venture in the name of Christ, and may it move out into the places of human need to bring the healing gospel of our Savior. We lift this prayer in humble faith and quiet confidence, knowing that all the good thoughts of our hearts are met and answered before we give them expression. We pray in the name of Christ.—Lowell M. Atkinson

Sermon: The Cross and the Face of God

Text: Ps. 40:1–3, 16–17; Phil. 2:5–11

One of the most powerful passages in the New Testament on the incarnation and death of Jesus Christ is found in Paul's letter to the Philippians, chapter two, verses 5 through 11. Without hesitation I would state that this passage is one of Paul's deepest theological insights. Some of his most profound thinking is reflected here, along with lofty eloquence. But this passage has also been a storm center of theological debate. As scholars have struggled with this difficult passage, controversy has surrounded them almost every time.

I. As we begin to examine the magnificent message found in this hymn, note that Paul first of all focuses on the divine nature of Christ—"Who being in the form of God," Paul stated, "thought it not robbery to be equal with God" (2:6).

a. The Greek language usually has several words to express one idea, while English usually has only one word. There are at least two words for *form* in Greek. One of these words means "appearance" or "shape." The other word means "what it really is in its essence." When I was born, I had a certain personality that was uniquely my own. This inner essence constitutes who I really am. As I grew, I changed from a baby to a young boy, from a teenager to a man, and have continued to change outwardly each year. But the essence of who I really am as a person remains the same. The word *form* that Paul used here about Jesus focuses on his inner essence.

b. In a special way Paul is saying that Christ shared in the essential quality of God's divinity. In his essence he was in the "form of God." I am not sure exactly what that means or how it is possible. There are several other places in Paul's Epistles, in other New Testament writings, and especially in the prologue to the Gospel of John where there are references to the preexistence of Christ (Col. 1:15; 2 Cor. 8:9; Heb. 1:1–4). "In the beginning was the Word and the Word was with God, and the Word was God" (John 1:1).

II. But notice also that Paul spoke about the humanity of Christ. He said Christ emptied himself. The Greek word for *emptied* refers to pouring something out of a container.

a. Scholars have wrestled with the self-emptying (*henosis*) of Christ, but the mystery has remained. I don't know how to explain the Incarnation, and it is not clear to me exactly what Paul is saying in this passage. But one thing is certain: Paul is focusing on the sacrificial nature of what God has done for us by identifying with us in human form.

b. Christ's self-emptying is revealed in his taking the form of a servant. Paul may have had in mind here the vision from Isaiah 53 in which the suffering servant takes upon himself our stripes and iniquities, and through his sacrifice we are healed. Christ became a bond slave. He was obedient unto death, even death on the cross. To be crucified on a cross was regarded as a great disgrace. No Roman citizen could be crucified on a cross and suffer that kind of indignity. It was against the law. It was criminals, slaves, and outcasts—the rejects of society—who were put to death on the cross. To die on a cross was the worst kind of disgrace a person could receive in ancient Biblical times.

c. God in Jesus Christ came to identify with us. He became a man and lived out his life within the limits of human frailty. Paul didn't say Christ pretended to be a man. Rather, he said that he emptied himself of divine glory and took on human flesh. As John wrote, "The word became flesh and dwelt among us" (John 1:14).

III. Paul stated further that Christ became the Exalted Servant. Paradoxically, Paul reminds us that the last has become the first.

The one who was the servant has become Lord.

a. Paul also indicated that Christ would have a name that is above every other name. Often in the Old Testament account of men's encounters with God, a man's name was sometimes changed because of that meeting. For example, Abram's name was changed to Abraham, and Jacob's name was changed to Israel. Jesus himself said that he would give us (Christians) a new name (Rev. 2:17).

b. Christ's new name was Lord. In ancient times, *lord* was a common title that might refer to a master, owner, political leader, emperor, or ruler, or to the Hebrew word for *Jehovah*. This means that Jesus Christ is Master, Owner, Ruler, Lord of Lords, and King of Kings. A person who is baptized in the name of Jesus Christ indicates by that act that he has pledged his oath to Christ and has promised to follow him as Master.

c. The hymn concludes with the universal appeal of the exalted Christ. All persons will fall down in worship before him. "Every knee," Paul said, "shall bow before him in heaven and earth, and under the earth. And every tongue shall confess that Jesus Christ is Lord, to the glory of God the Father" (2:10–11).

IV. To me, the most remarkable feature about this particular passage is the reason Paul wrote it in the first place. When Paul quoted or composed this hymn, he was not concerned with abstract theological treaties about God. This hymn was written to be directed toward a particular problem in the Philippian church. Their problem was disunity. The Philippian church was in turmoil because for some reason or another it was divided.

a. In the first part of the second chapter, Paul urged the members of the Philippian church to unify and stop their divisiveness. He challenged them to end their discord. He charged them to put aside all selfish ambition, the seeking of personal prominence, and all attempts at self-gratification. Their desire for pompous, self-serving, conceited ends divided the church. Paul's answer to this divisiveness was the example of the humility and sacrifice of Christ.

b. Paul was convinced that no Christian could be selfishly concerned about his or her rights, ways, interests, goals, or ambitions. As Christians we, like our Lord, have been called to be servants. Our primary concern should not be What can I get out of religion? but What can I give in ministry? Christianity is not a summons to sit around and admire the cross of Christ. The cross is a way of life—the path of sacrificial living.

IV. It is easy to reach low goals. What is your spiritual standard? The One who emptied himself, became incarnate, and died on the cross is our standard for love. His standard summons us to sacrificial love. His example calls us also to serve. "The greatest of all," Jesus said, "is the servant of all. I came not to be served but to serve." In his letter, Paul set the example of Christ in front of the Philippian church as the most powerful reason for ending their division. "Let Christ's mind be in you," Paul said.—William Powell Tuck

Illustrations

TRUE FELLOWSHIP.   Several years ago, in Milwaukee, a young man named Manuel Garcia had to undergo chemotherapy treatments for cancer. Like others who have had this treatment, his hair began to fall out in patches. His head was then shaved, and then he became very concerned about his appearance. His brother, Julio, recognizing Manuel's concern, shaved his own head. Julio enlisted fifty relatives, friends, and neighbors to do the same thing. Later, when visitors went to Manuel's hospital room, it looked like a bald-headed man's convention. This was one way Manuel's relatives and friends had to identify with him in his suffering and feelings of isolation.—W.P.T.

FITTING HUMILITY.   Years ago I visited Copenhagen and had the privilege of seeing some of the sculptures of the famous artist Thorwaldsen. One of his most noted statues is a figure of Christ who is standing with his head bent down so you cannot see into his face. When Thorwaldsen first finished this statue, Christ was erect, but the heat from the sun affected the newly shaped wax figure and caused the head of Christ to lean forward. The only way a person can look directly into the face of Christ is on bended knees before the statue. But isn't that the way we should always come before Christ? We must bow before the One we acknowledge as Lord of Lords.—W.P.T.

SUNDAY: NOVEMBER TWENTY-NINTH

LECTIONARY MESSAGE

Topic: Ready or Not, Here I Come!
TEXT: Matt. 24:36–44
Other Readings: Isa. 2:1–5; Ps. 122; Rom. 13:11–14

I can still remember, as a boy, playing hide-and-seek late into summer evenings. My brother, Rick, and I would get all of the neighborhood kids to play, sometimes numbering ten or more! We would hide just about anywhere we could squeeze, jam, or camouflage our bodies, including behind bushes, under cars, or high up in trees.

Now, imagine you are playing hide-and-seek with your friends one day. You've found a great hiding place behind some thick bushes in the backyard of a house. But the house is three down from the front yard where the base is located, and that means you can't actually see the base, hear the person counting, or know when that person has started to look for you. But the boy who is "it" never seems to finish counting and start looking.

So you just sit tight, knowing you have a great hiding place. It's an always-dreamed-of kind of hiding place—a "you'll never find me in a thousand years" kind of place. At first you feel great pride in not yet being discovered. But after a few minutes the feeling of pride starts to give way to curiosity (Why haven't I seen or heard him yet?). After a few more minutes, you start to get impatient (Where is he anyway?) and then anxious (Maybe he couldn't find me so he quit without telling me). Then, after what seems like an hour, what started out as pride has now turned to boredom. Finally, you just forget about the whole thing. After all, your favorite TV show is coming on and you don't want to miss it. So you come out of your hiding place and just go home.

Well, in a way, this lectionary text describes a kind of "cosmic" hide-and-seek game, only with a twist. For Jesus, you see, was about to leave his disciples, but he wanted them to know that he would return and they needed to be ready and waiting when he came back. He also told them that though he would come back, even he didn't know when; only God did.

So they waited and waited but he never came. They got married, had children, and eventually died. The children took their parents' place and waited for Jesus to return, but again they died before he came back. And so it has gone for generation after generation. Christians have been born into this world, lived their lives, waited and waited for his return, and died. And no Jesus. The game has gone on for centuries, with new players taking the place of the older ones. Waiting, wondering, and sometimes getting bored.

And honestly, isn't that where you and I find ourselves? Part of a "waiting game" that has gone on for nearly two thousand years? We are just waiting to hear those fateful words shouted from a heavenly home base, "Ready or not, here I come!"

I. *One, two, three, . . .* (v. 36). Jesus clearly told the disciples that no one knew the time of his return, not even him. Only God knew, and God wasn't telling. Many have predicted his coming, many have pointed to his imminent return, but all have been wrong. No doubt as this millennium rapidly draws to a close and another is born, there will be those who will confidently proclaim that Jesus will return on such-and-such a day or during this month or that year. But pay no attention to them. If Jesus didn't know when he would return, then surely they don't either.

Jesus, as it were, is still standing at home base counting. Only he doesn't stop at one hundred or five hundred or even one thousand! You see, Jesus can't come back until the Father says he can; so he just keeps counting. 1, 2, 3 . . . 153, 154 . . . 589, 590 . . . 1,212, 1,213, 1,214 . . . 10,998 . . . 182,280 . . . 2,945,153. . . .

II. *Ready or not, here I come* (vv. 37–44). In spite of the fact that Jesus didn't know the time of his return, he was very adamant: he would return. So he warned his disciples to "keep watch" and "be ready" so that when it happened it wouldn't catch them off guard and unprepared, as did the flood in Noah's day or as a thief might the unsuspecting home owner (see 1 Thess. 5:1–6).

In light of the extreme length of this cos-mic game, we modern-day disciples need to hear again Jesus' warning so we can be prepared, stand ready, and live expectantly. We need to guard against becoming so caught up in living out our lives (such as educational and career pursuits, marriage and family, recreation, and so on) that we forget about his return and thus let down our spiritual guard. Neither should we allow the seeming delay of Jesus' return cause us to become impatient, discouraged, or bored. Instead, we need to live lives that include an awareness of his coming.

Remember, Jesus will return, but it will be on God's time table, not ours (1 Pet. 3:8–9). This race of ours, after all, will not go to the swiftest but to the ones who stand firm and finish. There will come a day when we will all hear those fateful words, "Ready or not, here I come." Will you be ready, or have you already given up, quit the game, and gone home?—Michael M. Jones

Illustrations

A SURPRISING QUESTION.   Jürgen Molt-mann tells a story from the Talmud of a rabbi who was considering what questions a Jew would probably have to answer at the Last Judgment. What would the Universal Judge ask? First the rabbi thought of the obvious things: Were you honest in business? Did you seek wisdom? Did you keep the commandments? and so on. Finally a question came into his mind which surprised the rabbi himself. It was the question about the Messiah: Is that not the question Christians will be asked? Says Moltmann: "Did you hope for me? Did you keep hoping even when you nearly gave up? Did you endure to the end?"—Joan Delaplane, O.P.[9]

SOMETHING TO COUNT ON.   Dr. George Buttrick told about a man who was converted when he considered the miracle of gravity—that we are able to live on this planet and not be flung off into space. This man came to realize that there is something solid, reliable, and predictable that we can depend on, that there is *someone* out there, in there, down

[9] *The Living Pulpit.*

there, up there, everywhere that we can depend on. What he saw in nature was a sign pointing beyond nature itself to God. And that is precisely what John indicated was the purpose of the miracles of Jesus: they were signs. And John stated as the purpose of his Gospel: "That you may come to believe that Jesus is the Messiah, the Son of God, and that through believing you may have life in his name."—James W. Cox[10]

SERMON SUGGESTIONS

Topic: The Dimensions of the Christian Life
TEXT: Ps. 31:8

(1) Personal stature. (2) A great heritage. (3) A broad world. (4) The future—life tomorrow and for all eternity.—Elmer George Homrighausen

Topic: Bridges
TEXT: Luke 10:33–34

The making of a bridge to someone by (1) ending his loneliness, (2) healing misunderstanding, (3) loving him back to wholesome living and healthy laughter—or in a word, serving him.—Leslie D. Weatherhead

Hymn Suggestions: First Sunday of Advent

1. "Wake, Awake, for Night Is Flying," Philipp Nicolai (1599), translated by Catherine Winkworth (1858); "Wachet Auf," Nicolai, harmony by J. S. Bach (1731)

This venerable chorale could appropriately follow the reading from either Romans or Matthew. Because of its great length, the following procedure could be used: stanza 1, sung; stanza 2, read; stanza 3, sung.

2. "Awake, O Sleeper, Rise from Death," F. Bland Tucker (1980); "March Chapel," Max Miller (1983)

Also useful with either or both the Epistle and the Gospel reading is this contemporary hymn. It paraphrases a fragment of an ancient Christian hymn found in Ephesians 5:14.

3. "O God of Every Nation," William W. Reid Jr. (1958); "Llangloffan," Welsh Melody, harmony by David Evans (1927)

This modern prayer for peace echoes the prophecy of Isaiah that nation shall not take sword against nation nor learn war anymore.

4. "With Joy I Heard My Friends Exclaim," *Psalter* (1912); "Gonfalon Royal," Percy C. Buck (1918)

This paraphrase of Psalm 122 could well be used in place of the Psalter reading. Each stanza could be sung alternately by choir and congregation, with all joining together on the final "Alleluia."—Hugh T. McElrath

Worship Aids

CALL TO WORSHIP. "And the glory of the Lord shall be received, and all flesh shall see it together: for the mouth of the Lord hath spoken it" (Isa. 40:5).

INVOCATION. O God, we thank thee for the coming of thy Son Jesus Christ into our world and into our lives. He comes as a gift, for which we are joyfully thankful. Help us to prepare ourselves for that second coming, when he comes looking for the fruits of the Spirit. We ask this in the name of Jesus, our Lord, our Judge, and our Friend.—Theodore Parker Ferris

OFFERTORY SENTENCE. "Greater love hath no man than this, that he lay down his life for his friends" (John 15:13).

OFFERTORY PRAYER. In the spirit of the one who laid down his life for us, grant that the offerings we present to you may be used to bring life to those who are dead in trespasses and sins, and to renew life in us who have already received life eternal through our Lord Jesus Christ.

PRAYER. O merciful God, who didst come in Jesus Christ with saving power, to a world that walked in darkness and in the shadow of death: we praise and bless thee for all those who received him and gave to him the homage of their hearts and lives. For prophets who, in the face of tyranny, declared thy truth and thy righteousness; for psalmists who, in days of gloom, still believed in thy great goodness and sang praises unto thy name; and for innumerable simple folk who waited in patience and unfailing hope for the manifestation of thy glory—we raise to thee our grateful praise. Grant, we be-

---

[10]*Best Sermons*, Vol. 7.

seech thee, that we in this time may show forth thy salvation. Help us to put away all untruthfulness and all selfishness and greed, all malice and prejudice and cowardice. Let thy Holy Spirit cleanse us from all our sins, and teach us to love one another even as thou dost love us, that we may make manifest in our lives what thou canst do for thy faithful people.—Ernest Fremont Tittle

Sermon: Eagerly Waiting for What?

TEXT: Heb. 9:24–28

I feel compelled to ask if you often think about the Second Coming of Christ? Or maybe it would be more incisive to ask if you ever give serious thought to the sudden return of our Savior? Frankly?

I wouldn't be at all surprised to hear that many of us haven't given Christ's Second Coming much consideration at all. Because it's been my experience that in most mainline denominational congregations, pastors and people refrain from sober reflection on Christ's impending return—the creeping darkness covering personal and global realities notwithstanding! Do you wonder why that is?

I. Well, I'm not sure. But I can share with you some of the reasons I've been offered by selected colleagues and other Christians as objections to this doctrine.

a. I've been told by some that the doctrine of Christ's Second Coming is long outdated. And then these folk will go on to tell us that we should replace this worn-out belief with one of two options, neither of which I find compelling or appealing: on the one hand, some will tell us, we're pretty much on our own, so we must learn to rely on our own inner resources; on the other hand, some others would have us believe, it's within our power to build the Kingdom of God on earth, through successive and progressive steps. There is no end to historical development as we now know it.

Psychological readjustment, social reorganization, socioeconomic engineering, global reformation, ecological transformations, a "new world order"—and this, some would suggest, is the sum and substance of the world's ultimate salvation!

b. There are those Christians who would have us believe that any talk at all about the Day of Christ's return is tantamount to resurrecting a doctrinal dinosaur! They will argue that no contemporary Christian—least of all those willing to face the facts of modernity—could in good conscience believe in the physical return of Christ. Such folk are sure that this belief requires a sacrifice of one's sanity!

c. And finally there's the objection that seems to me to be the most pervasive among mainline Protestants. It's simply that our belief in our Savior's return is altogether impractical! That is to say, it doesn't deal with the day-to-day misery and misfortune of many people.

Instead, so the argument goes, the doctrine of Christ's return offers an escapist mentality from the pains, afflictions, and hardships of this world. Such objectors perceive this particular doctrine as the proposal of a mere fantasy—a "dream" created to sustain weakened faith.

II. Now I've no doubt that those who adhere to any one of these objections to the doctrine of Christ's return are sincere. But I'm also certain that they are sorely mistaken, because their positions are ultimately biblically indefensible and theologically unsound.

a. From my vantage point, to deny a place in the Christian faith to the impending return of Christ is to flirt with disaster. Without a firm faith in Christ's return, how can we ever hope to make sense of his promise to us in John's Gospel?

b. Jesus said: "Do not let your hearts be troubled. Believe in God, believe also in me. In my Father's house there are many dwelling places. If it were not so, would I have told you that I go to prepare a place for you? And if I go and prepare a place for you, I will come again and take you to myself, so that where I am, there you may be also."

c. Early Christians often expressed their belief in Christ's personal return. And they associated his return with a definite period of great wickedness on earth. But they also rejoiced in the conviction that Christ's return would mean the resurrection and transformation of their own bodies.

III. But maybe what is most important of all is that those same Christians claimed that belief in Christ's impending return had practical consequences! They were convinced that their lives should be lived on a higher plane, because they knew that their Savior was coming soon.

a. Take, for example, the letters of the apostle Paul. To the struggling and suffering Christians in the city of Thessalonica he once wrote: "For the Lord himself will descend from heaven with a cry of command, with the archangel's call, and with the sound of the trumpet of God. And the dead in Christ will rise first; then we who are alive, who are left, shall be caught up together with them in the clouds to meet the Lord in the air; and so we shall always be with the Lord."

b. What do you think? Was Paul merely pandering in wishful thinking? Or was he reaffirming the promise of Christ himself, who said, "I will come again and take you to myself"? You choose.

IV. But what, someone might ask, are the practical consequences of belief in Christ's Second Coming? That's a fair question. And I'll field it in this way.

a. I understand that there was a great social reformer in England who once remarked, "I don't think that in the last forty years I've lived one conscious hour that was not influenced by faith in our Lord's impending return." Here was a man who had devoted his entire life to the reform of social injustice and inequality, and his primary motivation was the conviction that Christ would soon return. I don't know about you but that seems to me to be pretty practical!

And I would add that when such conviction fails to make its impression on our thinking, it in no way influences the very practical dimensions of the daily discipline of faithful discipleship. But there's even more.

b. C. S. Lewis suggested that belief in Christ's impending return is like an ointment that lessens the pain of our current afflictions. It doesn't yet remove them—it helps us bear up under them! Beyond that, he was advocating that adherence to this belief is tantamount to a confession that our present condition is covered by Christ's Lordship, his care, and his compassion for his people.

V. The doctrine of Christ's return is a source of great comfort to those who suffer. Maybe for those first Christians—who were persecuted and suffered imprisonment—there was no more profound consolation than to remember Christ's promise: "I will come again and take you to myself."

a. The doctrine of Christ's return didn't afford them an easy escape from severe suffering. It did, however, provide them with a promise they could count on, and that promise gave them encouragement, which empowered them to endure, and endure, and endure. "I will come again and take you to myself!"

b. Christians today must sometimes suffer. They suffer the death of a child. They suffer from the most agonizing sicknesses. They suffer the pain of placing a loved one in nursing care. They suffer personal trials, temptations, deepening troubles, and turmoil of every kind. And comfort can still be found in that faith that believes that Christ has not, and will not, abandon his people to affliction. He has promised: "I will come again and take you to myself."

c. Christ first came to rob sin of its tyranny and its suffocating stranglehold on our lives. Obviously sin is still very much at large in our world—and in our lives. Even death and the devil are still quite active! But all of these have been robbed of their ultimate power over us. Their bothersome grip has been broken. By Christ's death and resurrection the devil has been deposed, the power of death has been destroyed, and sin has been defeated.

VI. As our world continues to experience change—sometimes drastic and disquieting change—we can always anchor our hearts and souls in the truth of Christ's impending return.

Whatever life or circumstances may bring, we can trust that as surely as Christ died for our sins, he lives for our support, and will return for our salvation!—Albert J. D. Walsh

Illustrations

THE RETURN OF CHRIST. "It seems to me impossible to retain in any recognizable form our belief in the Divinity of Christ and the truth of Christian revelation while abandoning, or ever persistently neglecting, the promised, and threatened, Return (of Christ)."—C. S. Lewis

NO FATAL WOUND. Even though we still carry about with us the remnants of sin, it doesn't rule over us. Even though we still feel its sting, it doesn't wound us fatally; because it is blunted and doesn't penetrate to the core of the soul!—John Calvin

SUNDAY: DECEMBER SIXTH

LECTIONARY MESSAGE

Topic: Repentance and the Religious—They Don't Always Mix!

TEXT: Matt. 3:1–12

Other Readings: Isa. 11:1–10; Ps. 72:1–7, 18–19; Rom. 15:4–13

Our gospel text introduces us to John the Baptist, seen by Matthew as the one who Isaiah had prophesied about so many years before (Isa. 40:3–5). The narrative opens with John in the desert, preaching a message of repentance "for the kingdom of heaven is near," and with people coming from the entire region to confess their sins and be baptized.

I. *Why did people venture out into the desert to hear John?* Maybe John reminded them of the prophet Elijah. After all, John looked the part, with his camel hair coat and leather belt (v. 4; see also 2 Kings 1:8). In fact, Jesus clearly identified John as "the Elijah who is to come" (Matt. 11:14).

Maybe the people realized that John was preparing the way for the Messiah and they wanted to be in on it. While Isaiah 40 tells of the preparation of the road for the coming of the Lord, Isaiah 35 speaks of the "highway of holiness" (Isa. 35:8–10). John was preparing the people spiritually to receive their king.

Maybe some of the people were curious about John's preaching and his message of repentance and baptism. Why, for instance, did John call for repentance? Was it because God was about to burst forth into history in a powerful way with the coming of the Messiah?

No doubt many came in order to obey John's message. Matthew recorded that people were confessing their sins and being baptized in the Jordan River (v. 6). But why? Wasn't the message a call to repent? Then why did the people proceed to confess their sins and submit to baptism? Could it be that without the admission of guilt and the confession of sins there can be no real repentance? After all, can people honestly change the direction of their lives and turn from sin if they never admit that their lives need changing and if they never confess just what sins they have committed? And just as confession was a vital part of repentance and the entire conversion process, so was baptism.

John's baptism was for repentance and the forgiveness of sins (v. 6; Luke 3:3).

II. *A strange and ironic turn in the story* (vv. 7–12). At this point the story takes a strange and ironic turn and really catches my attention, especially because I preach primarily to a Christian audience. John the Baptist came face to face with the religious leaders of his day, and fireworks erupted!

John's response to the presence of these leaders was one of utter contempt! He called them a bunch of snakes and warned them to truly repentant and demonstrate it by producing fruit that proved their repentance. In other words, they couldn't just "talk the talk," they had to "walk the walk."

How were the religious leaders short on "good fruit"? Basically, they made sure that their outward behavior appeared righteous while all the while they were inwardly impure. They were, Jesus argued, hypocrites to the core (Matt. 23:5–20). They had a hard outer shell with a dark inner core. They had a "righteous outer shell" for everyone to see but they were unrighteous and unchanged on the inside.

Then, anticipating their objections, John told them not to count on their religious lineage with Abraham to save them. Humorously John reminded them that God could just as easily turn rocks into children of Abraham. No, their religious heritage or traditions could not save them. Only a profound and life changing realization of sin in their lives and an attitude of repentance could prepare them for the coming of the Messiah and the salvation he would bring.

III. *What do they have to do with us?* So why am I so interested in this part of the story? Because it seems to me that we Christians have much in common with the religious leaders of Jesus' day. They were serious about their religion, and so are we. They read their scriptures for guidance, and so do we. They sought to please God, and so do we. And yet John had little use for them. So what about us?

My point is this: First, repentance is not easy. It involves honesty with ourselves and with God. It involves the admission and confession of sin to ourselves and to God. It involves changing the direction of our lives (behavior, thoughts, and attitudes). It involves living our lives in a way that demonstrates our repentance is real.

Second, it seems that religious folks, including Christians, have a difficult time repenting. For some reason we lose the ability to repent. And I am talking about people like you and me. We go to church, we pray, we sing, we grow up hearing about Jesus—and for some reason we become numb to it all. We become blind to our sins. We become comfortable in our religion and our routines. And before we know it, our lives have become fake—like the storefronts in a Hollywood western movie that are only facades propped up by wooden beams.

We can, like the Pharisees and the Sadducees, become hypocrites—too blind to see our own sins and too trusting in our own religious heritage and traditions. Many of us have grown up in Christian families, attended church, maybe even served as leaders in church—yet without much evidence of a changed life or without realizing that we have left the path and life of righteousness.

Someone has written that moral failure seldom comes about because of a blowout but usually because of a slow leak. The Pharisees and Sadducees trusted so much in their religious lineage and traditions that they could not see or hear their own moral "slow leak." We face the same danger today! The question is, what will our response be to God? Will we hear and heed the words of his prophet, John the Baptist, or will we, like the Pharisees and Sadducees, turn a deaf ear to him and, in essence, to God?—Michael M. Jones

Illustrations

PREPARATION.   As a reservist in the Air Force, I have been on bases that were in the middle of preparing for the arrival of an inspection team or a group of VIPs. One important aspect of that preparation was the spiffing up of the outward appearance of the base facilities, such as the buildings. As a result of this concern, the base commander almost always gave the order, "If it doesn't move, paint it!"

John the Baptist's orders were different, however. Instead of getting the people to be prepared for an inspection of their outward appearances, such as clothes or houses or the roads, he focused on preparing them for an inspection of their inward selves—an inspection concerned more with the condition of their hearts than with the condition of their hairstyles or their houses.—M.M.J.

REPENTANCE.   Repentance is . . . not only a realization of failure, not only a burst of contrition for having failed the good, not only a readiness to admit this failure freely . . . but also a determination not to fail the good again.—Douglas V. Steere[1]

SERMON SUGGESTIONS

Topic: Going His Way
    TEXT: Isa. 30:21
    How can we—you and I personally—know when we are going his way? (1) Surrender your will unconditionally to God's will. (2) Give your best thought to the study of his way. (3) Live a walking faith.—Ralph W. Sockman

Topic: Where Darkness Ends
    TEXT: 1 John 5:13
    Of all the places about which we would least expect to have substantial knowledge, the spiritual world is the most unlikely. We will never know everything about God, but God will give us light enough to live by, hope by, believe by, and love by. (1) We may know the love of God. (2) We may know the leadership of the Holy Spirit. (3) We can be assured of our share in eternal life.

Hymn Suggestions

    1. "Jesus Shall Reign," Isaac Watts (1719); "Duke Street," John Hatton (1793)
    The masterful Watts has turned Psalm 72—a prayer of David for his son Solomon—into a celebration of the conquests of Christ who is to come. In this remarkable transformation we have what is generally considered our first missionary hymn; its author envisaged the Great Commission of Christ realized and the Kingdom of God ushered in.
    2. "On Jordan's Bank the Baptist's Cry," Charles Coffin (1736), translated by John Chandler (1837); "Winchester New," *Musika-*

[1] *Door into Life.*

lisches Handbuch (1690), harmony by William H. Monk (1847)

Paralleling the story of John the Baptist in Matthew 3, this classic Advent hymn is a natural choice for the gospel reading for the day. Its singing should help worshipers prepare their hearts for the Christ to come.

3. "God Is Working His Purpose Out," Arthur C. Ainger (1894); "Purpose," Martin F. Shaw (1931)

Magnifying in its refrain the prophecy of Isaiah (11:9) that the earth shall be filled with the glory of God as the waters cover the sea, this hopeful hymn is quite appropriate for Advent worship.

4. "Hope of the World," Georgia Harkness (1954); "Donne Secours," *Genevan Psalter* (1551)

This contemporary hymn, reflecting the hopeful theme of the Epistle reading for this day, is especially suitable at this season when worshipers are looking toward a fresh coming of Christ into their hearts and lives.— Hugh T. McElrath

Worship Aids

CALL TO WORSHIP.   "Comfort ye, comfort ye my people, saith your God. Speak ye comfortably to Jerusalem, and cry unto her, that her warfare is accomplished, that her iniquity is pardoned" (Isa. 40:1–2a).

INVOCATION.   Dear Lord and Master of us all, may this Christmastide set the imprint of the message of the Scripture upon our minds and hearts so that thy Word may ever be central to our worship and shape the conduct of our lives. Help us to witness to the truth of thine everlasting gospel, which came to this world as glad tidings of great joy and causes us never to rest until all people everywhere from the least to the greatest will know Jesus Christ as Lord and King.—Donald Macleod

OFFERTORY SENTENCE.   "The silver is mine, and the gold is mine, saith the Lord of hosts" (Hag. 2:8).

OFFERTORY PRAYER.   God of grace, God of glory, help us to understand that we are recipients of your mercy. What we are your grace has made us. What we have your provi-dence has given us. And now, do your gracious work also in others through the gifts we bring.

PRAYER.   Eternal and almighty God, Gracious King, we come to your throne in this, your beautiful church, with the sparkling eyes of little children who have seen the greatest gift in the world, the babe in the manger, born to show us your will, to tell us that your Kingdom can come to us and through us to all the world. What a beautiful thought to know that the coming of our Christ was not just some distant event that took place once and has never been repeated. For the living Spirit of our Lord guides us in faith every day; walks with us in upright living, whispers like a still, small voice; abides in our minds with the vision of things eternal.

How thankful we are, O God, for this season and for your Spirit that moves us from carelessness to thoughtfulness, from selfishness to generosity, from being hard and callous to being kind and gentle, from indifference to concern and love. Help us to live and walk that way.

O God, we bring not just ourselves in this service of worship, but just now we bring others in prayer. So in silence we name and pray for one who we know is ill. . . . We name and pray for a doctor who we know has touched our lives, and we pray for one who we know is lonely at this time of the year. . . . And now we name and visualize and pray for one who dislikes us. . . . Now we name and pray for one who is a very precious friend.

Lord, we want to be open to receiving answers that you give for our prayers; and if we are to be part of your answer—to love the lonely, to visit the sick, to forgive an offender— enable us to hear your word of direction.

O God, at this time of year make of our souls a manger wherein the Lord of Life is born again, so that it is Christ who lives and reigns within us. In his beautiful Spirit, we pray together the prayer he taught to his disciples, saying, "Our Father. . . ."—George L. Davis

Sermon: The Skeletons in Jesus' Closet

TEXT: Isa. 11:1–10; Matt. 1:1–6, 17

I. The gospel lesson for this morning is from the first chapter of Matthew, the genealogy of Jesus.

a. Matthew is trying to impress Jews that

Jesus is the Messiah, the one prophesied, as we saw in the Old Testament lesson that was read for you this morning from Isaiah. "There shall come forth a shoot from the stump of Jesse." Jesse was David's father. "The stump of Jesse" means the royal family has been cut off, is no longer on the throne. But the Messiah, who was to be like a king, will come from this royal line, from the house of David. The Messiah must come from good people.

b. That's obviously why Matthew begins his gospel with the genealogy of Jesus Christ, the son of David. But Matthew wants to prove not only that Jesus was the Messiah but also that he was the Messiah for Gentiles as well as for Jews. So he goes back to the father of the Jews, Abraham. Jesus is the one who will bless all the nations of the earth. That explains the first line: "The genealogy of Jesus Christ, son of David, son of Abraham." He comes from royal stock. That's what a genealogy is supposed to prove—that he rules by virtue of blood. He comes from the right people.

II. So the genealogy starts out impressively, "son of David, son of Abraham." Then you read along through all the Aminnadabs and the Zerubbabels, all distinguished aristocracy and some royalty. And all men, because blood lines were always traced through the men. Then it hits you: there are some names here that are strange. I mean, they shouldn't be here. This is not orthodox genealogy.

a. Tamar, for instance. Tamar is a woman, and of questionable reputation. She is a seductress and a trickster. What's more, she is a Canaanite, not a Jew. What is she doing here?

Then Rahab, another woman. This one was identified in the Book of Judges as a prostitute. She hid some Hebrew spies in her house, thus making it possible for the Jews to defeat the Canaanites in the famous Battle of Jericho. She, too, is not a Jew but a Canaanite. She hid spies in her house, not her home—if you know what I mean.

And you read further and there's Ruth. Now, Ruth is a nice woman and of heroic qualities, but again a foreigner. Ruth was a Moabite.

And then you come across this line, "And David was the father of Solomon by the wife of Uriah." What a way to put it! You'd expect a genealogy to cover that up. Just say, "David was the father of Solomon." Or at least, if you have to mention the mother, say that she was the wife of David, not the wife of Uriah.

b. Why does the genealogy do that? You didn't have to mention women in genealogies. Not only does Matthew mention them, he mentions four unlikely women, none of them Jewish, and only one who you'd name your daughter after. Why are they there? There has to be a reason.

The obvious reason is because the fifth woman in Jesus' genealogy is also of questionable status in his background: his mother, Mary. She was, first of all, a peasant woman. She was not of the right stock. How could a king come from her kind of people? And second, the circumstance of Jesus' birth was a source of gossip—the virgin birth and all that. It was a problem then and is now.

Joseph was *betrothed* to Mary. He was not married to her. As you know, betrothed means they were engaged. They were going to get married. That was next. And here she shows up pregnant. That's the kind of situation that raises questions, and eyebrows.

III. Well, maybe the genealogy of Jesus according to Matthew is there to remind us how God works. You think it's strange that the Messiah should be the son of a peasant woman whose story is questioned. Matthew is saying with the genealogy, "That's the way God works sometimes." It's happened before. God doesn't always work in a way that we understand. In fact, I think you ought to be suspicious of anybody who says he understands the way God works.

a. I've grown accustomed to Christmas. For me it's a familiar story, a beloved story. I've told it and listened to it more than a hundred times through sermons, music, art, pageants, and plays. It's probably the world's most familiar story, so familiar that you and I are in danger of thinking that the way it happened was the way it was supposed to happen—but it was not.

b. It was not the way we would have done it, and it was not the way expected either, in spite of the prophecies. The prophecies that everybody took seriously did not say it would happen that way. They predicted a warrior coming with a sword, descending from heaven. The prophecies in Scripture that the Christians cited they found there after the fact, and they didn't convince anybody who didn't already believe. The fact was that Christmas was a surprise and a scandal. It was the way nobody imagined it would be.

IV. God does things his way, not ours. Have you ever said it couldn't happen because it's never happened before? Or have you said it's not going to happen because the odds are against it? Or how about, it can't happen because I'm not worthy? Psychologists tell us that an awful lot of people say that about themselves. It's not going to happen to me. Nothing good is going to happen to me because I am not worthy.

a. I bet that's what Mary said. The angel said, "Blessed art thou among women. God has chosen you among all the women of the world. Will you accept the honor and the ridicule and the responsibility?" And Mary said—I'm sure of this: "I'm not worthy."

She was just a girl. We can assume that. She was a teenager. Her people were not aristocrats, much less royalty. They were poor people. Nobody even knew who they were. In fact, nobody even really took the time to find out. Nobody cared about Mary. But the angel came. And Mary said, "I'm not worthy. The Messiah has to come from royalty. It can't happen because it's never happened before. The odds are against it happening, so it can't possibly happen now."

Then Mary listened to her heart, or to that sense deep inside of her that made her say, "Yes." That sense that says, "I know in my being that this is right. I must say, 'Yes.'"

b. You see, in the Bible there are two kinds of time. There is *chronos*—that's regular time, ordinary time. And there is *kairos*—that's special time, God's time, the right time. And God's time is not confined to our measurements, nor accessible to our reasoning. *Kairos* is when God is ready to act. It's the right time. And that time is known by intuition.

Actually, what Mary said was, "Let it be done unto to me according to your word." There was no sense to it. It was crazy. She was not qualified in any way. She should not have

been chosen. It would be misunderstood. There was going to be a scandal. She'd be hurt. But she said, "Yes."—Mark Trotter

Illustrations

GENEALOGICAL SURPRISE. The genealogy of Jesus is not the appointed lection for this Second Sunday of Advent; the story of John the Baptist is. But I have preached that story, I guess, about six times to this congregation, so I thought I'd try something that I have never done before and preach a text on the genealogy. When you reach my age, you have to manufacture excitement. And it's proven to be an exciting challenge, like finding a text in the phone directory. Who was it who said of the phone directory, "It has a great cast of characters but not much of a plot"? And the same thing can be said of the genealogy. So here we go, the genealogy of Jesus according to Matthew.—M.T.

THE IMPOSSIBLE TRUTH. Madeleine L'Engle, prizewinning writer of children's stories, is going to be here at the church next February. She's also a lay theologian, and a good one. She wrote that what bothers her about Christmas is not what bothers other people, not what they complain about—the commercialism, or the Santa Clauses with cotton whiskers, or the reindeer with electric bulbs or noses, or loudspeakers blaring neutered Christmas carols, or people pushing and swearing at each other in the stores. That's not what bothers her at Christmas. She says what bothers her at Christmas is God. Why would he do such a thing? Aren't there easier and better and more efficient ways to redeem the world? And what good did it do anyway? After Christ, things pretty much went back to the way they'd always been. And yet, it's Christmas, she says, that is her source of hope—hope borne of the very absurdity of it; the fact that it was not predicted; the fact that it was impossible, it couldn't happen that way. She writes, "The only God who seems to me to be worth believing in is impossible for mortals to understand."—M.T.

SUNDAY: DECEMBER THIRTEENTH

LECTIONARY MESSAGE

Topic: Are You the One? Are You Still the One?

TEXT: Matt. 11:2–11

Other Readings: Isa. 35:1–10; Luke 1:47–55; James 5:7–10

While John the Baptist was in prison, he heard what Jesus had been doing. While we are not told specifically what John had heard, apparently it raised some doubts in his mind as to whether Jesus was the Messiah. Why the doubts? Possibly it was because John was growing impatient. After all, where were the signs of imminent judgment of the wicked, and why was John still in prison when the Messiah was suppose to set the prisoners free? Or maybe it was because John had expected, along with most other Jews, the liberation of God's people through political and military means, yet Jesus' activities didn't show any promise of going in that direction.

I. *John's searching question* (vv. 2–3). So John sent his disciples to ask Jesus if he was "the one who was to come" or if they should expect someone else (v. 2). Again, his question was rooted in his impression that Jesus was not performing up to the standards of what the "real" Messiah would be doing. And John's question was of paramount importance because he wanted to know if Jesus of Nazareth was the Messiah, or if he and the others needed to look for someone else.

It is a question that we all must ask and answer for ourselves. Is Jesus really the Christ, the Messiah, the Son of God, the Savior of the world? Or was he just a great teacher, a prophet of God, a holy and righteous man? Or maybe Jesus was just a good man whom his followers built up and whose legend was and is bigger than his real life. For just as Jesus didn't meet all of John's expectations of what the Messiah would be like, so Jesus may fall short of our own expectations. After all, Jesus may not address certain social issues or injustices the way we think he should. He may not answer our prayers quickly enough or in the way we want or expect. He may even teach that we should do things that are contrary to our way of thinking or to the customs and practices of our culture. So just as John was forced to ask that searching question, "Are you the one?" we too must ask.

II. *Jesus' revealing answer* (vv. 4–5). In answer to John's question, Jesus pointed to the only two things that could truly bring about faith: what he had said and what he had done. He told John's disciples to describe to John just what they had heard and seen.

Jesus had been teaching and preaching all over the countryside and in the synagogues. His message was similar to John's: "Repent, for the Kingdom of heaven is near" (Matt. 4:17). In the Sermon on the Mount (Matt. 5–7), Jesus identified the sources of hypocrisy and showed how citizens of the coming Kingdom would need to live.

Jesus had not only been preaching, he had also been doing. In response to John's question, Jesus pointed him back to Isaiah 35 and then to Jesus' own ministry as proof that he was indeed the one to come. The blind could now see, the lame could now walk, the lepers were now healed, the deaf could now hear, and the dead had been raised (v. 5; Isa. 35:5–6). Jesus simply pointed to what he had said and done as proof positive that he was the one to come. John (as all of us must, for that matter) had to hear his words and see his deeds and then judge for himself.

But note what is absent here. Jesus didn't try to prove he was the Messiah by conventional (or expected) human means. There were no fighting armies to overthrow the government; no self-serving displays of supernatural powers, like lightning bolts striking down the enemy; no huge marching bands or political rallies to announce his arrival. Why are these things absent? Because they would not have fit in with what God had called the Messiah to do or to be. They would not have served the goals of Jesus, nor were they the primary focus of his ministry. Instead, Jesus said that "the Son of Man did not come to be served, but to serve, and to give his life as a ransom for many" (Matt. 20:28).

III. *Implications for his disciples.* Is there any significance to the signs given by Isaiah and fulfilled by Jesus, beyond the identification of the Messiah? Can these signs also offer us insight into the heart of God and what he cares about? Into Jesus' own focus for his ministry? And into what his disciples should be concerned about? I think the answer is a resounding "Yes!"

The signs of the "one to come" given by Jesus served not only to identify him as the Messiah; they also served as a clue to the focus of his mission and ministry. They further served as the guiding light for the ministry of Jesus' disciples. Note that in Matthew 10, Jesus sends out the Twelve to do exactly what he had been doing. They were instructed to proclaim that the Kingdom of heaven was near, and they were told to go among the people and heal them (Matt. 10:7–8). Later, in Acts, we find Peter and John doing just that (Acts 2–3). In essence, the disciples were to preach and teach the good news of the coming of the Kingdom of God and the way of salvation, and they were to serve others and not themselves (Matt. 20:20–28).

The implications for us are clear. Our focus, our reason for being, is to share the good news of Jesus Christ with others and to bring about healing in their lives. We may not all be gifted to do both, but surely we can do one or the other. Of course, the ability to do miraculous healing may be beyond us, but the ability to ease someone's suffering, the opportunity to share someone's heavy burden, or the gift of bringing joy and laughter into someone's life is not beyond us.—Michael M. Jones

Illustrations

EXPLANATION OF JOHN'S DOUBT. As Frederick Bruner forcefully points out, John doubted for good reason. "Why was John in doubt? Because John's Coming One in chapter 3, we recall, was mainly a figure of power, a bringer mainly of judgment, a carrier . . . mainly of 'fire,' with an ax in one hand to chop down the unfruitful tree and a shovel in the other hand to sift out the chaff in his granary (3:10–12). There is good reason to wonder if the Jesus *since* chapter 3 fit John's descriptions."[2]

FAITH AND DOUBT. Believers can be credulous, but disbelievers, too, can be gullible

[2]Frederick Dale Bruner, *The Christbook: A Historical/Theological Commentary, Matthew 1–12* (Waco, Tex.: Word Books, 1987), 408. For a fuller explanation of Bruner's argument, see pages 408–409.

fools. Don't join their company! Take a long look at Christ! The world desperately needs him. He is the way and the truth and the life.—Harry Emerson Fosdick[3]

SERMON SUGGESTIONS

Topic: The Church of Today
TEXT: Isa. 62:3
The prophet saw a glorious day ahead when the people of God would have entered into their ultimate earthly heritage. (1) This glorious Church belongs to and exists for the Lord Jesus Christ. (2) The New Testament churches were organized along functional lines. (3) The glory of the Church is in its holiness.

Topic: "More Room Still"
TEXT: Luke 14:22
God will not be content until the last soul on earth has had the opportunity to know him and enjoy his fellowship. (1) The curse of complacency. (2) The creativity of concern.

Hymn Suggestions

1. "Lift Up Your Hearts, Ye Mighty Gates," Georg Weissel (1642), translated by Catherine Winkworth (1855); "Truro," *Psalmodia Evangelica* (1789)
Written for Advent, this old hymn from German pietism exchanges the imagery of the Temple procession for the entrance of Christ into the hearts of the faithful, a place "set apart from earthly use."
2. "Come, Thou Long-Expected Jesus," Charles Wesley (1744); "Stuttgart," *Psalmodia Sacra* (1715), adapted by Henry Gauntlett (1861)
No Advent season should pass without the inclusion of this masterful hymn in the people's singing worship. It lends itself admirably to antiphonal singing line-by-line between choir and congregation.
3. "Tell Out, My Soul, the Greatness," Timothy Dudley-Smith (1961); "Woodlands," Walter Greatorex (1919)
The revolutionary song of the Virgin Mary is faithfully paraphrased in this contemporary version that has become quite popular

[3]*What Is Vital in Religion.*

in recent years. It could be sung in place of reading the Lucan text.

4. "O for a Thousand Tongues to Sing," Charles Wesley (1738); "Azmon," Carl G. Glaser (1828), arranged by Lowell Mason (1839)

The message that John the Baptist's disciples bore to their master (Matt. 11:4–6) was fulfillment of Isaiah's prophecy (35:5–6), both of which are celebrated in this stanza of Wesley's hymn:

Hear him, ye deaf; his praise, ye dumb;
Your loosened tongues employ,
Ye blind, behold your Savior come,
And leap, ye lame, for joy."

—Hugh T. McElrath

Worship Aids

CALL TO WORSHIP.   "Fear thou not, for I am with thee; be not dismayed, for I am thy God: I will strengthen thee; yea, I will help thee; yea, I will uphold thee with the right hand of my righteousness" (Isa. 41:10).

INVOCATION.   Stir up your power, O Lord, and with great might come among us; and because we are sorely hindered by our sins, let your bountiful grace and mercy speedily help and deliver us; through Jesus Christ our Lord, to whom, with you and the Holy Spirit, be honor and glory, now and forever.—*The Book of Common Prayer*

OFFERTORY SENTENCE.   "Every good gift and every perfect gift is from above, and cometh down from the Father of lights with whom is no variableness neither shadow of turning" (James 1:17).

OFFERTORY PRAYER.   Lord, as Jesus came into the world, to do the will of God, allow these gifts to bring new life to those in need, that light may forever shine because we dared to give as God asked, the God who blesses small things in great ways.—E. Lee Phillips

PRAYER.   "Wait for the Lord, take courage, be strong; wait for the Lord." What does it mean to wait upon you—you who are holy and eternal?

It is surely to wait in reverence—acknowl-edging who you are, realizing who we are. But yet, we can come in confidence, for we are not groveling slaves but your sons and daughters. We have been adopted into your family, the household of faith, not because of our merit but because of your grace—your unmerited love. The Spirit that we have received is not a spirit of slavery leading us back into a life of fear, but the Spirit that makes us your children.

To wait on you is to be silent until all our striving ceases. It is to be still. How still? To know that you are God. It is to be still so that above the clamoring of self-will we may hear the still, small voice of your will.

To wait upon you is to trust—to trust utterly. It is to let go and let you be God. But how difficult this is for us. We are all the time playing God. We come, even now, in our anxious activism thinking that we have to beat upon the door, or even knock it down to get your attention, when actually the door is always open and we but need to walk through it.

To wait upon you, O God, is to wait upon one another. If we are really listening we hear you saying: "Except your brother and your sister be with you, you shall not see my face." We do not see you except in the face of the other—whoever the other may be.

Let us wait in these moments with one another! For family solidarity threatened by alienation, we pray for persevering love, that reconciliation may come in the next few days. We pray for the ill among us. Where physical infirmity cannot be removed because of age or other disability, grant that strength of mind and of spirit that celebrates your wholeness even in the face of that infirmity. For those walking through the valley of the shadow of death we pray for the light of your countenance—the strength of the everlasting arms. To wait upon you is to be overtaken by a peace that the world cannot give and that the world cannot take away.

Enlighten and encourage the leaders of nations and the United Nations with the ways of justice and righteousness, that all peoples may live in peace.

To wait upon you is to come to know him who is full of your grace and truth. He is the way—may we follow him; he is the truth—may we trust him; he is the life—may we celebrate with him.

We thank you, God, that you are always waiting; may we learn to wait before you.— John Thompson

Sermon: The Sounds of Christmas

TEXT: Isa. 53:1–6; Luke 2:8–14

Listen! Listen! You can hear the sounds of Christmas everywhere.

Christmas has all kinds of sounds. We hear some of them, and others we do not hear because sometimes we do not want to hear them. But Christmas has always been filled with songs for those who know how to listen, for those who can hear.

Are you listening this Christmas season? What will you hear? What sound will you hear?

I. Listen! The angels came making a great declaration to the shepherds. These shepherds, some scholars think, may have been the special shepherds who tended the sheep for the Temple and provided the unblemished lambs for sacrifice.

a. God's angelic voices came to the shepherds, and they heard the message of good news. The message of good news told them of the birth of God's Son who was coming to transform the world.

Isaiah, the prophet, told of a *suffering servant*. The suffering servant bears the pain and sins of others and brings a redemptive means of healing. Isaiah pointed to One who would come and bear the sins of his people. The New Testament writers saw Jesus Christ as the one who fulfilled the good news about which the prophet wrote. He was the one who will bear us up, who will receive our stripes, and through his sacrifice we will find healing, redemption, and wholeness.

b. As we reflect on this good news again in this Christmas season, we need to hear it anew and receive the angels' message joyfully. The prophet reminds us of the power of God. This old story reminds us once again that it's not in your strength or in my strength but in the power of the One who is to come, the One who is to be born, who will bear your sins and my sins. So we face our sins not with our strength alone. We respond instead to the grace of God that comes into our life to enable us to find the inner strength from God in our life to transform us, redeem us, and make us whole.

II. Listen! Listen and you will hear the voice of the angels that give us words of hope. In the day of Jesus, people felt a great sense of hopelessness.

a. The message from the angel was words of hope. "Behold I bring you good tidings of great joy." Their hopes were not in vain. Oh, we live sometimes in a world in which it seems so hopeless to hope, so futile to dream, so useless to think that our lives or other lives, or our world, or our country, or other countries might be different. But if we give up hope, what then do we really have?

b. Those of us who may be in the darkest of the pits of despondence need to remember that the starlight presence of God is always there. It matters not how dark the circumstances are; we are not cut off from his presence, because he is there in the darkness with us to undergird us, to hold us up, to bear us up in our pain, to lift us up in our suffering. He doesn't always come and remove all pain, he doesn't do away with all suffering; but he is there with us, bearing us up in the midst of all our sufferings and trials. We need not give way to hopelessness. He sustains us and promises us the power of his presence.

III. Listen! Listen also to the angelic voices because sometimes we receive directions from them.

a. After hearing the angels, the shepherds acted on what they experienced in that great moment. And so must we. Sometimes the voices of the angels that we hear give us directions on what to do and say, and how to live in this confused world. We listen for guidance on how to be better individuals and how to live more Christlike in our world.

b. The words that come to us from the angels lead us to the Christ. They guide us to the Christ and point us toward him and a way of life with hope, newness, victory, and encouragement. Christ comes to us when we are in pain and gives us the assurance of his love, grace, and courage. He comes to us when our burdens are crushing us down, and we feel him lifting us up and helping us bear that load. He calls us to walk above the common way, to a higher way. He calls us to be more than we ever thought we could be, more than we have been. Because of his grace and his love, he comes to us and says to us: "I love you and I am with you and I will walk beside you." The good news is direction. Listen to it.

IV. When have you heard angelic voices? Have you ever? Angels represent the nearness and sustenance of the deepest unseen spiritual realities. Angels bring an awareness of the sense of the presence and power of God. I know, we have trouble hearing them, don't we?

a. There have been times I have been able to hear angelic voices. O, there were no trumpets. There was no chorus in the sky. There was no shouting, no verbal sound, but there was an intuitive sense within. There was a sense of the presence of God. There was a sense of being grasped and directed. I heard an internal whisper. Sometimes I have heard angelic voices through a friend who said: "Hey, Bill, hang in there" or "I'm with you" or "I'm praying for you." Sometimes I've heard the voice of God through reading a book, or listening to a lecture or a sermon.

b. Listen. Listen to the angels of God who are seeking to speak with you and me. They may come through persons or books. Sometimes we don't want to listen, because they may direct us to places we don't want to go. These messages may cause us to change our lives, habits, jobs, or relationships. The voices of God may challenge us, forgive us, change us, direct us, send us, and guide us. We are often afraid to listen because of what we may hear. Often we don't hear because we are spiritually tone deaf or because the sounds of the world have shut out these quieter sounds. But learn to listen. You and I may hear the voice of God.—William Powell Tuck

Illustrations

A STUNNING TESTIMONIAL.   Emory and Henry College is just a few miles up the road from where I was pastor in Bristol, Virginia. Saul Alinsky, a declared revolutionist and non-Christian, came to that campus to speak along with two noted clergymen. The two clergymen spoke about the Church, all its problems, and the many difficulties that the Church had within it. They focused primarily on what was wrong with the Church. Suddenly Alinsky jumped up and said, "You guys be quiet. I thought you were going to say a good word for the Church. Listen," he said. "It is doing a better job than education, business, or government, and you clergy ought to know this."—W.P.T.

JOINING THE CHORUS.   A group of Princeton University students went Christmas caroling and stopped outside the home of Albert Einstein, the great physicist. They had sung only a carol or two when he came outside and began to accompany them on his violin. Isn't that what should happen when we hear the angels—messengers of God? We are drawn out to become a part of those who, having heard, now respond by joining those who are seeking to bring peace on earth.—W.P.T.

SUNDAY: DECEMBER TWENTIETH

LECTIONARY MESSAGE

Topic: Christmas—Dispelling Any Doubts
TEXT: Matt. 1:18–25
Other Readings: Isa. 7:10–16; Ps. 80:1–7, 17–19; Rom. 1:1–7
Dispelling the smallest doubt. Such may be an accurate summarization of Matthew's account of Jesus' miraculous conception and birth. The reason is clear. Doubting the virgin birth isn't a new trend of our ultramodern, high-tech, instant, mobile, communications society. Quite the contrary, the Bible passionately and forthrightly addresses the tendency of humans to doubt the miraculous. However, accepting such events as accurate and believing them to be true is also very natural and very human. We need not doubt the Christmas story.

Let's face it: would you not doubt your fiancee if she told you she was pregnant with God's child? How about your daughter? Your sister? Your neighbor? Sure you would! In fact, most sane people—including Christians—already have!

Many of the world's well-known personalities, both actual and mythical, have made miraculous birth claims. Greek legend has it that Perseus was the son of Zeus (Jupiter) and his mother was the virgin Danae; that Zeus, king of the Roman mythological gods, was the son of Saturn, who lived on Greece's Mount Olympus as god of the heavens and the ruler of men.

Other Greeks claimed that Alexander the Great, the son of Philip of Macedon and Olympias, was begotten by a serpent. His mother fired young Alexander's imagination by telling him that he was a descendant of Achilles and that his father, Philip, was a descendant of Hercules. But such stories were not limited to the Greeks. According to Hindu myth, Krishna was the son of the virgin Davaki.

Closer to today's text, the Romans believed that Caesar Augustus, the first of the Roman emperors and the one sitting on Rome's throne when Jesus was born, was also conceived by a serpent as Augustus's mother lay asleep in the temple of Apollo. But such fables fail to compare, however, with the birth of Jesus Christ. Conceived by the virgin Mary through the power of the Holy Spirit, the Bible testifies that Jesus Christ is the Son of God and the sinless Savior of all mankind. And thanks to Matthew, we have at least four reasons to believe all the Bible says in regard to Jesus' divine beginnings.

I. *Matthew presents an accurate account* (v. 18). In the words of one unknown psalmist, "never put a question mark where God has put a period." This is exactly the advice that Matthew follows in his account of Jesus' beginnings. Without any question, without any doubt, and without any confusion whatsoever, Matthew is clearly and unapologetically saying, "This is how it happened!" His words are not an interrogative statement, but a simple statement of fact that speaks of Matthew's absolute assurance and firm conviction to report only the truth.

II. *Matthew presents Joseph's doubt as a reflection of our own* (v. 19). Society today often appears to be driven by pollsters, statistics, and majorities. As a result, supporting one's claim often means finding as many people as possible to champion our cause. Not so for Matthew; he presents a man who had doubts himself. But as a "just and righteous man," Joseph's desire to end his betrothal to Mary clearly demonstrates that, like you and I, the righteous can doubt the miraculous nature of significant Christological events and still benefit from God's helping us to overcome doubt.

While it would be too easy to think that Joseph responded as he did—accepting the story—because he overcame his doubt on his own, such is not the case. Matthew reports that it took the Word of the Lord, delivered through an angel, to convince Joseph that Mary was telling the truth. But to his credit, and unlike the vindictive Jonah, Joseph did not ignore the message, nor did he flee from God's will (vv. 24–25). As a result, his testimony assists believers in overcoming doubt with faithful obedience and careful attention to God's Word.

III. *Matthew propounds the testimony of an angel of the Lord* (vv. 20–21). "Do not be afraid"—these are the words used by the angel of the Lord to comfort Joseph's broken heart and alleviate his doubts.

Fear of the dark often causes us to doubt our safety. Fear of change often explains our doubting new ideas. Fear of the unknown quite commonly justifies our doubting medicines and vaccines. And fear of death regularly leads to our doubting a just and righteous God who must one day punish us for our sins. In addition, it may be our fear of being labeled a fanatic, a religious nut, a psychotic paranoia, or a sucker that causes us to doubt not only the Christmas story but much of the Bible. Fortunately, we need not be afraid; our fears and our doubts can be resolved!

Like Joseph, we can take the Christmas story for the miracle it is intended to be. Besides, having experienced firsthand the birth of my own four children, I well know the miraculous nature of any birth. And if God can reproduce the miracle of life, as he does every minute of every day, who am I to doubt an angel telling us that this same God can create life in ways we have yet to understand?

IV. *Matthew points to the testimony of the Old Testament* (vv. 22–23). While some may occasionally forget, the Bible of Matthew's day was our Old Testament. And it was just as important to them as our New Testament is to us. More so in fact! Like us, they memorized certain key passages of prophecy, and would surely have memorized and examined the claims of Christ found in their Old Testament Bible. They relied upon its truthfulness.

Old Testament references to the Savior's divine beginnings would not have gone unnoticed to fervent Jewish scholars of Jesus' day. In fact, as early as two hundred years before Christ's birth, the prophecy from Isaiah 7:14 was widely regarded as a special, unique sign of the Messiah.[4] Clearly Matthew's intention was to alleviate any doubt the people had by using their own Jewish prophet. And he helps to alleviate our doubts today.

Thanks in no small part to Matthew's accurate, reflective, heavenly inspired recognition of a fulfilled Old Testament prophecy, believers today need not feel ashamed or uncomfortable in believing the astonishing story of Christ's miraculous conception and birth. Even more important, we can believe without a glimmer of doubt that Jesus is indeed Emmanuel, "God with us!"

Merry Christmas!—Charles J. Williams Jr.

Illustrations

GOD'S PRESENCE.   A young Scottish presbyter was visiting an old lady who knew her Bible very well. At the end of the visit, the young man stood to leave the room but felt it his duty to leave some word of the Lord with his elderly friend. "What a lovely promise we have been given," he said confidently. "'Lo, I am with you always.'" To which the woman replied, "Hoot, man, it's not a promise—it's just a fact."—J. C. Ferdinand Pittman[5]

OVERCOMING DOUBT WITH TIME.   Following a recent trip to my doctor for a sore throat, I spent two days faithfully taking my prescribed medicine in just the right quantity. To my dismay, however, the sore throat seemed only to get worse. Doubting the medicine's effectiveness, I asked my doctor to give me a stronger prescription. Instead, she assured me that I needed to wait a day or two longer for it to kick in. She was right. I felt much better the very next morning. But the experience gave me a valuable lesson in life: that given a little time, many of our doubts will solve themselves.—C.J.W.Jr.

SERMON SUGGESTIONS

Topic: A Greater Splendor Than Expected
    TEXT: Isa. 60:1–12; John 1:9; 2 Cor. 4:6
    (1) The splendid but limited dream of the

prophet. (2) The glorious and universal fulfillment in Jesus Christ.

Topic: The Wonders of His Love
    TEXT: Eph. 3:14–21; Luke 2
    (1) The wonder of his love is that it comes to every one of us with no strings attached. (2) The wonder of his love is that it is personal. (3) The wonder of his love is that it will never stop, no matter what.—Hugh Litchfield

Hymn Suggestions: Advent IV

    1. "O Come, O Come, Emmanuel," twelfth-century Latin, translated by John M. Wade (1851); "Veni Emmanuel," Ancient Plainsong, adapted by Thomas Helmore (1854)
    Representing the general spirit of the prophets and of the psalmist (80:1–7) concerning the coming of Christ, this ancient song is now indispensable for Advent worship.
    2. "Hear Us, O Shepherd of Your Chosen Race," Bert Polman (1985); "Yorkshire," John Wainwright (1750)
    Stanzas 1, 2, and 5 of this modern paraphrase of Psalm 80 parallel the verses selected for the Psalter reading. The tune, often associated with the Christmas season, also has a relevance for this last Sunday before Christmas.
    3. "To a Maid Engaged to Joseph," Gracia Grindel (1983); "Annunciation," Rusty Edwards (1983)
    This unrhymed contemporary paraphrase of the announcement of the angel to Mary might be sung as follows: the first two lines of each stanza sung in alternation by two choirs or two sections of one choir with the congregation singing the last line. The hymn can supplement the reading of the gospel lesson.
    4. "Lo, How a Rose E'er Blooming," fifteenth–century German, translated by Theodore Baker (1894); "Es Ist ein Ros," German traditional melody, harmony by Michael Praetorius (1609)
    A beautiful hymn combining the themes of the prophecy of Isaiah, the Root of Jesse, the Virgin Mother, and Christ as the Rose dispelling darkness and death, this German song is particularly appropriate for this Sunday's worship.—Hugh T. McElrath

Worship Aids

CALL TO WORSHIP.   "Let us now go even unto Bethlehem, and see this thing which is

---

[4]Craig L. Blomberg, *The New American Commentary*, vol. 22, "Matthew" (Nashville: Broadman Press, 1992), 59–61.
[5]*Bible Truths Illustrated.*

come to pass, which the Lord hath made known unto us" (Luke 2:15b).

INVOCATION. Go with us now, O God, as we make our journey again along the familiar path to Bethlehem, and open our hearts to the ever-new experiences that can be ours as we enter more deeply into the meaning of the birth of Jesus our Lord, in whose name we pray.

OFFERTORY SENTENCE. "When they saw the star, they rejoiced with exceeding great joy; and when they were come into the house, they saw the young child with Mary his mother, and fell down and worshiped him; and when they had opened their treasures, they presented unto him gifts: gold, and frankincense, and myrrh" (Matt. 2:10–11).

OFFERTORY PRAYER. Our heavenly Father, we believe that no gift of ours is too large or too small to bring to you, if it is brought in the spirit of the love in which you gave your only Son and the love in which Jesus laid down his life for us. Make what we bring a blessing beyond all our imaginings, through your almighty power. To that end we bring and dedicate our offerings.

PRAYER. Loving God, as we come this last Sunday before Christmas, once again we pray that our minds may turn to the celebration of the coming of your Son into the world. Help us to make room for the Christmas celebration within our homes; may we pause and look inwardly that we might have a place within for you.

We thank you for this season and for its beauty. May we learn to use this time to pause and to think about you and your love. As we reflect on your greatness, may it remind us of our own impurity and cause us to confess our sins and seek to find release from the guilt and the selfishness that hold us down, and to find the peace and stillness that can come from your presence.

In this Christmas season may we once again be excited about the wonder of it. May we become as children as we reflect again upon our need for you and the great gift that you have given us through Jesus Christ our Lord. May our own giving reflect the fact that we have sensed and received the greatest gift of all that comes from you. May we celebrate this Christmas in a deeper and more meaningful sense because we have received that gift from you and your Son Jesus Christ. May he bring into our lives this Christmas a sense of newness and freshness, as we pray in the power of his strong name.—William Powell Tuck

Sermon: A Shout of Praise
TEXT: Matt. 2:7–12; Luke 2:20

At Christmas, it matters how we give—hopefully from love. But it also matters how we receive—hopefully, joyfully, and gratefully. Giving and receiving is what Christmas is all about. Christmas is the time when God, in love, gave us the gift of his Son, and the celebration of Christmas occurs when we receive his Son joyfully and gratefully. The most important questions for us to answer this Christmas are these: How have we responded to the coming of Christ? Have we received him or rejected him? Have we ignored him or followed him? What have we done with the gift God gave?

Hear the sounds of Christmas in our story. There's a sound of a prayer of worship being uttered by wise men who had been looking for the Savior for some time. They found him and fell on their knees and worshipped him. Then, if you listen, you can hear the shouts of praise coming forth from the mouths of the shepherds. They went to see, and when they saw him they went out "glorifying and praising God" (v. 20). He had come! Will Christmas become real for us? Will we receive God's gift at Christmas? If we do, what will it mean for us?

I. It is a gift of forgiveness for our past sins.

a. That was why God came. He came at Christmas to tell them that he loved them and would not give up on them. He would give them a new chance at life. He would begin with their sins. We know that the baby grew up to eventually climb a cross and die for their sins. He paid the penalty for them. He died the death that sin should have brought them. Through all of this, God was saying that rebellion was past history. It didn't matter any more. All that mattered was what they did today and from now on. The prayer of worship and the shout of praise came from the realization that their past sins were gone, and they had before them a new chance to obey God.

b. If we try to live by the wrong directions, if we try to follow our directions and not God's, it is guaranteed that someplace, sometime, somewhere, we're going to have an explosion on our hands. Life will fall in on us. We will discover that sin is too strong. It has more power than we thought. There are signs in our world today that sin has taken hold of us and that explosions have occurred.

c. At Christmas, God tells us what to do with our sin. Give it to him. That's what he came for, to tell us that on our own we cannot overcome sin. He will! What we need to do is to let our sins go and to receive his gift of forgiveness. When we give our sins to God, we can forget them and go on.

II. There is a gift of help for present troubles.

a. They had them, these shepherds. They struggled with all of the problems that we do: suffering and sickness, frustration and despair, loneliness, doubt, and death. They wondered how they could make it through the day, how they could make it through the night. Christmas came to tell them how God would help them. The God who came in Christ experienced and faced everything that they faced. He understands all of our problems. There was help for their problems. For their suffering and sickness there was healing or the strength to deal with it. For their despair and frustration, there was courage to go another step. Christ came to deliver them from their moment of trouble.

b. We need to hear that. We are no different. We struggle with these problems. Suffering and sickness hit us. Depression and frustration come often. Loneliness—have you ever felt that? Doubt—how many times have you wondered even about God? Death—far too many times we stand in the presence of that. How can we go on?

Christmas tells us how. With his help God moves in mysterious ways in our lives. He deals with all of us differently, but his grace does move. For some, he may speak through a friend. For others, it may be a sense of peace that overwhelms you. For others, it may be courage that you strangely find to stand up and go forward. For some, God may speak through worship or music. God speaks in his way. He works in his way. We need to be open to live our lives with the realization that

God is in it, and we must be open to receive the help that God gives us.

III. There is the gift of hope for future steps.

a. They clung to hope. The shepherds waited desperately for a Messiah to come and help them. The wise men scanned the skies for who knows how long for some sign that God was there. That's all it seemed they had to cling to, especially those shepherds. They had no wealth, no prestige, no power. All they had was hope that God would not forget them, that God was still in control of the world. That's all they had.

Christmas told them that it was enough. God would help. God was in control of the world and they could pray a prayer of worship and shout a song of praise because they could go back to all their difficult tomorrows with the assurance that the hope they lived by was true.

b. We live by hope, too. Sometimes in our world it seems the only thing we have left is hope. It seemed to me this Christmas that a lot of the Christmas trees were put up early this year, the lights went on earlier than I can remember in past Christmases. My feeling is that many people did it because they were desperately looking for some hope in the midst of the dark times we live in. Maybe bringing on the lights at Christmas reminds them of love and joy. Maybe if they turned on the lights the darkness wouldn't seem so dark.

c. Christmas tells us that a light has come into the world that can never go out, and the light is God. He has come to dwell with us and will always dwell with us. He has come to remind us that the hope we have is not in humanity; our ultimate humanity is in God and what he can do. What we know about God is that nothing—war, inflation, suffering, tragedy, death—nothing in the world can stop God from being God. Therefore, those of us who have put our hope in him can go forward to face whatever comes.

IV. These are the gifts that God has brought us at Christmas. I can imagine again that this Christmas, as in all others, God waits eagerly to see what we will do with his gifts. Here's forgiveness. Will we take it? Here is help for present troubles. Will we use it? Here is hope for future steps. Will we live by it?—Hugh Litchfield

Illustrations

THE WRONG RECIPE.   I read of a recipe book that had been recalled. You hear of cars being recalled but I never heard of a cookbook being recalled. This one was. It was recalled because they made a mistake in one of the recipes. In making a particular dish the way the recipe said to make it, they had neglected one of the basic elements: water. If you made it just as the recipe said, it would blow up in your face. They recalled the book to prevent that.—Thomas D. Lea[6]

UNTRAMMELED JOY.   Simon and Garfunkel, on the album *Parsley, Sage, Rosemary and Thyme,* sang the Christmas carol "Silent Night." Partway through the song the listener becomes aware of another voice reporting the seven o'clock news.

The news becomes louder until your attention leaves "Silent Night" and focuses on the news of murders, robberies, wars, and violence. The song of peace has been overpowered by the violence of our world. The song ends with a feeling of despair.

I would like to reverse the song. True, the news is not good. The world is violent and is torn by strife. But the news of Jesus' birth brings hope to the world. Like the angels who brought tidings of great joy, so do I—a Savior, who is Christ the Lord, was born in the city of David.—Robert A. White[7]

SUNDAY: DECEMBER TWENTY-SEVENTH

LECTIONARY MESSAGE

Topic: Expectations
TEXT: Matt. 2:13–23; 22:36–39; 27:37–39
Other Readings: Isa. 63:7–8; Ps. 148; Heb. 2:10–18

Human beings tend to expect great things from significant events: improved financial security from new jobs, happiness from new marriages, rest and relaxation from retirement. We expect greater parental responsibility with the birth of children, success to follow graduation, and spiritual growth with new pastors. These are but a few of the many expectations people face every day. In fact, such expectations seem only natural in a television society that gets a misguided glimpse of good at the end of what we watch.

Life seldom models the fictional world of television. Personal expectations are often shattered in the course of time. To quote a popular insurance commercial, "That's life!" But so is our learning to cope with shattered expectations. Discovering a better place to direct our faith is what Matthew's account of Jesus' early days is all about.

The birth of the Messiah, Israel's deliverer and redeemer, was a much awaited and much prophesied event in Jewish religious history. A time of peace, joy, prosperity, and return to the blissful state—albeit a Jewish one, described in the Garden of Eden. Unfortunately, such an interpretation of the ancient prophecies was premature given that Matthew clearly shows that a great many expectations were shattered.

I. *Expectations of the expecting* (vv. 13–15). Even before a child is born, parents harbor wondrous expectations of their child's appearance, behavior, attitudes, needs, successes, careers, and families. The messianic family was not immune to such behavior.

Put yourself in Mary's and Joseph's sandals. How would you react to the news? Would you not leap for joy, dream dreams, plan plans, and ponder fascinating expectations if an angelic messenger told you your child would one day be great: a national political leader, a professional ball player, a prominent world scientist, or a Fortune 500 executive? Sure you would! Now, how would you react if you were told your child would save the world from its sins? Mary and Joseph lived with this promise and expected it to occur. Still, who would have expected that the Messianic family would have to flee for their lives into a foreign country? Surely not the awestruck Mary and Joseph. Their expectations for Israel's salvation seemed shattered by the second angelic announcement—flee to Egypt!

II. *Expectations of Bethlehem's mothers* (vv. 16–18). In spite of the announcements, the songs, the visits, the praise, and the absolute awe surrounding the birth of the Christ child, the event was not a global celebration. In fact, one person in particular—the vile, cruel, ambitious Herod the Great—became so jealous and so filled with hate that he ordered the senseless slaughter of Bethlehem's sons two years old and younger.

Scholars do not know how many children were sacrificed for Herod's political prestige, but one thing is certain. For every innocent life lost, for every precious drop of blood spilled, and for every suffering soul released, there was a mother—a mother like Mary and a mother like yours and mine—who wailed and lamented the unbelievable and inescapable horror. Their parental expectations had been shattered!

Who would have expected suffering and death to be a result of the Messiah's birth? Not Mary, not Joseph, and certainly not those parents who suffered the shattered expectations of dead children.

III. *Expectations of an uninformed world* (vv. 19–23). In spite of its triumph, the birth of Jesus the Savior was nevertheless an obscure dot virtually unnoticed by history and the world for many years. Obscure like the lost names of the dead innocents. Obscure like the private parental expectations of the messianic family. Obscure like most news of that day. Obscure, that is, except for the gospels, where it receives its due attention and understanding in the context of holy writ.

Relative to the birth, the hurried retreat, and the senseless massacre, the years passed like any other; buildings were built, streets were strewn, waterways were dredged, battles were won, governments were lost, many were born and many died. And alas, Herod did finally perish like the mortal he was, and was replaced with his own sons and a crumbling order. Ironically, it was Herod's sustained oppression that helped to propel the people's expectations for messianic deliverance. Misunderstanding continued as well—despite the signs so clearly and consistently painted by the ancient prophets and studied by the religious leaders.

The people expected the Messiah to be a mighty king, a military master who would raise a Jewish army in the tradition of David. Who would have expected an obscure carpenter with obscure followers—an obscure means of deliverance from an equally obscure little town? Surely not those who interpreted the Old Testament scriptures—and surely not the people of the world today. And although our societies seem worlds apart, the lost and despondent of every age share a common need: to have their carnal expectations shattered.

Christ came into this world not as an exalted leader, as some expected he would, but as a babe in swaddling clothes. He did not rise to political power but simply grew like a man—one step, one day, one meal, one task, one trial at a time. And Christ came not with wealth but with wisdom—the wisdom of a simple message to love the Lord with all your heart and with all your soul and with all your mind, and to love your neighbor as yourself. Many expectations were shattered when Christ emerged from obscurity to proclaim these words. But in doing so, he replaced each shattered expectation with a fuller revelation of himself as the living Lord.

May we begin this year with high hopes and great expectations. But let us not expect God to bless all that we do. The Almighty often has different plans, and we should expect him to reveal them in simple, uncomplicated, and unassuming ways. Where can we find this plan? Where can we find that inescapable hope that guides us through the hard times and shattered expectations waiting in the year to come? We can find it first in parents fleeing for a baby's life, amid the backdrop of murdered children; then in a man emerging from obscurity to die in public disgrace on Calvary's hill. His name is Jesus Christ, and he knows what to expect for you and for me.

We may not know what the future holds but we can know the one who holds the future in the palm of his nail-scarred hand. May you expect no less in the year to come. *Soli deo gloria*—to God's glory alone!—Charles J. Williams Jr.

Illustrations

NO HELP FROM HEAVEN.   On a wall in the Alte Pinakothek museum in Munich, Germany, hangs a highly respected rendering of Herod's cruelty entitled "The Slaughter of the Innocents." The work, by one of the most notable artists of his time, Peter Paul Rubens, magnificently captures the gripping rampage. "[Rubens] has organized his depiction in a great spiral of overlapping activity . . . a regally dressed woman in the center, her outstretched arms leading the viewer to the angels who are waiting, ready to receive the children into heaven. Fathers behind the women [threaten] with stones as mothers wail and plead. One of the latter tries to scratch out the eyes of a soldier; another grabs an attacker's hair; a third bites a murderer's arm. Children scream, thrash out, and are piled up like carcasses from the hunt, while soldiers bare their ugliest faces and flex muscular arms and legs against the unexpected strength of the women."[8]—C.J.W.Jr.

ROSES WILL BLOOM AGAIN.   Shattered expectations need not be a negative event. One of the great sermons by R. G. Lee, "Roses Will Bloom Again," echoes this universal truth in describing the desert: "The desert, the desolate desert, the dreary desert, with the cracks in the ground that seem like parched lips that cry for rain; the desert, desolate without a flower or fountain in all of its weary miles; the desert, with its hot sands that burn the eyes as the wind blows across them; the hot desert, the desolate desert, the dreary desert, the desert without pools of water, the desert without flowers, the desert with the jackals that howl and the wolves that prowl, and the serpents that crawl."[9]

Who would imagine such a place bursting into beauty like a rose of the garden? Dr. Lee did, and so did the prophet Isaiah when he wrote, "The desert shall rejoice, and blossom as a rose" (Isa 35:1). The same God who turns the dry terrain into a beautiful garden can surely turn your shattered expectations into something wonderful.—C.J.W.Jr.

[8]Richard Mühlberger, "The Bible in Art: The New Testament" (New York: Portland House, 1990), 46–47.

[9]Robert Green Lee, "Roses Will Bloom Again." In *Payday Someday and Other Sermons by Robert Green Lee,* Baptist Classics Series, edited by Timothy and Denise George (Nashville: Broadman, 1995), 233–247.

SERMON SUGGESTIONS

Topic: The Martyrs

TEXT: Isa. 26:16–21; John 16:21; 2 Cor. 4:17

Theme: Come, my people—hide yourselves for a little while until the wrath is past. (1) When in distress, seek the Lord in prayer. (2) Recognize that there may be an element of divine chastening in every bitter experience of life, and let it draw you to the Lord in faith rather than drive you from him in unbelief. (3) Look for an end to "the wrath" or "the indignation" that now causes so much blood to be shed on the earth.—John P. Milton

Topic: After Christmas, What?

TEXT: Matt. 2:12

(1) After Christmas, we ought to gain a new perspective and appreciation of life and everything we do in it. (2) After Christmas, we ought to live with a renewed confidence that God can help us face and handle the unexpected occurrences. (3) After Christmas, we ought to have a deeper commitment to Christ.—Hugh Litchfield

Hymn Suggestions: First Sunday After Christmas

1. "Go Tell It on the Mountain," African American Spiritual, John W. Work Jr. (1940); "Go Tell It," harmony by John W. Work III (1940)

This spiritual, in unaffected words and music, joyfully proclaims the Savior's birth. A soloist or choral group could sing the stanzas, leaving the unison refrain for congregational singing.

2. "Praise the Lord, Ye Heavens, Adore Him," Anonymous, *Foundling Hospital Psalms and Hymns* (1797): "Hyferdol," Rowland H. Prichard (1830)

This eighteenth-century hymn, the first two stanzas of which are based on Psalm 148, voices praise to both the God of creation and the God of salvation. It could effectively be sung antiphonally line-by-line between choir and congregation.

3. "In Bethlehem a Newborn Baby," Rosamond E. Herklots (1909); "In Bethlehem," Wilbur Held (1983)

The flight into Egypt, as recorded in the

gospel reading for this day, is the subject of this contemporary hymn. The simple folk-like tune could appropriately be accompanied on a guitar.

4. "O Come, All Ye Faithful," John F. Wade (1743), translated by Frederick Oakeley (1841); "Adeste Fidelis," John F. Wade (1751)

Scores of Christmas carols and hymns could be chosen for this Sunday's worship. Possibly none is better known and loved than this one, which invites every worshiper to join in the adoration of the Christ Child.—Hugh T. McElrath

Worship Aids

CALL TO WORSHIP. "Great and marvelous are thy works, Lord God Almighty; just and true are thy ways, thou King of saints. Who shall not fear thee, O Lord, and glorify thy name? For thou only art holy; for all nations shall come and worship before thee; for thy judgments are made manifest" (Rev. 15:3b–4).

INVOCATION. O Lord, let this be a time of reflection and confession and thanksgiving; a time of renewal of faith and hope and love. By your very presence and in the power of the Holy Spirit may this prayer be answered.

OFFERTORY SENTENCE. "For ye know the grace of our Lord Jesus Christ, that, though he was rich, yet for your sakes he became poor, that ye through his poverty might be rich" (2 Cor. 8:9).

OFFERTORY PRAYER. As you have enriched us with your boundless grace in so many ways, O God, grant us also the blessing of courage to follow the example of our Lord in giving and serving.

PRAYER. Eternal God, on this Sunday after Christmas many of us are like the young man in one of Jesus' stories who went and spent all he had, and finding himself in want, returned to his father's house. Some of us have spent all of our money, even money we didn't have. Bless us for our generosity and good intentions. Some of us have spent all of our energy. Give us rest and peace and refreshment of soul. Some of us have also spent

our hope, love, and excitement about life. Give us a renewal of our faith and a capacity to share in the fellowship and dreams of the Christian community.

As the year draws to a close, help us, loving God, to remember with thankfulness the good moments that it has held, and to lay to rest without fear or guilt the bad ones. Usher us into a new year with the will to find new insight and to live with new strength. You are the living water; teach us to drink deeply from your well. You are the bread of life; teach us to eat daily until we are filled. Give peace to the troubled, wholeness to the sick, companionship to the lonely, resourcefulness to the shallow, commitment to the faint-hearted, and joy to those who are broken in spirit.

Bless the months before us; bring rest to our weary world and hope to millions who dwell in darkness. Use us, who wait before you, to accomplish your will through devotion, imagination, and love. In Jesus' name we pray.—William Powell Tuck

Sermon: Living on the Wrong Side of Christmas

TEXT: Ps. 72:1–8; Acts 8:26–40

There are many people who live on the wrong side of Christmas. The revolution that has come through the life of Jesus Christ has transformed our world. But many people live as though it had not happened at all. We have just celebrated the birth of Christ—Christmas—but it does not take much insight to realize that the life and teaching of Christ have not fully had their sway in our world.

I. Some people live on the wrong side of Christmas because they still live in anticipation of its coming.

a. The Old Testament is filled with anticipation. The Ten Commandments offer guidelines for relating to God and others. The teachings of the great prophets like Micah, Amos, Hosea, and others instruct us in the areas of righteousness and justice. The Old Testament writers are constantly pointing toward the future for the fulfillment of their teachings. They are reaching forward in anticipation to something—someone—to complete their hopes and dreams.

b. The seventy-second Psalm is an example of this spirit of anticipation. This royal psalm was most likely written in connection with the coronation of a king. The writer prayed that the new king would rule with God's justice and righteousness, be a defender of the poor, and reign a long time with peace and prosperity. The Jewish people lived in anticipation of the king who would one day come and reign as envisioned. The prophet Isaiah wrote about one who would lay down his life for his people. He, too, was looking to the future in anticipation of a Savior.

c. Many are still living in anticipation of the coming of Christ. They are still looking for God to come, and they do not see his presence in our world.

II. There are others who spend their lives on the wrong side of Christmas because they only look backward.

a. They look back to Christ's birth, life, teachings, death, and Resurrection. We, of course, have to look back to study who he was and what he said, but these persons spend all of their time looking to the past. Christ for them is like one of those small bubblelike Christmas scenes you can shake to see snow whirl all around when you set it down. The Christmas scene is self-contained and artificial. It may be beautiful, but it offers no life—only fantasy. For some people, this is their concept of Christ. He is a distant person in the past. They believe he gave us good teachings, lived a good life, and did some marvelous things, but that he is confined to the past.

b. We all focus a great deal of our Christmas celebration on the past, don't we? There are, of course, many rich heritage's from the past that we want to hold on to. But for some of us, Christmas is nothing but nostalgia. We become absorbed in looking back and thinking about the time when we were small children and sat in front of the fireplace with mother and father. Christmas for us is primarily a time of looking back to the past. There is no sense of the present in it at all for us today.

c. Christmas is not just a past event. The past should become a stepping-stone to enable us to realize the deeper meaning of Christmas, so that we will not live with our focus in the wrong direction. We draw on the past to live more creatively in the present.

III. Some others live on the wrong side of Christmas because their vision is directed primarily towards the future.

a. You have seen the signs as you drive down the highway: "Prepare to meet your God," or "Jesus is coming soon." The chief emphasis here is on a Jesus who is to come. He is the distant Christ, the One who will come sometime in the future. These persons spend all of their time speculating about when Jesus will return, how it will happen, what our condition will be, and what we might be doing. Everything focuses on a Christ who is still in the future. That is focusing on the wrong side of Christmas, too. This is not to say that the Second Coming has no place in our theology. Of course it does. But when it is our primary focus, then the emphasis is in the wrong place.

b. This does not mean that we are to live without some sense of expectancy toward the future. Too many live without any real expectations about the future. That is the reason some persons accomplish so little in their lives. They have no expectation, no sense of doing anything with their life. Meaningful living arises out of having expectations for our future and genuine goals. We are constantly reaching toward fulfillment. We live with an openness toward Christ to guide us in his way.

IV. How then are we to live in the light of Christmas? We have to learn to live in the present.

a. At this point the characters from the book of Acts enter our story. Earlier, Philip had given his life to Christ and become his disciple. There are some lessons in the story on the encounter of Philip with the man from Ethiopia that may offer guidance for us in learning how to live in the present. One day a messenger from God came to Philip and said, "Arise and go to the road from Jerusalem to Gaza." And you notice what he did: immediately he followed the guidance of God's spirit.

b. Notice that his meeting with the traveler along this busy road to Gaza seemed to happen by chance. It was not planned or thought through. God may sometimes work in our lives or through a "chance" encounter we have with someone else to accomplish his will. Through that chance meeting we may have an opportunity to help another person, or they may influence us.

c. The man Philip met was reading a passage of Scripture from the fifty-third chapter of Isaiah. When Philip found out that the man did not know the meaning of the passage he was reading, he took time to start where he was and guided him into understanding its meaning. Verse 35 indicates that Philip shared the good news of the gospel with the man, which may have taken some lengthy period of time. But he began with the man where he was. That's where God always begins with us. He meets us when we are hanging on the end of the rope of our frustrations, or in our failures, sorrows, pains, joys, hopes, ignorance, and wisdom. Wherever we are, God begins with us there and gently guides us further into truth.

d. After the Ethiopian eunuch had heard the message of Christ and realized that Isaiah's prophecy about the suffering servant was fulfilled in Jesus' coming, he saw water near them and asked Philip: "Look, here is water. What is there to prevent my being baptized?" At that moment he was baptized and arose from the water to live for Christ. When you surrender your life to God, you begin to live for him right at that moment—not sometime in the future, but right then. At any moment, in any place, God can touch your life through a friend or stranger and challenge you to live for him. Having been changed by his spirit, you are to begin living for him today.

V. God has given us this day. Live today. Utilize it well. Accept it as the gift that God has given you. This is the time we know we can live for the Christ. Remember the words of the prophet: "He shall be called Emmanuel, which means 'God with us.'" God is with us now—not just in the future, not only in the past, but in the present. He is Emmanuel—God with us now.—William Powell Tuck

Illustrations

INDICTMENT. Someone once asked the renowned Jewish theologian Martin Buber why he had not accepted Jesus as the Messiah. "When my Messiah comes," he responded, "there will be a reign of peace, justice, and righteousness for all mankind. Your Christ has not brought this into the world." Friedrich Nietzsche was asked why he had not become a Christian. "When I see one," he replied, "I will become one." Both of these persons have issued a strong indictment on how far removed our daily living is from the teachings of Christ and how little Christ has really penetrated our lives.—W.P.T.

PROSPECT. A young man sat in my study a number of years ago. He had reached the bottom of his life and seemed to be hanging onto a knot in the rope of his life. He poured out the ills that he felt were in his life and exclaimed that he didn't know where to turn. I tried to turn him to God. I pointed out the good things I saw in him. I noted the high virtues and spoke about the dreams, hopes, and possibilities he had. He still had great promise. Unless a person can see the possibilities in his or her life, then that life remains anchored to the past and that individual cannot really grow or reach his or her potential. The power of God is never released in you without some vision of what you can become. You cannot live a productive life with your eyes focused only on the future, but you do need to have some sense of expectation as you move forward into tomorrow.—W.P.T.

SECTION III.
Messages for Communion Services

SERMON SUGGESTIONS

Topic: How to Enjoy a Meal

TEXT: 1 Cor. 11:17–26

I. In our text for this morning, Paul instructs the Corinthians on how to receive Holy Communion. He makes it clear that they are not doing it right! "In what I am about to say, I do not commend you." That is to say, they had it all wrong. He says, "You come to gorge yourself, and you do not think of those who are with you at the same meal. You have it all wrong."

It sounds like he is reminding them, in the way that parents brief their children before the guests arrive, to have good table manners, saying, "Don't grab the food; pass it to your neighbor; don't speak with your mouth full." But that's not exactly what Paul is doing. This is a sacred meal, not an ordinary meal, and the Corinthians knew that. They were Greeks, recently converted from what were called "mystery religions," in which the central act of worship was a sacred meal. But, Paul says, "this is a different meal than the one you are accustomed to." In the mystery religions, the food on the table somehow, by magic, was changed into heavenly food, and the purpose of eating was to be transported out of this world into a heavenly state. The purpose of the meal was to get "high," —to be transported into another realm of consciousness. The Greek word for this was *ekstasis*, from which we get our word *ecstasy*, and it means to get outside of your body. That was the purpose of the meal in the mystery religions. They came to gorge themselves on the premise, I suppose, that the more you eat

and the more you drink, the higher you get. They thought that Communion in the church, another sacred meal, was of the same nature.

"You have it all wrong," Paul says. "When you meet together, it is not the Lord's Supper that you eat." And then he describes the nature of the Lord's Supper. He says that its essence is remembrance: we meet to remember what happened at the Last Supper, to remember that Jesus took the cup and the bread, gave thanks, and then passed them to his disciples and said, "These are symbols of what I am about to do for you"—in other words, that he was about to bear the cross for us. Paul leaves no doubt about what it means to say that Jesus bore the cross for us. To the Corinthians, later, he will say it means this: "God was in Christ reconciling the world unto himself, and calling us to be ministers of reconciliation." So, when you come together for this meal, remember what he did, and act as though what he did did some good. That is, be *reconciled*, act like you're a family. Eat together as one body, be one, be reconciled. That's his message.

II. There's been a debate in the Church ever since the Middle Ages about the presence of Christ in the Communion: how is Christ present here? The debate focused on the elements, asking, Do they really become the body of Christ? There are several theories that try to explain the mystery of why we can say that Christ is present with us in the Holy Communion. In a way, these theories have served as a distraction. They focus on the wrong thing. They ask, *when* do the elements become the actual body of Christ? The answer Paul gave to the Corinthians was, when we are one, when we are reconciled with each other, when we can come to the table as one family.

a. It's true that in Communion a miracle takes place, but not the one the Corinthians thought took place, and not even the one that some Christians think takes place. The miracle was not in the elements, according to Paul. The miracle was in the congregation. In this world that is divided by race, clan, nation, gender, age, and a whole score of other fences that we build between one another, Paul says to the Church, "Knock the fences down and be *one*. Be like a family, sit together at one table, with one loaf and one cup. Act as though what he did for you did some good."

That's why from the beginning the members of the Church were instructed to greet one another with a kiss. In the Communion that's called "passing the peace." It was to be done before they came to the table. Its purpose was to make sure that there were no enemies at the Lord's Table, nor even any strangers. The custom has dropped out of most churches today, although it's making a comeback, I understand, in some churches. We do something like that, incidentally, you know, at the end of the service in this church. But at Communion it ought to come before the meal, just as when you are invited to a dinner party you meet the guests before you sit down at the table so that there is fellowship among you. We're going to do something like that this morning. Don't worry. I'm not going to ask you to lose your inhibitions; we would not be Methodists, would we, if we lost our inhibitions. But neither would it be right for us to celebrate Holy Communion in this church as strangers, because the miracle of Holy Communion is not what happens on the altar, it's what happens in the nave. It's not the elements that become the body of Christ, it's the congregation that becomes the body of Christ.

b. This passage contains another important instruction that we often overlook. Paul says that we are to celebrate this meal until Jesus comes again. That means that as we gather here we are to remember not only what happened in the past, but also what will happen in the future. That makes us different than most people. Most people base their behavior in the present only on what has happened in the past. They say they are realistic

in doing that, that what has happened in the past is going to determine what happens in the future, or what has happened in the past will be repeated in the future. So they say, "There will always be wars, there will always be hatred, there will always be those people you cannot trust." Or they say, "I can never change." They base the present only on their knowledge of what has happened in the past and call it realism. Most people live that way. They let the past determine the present.

But Christians are different. We're to base our behavior in the present on what will happen in the future. In fact, we believe that the future has already begun, because Jesus Christ has already been here and the Kingdom has already been established. We are instructed to live as if his Kingdom were already here. We're to get our instruction not from the past so much as from the future.

We're different from others in some ways, we Christians, because we let what *will be* determine the way we live now. We have, in Holy Communion, that vision of the time when we'll all be one, when we'll be like a family. We'll all be at one table, and no one will be turned away.

If we can live like that now, in this kind of world, that's a miracle—the miracle of Holy Communion, when Christ is really present.— Mark Trotter

Topic: Is Human Forgiveness Possible?
TEXT: Matt. 18:21–22

I. It has generally been understood that forgiveness is something Christians do naturally and that the church helps them to do it. The Lord's Prayer, for example, speaks of forgiving our debtors as God forgives our debts (Matt. 6:12). Nevertheless, what I hear again and again in my pastoral counseling is, "I just can't forgive her (or him) for what she (or he) has done." Apparently, there are some issues that simply cannot be resolved by merely trying harder.

Today's text indicates that Peter was apparently struggling with this matter. Jesus had just warned his followers about the evil of leading others to sin (Matt. 18:1–9). Instead of becoming the cause of someone else's ruin, every believer should make it his or her business to find the sheep that has gone astray and bring it back to the fold (Matt. 18:10–14).

Suppose, however, that the shoe is on the other foot. Suppose that I am neither the sinner nor the one who has caused another to become involved in sin. Suppose instead that I am the one sinned against. What then? Am I to assume that it is my responsibility to put things right again?

In Matthew 18:15–20, Jesus presented the whole scheme for mending broken relationships among Christians. In summary what he said was: "If anyone sins against you, spare no effort to immediately get things right again."

Upon hearing Jesus' teaching, Peter apparently realized that he must forgive a brother who has sinned against him (Matt.18:21). But if he were to take the initiative in bringing about this reconciliation, how often must he reveal this merciful attitude? How long must he be patient? Is "up to seven times" adequate—even admirable?

There was something wrong with Peter's approach, however. It sounded as though a forgiving spirit was a commodity that could be weighed, measured, counted, and packaged. It suggested that forgiveness could be parceled out little by little up to a certain well-defined and predetermined limit. Peter apparently believed that beyond a certain point forgiveness ought not to be expected, or even required.

II. What, then, is forgiveness? If it is not condoning or excusing what someone else has done, what is it? If it is not an admission that my hurt was self-inflicted and thereby diminished your responsibility for my pain, what is it? If it is not the surrender of some kind of fantasized power over you that I have grown to treasure dearly, what is it? If it is not forgetting, then tell me, what is forgiveness?

What happens when a hurting person forgives the person who caused the injury? What happens when God forgives a sinner?

The bottom line is that forgiveness is a miracle. Forgiveness is a new beginning. Forgiveness is starting over and trying again with the person who caused you the pain.

Take God, for instance. When God forgives, he offers us a new start with him. He holds out his hand and says, "Come on. Take it. I want to be your friend again. In spite of everything, I want to be with you. I want to be over you, and under you, and in you as the loving power of your existence. I am not go-

ing to let anything you do get in my way. So, let's begin again."

That is what God does when he forgives us. He breaks down the walls we build. He gets into the backyard of our souls and takes the initiative in building a new relationship with us. We can do it, too, with one another.

You start where you are, not where you wish you were, not where you would have been if the bad things had never happened. You start wherever you are now, with any person who has hurt you, and you take the initiative in making a new beginning.

You hold out your hand and say, "I want to be your friend again. I want to be your father again, your daughter again, your husband, your wife, your son again. Let's start over." This is what forgiveness is!

Forgiveness is the creation of a new beginning. It does not always take away the hurt. It does not deny the past injury. It merely refuses to allow it to stand in the way of a new start.

You do not have to understand why the other person caused you such pain. You do not have to get the whole story straight—to piece together all the loose ends so you can be sure there are no secrets left. You certainly do not have to squeeze every ounce of guilt from the soul of the person who did you wrong.

You just begin where you are in the mutual pain. Both of you hurt, and you begin at the point of that shared hurt. That is the starting line for a new relationship. And from there you walk together into the future.

Some of us have to forgive people who are beyond our reach. You may have to forgive a former husband who still hates you so much he would stuff your forgiving spirit down your throat. You have to forgive a neurotic mother long dead, and begin again with only a memory of her.

Forgiveness does not deny the past. It can only create a new future. Sometimes we must forgive in absentia, letting go of our resentment and spite and starting over with the free spirit inside us, leaving the other person to God.

It is hard, perhaps the hardest thing you have ever tried to do. In fact, it is so hard you may wonder why you should even try. Once you have been stung by somebody's brutal unfairness, you have incentive enough to never forgive—never, never, never!

The logic of sheer justice is on your side. You were treated unfairly—wrongly. It is not fair to forgive. He did you dirt. He made you feel so unlovable that you felt less than human. All that you owe him is your contempt!

Let him feel the frigid blast of your scorn. Why should he get anything from your hurting heart but the hatred that you genuinely feel? Let him sleep in his misery! The only clout you have with him anymore is the clout of your contempt. You want him to feel its full force!

Why should you forgive him?

The primary reason is the wooden cross dug into a hill where a man once died in pain for sins he did not commit. God invented forgiveness as the only way to keep alive the relationship that is most precious to him—the relationship with the children he created but who turned against him.

If God had not found inside himself the power of love to forgive, there would be no future for the likes of us. But he found it, and the hope of the whole world is vested in his readiness to make a new beginning with us—a million new beginnings if they are needed.

He never shuts the door to us. He will always forgive. He does not merely forget. He does not merely understand. He puts himself at our side and says: "Let's start over. I will be your father again. I will be your friend again. I will be your savior forever. Let's start over."

Every time an ordinary person like you or me discovers the power to begin again in a relationship with someone who caused us needless pain, that person walks in stride with the living God.

That, I believe, is the crux of the matter. Human forgiveness is possible only if we are freed by God's forgiveness. And then, when we forgive, we are even more free. We are free to make a new beginning and know in our hearts that life will be all right again even when someone has made everything unspeakably wrong for us!

Yes, human forgiveness is possible! It's up to you, however, to make it happen!—Gary C. Redding

Topic: Taking the Cross

TEXT: Mark 8:31–38

All of the talk about suffering and dying in today's text sounds like a message for a hos-

pice or a funeral parlor. One might suggest that it is a word for the aged and the dying, but the disciples were in their prime. They were planning for life. The numerous inquiries about life indicate that people were attracted to Jesus' promises of life in abundance, life with eternal dimensions. Thus Jesus' conflict with Peter makes sense. Peter's confession, "You are the Christ," is the high point in the gospel; it was more than a discovery—it was a revelation! He had just identified the Messiah, and now he was expected to accept a total revision of the role of the Messiah. The common expectation was that the Son of man would come on clouds of victory, but Jesus revised the script. The Son of man would suffer. The twelve disciples had to be prepared for what was coming—rejection, suffering, and death at the hands of elders, priests, and scribes. Do you blame Peter for protesting? He had come to Jesus for life rather than death, for victory rather than failure, for reward rather than punishment.

I. The cross deals in truth. One would think that at about this time a wise leader would have realized that he had taken his disciples too far, that they couldn't handle talk of suffering and death, that it was time to leap over the pain and speak only of the resurrection. Instead, Jesus extended the message of the cross. He credited the disciples with the maturity to deal in truth; he called all would-be disciples to deny self, take up the cross, and follow him. At this point in the gospel, the cross becomes more than an event in history. It does not end with the death of Jesus. The cross is the norm of discipleship. Unlike demons and denari, it is not disposable—not a part of ancient culture that can be discarded the moment we leave the first century. The cross has become the symbol of Christian life. Both baptism and the Lord's Supper focus on the cross of Christ as the symbol of redemptive suffering. We cannot hide from the unpleasant truth of the gospel.

My son had surgery for a small hernia at the age of four. We were referred to a pediatric surgeon, who made an indelible impression on me and my son. He treated the child as if he could understand pain and surgery. He spoke to the child rather than to the father. He gave details right down to needle sticks, funny green suits, and waking up with pain. But his tone of voice reassured both father and son that this was going to be OK, and so it was.

Peter wanted Jesus to avoid the suffering, or perhaps to avoid the truth. Why should Jesus speak of suffering, death, and the cross? Why not let sleeping dogs lie? The bad will emerge soon enough. There is a general truth here. Suffering and death are a part of life that can neither be avoided nor ignored. The truth hurts, but the truth also prepares; the truth strengthens and sets us free.

II. The cross points toward hope. The word of the cross is good news, not bad. Peter did not understand this, and his misunderstanding has become a basic problem for the church through the ages. That Jesus died is not so difficult as how he died. The scandal of the cross is multiplied by the extended expectation that we too should take up the cross. The way of the cross is an absurdity that works out to make perfect sense in real life. Nothing worthy of our best comes without cost. You cannot love without pain. The commitment to love another person is a door to suffering. To love is to be present, to be vulnerable, to care, to be involved. The pain of love is like the pain of birth. It has meaning. It brings life. The Incarnation, the Word become flesh, is the way of God. The redemptive love of God sent the Son into the world. In Christ, the absurdity of the cross was transformed into perfect sense because it was perfect love.

Dietrich Bonhoeffer called the cross "the cost of discipleship": "When Christ calls a man, he bids him come and die." It may be a death like that of the first disciples, who left home and work to follow Jesus, or it may be a death like Martin Luther's, who left the monastery and went out into the world. But it is the same death every time—death in Jesus Christ, "the death of the old man at his call." The word of the cross stands for all time as a landmark of Christian love—there is no cheap grace. There is no way to become Christian and avoid the cross. There is no place for disciples who are not followers.—Larry Dipboye

Topic: The Great Hinges

TEXT: 1 Cor. 16:8–9; 2 Cor. 1:8–10

In the last chapter of Paul's first letter to the church of Corinth, we come upon some interesting words: "But I will stay in Ephesus until Pentecost, for a wide door for effective work has opened to me, and there are many adversaries" (1 Cor. 16:8–9 RSV). *The New English Bible* makes the message even clearer: "A great opportunity has opened for effective work, and there is much opposition" (v. 9).

Haven't you found it true in your own life? The things that mean the most to you were purchased at a very great price. Good things never come easy. That baby you almost lost— or thought you'd never have—is a special child because of the pain and the difficulty you experienced. That marriage of yours means much to you because of the struggle you both had to go through for what seemed at the time a million years. That faith that carries you means more than you could ever begin to put into words because back there was a dark night of the soul when you thought you'd lost it all. Yet somehow you made it—and here you are.

Some of you savor life in a way that most of us know nothing about. You almost lost it back then, and now every day is a special grace. You may be in real estate, banking, or teaching, and what you do means a great deal because of the sacrifices and years of hard work it took to get you where you are. So, many here know the truth of our Scripture today: "A great opportunity has opened for effective work, and there is much opposition."

Doesn't this verse run counter to so much of the religion we hear on all sides? According to this religion, you're in God's will if everything works out all right. Good people have untroubled marriages. Good people do not get divorces and do not fuss. Good people do not have doubts within the faith journey. Good people have things work out to their advantage. Good people don't suffer or have emotional problems or financial worries. Good people find that everything works out just fine.

And down beside that subtle heresy we place today's Scripture: "A great opportunity has opened for effective work, and there is much opposition." Is there a more universal truth?

I. *Great opportunities come to us all.* Paul would stay in Ephesus, he said. Piecing the record together, we find that he was there, on and off, for at least three years. Ephesus was a large seaport city in the Roman province of

Asia; it was a commercial and religious center; it was the number one city in the province; and as A. T. Robertson put it, "After years of hard work, a door, great and powerful, stands wide open." Paul recognized that if the gospel could take root in Ephesus, it could spread like a wildfire across the whole of Asia.

All of us have some Ephesus, some great challenging opportunity, that could change us for the rest of our days. I never will forget my father telling about that man in the 1930s who knocked on my father's door more than once, trying to talk him into buying a few shares in a new drink they were peddling in Columbus, Georgia. The concoction had a strange name: "Coca Cola." Many who picked up that stock are millionaires today. We all have let some opportunity slip by that cannot be called back.

But Paul, much wiser than most of us, saw in his Ephesus an open door—and so he walked through it. In Shakespeare's *Julius Caesar,* Brutus speaks: "There is a tide in the affairs of men, / Which taken at the flood, leads on to fortune; / Omitted, all the voyage of their life / Is bound in shallows and in miseries; / And we must take the current when it serves, / Or lose our ventures."

Open your eyes to the doors that are open to you. What is your Ephesus? If you are father or husband, it may have something to do with giving yourself to those closest to you in meaningful ways. If you are a teenager, Ephesus may mean getting to know your parents as people and not just as parents. If you are a student, what you do in the next four years may determine the rest of your life. If you are on the edge of retirement, your Ephesus may be to see life not as a finished thing but as only the beginning of a new adventure.

II. *Great opposition goes hand in hand with great opportunity.* We are not uncertain of the opposition at Ephesus. In 1 Corinthians 15:32 Paul spoke of the "beasts" he had to battle at Ephesus. In 2 Corinthians 1:8–9 he talked about how he was under the sentence of death in Asia. We know that the silversmiths at Ephesus had a pretty good business forging their shabby little silver statues of the great god Artemis. They saw in Paul's word a threat to their business. When you tamper with a person's pocketbook, you usually get a

rise out of him. But the point? When the great hinges open, often there is opposition, adversity, difficulty.

In my experience at least there are two kinds of enemies. There is the enemy within. My own insides can immobilize me. Fear of the unknown, of the unsure, of making a fool of myself, can be a powerful adversary. The weight of my past and the fragile little ego bequeathed to me can make it hard to walk through when the great doors of opportunity open. It is so much easier to drift, procrastinate, or evade than to walk through those challenging doors. The enemy, for me, has been within.

But the enemy, for me, has also been without. Circumstance can make life more difficult. Being in the wrong place at the wrong time can make it more complicated. Not having the advantages that somebody else has muddles the matter. We have all played that sad little game: "if, if, if." If sickness had not come. If turmoil had not happened. If I had not been passed over for that job. If my boss was not so mean. If that lump had not appeared. If those corpuscles had been normal. If I hadn't been born with freckles. If I had more money. If, if, if. "A great opportunity has opened for effective work, and there is much opposition."

Always there is opposition. Trouble comes with the territory. Nothing good has ever come to any of us with a small price tag attached. When will we ever learn that the only things we ever get at bargain-basement prices are trinkets best left in the basement?

III. *We do not lose heart . . . we stay in Ephesus.* So what are we to say? Paul said: "I will stay at Ephesus at least until Pentecost." There was a great door and there were many adversaries. And he chose to stay.

And you, what will you do? Stay or run away? It comes down to that choice at the end, doesn't it?

Winston Churchill said that the secret of success could be discovered in six little words: "Never, never, never, never give up." These words helped him and the people of England through the dark days of World War II. Aren't they what Paul said?

Skip from the last chapter of 1 Corinthians to the fourth chapter of 2 Corinthians. Many in that church did not understand Paul's motives. Some would not speak to him. Some doubted his word. But the apostle did not turn back. "Therefore, having this ministry by the mercy of God, we do not lose heart. We have renounced disgraceful, underhanded ways; we refuse to practice cunning or to tamper with God's word . . ." (vv. 1–2). Now skip down to the eighth verse of that fourth chapter: "We are afflicted in every way . . . perplexed . . . persecuted . . . struck down." But in between all those adversities, Paul weaves a golden thread: "We are not crushed . . . we are not driven to despair . . . we are not forsaken . . . we are not destroyed." In the sixteenth verse he comes full circle: "So we do not lose heart." Though our outer nature is wasting away, our inner nature is being renewed every day.

Back now to 2 Corinthians 1:8–10, in which the apostle speaks of Ephesus. "For we do not want you to be ignorant, brethren, of the affliction we experienced in Asia; for we were so utterly, unbearably crushed that we despaired of life itself. Why, we felt that we had received the sentence of death; but that was to make us rely not on ourselves but on God who raises from the dead; he delivered us from so deadly a peril, and he will deliver us again." When facing the open door—adversaries and all—we need not run away in fear or despair. God will be with us in it.

I do not know what you have on your heart. There may be myriad opportunities you have let slip through your fingers. There may be some Ephesus toward which you have failed to walk. There may be a host of adversaries that have crippled and drained you of so much that makes life good. But remember that Paul, in writing to a fussy, troubled church, burned into their hearts: "A great opportunity has opened for effective work, and there is much opposition. But I will stay in Ephesus. . . ."—Roger Lovette

Illustrations

THE WARMEST PLACE.   Once in a group we were asked to name the warmest room in the house where we grew up. The leader wanted us to describe the room where we felt safest and most secure, the room, I think, that represented home. As we moved around the circle, it was amazing to hear the answers. Almost everybody named the kitchen. We felt warmest in the place where we sat down and ate together. The church has gathered around a table for two thousand years and found a family and bread and a cup for the journey and a place of incredible warmth.—Roger Lovette

FROM SYMBOL TO SACRAMENT.   The fact that the bread and wine, though they are only symbols, have so often served as the acknowledgment of God's sacramental presence is probably the reason why, by metonymy, we call the Holy Supper *the* sacrament. We all remember those blessed times when God has been much more than a conception in our worship. Whenever he has left a result upon us, whenever we have risen from the table with a deeper insight, a heightened vision, a firmer resolve, the symbols we have used as an acknowledgment that God once appeared in history have been taken in hand by the Creator and Redeemer himself and made very present sacraments.—Douglas Horton[1]

CHRISTIANS AS THE GOSPEL.   Theologically, we have been discovering anew that the Church is not an appendage to the gospel; it is itself a part of the gospel. The gospel cannot be separated from that new people of God, in which its nature is to be made manifest. Practically, this has always been known to everyone who has ever attempted to talk with the adherents of faith other than his own. Even where it is only two individuals who meet to talk, each brings with him the whole of what he is and of what his faith has made of him. The community is implicit in the individual, the Church in the believer. We may feel that the gospel towers over us, judging us; yet as far as the world is concerned, we are ourselves the gospel; there is no other.—Stephen Neill[2]

A GOOD COMMUNION.   Our Lord did not say, "Come unto me all ye faultless"; neither did he say, "Be sure you tear yourselves to pieces first." There are only three necessities of a good Communion—faith, hope, and charity. To rely utterly on God and be in char-

[1] *The Meaning of Worship.*
[2] *Christian Faith and Other Faiths.*

ity with the world—this is essential. What you happen to be feeling at the moment does not matter in the least.—Evelyn Underhill[3]

FORGIVING OTHERS.   He that cannot forgive others breaks the bridge over which he himself must pass if he would ever reach heaven; for everyone has need to be forgiven.—George Herbert

[3] *Letters.*

SECTION IV.
Messages for Funeral Services

SERMON SUGGESTIONS

Topic: Easter and Our Sorrow

There was the testimony of Jesus that his [God] was the God of the living and not [of] the dead. And there was his sure word, "I am not alone, for the Father is with me." There was the steadying reminder, "Be of good cheer, I have overcome the world." Here was the promise of the Son, which was meant to bring strength and courage and victory.

Suddenly he was in their midst—alive! The dead Jesus now the living Lord! He comes— the message of Easter—triumphant over the grave when everything is lost. He comes— when sorrow is the heaviest! He comes—when destruction is the greatest! He comes—and salvation is the nearest! Hear him speak to every disciple in every age: When your world comes to an end, I will come to you. When catastrophe engulfs you, I will enfold you. When your heads are bowed in sorrow, lift up your hearts in joy!

He reveals the Word in the one Word we long to hear: those who belong to Christ will live! "We say, 'In the midst of life we die.' God answers, 'Nay, in the midst of death we live.'"[1] Death is our enemy and would be to the end. But Christ comes! When he guards us and keeps us, he transforms death from defeat into victory, from despair into hope, from destruction into completion. "The death which they thought to inflict on Him as dishonour and disgrace has become the glori-

ous monument to death's defeat."[2] So—bless his name—death becomes not the end but the beginning. It is not the end of the way, but the way of the beginning. For Christ brought the end of death and the beginning of life!

And let all our frail and needy hearts remember that . . . Christ finds those who need him most. He . . . calls us by name as he called Mary that first glad day in the long ago. Forgiving our sins and offering us life, he finds us. We could never reach up to God, but he has already reached down to us. This is the gladsome news of Easter!

So, lift up your hearts! Hope for the future lies in what God did long ago when he raised Christ triumphant from the grave. And the Spirit of God abides in our hearts in this present hour to empower us and to assure us: there will be a last day, a Great Day of the Lord, for all who are kept in Christ's hand. So, lift up your hearts! "If you have heard the Easter message, you can no longer run around with a tragic face and lead the humorless existence of a man who has no hope."[3]

When trouble steals upon you, sing, "He's got the whole wide world in his hands." When night comes, pray, "Lead, kindly Light! amid th' encircling gloom." When there is no place to stand, sing, "How firm a foundation, ye

[1]Roland Bainton, *Here I Stand: A Life of Martin Luther* (Nashville, Tenn.: Abingdon Press, 1950), 370.

[2]Athanasius, *The Incarnation of the Word of God, Being the Treatise of St. Athanasius,* translated by a religious of C.S.M.V., S.th (Old Tappan, N.J.: Macmillan, 1946), 54.

[3]Karl Barth, *Dogmatics in Outline,* translated by G. T. Thomson (London: SCM Press, 1955), 123.

saints of the Lord!" And when there is no abiding city, remember, "Jerusalem, the golden, with milk and honey blest!"

Be possessed of Christ, and you will know that through the tender mercy of God the dayspring from on high has visited us, to give light to them that sit in darkness and in the shadow of death and to guide our feet into the way of peace.

In the midst of our days and years Christ confronts us as surely as he did his sorrowing disciples long ago. And, Lord of life, he cries: I *died* and I *live* for you!—Raymond Bryan Brown[4]

Topic: The Candle of the Lord

TEXT: "The spirit of man is the candle of the Lord." Prov. 20:27

The essential connection between the life of God and the life of man is the great truth of the world, and that is the truth which Solomon sets forth in the striking words which I have chosen for my text this morning. The picture which the words suggest is very simple. An unlighted candle is standing in the darkness and someone comes to light it. A blazing bit of paper holds the fire at first, but it is vague and fitful. It flares and wavers and at any moment may go out. But the vague, uncertain, flaring blaze touches the candle, the candle catches fire, and at once you have a steady flame. It burns straight and clear and constant. The candle gives the fire a manifestation point for all the room which is illuminated by it. The candle is glorified by the fire and the fire is manifested by the candle. The two bear witness that they were made for one another by the way in which they fulfil each other's life. That fulfillment comes by the way in which the inferior substance renders obedience to its superior. The candle obeys the fire. The docile wax acknowledges that the subtle flame is its master and it yields to his power; and so, like every faithful servant of a noble master, it at once gives its master's nobility the chance to utter itself, and its own substance is clothed with a glory which is not its own. The disobedient granite, if you try to burn it, neither gives the fire a chance to show its brightness nor gathers any splendor to itself. It only glows with sullen resistance

and, as the heat increases, splits and breaks but will not yield. But the candle obeys, and so in it the scattered fire finds a point of permanent and clear expression.

Can we not see, with such a picture clear before us, what must be meant when it is said that one being is the candle of another being? There is in a community a man of large, rich character whose influence runs everywhere. You cannot talk with any man in all the city but you get shown, in that man's own way, the thought, the feeling of that central man who teaches all the community to think, to feel. The very boys catch something of his power, and have something of his power, and have something about them that would not be there if he were not living in the town. What better description could you give of all that, than to say that that man's life was fire and that all these men's lives were candles which he lighted, which gave to the rich, warm, live, fertile nature that was in him multiplied points of steady exhibition, so that he lighted the town through them?

Or, not to look so widely, I pity you if in the circle of your home there is not some warm and living nature which is your fire. Your cold, dark-candle nature touched by that fire burns bright and clear. Wherever you are carried, perhaps into regions where that nature cannot go, you carry its fire and set it up in some new place. Nay, the fire itself may have disappeared, the nature may have vanished from the earth and gone to heaven; and yet still your candle life, which was lighted at it, keeps that fire still in the world, as the fire of the lightning lives in the tree that it has struck, long after the quick lightning itself has finished its short, hot life and died. So the man in the counting room is the candle of the woman who stays at home, making her soft influence felt in the rough places of trade where her feet never go; and so a man who lives like an inspiration in the city for honesty and purity and charity may be only the candle in whose obedient life burns still the fire of another strong, true man who was his father, and who passed out of men's sight a score of years ago. Men call the father dead, but he is no more dead than the torch has gone out which lighted the beacon that is blazing on the hill.— Phillips Brooks

[4] *The Fire of Truth.*

Topic: The Pillar in God's Temple

TEXT: Rev. 3:12. "Him that overcometh will I make a pillar in the temple of my God, and he shall go no more out; and I will write upon him the name of my God, and the name of the city of my God, . . . and my new name" (KJV).

There can be no end of the universe where God is, to which that growing temple does not reach, the temple of a creation to be wrought at last into a perfect utterance of God by a perfect obedience to God.

Oh, my dear friends, that is the victory that is awaiting you. Slowly, through all the universe, that temple of God is being built. Wherever, in any world, a soul by free-willed obedience catches the fire of God's likeness, it is set into the growing walls, a living stone. When in your hard fight, in your tiresome drudgery, or in your terrible temptation you catch the purpose of your being and give yourself to God, and so give him the chance to give himself to you, your life, a living stone, is taken up and set into that growing wall. And the other living, burning stones claim and welcome and embrace it. They bind it in with themselves. They make it sure with their assurance, and they gather sureness out of it. The great wall of divine likeness through human obedience grows and grows, as one tried and purified and ripened life after another is laid into it; and down at the base, the cornerstone of all, there lies the life of Him who, though He was a son, yet learned obedience by the things which He suffered, and, being made perfect, became the author of eternal salvation unto all them that obey Him.

In what strange quarries and stone yards the stones for that celestial wall are being hewn! Out of the hillsides of humiliated pride; deep in the darkness of crushed despair; in the fretting and dusty atmosphere of little cares; in the hard, cruel contacts that man has with man; wherever souls are being tried and ripened, in whatever commonplace and homely ways—there God is hewing out the pillars for his temple. Oh, if the stone can only have some vision of the temple of which it is to lie a part forever, what patience must fill it as it feels the blows of the hammer and knows that success for it is simply to let itself be wrought into what shape the Master wills.

Upon the pillar thus wrought into the temple of God's loving kingdom there are three inscriptions. I can only in one word ask you to remember what they are: "I will write upon him the name of my God, and the name of the city of my God, and my new name."

The soul that in obedience to God is growing into his likeness is dedicated to the divine love, to the hope of the perfect society, and to the ever-new knowledge of redemption and the great Redeemer. Those are its hopes, and reaching out forever and ever, all through eternity, those hopes it never can exhaust. Those writings on the pillar shall burn with purer and brighter fire the longer that the pillar stands in the temple of Him who Jesus calls "my God."

May all this great promise ennoble and illumine the struggle of our life; keep us from ever thinking that it is mean and little; lift us above its details while it keeps us forever faithful to them; and give us victory at last through Him who has already overcome.—P.B.[5]

Illustrations

THE LAST WORD.   When Henrik Ibsen, the Norwegian dramatist, came to die, his last word was, "Nevertheless." He was a great critic of the society in which he lived, a great objector and debater. It was fitting that this should be his last word. Just as he started to say something in rebuttal to what had been said, he got out the word, "Nevertheless," and then death struck suddenly.

A good word for the last word, "Nevertheless." In a very real way that is what Christian faith is all about. It takes an honest look at all the evil in the world. It faces all of life's confusions, its frustrations, its suffering, its disaster, and says, "Nevertheless." It was true in the very beginning of Christian history. In the Crucifixion of Jesus, all the agents of evil had done their utmost: Judas, Caiaphas, Pilate, and the mob. "Nevertheless," on the first day of the week, "as it began to dawn. . . ." There is a beautiful picture of that in an Edinburgh cemetery, at the grave of the little daughter of Sir James Simpson, the discoverer of chloroform. On her tombstone are carved her name and the words: "Nevertheless I Live."—Halford E. Luccock[6]

---

[5] *Candle of the Lord and Other Sermons.*
[6] *Unfinished Business.*

TEARS.   God washes the eyes by tears until
they can behold the invisible land where
tears shall come no more. O love! O affliction! Ye are the guides that show us the way
through the great airy space where our loved
ones walked; and, as hounds easily follow the
scent before the dew be risen, so God teaches
us, while yet our sorrow is wet, to follow on
and find our dear ones in heaven.—Henry
Ward Beecher

GOD'S PROMISES.   We have the promises
of God as thick as daisies in summer mead-
ows, that death, which men most fear, shall
be to us the most blessed of experiences, if
we trust in him. Death is unclasping; joy,
breaking out in the desert; the heart, come
to its blossoming time! Do we call it dying
when the bud bursts into flower?—H.W.B.

FROM DEATH UNTO LIFE.   Jesus did not
answer questions directly; he did something
better and wiser. He taught—nay, he revealed—the triumph of personality, but he
left the details of the afterlife in discreet
silence, lest they interfere with the life that
now is. He confirmed faith without satisfying
curiosity.

Must we admit, then, that we know nothing at all about life after death, and that we
are left in a world of dim hints and cryptic
analogies, with no glad assurance? Far, very

far from it! We know much, very much,
about life after death, both as to its realities
and its conditions; all, in fact, that we need to
know, if we are wise enough to lay the facts to
heart.

Now take thought: All the realities that
make life great, deep, and rewarding, giving
it meaning here and value hereafter, abide
untouched by time and death. They are both
realities and prophecies, and if we ponder
them deeply they light up the future while
they bless and guide us here.

Just consider: God lives here, hereafter, and
unto everlasting: "In him we live, and move,
and have our being." In him there is no
death, no darkness, no distance. Pray, what
more do we want or need to know? To know
God, Jesus told us, is life eternal: "All live
unto him!"—Joseph Fort Newton[7]

IMMORTALITY.   One of the most striking
and impressive things ever said on the subject of immortality and man's need for it was
what Hortense, daughter of Napoleon's
Josephine and mother of Napoleon III,
wrote to her son when he was for a brief time
in America. He was seriously ill and she did
not expect to meet him again in this life. But
she wrote: "Believe that certainly we shall
meet again. Have faith in this consoling idea.
It is too necessary not to be true."—Clarence
Edward Macartney

[7]*Everyday Religious Living.*

SECTION V.
Lenten and Easter Preaching

SERMON SUGGESTIONS

Topic: Temptation

TEXT: Matt. 4:11

As we travel through this Lententide, it is to our advantage that we do so mindful that Jesus came to confront life as we must. It is in his experience dealing with temptation, uncertainty, infidelity, blindness, death, and fickleness that we discover how we can face up to these challenges ourselves. Today we meet Jesus dealing with the most universal test of all: *temptation!*

What the Bible calls "temptation" is in fact something different than being lured or seduced into an evil act. God does not tempt us in that sense. The Greek word *peirazein,* which the evangelists use regarding Jesus' experience after his baptism, does not mean "to entice a man to do wrong," but "to test." The devil *tempts,* luring us into his trap. But Jesus was *tested.* Why?

The Lord had just launched his mission. His Baptism by John in the River Jordan was the ordination event that propelled Jesus into his all-too-brief ministry. He had heard the wondrous words of the Father saying, "This is my beloved Son, with whom I am well pleased." The Spirit of God had descended upon him like a dove. He was at the peak of spiritual ecstasy. Enthusiasm for his mission surged within.

But before he could really get going, all his years of preparation needed to be checked out. Thus we read that "Jesus was led up by the Spirit into the wilderness to be *tempted* by the devil." That should read "tested"! *Tested* by God; *tempted* by Satan.

Why would God do such a thing to his Son? To himself? It is not easy to figure that one out, unless one thinks that God himself determined it was essential that Jesus—who though fully God but who had relinquished some of his authority and was perhaps now weakened by being fully human—needed to "test drive" his newness. As Paul taught the Philippians, Jesus "did not count equality with God a thing to be grasped, but emptied himself, taking the form of a servant, being born in the likeness of men" (2:6–7). In short, this was a practical exercise, on-the-job *testing,* so to speak, so that Jesus himself could be assured that he could stand up to the future tests to be imposed upon him—the greater tests of crucifixion and death that were ahead!

And from whom does this information come? None of the disciples were present with Jesus in the wilderness. Jesus was alone, therefore he himself shared with the Twelve what has been recorded for us so that we may know what he went through. The purpose of sharing his experience with us was to give us courage and hope when we seem pinned against the wall. James Stewart writes, "It means that Christ's temptation was real, literally, desperately real. . . . Jesus told this story because the titanic struggle of the desert days and nights had marked His soul forever, and He could never forget." The writer to the Hebrews emphasizes, "Because He Himself has suffered and been tempted, He is able to help those who are tempted" (2:18). Jesus shared this story for *our* benefit.

Thus, in the arid wilderness, that ragged, rugged desert—that place called "The Desolation" by many—when Jesus was physically weakened by a more-than-six-weeks' lack of nourishment, the Spirit of God led him to be tested.

And who was it that tested him? None other than the old tempter, the devil, Satan. As cunning as he was in the Garden of Eden in luring first Eve and then Adam into his evil plan to disobey God, so he sought to entice Jesus. Here is the second meaning of the word *peirazein:* God permitted his Son to be *tested.* Satan, however, was eager to seduce Jesus into submission, and thus to *tempt* him not only to disobey God but to deny His mission—to be lured into Satan's trap.

Satan appealed to Jesus' *physical* needs. "If you are the Son of God, command these stones to become loaves of bread," he demanded.

As famished as he was, Jesus knew more than hunger for food; he knew also hunger for God's Word and God's purpose. "One does not live by bread alone, but by every word that comes from the mouth of God," he said.

Because the appeal to Jesus' bodily, physical needs was rejected, Satan perhaps thought he could appeal to Jesus' *spiritual* urges. Taking Jesus to the heights of the Temple, Satan ordered, "If you are the son of God, throw yourself down; for it is written, 'He will command his angels concerning you,' and 'On their hands they will bear you up, so that you will not dash your foot against a stone.'" This was an attempt to challenge Jesus' faith and egg him on to a foolish decision.

The devil quoted Scripture beautifully—but not thoroughly. Jesus resisted the temptation and passed the test once again. "Again, it is written, 'Do not put the Lord your God to the test,'" quoted the Savior adroitly.

If satanic appeal to physical and spiritual needs are repudiated, it might work to appeal to Jesus' ego—to lust for the power every human possesses, to political vigor and calculating might. Ascending to a loftier height than the Temple, to a mountain from which could be viewed many nations stretched out below, Satan exclaimed, "All these I will give you, if you will fall down and worship me."

Many a human would give his soul for less than that—unfortunately. And unfortunately many have. Jesus was not about to fail this test, however, as he had not failed the other two. "Away with you, Satan, for it is written,

'Worship the Lord your God, and serve only him.'"

The tempter, the evil-minded devil "left him, and suddenly angels came and waited on him." Jesus had, at his weakest moment, passed the rigors of the most taunting of tests. Material, spiritual, and political enticements were not enough for Jesus to abandon His cause.

You and I are not Jesus. We deal with these allurements every day to a lesser degree. We want more than bread! We are eager to manipulate others as well as to try that tactic with God! We seek control over others lest they have control over us! Are these not common, everyday issues with us?

It is for us to learn that although we may make many bad choices, if we listen to the counsel of Scripture we will make fewer wrong ones. If we understand the intent and spirit of God's Word, and not just know a few of its passages, as does the devil, we will make better choices. If we face confrontations with the devil knowing that Jesus is at our side, we will not falter. If we strive to remain loyal to our purpose for being, we shall give better answers to the test of life than what Satan seeks. We will not be perfect. We will continue to make bad choices—but hopefully, if we are attentive to God's Word, we will make fewer of them.

Thus, when you confront the enticements not only of bread but of bounty, weigh the fact that we do not live by bread alone.

When you meet the allurements of sensational opportunities that go beyond faith as well as reason, do not test God, but transform such fantasies into trust. Let God rather than your mirages lead you.

When you meet the attraction of power for the sake of selfishly dominating others, resist it. Jesus subscribes to a greater power, and so should we. This power enables us to be like the llama, that South American cousin to the camel, which fears nothing. Colorado sheep farmers were losing their flocks to coyotes until they brought in the "aggressive, funny-looking, afraid-of-nothing llama." The llamas seemingly believe the words of James, "Resist the devil and he will flee from you" (4:7). Sheep losses were cut drastically because the llamas were unafraid of the cowardly coyote. God's Word is our llama. Let it shield you.

The net result will be that you will discover

the devil disappearing, and you will also sense God's angels attending to your needs. You will feel the warmth of God's love and know the wonder of his forgiveness.

Although the devil left Jesus, it was not for all time. Luke says, "He departed . . . until an *opportune* time" (4:13). He would return. He would return and tempt Christ's followers. He would return and twist the minds of the religious authorities and political leaders so that justice would be denied. He would come again to infest us with his malignant ideas.— Richard Andersen

Topic: How to be Moral While Living in Sodom

TEXT: Rom. 12:1–2; Gal. 5:19–24

Do you sometimes have the feeling that you live in Sodom? Sodom and Gomorrah are something of the biblical paradigm for sinful society. The city of Sodom was notorious for its insensitivity to human values, its crass manners, its gross violations of basic standards of human decency. The men of Sodom violated and abused visitors to the city. When angels visited Lot without securing a visa from the city elders, they were threatened with the most humiliating and degrading acts to their bodily and spiritual integrity. What a place! Sodom was so notorious that Abraham bargained with God for its survival. God promised that Sodom would be spared if only a handful of righteous people could be found there. But its wickedness was so profound, the city was destroyed.

There are times, I suppose, that we all feel we live in Sodom. We may call it Louisville or Lumberton, but it may seem like Sodom. The news is often bad. No city deserves to be thought of as Sodom. For every bad person, we can find hundreds of honorable and decent people we love and respect.

But the question Paul dealt with is still important: how can we live with integrity in a Sodom-like world? There is a shadow side to America the Beautiful. An evil permeates every level of society. An ugly and demonic face appears to mock our image of peace and prosperity.

Paul was talking to people who were afraid they were living in Sodom. They lived in Rome and Galatia, but these cities seemed like Sodom. The problem was how to live within a pagan society with integrity. How could they

be moral when they were surrounded by decadent thoughts and patterns of behavior?

Paul's counsel was simple and straightforward. To the Romans he said: "Present your bodies as a living sacrifice. . . . Do not be conformed to this world, but be transformed by the renewal of your mind." The point was to live in such a way that one's life becomes a living worship—an expression of one's commitments to the living Christ.

His counsel to Galatia was similar. He contrasted the "works of the flesh" with the "fruits of the spirit." The task was simple to describe: weed out the vices and develop the virtues. The vices of which he spoke sound terribly contemporary: immorality, impurity, licentiousness, idolatry, sorcery, enmity, strife, jealousy, anger, selfishness, dissension, party spirit, envy, drunkenness, carousing, and the like. Such features of the mind and heart should not be allowed into the mind and heart of the conscientious Christian. Then Paul spelled out the virtues that should be cultivated: love, joy, peace, patience, kindness, goodness, faithfulness, gentleness, self-control. Then he added a classic statement: "Against these there is no law." These are the signs of the work of the Holy Spirit in the Christian's life.

Paul's counsel reminds me of an essay by Benjamin Franklin, "How I Became Perfect." Franklin, I am aware, was being sarcastic. He was poking fun at Puritan types who acted as if they had all virtue and no vice. He made a point that is well taken: if you think you are perfect, you aren't. No one is.

Even so, the exercise is necessary. Identifying the kind of people we should be is necessary to avoid becoming the kind of persons we should not be. Paul provides helpful guidance for our own integrity while living in Sodom. He is as relevant to our situation as to the situations in Rome and Galatia. The message is straightforward and timely.

I. *Do not be conformed to the dominant divisions. Be transformed by a new image of how life should be lived by people of integrity.* I am somewhat reluctant to speak of the vices of our time that make us Sodom-like. Our lists usually are too short and contain the wrong vices. We are inclined to list vices that do not affect us. Attacking those vices in which we do not participate may be a cheap way to imply we are above it all: I do not use alcohol,

I am not sexually permissive, I am not a carouser, or I am not violent, and so on. But there are vices in which we do participate—ways of thinking that perpetuate the tragic divisions that always threaten to tear apart the social fabric.

Our world is a place of violence, of greed for power, and of insatiable lust. We are deeply divided, hostile, and paranoid. We lack a sense of community, show little compassion toward the needy, and can hardly trust one another.

We are also confused about sex, as was Sodom. Sex is both pervasive and puritanical; we have a widespread permissiveness compounded with a profound prudery. Sex sells everything and seems to dominate television, advertising, the movies, and business. We are a sex-saturated society, but it is not healthy sex. Our children and teens get a confusing message: sex is okay but unacceptable. They are caught in a tragic Catch-22. Their hormones are raging and the cultural message to engage in permissive sex is powerful and often irresistible. Birth rates among unmarried teens are scandalous. The increase of AIDS and other sexually transmitted diseases among teens spreads the disastrous tragedy of misguided attitudes ever wider.

Sodom is never far from us. Unless we live with integrity, we fall prey to destructive forces, both personal and social. The task is not to conform but to be transformed by the renewal of our minds. The issue is to think in different ways, adopt a different way of life, be a living sacrifice so that our life or way of being before God is one of worship. Christian faith is proper living.

Paul provided the Galatians with a different image than the one that perpetuates the profound divisions of society—that divides us and creates hostility and results in violence and tragedy. "In Christ," he said, "there is neither Jew nor Greek, neither slave nor free, neither male nor female" (Gal. 3:28). There it is, a new way of thinking that abolishes the distinctions of race, gender, and class that society seems to embody.

II. *Be people of integrity.* Being transformed is an inner discipline. It has to do with the springs of action rooted in thought and motive. Before we can act ethically, we must want to be ethical persons. The issue is one of character, or integrity.

Our moral crisis is a crisis of moral modeling and personal integrity. Society suffers from a pollution of the moral springs from which we all drink. To whom might our youngsters look for guidance when the adults seem confused about moral integrity?

Paul once challenged Christians at Philippi to "imitate me just as I am an imitator of Christ." Having "the mind of Christ" (Phil. 2:5) will cause one to live in such a way that action flows from the deep springs of righteousness. Right action follows from the inner life of virtue.

One of the favorite sports of our time is to criticize young people as if they have abandoned all moral concerns. The problem has persisted throughout history. Adults write the books and sermons, and youngsters come off as if they are the bad guys. But the problem is among adults—we hardly provide an exemplary example for the young. Their primary moral models are those in the professions and in sports. But many of these heroes have feet of clay—an interior life that mocks their outward display of success.

And what of the professions? Scandals tarnish us all: physicians who betray the patients' trust and exploit their vulnerability, ministers whose dalliance leads to moral scandal, and attorneys whose ways raise questions of integrity. I think of the Virginia gynecologist who took advantage of his patients. Our business leaders also exploit workers and continue to despoil our environment.

There are times we do well to fear we live in Sodom. When our trusted servants can no longer be trusted, society comes nearer to destruction.

The irony is that this is also a time of religious fervor. We take pride in being a "Christian" nation and in Christianity as the dominant religion. While we talk of being religious, it amounts to a piety of language rather than a righteousness of life.

In Sodom we are cursed with loophole religion. The capacity for rationalizing even the most ungodly of actions is what I call the original sin. People can rationalize—that is, give what they think are good reasons for—any act from murder to theft.

III. *Do not be conformed to the notion that money is all important.* We are tempted to think that the way to measure life and others is by where people live and how big their house is and how much money they make. We need to be transformed by a renewed mind: greed is at the heart of the ethic in Sodom.

Sodom was (is) a place of confusion about ethics—and that is our problem. We are tempted to believe that the cynic was right when asked whether he knew the Golden Rule. "Of course," he said, "the one with the gold makes the rules."

Remember Jesus' question: "What will it profit you if you gain the whole world and lose your own soul? Or what would you give in exchange for your soul" (Luke 9:25)? Who can buy the admiration of friends and peers? Who can buy the great gift of a clean conscience, of a mind untormented by guilt? Who can buy a reputation of a person of integrity?

The ways of Sodom are never far from us. They tempt us to settle down and live a life of conformity to cultural norms, to be part of the culture.

Paul has an answer to that temptation. The challenge for Christians is to live with integrity even if you live in Sodom. Living there may be unavoidable, but losing our integrity there is not necessary. Here is the rule: do not be conformed to the ways of the world, but be transformed by the renewal of your mind. That is how to live in Sodom without losing your integrity.—Paul D. Simmons

Topic: The Jerusalem Road (Cruel Road of Crucifixion)

Text: Matt. 21:1–11

The week before Jesus' Crucifixion, he rode triumphantly into Jerusalem. What an extraordinary way for him to demonstrate his kingship. Perhaps most of his followers expected him to demonstrate his kingship in a bold, dramatic way, charging into Jerusalem on a white horse in a blaze of glory to announce that the Messiah had arrived.

What happened was just the opposite. As Jesus drew near Jerusalem, he sent his disciples ahead to get a donkey for him to ride into the city. This was the way he made his triumphal entry. Jesus used this opportunity to show what his kingship was all about.

The "Jerusalem road" demonstrated a fourfold purpose:

I. *It was a road of humility* (vv. 1–3). How could Jesus be the King of Kings and the Lord of Lords and display such humility? He had always stated that his kingship would be one of servanthood and humility. Many of the Jews had the idea that the Messiah would be a triumphant ruler who would overthrow the Roman government and restore Israel to its former glory under King David. But Jesus did not come as a conquering king; he came as a suffering servant. To a large extent, that was why the Jews rejected him. He did not meet their expectations. He said to his own disciples, who were arguing over who was going to be the greatest in the Kingdom, "Whoever wants to be first must be slave of all" (Mark 10:44 NIV). Servanthood is greatness in God's Kingdom.

During that week, Jesus went to the upper room on the night he was betrayed to observe Passover with his disciples. There they all sat with dirty feet. They had no servant to perform the menial task of washing their feet. So Jesus assumed the role of host and servant. He washed his disciples' feet (John 13). This was the road of humility.

Paul spoke of this humility: "And being found in appearance as a man, he humbled himself and became obedient to death—even death on a cross" (Phil. 2:8 NIV). Humility was a necessary part of Jesus' travel on the road leading to Jerusalem and crucifixion.

II. *It was a road of obedience* (vv. 6–7). The disciples obeyed the Lord when he told them to get the donkey for him. The obedience demanded of Jesus was far greater. It was an obedience he had demonstrated throughout his earthly life. At the age of twelve, when Jesus was in the temple in Jerusalem discussing with the learned men there, his parents returned and scolded him for failing to be with the family when they left town. Jesus said, "I must be about my Father's business" (Luke 2:49). Jesus' first loyalty was to his heavenly Father. "I have come down from heaven not to do my will, but to do the will of him who sent me" (John 6:28 NIV). Jesus obeyed his heavenly Father, and everything he did was lived out of that obedience.

Later in the week, in the agonizing moments before his betrayal and arrest, Jesus struggled with the ultimate test of obedience. In the garden of Gethsemane, he poured out his heart to his heavenly Father, saying, "Father, take this cup." Still, he realized that there was only one way for people to be reconciled to God. Jesus, in a statement of total submission to the Father's will, said, "Not my will but yours be done" (Matt. 26:39). Jesus submitted to the plan that led to his crucifixion because he knew it was the only way.

III. *It was a road of destiny* (vv. 10–11). The people responded to Jesus' entry into Jerusalem by spreading their clothes and the branches from trees on the road. They very likely believed that the time had come for Jesus to declare himself and to liberate and lead them toward a future of prosperity and success.

The Bible tells us that Jesus was a lamb slain from the foundation of the world (Rev. 13:8). Crucifixion was his destiny. He was going to die a criminal's death between two thieves, humiliated, naked, and exposed to those who taunted and jeered him in the final moments of his life. It seemed a cruel destiny.

As he rode into Jerusalem, who would have thought he would be crucified before the week was over? As they hailed Jesus as their king, the crowd shouted, "Hosanna in the highest" (v. 9 NIV)! Kingship of this world was not Jesus' destiny. The mocking glory of his triumphal entry was demonstrated later in the week when the crowds cried, "Crucify him."

Pontius Pilate thought he could change the crowd's mind. He brought our Barabbas, a murderer he had in prison. Pilate thought, *Certainly they won't choose this criminal over this innocent man.* But Jesus' opponents moved through the crowd saying, "Choose Barabbas, choose Barabbas." When the two men were brought before the Jews, Pilate offered to free one. To his disbelief, the crowd shouted, "Give us Barabbas!" Pilate freed Barabbas, and Jesus—the perfect Son of God, totally righteous, supremely holy, completely innocent of any crime—was sent to die the most horrible death of his day.

Jesus said, "My Kingdom is not of this world" (John 18:36 NIV). That became increasingly apparent as the week progressed. Ever since then, people of the Kingdom have known that they cannot establish his Kingdom in this world with this world's means, certainly not by force of arms. We become people of his kingdom when we receive him into our hearts. The world will not come under his complete dominion until his second coming: "They will make war against the Lamb, but the Lamb will overcome them because he is Lord of lords and King of kings and with Him will be His called, chosen and faithful followers" (Rev. 17:14 NIV).

One day we will reign with Christ. Meanwhile, we realize that just as Jesus' destiny led him to the cross, we also must be people of the cross. We live in a world of suffering, heartbreak, and disappointment. When you are a Kingdom person, it is hard to understand why you must be a part of this. We imagine that life should be easier, not harder, for us since we have received eternal life through Christ. Yet we are called to share the fellowship of his suffering (Phil. 3:10). We cannot separate ourselves from that. He set the example of self-denial for us to follow as he traveled the Jerusalem road, a destiny that included taking our sins and punishment on himself.

IV. *It was a road of fulfillment* (vv. 4–5). Jesus' entry into Jerusalem was the fulfillment of prophecy: "See, your king comes to you . . . gentle and riding on a donkey" (Zech. 9:9 NIV). This is just one of the many prophecies in the Old Testament regarding Jesus' arrest, trial, and crucifixion. He was betrayed by a friend (Ps. 41:9) and sold for thirty pieces of silver (Zech. 11:12). False witnesses accused Him (Ps. 27:12). He was silent when accused (Isa. 53:7), struck, and spit on (Isa. 50:6). He was hated without a cause (Ps. 69:4) and suffered vicariously (Isa. 53:4–6). His hands and feet were pierced (Ps. 22:16). He was mocked and insulted (Ps. 69:21). He prayed for his enemies (Ps. 109:4). His side was pierced (Zech. 12:10). Soldiers cast lots for his clothes (Ps. 22:18). Not a bone was broken (Ps. 34:20), and he was buried with the rich (Isa. 53:9). These are a few of the prophecies that came true when Jesus fulfilled his mission of redeeming humanity through his atoning death by crucifixion.

Do you see how Jesus' Crucifixion was central to fulfilling God's plan for humanity? Every step toward the cross occurred in the will of his heavenly Father.

Jesus traveled that cruel road of crucifixion because he knew a better day was coming. It could come only through his death. Hebrew 12:2–3 states: "Let us fix our eyes on Jesus, the author and perfecter of our faith, who for the joy set before Him endured the

cross, scorning its shame, and sat down at the
right hand of the throne of God. Consider
him who endured such opposition from sinful men, so that you will not grow weary and
lose heart" (NIV).—Larry Michael

Topic: The Love That Conquers Death
TEXT: John 20:1–18

The good news is not that all men die. We
knew that. The good news is that through the
love of God all can be made alive! This is why,
after giving so little space to the Crucifixion,
the Gospel writer allots two whole chapters to
stories about the Resurrection.

One of them is this lovely narrative about
Mary Magdalene and Peter and John coming
to the tomb and finding it empty and realizing for the very first time that the Savior who
had spoken about living in love, about abiding in him, had been raised from death.

The story is blessedly familiar. Mary, unable to sleep and drawn by her attachment to
the Master, arises long before dawn and
comes to the garden where the tomb is. Finding the tomb disturbed, she runs back to
Peter and John and awakens them. They race
to the tomb, and Peter, impetuous man that
he is, dares to go inside, followed by young
John. Jesus is gone but the burial clothes are
there, neatly folded on the shelf of the rock
where the corpse had lain. Peter and John
race back to tell the other disciples, but Mary
lingers near the open tomb. Filled with wonder, she looks inside and sees two angels sitting on the stone shelf. They mark her tears
and ask why she is weeping. She says, "Because they have taken away my Lord." And at
that moment she looks around and sees
someone standing near her. Confused, her
eyes still filled with tears, she mistakes him
for the keeper of the garden. "Oh, sir," she
says, "what have you done with him? If you
will tell me, I will go and take care of the
body." And the vision says: "Mary." She knows
instantly who it is, and all the stars of heaven
shine in her eyes and the melody of ethereal
harps is in her voice as she says, "Master!"

To me, there is no story more beautiful in
all the world.

Mary.

There is more theology in the calling of
that name than in all the other books of the
Bible put together. What it says is that love
and intimacy are what the Christian faith is

all about. The Shepherd knows his sheep by
name and his sheep know his voice when
they hear it. Our relationship to God is not
impersonal, and we are not lost in the masses
that have inhabited the globe since the
beginning of time. Each of us matters individually to God, and in that mattering is our
salvation.

Buddhism teaches the renunciation of
personal identity until all are absorbed in the
whole, and there is no Mary, or Tom, or Susan,
or Dick. Scientific materialism teaches the
same thing, that everyone consists of atoms
that at death return to the state of nature,
making personality illusory and evanescent.
It is the same in the official doctrines of Communism: the individual soul does not exist
apart from a concatenation of atoms that will
be dispersed at death. But not so with Christianity! Christianity says that all these under-
standings are wrong. The person *is* important. The person *does* survive. And nowhere is
this basic teaching of Christianity more significant than in the face of death and separation from loved ones.

"How can God permit us to be separated
from those we love?" asks a mother whose little child is being buried. "Isn't it all a lie?"
No, it isn't all a lie. She will understand when
the first pain of absence has left her. The
separation is not forever. And it may not even
be as complete as we sometimes think it is. It
is only momentary, and it may be only apparent rather than actual, as this story of Jesus
and Mary suggests. The veil that separates us
from our dear ones, if we live in love, is very
thin indeed.

This is what the writer of the Fourth Gospel saw. The apostle Paul, trained as a philosopher with the Greeks and the Romans, had
a slightly different vision, which included the
sleep of the dead until the time of a second
coming of Christ. So did the writer of Revelation, who was clearly not the same as the
author of the Gospel of John. But John—
who had been with Jesus and knew him, who
had sat by his bosom at the Last Supper and
heard his words about love, who saw him die
and then beheld him in his transfiguration
beyond death—knew the truth: there is no
real separation for those who abide in God's
love. God *is* love, he said in one of his letters,
and that is the guarantee, that is the assurance, that is the bottom line. God is love, and

as God is also the source of all true life, those who abide in God can never die but only pass into eternal life, a life whose quality we can but dimly estimate.

A woman I met in Nashville told this little story to me. Her father, who had lived as a derelict most of his life, had been converted to Christ a few years before his death. Those last years had been happy, good, productive years. Then one day he had been caught in a fire and badly burned over most of his body. His suffering was intense, but he seemed not to mind it. And at the end, in the final moments of his life this side of the grave, the daughter was in the room at the hospital as he raised his arms, the charred bits of flesh literally falling off them as he did, and sang in a wavering but devoted voice, "Amazing grace how sweet the sound, that saved a wretch like me; I once was lost but now am found, was blind but now I see."

He saw the lights. He heard his name. He knew the love that conquers death and the Savior whose name is life.

That is what our faith is about, for all of us. Not death, but life.—John Killinger

Topic: Power for the Powerless

TEXT: John 20:1–8

The message of Easter morning is that we are not condemned to live a defeated life. God is willing to roll away all the stones that have seemed to seal our fate.

Too good to be true, you say? That is such a typical response. The fact is that we are always more inclined to despair than to hope. We frequently declare ourselves down and out and our undertakings over and done with before the final verdict is in. We are much more easily susceptible to believing the worst—even about ourselves—than to count on the best.

Sadly, the world is more apt to believe in its heroes' ability to snatch victory from defeat than Jesus' followers are to believe the same about their Lord. Fortunately, Jesus' resurrection did not depend on the faith of his disciples; if it had, it likely would never have occurred. Nor do his victories in the twentieth century depend on our faith, but only on the power of God.

Nevertheless, Jesus' resurrection victory was not complete until his defeated disciples shared his triumph. That explains why he made such deliberate attempts to show himself to so many. Only in that way could his resurrection become their personal triumph—over fear! Apparently there was nothing that Jesus felt compelled to challenge more than fear.

At the last supper he had said to them: "Peace I leave with you; my peace I give to you; not as the world gives do I give to you. Let not your hearts be troubled, neither let them be afraid" (John 14:27). Even so, they fled the garden when he was arrested. Most apparently stayed away from his execution, fearing, no doubt, the same fate. After his burial, they hid out.

Responding to the disciples' fate, the angels' first words each time they announced Jesus' resurrection were "Fear not." And that was the meaning of the first Easter: do not be afraid. He is not here. He is risen, just as he told you. There is no more reason to be afraid.

We, too, are so consumed by fear. Our fear ranges from a vague uneasiness and anxiety about everything in general to nothing in particular. We fear specific things: disease, old age, loneliness, parenting, marriage, strangers, being hurt, causing hurt, failure, punishment, germs, nightmares, bankruptcy, responsibility, death, and the dark. We are afraid of what God will allow to happen to us. What if he allows the same things to happen to us that happened to his own Son?

The worst that could happen to us is death. Because of the resurrection of Jesus, however, there is no reason to be afraid of that. Paul wrote to young Timothy: "God did not give us a spirit of fear, but one of power, love, and a sound mind" (2 Tim. 1:7). The Resurrection of Jesus has overcome even the worst that can happen to us—even death! Not even death can snatch us from the Savior's hand. His Resurrection can also become our personal triumph over inability and handicap.

Probably no other disciple felt the sting of Jesus' death more than Peter. Jesus had called him the rock, perhaps counting on him to be steady as a rock. Yet in the end Peter had proven to be only hardheaded, not dependable. Egotistically, he had declared that even if everyone else denied the Lord, he would never (Mark 14:26)! Then, before the sun came up, he had denied any connection at all with Jesus—and not once but three times.

How do you live with yourself after you have done something like that? How do you ever again look squarely in the face of the one you have denied?

Jesus' love does not fail no matter how much we fail him. Interestingly enough, we often fail him though we genuinely love him. Still, what we learn from it all is what Peter discovered: our relationship with him does not depend on our ability but on his faithfulness.

Peter was not the only one ever to fail the Savior. James and John had confidently declared their ability to earn the places of leadership in the kingdom of God that they had so ambitiously and publicly sought (Mark 10:38). Time and again, they had all failed.

Still, they were the first ones Jesus wanted to see after his Resurrection. Scattered, fearful, and despondent though they were, he wanted them gathered together. Failures, weakness, and all—they were the ones he would use to take on the world in the power of the Resurrection.

It could be the best day of your life when you finally learn to accept certain limitations and inabilities. Indeed, there is so much about yourself and your circumstances that you are powerless to change. And that is the reason for the cross and the promise of the Resurrection. What you are not able to do, he always can!—Gary C. Redding

Topic: Surprised by Galilee
TEXT: Matt. 28:1–10

Voltaire, one of the architects of eighteenth-century Enlightenment thought, once described Easter as "a feast celebrated by Christians in remembrance of a God who was hanged." He was right, of course, except that it's really not "in remembrance." Resurrection is a firm reminder that God's name is not "I Was" but "I Am." We are not here to commemorate a story from the past. Rather, we have come to celebrate a love so strong that it has endured the cross and the centuries to strengthen us—now! At Jesus' tomb, men wrote "the end," but God wrote "to be continued." And what Jesus started has continued, not because of a memory but because of a presence.

There is a surprise in the biblical account, however. Verse 10 of Matthew's account says,

"Then Jesus said to them, 'Do not be afraid: go and tell my brethren to go to Galilee, and there they will meet me.'"

"Go to Galilee, and there they will meet me"—but he had died in Jerusalem! Jerusalem was the heart of Hebrew faith and history; it was the seat of the Roman power in the southern province; it was the backdrop against which all of Jesus' last week had been lived out. If Christ is alive—triumphant over death and evil—why not meet him in Jerusalem, or Rome, or even Athens? There was nothing exciting about Galilee—neither religiously nor politically nor socially. The disciples had already put in their time there; Jesus had spent almost all of his early ministry in that northern province.

For Easter to be so earthshaking, Galilee seems so mundane.

For God's power to be unleashed in the Resurrection, Galilee seems so anticlimactic.

Come to think of it, we might have guessed that this would happen. It's typical. "Unto you is born this day a Savior which is Christ the Lord"—but there was only a barn and a bed of straw! "The Word became flesh and dwelt among us. We have beheld his glory, glory as of the only Son from the Father"—but there was just a carpenter and an itinerant rabbi in an out-of-the-way Syrian province. And this: "He is not here; he is risen from the dead!"—but there were instructions to go back to Galilee.

God at work in the ordinary.

He seems to choose that way so often—but that approach feels weak after Easter. The Resurrection of Christ sets off deep charges of hope and promise inside us. If God can do this, he can do anything. So we thrust our shopping list on God.

We want him to change the world.

We want him to alter our circumstances perceptibly.

We want him to reshuffle the deck of life and deal us a new hand.

That's what we want, and what we get is, Go back to Galilee, back to the commonplace, the ordinary, the everyday. And we feel, Nothing has changed there because of Easter.

But at the very best, maybe we can be changed, and that will change how we understand Galilee, and live in Galilee, and relate to all that is ordinary or terrifying there.

I. For instance, *humanity* is there for all of us in the ordinariness of Galilee, and that's the biggest part of our struggle. Cassius said it, in Shakespeare's play about Julius Caesar: "The fault, dear Brutus, is not in our stars, but in ourselves, that we are mortal." And humanity is okay except that our humanness includes our sinfulness. We think and scheme and do the wrong and the selfish.

But Jesus Christ crucified and alive again means that our sins and scars are not too much for God. Forgiveness can be more than a word; with Christ alive, it can be an experience.

The sort of seedy characters with whom Jesus was most comfortable *before* the cross and the Resurrection—outcasts, the lame, the devious, and hypocrites—he didn't reject *after* the empty tomb.

It's okay to be human. God calls us to forgiveness and to the fullest humanity that is possible, and a risen Christ will point the way. It's okay that we're not angels—who wants to be an angel? It's okay to risk living out of forgiveness and by love. We walk with one who draws us on toward the wholeness of our humanness.

"Go to Galilee where there's humanity. I will meet you there," he said.

II. Also present in Galilee is *routine*. And that can be a real problem—that life is as boring as it is painful, that it's as much mundane as it is tragic or eventful. We spend a lot of our days, as one man put it, caught up in "the thick of thin things." In such a life it's hard to see the exciting hand of the risen Christ—because we're looking for it in the wrong places.

In the New Testament, after Easter, a community of faith took hold and exciting things started to happen. But it wasn't *all* missionary journeys and miracles and great revivals and dialogue with the philosophers and trips to the center of the world in Rome. Mostly it was old prejudices about Gentiles and Jews slowly withering. It was long nights in jails with certain death on some future day. It was struggling little churches fussing over how to eat and drink, how to worship, and how to make this new faith work in a culture of slavery and dictatorship.

When you get to the end of almost every one of Paul's letters in the New Testament, there's a list of names you can hardly pronounce, people you never heard of, who just gave a little money and offered some simple hospitality and shared what little they had with others—and Paul calls them blessed and memorable folks, men and women who found ways to serve the risen Christ in the routine stuff of living.

So many things we *have* to do, so much we'd rather *not have* to do, but this may be the most significant work we ever do. Who knows what the risen Lord may do with the deadening, dull work of our lives? George Herbert (1593–1633) wrote these lines in a hymn:

Teach me, my God and King,
In all things there to see;
And what I do in anything,
To do it as for thee.

It's hard to do that consistently. But knowing that Christ is present in *all* things helps a lot.

"Go to Galilee," Jesus said. "I will meet you there, in your routine and your humanity."

III. But *trouble* is there for us all as well. The predictable and the unexpected, the physical and the emotional—there's always trouble in Galilee. Being a Christian, living in partnership with a risen Christ who meets us there, doesn't eliminate the trouble; but it does help us deal with it when it comes.

When there's trouble and pain in Galilee, the choices are two: either you have something to hold on to, or you have nothing. Resurrection says we have someone to hold on to—someone alive and present and standing beside us. Because Christ lives, God's overcoming love—and *not* our troubles—is life's ultimate reality.

"Go to Galilee—to its trouble—and I will meet you there."

IV. *Death,* too, is present in Galilee, always. But Christ risen from death changes it. Clement of Alexandria, an early Church father, said, "Christ has turned all our sunsets into dawns." Not quite—that makes it a bit too simplistic. Christ risen does not take away the pain and grief of separation from someone we love. The loss and loneliness are real. His Resurrection does not subtract the hurt; it *does,* however, add the dimension of life beyond the silence, and that changes the face of death—radically, clearly, eternally.

"Go to Galilee. I'll meet you there, and we'll deal with death together."

V. One other thing—*religion* is there/here in Galilee for each of us. And after the empty tomb, religion can never again be dead ritual or empty form. Worship cannot be Christian worship if it is just "in memoriam," or if it's withdrawn from the realities of daily living.

"Go to Galilee," he said, "I'll meet you there in worship and fellowship and ministry that will mean something."

The clue to all I'm saying is in verse 9 of our text: "And behold, Jesus met them and said, 'Hail!'" The Greek word translated as *hail* is a word of greeting like *hello,* or as we Texans might say, *howdy.* The first word Jesus speaks after the Resurrection is as casual as, "Howdy, what shall we do now?" The faith that follows this risen Christ is in constant engagement with life, in constant dialogue with things like humanity and routine and trouble and death and religion. It's not lifeless and detached.

And if the Resurrection can change us, we can begin changing Galilee. It won't happen quickly or easily, and the change may seem imperceptible. But Christ-in-us and Christ-with-us will make the difference.

"Go to Galilee—there you will meet him."

It's a good thing, because, come to think of it, that's exactly where we need him!—William L. Turner

Illustrations

ON BEING AFRAID OF LIFE. He who is anxious and knows Christ may be assured that he is not alone in his anxiety, but that Christ, too, has gone through it. And this means a completely new attitude toward the future; no longer is the future a befogged landscape into which I peer anxiously because all kinds of obscure perils are brewing there for me. No, everything is changed: we do not know what is coming, but we know *who* is coming. And he who possesses the last hour no longer needs to fear the next minute.—Helmut Thielicke[1]

IMPACT OF THE CROSS. We live so far from the cross that it is hard for us to see it for what it was. Certainly it was nothing like the burnished crosses that we put in our chancels. How much more appropriate it would be if we had a rough-hewn, blood-stained, wooden cross above that table, and if we must have a picture, to have men of our own day around that cross: farmhands and fisherfolk, steel puddlers and sharecroppers, clerks and taxi drivers, preachers and priests, and business men, engineers, and soldiers. For we all had a hand in it. The cross, unhappily, seems so far off and so unreal when really what it is and what it does is so contemporary. The people about it were people like us.—Clayton E. Williams

GOD'S VICTORY. The workings of love are not smooth or suave or sedate; they are anguished, awkward, incongruous. But above all they have within them the seed of the splendor of victory, for if God is love, there can be, even in the most awkward squeezing of himself through the narrow slits of our impoverishment, no point at which he is not omnivictorious in the anguish of his self-attenuation. So to be surprised by a joy far beyond what we could ever by ourselves generate or sustain is to know God as surely as he can be known in this our very fleeting life in which we are all running forward to death.—Geddes Macgregor[2]

GOD'S COSTLY LOVE. The passion and death of Jesus are not God's punishment, anger, or revenge directed at an innocent human victim. On the contrary, the crucified Jesus is the unsurpassable expression of God's costly love for the world. As Jürgen Moltman explains, all of the world's suffering is taken into the life of God on the cross. In the Incarnation and its climax in the Crucifixion, God the Father gives his Son to the world and experiences the grief of losing his beloved. Jesus' gift of himself is also an act of free, self-giving love.—Daniel L. Migliore[3]

MARY'S ROLE IN REDEMPTION. Jesus Christ—true God and true man—knew he could rely on his mother as he pursued his mission within the framework of his all-important duty and thus carried out the will of the Father. He knew he could rely on his mother. . . . He was sure of her heart, that heart which helped him to express, in hu-

[1] *Christ and the Meaning of Life.*

[2] *He Who Lets Us Be.*
[3] *The Power of God.*

man fashion, in terms of human thoughts and feelings, the great heart of the Father. This motherly heart did not fail him at the testing time of Gethsemane and Calvary. It was close to him on the road from Pilate's praetorium to Mount Calvary as he carried his cross, and it was close to him when he drew his last breath. She was there; and with her were John the Apostle and Mary Magdalen (John 19:25–26). And even from the cross, Jesus once again firmly asserted his mother's role in the mystery of redemption and of the Church, saying to John, "Behold your mother," and to his Mother, "Behold your son" (John 19:26–27). These words belong in his testament.—Pope John Paul II[4]

---

[4]*Sign of Contradiction.*

SECTION VI.
Messages for Advent and Christmas

SERMON SUGGESTIONS

Topic: The Future Is Different Now

TEXT: Jer. 33:14–16; Luke 21:25–36

Jesus had a lot to say about the future. He described a time when "there will be signs in the sun, the moon, and the stars, and on the earth distress among nations confused by the roaring of the sea and the waves. People will faint from fear and foreboding of what is coming upon the world, for the powers of the heavens will be shaken. They will see the Son of man coming in a cloud with power and great glory. Now, when these things begin to take place, stand up and raise your hands, because your redemption is drawing near." The second coming of Jesus and the end of time are at the center of the Christian faith. Every Sunday we affirm our belief in the future Jesus promised when we say in the Apostle's Creed, "He shall come to judge the quick and the dead." Jesus is coming again, and because of that the future is now different than it would have been if he had not come at all.

But there are some real difficulties with this forecast. In fact, I think it's fair to say that most of us are kind of uncomfortable with all this talk about Jesus' second coming. After all, it's taking an awfully long time for the future Jesus promised to get here.

So every year during Advent we read these passages about the second coming of Jesus, and it makes us a little uncomfortable. After all, Jesus said, "Truly I tell you, this generation will not pass away until all things have taken place." But quite a few generations have passed since Jesus said those words.

If God measured time the way we do, we would have a problem. We'd be faced with the choice of either believing that the end of time is upon us or dismissing Jesus' promise as a mistake.

A lot of people don't realize that the way God thinks about time is different from the way we think about time. You've heard from those folks. They hear on the news about plagues in India and assume that those are the plagues that Jesus said would happen just before he came again. There is a series of earthquakes in California and these people are sure they are the signs of the end that Jesus foretold.

If our perception of time changes over a few decades, just think how God, who has been around for billions of years, must view time. When the Bible says that Jesus is coming soon, it may mean just a few short millennia. Or it may mean tomorrow. But to say with utmost conviction that Jesus will come in our lifetime is to impose our conception of time on God. When Jesus talked of "this generation" passing away, I believe he meant the generation of all those who have lived and will live since his resurrection, not a literal generation the way we understand it.

The kind of time that Jesus talked about isn't the kind of time we measure with a watch. That's the kind of time we mean when we say, "It's time for the movie to start," or "It's time for the train." The kind of time that Jesus talked about is more like what we mean when we say, "It's time to get serious about school," or "It's time we got married." It's a kind of time that is "the right time," that's not dependent on the hour or the day or the year.

There are signs that the promise Jesus

made is coming true, signs that his kingdom is coming, just as we pray for it every Sunday in the Lord's Prayer when we say, "Thy kingdom come." What are some of those signs? Our gathering here is one. Every Sunday when we gather to worship God we are a sign that the promise Jesus made is true. Every once in a while, regimes that oppress minorities or rule with cruelty fall, and that is a sign of the promises Jesus made. None of these events, however, is a sign that Jesus' return is right around the corner as we measure time by the clock. But each of them is a sign that Jesus' promise is true, that he will come in his own due time.

The signs are all around us, if we can perceive them—signs that what Jesus promised is true, that he will come again to make everything right and to fulfill the deepest longings of the human heart. He will come to finish what he started, to complete the work we are doing.

To do that, he will shake the very foundations of the earth and do away with all greed and violence and anger. Our world is so wedded to violence and greed and dishonesty that it will be a violent upheaval when Jesus comes to do away with all those things. But to those of us who know what's going on, who know that the upheaval is just the birth pangs of a new creation, those are signs of hope, not fear.

We don't know when all that will happen, but we know it will. And knowing that Jesus is going to come again to complete what he began gives us hope to carry on. When we're tempted to give up on trying to change the world into a better place and to just look out for ourselves, we can remember that our efforts to help others are signs of what Jesus promised. When it seems that it's a waste of time to live as Jesus wants us to live, we can know that he will eventually have the upper hand.

The future truly will be different—different than it would have been before Jesus came into the world and started the process of changing the world. Knowing what God holds in store, what choice do we have but to live every day getting ready for it?—Stephens G. Lytch

Topic: What's Taking God So Long?
TEXT: Isa. 52:13–53:12; Matt. 11:2–6
I hate to wait! In fact, one of my recurring images of hell is an eternity of standing in line. And, like you, I'm forced to wait several times each week.

We wait for the mail, the delivery truck, the service technician. We wait for someone to return our call, for the hostess in the restaurant to call our name or number. We wait for the plane to arrive or the train to pass the crossing. We wait for the morning after a long, sleepless night.

And there are other, more acute times of waiting. A childless couple waits for a baby. A patient waits anxiously for the test results or the diagnosis. A single person waits for marriage, or whatever is next. The chronically ill wait for health. The emotionally scarred wait for peace of mind. Men and women in dead-end careers wait for a breakthrough. Those caught in unhappy marriages wait for relief, redemption, or escape. Students wait to get on with life. The lonely wait to belong.

Still, for all the waiting we do, we are not very good at it.

Advent reminds us that God's people have always waited for him. The people of Israel waited for four hundred years in Egypt for God to deliver them. Then for forty more years they waited on the doorstep of Canaan for God to make good his promise about the land flowing with milk and honey.

But even when they finally entered the promised land, the waiting was not over. There were all those other interminable years of waiting—through wars, oppression, exile. The prophets kept telling them to hold on. God would soon send the Messiah—a mighty deliverer. But it didn't happen.

And finally, it was almost as if even the prophets themselves grew tired of waiting. There were four hundred long years when even they became silent.

Waiting does that to you sometimes. It's possible to wait for so long—to be put off so many times—that you can grow discouraged, disillusioned, and unbelieving.

What takes God so long? Why does he make us wait? What is God up to? Frankly, God's patience sometimes looks like cold indifference. His deliberate pace is so maddening. He acts as if he has all eternity to work out his purposes. Why, he sometimes acts as if he's not even aware of how valuable our time is—or how short.

But Advent reminds us that God is not

absent. He's simply patient. And what is called for in the face of all this waiting is faith, not frustration.

Simeon was a model of patient expectancy (Luke 2:25–35). He was an aged, spiritually devout, and morally upright person. He is also identified as one who lived out his days looking for—believing that he would live to see—the coming of "the consolation of Israel." (That was a phrase used by many Jews to describe the fulfillment of their messianic hope. See Isa. 40:1; 52:10.)

Simeon also is characterized as one who was particularly endowed with the Holy Spirit. When he entered the Temple "in the Spirit," Simeon took the baby from Mary and Joseph and recognized that he held in his arms the promised Messiah. He then declared that he was ready to die because God's promise to him had been fulfilled. He could depart in peace, without regret or a sense of frustration. Simeon was one of those fortunate people who had come to the end of the way with the conviction that life could not have been more rewarding and meaningful—because he had patiently waited upon the lord to keep his Word.

Do you see it? Faith is as much a way of waiting as is frustration. We should never give up too quickly when everything seems to go wrong. We should never give up too quickly on a troubled marriage. We should never give up too quickly on our troubled children. We should never give up too quickly on our troubled selves.

Everything does not have to be all right today. Give God time, just as he has given plenty of time to us.

There are two words in the New Testament for time. One is *chronos*. It indicates time that can be measured by the clock. But then there's *kairos*. It indicates the dramatic moment when life takes on new meaning, the light bulb comes on, God speaks to you loud and clear. It's the "aha!" moment when you finally see what you've been struggling to see for what seems to be a lifetime. It's the moment of new insight, new learning—the excitement of a new discovery, the thrill of a new idea.

Kairos is the moment that touches us deeply and that changes us for a lifetime.

Kairos is the time in which God works. It's the moment the apostle Paul described when he wrote: "And when the time had fully come, God sent forth his Son, born of a woman . . . to redeem those who were under the law, so that we might receive adoption as sons" (Gal. 4:4–5).

Kairos is the moment when you are moved to do something—when God touches you and calls you to a special job.

Perhaps our greatest problem is that we live by the *chronos* clock and God operates according to *kairos* time.

How's your clock set? This is a particularly important question during Advent. For here we are, waiting for God to do it again. We're waiting for him to interrupt our hectic, hurried lives, measured according to *chronos* time—waiting for him to transform our lives and time into *kairos*—times of life-changing encounter.

Life is packed with *kairos* moments. Advent is full of them. My prayer is that we won't miss them—that we will be warmed by them, that we will hold on to them, and celebrate them, and never throw them away.—Gary Redding

Topic: Away with the Manger
TEXT: Luke 2:1–20

She gave birth to her firstborn and wrapped him in bands of cloth and laid him in a manger, because there was no place for them in the inn.

At that moment, time began to be healed by eternity. The most significant ever intersection between the needs of humanity and the grace of God met here, in a stable.

Now, there is some question historically about exactly which census was being taken, but Joseph and Mary wound up with a feeding trough for a crib and a barn for a delivery room. Was there no family left in Bethlehem? Couldn't the innkeeper have made room for them off his courtyard somehow?

The truth is that the innkeeper, or a family member, gave them what the Jewish law required—namely, absolute privacy. We can't impose a twentieth-century understanding of obstetrics on first-century Palestine. The woman was considered ceremonially unclean for forty to eighty days following the birth of a child. To have her deliver in a crowded inn, in one of those open cubicles off the courtyard, would've made everybody in the place ritually impure—restricting both worship and social activities for a while. Unless he had been willing to evacuate the whole inn, the innkeeper did the best he could for the young couple.

So Jesus came into the world in the privacy of a cave-barn; Mary wrapped him in bands of cloth to keep his body straight for proper growth; some shepherds came for a brief visit; eight days later the child was circumcised and named—and that was that.

Yet every year at Advent and Christmas, we pay a return visit to that manger—and the fantasies about it bloom and rebloom, all the way from talking animals to the lyrics of John Thomas McFarland:

> The cattle are lowing
> The baby awakes
> But little Lord Jesus
> No crying He makes.

I doubt that!

When you strip away the fantasy, you're left with a barn and a feeding trough. What's that worth?

Not very much, if you take the New Testament seriously. Luke's the only writer to even mention it, and in verse 19 he writes, "Mary treasured all these words and pondered them in her heart." Later on, I believe, she told them to Luke—maybe *much* later, because she would have understood them, they *all* would have understood them, more completely in the light of how this baby turned out.

Dag Hammarskjold, former secretary-general of the United Nations, is well known for the statement that, having seen the future, we now see that the "manger is situated on Golgotha, and the cross has already been raised in Bethlehem." But nobody knew that until they'd lived into it.

So Mary remembered and kept and one day told to Luke this manger story, and in retrospect it fits.

Could we do without the manger? Yes, if we're looking for the *main* chapter in the Jesus story—his ministry, his death and Resurrection, his promised return. Coming to the story of the manger every December, we must not get snared and stopped in a web of nostalgia and sentiment. It's part of the story we would never have heard except for the quality of life that grew out of it. It's worth repeating—the people who first wrote his

story point, by the scant attention they give his manger, to the larger meaning of life.

Don't get stuck at the manger, or you'll miss the real story.

But I'm not ready to throw the manger away. It's only a small part of the drama, but it's there. So what's there in that manger for us?

I. *Simplicity,* for one thing. "This will be a sign for you: you will find a child wrapped in bands of cloth and lying in a manger" (v. 12).

What a sign! Another baby born to another ordinary couple—a child in a feeding trough—it's remarkable that the shepherds even bothered going into town. Angels and hosannas in the night sky are momentous, but the "sign for you" was so very plain and commonplace. Caesar Augustus was a wonder, all right—savior, son of God, colossus of the world, bigger than life. But somehow all that the Caesar-saviors promised and all the grandeur that Rome offered was not enough and did not satisfy. Slavery and chauvinism and cruelty were ever-present facts of life. So sated with emptiness, so bloated with restlessness were people, sixty-six days of every year were public holidays, and the number of holidays grew under each emperor.

The bigness and breadth of Rome somehow wasn't working!

And then God did this simple thing in Bethlehem as if to say, "Look here! The deepest longings, the hopes and fears of all the years are met, not in the grandiose but in the ordinary." The manger slows us down, and reminds us that God often works quietly, simply. He's taken a life born in the straw to show us how to live! No power plays, no grasping, no conniving—just the simple, leavening strength of love and truth—and Jesus of Nazareth became the Savior that no Caesar could ever be.

I see this manger as a symbol, a parable, that says that simplicity is God's tool of choice in the remaking of our lives and our world.

Oh, the crudeness and simplicity of the manger! How it pales in comparison to our big, busy world! But God is still trying to tell us something there, I think—that what our size and our secularism seem never able to do for the hunger in our hearts, this Savior birthed in utter simplicity *can!*

II. *Feelings* are there. If this whole story is true—the invasion of human history by a loving and forgiving God; the one life uniquely designed to straighten out our lives and our relationships; peace on earth among those who will favor that and choose that; the healing of time by eternity—if that's what was under way at this manger, we should make like a jumping Toyota commercial: "Oh, what a feeling!"

James Stewart of Edinburgh used to say that we do need times when the glory of the Christ thing just *grips* our hearts and *blinds* our eyes with tears and *fires* our wills for service. Advent is such a time—the manger is such a place!

Now, encounter with God is more than emotion, but that's part of it, because feelings are a part of us! In a callous and sophisticated world, the manger invites us to realize what's happening here. God has come to set us free and make us new. Consider that, feel that, rejoice in that!

III. There's one other thing in this manger for us: *equality* is there. Reaching far back into the Jews' history, there were those messianic hopes. In the worship of the Temple, in the preaching of the prophets, the expectation would not be extinguished. Now, there is this: "The angel said to them, 'Do not be afraid; for see—I am bringing you good news of great joy for all people: to you is born this day in the City of David a Savior, who is the Messiah, the Lord'" (vv. 10–11).

And that hopeful, inextinguishable, long-awaited Word came to *shepherds*!

Can you believe it? No holy men, no prophets, no scribes—the first Word came to some religious pariahs, outcasts of the religious establishment. The shepherds' lifestyle made it impossible for them to be ritually clean very often. Their reputations in first-century society were not good. So questionable was their integrity as a group that they were rarely allowed to give testimony in a court of law.

So, to whom did the angels of heaven announce good news of a great joy? To shepherds, of course—maybe because it was good news that shall be to *all* people.

So the poor and the rejected hear the good news first, and they are at home with a stable. That God's love is lying in that manger is believable for "their kind." Besides, there are no barriers in a stable. All our fussy ideas about race and class and position are irrelevant here. There is an equality of *need* there.

Who do we meet in Luke's story? A Roman emperor, a Syrian governor, a Nazareth couple, a Bethlehem innkeeper, and Judean shepherds. All stand on the level ground of spiritual need. No one lives and breathes, then or now, who doesn't need the good news of a great joy—the forgiving and empowering love of God in Christ Jesus.

There is also an equality of grace here. Who knows whether any of these first participants came to understand and to believe? Who knows whether they found the good news and the peace it promises? What I do know is that it's there for everybody and anybody—for you and me.

A three-year-old was lying on her stomach and gazing at the nativity scene beneath the family Christmas tree. Suddenly she jumped up and ran to her mother. "Mommy, guess what? God's my size!"

Yes! Grace is *your* size, for *your* need.

Away with the manger? I think not. That manger—as plain and crude as it is—is one of history's reminders of that need, of that grace, of our joy, of our hope.—William L. Turner

Topic: And Joseph Named Him Jesus

TEXT: Matt. 1:18–25

I'd like to talk about one of the best loved but least known people in the Bible. Every year Joseph shows up on our Christmas cards and in our manger scenes, but we really know very little about him. Outside of the Christmas stories, his name appears only four times in the whole New Testament, and even then it's only to identify Jesus, in phrases like "Jesus, the son of Joseph." Except during those few months when he helped Mary through her pregnancy and the birth, the Bible almost completely ignores Joseph. He appears on the scene briefly, does his part, and then vanishes into the background of the New Testament story.

There's a lot we don't know about Joseph, but one thing we do know is that he was a righteous man. That's how Matthew describes him. Now, righteousness is one of those big religious words that keep coming up in the Bible. We know we should be righteous, but we would be hard pressed to say exactly what it means. It's a word that fares well on Sunday morning in church, but we're not quite sure what to do with it on Monday morning at work.

Part of being righteous is, very simply, doing what is right. Joseph was a man who always tried to do what was right. That's why Joseph resolved to break his engagement to Mary when he found out that she was expecting a child. In those days, an engagement to be married was even more important than it is today. Once a man and a woman were engaged, it was almost as if they were actually married. The wedding ceremony still had to take place, but there was nothing tentative about an engagement. It was a legally binding agreement. If a woman engaged to be married was found to be with child by someone other than her fiance, Jewish law required that the fiance break off the engagement. It didn't allow the man to forgive and forget. And since Joseph was a man who always did what was right, he resolved to end the relationship.

According to the law, Joseph was supposed to break his engagement to Mary, but he could have done more than that. He was entitled to make her pay for the disgrace he felt. The law allowed Joseph to have Mary stoned to death, but even if he didn't want to go that far, he could have made a spectacle out of Mary and humiliated her in public. He could have played it to the hilt and gotten lots of sympathy for being the innocent party who was grievously wronged.

But that's not the kind of man Joseph was. He wanted to do what was right, but he was also kind, so he resolved to put her aside quietly, to say nothing in public, to spare her some of the humiliation and shame. Joseph not only wanted to do the right thing, he was also a man of compassion. He was a righteous man.

But Joseph's righteousness was more than doing right and having compassion. His goodness and kindness grew out of his relationship with God. And it was because of his relationship with God that an angel appeared to him and gave him a part in the most amazing thing that God has done since the creation of the world. Joseph, a righteous man, was able to see what God was doing and he was willing to take an active part in it.

We remember Joseph at Christmas because Joseph responded to an invitation to be a part of God's plan.

If Mary's child would be Israel's king, he had to be a member of the house of King David. God had promised that the Messiah would be a descendent of David, with whom God had made a covenant a thousand years before. Joseph was of the house and lineage of David, and God asked Joseph to name Mary's child. In naming the child, Joseph played a part in fulfilling God's promise. Joseph named him the name by which the whole world has come to know him—Jesus, which means Savior. Just when Joseph would have receded into the background, he played his most important part in God's plan. Joseph was a righteous man.

It's a humbling thing to be asked to play a role in what God is doing. And few of us are ever presented with the chance to play a dramatic role in God's work. Certainly we're never asked to play a part as momentous as Joseph did when he named the Messiah. And usually we have to discern God's invitations without the help of an angel appearing to us. But we do have opportunities to be righteous, to stand up for what is right, to show God's love, to have a part in what God is doing in this world Christ came to save.

This church is carrying on in the tradition of Joseph when we teach our children how God is involved in their lives, when we help each other see God at work among us, when we stand here as a beacon of light in a world that desperately seeks an alternative to the way things are.

A righteous person is one who earnestly tries to do what is right. A righteous person is one who does everything with compassion for others and humility before God. But above all else, a righteous person is one who responds to God and allows God to work through him a piece, however small, of the eternal plan. It won't be as miraculous a piece of the plan as God worked through Mary, conceiving in her a child by the Holy Spirit. It may not seem as momentous as what God worked through Joseph, calling on him to name the savior of the world. But it's through people who are ready to hear God calling to them, calling to them in ways that may be subtle and unsuspected, that God keeps working out the plan of peace and forgiveness and new life that began at the creation and was revealed in the manger in Bethlehem. A righteous person is someone who is open to God working in his or her life, in ways both great and small. It's as simple—and as complex—as that. May the one who was named Jesus, Savior, by Joseph fill you with righteousness this Christmas. In him may you find your place in God's holy Kingdom.—Stephens G. Lytch

Topic: The God of the Lowly
TEXT: Luke 1:46–55

We want to remember that Christmas without Christ is not Christmas at all. Hear the song of Mary, that simple, devout, peasant girl who grew up in Nazareth. Many scholars feel that she was twelve years old when she discovered that she was going to be the mother of the Christ child. It was an overwhelming experience for her, as you might imagine.

From her joy she sang the song we call the Magnificat. She rejoiced in the God that she had discovered in her experience. The interesting thing is that the God she discovered was a God who was for the lowly. Throughout the song she described a God who was concerned about those no one else seemed to be concerned for.

If we're ever going to celebrate Christmas right, we've got to understand the kind of God who came. We need to look at her song and see how God is a God for the lowly.

I. *He is a God who came to love the forgotten.* "He has helped," she said, "his servant Israel" (v. 54), that ragtag group of Jewish people who had rebelled so many times and were scattered abroad and seemed so helpless.

It is interesting at Christmas that we do seem to have concerted efforts made to meet the needs of the poor and the less fortunate. It's so sad that the rest of the year these same needs are often ignored or forgotten. This is why Christ did come. He came to go to those who felt themselves unworthy, to go to those who felt themselves forgotten and left out, and to tell them they were not left out. They were cared about and they were understood. He came to identify with them.

In a sense this is what God has come to say at Christmas. The same concern he has for the rich he has for the poor. The same concern he has for the "up and ins" he has for the "down and outs." The same concern he has for the powerful he has for the weak. Everyone is precious to him. That means, thank God, you and me.

II. *God is a God who comes to have mercy on the needy.* This was another part of Mary's song. He has mercy on "those who fear Him" (v. 50). Those who trusted him, those who believed in him, those who committed themselves to him—God was merciful to them. They needed it.

These Jewish people had rebelled so many times, broken the heart of God over and over, but there were still those who clung somehow to the belief that God would not forget them; God would still come and make out of them something worthwhile. Mary knew that God would. They could have another chance; they could get up and go on again. Coming at Christmas was a God who would start all over again with those who wanted him to.

III. *He is a God who came to exalt their righteous.* All the way through Mary's song there was an affirmation of victory, that God was a God who would honor Abraham and the promise he made. That promise was that if they trusted him and did his will, he would make out of them a great nation; they would be part of his kingdom.

What Mary was singing was that God would do that. Those who loved him and followed him would be the victors. It didn't seem like it, but this is what Mary said: "He has scattered the proud in the imagination of their hearts, he has put down the mighty from their thrones . . . the rich he has sent empty away" (vv. 51–53). Now these were the ones who seemed to be on top of things: the rich, powerful kings, those who had money, those who had power, those who could snap their fingers and people would jump. They were the ones who seemed to be the victors—not some ragtag bunch of Jewish people singing about God coming, not poor and needy people who had little power and prestige.

But Mary sang of the little people. He has "exalted those of low degree; he has filled the hungry with good things" (vv. 52–53). In other words, Mary said that those who love the Lord will not be disappointed, will not be forgotten. They will share in his kingdom.

God blesses those who, in the way they can, seek to follow him and to do his will in the places where they live.

Only when we give will we find. Only when we lose will we receive. Only when we love will we be loved. Only when we do his will we truly live.

This is what Christmas says: Christ comes again to look you in the eye and to say, "I love you." All the celebrating that we do at Christmas is our opportunity to look him back in the face and say, "We love you." God is trying to find you again. I hope this Christmas you will make sure he does.—Hugh Litchfield

Illustrations

ADVENT. During these last days of Advent, the Church gives us a series of antiphons to the Magnificat, drawing attention to and adding special urgency to that sense of expectation which closes in on us as the great feast draws near. They address our blessed Lord under various titles given to him by the old Jewish prophets before the world was saved. Now he is the Branch that grows, suddenly and belatedly, from the trunk of Jesse, from the royal dynasty of Israel, hardly more than a memory in the great lumber room of the past. Now he is the Key of David, the providentially designed instrument which fits into the lock of our sad human experience, the one instrument that can provide the answer to all our puzzles, give freedom to all our inhibited aspirations. But the metaphor under which we greet him this evening, the twenty-first of December, is perhaps the most primitive of all. "O Day-star, radiance from the eternal Light, Sun-rise that is the world's amending, come and enlighten us as we sit here in darkness, under the shadow of death."—Ronald A. Knox[1]

THE DESIRE OF ALL NATIONS. The hope of the world lies in the Christmas message: Immanuel, God with us. Today some are looking to political machinery to fashion a new earth, some to social security, some to humanitarian sentiment and ethical endeavor. We need these things indeed; but unless there is a surer foundation we shall be heading straight for disillusionment. Not man is self-sufficient, but God's redemptive action, not mere human planning on the horizontal level but the inrush of a new power from the beyond, is our supreme need now. In short, Christ is (albeit often unrecog-

nized) the desire of all nations, the hope of the ends of the earth.—James S. Stewart[2]

THE MEANING OF CHRISTIANITY. It will be generally recognized that to speak of the meaning of Jesus Christ is to speak of what is most distinctive and most decisive in Christian life and faith. The Christian religion, in whatever form, finds its center and, it might almost be said, its circumference also in Christ. It is Christ who both distinguishes and unites the church. In so far as the church is one and in so far as it has a distinctive message to impart and a distinctive gift to bestow, Christ is the principle of both the distinctiveness of its service and the unity of its life. In a word, the whole essential meaning of Christianity is not less, or more, than the meaning of Christ.—John Knox[3]

CAN I KNOW GOD? The one desolating doubt I have had in my adult religious life was on this question. It was midnight in my soul, but I emerged more sure than ever, and the passing years deepen my conviction. I am quite sure now. Christ was incarnate God. He is utterly trustworthy. Travel with him and travel with confidence. (Forgive me if I sound presumptuous but I have tested him and been tested, in many ways.) I am in no doubt that God spoke through the Hebrew prophets and the Eastern sages, but his fullest final word was Christ. All men must come to him at the last. He has the answer to the problems of our private lives, our families, our business, our civic and national affairs. Apart from his triumph I see no hopeful prospect for our race.—W. E. Sangster[4]

THE HUMANITY OF JESUS. The mystery at the heart of the Christ-event is that Jesus is, in some paradoxical way, God-man. He is a historical being, a man among men. Yet his life, death, and Resurrection are, for Christian believers, a saving disclosure of God, effective in their lives. He is a human being who is also a divine act. The Christ is history and yet He transcends history. But of course Jesus is

---

[1] *The Pastoral Sermons of Ronald A. Knox.*
[2] James S. Stewart, in Paul Butler, *Best Sermons: 1947–48.*
[3] *The Meaning of Christ.*
[4] *Can I Know God?*

more than man. He is not just a strange and haunting figure of the past. His historical humanity accompanies all history. He is no "far-off mystic of the Galilean hills," to use Lord Morley's phrase, but rather he is our living contemporary. We read the Gospel story and find him standing forth and judging us, searing our conscience and challenging us with his self-giving love. In Richard Jeffries' classic story of boyhood, *Bevis,* he tells of a boy reading the Gospel story. "The Crucifix-ion hurt his feelings very much; the cruel nails; the unfeeling spear; he looked at the picture a long time and then turned the page saying, If God had been there, he would not have let them do it!" But God was there! This is the mystery of Jesus. The historicity of Jesus is the historicity of God. The humanity of Jesus is the humanity of God. The life of Jesus is eternal life, for it is the life of God in man, the life of God wrought into the texture of our human story.—Eric C. Rust[5]

[5] *The Word and Words.*

SECTION VII.
Evangelism and World Missions

SERMON SUGGESTIONS

Topic: God Has Three Sons

TEXT: Luke 15:11–32

This sermon is one of thousands based on Jesus' best-known story—the parable of the prodigal son, as we have titled it. It is in this story that Jesus first suggested that God has three sons.

I. Jesus first told this story in response to the charge that he was mixing with the wrong crowd. In his day it was every bit as important as it is in our time for one who wanted to be thought of as a good person to run with the right people. One was most definitely judged by the company one kept, and since Jesus had begun to keep company with known sinners, some of the more judgmental and critical members of his society questioned his morality.

Jesus took that criticism as an opportunity to explain why he had come in the first place: to reach those who needed reaching, to heal those who were in need of healing, and to find those who had gotten lost. It was that last purpose—to find those who had gotten lost—that Jesus was illustrating with the parable of the prodigal son. But in the course of explaining that he'd come for the lost, he revealed that God has three sons.

You see, the father in the parable represents God. When his children leave him, he patiently waits for them to come back home. Through this story, Jesus is saying that in his association with sinners he is doing what God, the Father, does. He is seeking those who have wandered off in their foolishness and gotten lost.

II. Well, if the father in the story is God, who are the two sons? Who does Jesus want us to think of when we hear this story?

I think the sons are representative of all people. In one sense, all people are God's children. He is the Creator. He is responsible for all life. Therefore he is the Father of all mankind.

There is another way we can tell that the two sons in Jesus' story represent all people. It is the way they believe. The youngest son, who asked for his inheritance early then went off to a far county where he squandered all of it in loose living, represents all the rebellious, selfish people of the world.

Notice that this son does not deny his relationship with his father. He does not repudiate his heritage. It just doesn't mean all that much to him. He knows a better way. He is strong enough and smart enough to avert even the most common pitfalls. He can make it, even if no one else can.

Some of us are beginning to recognize the youngest son in Jesus' story. He has walked among us. We've talked with him. We've observed firsthand his foolish selfishness. We've taken note of his self-destructive attitude. Why, we may have even seen his face in the mirror. The youngest son exemplifies all the people of all time who have ever acted on the belief that rules don't apply to them—all people who have ever turned up their noses at God's commandments.

III. The older son in Jesus' story represents the faithful but resentful people of the human family. These are the people who can be counted on to be true through thick and thin. They are not motivated to chase personal dreams, if indeed they have any. They do not think of themselves as much as they think of others around them, especially those for whom they feel responsible.

Now, you may be impressed with what appears to be exemplary love by the older son for his father, but look again. Jesus tells us more about him. True enough, he stayed home to do his rightful part in the family, but that does not necessarily mean his motivation was love. He may simply have felt obligated to care for his father in his old age. He may have been sympathetic to his father's grief, or he may have just been afraid to venture out from home alone.

One clue to the older son's true feelings was his reaction when his younger brother returned home. He resented the fact that although his brother had acted irresponsibly, he was received home so cheerfully, while the older son had served the father with great dedication yet had never had such fuss made over him. Is there no justice? Isn't the basic rule of justice that the faithful are rewarded and sinners are punished? Then how does the father explain the welcome home party for the younger, selfish brother?

Does it ever grate on you a little bit to see your neighbor prosper when you have to scrimp and scrape to get by? Is there no justice?

Now you can see that the older son in Jesus' story is alive and well today, and he lives right here.

IV. This is where the parable reported in Luke 15 ended—but it was not where the story ended. The story was finished by the teller of the parable. He was not just the narrator of the story; he was, and is, its principal character.

God had *three* sons. Two of them were sons of earth, children of his creation; the other was the Son of heaven, begotten by God's abiding grace. The younger son of earth forgot his true home and through pride of the flesh sank into shame. The older son of earth, though not unmindful of his heritage, began to despise his brother and so grew hard through pride of the mind. The Son of heaven lived always in his Father's joy. But a shadow fell over both the Son and the Father whenever they thought of the children of earth.

The Father said: "I will send the Son of my abiding grace to appeal to them." The Son of heaven said: "I will go that my brothers may come home and that my Father may no longer grieve." So the Son of heaven took flesh and walked the winding, treacherous roads of earth. He found the younger prodigal, ate his husks, and shared his shame. But the prodigal was deaf and blind. "No brother of mine," he said, "and God is only a name." Then the Son of God's abiding grace found the elder prodigal, who was in church, but he was also hard of heart. "Why should you seek my brother?" he asked bitterly. "He is a wastrel and it looks to me that you are no better than he!"

Then happened the most cruel thing the earth has ever known. The two prodigals killed the Son of God's abiding grace, for his light was pain in their afflicted eyes. In hate they nailed him to a cross. But—*but*—he prayed for them as he died. The younger prodigal said, "I would return to the Father if I had not killed his only begotten Son, but now. . . .'" The older prodigal said: "I never knew my lovelessness 'til I saw his love, but I have killed him, so now. . . ."[1]

And both prodigals knew he was with them.

This is the point of the story—the larger story of which the parable reported in Luke 15 is just a part: God has *three* sons. It is the Son of heaven, the Son of God's abiding grace, who is also the Son of the cross, who makes it possible for both prodigals to come back home and stay.—David W. Crocker

Topic: Where in the World Is God?

TEXT: Ps. 139:1–18; Rom. 11:33–36 NRSV

The statement by NASA some time back regarding the possibility of life on Mars ignited debate in the religious community.

The possibility of life on other planets does indeed raise some questions about the nature of the world we live in, the nature of humankind, the nature of Jesus, the nature and extent of salvation, and most assuredly, the very nature of God. The possibility of life on other planets, or even more mind-boggling,

---

[1]This passage is paraphrased from Walter Russell Bowie and others, "The Gospel According to St. Luke," in George A. Buttrick, (ed.), *The Interpreter's Bible*, vol. 8 (Nashville: Abingdon, 1952), 272.

the possibility of life in other solar systems, causes me, at least, to ask the question, "Where in the world—no, let me rephrase that—where in the *universe* is God?"

This is a question the psalmist wrestled with thousands of years ago. And contemplating the nature of God, the apostle Paul was led to exclaim, "Oh the depth of the riches and wisdom and knowledge of God! How unsearchable are his judgments and how inscrutable [difficult to fathom] his ways" (Rom. 11:33)!

I. *One of the great mysteries of life and faith is that there is no place where God is not.* If it were possible for us to dig to the center of the earth, when we got there we would find the presence of God. If we were able to search out the deepest hole in the deepest sea, when we got there, we would find evidence of God. If we were able to travel to—and we know we cannot and probably will never be able to—the farthest, darkest spot in all the universe, there we would feel the presence of God. Who can understand it? And who can try to explain it? Such thoughts caused the psalmist to cry, "Where can I go from your spirit? Or where can I flee from your presence?"

"Who can hide in secret places so that I cannot see them? says the Lord" through the prophet Jeremiah. "Do I not fill heaven and earth?" (Jer. 23:24).

The truth is, we can never hope to fully understand God. All attempts to put God into a neat theological box are futile, if not downright sacrilegious. The ways and nature of God defy human comprehension; it is a fact of life.

II. *And yet the other side of the great mystery of God is that the same God whose presence graces the farthest star in the universe is also right here with us.* Hear what the psalmist says at this point:

O Lord, you have searched me and known me.
You know when I sit down and when I rise up;
you discern my thoughts from far away.
You search out my path and my lying down.
You are acquainted with all my ways.
Even before a word is on my tongue,
O Lord, you know it completely (139:1–40).

There are those who would contend, and perhaps rightly so, that in searching for God we need not look outside ourselves, but rather, deep within ourselves, within our own hearts.

All of us come to points in our lives when we ask, Where is God? Where is God when I need him most? Where is God when there is sickness? Where is God when there are family conflicts or financial troubles? We have all said it—or at least we have thought it. Like children who feel separated or far away from their parents because of the darkness, even though our parents are just across the hall or on the other side of the wall, we often feel separated from God by life's dark clouds. But the truth is, God is *always* right here with us. God can never desert us. It is a contradiction in terms. "Wherever you are, He is with you" (Koran 57.4). Let us not forget that the apostle Paul preached to the Athenians that God "is not far from each one of us. For 'In him' we live and move and have our being'" (Acts 17:27–28).

As the poet Alfred, Lord Tennyson so aptly phrased it:

Speak to Him thou for He hears,
and spirit with spirit can meet—
Closer is He than breathing,
and nearer than hands and feet.

Where in the world, or where in the universe, is God? God is on the highest mountain peak and in the lowest pit of the sea. He is at the farthest and darkest spot in space, and he is on Mars, and Saturn, and Pluto. In the words of the Koran, "Whichever way you turn, there is the face of God" (2.109). But the really good news is, God is right here with us, deep within our own hearts.—Randy Hammer

Topic: God's Chosen Instruments

TEXT: Acts 9:1–20

Somehow or other, Saul's experience on the road to Damascus seems to be the standard by which we judge conversion experiences. Lots of folks think that the goal of evangelism is to create some kind of dramatic turnaround, complete with blinding light. This is the kind of conversion experience that gets the most press—the one that reminds you of the story of Saul, in which a person who was living one way had a life-changing encounter with Christ and—Boom! He's turned around 180 degrees and is now going in the opposite direction.

These kinds of stories are good. They happen all the time. Some of you have had a life-changing encounter almost like Saul's on the road to Damascus, and I praise God every time I hear a story like that. But they make me feel inadequate. My story isn't one that would be written up in a magazine.

So, we may hear of Saul's conversion and feel like we don't have anything to say. We may focus so much on Saul that we overlook the character in the story with whom we may have the most in common. Instead of feeling guilty that we've never had a conversion experience like Saul's, maybe we should take a little more notice of Ananias. For most of us, evangelism isn't so much relating our stories of dramatic encounters with Christ or preaching before large crowds. Instead it is the practice of being with someone at the right time to help that person make sense out of what God is doing in his or her life.

A lot of people are trying to do what Saul was trying to do. They're trying to earn their self-worth. When he went from city to city rounding up Christians to bring them to trial, he wasn't trying to be some evil, godless person. He was trying to show how good he was, how important it was to him to uphold the religious laws. He really thought he was doing the right thing, working hard to find favor with God.

Many of the people we know may not think of what they do in religious terms the way Saul did, but they're trying just as hard as he was to earn their self-worth. Now there's nothing wrong with hard work or giving yourself generously to others. The problem comes when we try to earn our well-being the way Saul was trying to please God by keeping strictly to the letter of the law.

It was only when God struck him blind in the middle of the road that Saul realized how helpless he really was. Before he could do what God wanted him to do, he had to give up trying so hard.

Sometimes we have to be struck down in the middle of the road before we're ready to hear what Jesus has to say to us. It's not always God who does the striking. Sometimes we put ourselves in a difficult situation, or sometimes we just have bad luck. But sometimes we have to find ourselves in a place like that in which Saul found himself—feeling helpless and at the end of his rope—before we can hear what Jesus is trying to tell us.

Jesus often comes to us at turning points in our lives, times when we really don't have any place else to turn but to him.

Sitting there in the darkness in Damascus, Saul didn't know which way to turn. Jesus had spoken to him, but he didn't know what to do about it. That's when Ananias came to him. Ananias didn't berate him for what he'd done in the past. He didn't threaten him with hell-fire unless he changed his ways. He just very quietly and simply explained to Saul what was going on. He pointed out to him how Jesus was giving Saul strength in his weakness. God did the work. God did the converting. All Ananias did was help Saul understand what was going on and introduce him to the community of believers in Damascus.

Part of the reason that evangelism is such a hard thing for so many people to do is that we think of it as trying to talk people into believing something they may or may not want to believe. Really, evangelism is helping other people to respond to Jesus' call to them. Some people have a special gift of standing up in public places and proclaiming the gospel to whoever will hear. Saul had that gift, and he used it to help thousands of people respond to the Lord. But for many of us, our call to be evangelists is more like Ananias' call: we help others understand what's going on in their lives and show them how to respond to Christ.

We have to listen very carefully to people and understand where in their lives Christ may be knocking. This may mean sharing what Christ has meant in your life, how he has helped you through your transitions and difficulties. Or it may mean something as simple as inviting someone to church so they can experience what it's like to be a part of the body of Christ.

But remembering that the initiative lies with Christ relieves us of much of the anxiety of being evangelists for him. The actual turning of the heart lies with him.

When Christ chooses us to be his followers, he chooses us to be instruments to spread the good news of eternal life. Each of us is a different kind of instrument, but each of us is chosen to help spread the word. It's good news we're supposed to share. Every believer is called to be an evangelist.—Stephens G. Lytch

Topic: Service or Serve Us?

TEXT: Mark 10:35–45

One of the principles of excellence in the best-selling book on the best-run companies in America, *In Search of Excellence*,[2] was an obsession with service. Folks like being appreciated even if the objective is just business. They like being served. This principle is not so much about a real benefit as it is about conveying to the customer, "You are important."

I. *The Kingdom standard of service is costly.* What about the church? Do strangers who come into this place receive a level of attention comparable to that received in a Japanese service station? Surely we have a greater mission than a gas station, and a higher concern for the needs of people. Do the members of this church receive quality time and energy from the ministers, deacons, teachers, and other caregivers? George Barna writes about "marketing the church" and "user-friendly churches." He uses business language to describe and evaluate churches, and sometimes one gets the impression that profit is the motive. One of the largest Southern Baptist churches in the country was featured in *The Wall Street Journal* a few years ago. Ushers and parking attendants were schooled by Disney World on the best techniques in courtesy and people management.

Mark was brutally honest about the humanness of the Twelve. Sibling rivalry, competition, jealousy, and anger sometimes distracted them from their mission. Mark threw in a story about James and John that sounds like a page from Peters and Waterman's book. In the world of business, the sons of Zebedee might be lauded for their determined ambition, but in the community of discipleship such behavior was shameful (Matthew attributed the whole embarrassing incident to their mother). James and John asked Jesus for the best seats in the house. They wanted to be close enough to share the glory when the movement arrived and the Kingdom was

established. The other disciples were furious with the ambition of James and John, and Jesus reminded the Twelve that their community was not about being served but about serving: "For the Son of Man came not to be served but to serve and to give his life a ransom for many." Sharing the cup and the baptism of Jesus meant sharing the pain. Discipleship is about "serve others" not "serve us."

II. *Who is the customer?* This is a common question in business circles today. One has to focus all energy on the customer in order to sell widgets and grow the business. The only real problem with James and John was a total misunderstanding of the mission of the Kingdom. They thought of themselves as customers. Jesus gently turned them around to see that they were the servants. They survived the ordeal, perhaps with a little resentment from their colleagues, and with a whole lot more wisdom about the meaning of Kingdom service. They needed to learn that Jesus was not involved in a big giveaway promotion. Any resemblance between the grace of God and the free offers in the mail from real estate brokers in Florida is in the eye of the beholder. This is a community of grace. We are not in a race with one another for the best seats in the Kingdom.

Walter Rauschenbush was a Baptist pastor at the turn of the century whose reading of the gospel led him to ministry in Hell's Kitchen, a ghetto of poverty in New York City. He took seriously the challenge of Jesus to feed the hungry, to clothe the naked, and to visit the sick and imprisoned. The focus of Christian service is on the weakest and the least in the society in which we live. Rauschenbush saw the social injustice of his time to be the mission of the church. The customer was measured by need rather than by profit. The energies of the church existed for the salvation of the world, and the church's resources had to focus on the socially and economically lost as well as on the spiritually lost.

I believe that we need a good dose of the social gospel in the Church today. There is entirely too much competition among churches, much like the competition among the disciples over the chief seats. The appeal of the church and the understanding of service sound too much like pitching soap or selling burgers. Those that are the biggest and that offer the most are judged to be the

[2]Tom Peters and Robert Waterman, Jr. (New York: HarperCollins, 1982).

best. Hear the word of the gospel. Jesus said that the greatest is the servant, that the first must be the slave of all.

III. *Service pays.* These days, volunteer organizations like churches are being reminded that people work for pay. If you cannot pay them in money, you had better find another means of reward, even if it is an occasional pat on the back. It seems that nobody works for nothing. Now, there is nothing wrong with wanting to be appreciated. James and John were not demons. They were much like you and me. They expected something besides the statistical value in following Jesus. Maybe they were selfish and inconsiderate of the others when they asked for the best places, but people often say one thing and mean another. Have you noticed how often children will make a major issue of wanting a cookie when all they really want is for Mom and Dad to embrace them and say, "I love you"? Sometimes the only pay we receive in life is being loved and appreciated.

The whole discussion of work ethic in our time revolves around the meaning of pay. When people work only for money, they are usually very poor workers. Something else has to motivate and drive our interest. Jesus calls us to service, not to "serve us." The church is where one finds the meaning and reward of service not only when one is down, but in the joy of giving a cup of cold water in the name of Jesus.—Larry Dipboye

Topic: What to Say About Jesus

TEXT: John 1:43–51

What do you say about Jesus? The first time I ever had to wrestle with that question was in the seventh grade, out by the bike racks behind the junior high school. I'd grown up in a church-going family, vaguely aware that there were people out there who didn't believe in Jesus (something that puzzled me), but it didn't really came home to me until one spring afternoon. I'd stayed after school for some extracurricular activity. Five of us boys were unlocking our bikes to go home when Pat, a Roman Catholic, said he was on his way to confirmation class.

"Do you really believe in Jesus?" one of the boys, who was Jewish, asked him.

"Sure," Pat replied.

"But why? What's so special about him?"

"He's the Son of God," said Pat.

"How do you know that?"

"Well, Jesus did miracles. He healed sick people."

"Can you prove it?" the skeptic asked.

"It says so in the Bible."

"But the Bible's just another book," another one of the boys said. "What makes it so special?"

I was starting to get uncomfortable. Here was Pat, telling all the things I'd learned as gospel truth in Sunday school, and they weren't having a bit of effect on the three boys who didn't believe. I figured I'd better say something. I didn't really have anything more convincing to say than Pat did but I was starting to fear that God was going to hold me accountable if I didn't say anything. So Pat and I pulled out every argument we could think of to convince those three boys they should believe in Jesus. We didn't seem to be changing any minds.

Finally, in desperation, Pat asked, "If Jesus wasn't who he claimed to be, then why do so many people believe in him?"

"Well, a lot of us don't," one of the skeptics scoffed as he wheeled away on his bike.

As I rode my bike home, I felt angry, confused, and pretty inadequate. I felt angry at the boys for not believing, confused because I had to admit that their arguments made sense, inadequate because I felt like I'd let Jesus down by not defending him well enough. I'd always thought that everything I believed about Jesus was so self-evident that anybody who heard about him couldn't help but believe. I couldn't seem to come up with any argument that would convince someone to believe in Jesus.

And, you know, it hasn't changed a whole lot. Oh, I know a lot more about the Bible now. I have three seminary degrees hanging on the wall in my study, and I can read the New Testament in Greek. I've read most of the arguments people can make against the Christian faith, and I've developed some rather sophisticated responses. But I've still never been able to prove to anyone why they should believe in Jesus.

Just last week I was talking with someone who was despairing that his life was hopeless. In fact, he was thinking about suicide. He's read books about why he should believe; in fact, he knows his Bible pretty well. "I'm just not worthy of God," he told me.

I resisted the temptation to argue with him and give him reasons why he was worthy. He'd heard the lecture before and he knew the facts, but knowing the facts wasn't what was going to give him a purpose for staying alive. All I could say was, "I don't know you that well, but I do know God. And I don't think God's love for you has changed." And I had to leave it at that, trusting God to do the rest.

You see, believing in Jesus isn't a matter of weighing all the arguments and deciding whether Christianity is right or wrong. Believing in Jesus isn't like shopping for a new car, where you evaluate the claims of the salesperson, take the car for a test drive, figure how much you can afford, then decide whether or not it's right for you.

To believe in Jesus isn't just agreeing to a list of creeds and affirmations. It's entering into a relationship with him. And relationships aren't made by what somebody tells us but by firsthand encounters. I can tell you that Beth is a wonderful person, someone who's compassionate and winsome and fun to be around and someone you should really get to know. I can tell you enough so that you will want to meet her. But I can't create a relationship between the two of you just by telling you about her. Until you actually meet her and get acquainted and spend some time with her, you don't really know her. The best I can do is point you in the right direction and introduce you to her.

That's what Philip did for his friend Nathanael. Philip told Nathanael what a wonderful person Jesus was. He shared the excitement of his new relationship. "We have found him about whom Moses in the law and also the prophets wrote, Jesus son of Joseph from Nazareth." But Nathanael, like the boys around the bike rack, wasn't convinced. All he had to say was, "Can anything good come out of Nazareth?" Nazareth, that provincial town, far removed from the center of worship in Jerusalem, a common place that would never be the kind of town to produce the Messiah. For sophisticated Nathanael, Jesus' hometown was enough reason not to believe in him.

Philip could have gotten into a long discussion with Nathanael. He could have told him all the reasons that Jesus is who he said he is; he could even have come to the defense of the town of Nazareth. But he didn't do that. All he said was "Come and see"—a simple invitation to meet the man himself. Philip had the good sense to know that he couldn't convince Nathanael to believe. Only Jesus himself could do that.

And Jesus didn't try to argue Nathanael into believing. He didn't give Nathanael a sermon on why he should give his life to Jesus or how much better off he'd be if he became a disciple. Listen again to what happened: When Jesus saw Nathanael coming toward him, he said of him, "Here is truly an Israelite in whom there is no deceit." That struck a chord with Nathanael. He was a man who prided himself on saying exactly what was on his mind. Maybe he was one of those insufferable people who you wish would keep their opinions to themselves. So Nathanael asked, somewhat suspiciously, "Where did you get to know me?" And Jesus replied, "I saw you sitting under the fig tree before Philip called you." Nathanael responded, "Rabbi, you are the Son of God! You are the King of Israel!"

And isn't that how so many of us have come to profess Jesus as Lord, because in him we have experienced a profound sense of being known? Jesus knew everything about Nathanael, even before Nathanael met him. Jesus knew his character, that he was an honest person with no deceit. He even knew the smallest details, like where he had been sitting before Philip called him.

Now, that doesn't mean that Jesus is the divine snoop. So often his profound knowledge of us has been used by well-meaning evangelists as a threat, like a prosecutor trying to twist a confession out of a suspect. "We've got the goods on you. Confess and believe or you'll be punished forever." How many times have you heard that hellfire and brimstone sermon trying to scare you into faith, saying that there is no place to hide from Jesus?

But that's not how Jesus convinced Nathanael to believe. He didn't see him coming and yell, "I know you, you sinner. You're full of pride and you're going to hell." No, Jesus saw what was good in Nathanael. Maybe he saw something that no one else had ever seen. Jesus has a way of seeing what's good in a person, of knowing us so well that he thinks more of us than we do of ourselves. A few days after he met Nathanael, Jesus came across a Samaritan woman drawing water from a well. After a conversation, he told her to go get her husband. She said that she didn't have a husband, and he said, "You are right. You have had five husbands, and the one with whom you live now is not your husband." He wasn't belittling her or shaming her, just letting her know that he knew her. And there's something very powerful about being known.

That's one reason that listening is one of the most important ministries of the church. Much of what we're about is listening to each other. We listen when we share with each other in our Sunday school classes or small groups. We go to a pastor for counseling in the hope that he or she will really listen and understand our problems and help us understand and cope with them. Our church has enrolled in the Stephen Ministry so we can become better listeners to those who are going through rough times. When we listen compassionately to others, it's as though Jesus is listening through us. When others entrust some of who they are to us, when they let us get to know them, they might come to realize that Jesus knows them, too, even better than they know themselves.

There's no way we can learn enough theological arguments to convince someone to enter into a relationship with Jesus. The best we can do is introduce someone to him. People who have studied what makes churches grow have taken surveys and discovered that it's not the particular doctrines of a church that make people join. It's not their high-profile advertising. It's not even, I'm disappointed to say, the sermons of the pastor. Seventy to 90 percent of the people who join a church do so because a friend or a relative invited them. Those friends didn't have seminary degrees or consider themselves biblical scholars. All they did was give an invitation, something as simple as saying, "Come and see what's going on."

In the tenth chapter of John, Jesus describes himself as the Good Shepherd. He says that he knows his sheep and his sheep know him. His mission on earth is to gather all those who belong to him, those he already knows. Not everyone is going to accept that invitation the first time it's offered. Some need to hear it for years before they finally

respond. And there are some who, for whatever reason, may never accept it, who have their own reasons for not wanting to be known by Jesus and have him as a friend. But I think the story of Nathanael can take off of us some of the pressure we feel to know all the answers before we can say anything about Jesus. All we really have to know is what we've seen, and all we really have to say is, "Come and see." If we do just that much, Jesus can take care of the rest.—Stephens G. Lytch

Illustrations

THE UNIQUENESS OF JESUS.   Some men drifting in a rubber boat on the vast Pacific said that the greatest source of strength and hope that came to them during those torturous days was the assurance that they were being sought. Such is Jesus' picture of God— one who seeks the lost. And it was a new picture! Montefiore, the Jewish scholar, said: "The Rabbis . . . welcomed the sinner in his repentance. But to *seek out* the sinner, and, instead of avoiding the bad companion, to choose him as your friend in order to work his moral redemption, this was, I fancy, something new in the religious history of Israel."— Howard Cooke Phillips[3]

THE HOPEFULNESS OF CHRIST.   How to be faithful and at the same time hopeful is sometimes one of the most difficult of problems—how to be true to our own sense of truth and yet at the same time to keep hope alive. And I say that as you read the life of Jesus you are amazed at his solving of that problem, for never was he less than perfect truth, yet did he always quicken into hope. Never was a man so faithful as the Lord, never one who could so pierce the depths. He never uttered a single word of compliment. He never said anything because it sounded kindly. And the amazing thing is that with that fine fidelity to all that was saddest and all that was most tragical, chords that were broken began again to vibrate under the thrill and music of his speech. Poor women who had fallen to the streets began to hope again, they knew not why. The thief on the cross, after a lawless life, awoke

[3] *The Timeless Gospel.*

to feel that *he* might be remembered. In the very hour that they were self-exposed, and found themselves judged as man had never judged them, in that very hour they began to hope. That is always the wonder of Christ's hopefulness. It leans on the bosom of a perfect knowledge. It sees the vilest, and yet does not despair. It knows the worst, and yet it hopes the best. And that is why the hopefulness of Jesus is still moving and mighty in the world, when other hopes that were all golden once have passed, broken, into the glen of weeping.—George H. Morrison[4]

TO BE A CHRISTIAN.   Many people wonder what it means to be a Christian—not just a nominal Christian but a *real* Christian, a committed Christian, one who takes his allegiance to Christ very, very seriously.

Sometimes being a Christian is thought to mean "going to church." That is important, but it can hardly be called the definition of Christian belonging. Sometimes it is taken to mean acceptance of this or that creed or set of doctrines. Firm belief is important but in itself is not the definition of a Christian. Reading the Bible, saying one's prayers, these two are sometimes assumed to make one a Christian. Again, these are important, but they do not define a Christian. Let me propose an answer to the question, What does it mean to be a Christian? which not only makes sense of my own Christian allegiance but also is founded on the New Testament witness and therefore ought to have a compelling quality for anyone who dares to profess and call himself Christian.

To be a Christian is *to be caught up into life in Christ.* Life in Christ gives the importance to church going, doctrines, creeds, Bible reading, prayer—and maybe above all to the effort to live day by day with one's fellow men in a fashion befitting the man or woman who would be a disciple of Jesus.—Norman Pittenger[5]

CHRISTIAN FREEDOM.   Christian freedom puts me in the position where I stand before God himself, answerable to Him alone, yet in humility I must give due consideration and

weight both in my thinking and behavior to what is the general public opinion of Christendom. In estimating this I must bear in mind not only the teaching of the Bible but also the tradition of the past, of Christian history. I must open my mind to be influenced not only by academic argument and thought but also by the spirit of Christian worship, and by the accumulated experience of Christian living. Then I am free—free to obey my conscience, to exercise my private judgement, and to stand fast in the liberty wherewith Christ hath made me free.

Christian freedom is both dynamic and purposive. It is not only *freedom from* or *freedom in.* It is primarily *freedom for* God's service. We are to be released from all bondage so that all our powers and the depths of our personality may be set free to be given gladly and used fully by him who has made us free.—Bryan Green[6]

THE CHURCH EVANGELISTIC.   Let me say to all ministers, you will find you must have your church act with you if you are going to do any evangelistic work. And to church members, it is no use wasting breath in the criticism of a minister because he is not doing evangelistic work. Let the church fall into line. One of the first missions of the ministry will be to bring the church into sympathy, and that will often need a great deal of common sense and patience.

No church ought to be allowed to exist that has not added to its membership by confession of faith. If a church is existing only by letters of transfer, it is time the doors were closed and "Ichabod, the glory of the Lord has departed" was inscribed across them.—G. Campbell Morgan[7]

HOW LORIMER WAS LED.   Dwight L. Moody, America's greatest evangelist, was led to Christ by a Sunday school teacher, Mr. Kimberly, in the rear of a shoe store on Court Street in Boston. Dr. George H. Lorimer, perhaps the most famous of the pastors of Tremont Temple, Boston, and whose son became editor of the *Saturday Evening Post,* began his career as a theatrical man. He was

[4] *The Greatest Sermons of George H. Morrison.*
[5] *Life in Christ.*
[6] *Saints Alive.*
[7] *A Treasury of G. Campbell Morgan.*

won to Christ in Louisville when some women went to their pastor, Dr. Everetts, and suggested that invitations to church service be passed out at neighborhood doors. The women passed an invitation card to Dr. Lorimer, but he replied, "No, you haven't any use for me. I'm a theatrical man." The women were so courteous, however, that he could not refuse their invitation and came to church. Dr. Everetts's sermon was: "The summer is ended, the harvest is passed, and I am not saved." Lorimer was saved in church that Sunday and later became pastor of Tremont Temple, Boston. One of the young lawyers who listened to his preaching was Russell H. Conwell. Dr. Lorimer led Conwell to accept Christ. Conwell went to Philadelphia and built the great Temple University and the Grace Baptist Temple there.—Benjamin P. Browne

SECTION VIII.
Preaching from Great Old Testament Texts

BY THOMAS G. SMOTHERS

Topic: The Worth of a Human Being

TEXT: Ps. 8

If you ask people what they are worth, they will likely give you an answer in terms of dollars and cents: so much in cash, so much in houses and land, so much in stocks and bonds. What a trite, superficial estimate of a person's life. This psalm, by affirming that persons are located at the center of God's care, helps us to focus on who we are and on what we are really worth.

The psalm begins with an ascription of majesty to God, as every psalm of praise must do. The psalm, however, is about people and about their value in God's sight. It is good news to those who feel they are worthless. It is an unwelcome message to the centers of power, which are able to maintain their power by asserting their control over persons.

I. *God's providential care.* "When I look at your heavens, the work of your fingers, the moon and the stars which you have established, what are we that you should care for us?"

Reflecting on his tiny niche in the scheme of things, the psalmist raised the question with a profound sense of awe. But the question itself is as strong an affirmation of divine providence as we can find in the Bible.

In 1969 we watched the television screen intently, waiting for Apollo 11 to emerge from behind the moon. All communication with the astronauts was lost during those long moments. When the capsule had completed its turn, its cameras were focused on tiny earth, turning in the immensity of space, and we were struck by how vulnerable we are on planet earth. How easy it is to feel despair!

But the psalmist reminds us that God cares for no one more than he cares for you and me. We have not been abandoned, nor have we been forgotten. Eric Rust used to remind his theology students that God's greatness is seen best of all in that the one who is so infinitely great loves us, who are so infinitely small.

That may seem a stupendous claim to make, and yet the faithful through the ages have given living testimony out of their experiences to God's providential care. Despite disappointments and loss, and in the midst of pain, they have testified that underneath us are the everlasting arms.

How much are you worth? At least this much: that there is nothing you can ever do to make God not love you.

II. *The unique place of persons.* The text reads: "You have made them to be a little less than God." The words "a little less than" maintain the gulf that separates us from God, which can be bridged only by the grace of God. But at the same time they affirm the special and unique place that God has granted to each of us.

"You have crowned them with glory and honor and have given them dominion over your creation; you have put everything under their feet." Note the language: "you have crowned them," "glory and honor," "dominion." This is royal language, the most exalted mode of expression available to the psalmist.

The unique place of humans in God's intent is astounding. This text came as good news at a time when the religious systems surrounding Israel had a discouragingly low view of the worth of persons. In Egypt, people were to work the soil, build the monuments, question nothing, innovate nothing. Only the pharaoh had dignity and status, because he was worshiped as a god. In Mesopotamia, people often felt themselves at the mercy of capricious gods. They thought that the only ways to find dignity were somehow to become divine themselves or to make an eternal reputation for themselves.

Psalm 8 flatly rejects all such low estimates of the value of persons. The Bible affirms that humans were created with built-in dignity, a dignity to be respected. People are not playthings of the gods; rather, all people have been invited to be coworkers with God.

In the same way, this psalm challenges all contemporary views that would make human welfare secondary to any cause or ideology. Human beings form the locus of value: what is good and of lasting value is that which upbuilds human life. Each political philosophy, each theology, each government program, and each economic system has got to be judged finally in light of its effect on the needs of persons. No one has the right to lord it over another person, or to deny another the right to enjoy the benefits of God's good earth. H. W. Wolff has reminded us that dominion over the world has not been given to great individuals alone but to the entire community of human beings, not to us alone as the people of God but to all people, not to men alone but also to women, and not to the powerful alone but also to the weak. Humans are commissioned to rule the natural order; they are forbidden to rule one another. The lordship of one person over another is a falsification of the image of God. Basic human rights are a right of creation, not favors granted by governments.

This text is heard as good news by the oppressed. Christian witness must speak the prophetic Word against all systems that deny to so many of the world's people any chance for a life of dignity. "You have made them to lack only a little from God."

III. *Human responsibility in the world.* This is a comprehensive responsibility: "over the birds of the air, the beasts of the field, the fish of the sea." There is no room for any kind of humanism here. This glory and honor that we have, have not been grasped or stolen but rather graciously given for the purpose of keeping the creation healthy. The earth is ours, not to plunder or to consume but to preserve.

Our word *ecology* is derived from the Greek word for *house.* The earth is our home, our house, and yet we are like the person tearing down his house while trying to live in it. Our planet is dying, not because we *cannot* keep it alive but because we *will* not. Our polluted air and water are not just technological problems, they are fundamentally spiritual problems. We are responsible not only for the people in the house but also for the house.

IV. *Christ as the realization of God's intention.* The psalm takes us to exhilarating heights. God intended so much for us: all the dignity and glory short of divinity; and God has entrusted so much to us: the care of souls and the health of the world. But the story of our life as the human family is the story of our rejection of that glory for ourselves and the denial of it to others.

The writer of Hebrews reflected on these verses in Psalm 8 and sadly noted human failure to fulfil God's intention. He wrote in Hebrews 2:8: "As it is we do not yet see everything in subjection to him." Here is the high calling and the lost opportunity. But the writer was not finished. He wrote: "But we see Jesus . . . crowned with glory and honor because of the suffering of death . . . to bring many sons to glory."

In Christ we see the realization of God's intention. Through Christ the worth and dignity of persons are reclaimed, and the right relationship of people with God and with their brothers and sisters can be regained.

Topic: Food for the Journey

TEXT: 1 Kings 19

I used to preach this text as a warning to cowardly servants of God, and I thought that God solved Elijah's crisis of faith by speaking to him in the still small voice. In recent days I have been a resident of Elijah's wilderness. I have spent a lot of time sitting under my own broom tree. So have many others. I have discovered that you don't have to be a runaway to find yourself in such a wilderness, with no strength or will of your own to continue. I now read this text in a different way, and it has brought to me a powerful Word. If you find yourself in Elijah's wilderness, there is good news for you here.

If you seek to serve God with all your heart

and you are without enemies, there is something wrong in the quality of your service. Do you really think that you can preach God's good news and escape the threats of the Jezebels? Do you think you can stand for justice, for peace, for the rights of all persons and escape the undying hatred of almost everyone, including the religious leaders? It must be said in Elijah's favor that he had the right enemy. There will always be a Jezebel, someone or something that seeks to brutalize you, to render you powerless. That it was Jezebel who hated Elijah should have been a powerful affirmation of the rightness of his course. But his fear blurred his vision.

Elijah was plunged into a paralyzing depression. He asked that he might die. I have never been that far down, but I know that the lack of normal emotions, the lack of caring deeply about anything, can be frightening and devastating. This was classic depression.

One might have expected God to confront Elijah with his failure. But there is no accusation in this text. Note, instead, the gentleness of God. There were provided for Elijah what he in his depression needed most: food, water, and the healing gift of sleep. The angel touched him and said, "Arise and eat, or the journey will be too great for you"—as though to say: your running away is a long journey, Elijah, you will not finish it soon, and the worst days are still to come.

Many people discover this truth for themselves, that there is, after all, food for this journey of the soul. There is the nourishment that memory brings, the memory of better days when God did not seem so distant, when there was so much joy in trying to serve God. There is the food provided by words of appreciation, by the gentle hand on the shoulder that conveys that someone cares. There is the strength provided by the straight talk of a respected friend who helps you to see your hurt from another perspective. There is the nourishment provided by the strong faith of a fellow pilgrim who has stayed a while in your present wilderness and emerged a stronger person.

Elijah's journey was away from his calling, away from his people, away from the place where he was needed. But it was also a continuing journey into the dark night of the soul. The remarkable thing is that God let him run, and that God strengthened him to

run further. The terrible thing has got to run its course, and no easy solutions are lasting ones.

In *The Pilgrim's Progress,* when Christian left the City of Destruction, Bunyan had Obstinate and Pliable go with him. Obstinate called Christian a fool and turned back. But Pliable was willing to go along for a while. Soon Christian and Pliable fell into the Slough of Despond. Pliable said, "Is this the happiness you have told me about?" And with that he climbed out of the slough on the side that was next to the City of Destruction. But Christian continued to struggle to the side of the slough that was next to the Wicket Gate, above which the light was shining. A man named Help drew him out of the mire. Christian said, "Why is not this plot mended?" Help replied, "This miry slough is such a place as cannot be mended. For 1600 years the king's surveyors have been employed about this patch of ground, so that it might be mended, but it is the Slough of Despond still, and so it will be, when they have done what they can." And even when Christian got out of the Slough of Despond, he still had his burden on his back. There was still a long journey ahead.

And so Elijah kept on running, all the way to Mt. Horeb. There he lodged in a cave. This was the place where God had appeared to Moses in lightning, thunder, and storm cloud. Was Elijah expecting a similar experience, an overpowering display of God's might that would solve all his problems? The Lord asked, "What is it with you here, Elijah?" Instead of seeing this as an accusing question, see it as an invitation: "Elijah, do you want to talk about it?" Elijah's response was embarrassing, a violent rush of words: "Lord, I have been zealous for you, but your people are faithless, and I am the only one left and they are trying to kill me."

"Elijah, get out of your cave and stand on the mountain." The Lord passed by and a great wind smashed the rocks, but the Lord was not in the wind. And after the wind there was an earthquake, but the Lord was not in the earthquake. And then there was a fire, but the Lord was not in the fire. After the fire, there was a sound of quiet stillness.

It is difficult to interpret these verses. If Elijah expected a revelation in the midst of fire and storm, he did not get it. Perhaps he needed to be reminded that the Lord has all the power—not Ahab, not Jezebel, and not Elijah. I do not know what the sound of quiet stillness was. The text does not say that it was the still, small voice of God. What it says is that after the crashing of the storm there was abrupt silence. Elijah's mind was certainly not set at ease. There is no promise here, no encouragement, not yet.

In the silence Elijah emerged from his cave, his face wrapped in his cloak. And a voice said, "What is it with you here, Elijah?" Elijah still blustered. He was not changed. He still sought to justify himself before God: "I have been zealous for the Lord of Hosts."

But then there came not a promise but a command: "Go, anoint Hazael king over Syria, Jehu king over Israel, and Elisha to be prophet in your place." The command had shock value. There was no promise of personal safety. Elijah was sent on a mission as dangerous as any in the past. He wanted the powerful side of God: dramatic defeat of enemies once for all. But he had to learn that the battle with Baal is long and dangerous, and that Baal sometimes wins. The victory at Mt. Carmel was not the end of the struggle.

But of course God's new commission was the ultimate word of encouragement: "Elijah, your life is not over, there is work for you to do." And he was told that he would not have to struggle alone, that God had left seven thousand who had not bowed the knee to Baal nor kissed him.

Revelation did not come in fire, storm, or even in the silence. The revelation was found in the new call to service: "Go!" Here is the needed word. It is the future that conveys meaning to the present. The great prophet of the exile declared, "Remember not the past. God is doing a new thing. Can you not hear it? Can you not see it?" (Isa. 43:18–19). God's purposes are still running. What Elijah got was not a solution to all his woes. What he got was something better: a renewed vision for his life. All of his past victories for God would not redeem the present. Elijah could not get out of his slough of despond on the side of the past. He had to struggle on across in the direction of the call of the future, and with the burden still on his back.

If anything is to redeem the troubled and confusing present circumstances it must be the call of God to the ministry of the future. A church may have a rich heritage and a glorious past. That heritage can instruct us and inspire us, but it cannot get us out of the slough of despond, or else it would have done so long ago. We have sat under our broom trees long enough. This is not the time to bemoan the woes of the past. It is the time to dream our greatest dreams. It is the time to catch the vision of what God is just about to do. Can you not hear it? Can you not see it?

Topic: Hope in God

TEXT: Isa. 40:27–31

This text begs to be preached. It has the ring of authenticity. It speaks powerfully to the people of God in all periods of time when they are in danger of losing their bearings.

This Word was addressed to a discouraged, dispirited people who lived in exile. Jerusalem, the Golden, had been smashed to ruins by the Babylonian conqueror. The people had lost all the symbols of their faith that they thought were essential. There was no longer a temple, no altar of sacrifice, no table of shewbread, no ark of the covenant. Some had begun to worship the gods of Babylon. After all, had not Babylon won the war? Surely it meant that the gods of Babylon were more powerful than their God.

When this great prophet pleaded with the exiles to hold onto their faith, they complained bitterly: "My way is hidden from the Lord, my justice passes by my God unnoticed."

The prophet used every device at his disposal to reach them in their discouragement. He used irony and sarcasm to shame them, invective to insult them. He painted marvelous word pictures of the sublime future that God had in store for them, in order to awaken hope in their hearts. The prophet is seen at his best in this text, with the message that *waiting is hope*.

But the people wondered how the prophet could speak of hope when the Lord was back in Jerusalem. How could they sing the songs of Zion in a foreign land?

This text suggests three things about placing our hope in God.

I. *Hope is kindled by remembering the past.* The prophet said, "Have you not known? Have you not heard? The Lord is the everlasting God." The Lord is the God of *olam*:

eternity, the universe. Do you not remember your history? "Look to the rock from which you were hewn, and to the quarry from which you were dug" (51:1). Don't you remember how God brought your ancestors out of Egypt and to a new land? Don't you remember how God bore you as on eagles' wings? Don't you remember how you used to sing: "The eternal God is our dwelling place, and underneath are the everlasting arms?"

How can you say, "My way is hidden from the Lord"? The Lord is the everlasting God and has not abandoned you. Remember your history. It is a history of divine providence.

The prophet would remind us that hope is not built on temporary circumstances, or upon human feelings. Hope is built on the reality of God's faithfulness. When I go fishing I hope I will catch the big one, but I know that it is a hope against hope. Our hope as the people of God is not like that. It is a living hope based on the events of our history, that as God has been faithful to us in the past, so God will be faithful in our present moment of greatest need. It is surely the greatest ingratitude to blame God for apparent inactivity during times of hopelessness while we forget the whole history of God's grace. How many volumes would be required to record all of God's mercies to each of us? The memory of God's faithfulness can bear us through many a dark valley until the dawn of a better day.

Here is the beginning of hope. The prophet pleads: remember your past. Do not forget the God who has brought you safely thus far. Do not forget the rock from which you were hewn. Hope is built on the solid foundation of the memory of God's faithfulness.

II. *Hope is sustained by the fact that the everlasting God is still working in our lives.* "The Lord is the everlasting God, the creator of the farthest bounds of the universe." The word translated "creator" is a participle, indicating action in the present, action that is ongoing. The God who created is creating still.

The prophet's constant theme is that God is always doing a new thing (42:9; 43:18–19). In the midst of your despair, get ready, for God is about to do a new thing.

The new thing from God for which the prophet begged Israel to prepare was a reversal of fortunes, the return from exile. There

would be a new Exodus, this time so awesome that the original Exodus would pale in comparison.

The Lord does not faint or grow weary. Old people may grow weary, and even the young may grow faint, but God never does. It is God who gives power to the weary and strength to the faint. The Lord is still at work, and those who are waiting on the Lord, those who are hoping in the Lord, shall renew their strength in the midst of their hopelessness.

Most of us have known those terrifying times when in the darkest night of the soul it seemed that God had fallen silent, and batter as we might against heaven's gates with tears in our eyes, with cries, and with prayers, there seemed to be no voice, none to answer. C. S. Lewis wrote honestly about his feelings following his wife's death from cancer. He wondered where God was in that worst of all hours. He wrote: "Go to God when your need is desperate, when all other help is vain, and what do you find? A door slammed in your face, and a sound of bolting and of double-bolting on the inside." But time passed, and God continued to work, to the extent that Lewis came to feel that the door was no longer locked against him. He wrote: "Perhaps your own cries deafen you to the voice you hoped to hear. I turned to God once more, and I no longer met that locked door."

God, the creator of the universe, is still creating, still working, still building. And those who are hoping in God will renew their strength.

III. Notice what this text promises. It does not promise everything. It provides no instant solutions, no easy resolutions to intractable problems, no shining light during the darkest watch of the night, no instant reversal, no final answers to life's mysteries.

What is promised here is what is needed most: the renewal of strength for the crises ahead. Here is comfort: the promise of strength to endure, to last, the strength to hold on until it is time for a new chapter in life. One can take new heart for the struggle.

Here is the promise: that the people of God, though few in number, can renew their strength to do the right thing because it is right, to reject compromise with the cheap and the tawdry.

Here is the promise: that those who suffer the sting of mindless discrimination on the basis of race or national origin, who know that Christ came to demolish the hateful walls of distinction that make so many people less valued, can renew their strength.

Here is the promise: that those who are oppressed, denied justice, starved, and marginalized can renew their strength to sing the praises of God in a new key, can hymn into existence the world as the Creator meant it to be, and with their newfound strength can lead reality to where it has not yet been.

There is no hope in human beings, no hope in plans or councils, no hope in institutions. These all fail and disappoint. But the everlasting God never grows weary. God gives power to the faint.

When dreams are blasted, when hope seems denied, when your bones seem turned to water and there seems to be no reason to endure, get ready. Get ready for the new thing the Almighty is about to do.

Topic: A Challenge to Popular Religion
TEXT: Jer. 7:1–15

Good king Josiah was honored by the historian for his piety and religious reform. Though well intentioned, Josiah's reform dealt only with religious forms and practices and with nationalistic hopes. It seems to have lacked the spiritual depth to engender true repentance in the population. When Josiah was killed in 609, Judah found itself in crisis. The hopes fostered by Josiah died with him. A new world order was emerging in Babylonia. The people of Judah sought security and a basis for the continuation of nationalistic hope. This hope was centered on the Temple and traditional religion.

Jeremiah appeared at the Temple to challenge popular religion and the false hopes associated with it. His task was to remove all false hope so that true hope could emerge. It almost cost him his life.

Today is little different from that day in that widely differing views of "true religion," all claiming the mantle of orthodoxy, perplex the people. Jeremiah's Temple sermon and the circumstances prompting it provide a chance to ponder anew the basis on which genuine hope may be built.

I. *Popular religion.* Perhaps partly out of traditional piety and partly as the result of Josiah's cultic centralization, the people viewed the Temple as the guarantee of God's presence. It was unthinkable that God would allow the temple to be destroyed, for that would mean the end of the state. Popular religion is stubbornly conservative, with a sincere desire to trust in the efficacy of religious symbols. But this was a religion of form, lacking a proper ethical sensitivity and equated with nationalism. A religion of unchanging symbols and forms may encourage people to face an uncertain future with a false confidence. The tragedy is that it may not enable people to have a realistic view of present circumstances. The popular faith of Jeremiah's day was true in part, and it could appeal to scripture and tradition. For instance, the tradition based on 2 Samuel 7 promised stability of the Temple and the worship system, and the tradition associated with Isaiah 33:20 and 37:33–35 proclaimed the inviolability of Zion. Did Jeremiah believe that God was no longer able to safeguard Zion?

As the parallel in Jeremiah 26 shows, the priests and prophets were allied with the people against Jeremiah. It is not at all clear that the religious leaders intended to lead the people astray. They seem to have been intent on encouraging confidence in God. But theirs was a hidebound orthodoxy, impervious to change, shallow in moral perception, and unable to discern the times.

II. *The religion of a prophet.* Jeremiah was a revivalist in the truest sense. His task was to call the people back to their original covenant obligations as found in the Torah. Covenant stipulations called for justice for the neighbor—care for the vulnerable people in society, represented by the resident alien, the orphan, and the widow. But the population was guilty of not only failing only in these responsibilities but of much worse as well. At least five of the ten commandments are alluded to as having been violated, resulting in murder, idolatry, stealing, swearing falsely, and adultery. Such actions constituted willful breach of covenant that put the nation outside of any hope of deliverance. The people's arrogance was staggering. They thought they could do as they pleased and then enter the Temple precincts and declare: "We are safe!" This unfounded confidence in the Temple as the guarantee of national security cut the nerve of moral effort.

Jeremiah 7:3 must be rendered: "Amend your ways and your doings so that I may dwell with you in this place." The question was not whether the Lord would continue to let the people dwell there, but rather whether the deeds of the people would allow the Lord's presence to continue to dwell with them.

The prophet gave a lesson from history to remove their unfounded hope in the existence of the Temple. The temple at Shiloh, where the Lord had first made the divine name dwell, had been destroyed by the Philistines, and the Lord had suffered no damage. The Lord never needed a temple. And now the present Temple in Jerusalem, in which the people trusted, was to suffer the same fate as the sanctuary at Shiloh.

The Lord is not a God of place. Sacred places can be helpful, but they are never essential. The Lord is wherever the people of God are, in whatever condition. This ancient ideal was a reality in the days of the wilderness wanderings, when all the sacred furniture and the tabernacle were portable. Every place was sacred if the Lord was there. The people of God are at their best when they remember that they are called to be a wandering people, on the way to a homeland and having no certain home in the world. The people in Jeremiah's day were to lose all the symbols of their faith in which they trusted: temple, city, monarchy, altar. They were to discover that finally all they had left was all they ever needed: the fact of God's presence in a foreign land of exile. Jeremiah labored to help them learn how to live among the ruins. Real hope lay in a return to the Lord alone.

III. *The perplexity of the people.* The people of Judah were overwhelmed by conflicting opinions about how to survive the approaching menace. Who to believe? Who was the true prophet? They had to decide crucial questions before all the evidence was in. Their confusion is clearly reflected in Jeremiah 26.

It is no easier today to decide who is the true prophet. There is no final criterion that will provide the definitive answer. But Jeremiah's insistence on repentance, on a return to the covenant, has the ring of authenticity.

Topic: How to Repent

TEXT: Hos. 6:1–6; 14:1–8

Although the theme of the love of God dominates the book of Hosea, it is important to see that the emphasis on repentance is no less focused. Hosea spoke and wrote with great passion about God's unimaginable love continually offered to restore a broken relationship. But the prophet also emphasized what the people had to do from their side to restore the relationship: repent. It was not the prophet's job simply to denounce; it was equally his job to engender repentance in the hearts of a people whom he loved.

Hosea's idea of repentance is highlighted and defined in 10:11–15, where once again he used the metaphor of Israel as a draft animal, plowing wickedness only to reap evil and to feast on the fruit of lies. It was time to seek the Lord if they wanted a reversal of fortunes. Israel would have to learn to plow again, to break up fallow ground (the neglected, unused, or untried land), and to sow righteousness if they expected to reap the benefits of the covenant promises. In other words, repentance was being willing to start over again, to learn again, to master the old disciplines, to make a new commitment.

I. *An incomplete repentance.* Hosea 6:1–3 contains a call to repentance along with some statements that seem to be appropriate for a ritual of repentance. The confession that the Lord has sent judgment is balanced by the confident assertion that the Lord will bind up and heal. The initial call to return to the Lord is paralleled in 6:3 by the call to press on to know the Lord. The Lord's dependability is likened to the inevitable dawn.

These verses contain nothing that is patently improper to repentance. The confidence expressed in the Lord's ability to heal and to restore is altogether worthy. The Septuagint ended 5:15 with the word "saying," clearly making 6:1–3 a continuation of the Lord's speech in which the Lord supplied statements for Israel to use in repenting. If one accepts the Hebrew text, which lacks "saying" in 5:15, then 6:1–3 would be understood as words initiated by Israel.

If the words of 6:1–3 had been acceptable to the Lord, the book of Hosea could have ended at 6:3. But 6:4–5 indicates their unacceptability. One may wonder whether they were not acceptable because they lacked a confession of sin, or whether they were presumptuous words, asserting that the Lord would always rescue them no matter what they did. Hosea 6:4 and 6, however, provide the right emphasis: Israel's commitment to covenant fidelity, despite words spoken at a spiritually charged moment, was as flimsy and insubstantial as the morning dew. Words alone, no matter how artful, could not suffice.

II. *A ritual of repentance.* Hosea 14:1–3 contains a call to repentance that is best understood as a liturgy of return that focuses on the spoken part of the ritual. In contrast to 6:1–3, the words of this approved liturgy emphasize the confession of guilt. Israel was to acknowledge failure in three areas: her dependence on foreign alliances, which provided the potential for religious syncretism; her trust in military might; and her idolatry. These transgressions are representative of the whole list of failures. The ritual ends with a confession that is deceptive in its simplicity, for it is nothing less than a statement of complete trust in the Lord as the only one who can provide mercy.

The ritual of confession and repentance is followed by an oracle of forgiveness (14:4–7). This part of the ritual would customarily be spoken by a priest or a prophet. There is the promise that the day of wrath would be turned away and that the Lord would heal their turning away and love them unstintingly. In 14:5–7, the poet waxes eloquent, using eight similes in three verses to liken the people's restoration to the extravagantly verdant life of nature. Israel would return to life and recover her glory.

III. *Insight from Hosea on repentance.* Repentance requires saying something. It needs to be verbalized, and the right words are crucial. The words should be carefully considered so that they will be an adequate and worthy expression of the sentiments of the heart.

But repentance is also something one is to do. The right words are important, but the deeds worthy of repentance put the seal of authenticity on the words. Genuine repentance can be verified empirically.

Repentance is willingness to give up orientations that do not lead to life, to the knowledge of God. It is the willingness to be led back to the beginning, to cancel out a lifetime of "best-laid plans" and to accept the thrilling power of a new commitment that embraces all of life's choices.

SECTION IX.
Health-Giving and Health-Destroying Preaching

BY WAYNE E. OATES

For much of my ministry, my preaching, teaching, and pastoral work have been with mentally sick people, individually, in small groups, and within large congregations. Their blunt feedback has made me appreciate the original meaning of 2 Timothy 4: 3–4: "For the time is coming when people will not put up with sound doctrine."

Countless groups of people seem to have interpreted the words *sound doctrine*—from translations of the Bible into English, from the King James Version to the New Revised Standard Version—to mean correct dogma, theological orthodoxy, and doctrinal conformities to systems. But the original Greek does not give that meaning. The transliteration of the Greek is *hygiainouses didaskalias*, literally meaning "hygienic" or "health-giving teachings." Its interpreted meaning is "be in good health," or "be healthy." The good news of Jesus Christ focuses not merely on the creeds and ideologies that people "with itching ears" like to dispute, but on the total well-being of listeners to whom we preach, on the functional integrity of the whole person day in and day out.

The sermon that focuses on the total well-being of people in the audience is an *audience-centered* sermon. It is not primarily concerned with abstractly peddled partisan doctrines, which are likely to precipitate severe self-condemnation or emotional illness. To the contrary, an audience-centered sermon brings unity, wholeness, and well-being as a result of its "hygienic" or health-giving teaching. Such preaching is concerned with the well-being of whole persons before God in Jesus Christ.

Some Themes for Preaching Health-Giving Sermons

BELIEF THAT ONE HAS COMMITTED THE UNPARDONABLE SIN.   A persistent theme of health-giving preaching is *forgiveness*. One of the besetting obsessions of hospitalized psychiatric patients is that they feel they have committed "the unpardonable sin." Many people trudging about outside hospitals feel this, too. Often a patient will say that the precipitating factor in their illness is that they heard a sermon on the unpardonable sin. To verify their feelings, they may quote Scripture, such as Matthew 12:31–32, in which Jesus says: "Therefore, I tell you, every sin and blasphemy will be forgiven [you], but blasphemy against the Spirit will not be forgiven. Any whoever says a word against the Son of man will be forgiven; but whoever speaks against the Holy Spirit will not be forgiven, either in this age or the age to come."

This passage is the text most often mentioned by persons in and out of the hospital who feel that they have committed the unpardonable sin. Often they cannot be specific about what they said or did to commit the unpardonable sin. They simply are convinced that they have done so.

This passage is both bad news and good news about forgiveness for us. The context of the text must be taken into consideration. In Matthew 12:22, Jesus healed the blind and mute demoniac. The man "spoke and saw." The crowd asked: "Can this be the Son of David?" But the Pharisees, when they heard about it, said: "It is only by Beelzebub, the prince of demons, that this man casts out demons." Beelzebub, in the Old Testament, was a pagan Phoenician god consulted by King Ahaziah (2 Kings 1:2–18). In Hebrew the name means "Lord of Flies." In the New Testament, Beelzebub is directly related to idolatry and associated with the substitution of the worship of Satan for the worship of the Holy Spirit. This is idolatry, which must be present to spawn a demon. One has to have an idol before he or she can become demonic, because to worship anything less than God or the Holy Spirit is idolatry. In this text's meaning, it is blasphemy. Today we call idolaters "compulsive obsessional persons."

In context, Jesus means that to worship Satan or Beelzebub instead of the Holy Spirit is blasphemy and is unpardonable. That is the bad news.

The good news is that the Pharisees, having said that Jesus was a worshiper and servant of Beelzebub or Satan, would be forgiven. But to say such against the Holy Spirit is a blasphemy that will not be forgiven. Jesus was very forgiving himself, but he implies that to blaspheme against the Holy Spirit was to become an idolater of Beelzebub or Satan, which was unpardonable.

Consequently, this text is very difficult for the modern churchgoer to understand in its textual and contextual meaning. It is very complicated to interpret it adequately in a present-day sermon—that is, in a thirty-minute one-way lecture to a large crowd. This text is best addressed in dialogue with a small group in which all the members can respond and ask questions of the pastor and each other. "Idolatry of Satan" can be translated into "compulsive obsession with controlling powerful fear."

A digression has been implied here. I said that the sermon form—which is a postbiblical form of communication—has definite limitations of time and direction of communication. People cannot interrupt a sermon and make comments or ask questions. An already-depressed person could not and would not get individual attention. Such persons may need even more than a small group. They may need individual, one-on-one attention. As a spiritual director, a pastor needs to provide that time for people to discuss their spiritual dilemmas, especially if they think they have committed the unpardonable sin.

In such spiritual direction, a pastor listens, encourages more sharing, and enables persons to unfold their life story. This gives them an opportunity to unburden themselves of realistic and unrealistic experiences of shame and guilt. Out of this unburdening will appear some very realistic temptations that are bothering them.

One of the most common burdens is that of unforgiving attitudes toward people who have severely damaged the person. This reveals a far less complicated explanation of the unpardonable sin in Jesus' teachings. In Matthew 6:11 and 14, the Lord's Prayer says:

and forgive us our debts
as we also have forgiven our debtors . . .
For if you forgive others their trespasses
your heavenly Father will forgive you;
but if you do not forgive others,
neither will your heavenly Father forgive
     you.

This is a concrete, interpersonal explanation of why God refuses to forgive people. It is extremely applicable to a congregation because members often have grudges against one another that they nurse for decades. Furthermore, a pastor can preach on this text and be of positive help to a person who feels they have committed the unpardonable sin. The pastor can also ask a person directly about anyone they cannot forgive.

Another possible cause of people being burdened with the feeling that God will not forgive them is that they have been verbally, physically, and/or sexually abused by a parent or a sibling or both. They carry a burden of shame and self-loathing, and often feel responsible for their sordid history. They can never pray to God to have mercy on them as sinners nor can they forgive the perpetrators.

A gentle but firm encouragement of them to forgive the perpetrator is in order. They need not feel it necessary for the perpetrator to *ask* them for forgiveness. Then, too, they may have to forgive the person repeatedly. The disciples asked Jesus how many times they should forgive someone—seven times? Jesus answered: "Not seven times, but I tell you, seventy times seven" (Matt. 18:21). Thus, forgiveness is like washing your shirt, blouse, or hair—the dirt reappears and one has to wash it again and again. Forgiveness becomes a way of life rather than self-condemnation.

The person you hate can be a real barrier between you and God.

A more ancient source of the feeling that one has committed the unpardonable sin is the temptation to commit suicide. Throughout history many Christian churches have taught that a person who commits suicide goes straight to hell. There is no forgiveness for them. One young man said to me that he wished there would be a building tall enough that he could jump off and get forgiveness from God before he hit the ground! The Catholic Church for many centuries refused to permit a person who had committed suicide to be buried in consecrated burial grounds. Protestants have carried this belief also. However, the Scriptures do not teach this at all. It is not in the teachings of Jesus, the apostle Paul, or other writers of the New Testament. The only biblical teaching is an extrapolation of the fifth commandment: "You shall not murder" (Exod. 20:13). The most vivid association of suicide in the Bible is Judas' hanging of himself. Because Judas betrayed Jesus, suicide can, again by extrapolation and by stretching the imagination, be looked upon as betraying Jesus Christ. This would be unpardonable. But it is not what Jesus meant by the unpardonable sin. Hence, the belief that suicide is the unpardonable sin is a distortion of the gospel.

In the context of spiritual direction, suicide may be what people are contemplating when they say they have committed the unpardonable sin. A pastor can hopefully draw this out of the troubled person. As Proverbs 20:5 puts it, "The purpose in a person's mind is like deep water, but a person of understanding [tebunah] will draw it out."

Thus, the feeling that one has committed the unpardonable sin is a symptom of a dangerous depression. The person may be suicidal. He or she needs both close pastoral attention and immediate psychiatric care.

BELIEF IN A MALICIOUS GOD.   Deeply disturbed people, severely grieving people, people under constant abuse, suffering, and pain often perceive God as a malicious tyrant who has inflicted these sufferings upon them. But as Einstein said, "God is subtle, but he is not malicious."[1] For example, a young mother

whose baby had died suddenly asked me, "Why did God kill my baby?" To answer such a question is to engage in theodicy, that is, justifying or explaining how if God is good and can only do good, why evil things happen to people. In Rabbi Kushner's words, "Why do bad things happen to good people?"

It seems as though it is woven into our very nature as human beings to think of ourselves as exceptions to all forms of suffering, to think that if we do what is good in our own eyes, God will see to it that no bad thing happens to us. If our son or daughter is permanently handicapped by war wounds or a car accident, to many this means that God caused it, possibly because of some wrong doing by us.

But Jesus said, "Your . . . Father who is in heaven . . . makes his sun to rise on the evil and on the good and sends rain on the just and the unjust" (Matt. 5:45). Our goodness or evil does not make us exceptions either to the sun and rain on our gardens or to the tornado that can kill us. The issue seems to revolve around reconciling the goodness of God with the indifference of the laws of nature to our goodness or evil. The wicked prosper and the righteous suffer. It was Mother Nature, not God. The answers to our questions about "Why?" are wrapped in mystery. This is why the patient asked me, "Why did God kill my baby?"

We are filled with terror when we try to think of God apart from the Lord Jesus. He said: "I and my Father are one" (John 10:30). We can ask the young mother: "Can you imagine the Lord Jesus killing your child?" He blessed children and pronounced doom on anyone who caused a child harm or to stumble (Matt. 18:1–6). As for me, I have seen God in the face of Jesus Christ. This means that God does not will that we perish, and that when death does come, since God has raised Jesus Christ from the dead, death itself is dead. He will raise us from the dead. In this is our hope in the presence of suffering and death.

But when, in our grief, we are overwhelmed with anger that we have lost someone, especially an irreplaceable child, it is easy to be *angry* at God, as the young mother was. In fact, we are angry at the whole world. But we need to remember the patience of God in Jesus Christ. When we are angry at God, God

[1]Ronald Clark, *Einstein* (New York: World Publishing, 1971), 390.

can take it. If we condemn ourselves for being angry at God, God forgives us. As 1 John 3:20 tell us, "Whenever our hearts condemn us, God is greater than our hearts and knows everything." Not a thought is in us but that God knows it. God understands us and loves us even when we are angry.

The theme of being angry at God for our misfortunes is one that calls for sermons of interpretation and encouragement for congregations. A good set of texts is Psalm 139, Matthew 5:45, 1 John 3:30, and Ephesians 4:26. Anger is a basic human emotion arising out of many human situations, such as injustice, frustration, helplessness, and being hurt. These words are almost synonyms for anger. A pastor can cushion the sermon with these words.

One antidote for anger is humor—humor without sarcasm, vindictiveness, or ridicule. We often do not lose our temper as much as we lose our sense of humor. But life hits us with overwhelming events in which nothing is humorous. The sudden death of a loved one, especially a child; the loss of a very good job after many years of faithful service to an employer; abandonment by a spouse through divorce; or a severe conflict in a church fellowship—these and many other situations are occasions for us to rail at or question God. They raise the questions about whether God cares for us, whether any such care is in God.

In sermons on anger toward God, the pastor need not be concerned with the limitations of the sermon form—brevity of time and the fact that the sermon does not allow for questions and answers from the audience. One reason for this is that numerous everyday, hard-working people walk around and do their regular day's work, but in their meditation as they work they ask God why he has done awful things to them and their loved ones. What the sermon does not allow, private meditation makes possible and helpful.

THE REALITY AND WORK OF THE DEVIL. A third emotional health concern for people is their feelings about the devil's dealings with them. One patient to whom I had extended care told me that the devil had told him to kill himself. I asked him if he knew what Jesus said about the devil. He said that he did not know. I quoted for him these words from John 8:44: "[The devil] was a murderer from the beginning and does not stand in the truth, because there is no truth in him. When he lies, he speaks according to his own nature, for he is a liar, and the father of lies."

I told my patient, who had now become my friend, "You have been told to kill yourself by the great deceiver; a liar and the father of lies told you to kill yourself. Don't be deceived by the devil. Listen to the truth from the Lord Jesus Christ who loves you, speaks the truth, and wants you to live."

This friend's dire circumstance reveals the other side of the problem of evil. The belief in the devil has always been the alternative for believing in the goodness of God, the God and Father of our Lord Jesus Christ.

I do not hear or read many sermons about the devil. The text from John 8:38–59 is a good one for preaching about the devil. It provides Jesus' contrast between himself and the devil. Jesus said that he came from God, who sent him. The Pharisees claimed God as their only Father. Then Jesus said that if this were true they would love Jesus because he came from God. But, he said, they were from their father, the devil, and described the devil as the father of lies.

The Pharisees responded and called Jesus a Samaritan who had a demon, and that he was posing as being greater than Abraham because he said that the person who keeps God's Word would triumph over death.

This text, which reveals Jesus wrestling with the devil and the demonic in his opponents, is the strong meat and not the milk of the Scriptures. If a pastor preaches on this text, he or she may be sure that it conveys the strong belief of Jesus in the existence and deceptiveness of the devil. It was the devil who tempted him in the wilderness (Matt. 21: 1–11; Luke 4: 1–14).

The devil has a strange history in the Christian community. In the Old Testament, the devil was known as *Satan*, or the adversary. In these days of inclusive language, do we call the adversary "he" or "she"? In Genesis 3:1ff, the adversary, disguised as a serpent, is called "he." But in later Christian history, two leaders of the Inquisition were Johannes Sprenger and Hendrick Kraemer. They used a handbook called *Malleus Maleficarum,* or *The Witches' Hammer,* to persecute mentally disturbed persons, usually women, as witches. This handbook was written by a man named Trithemos between 1487 and 1489 A.D.[2]

To return to the Scriptures, Yahweh was originally assumed to be good, but in his anger he could wreak evil upon people. An example of this is found in Exodus 4:24–26, in which Yahweh sought to kill Moses but changed his mind and "let him alone." But as Jeffrey Buron Russell says, "In time, good qualities came to be ascribed to God, evil being attributed to Satan."[3]

In the New Testament, the devil is the tempter of Jesus, the prince of the old era prior to the fulfillment of Christ's rule. He is the enemy that sows tares in the good wheat field (Matt. 13:39). The devil, or Satan, seems to work on the principle of incarnation, imitating the work of God who enfleshed himself in the person of Jesus Christ. Jesus said to Simon Peter, "Get behind me, Satan" (Matt. 8:33 and Matt. 16:23). Luke 22:3 tells us that "Satan entered into Judas" to betray Jesus. Peter said to Ananias, "Satan has filled your heart to lie to the Holy Spirit" (Acts 5:3). And Paul says in 2 Corinthians 11:14 that "even Satan disguises himself as an angel."

Revelation 2:9 and 3:9 say that even a synagogue or, today, a church can become at least an instrument or at most an incarnation of Satan. Overall, the New Testament depicts the devil as an "oppressor" (Acts 10:38), as one who has the "power of death" (Heb. 2:14), and as "an adversary that prowls around" (1 Peter 5:8). Revelations 12:9 and 20:2 say that the devil is the ancient serpent.

Such texts are vivid material for a pastor to use if he or she chooses to preach or teach about the devil or Satan. The central feature of the devil or Satan is *deception* as opposed to the truth—either truth in people or in God. Ananias lied to the Holy Spirit as an instrument of the devil. My own inclination in preaching would be to emphasize this deceptiveness in our relationships with ourselves, with others, and with God. As O.T. Binkley, a

revered professor of mine, used to say, "If we limit ourselves to speaking only the truth in love [Eph. 4:15], we will have half as much to say, but what we do say will have twice the influence." This is a "health-giving" way to go. Deception is the illness way to go.

A homiletical approach to considering the repeated references to the devil or Satan is to focus on the healing power of truth spoken in love and the destructive power of deception—self-deception, deception of others, and attempts at deception before God. The way of truth spoken in love is the way of Jesus Christ. The way of deception spoken with a forked tongue is the way of the devil or Satan, whether we consider the devil a personified being or a symbol for deception, the "father of lies."

THE SPIRIT OF GOD HAS LEFT ME.   The feeling of being abandoned by God is another pathology of the spirit that plagues mentally ill persons. I have experienced repeated instances of patients telling me that the Spirit of God has left them. In many instances, quite a few if not all of the people that were near them have left them as well. They are in the middle of the process that follows broken relationships described by John Bowlby. In a three-volume set on attachment and loss, Bowlby reports on the behavior of infants who have been left by, abandoned by, or alienated from their parents. He says that they go through three stages: protest, despair, and detachment. In the stage of protest, the child "cries, loudly shakes his [or her] cot, throws himself [or herself] around, and looks eagerly towards any sight or sound that might prove to be his [or her] missing mother."

In the stage of despair, the child expresses signs of "increasing hopelessness." The child is quiet, undemanding, "withdrawn and inactive" and is in "a state of deep mourning."

In the stage of detachment, which is often misunderstood by others as improvement, a child acts as if neither "mothering nor contact with humans has much significance." This behavior could be called apathy or being past feeling. The child becomes concerned with objects and food. Logs and food are immobile. They can't leave you.[4]

[2]Gregory Zilboorg, *A History of Medical Psychology* (New York: Norton, 1941), 140ff.

[3]See Alan R. Richardson and John Bowden (eds.), *The Westminster Dictionary of Christian Theology* (Philadelphia: Westminster Press, 1983), 156–157.

[4]John Bowlby, *Attachment.* Vol. 1 of *Attachment and Loss* (New York: Basic Books, 1969), 27–28.

I am persuaded that adults can go through these same stages when faced with abandonment, loss, or alienation. I do not think that adults move through these stages automatically, although it may be that an infant does, as Bowlby says. Adults, I think, can get "stuck" in any one of these stages.

For example, I have seen adults stay in a chronic state of depression. They may stay in a conviction that the Spirit of God has left them. These feelings may have originated in one major trauma after another. I have counseled numerous Vietnam veterans and have seen them stuck in depression about having lost comrades in the war and then come home to receive ridicule and rejection by many people. They may then have been rejected by more than one wife, and so on, and have stayed both depressed and detached. Many of them have become homeless and dysfunctionally related to God. Even the Spirit of God seems to have left them.

This condition of veterans' abandonment by God is wide open for the attention of the pastor as a preacher and as one who reaches out to people in visitation and counseling. These persons have lost initiative. Their families may be steadfast members of a pastor's congregation. They may never come to church themselves. Outreach is needed, not ignoring them or allowing them to become out of sight, out of mind.

Pastors who work in hospitals, outpatient clinics, and shelters for the homeless see these alienated ones regularly. The steadfastness and encouragement of the Scriptures is what they need. When we turn to the Scriptures for an example of the Spirit of God having left someone, it can be found in the story of Saul in 1 Samuel 16:14–25. The story begins: "Now the Spirit of the Lord left Saul, and an evil Spirit from the Lord tormented him." Now, that poses a dilemma that a careful builder of sermons cannot wisely ignore. Does the Lord send evil spirits to torment us? A severe depression, as we call it today, is certainly an evil spirit, but does it come "from the Lord"? We have already in this chapter struggled with the source or sources of evil. In other places in the Scriptures, especially in the four gospels, evil spirits are said to come from the devil. As we have seen, many people today think so, too. But then again, they may attribute evil spirits to the Lord.

I recall visiting a man in my first parish. He was not a Christian. I told him of how my life had been blessed by God, delivered from many dangers, and so on. His reply to me was, "The Lord may have done all those things for you, but he has ruined me!" Whether we know or like it or not, many people today feel as this man did: God has ruined them. The move from experiencing God as an empty void to thinking of God as an enemy to thinking of God as a friend is a long journey.

Nevertheless, the Scriptures tell us that "the Spirit of the Lord left Saul and an evil spirit from the Lord tormented him." The patients with whom I work who say the Spirit of the Lord has left them are certainly tormented by a spirit of hopelessness and depression. Could this evil spirit in the Scripture be the "spirit of heaviness" (Isa. 61:3 KJV). I assume, based on painful experience with others who have killed themselves, that such persons are suicidal. We must remember that Saul finally killed himself when his armor bearer would not kill him (1 Sam. 31:5).

Robert Browning provides the preaching pastor excellent material in his long poem, "Saul," on Saul's experience of the Spirit of the Lord leaving him. He says that Saul "sinks back" on life. His servants called David to play music to him and talk with him. David played music that enchanted sheep, other music that quails responded to, music that was the "help-tunes" of the reaper, and the marriage song. Nothing moved the motionless Saul.

Then he called him by name—"Saul"— and Saul began to move about. Then he resorted to prayer to God, saying, "O, speak through me now!" His prayer continued. He said: " 'Tis weakness in strength that I cry for in my flesh in the God head. I seek and I find it." Then he said: "O Saul, it shall be a Face like my face that receives thee; a Man like to me, thou shalt love and be loved by, forever: A Hand like this hand shall throw open the gates of new life to thee! See the Christ stand!"

This long poem can be useful in sermon preparation. It can be found in *The Poems and Plays of Robert Browning* (New York: The Modern Library, 1934), pp. 40–54.

In terms of pastoral care, persons who feel that the Spirit of God has left them are prone to suicide and need psychiatric care in today's world. Be sure and find a psychiatrist to whom you would be willing to send your dearest loved one. Hopefully your family physician or internist can help you find one. The hazard of suicide, as I have said, is very high. One or more of the modern psychiatric medications can make a vast difference. We do best when we pay attention to the whole person. They have need of a physician as well as the divine.

CRUCIFYING CHRIST AGAIN.   A fifth and final obsession of seriously disturbed persons is their conviction that they have "fallen away and are crucifying Christ again." The pastor immediately recognizes these words as coming from Hebrews 6:4–6: "For it is impossible to restore again to those who have been once enlightened, and have tasted the heavenly gift, and have shared in the Holy Spirit, and have tasted the goodness of the word of God, and the power of the age to come, and have fallen away, since on their own they are crucifying again the Son of God and holding him up to contempt."

Here again, persons who are obsessed and depressed think they have committed apostasy, sinned away the days of grace, and crucified Christ again. They feel they have no future in the God and Father of our Lord Jesus Christ.

I have seen patients who have told me, quoting Hebrews 4:8, that they have sinned in this way. One patient, a fifty-year-old married woman, attempted suicide by slitting her wrist. When that failed to kill her, she drove to a nearby river bridge to jump off, but a traffic jam prevented it. When that failed, she came back home and chopped her hand off at the wrist. Fortunately her husband came home very soon from work and got her to one of our hospitals that has a world-renowned hand clinic. They reattached the hand to her arm with success. I was asked by the psychiatric consultation team to see her. She told me that she had "fallen away from God, crucified Christ again, and it was impossible to restore her to salvation in God's Son." She was beyond reasoning. She was psychotically depressed and felt completely hopeless. She refused to specify what she had done or how she had learned this rather obscure pas-

sage of Scripture. My only assumption is that someone among the Sunday school teachers or home Bible study groups or some sermon she had heard had taught her this passage. They did not have any way of knowing how depressed and deathly ill someone in their audience was.

This passage is one of the few passages in the New Testament that strips all hope from such a person. It is the favorite apostasy passage of some pastors I have known well. It is often the chosen passage of acutely suicidal patients I have met in mental hospitals. Personally, I would suggest that it not be used as a sermon text. It is the epitome of hopelessness.

I would prefer to preach on Romans 5:1–5, using a title such as "The Process of Hoping."

Conclusion

In fact, all of the passages I have quoted convey hopelessness. But "faith is the assurance of things hoped for, the conviction of things not seen" (Heb. 11:1). This assurance and this conviction are a healing grace engendered by the love of God in Christ. Having spent twenty-five years of my life ministering to mentally ill persons, I have found this passage most useful. According to 1 John 3:20: "Whenever our hearts condemn us, . . . God is greater than our hearts, and he knows everything." We pave the way to hopelessness when we obsessively worship a guilty conscience, whether the guilt is real or imagined.

Isolated passages of the Scripture can be the fuel on the already burning sense of hopelessness that people are carrying around with them. These texts are very informative and helpful if studied carefully in their context and in the light of the whole truth of the whole Bible. Jerked from their context and alienated from the drama of redemption in the Bible, they can be latched onto by desperately mentally disturbed people.

They bring not a health-giving doctrine but a message of hopelessness in the name of God to people who are already filled with hopelessness and devoid of resources to rekindle hope. Collaboration among pastors, chaplains, personal physicians, and psychiatrists is needed to bring all of the resources of hope in the gospels and in the vast pharmacopoeia of medicine to bear upon the desperation of these persons. Again, they have need of physicians as well as the divine. In the contemporary surge of interest by physicians in the relationship between spirituality and healing, my own conclusion is that nothing is more important than hope and nothing is more hazardous than abject hopelessness.

SECTION X.
Children's Sermons and Stories

January 4: First Sunday of the Year

Good morning, boys and girls. I hope you all had a good Christmas. You know, Christmas is when we celebrate the birth of the baby Jesus. Today I want to tell you a story about what happened to the baby Jesus after he was born.

You all know the story of the three wise men, right? You remember that they came to see the baby and brought him some very precious gifts. Did you know that they had to stop for directions along the way? The wise men were kings, you know, and they thought that the best person to ask for directions would be another king. So they found the king of Israel, a man named King Herod, and asked him if he knew where to find the baby who was born to be king of the whole world. Now, the wise men didn't know it but Herod was a bad king. He had never heard of Jesus, but when he heard that a baby had been born to be king of the world, he became very upset. He didn't want any little baby around who was more important than he was. So he sent the wise men on their way and asked them to let him know when they found the baby Jesus. What he didn't tell them was that he wanted to kill Jesus.

God warned the wise men in a dream what Herod was going to do. So after they gave Jesus their gifts of gold and frankincense and myrrh, they got on their camels and went home without ever seeing Herod again.

But Herod, mean king that he was, wasn't about to take a chance that the baby king would grow up and become more important than he was. So do you know what he did? He ordered his soldiers to go through the whole country and kill every child that was under two years old. Can you imagine that? Wasn't that awful?

But he didn't get baby Jesus. You see, an angel came to Joseph one night and told him to put Mary and the baby Jesus on a donkey and go to a far away country called Egypt. So by the time mean old Herod's soldiers came around looking for Jesus, he was long gone.

Jesus and Mary and Joseph stayed in Egypt for a good long while, until they heard that Herod was dead. Then they saddled up their donkey and went back to the land of Israel. But they didn't go back to Bethlehem. Instead they went to a town called Nazareth. Joseph opened a carpenter shop there, and that was the town where Jesus grew up. Jesus lived there until he became a man.

It's a good thing that angel came to Joseph, wasn't it? Otherwise, mean old Herod might have gotten the baby Jesus. But God was looking out for Jesus. You know, God is looking out for you too.—Stephens G. Lytch

January 11: Holding the Ladder

TEXT: Phil. 4:14, 16

Object: Drawing of workers on a ladder

This is a simple picture of three "stick" people working on a ladder. The first figure is up the ladder that is leaning against the wall, a second person is holding the ladder at the bottom, and a third person is standing nearby ready to run any errands. The person on the ladder has to be willing to climb high up the wall. He or she has to be free from fear of heights. The one holding the bottom of the ladder is required for safety purposes. If the bottom of the ladder slips, the person on top could fall and be seriously injured. The third person is ready to get whatever the person up the ladder needs. If the third person were not involved, the one up the ladder would have to climb down and up the rungs each time something was needed. That would waste a lot of time.

Working on a ladder is a lot like mission work. Someone has to be willing to go into the mission field, and many others are required to support the missionary. Missionaries need and appreciate all the encouragement and support that comes from their home base.

A man named Paul was a missionary over almost two thousand years ago. He wrote a letter to the church that was supplying his practical needs. Listen to these two verses.

Mission work has not changed since Paul was a missionary. There must be many people holding the ladder of the missions effort. Missionaries request prayer for the challenges they face. Financial support is needed so that those in foreign and local fields won't have to worry about paying their bills. Missionaries like to get letters from their friends back home. Such support assures missionaries that somebody is holding the bottom of their ladder.

The Lord may call some of us to mission work. Mission work can be in a foreign land or in our home area. If we are not called to be a missionary, we must participate in missionary support. Everyone must be involved in mission work.—Ken Cox

January 18: Martin Luther King's Birthday

Has anybody ever treated you badly because you were different from him or her? How did that make you feel? When I was little I was chubby, and I remember one winter day when I was walking home from school some boys threw snowballs at me and shouted, "Fatty, fatty, two by four, can't get through the bathroom door." That made me feel very bad.

It's not right to treat people who are different from us badly. It used to be that many people whose skin was white treated people with black skin very badly. Some white people wouldn't let black people eat in the same restaurants they did. They couldn't drink from the same water fountains. Whenever a black person rode the bus, they had to sit all the way in the back.

One day, in a town called Montgomery, Alabama, Mrs. Rosa Parks, a lady whose skin was black, got on a city bus. She was very tired. A white man got on the bus and ordered her to get up and give him her seat. She refused, and there was a lot of trouble. The news got out that Mrs. Parks had been treated badly because she had black skin, and other black people in Montgomery decided they wouldn't ride the buses anymore until the white people treated them right. For 382 days they stayed off the buses.

A minister named Martin Luther King Jr. was a new pastor in Montgomery. He heard about Mrs. Parks. He was a black man, and he knew that Jesus told everyone they should treat people fairly, whether they were like them or different. He told all the people what Jesus had said. After a long time, the white people let the black people sit wherever they wanted to sit on the bus.

Dr. King became famous for helping the black people in Montgomery. After that he went many places and told everybody that God wants us to treat people nicely, whether they're like us or not. Tomorrow we celebrate Dr. King's birthday. You can celebrate it by remembering to treat everybody kindly and by not being mean to anybody just because they're different from you. It hurts us when people treat us badly because we're different from them. And we hurt other people if we are mean to them because they're different from us. God loves everybody, no matter what they look like. And God wants us to love everybody too.—S.L.

January 25: The Turtle Tribe

Is there anyone here who does not know what a turtle looks like? The turtle is a very unusual little creature, for he carries his house around with him. Whenever he is scared or needs to get away from something, he simply pulls himself into his house. This is the way he solves his problems in life. In a sense, he goes into a small room all by himself and hopes that whatever is bothering him will be gone when he comes out.

Now, there are many people who are like the turtle. I call them "the People of the Turtle Tribe." They are the people who simply withdraw from the world when they are faced with a problem. They do nothing to help solve the problem except to close their eyes and hope the problem will go away by itself. They do nothing to help themselves or anyone else.

Christians, however, are not turtle people. When they are faced with a problem, they try to take care of it. They pray to God for guidance. Because they are part of a church family, they have people around them to whom they can turn for help. Because they believe that the Bible gives us instructions on how to live, they turn to the Scriptures for guidance. For example, if you are having a problem with other people, the Bible tells you how to get along with others. In Romans 12 we read about living in harmony with one another and overcoming evil with good. And Jesus taught us to "do to others what you would have them do to you" (Matt. 7:12 NIV).

A Christian is one who goes out of self to God and to all the people we are called to love. A Christian is not a member of the turtle tribe.—Kenneth Mortonson

February 1: Under Construction
TEXT: 1 Thess. 5:1–11. "Therefore encourage one another and build up each other" (v. 11).

Object: Building blocks

How many of you like to play with building blocks? [*Let them answer.*] I always enjoy building things and it looks like many of you like to build as well. All through life people like to build things. That is why so many buildings get built. Some people build careers. Others build the community where they live. Churches are built by people. Today, however, I want to talk about building something that most of us might not think about. I want to talk about building people.

Now, God makes people, and God makes us grow and learn. But we all help add to each other or take away from each other. We can help build people or we can tear people down.

How can we tear people down? [*Let them answer.*] We can be critical and mean with others and that tears them down. It makes people think less of themselves. We might not see any difference in a person who has been criticized, but there is a difference. When we tear people down, the tearing down begins on the inside of that person. That is why sometimes we are mean to people and think nothing of it. It's not like building a tower from these blocks and then

knocking them down—we can see that. With people, the difference is on the inside.

Now, let me ask: Do you think God wants us to tear anybody down? [*Let them answer.*] No, God wants us to build each other up. How do we do that? [*Explore various ways of building each other up.*] Compliments help. When we see that a person is acting in a very pleasing way, we can say so. When someone does something exceptionally well, we can tell that person what a good job she or he did. We have many ways of building people.

We're all people builders. We're all in the construction business! Imagine that!—Dennis R. Fakes[1]

February 8: Jesus' Valentine
TEXT: John 15:13

Object: A heart and a cross cut out of red paper

From this folded piece of red paper we can cut out a heart, like this. On Valentine's Day people will be showing their love for each other by giving valentines. On just about every valentine card is a heart. Giving our hearts is very special. The heart is the center of our feelings and decisions. If we give someone a heart like this, it is the same as saying that we are giving our lives to them.

Jesus said that the greatest way to demonstrate our love for one another is to give of ourselves. That's what Jesus did when he died on the cross for the sins of the world. Listen to this verse.

Now, let me cut one more thing out of this heart. If I fold the heart and cut this way and that, a cross is taken out of the middle of the heart we made just a moment ago. I like to think of this heart with the cross out of its center as Jesus' valentine to the world.

On Valentine's Day, let's remember the greatest valentine that has ever been given to the world: Jesus' valentine. We can give a valentine back to Jesus each day as we give our lives in service to him.—K.C.

February 15: Potluck
Object: Envelopes containing various small items

Have any of you ever been to a potluck? Can you tell us what it is? Right, it is a meal to

[1] *CSS Plus.*

which each family brings a dish to share. It might be something you like or something that you would just as soon not eat. That's why it is called a potluck, because you never know what everyone else will bring. You have no control over what is served at the meal.

A potluck represents something that happens to us all the time. Some people express it this way: "You never know what the day might bring forth." For example, I heard of a lady who lived out in the country who went to look for something and accidentally stepped in a foxhole and broke her leg. Suddenly her life was changed for many days to come.

Now, while it is true that we have very little control over these unexpected things that can happen to us, that is only half of the story. We may not have much control over what may happen to us, but we do have a great deal of control over how we *respond* to whatever happens to us.

For example, if someone teases you, you can get angry at them or you can just ignore them. If someone won't share with you, you can cry or you can say, "OK, that's all right. I'm not going to let that upset me and make me unhappy."

I have a number of envelopes here. Inside each envelope is something different. There might be a piece of blank paper, or a bookmark, or a coupon for a free ice cream cone [*or whatever you might be able to get from a local fast-food store*] or some money (a penny or nickel or dime). It could be anything. Now, you have no control over what you get, only over how you respond to what you get. Just don't feel bad if you get nothing. [*You could be sure that there is something valuable in each envelope.*]—K.M.

February 15: God Takes Care of Jonah

TEXT: Jonah 1:17

Object: A life preserver

Life preservers like this keep folks from drowning when they fall into deep water. The Bible tells us that God kept Jonah from drowning by using a whale.

Jonah was a prophet of God. That means the Lord gave Jonah special messages to be delivered to his people. The Lord also told Jonah where to go and speak. On one occasion, God gave Jonah a sermon to be preached in a city named Nineveh. Jonah didn't want to go to Nineveh because he didn't like the people there. He tried to run away from the Lord by taking a ship to a foreign land. While on the voyage, God disciplined Jonah and also saved his life.

The Bible says that the dangerous seas grew rough and frightening on that runaway voyage. Jonah knew the storm was his fault because he had not done what God asked him to do. After the other men threw him into the water to save the ship, the Lord kept Jonah from drowning. Listen to this verse.

Being in the whale was a lesson to Jonah. It's like being punished at home. While we go without certain privileges we have time to think. While Jonah was in the whale, he thought and prayed to God for forgiveness. The whale saved Jonah from drowning in the storm and played a part in putting Jonah back on the right track.

After Jonah was out of the whale, he went to Nineveh and preached. Jonah's sermons helped a lot of people. When we do what the Lord wants us to do, we avoid being disciplined for our disobedience. If we are wise we will always be obedient as soon as we possibly can. When we are obedient to God we discover that we can have joy.—K.C.

March 1: The Small Cut That Destroys

Object: Large red apple

This big red apple seems to be in wonderful condition, but it is badly bruised. The wound is not big. In fact, most people would probably overlook it. Yet it is there just the same. Can anyone see it? The fatal cut is at the end of the stem, and because this apple has been cut off from the living tree that provided its nourishment, it will grow no more, because it cannot maintain itself alone.

The same is true in our God-given life. Jesus said, "I am the vine; you are the branches. If a man remains in me and I in him, he will bear much fruit; apart from me you can do nothing" (John 15:5). We cannot live the truly abundant life that God desires for us when we cut ourselves off from the true vine that nourishes us. I encourage you to hold onto that vine so that you can produce much good fruit.

There are many ways in which you can hold onto the true life that is found in Jesus. Sunday school is important. Worshiping each Sunday with your family is important. Reading your Bible regularly is another way to cling to the vine that gives true life. And doing what you know is right is the way that you bear good fruit and show the world that you are a part of the living vine, that you are a Christian.

But also remember that it takes time to discover the true life God offers us. Don't let impatience cause you to break away from the true vine, because although the break may seem small to you now, it will destroy the fruit. [*Hold up the apple.*] It is not good enough just to look good for awhile. We are called to live well, all of our lives, and to live we must be nourished and we must keep on growing.—K.M.

March 8: The Narrow Road to Life
TEXT: Matt. 7:13–14
Object: A map and drawing of a fork in the road

This road map is a good thing to have on long trips. It shows which road to take and prevents folks from getting lost. Living each day is like a journey. The map that God has given us is the Bible. The Bible points us in the right direction. On life's journey we often come to special instructions that require brave decisions.

This picture is of a fork in a road. See, the road comes to a place where either this route may be taken or the other way may be selected. Jesus said that we must be careful about the decisions we make when we come to a fork in the road. Listen to these verses.

When we are living to please Jesus we must make some difficult choices. Some forks in the road have one way that is being taken by many people. For instance, some friends may steal some candy from a store and dare you to do the same thing. These popular ways may appear smooth and happy. However, there is reason to refuse that way because taking such a road requires us to do something that we know does not please Jesus.

The road that Jesus leads us to take may appear very narrow. There are only a few people traveling the right road, and we are tempted to go with the crowd. Even though we know that the less traveled way pleases Jesus, it takes a courageous decision to trust the Lord and go it alone.

A road map keeps us from getting lost on long journeys over unfamiliar highways. The Word of God will direct us to the proper destination for our lives. However, from time to time we will come to a fork in the road that requires us to make a brave decision. Let's always be strong and travel the road that will lead to life.—K.C.

March 15: The Importance of Names
TEXT: Exod. 3:13–20
Object: A book for expectant parents that lists names and their meanings

There's a lot of excitement in our house these days. We're expecting a new baby any day now. One thing we're trying to decide is what we should name the baby. We've been thinking for months about what would be a good name for the baby and there are so many nice names that it's hard to decide. I'll bet your parents thought a lot about what they wanted to name you before you were born.

One thing we've learned as we've been thinking about names is that names mean something. For instance, my name, Steve, means garland, which is a kind of crown made from leaves that you wear on your head. [*Show the book.*] We've been looking through this book of names that tells what some names mean. How would you like to find out what your name means? Let's look in the book and see if your name is in here.

[*Look up children's names.*]

We've talked about Moses before, and you know who he was. The Bible tells us that one day Moses was out in the desert watching his sheep and he saw a bush that was on fire but it wasn't burning up. God spoke to Moses from the bush and told him to go lead the Hebrew people out of Egypt. While Moses was talking to God, he wanted to know what God's name was. It's hard to talk to somebody if you don't know their name. So God told Moses his name. God's name is YHWH. YHWH means "I am." God's name told Moses something that was important to know. God's name means that God is with us all the time, wherever we are.

Names are important. Whenever we talk to our friends we always call them by name. I don't say, "Hey you." I say, "Hello Lindsay," "Hi Sam." When we talk to God, we talk to him like he's a friend. We can call him by lots of names: YHWH, Jehovah, Lord, Jesus, Christ. But whatever name we call God, God loves us and is still always watching over us. God's name means he's with you.—S.L.

March 22: Throwaways

One day, a young man on a bicycle was riding down a street. He had been drinking from a soda pop can, and when he finished with it, he simply threw it onto someone's front lawn. Why do you think he did that? [*Because the can was empty and he didn't need it anymore.*] True, the can needed to be disposed of, but what do you think about the idea of just throwing it anywhere? What do you think the owner of the house will do when he finds the can on his front lawn? [*He will take it and put it in his garbage can.*]

So, what the young man on the bicycle was doing by his action was saying to that homeowner, "Here, you take care of my garbage for me—whether you want to or not."

Passing a responsibility on to someone else without even asking if it is all right is not a very nice thing to do. But that is what people do when they take things they don't want and throw them on someone else's property. Such people are being very thoughtless. And one of the worst cases is when a person throws away their chewing gum in a public parking lot. What a mess it makes when someone else steps on that sticky chewing gum.

It is so easy for people to be so wrapped up in what they are doing that they fail to stop and think about what they are doing to other people. Part of being a Christian is to love our neighbors and that means being thoughtful of all the people who live around us, even the stranger we never see.—K.M.

March 29: Bragging Hurts Feelings

TEXT: Prov. 29:23

Object: A yardstick

This is a yardstick. If we had time, we could measure how tall all of you are. Some boys and girls who are tall for their age brag about their height. When we tell others about something special in our lives in a boastful way, we are guilty of bragging. For instance, I could look at every one of you and say, "I'm taller than all of you, ha, ha, ha. You are all a bunch of shorties." Saying that would make it sound like I'm better than you. Such bragging would be silly. After all, I'm an adult and all of you are still growing.

God has made some persons smarter, faster, stronger, prettier, or more handsome than others for a special purpose. We are not to brag about or use selfishly what God has graciously done for us. The Lord wants us to build others up, not tear them down by boasting. All that we are or possess should be used to help others. Listen to this verse.

People who brag become very unhappy. We boast when we are not sure of ourselves. Braggarts think they will feel better after the confidence of others has been torn down by their words. Nobody likes to feel they aren't as good as somebody else. When we hurt others, in most cases angry feelings are shown to us in return. The braggart eventually discovers that standing on the broken feelings of others doesn't lift them up at all.

When we are gentle and quiet about the gifts God has given us, we are always happier on the inside. And the more we help others by what we say, the better we like ourselves. Let's remember that God wants us to be encouraging to others in all that we do.— K.C.

April 5: Jesus Died for Our Sins

TEXT: Phil. 2:8

Object: A crucifix

There are two representations of the cross. One is like this, called a crucifix, with Jesus still on the cross, and the other is an empty cross. Both portrayals are important. The crucifix emphasizes that Jesus died on the cross as he willingly gave his life for the forgiveness of our sins. Listen to this verse.

Jesus gave, or sacrificed, his life so we could live in close friendship with God. Jesus gave us a good example of giving so others can have.

It is very easy to have a "me first" attitude that makes us want to go first and have the biggest piece of cake at birthday parties. If we live with a "me first" attitude all the time, we begin to become very small. We are afraid to let others go first because we are scared that we won't get our share. The Bible teaches that the more we take, the less we have.

Jesus calls for his children to be like him. He tells us to take up our crosses and follow him. He teaches us that as we give we will find our cups filled to overflowing.

Sacrifice accomplishes a lot. When Jesus died on the cross, he was giving his life so we could have eternal life. When we give of ourselves, others benefit from our abundance and we don't seem to run out. Also, we find joy in living. Deep down inside we become happy with ourselves. So, let's not be afraid to give ourselves. When we see a crucifix, we can consider how much Jesus gave to us, and we can remember to be generous to others.—K.C.

April 12: The Empty Cross

TEXT: Phil. 2: 9–11

Object: A cross

There are two representations of the cross. One is like this, called an Easter cross or an empty cross. The other type of cross is a crucifix, which portrays Jesus still on the cross. The Easter cross is a symbol of life because it is empty. When we look at this cross we know that Jesus has left the place of death to rise to life.

A burial tomb was used in the days of Jesus instead of a cemetery. A tomb looks like a cave or a hollow place in a rocky hill. In those days the people carved out a place in the hills and placed their loved ones there when they died. After Jesus died on the cross, he was taken down and placed in a tomb.

On the third day after Jesus died on the cross, his followers went to visit the tomb. They discovered that Jesus was not there. The angels announced that Jesus had been raised from the dead and had gone to heaven. Jesus was given the place of highest honor because he had accomplished God's purpose for his life. Listen to these verses.

Jesus is not only alive in heaven, he is alive in us. That is the victorious message of Easter. When we accept him as Savior, his spirit begins to live in us. We are able to live lives that are pleasing to him because his life is in us.

The cross is a reminder of the death of Jesus for our sins. The Easter cross is also a reminder that he is alive in our world. One day we will be raised and go to heaven where Jesus is. We will see him face to face on that special day.—K.C.

April 19: Easter—One Great Hour of Sharing Offering

TEXT: John 21

This morning I want to tell you a story about something that happened a few days after Jesus rose from the dead. After Jesus had died, his closest friends, the disciples, had gone back to their homes in a land called Galilee. Now, Jesus' friends had been fishermen. They were very sad because Jesus had died, so sad that they had gone back to their old jobs of catching fish.

The disciples used to fish on a great big lake that is called the Sea of Galilee. They went fishing at night because that's when the fish were easiest to catch. They didn't fish with fishing poles, the way you and I might fish. Instead, they used big, huge nets. They would throw their nets over the side of their boat and then pull the net back in. All the fish that were in the way of the net would be caught and brought back into the boat.

On this one night, Jesus' friends had been fishing all night long without any luck. Just as the sun was rising in the morning, they happened to look over at the shore of the lake and saw a man standing there. They didn't know who the man was, but he called out to them and asked if they had caught any fish. They called back and said no, they hadn't. So the man on the shore told them to throw their nets over the other side of the boat and see what happened. They did, and they caught so many fish that they couldn't haul them all into the boat.

Then one of Jesus' friends, a man named Peter, recognized that the man who had called to them from the shore was Jesus. Peter was so excited that he jumped into the water and swam to the shore. The other disciples brought the boat back to the shore. It was so loaded down with fish that it could hardly move.

When they got to the shore of the lake, Jesus was sitting by a charcoal fire cooking some fish for breakfast. He told the disciples to come and have some with him.

After breakfast he asked his friend Peter, "Do you love me?"

"Yes, Lord." Peter replied. "You know that I love you."

"Then feed my lambs," said Jesus.

Jesus asked Peter that question, "Do you love me?" three times, and each time Peter told him that he did love him. And each time Jesus told him to feed his lambs.

Now, when Jesus told Peter to feed his lambs, he meant that he wanted him to care for Jesus' friends, all the men and women and boys and girls whom Jesus loves. And that's what Jesus wants each of us to do, to care for all the people he loves by sharing with them what we have.

And that's exactly what you did with these boxes you brought to church filled with coins. The money that you've put into these One Great Hour of Sharing boxes is going to be used to feed people all over the world. Part of it is going to buy food for people who are starving. Part of it is going to be saved until there is some great disaster like a hurricane or an earthquake. Then it will be used to buy food and medicine and clothing for people who have lost their homes. Part of it will go to teach men and women how to make a better life for themselves by being better farmers or digging better wells.

After Easter, Jesus' disciples met him when he gave them fish to eat by the shore of the lake. People around the world are going to know the love that Jesus has for them because of the offerings you bring this morning. You're helping to feed God's people. That makes Jesus very happy. I hope it makes you happy too.—S.L.

April 26: Trusting What You Can't See

TEXT: John 20:24–29

Has anyone told you something that you had a hard time believing? For instance, if somebody told you that they had alligators in their basement, you'd want to see it before you believed it, wouldn't you? If I told you that I could run faster than a car, you'd want to see me do it before you believed me, wouldn't you?

But, you know, there are some things we believe without seeing them. I believe that some of you go to kindergarten, even though I've never been to your class. And I believe that God loves me, even though I've never seen God.

This morning I want to tell you a story about someone who had a hard time believing something unless he saw it. This man's name was Thomas. He was one of Jesus' disciples.

This story happened the evening after Jesus had risen from the dead on Easter morning. Jesus' disciples were all together in a room. They were all afraid of what was going to happen to them now that Jesus wasn't around anymore. They hadn't seen Jesus since he had risen, and they weren't quite sure whether or not to believe that he was alive. They were all talking with one another when, to their surprise, Jesus was standing right there among them. They were all startled to see him and wondered how he had gotten there. But he said some kind words to them that put them at ease. Then, once he had assured them that he was indeed alive, he left them just as mysteriously as he had appeared.

One of the disciples, a man named Thomas, wasn't with them when they saw Jesus. When the other disciples told him that Jesus had risen from the dead and come to see them, he didn't believe them. "Let me see the scars in his hands and put my finger in the cut on his side where they stabbed him. Then I'll believe," he said.

The following week the disciples were all together again in the same room. This time Thomas was with them. All the windows were closed and the doors were locked, but suddenly Jesus was right there among them. He said to Thomas, "Here, Thomas, put your finger on my palm where they nailed me to the cross and touch my side where they stabbed me. Then you'll believe that I really was dead and that God raised me up on Easter."

Well, Thomas was shocked. He fell down at Jesus' feet and said, "My Lord and my God!"

Then Jesus said to him, "You believed because you saw me. Happy are those who don't see me and still believe."

We've never seen Jesus face to face. We've never touched him the way Thomas did. But we believe that he loves us and cares for us in ways we can't always see. He's always with us, even when we can't see him.—S.L.

May 3: Accent

Object: Jar of Accent

Do any of you like to cook? What do you cook? Have you ever seen a bottle like this in your kitchen? This is called "Accent." It is sprinkled on meats and other foods to bring out the good flavor of the food. It does not make the food better for you, it just makes it taste better, according to the manufacturer.

This morning I want to remind you of something that we all need to add to life that is like this Accent. It does not increase the material blessings of life, but it is something that brings out the good "flavor" of living with one another. The accent I am thinking of is called gratitude. It is that little sprinkling of life with words of appreciation.

Remember that day we call Mother's Day?

Next Sunday it is expected that you will express, in some way, that you are thankful for all that your mother has done for you. But for this expression of gratitude to be meaningful it should be added each day of life.

What I would like you to do this week is to put this to the test. Watch your parents and when you see either your mother or your father doing something for you, say "Thank you." Think of it as a time when you are sprinkling a little Accent on your unique relationship with your parents. See how you feel and watch for the effect on your mother and father. In fact, if you have a brother or sister, try it on them, too. Why you can even use the gratitude Accent on your teachers at school. Sprinkle it around throughout your day. I think you will find that it will have a good effect on your life and on the life of the people around you.—K.M.

May 10: The Star

TEXT: Prov. 31:28, 31

Object: Picture of a star athlete

This is a picture of [*name of athlete*]. He is [*tell his position on which team*]. He is an outstanding athlete and helps his team win games. He is paid a huge salary and has a fan club that writes him adoring letters. Wherever he goes, people line up and ask for his autograph. They get him to sign footballs, pictures, programs, just about anything. That "star" treatment must make him feel very important.

There is a star in your life that is easy to overlook. This is the day of the year we have set aside to honor our mothers. Mothers work very hard and play a vital role in making their children winners, but mothers don't receive salaries for their work. Few people line up to get their autographs. In fact, in most families the hard work and valuable contributions of mothers are taken for granted. That means we rarely pause to thank them for all they do. We just think that mothers are here to care for us like a very efficient robot.

The Bible commands us to make our mothers feel special. We are to give them credit for their hard work. Listen to these verses.

So, today is the day to make your mother feel like a star. The wonderful thing is that making moms feel special is a simple thing to do. All mothers desire is a word of thanks

now and then. If you can fix up a simple card that expresses your gratitude for her, or just tell her that you appreciate her, she will feel like a star. And don't think that Mother's Day is the only time to make your mom feel special. Every now and then tell her that you love her and are grateful for her loving care. When you see her eyes light up you'll know she feels like a star!—K.C.

May 17: Great Faith!

TEXT: Matt. 15:21–28. "Woman, great is your faith!" (v. 28).

Object: A pole

Good morning! Have you ever been to a circus? [*Let them answer.*] Do you like circuses? [*Let them answer.*] What is your favorite part? [*Let them answer.*] One of my favorite parts is when the high-wire acrobats climb way up high and walk on a narrow wire. How do they do that? I wonder.

Once there was a high-wire artist who was amazing. [*Here you can take your pole and mimic a high-wire artist with a pretend wire on the floor.*] He did all kinds of things on the high wire—without a net under him. If he had ever slipped, it would have killed him because he was so high up.

After one amazing performance, he climbed down and asked the people in the audience if they believed he could walk on the thin high wire with a man on his back. The people there that day answered, "Yes!" Then he turned to a man sitting on the front row. "How about you, sir? Do you believe I could walk on that wire up there with a man on my back?" "Yes," the man said. "Then prove it," the acrobat said. "I want you to get on my back as I climb back up there and walk across."

Now, what do you think the man said to the high-wire artist? [*Let them answer.*] The man from the audience would need a lot of faith in the high-wire artist to actually entrust his life to the man.

One day a woman met Jesus and asked him to heal her daughter. He was amazed that she trusted him so much. She was like the man from the audience—she really believed in Jesus. Jesus said to her, "Woman, great is your faith." And then he healed her daughter!

We also can trust Jesus. We know that Jesus can do wonderful things. He can heal and he can do many things we cannot do. I would not trust myself to a man walking on a high wire, but I do trust Jesus with my life. That kind of trust is called faithfulness. Jesus wants us all to trust him, to have faithfulness like the woman he met a long time ago.—D.R.F.[2]

May 24: When a Friend Moves Away

Have any of you ever moved away? Did you used to live someplace else before you lived here? [*Let them answer.*] Moving can be kind of sad, can't it? You leave behind old friends. But moving can be happy, too. You get to make new friends. If you hadn't moved here, I wouldn't know you, so I'm glad that you live here.

Have any of you ever had a friend move away? [*Let them answer.*] It's sad when our friends move away, because we don't see them as often as we did when they lived near by. But whenever I'm sad because friends have moved away, I try to think of all the new friends and the new house or school they will have in their new home, and that makes me happy for them.

There's a lot about moving in the Bible. Have any of you ever studied about Moses in Sunday school? Moses led the Hebrews out of Egypt to a new place called Israel. And Jesus moved from place to place. I'm sure there were many towns he visited where the people wanted him to stay with them all the time. But Jesus had to go teach other people in other places about God, so he was moving around all the time.—S.L.

May 31: Different Parts, Yet One

TEXT: Rom. 12:1–8. "We, who are many, are one body in Christ" (v. 5).

Object: A picture of your church building

Good morning! This morning I want to see if we can think of all the rooms in this church building. Let's start. We can begin here. What is this room called here? [*Let them answer.*] Now, let's think of every room in this building. Who would like to name a room? [*Let them answer. You could list each name on a blackboard, clipboard, or large sheet of newsprint.*] Every one of these rooms is important. We have this room where we worship. That is important. We have the room where we meet for Sunday school.

That certainly is important. We have closets where we keep things stored. Those rooms are important. We have restrooms. Those rooms are important. Do we have any rooms that are not important? [*Let them answer.*] Every room is good for something. If we didn't have a heating room, for example, we would get cold in the wintertime. If we didn't have a church kitchen, we couldn't serve meals at fellowship time. Every room in our church building is important.

In the same way, each person here is important. We all do different things. I do the children's sermon this morning. Our organist plays the organ. Our pastor preaches the sermon. Our choir sings the choir anthem. The congregation sings the hymns. We all fit together. A long time ago the apostle Paul said that we all belong to one another. Each one of us is important to one another. We all need each other. Each one us is important! I belong to you and you belong to me. If I hadn't come this morning, we wouldn't be doing what we are doing right now. If you hadn't come this morning, I would really miss you.

The apostle Paul said that we are all together in one church even though every one of us is different. You and I are the church! This is just the church building. The church building has different rooms for different things; the church—you and I—have different talents and abilities. We are all different, but we belong together. I belong to you and you belong to me. I would really miss you if you weren't here, just like the church building would be really strange if this room were not part of the church building. I'm glad I have you and you have me and that, together, we have a God who loves us.—D.R.F.[3]

June 7: Make an Appointment with God

TEXT: Ps. 29:2

Object: An appointment calendar

This is my calendar for the week. Marked on the calendar are the appointments I have made. An appointment is a time set aside for a special person. If you call me and make an appointment to see me, I will write it down so I won't forget it. When you come at the time

[2] *CSS Plus.*   [3] *CSS Plus.*

of your appointment, I will be ready to meet with you. No one else will be able to see me during that time. The appointment time will be reserved especially for you.

We have to make appointments to meet with the Lord. Because our schedules are so busy, we must set aside a day and special times on that day to meet with the Lord. If we don't make a special time for the Lord, a friend may come by and ask us to do something else on the spur of the moment, or we might start watching a television show and miss a time that we should meet with the Lord.

Our worship times with the Lord should be high-priority times; that means we will not let anything interfere with them. Listen to this verse.

A *standing appointment* is an appointment on the same day each week at the same time of day. We need to make a standing appointment each Sunday to worship the Lord. Remember, if we don't make appointments to meet with the Lord, something else will slip into our schedule to rob us of that time. Let's make and keep our appointments with Jesus.—K.C.

June 14: How to Treat Others

TEXT: Luke 6:31. "Treat others just as you want to be treated" (CEV).

During World War II, I spoke at one of our largest airfields, at Rantoul, Illinois, and during my stay there the commandant courteously took me on an inspection tour and showed me everything that was not a strict military secret. The most interesting room he showed me was the room were hundreds of soldiers were inspecting parachutes.

I noticed the meticulous care with which they worked on those chutes, and asked permission to talk with some of the soldiers.

"You men seem to bestow great care on those chutes. You work just as if you were going to have to drop in one of them yourselves."

One soldier grinned and replied: "Sir, that is exactly what we have to do. The rule around here is that each fellow who works on one of these chutes has to take the first jump in it. You're right! I'll say we give them careful attention. I suppose they have that rule so that we'll be very careful in our work on them. When you have to drop in the one you yourself inspect, you're careful in your inspection."—William L. Stidger

June 21: Don't Misunderstand Your Father

TEXT: Exod. 20:12

Object: A packed bandana tied to a stick

In a *Dennis the Menace* cartoon, Dennis was running away from home. He had a stick like this on his shoulder, and tied in the handkerchief was everything he needed, like a candy bar and crackers. Dennis's dad was on the porch watching Dennis as he was leaving their front yard. I don't think Dennis was gone long. He was probably home soon and glad to be where he was loved.

Dennis the Menace was running away because his father was always telling him what to do and making up rules. When I was growing up I felt the same way. My father was always correcting me and making me do chores around the house. It was enough to make me angry at times. Years later I realized that my dad loved me and was helping me every time he got involved in my life, even if it was just to correct me and make up a bunch of rules. I have thanked him many times for telling me how to live.

Fathers can be misunderstood by their children. The Bible tells us to honor or to be obedient to our parents. Listen to this verse.

Honoring fathers means being obedient even when we don't fully grasp why we should be obedient. The Lord gave us this commandment because all kids tend to rebel against instruction only to look back years down the road and actually appreciate the rules and instructions that they once disliked.

This is the day we pay tribute to our dads. Be sure to tell your father today that you appreciate and love him. The Lord is pleased with us when we are obedient to our fathers and honor them with grateful words. This Father's Day remember that Dennis the Menace discovered that his dad was right. One day you will too.—K.C.

June 28: Did It Just Happen?

One day, two scientists were walking along a country road looking at the beauty of nature. One of them asked the other if he believed that the grass and flowers and trees grew by mere chemical force. In other words, did he believe that the things of nature just happened. "No," replied the other scientist, "No more than I could believe that the books of botany describing them could grow by mere chemical force."

We look at any book and it is obvious that someone had to compose the words and put them together in a proper order so that they would make sense. The same is true of the things we see in nature. When we see the beauty of nature and begin to understand how all the cells within a living thing fit together to a make a flower or a tree or a blade of grass or anything else, then we know that it didn't just happen. In faith we say that God composed it all. As the psalmist reminds us, "The earth is the Lord's and everything in it, the world, and all who live in it" (Ps. 24:1 NIV).

We have churches so that boys and girls and men and women can come together and learn about the source of all beauty and wisdom and goodness in life. And as they learn about the source of all truth, they find that God is not only the force of creation but also our parent, and as such he seeks to live with us and to show us how to live with one another. We find this personal God in Jesus, who taught his disciples: "Anyone who has seen me has seen the Father" (John 14:9 NIV).—K.M.

July 5: God's Care for Us

Text: Matt. 10:29–31

Saturday was a very sad day in our house. Our little parakeet, Pepper, died. He was a pretty green and yellow bird who liked to chirp loudly and do funny tricks with the toys in his cage.

Saturday morning I noticed that something was strange about him. He looked weak and sick. We took him out of his cage and put him on the kitchen table hoping he would be more comfortable. Then we called the veterinarian to see if she could help.

The veterinarian said to bring him right over. But she said it would cost $50.00 to look at him. My daughter and I talked about it. We had paid only $19.00 for Pepper. For the $50.00 we would pay to take him to the veterinarian we could buy two brand new birds and have money left over. But we didn't think about it very long. We loved Pepper, and we were willing to spend that much money to help him.

Unfortunately, by the time we got Pepper to the veterinarian it was too late. Saturday afternoon we invited the neighborhood kids to our house and had a little funeral for Pep-

per and buried him in the garden outside the kitchen. And at the service we read these words that Jesus said: "For only a penny you can buy two sparrows, yet not one sparrow falls to the ground without [God's] consent. As for you, even the hairs of your head are all counted. So do not be afraid; you are worth much more than many sparrows!"

What a wonderful thing to know! God cared for little Pepper, and I'm sure that God was sad with us because Pepper died. And if God cares for a little bird, how much more does God care for you! If you're afraid or sick or lonely or sad, God cares for you even more than we cared for Pepper. God cares for you as much as your Mom and Dad, who love you more than anyone else in the world.

Don't ever think you're small and unimportant. God who loves the little birds loves you even more.—S.L.

July 12: The Weapon of Our Mouths

Text: Prov. 12:18

Object: A toy gun or knife

All of us have a very powerful weapon in our possession. It is not a gun or knife like these toys, it is our mouth. The words that we speak are very powerful, and therefore we must be careful with what we say. Listen to this verse.

The Bible instructs us always to tell the truth. Telling the truth is the ninth of the Ten Commandments. We must come to love the truth and always tell the truth. When we tell the truth in care and love, we will be speaking correctly.

If we are not careful about what we say we can seriously harm someone. Listen to a story about a boy named Eddie. A new girl named Sarah was placed in Eddie's second grade class. Sarah was very quiet. Some of the pupils in the class started noticing that their pencils were missing. Eddie had a pencil taken from him. Eddie told one of his friends that he thought the new girl was taking the pencils. Eddie's friend told some others and pretty soon everyone was blaming the shy Sarah of stealing. Sarah was embarrassed and ashamed for being accused of theft. As it turned out, someone else had taken the pencils and Sarah had nothing to do with it. Eddie felt bad after he learned the truth. After apologizing to Sarah, he had learned the power of the things he had said.

For our society to operate for the best, we should always tell the truth and be careful in the use of our words. The words that come out of our mouths are very powerful. Let's be certain that our words are powerful tools for good and not for harm.—K.C.

July 19: Forgiving a Debt

Text: Matt. 18:21–35. "How often should I forgive?" (v. 21).

Object: A wrapped gift, complete with bows

One day Peter came to Jesus and said, "How many times should I forgive someone who does me wrong?" What do you suppose Peter wished Jesus might say as an answer? [*Let them answer.*] I can imagine Peter wished Jesus would have said, "Get even with those who do you wrong. If someone hurts you, hurt them back. If someone steals from you, take from them." But Jesus didn't say that. Who knows what Jesus said to Peter? [*Let them answer.*] Jesus said, "Don't forgive a person seven times, but seventy-seven times." In other words, keep on forgiving.

When I think of forgiving, I think of *giving*. This present I have might be an example of giving. If I got a present all neatly wrapped like this, I would be quite thrilled. Forgiving is like giving because forgiving is a gift we give to ourselves. Let me explain.

When someone does us wrong, we usually get upset and angry with that person. Does that hurt the person? No, it hurts me. I'm the one all upset and angry. The best thing I can do for myself is forgive the other person. Then I'm no longer upset and angry. It's like giving a gift to myself. That's how forgiving is like giving.

Besides that, God wants us to forgive others. Jesus told Peter a story about forgiveness. He said a man owed his king lots of money. Let's say he owed him a thousand dollars. The king was a good king and he said to the man, "I forgive you your debt. You don't have to pay me back." Now, this man had another man who owed him some money. He didn't owe him as much, but he did owe the money. Let's say he owed him a dime. Even though this man had been forgiven a thousand-dollar debt by the king, he would not forgive the man who owed him just a dime.

God forgives us and expects us to forgive others. That is the point Jesus was trying to make with this story. Forgiveness is very im-

portant to God because God knows it makes us feel better. It's a gift we give to ourselves and others. Maybe that's why it's called for-*give*ness."—D.R.F.[4]

July 26: A Blade of Grass

Object: A blade of grass

Summertime is a wonderful time of the year. There are so many fun things we can do outside. What do you like to do in the summer? [*Let them answer.*] There are also many things we can learn during the summer, if we take the time to look at what is happening around us. For example, as you look at this blade of grass, what can you tell me about it? First, we can notice its color. It is green, and that means it is growing properly. This is also true about people. The growth that takes place in us will be seen, if it is true growth.

Now, when the grass grows around your house, what happens to it? Look again at the blade of grass. See, it has been cut off at the top. For a lawn to look nice, the grass must be cut so that all the blades of grass are about the same height. In a sense, we can say that the grass is being disciplined. Certain restrictions are placed upon it so that it can fulfill its role in life. We plant grass around our homes and we keep it cut so that it will have a pleasant appearance.

The same thing applies to you and me. We must discipline ourselves, or be instructed by others so that we can learn how to make the best use of life. As Christians, we believe that we have a role to fulfill to life; that is, we are here for a purpose. And just as the grass needs to be cut often to maintain a good looking lawn, so we need to be continually trained by life as we continue to grow. We need the discipline of eating properly each day. We need to go to bed at a certain time to get proper rest. We need to work and exercise our mind and spend time with friends. Each one of us needs to decide what we will do to grow into the beautiful person God wants us to be.—K.M.

August 2: All Moses Needed Was His Staff

Text: Exod. 4:2,17

Object: A long, thick stick

Moses was a shepherd a long time ago.

[4]*CSS Plus.*

Like all shepherds, Moses had a staff like this. This may look like just a big stick to you, but in the hands of a shepherd a staff is used to direct, protect, and control his sheep.

The Lord called Moses to do a very big job. God's people were being held in slavery in Egypt, and Moses was instructed to rescue them from that cruel captivity. Moses was accustomed to taking care of a small herd of sheep. It must have been a shock to be told that he was to lead millions of people for the Lord. Moses wondered if he needed something special to do his job. God told Moses that all he needed was what he already had: his staff, and a willingness to trust God. Listen to these verses.

When Moses arrived in Egypt he did need special help. Pharaoh didn't want to release God's people from slavery, and he had a huge powerful army that followed his commands. But Moses was obedient and made use of his staff. Moses struck the Nile river with his staff and the water turned into blood. He held his staff out over the Red Sea and it divided in two so the Israelites could walk through the sea on dry land! Moses discovered that all he needed was what he already possessed: a staff.

When the Lord gives us something to do, he will make sure that we have everything we need to complete the job. When we serve the Lord, we discover that he has been preparing us for whatever he calls us to do. And instead of expecting God to use someone or something else, all we need to do is be ourselves and use whatever we have. We must be willing to do great things for God. All Moses had was a staff, and that was all he needed, with God's help.—K.C.

August 9: Two Twigs

Object: Two small branches, one from a dead tree and one from a live tree

This morning I want you to take a moment and look at all the people who are here today. We can assume they are all Christians because they have come to a Christian service of worship. But we really cannot tell if someone is a Christian just by looking at that person. And it is probably not a good idea for us to try and judge other people. Maybe we should just think about ourselves.

What does it take for you to be a Christian? Jesus said, "If you hold to my teachings, you

are really my disciples. Then you will know the truth, and the truth will set you free" (John 8:31, 32 NIV). What Jesus wants us to do is learn what he has to teach us and hang on to it and live by it. When we do that, we will find the truth about his way of living and will be set free to live our true God-given life. We will also find out the truth about who Jesus is.

Let me see if I can show you what that means. Here are two twigs. They look pretty much alike. But they are different on the inside and that is seen when I bend them. One is stiff and breaks when bent. The other is flexible and after it is bent it returns to its original shape. The branch that broke is from a tree that has been dead for a long time. Since it is no longer growing, it is set in its ways. The other branch came from a live tree and the signs of life are still in it.

As we learn what Jesus has to teach us and take hold of his ways and live by them, we are given a new spirit inside that helps us to find our true, God-given life. It also helps us to know that in Jesus, God is with us.—K.M.

August 16: God Supplies Our Needs

TEXT: Exod. 16

Do you know one of the things I like best about the summer? I love all the fresh fruits and vegetables you can get. At our house we have corn on the cob almost every night, and fresh tomatoes and peaches. Do you eat any of those good things at your house? [*Let them answer.*]

And do you know who makes all that good, fresh food grow? That's right. God. God makes sure we have everything we need every day. But sometimes it's easy to forget that it's God who gives us all that good food. Let me tell you a story about some people who almost forgot that it's God who gives us everything.

Moses and the Hebrew people were slaves in the land of Egypt. They had to do everything that the Egyptians told them to do. But one day God led the Hebrews out of Egypt so they could be free. God led them out into a desert.

Now, out in that desert there were no motels where they could sleep, or restaurants where they could eat, or stores where they could buy food to cook. They had to eat the food they had brought with them when they ran away from Egypt. But before long all that food was gone. They started to complain.

"I wish we had never come," one man said.

"I wish we were back in Egypt," said somebody else. "They were mean to us there, but at least we had enough to eat."

Everyone began to fuss.

Moses heard their grumbling. He knew that God hadn't brought his people out into the desert to forget about them. So Moses called all the people together and said, "Stop your complaining. God will take care of us and give us everything we need."

That evening a big flock of birds called quail flew into the camp. The people caught the quail and cooked them. Boy, did that meat taste good!

The next morning a heavy dew covered the ground. When it dried up, there were lots of white wafers all over the ground like snow. "What is it?" the people asked. The Hebrew word for "What is it?" is *manna*, so they called the bread manna.

"It's like bread," Moses said. "Taste it."

The people tasted it, and it was delicious. It tasted like crackers and honey.

"God has given us all we need," Moses said. "The birds will come every evening, and the "what is it" bread called manna will come every morning."

That night everyone was happy. They knew that God cared for them. God had put them out in the desert, but he hadn't forgotten about them. God gave all they needed.

Every day for the next forty years, until they arrived at their new home, the Hebrew people woke up every morning and went out and gathered the "what it is" bread, or manna. They knew that God would give them everything they needed. Just like God gives you and me all we need.—S.L.

August 23: The Seesaw

I think that just about everyone at one time or another has played on a seesaw or teeter-totter. All you need to make a seesaw is a long, strong board and something that will hold the center of that board up off the ground. Then, when you get on the board with another person and one of you is seated at each end, you can have a lot of fun going up and down and trying to hold the other person in the air.

I have a story to tell you about a group of girls who were out camping and having a lot of loud fun with a group of seesaws. But there was a problem. First, let me tell you about how the girls came to play on the teeter-totters. About thirty Girl Scouts came to the camping grounds in a state park. One night at about 10:30 these girls were all sent off by their counselors to the shower building so they might bathe before going to bed. The only problem was that there were too many of them and some of them had to wait their turn. Now, the teeter-totters were near the showers. It was a fun place to wait. Suddenly, the stillness of the night in the campground was shattered by the squeaking of the seesaws and the laughter of the girls. Now, there was nothing wrong with the girls having fun. The only problem was they had forgotten that other people in the camp were trying to go to sleep.

This illustrates a problem common to many people. It is very easy to become so involved in something that all we can think about is our own pleasure. When that happens, it means we have failed to consider the effects of what we do on other people. Jesus taught us to love our neighbors. That means we are to be considerate of them and not have fun at the expense of someone else. It is a lesson we all need to remember.—K.M.

August 30: The Water of Life

TEXT: Rev. 22:17

Object: A bottle of water

Bottled water has become very popular. Concession stands at ballparks used to offer a variety of sodas: root beer, colas, orange, and strawberry. Now those same concession stands are also selling plain water. Water is good for quenching thirst. Plain, pure water is valued because it lacks chemical additives and contaminants. Pure water takes away our thirst but does not add any impurities to our bodies.

In Jesus' day, rainwater was channeled into underground storage areas called cisterns. Cistern water would get an unsavory taste and smell after it had been in storage for several months. The people then valued "living water," or water that flowed in a stream or river. That water never tasted stale or bitter. Living or flowing water was fresh and clean and quenched thirst with a delicious taste.

Jesus taught that when people trusted in

him as Savior they were drinking the water of life. Listen to this verse.

Jesus is like pure bottled water. The water of life meets the thirst of our lives and there is no charge for all that we wish to drink. God gives living water to us freely. When we drink from the well of life our sins are forgiven and abundant life is granted to us. Furthermore, after we have quenched our thirst, living waters flow from within us as we tell others about our faith in Jesus Christ [see John 7:38].

Pure water, like this bottled product, meets our physical needs better than any other liquid. Jesus as living water quenches our spiritual needs and allows us to share the secret of abundant life with others.—K.C.

September 6: Listen!

Object: A clock or watch that makes a ticking sound but does not have a second hand

If this clock were placed in your hand there would be two ways in which you would be able to tell whether or not it was working. Does anyone know what those ways are? [*Let them answer.*] One way would be to listen to it, and if you could hear the tick, tick, tick, you would know it was running. The other way would be to look at the face of the clock and watch its hands. If they moved, the clock would be working. But because this clock has no second hand, you would have to watch for several minutes to be sure it was running. For this kind of clock, the quickest way to know it is working is to listen to it.

The same applies to our Christian life. In a matter of a few seconds, people hear what we say. And from the words we speak, they know what kind of spirit is in us. If our words are kind and gentle, they know we are a loving person. If our words are angry or hurtful, they think that we are mean.

Maybe you have been in a church where a minister says a little prayer before he preaches. It goes something like this: "May the words of my mouth and the meditations of my heart be acceptable in thy sight, O Lord, my Strength and my Redeemer." That is a good prayer for everyone to say at the beginning of each day. We want our thoughts and words to help, not hurt, the people around us. It sometimes helps if we stop and listen to our words as we speak to other people.—K.M.

September 13: God Gives Us Instructions
TEXT: Ps. 32:8

Object: A car model kit

As I take the lid off this car model kit we can see a bunch of little pieces. These plastic parts are just like the metal and chrome parts on a real car. Because I don't know how to take apart or put together a real car, I can't assemble this model either. I guess I could figure out where everything goes if I had several months, like putting together a big jigsaw puzzle. To make things easier, the manufacturer has put these in. They're the instructions. The instructions give a diagram of a step-by-step process to put the model together.

Our lives are even more complicated than this model. We have many days, weeks, months, and years to live. To know how to live the best way is impossible on our own. There are so many decisions to make. Just like the manufacturer of this complicated model, the Lord has given us instructions to guide us. The instructions are contained in the Bible. Listen to this verse.

If we were to put this model together without instructions it would probably look funny, and we might have some important parts left over. But if we follow these instructions, the model will turn out looking like the snazzy picture on the box. Our lives are like that, too. If we try to live according to our own wisdom, our lives end up missing some very important parts. Our lives may even look like a mess. When we follow God's instructions for our lives, we have days and years that are blessed.—K.C.

September 20: Watch the Leaves Change

Wonderful things are happening outdoors. The leaves on many trees are changing. It is beautiful, but it won't last. Soon the leaves will be dropping off the trees.

A naturalist in the Smoky Mountain National Park once told a group of people that one of the reasons the leaves change colors is that at this time of the year the days are getting shorter. With less sunlight, less chlorophyll is manufactured in the leaves and so the greenness slowly fades away.

There is an important lesson here for us. Like a tree, a Christian's life cannot be as it should be without sufficient spiritual light from God. One way to get that light is to worship God. Through regular worship the awareness of God remains alive within us and our life reflects the true colors of being a Christian. But when we stay away from the light, when we fail to sing his praises and hear his word, then the reality of God seems to slowly fade and life turns toward another center and takes on another color.

When we see a green tree, we know that it is alive and healthy. When the fall comes and the leaves change and fall off, we cannot know the true condition of that tree until it begins to grow again in the spring. Then we know it is alive when the green leaves return.—K.M.

September 27: Getting in God's Way
TEXT: Matt. 16:21–28. "Get behind me, Satan!" (v. 23).

Object: A football

When I think of today's story, I think of football. Let me explain myself. Today's story is about the time when Jesus tells his disciples that he is going to Jerusalem to suffer and die. Peter, the leader of the disciples, said to him, "God forbid it, Lord! This must never happen to you."

I can understand why Peter might say that, can't you? Peter loved Jesus and did not want Jesus to suffer and die. Whenever we love someone, we never want them to suffer and die. That's the way Peter was. He could not understand suffering and death.

But Jesus tells Peter, "Get behind me, Satan!" Wow! That sounds strong, doesn't it? When I think of Satan I think of the devil— of someone who stands in God's way. That is what Jesus meant. "Peter, you are standing in God's way. I must suffer and die. I don't want to and you don't want me to, but that is what God wants me to do. It is God's will."

When football players have a football, they want to run it all the way to the end zone to make a touchdown. But there is a problem that's keeping them from doing that. What might that problem be? [*Let them answer.*] The problem is that there is a defensive team standing in the way!

Peter was a good person who loved the Lord Jesus. But he was standing in Jesus' way. That is why Jesus called him "Satan." Peter was like the defensive football team that prevents the quarterback from making a touchdown. Peter was not a "bad" person, just like the opposing football team is not a "bad" team. It's just that Peter was in the way.

Sometimes very good, churchgoing people get in God's way as well. Some of God's most faithful people are the very ones who stop the church from accomplishing much. That's why we always pray for God's will to be done. We want things to go God's way—even when we can't understand why. It must have been hard for Peter to understand why Jesus had to suffer and die. It's hard for us to understand that, too. There are many things we do not understand. But we always pray that we not be in God's way, blocking the kingdom.—D.R.F.[5]

October 4: Jesus Meets All Our Needs
TEXT: John 6:35

Object: A slice of bread

If I were to say that bread would be the only food for lunch today, like this slice, we would groan with disappointment. Because of the wide variety of foods that we are blessed with and enjoy every day, we would think we had fallen on hard times if all we had to eat was bread.

The flour that has gone into making this slice of bread has been highly refined. The process is carried out so that the bread can be white and the texture very smooth with no holes or rough spots. The refining of flour removes some of the nutrients that were not taken out in Jesus' day. In Jesus' day, eating bread provided most of what was needed for good nourishment. Of course Jesus' family enjoyed fish from the sea of Galilee, and fruit and vegetables, too, but bread was a chief part of, and in some cases the only food, in their meals. Jesus taught his disciples to pray for their daily bread because that was all they really needed to eat.

Jesus called himself the bread of life. Listen to this verse. Jesus called himself bread because if a person had Jesus, they had all that was really needed in life. When someone has faith in Jesus, they have salvation and the promise of a home in heaven. When we trust Jesus as our Lord, we have the promise of his care, protection, and guidance, like a shepherd cares for his sheep.

It's easy to make life very hectic and complicated. We may have enough money but we want more. We might see someone with

[5] *CSS Plus.*

something we don't have and we just have to have one, too. Certain folks might laugh if we said that Jesus is all we really need in life. Some persons would rather have lives that are complicated by worry and fear instead of a simple life of trust in a loving God. A lot of the things we want in life are not absolutely necessary. These are things we only think we need.

This slice of bread may not look very appetizing, but when prepared correctly, bread supplies all we really need in the way of food. Jesus is all we need for our spiritual lives. When we have Jesus, we have all we need. We have the bread of heaven when we trust Jesus.—K.C.

October 11: The Apple and the Moon

Object: A small ball attached to a three-foot string

Isaac Newton was a scientist who was born in 1642. One day he was sitting in an orchard thinking about the universe and wondering what kept the moon in its place. As he sat there, an apple fell off the tree, and he remembered that a scientist before him had said that the earth has a power within it that pulls to itself everything that is left in the air without any support. "Then why doesn't the moon fall to the earth?" wondered Isaac. "Could it be that the earth pulls just hard enough to keep the moon going around and around and yet not hard enough to pull it in?"

We see how this works when we take this ball and spin it around on this string. The ball represents the moon, and the string is like the pull of the earth on the moon. The ball traveling around wants to fly away as it would if I let go of the string. But as I hold the string, it applies just the right force to keep the ball in place. The same thing happens with the earth and the moon and the pull of gravity between the two.

God, by the power of his great wisdom, created the earth and the moon and the sun and all the great world in the sky as magnets, each drawing the other to itself yet also moving around in the sky. By the powers that God has put within them, all the parts of our universe are held together and work together to maintain God's creation.

The same thing applies to each one of us. God has given us special powers. We also are to work together to fulfill his holy will. "The earth is the Lord's, and everything in it, the world, and all who live in it" (Ps. 24:1 NIV).— K.M.

October 18: God Cleanses Our Hearts

TEXT: Ps. 51:1–2

Object: A bar of soap

This is a bar of soap. When we wash with soap we get really clean. I once saw two boys playing in a sandbox. They were having a great time digging tunnels and pouring sand all over each other. When their moms called them to go home, they had sand everywhere: stuck to their sweaty legs, down their backs, even in their hair. I imagined that those two rowdy boys looked forward to taking a bath and getting clean. It's hard to imagine anyone crawling into clean sheets at bedtime with sand on their legs, back, and hair. Yuck.

The Bible teaches us that we can get dirty in other ways. When we do something that is wrong, like stealing or hurting a friend by mean remarks, we don't feel good inside. This sadness that we feel deep in our thoughts is called a dirty conscience. Only God can give us a clean conscience. Listen to these verses.

God gives us a clean conscience by forgiving us. Whenever we do something wrong, it is a sin against God. We may throw a rock and hit our sister, but the Lord experiences pain, too. So the Bible instructs us to tell the person that we have wronged that we are sorry. If we have taken something from them, we must give it back. Then we are to tell or confess our feelings through prayer to Jesus. When we ask God for forgiveness, and set the matter right with the ones we have wronged, the Lord is faithful to heal our inward bad feelings.

It's hard to imagine climbing into clean sheets at bedtime covered with sand. We shouldn't try to go to sleep with a dirty conscience either. Whenever we do something wrong we must tell the person we have wronged that we are sorry, and ask God to forgive us. Sleep is sweet when we go to bed after a bath, in fresh sheets, with a clean conscience.—K.C.

October 25: A Lesson from the Pumpkin

Object: A carved pumpkin, real or artificial

We have seen a lot of changed pumpkins recently. The top has been cut off, the inside has been cleaned out, and a light has been placed inside after the front has been cut open.

Now, what can we learn from this pumpkin? First of all, we know that before the light can be placed in it, the seeds inside have to be cleaned out. Then, if the light is to be seen [*turn the back of the pumpkin toward the group*] the front must be cut out [*turn the front toward the children*].

The same thing applies to our life as Christians. Jesus said, "I am the light of the world" (John 8:12 NIV). He also said, "Let your light shine" (Matt. 5:16 NIV). If we are to receive the light from God, as given to us in Jesus, then we must seek to remove all those things that would prevent us from receiving that light, or that would make the light go out once we have it. Laziness, indifference, and ignorance of what is in the Bible are just a few of the things we must remove.

Then, as we receive the light of God, we must give our own special expression to what we have received. Each one of us has our own unique way of being kind and showing concern for others. We take God's Word, God's Light, and we look for its special meaning for us. Then, as we live with others, they see who we are by what we do with the light. The Bible tells us to "be doers of the word, and not hearers only" (James 1:22 NIV). When we hear or read, we receive. When we do the right things, we take the light and let it shine out to influence the lives of everyone around us. The lesson of the pumpkin is for all seasons.—K.M.

November 1: Listening to God

TEXT: 1 Sam. 3:10

Object: A sign that says "Quiet"

Signs like these are posted in some libraries. The signs instruct the visitors in the library to be very quiet so folks who are reading, studying, and thinking will not be disturbed. In church we are to be quiet, too. Have you ever been "shushed"? There is a friendly "shush" like this [*demonstrate*] and a rough, commanding "shush!" like this [*demonstrate*]. When I was growing up I got "shushed" all the time. Years later I understood why I needed to be quiet in church.

We are to be quiet and reverent in church because in this special place we hear from the Lord. The Lord speaks to us through songs, scripture readings, and preaching. It is hard to hear the Lord if others are making distracting noises all around us, like talking, giggling, or paper rattling. Also, we cannot hear from the Lord unless we are in the proper attitude of listening. Being willing to hear the Lord is very important.

This passage describes an episode late at night. God had spoken to young Samuel twice after bedtime, but Samuel didn't know who was trying to talk to him. An older man told Samuel that it was the Lord and to be quiet and get ready to listen. Then, with Samuel in the proper attitude and during the quietness of the night, the Lord delivered the message to young Samuel. Listen to this verse.

The Lord has a message for all of us. Let's make sure we are quiet and ready to hear from the Lord whenever we come to church.—K.C.

November 8: Ever Ready

TEXT: Matt. 25:1–13. "Keep awake therefore, for you know neither the day nor the hour" (v. 13).

Object: A flashlight with fresh batteries and an exit sign

Most of us have flashlights at home. We don't use them very much because we usually don't need to. The electricity keeps our lights on and so we don't need a flashlight. But have any of you been at home when the lights went out because the electricity stopped? [*Let them answer.*] If that happens, it's good to have a flashlight around. But flashlights need something to make them work. What do they need? [*Let them answer.*] They need fresh batteries. If the batteries are old, the flashlight won't work well and won't work long. Having a flashlight ready and fresh batteries is one way of preparing for something that might not happen for a long time. But we like to prepare—just in case the lights go out soon.

Now, let me ask you about another kind of preparation. See those signs over the doors of our church? What do they say? [*Let them answer.*] They say "EXIT." What do they mean? [*Let them answer.*] In other words, an exit sign tells us where to go if the building were on fire or something. Does the building usually catch fire? [*Let them answer.*] It doesn't, but we need to have signs up to be prepared should that ever happen. We hope it never, ever happens. But the signs are there—just in case.

One time Jesus told a story about being prepared. He told about being prepared for his return. Someday Jesus will return to earth to take us to heaven. Life on earth is a wonderful gift, but we will not live on this earth forever. Someday we shall go to heaven to live with God. Jesus will come and get us and it will be a wonderful day. The problem is we have no idea *when* Jesus will return. So we always want to be ready. We want to be prepared. We live every day as if this were the day Jesus was coming to get us to be with him in heaven.—D.R.F.[6]

November 15: Using Your Bibles

Occasion: Distribution of Bibles to third graders

Object: A Bible that appears well used

This is a very special day in our church. This is the day we give Bibles to the third graders. I'll bet all of you have a Bible in your house, and I'll bet your parents read it to you.

Why is the Bible such a special book? [*Let them answer.*] That's right. It tells us about Jesus. It's full of stories that let us know what God is like and how much he loves us. It tells us how God wants us to live.

The Bibles that the third graders are getting today look nice and new. They have shiny covers and the pages are all straight and clean. But I hope they don't look that way always. Oh, I want you to take care of them and treat them kindly, but I hope that one day these Bibles will look like mine. [*Hold up well-worn Bible, with signs of wear such as a loose binding, scuffed corners, or dog-eared pages.*] This Bible has been lots of places. It's been in backpacks and suitcases. It's been in airplanes, boats, trains, and cars. It's been opened and shut hundreds of times. There are even pencil marks in it where I've underlined things. It looks like this because it's been well used.

Your new Bible isn't meant to sit on a shelf in your room. It's not just to bring to Sunday School. Now that you're in the third grade, you're able to read very well. Bibles are meant to be used. I hope that one day yours will look like mine.—S.L.

[6]*CSS Plus.*

November 22: Are Little Wrongs Okay?

TEXT: Matt. 25:21

Object: A sugar packet

This little sugar packet was purchased in the supermarket. These little packets are seen mostly in restaurants, where they are provided for people to sweeten their tea or coffee.

It would be easy to think that it is okay to take a few extra packets from the restaurant and use them at home. It's just a little package that couldn't cost but a few cents. But it is wrong to take a package of sweetener home. Even though we are welcome to use as many packets as we wish while in the restaurant, we are guilty of taking something that doesn't belong to us when we take them home for personal use.

This may sound picky—after all, what is a few cents to a restaurant? There is a principle involved here, however. Whatever we do with small things, we soon begin to do with big things, whether good or bad. Listen to this verse.

On snowy hillsides when the conditions are just right, a small snowball rolls until it gets bigger and bigger. Finally, what started out as a harmless snowball results in a catastrophic avalanche. The same thing is true with honesty. If we are dishonest with small things, we soon become accustomed to being dishonest with bigger things. Our actions snowball. On the other hand, if we are honest with little things, we learn to be honest with big things.

Our whole country is linked together in a group called a society. When someone does something wrong, even if it is little, it affects all of us. Let's remember the lesson of being honest with small things.—K.C.

November 29: Patience

Object: A bag of individually wrapped candies

Has anyone ever asked you to be patient? Can anyone tell me what the word means? [*Let them answer.*] Right. It means learning to wait. Let me give you an example: Your mother is talking on the telephone, and you want to ask her something and you start to talk. Now, she cannot listen to you and the person on the phone at the same time, so she may ask you to wait without being upset about having to wait—that is, to be patient. Or you are doing something and your Dad calls you for supper and you say, "Just a minute," while you finish what you are doing. That is asking your Dad to be patient. Another example is when you came to church this morning. You know that the service will last about one hour. You may have other things you want to do, but you must wait until the service is over before you can leave. Being patient is being willing to wait until the time is right for you to move on to something else. You show you are willing to be patient by sitting still and listening to what is going on and being willing to participate when you can.

Being a patient person is not always easy, but it is something that everyone has to learn to do, and the sooner you learn about it, the happier you will be. Also, being patient is part of what it means to be a Christian. Paul taught us, simply, to be patient with everyone (1 Thess. 5:14).

Now, today I would like to give you all the opportunity to learn patience. [*Give each child a piece of wrapped candy.*] I assume you like candy, but I want you to wait until after lunch before you unwrap it.—K.M.

December 6: The Light of God's Presence

TEXT: Exod. 27:21

Object: A menorah (candle holder)

This candle holder holds seven candles and is called a menorah. The original menorah was very big and held olive oil that burned with a wick. Some priests were given a job of keeping the menorah's light burning at all times. Listen to this verse.

The constant light of the menorah stood for the presence of God. In the day of Moses, the worship center for God's people was a big tent. The big tent was called the tabernacle. The tabernacle was in the center of the camp. Whenever the people would look toward the tabernacle during the night, there was always a glow coming from the large menorah. This continual light reminded the people that God was always with them.

The light of the menorah also removed darkness. Darkness is symbolic of all that is wrong or evil in our world. Whenever the electricity goes off at night and candles are lit, everyone in the house hurries to where the light is. Darkness makes us uncomfortable and we want to be in a room that is full of light. In the same way, evil actions trouble us and we desire to be in a wholesome environment.

God has promised to be with us always. Our faith in the promise of God to abide with us should glow brightly, just like a candle. Also, as we live for the Lord, allowing our actions to voice our obedience to the Lord, we will dispel the darkness of evil that is around us.

The menorah was to be kept burning through darkness. God's presence should light up our lives by dispelling loneliness and bad actions.—K.C.

December 13: Better Than Money

In our village there is a Jewish druggist I like. He is round and fat and friendly, and when I go into his store I feel that he is glad to see me. In fact, he makes me feel so much as if mere business is a personal matter that I pass ten drugstores to get to his store every day of my life. One day I said to him: "Mr. Dorenbaum, I don't want to buy a thing today. I tried to think up an excuse to come in here just to talk with you. I like to come into your store."

He smiled and replied: "That's the way I feel about your coming in, doctor. It's good to see you every day. It makes my day better." Then he added thoughtfully: "Friends are better than money any day with me."—William L. Stidger

December 20: Advent/Christmas

Do any of you boys and girls have a bird feeder in your backyard? [*Let them answer.*] I love to watch the birds come to our bird feeder during the winter. I like to see their pretty colors and watch the way they eat seeds and do funny things.

Last week a brilliant red cardinal came to our feeder. As I watched him through my kitchen window, I realized that he didn't know that I was watching him. He didn't even know that I was the one who had given him food. I found myself wishing that I could talk to that pretty cardinal. I wanted to know what it was like for him living in the woods behind our backyard. I wanted to let him know that he should be careful because the new neighbors have a cat that likes to hunt birds. I wanted to tell him how much I enjoyed his beautiful feathers, and how cheerful his chirp, chirp, chirp sounded to me on a cold winter day.

But I couldn't tell him any of those things

because he didn't know me. He didn't know my language. If I were to go out the door and try to talk to him, he would fly away because I am so much bigger than he is. I knew that the only way I could talk to that cardinal so he would listen would be if I became a bird myself, which of course I can't do.

Long, long ago, God must have felt the way I did as I was looking at the cardinal in my backyard. God has many things he wants to say to us, but God is so much greater than we are that we can't understand him. God wants to tell us how much he loves us. He wants to help us when we're in trouble. He wants to let us know that he's the one who gives us everything we need. But God is so much greater than we are that it's hard for us to understand, just like it's hard for a bird to know what I want to say. But God, who can do anything, had a way of letting us know him. God became one of us. God sent his Son Jesus to come among us as a person. Jesus was born at Christmas, he was a child just like you are, and he grew up to become an adult. Jesus tells us about God in ways we can understand. That's what's so special about Christmas. In Jesus, God comes to you and to me and shows us that he is our friend.—S.L.

December 27: A Haunting Reminder

A writer of many years ago used his excellent powers of imagination to picture the return of Jesus to heaven and the concern of the chief angels that his sacrifice on earth not be lost in any way. One of the angels is reported to have asked, "Master, what plan did you leave on the earth whereby the people shall come to know of the salvation which you made possible?" The writer imagined that Jesus, smiling confidently, replied, "I left Peter, John, and the other faithful disciples; they will tell others about me, and those others will tell others." One of the chief angels, not quite satisfied that the gospel would get through, persisted: "But, Master, what if those followers fail you?" The writer pictures Jesus' smile of confidence in replying: "If my followers fail me, I have absolutely no other plan."—Chester Swor

ACKNOWLEDGMENTS

Acknowledgment and gratitude are hereby expressed for kind permission to reprint material from the books and periodical listed below. Each of these selections is used by permission.

Excerpts from C. Ferris Jordan in James C. Barry, ed., *Award Winning Sermons*, Vol. 4, pp. 41–51, © 1980, Broadman Press

Excerpts from Allen F. Harrod in James C. Barry ed., *Award Winning Sermons*, Vol. 3, pp. 43–48, © 1979, Broadman Press

Excerpts from Hugh Litchfield, *Preaching the Christmas Story*, pp. 57–63, 115–120;, © 1984, Broadman Press

Excerpts from Roger Lovette in James C. Barry, ed., *Award Winning Sermons*, Vol. 4, pp. 26–27, © 1980, Broadman Press

Excerpts from Raymond Bryan Brown, *The Fire of Truth*, pp. 26–27, © 1982, Broadman Press

An excerpt from Larry Michael in *Proclaim*, April–June 1995, pp. 35–36, © 1995, The Sunday School Board of the Southern Baptist Convention

INDEX OF CONTRIBUTORS

SERMON TITLE INDEX

Children's stories and sermons are identified as (cs); sermon suggestions as (ss)

SCRIPTURAL INDEX

346

INDEX OF PRAYERS

INDEX OF MATERIALS USEFUL AS CHILDREN'S STORIES AND SERMONS NOT INCLUDED IN SECTION X

INDEX OF MATERIALS USEFUL FOR SMALL GROUPS

TOPICAL INDEX